General Motors N-Cars Automotive Repair Manual

by Bob Henderson and John H Haynes

Member of the Guild of Motoring Writers

Models covered:

1985 thru 1987 Buick Somerset
1985 thru 1990 Pontiac Grand Am and Oldsmobile Calais
1986 thru 1990 Buick Skylark

(9T3 – 1420)

ABCDE
FGHIJ
KLM

Haynes Publishing Group
Sparkford Nr Yeovil
Somerset BA22 7JJ England

Haynes North America, Inc.
861 Lawrence Drive
Newbury Park
California 91320 USA

Acknowledgements

We are grateful for the help and cooperation of General Motors Corporation for their assistance with technical information, certain illustrations and vehicle photos, and the Champion Spark Plug Company who supplied the illustrations of various spark plug conditions.

© **Haynes North America, Inc.** **1988, 1990**
With permission from J. H. Haynes & Co. Ltd.

A book in the **Haynes Automotive Repair Manual Series**

Printed in the USA

ISBN 1 85010 638 X

Library of Congress Catalog Card Number 90-82728

Contents

1985 Pontiac Grand Am

About this manual

Its purpose

The purpose of this manual is to help you get the best value from your vehicle. It can do so in several ways. It can help you decide what work must be done, even if you choose to have it done by a dealer service department or a repair shop; it provides information and procedures for routine maintenance and servicing; and it offers diagnostic and repair procedures to follow when trouble occurs.

It is hoped that you will use the manual to tackle the work yourself. For many simpler jobs, doing it yourself may be quicker than arranging an appointment to get the vehicle into a shop and making the trips to leave it and pick it up. More importantly, a lot of money can be saved by avoiding the expense the shop must pass on to you to cover its labor and overhead costs. An added benefit is the sense of satisfaction and accomplishment that you feel after having done the job yourself.

Using the manual

The manual is divided into Chapters. Each Chapter is divided into numbered Sections, which are headed in bold type between horizontal lines. Each Section consists of consecutively numbered paragraphs.

At the beginning of each numbered section you will be referred to any illustrations which apply to the procedures in that section. The reference numbers used in illustration captions pinpoint the pertinent Section and the Step within that section. That is, illustration 3.2 means the illustration refers to Section 3 and Step (or paragraph) 2 within that Section.

Procedures, once described in the text, are not normally repeated. When it is necessary to refer to another Chapter, the reference will be given as Chapter and Section number i.e. Chapter 1/16). Cross references given without use of the word ''Chapter'' apply to Sections and/or paragraphs in the same Chapter. For example, ''see Section 8'' means in the same Chapter.

Reference to the left or right side of the vehicle is based on the assumption that one is sitting in the driver's seat, facing forward.

Even though extreme care has been taken during the preparation of this manual, neither the publisher nor the author can accept responsibility for any errors in, or omissions from, the information given.

NOTE

A **Note** provides information necessary to properly complete a procedure or information which will make the steps to be followed easier to understand.

CAUTION

A **Caution** indicates a special procedure or special steps which must be taken in the course of completing the procedure in which the **Caution** is found which are necessary to avoid damage to the assembly being worked on.

WARNING

A **Warning** indicates a special procedure or special steps which must be taken in the course of completing the procedure in which the **Warning** is found which are necessary to avoid injury to the person performing the procedure.

Introduction to the General Motors N-cars

The General Motors N-cars include the 1985 through 1990 Pontiac Grand Am, Buick Somerset and Oldsmobile Calais and the 1986 through 1990 Buick Skylark. These models are available in 2-door coupe and 4-door sedan body styles and feature four coil suspension and front wheel drive.

The cross-mounted inline four-cylinder or V6 engines are equipped with either throttle body or mult-port fuel injection and some later models are turbocharged. The engine drives the front wheels through either a manual or automatic transaxle by way of unequal length driveaxles. The power assisted rack and pinion steering is mounted behind the engine.

The brakes are disc at the front and drum-type at the rear with power assist as standard equipment.

Vehicle identification numbers

Modifications are a continuing and unpublicized process in vehicle manufacturing. Since spare parts manuals and lists are compiled on a numerical basis, the individual vehicle numbers are essential to correctly identify the component required.

Vehicle Identification Number (VIN)

This very important identification number is located on a plate attached to the top left side corner of the dashboard of the vehicle (see illustration). The VIN also appears on the Vehicle Certificate of Title and Registration. It contains valuable information such as where and when the vehicle was manufactured, the model year and the body style.

Body Identification plate

This metal plate is located on the top side of the radiator support (see illustration). Like the VIN, it contains valuable information concerning the production of the vehicle as well as information about the way in which the vehicle is equipped. This plate is especially useful for matching the color and type of paint during repair work.

Engine identification numbers

The engine ID number on the 2.5 liter four-cylinder engine is located on a pad on the engine block under the exhaust manifold or at the rear of the cylinder head (see illustrations). The 2.0 liter OHC four-cylinder engine ID number is found on the left front side of the block, on the casting to the rear of the exhaust manifold (see illustration). On V6 engines, the ID number is located on a pad at the front surface of the engine block, adjacent to the water pump or on the edge of the cylinder head (see illustrations).

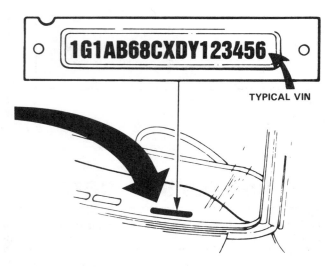

TYPICAL VIN

The Vehicle Identification Number (VIN) is on a plate attached to the left top of the instrument panel where it can be seen from outside the vehicle

The body identification plate is located on the radiator support

The 2.5L four-cylinder engine ID number can be found on the engine block under the exhaust manifold (arrow)

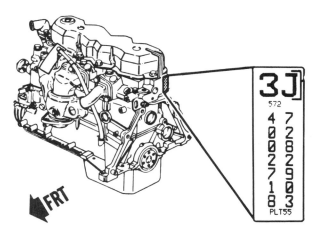

Alternate 2.5L four-cylinder engine ID number location

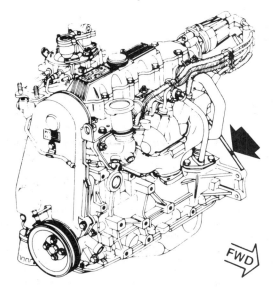

Location of the 2.0 liter OHC engine ID number (arrow)

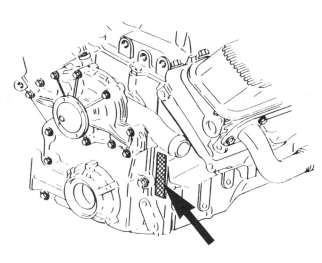

V6 engine ID number location (arrow)

Alternate V6 engine ID number location

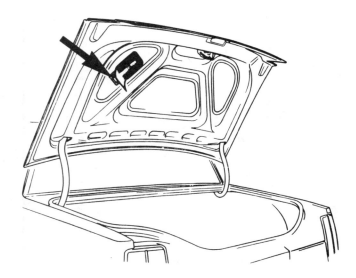

The service parts identification label is located on the trunk lid (arrow)

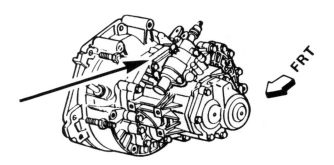

Manual transaxle ID number location (arrow)

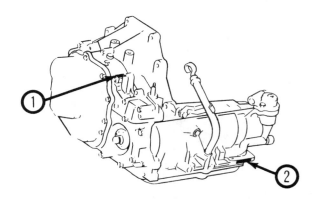

Automatic transaxle VIN (1) and model code (2) number locations

Service parts identification label

This label is located inside the trunk lid **(see illustration)**. It lists the VIN number, wheelbase, paint number, options and other information specific to your vehicle. Always refer to this label when ordering parts.

Manual transaxle number

The manual transaxle ID number is located on a pad on the forward side of the transaxle case **(see illustration)**.

Automatic transaxle numbers

The identification number is located on a flange pad at the top of the transaxle case and the model code is on the lower front edge near the dipstick **(see illustration)**.

Vehicle Emissions Control Information label

The Vehicle Emissions Control Information label is found under the hood, usually on the air cleaner intake (see Chapter 6 for an illustration of the label).

Buying parts

Replacement parts are available from many sources, which generally fall into one of two categories – authorized dealer parts departments and independent retail auto parts stores. Our advice concerning these parts is as follows:

Retail auto parts stores: Good auto parts stores will stock frequently needed components which wear out relatively fast, such as clutch components, exhaust systems, brake parts, tune-up parts, etc. These stores often supply new or reconditioned parts on an exchange basis, which can save a considerable amount of money. Discount auto parts stores are often very good places to buy materials and parts needed for general vehicle maintenance such as oil, grease, filters, spark plugs, belts, touch-up paint, bulbs, etc. They also usually sell tools and general accessories, have convenient hours, charge lower prices and can often be found not far from home.

Authorized dealer parts department: This is the best source for parts which are unique to the vehicle and not generally available elsewhere (such as major engine parts, transmission parts, trim pieces, etc.).

Warranty information: If the vehicle is still covered under warranty, be sure that any replacement parts purchased – regardless of the source – do not invalidate the warranty!

To be sure of obtaining the correct parts, have engine and chassis numbers available and, if possible, take the old parts along for positive identification.

Maintenance techniques, tools and working facilities

Maintenance techniques

There are a number of techniques involved in maintenance and repair that will be referred to throughout this manual. Application of these techniques will enable the home mechanic to be more efficient, better organized and capable of performing the various tasks properly, which will ensure that the repair job is thorough and complete.

Fasteners

Fasteners are nuts, bolts, studs and screws used to hold two or more parts together. There are a few things to keep in mind when working with fasteners. Almost all of them use a locking device of some type, either a lockwasher, locknut, locking tab or thread adhesive. All threaded fasteners should be clean and straight, with undamaged threads and undamaged corners on the hex head where the wrench fits. Develop the habit of replacing all damaged nuts and bolts with new ones. Special locknuts with nylon or fiber inserts can only be used once. If they are removed, they lose their locking ability and must be replaced with new ones.

Rusted nuts and bolts should be treated with a penetrating fluid to ease removal and prevent breakage. Some mechanics use turpentine in a spout-type oil can, which works quite well. After applying the rust penetrant, let it work for a few minutes before trying to loosen the nut or bolt. Badly rusted fasteners may have to be chiseled or sawed off or removed with a special nut breaker, available at tool stores.

If a bolt or stud breaks off in an assembly, it can be drilled and removed with a special tool commonly available for this purpose. Most automotive machine shops can perform this task, as well as other repair procedures, such as the repair of threaded holes that have been stripped out.

Flat washers and lockwashers, when removed from an assembly, should always be replaced exactly as removed. Replace any damaged washers with new ones. Never use a lockwasher on any soft metal surface (such as aluminum), thin sheet metal or plastic.

Fastener sizes

For a number of reasons, automobile manufacturers are making wider and wider use of metric fasteners. Therefore, it is important to be able to tell the difference between standard (sometimes called U.S. or SAE) and metric hardware, since they cannot be interchanged.

All bolts, whether standard or metric, are sized according to diameter, thread pitch and length. For example, a standard 1/2 — 13 x 1 bolt is 1/2 inch in diameter, has 13 threads per inch and is 1 inch long. An M12 — 1.75 x 25 metric bolt is 12 mm in diameter, has a thread pitch of 1.75 mm (the distance between threads) and is 25 mm long. The two bolts are nearly identical, and easily confused, but they are not interchangeable.

In addition to the differences in diameter, thread pitch and length, metric and standard bolts can also be distinguished by examining the bolt heads. To begin with, the distance across the flats on a standard bolt head is measured in inches, while the same dimension on a metric bolt is sized in millimeters (the same is true for nuts). As a result, a standard wrench should not be used on a metric bolt and a metric wrench should not be used on a standard bolt. Also, most standard bolts have slashes radiating out from the center of the head to denote the grade or strength of the bolt, which is an indication of the amount of torque that can be applied to it. The greater the number of slashes, the greater the strength of the bolt. Grades 0 through 5 are commonly used on automobiles. Metric bolts have a property class (grade) number, rather than a slash, molded into their heads to indicate bolt strength. In this case, the higher the number, the stronger the bolt. Property class numbers 8.8, 9.8 and 10.9 are commonly used on automobiles.

Strength markings can also be used to distinguish standard hex nuts from metric hex nuts. Many standard nuts have dots stamped into one side, while metric nuts are marked with a number. The greater the number of dots, or the higher the number, the greater the strength of the nut.

Metric studs are also marked on their ends according to property class (grade). Larger studs are numbered (the same as metric bolts),

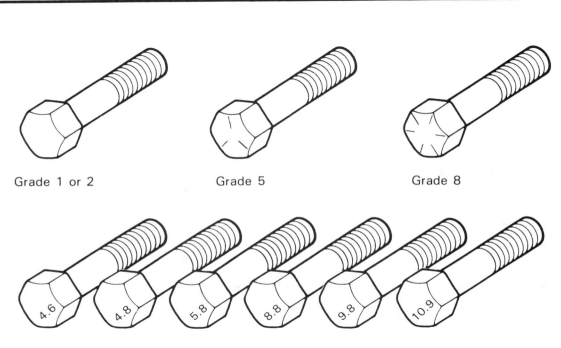

Grade 1 or 2   Grade 5   Grade 8

Bolt strength markings (top — standard/SAE/USS; bottom — metric)

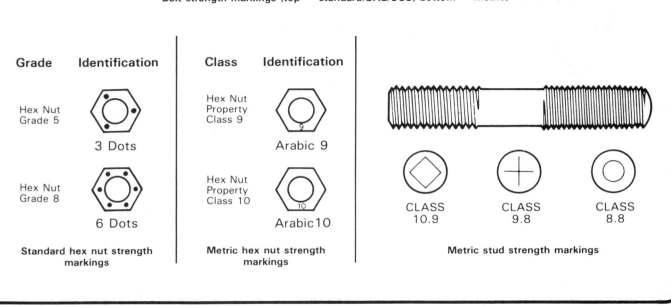

Grade	Identification
Hex Nut Grade 5	3 Dots
Hex Nut Grade 8	6 Dots

Standard hex nut strength markings

Class	Identification
Hex Nut Property Class 9	Arabic 9
Hex Nut Property Class 10	Arabic 10

Metric hex nut strength markings

CLASS 10.9   CLASS 9.8   CLASS 8.8

Metric stud strength markings

while smaller studs carry a geometric code to denote grade.

It should be noted that many fasteners, especially Grades 0 through 2, have no distinguishing marks on them. When such is the case, the only way to determine whether it is standard or metric is to measure the thread pitch or compare it to a known fastener of the same size.

Standard fasteners are often referred to as SAE, as opposed to metric. However, it should be noted that SAE technically refers to a non-metric *fine thread* fastener only. Coarse thread non-metric fasteners are referred to as USS sizes.

Since fasteners of the same size (both standard and metric) may have different strength ratings, be sure to reinstall any bolts, studs or nuts removed from your vehicle in their original locations. Also, when replacing a fastener with a new one, make sure that the new one has a strength rating equal to or greater than the original.

Tightening sequences and procedures

Most threaded fasteners should be tightened to a specific torque value (torque is the twisting force applied to a threaded component such as a nut or bolt). Overtightening the fastener can weaken it and cause it to break, while undertightening can cause it to eventually come loose. Bolts, screws and studs, depending on the material they are made of and their thread diameters, have specific torque values, many of which are noted in the Specifications at the beginning of each Chapter. Be sure to follow the torque recommendations closely. For fasteners not assigned a specific torque, a general torque value chart is presented here as a guide. These torque values are for dry (unlubricated) fasteners threaded into steel or cast iron (not aluminum). As was previously mentioned, the size and grade of a fastener determine the amount of torque that can safely be applied to it. The figures listed here are approximate

Metric thread sizes	Ft-lb	Nm/m
M-6	6 to 9	9 to 12
M-8	14 to 21	19 to 28
M-10	28 to 40	38 to 54
M-12	50 to 71	68 to 96
M-14	80 to 140	109 to 154

Pipe thread sizes		
1/8	5 to 8	7 to 10
1/4	12 to 18	17 to 24
3/8	22 to 33	30 to 44
1/2	25 to 35	34 to 47

U.S. thread sizes		
1/4 — 20	6 to 9	9 to 12
5/16 — 18	12 to 18	17 to 24
5/16 — 24	14 to 20	19 to 27
3/8 — 16	22 to 32	30 to 43
3/8 — 24	27 to 38	37 to 51
7/16 — 14	40 to 55	55 to 74
7/16 — 20	40 to 60	55 to 81
1/2 — 13	55 to 80	75 to 108

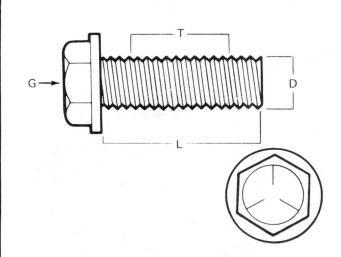

Standard (SAE and USS) bolt dimensions/grade marks

G   Grade marks (bolt strength)
L   Length (in inches)
T   Thread pitch (number of threads per inch)
D   Nominal diameter (in inches)

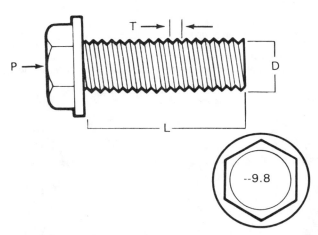

Metric bolt dimensions/grade marks

P   Property class (bolt strength)
L   Length (in millimeters)
T   Thread pitch (distance between threads in millimeters)
D   Diameter

for Grade 2 and Grade 3 fasteners. Higher grades can tolerate higher torque values.

Fasteners laid out in a pattern, such as cylinder head bolts, oil pan bolts, differential cover bolts, etc., must be loosened or tightened in sequence to avoid warping the component. This sequence will normally be shown in the appropriate Chapter. If a specific pattern is not given, the following procedures can be used to prevent warping.

Initially, the bolts or nuts should be assembled finger-tight only. Next, they should be tightened one full turn each, in a criss-cross or diagonal pattern. After each one has been tightened one full turn, return to the first one and tighten them all one-half turn, following the same pattern. Finally, tighten each of them one-quarter turn at a time until each fastener has been tightened to the proper torque. To loosen and remove the fasteners, the procedure would be reversed.

Component disassembly

Component disassembly should be done with care and purpose to help ensure that the parts go back together properly. Always keep track of the sequence in which parts are removed. Make note of special characteristics or marks on parts that can be installed more than one way, such as a grooved thrust washer on a shaft. It is a good idea to lay the disassembled parts out on a clean surface in the order that they were removed. It may also be helpful to make sketches or take instant photos of components before removal.

When removing fasteners from a component, keep track of their locations. Sometimes threading a bolt back in a part, or putting the washers and nut back on a stud, can prevent mix-ups later. If nuts and bolts cannot be returned to their original locations, they should be kept in a compartmented box or a series of small boxes. A cupcake or muffin tin is ideal for this purpose, since each cavity can hold the bolts and nuts from a particular area (i.e. oil pan bolts, valve cover bolts, engine mount bolts, etc.). A pan of this type is especially helpful when working on assemblies with very small parts, such as the carburetor, alternator, valve train or interior dash and trim pieces. The cavities can be marked with paint or tape to identify the contents.

Whenever wiring looms, harnesses or connectors are separated, it is a good idea to identify the two halves with numbered pieces of masking tape so they can be easily reconnected.

Gasket sealing surfaces

Throughout any vehicle, gaskets are used to seal the mating surfaces between two parts and keep lubricants, fluids, vacuum or pressure contained in an assembly.

Many times these gaskets are coated with a liquid or paste-type gasket sealing compound before assembly. Age, heat and pressure can sometimes cause the two parts to stick together so tightly that they are very difficult to separate. Often, the assembly can be loosened by striking it with a soft-face hammer near the mating surfaces. A regular hammer can be used if a block of wood is placed between the hammer and the part. Do not hammer on cast parts or parts that could be easily damaged. With any particularly stubborn part, always recheck to make sure that every fastener has been removed.

Avoid using a screwdriver or bar to pry apart an assembly, as they can easily mar the gasket sealing surfaces of the parts, which must remain smooth. If prying is absolutely necessary, use an old broom handle, but keep in mind that extra clean up will be necessary if the wood splinters.

After the parts are separated, the old gasket must be carefully scraped off and the gasket surfaces cleaned. Stubborn gasket material can be soaked with rust penetrant or treated with a special chemical to soften it so it can be easily scraped off. A scraper can be fashioned from a piece of copper tubing by flattening and sharpening one end. Copper is recommended because it is usually softer than the surfaces to be scraped, which reduces the chance of gouging the part. Some gaskets can be removed with a wire brush, but regardless of the method used, the mating surfaces must be left clean and smooth. If for some reason the gasket surface is gouged, then a gasket sealer thick enough to fill scratches will have to be used during reassembly of the components. For most applications, a non-drying (or semi-drying) gasket sealer should be used.

Hose removal tips

Warning: *If the vehicle is equipped with air conditioning, do not disconnect any of the A/C hoses without first having the system depressurized by a dealer service department or an air conditioning specialist.*

Hose removal precautions closely parallel gasket removal precautions. Avoid scratching or gouging the surface that the hose mates against or the connection may leak. This is especially true for radiator hoses. Because of various chemical reactions, the rubber in hoses can bond itself to the metal spigot that the hose fits over. To remove a hose, first loosen the hose clamps that secure it to the spigot. Then, with slip-joint pliers, grab the hose at the clamp and rotate it around the spigot. Work it back and forth until it is completely free, then pull it off. Silicone or other lubricants will ease removal if they can be applied between the hose and the outside of the spigot. Apply the same lubricant to the inside of the hose and the outside of the spigot to simplify installation.

As a last resort (and if the hose is to be replaced with a new one anyway), the rubber can be slit with a knife and the hose peeled from the spigot. If this must be done, be careful that the metal connection is not damaged.

If a hose clamp is broken or damaged, do not reuse it. Wire-type clamps usually weaken with age, so it is a good idea to replace them with screw-type clamps whenever a hose is removed.

Tools

A selection of good tools is a basic requirement for anyone who plans to maintain and repair his or her own vehicle. For the owner who has few tools, the initial investment might seem high, but when compared to the spiraling costs of professional auto maintenance and repair, it is a wise one.

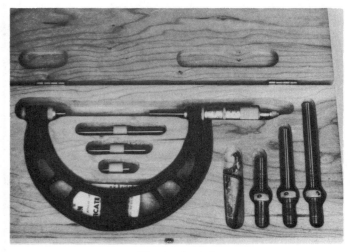

Micrometer set

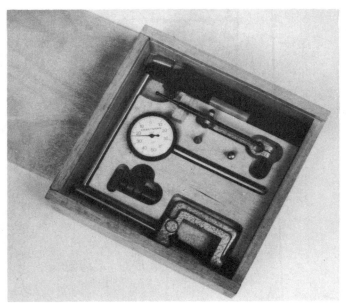

Dial indicator set

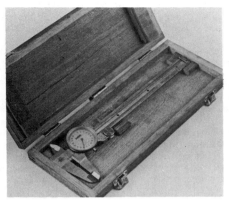

Dial caliper

Hand-operated vacuum pump

Timing light

Compression gauge with spark plug hole adapter

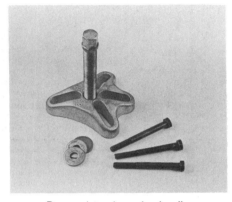

Damper/steering wheel puller

General purpose puller

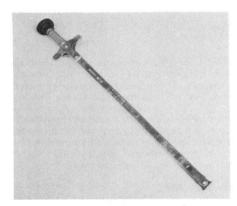

Hydraulic lifter removal tool

Valve spring compressor

Valve spring compressor

Ridge reamer

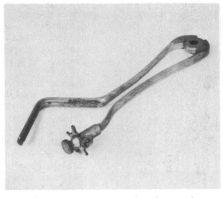

Piston ring groove cleaning tool

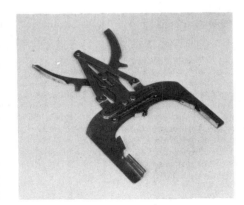

Ring removal/installation tool

Ring compressor

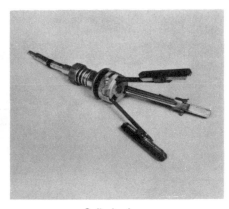

Cylinder hone

Brake hold-down spring tool

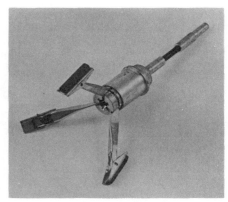

Brake cylinder hone

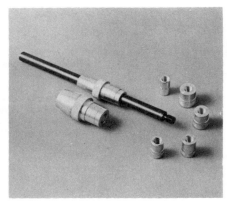

Clutch plate alignment tool

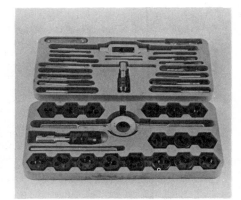

Tap and die set

To help the owner decide which tools are needed to perform the tasks detailed in this manual, the following tool lists are offered: *Maintenance and minor repair, Repair/overhaul* and *Special.*

The newcomer to practical mechanics should start off with the maintenance and minor repair tool kit, which is adequate for the simpler jobs performed on a vehicle. Then, as confidence and experience grow, the owner can tackle more difficult tasks, buying additional tools as they are needed. Eventually the basic kit will be expanded into the repair and overhaul tool set. Over a period of time, the experienced do-it-yourselfer will assemble a tool set complete enough for most repair and overhaul procedures and will add tools from the special category when it is felt that the expense is justified by the frequency of use.

Maintenance and minor repair tool kit

The tools in this list should be considered the minimum required for performance of routine maintenance, servicing and minor repair work. We recommend the purchase of combination wrenches (box-end and open-end combined in one wrench). While more expensive than open end wrenches, they offer the advantages of both types of wrench.

Combination wrench set (1/4-inch to 1 inch or 6 mm to 19 mm)
Adjustable wrench, 8 inch
Spark plug wrench with rubber insert
Spark plug gap adjusting tool
Feeler gauge set
Brake bleeder wrench
Standard screwdriver (5/16-inch x 6 inch)
Phillips screwdriver (No. 2 x 6 inch)
Combination pliers — 6 inch
Hacksaw and assortment of blades
Tire pressure gauge
Grease gun
Oil can
Fine emery cloth
Wire brush

Battery post and cable cleaning tool
Oil filter wrench
Funnel (medium size)
Safety goggles
Jackstands (2)
Drain pan

Note: *If basic tune-ups are going to be part of routine maintenance, it will be necessary to purchase a good quality stroboscopic timing light and combination tachometer/dwell meter. Although they are included in the list of special tools, it is mentioned here because they are absolutely necessary for tuning most vehicles properly.*

Repair and overhaul tool set

These tools are essential for anyone who plans to perform major repairs and are in addition to those in the maintenance and minor repair tool kit. Included is a comprehensive set of sockets which, though expensive, are invaluable because of their versatility, especially when various extensions and drives are available. We recommend the 1/2-inch drive over the 3/8-inch drive. Although the larger drive is bulky and more expensive, it has the capacity of accepting a very wide range of large sockets. Ideally, however, the mechanic should have a 3/8-inch drive set and a 1/2-inch drive set.

Socket set(s)
Reversible ratchet
Extension — 10 inch
Universal joint
Torque wrench (same size drive as sockets)
Ball peen hammer — 8 ounce
Soft-face hammer (plastic/rubber)
Standard screwdriver (1/4-inch x 6 inch)
Standard screwdriver (stubby — 5/16-inch)
Phillips screwdriver (No. 3 x 8 inch)
Phillips screwdriver (stubby — No. 2)

Pliers — vise grip
Pliers — lineman's
Pliers — needle nose
Pliers — snap-ring (internal and external)
Cold chisel — 1/2-inch
Scribe
Scraper (made from flattened copper tubing)
Centerpunch
Pin punches (1/16, 1/8, 3/16-inch)
Steel rule/straightedge — 12 inch
Allen wrench set (1/8 to 3/8-inch or 4 mm to 10 mm)
A selection of files
Wire brush (large)
Jackstands (second set)
Jack (scissor or hydraulic type)

Note: *Another tool which is often useful is an electric drill motor with a chuck capacity of 3/8-inch and a set of good quality drill bits.*

Special tools

The tools in this list include those which are not used regularly, are expensive to buy, or which need to be used in accordance with their manufacturer's instructions. Unless these tools will be used frequently, it is not very economical to purchase many of them. A consideration would be to split the cost and use between yourself and a friend or friends. In addition, most of these tools can be obtained from a tool rental shop on a temporary basis.

This list primarily contains only those tools and instruments widely available to the public, and not those special tools produced by the vehicle manufacturer for distribution to dealer service departments. Occasionally, references to the manufacturer's special tools are inluded in the text of this manual. Generally, an alternative method of doing the job without the special tool is offered. However, sometimes there is no alternative to their use. Where this is the case, and the tool cannot be purchased or borrowed, the work should be turned over to the dealer service department or an automotive repair shop.

Valve spring compressor
Piston ring groove cleaning tool
Piston ring compressor
Piston ring installation tool
Cylinder compression gauge
Cylinder ridge reamer
Cylinder surfacing hone
Cylinder bore gauge
Micrometers and/or dial calipers
Hydraulic lifter removal tool
Balljoint separator
Universal-type puller
Impact screwdriver
Dial indicator set
Stroboscopic timing light (inductive pick-up)
Hand operated vacuum/pressure pump
Tachometer/dwell meter
Universal electrical multimeter
Cable hoist
Brake spring removal and installation tools
Floor jack

Buying tools

For the do-it-yourselfer who is just starting to get involved in vehicle maintenance and repair, there are a number of options available when purchasing tools. If maintenance and minor repair is the extent of the work to be done, the purchase of individual tools is satisfactory. If, on the other hand, extensive work is planned, it would be a good idea to purchase a modest tool set from one of the large retail chain stores. A set can usually be bought at a substantial savings over the individual tool prices, and they often come with a tool box. As additional tools are needed, add-on sets, individual tools and a larger tool box can be purchased to expand the tool selection. Building a tool set gradually allows the cost of the tools to be spread over a longer period of time and gives the mechanic the freedom to choose only those tools that will actually be used.

Tool stores will often be the only source of some of the special tools that are needed, but regardless of where tools are bought, try to avoid cheap ones, especially when buying screwdrivers and sockets, because they won't last very long. The expense involved in replacing cheap tools will eventually be greater than the initial cost of quality tools.

Care and maintenance of tools

Good tools are expensive, so it makes sense to treat them with respect. Keep them clean and in usable condition and store them properly when not in use. Always wipe off any dirt, grease or metal chips before putting them away. Never leave tools lying around in the work area. Upon completion of a job, always check closely under the hood for tools that may have been left there so they won't get lost during a test drive.

Some tools, such as screwdrivers, pliers, wrenches and sockets, can be hung on a panel mounted on the garage or workshop wall, while others should be kept in a tool box or tray. Measuring instruments, gauges, meters, etc. must be carefully stored where they cannot be damaged by weather or impact from other tools.

When tools are used with care and stored properly, they will last a very long time. Even with the best of care, though, tools will wear out if used frequently. When a tool is damaged or worn out, replace it. Subsequent jobs will be safer and more enjoyable if you do.

Working facilities

Not to be overlooked when discussing tools is the workshop. If anything more than routine maintenance is to be carried out, some sort of suitable work area is essential.

It is understood, and appreciated, that many home mechanics do not have a good workshop or garage available, and end up removing an engine or doing major repairs outside. It is recommended, however, that the overhaul or repair be completed under the cover of a roof.

A clean, flat workbench or table of comfortable working height is an absolute necessity. The workbench should be equipped with a vise that has a jaw opening of at least four inches.

As mentioned previously, some clean, dry storage space is also required for tools, as well as the lubricants, fluids, cleaning solvents, etc. which will soon become necessary.

Sometimes waste oil and fluids, drained from the engine or cooling system during normal maintenance or repairs, present a disposal problem. To avoid pouring them on the ground or into a sewage system, pour the used fluids into large containers, seal them with caps and take them to an authorized disposal site or recycling center. Plastic jugs, such as old antifreeze containers, are ideal for this purpose.

Always keep a supply of old newspapers and clean rags available. Old towels are excellent for mopping up spills. Many mechanics use rolls of paper towels for most work because they are readily available and disposable. To help keep the area under the vehicle clean, a large cardboard box can be cut open and flattened to protect the garage or shop floor.

Whenever working over a painted surface, such as when leaning over a fender to service something under the hood, always cover it with an old blanket or bedspread to protect the finish. Vinyl covered pads, made especially for this purpose, are available at auto parts stores.

Booster battery (jump) starting

Certain precautions must be observed when using a booster battery to start a vehicle.

   a) Before connecting the booster battery, make sure that the ignition switch is in the Off position.

   b) Turn off the lights, heater and other electrical loads.

   c) Your eyes should be shielded. Safety goggles are a good idea.

   d) Make sure the booster battery is the same voltage as the dead one in the vehicle.

   e) The two vehicles MUST NOT TOUCH each other!

   f) Make sure the transmission is in Neutral (manual) or Park (automatic).

   g) If the booster battery is not a maintenance-free type, remove the vent caps and lay a cloth over the vent holes.

Connect the red jumper cable to the *positive* (+) terminals of each battery.

Connect one end of the black jumper cable to the *negative* (–) terminal of the booster battery. The other end of this cable should be connected to a good ground on the vehicle to be started, such as a bolt or bracket on the engine block **(see illustrations)**. Use caution to ensure that the cable will not come into contact with the fan, drivebelts or other moving parts of the engine.

Start the engine using the booster battery, then, with the engine running at idle speed, disconnect the jumper cables in the reverse order of connection.

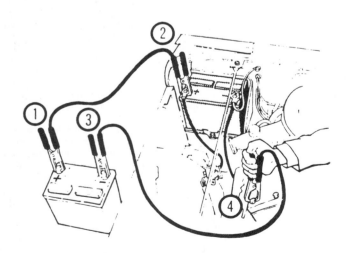

Make the booster battery cable connections in the numerical order shown (note that the negative cable of the booster battery is NOT attached to the negative terminal of the dead battery)

Adapters designed to make jumper cable connections to side terminal batteries safer and easier are available from auto parts stores

Jacking and towing

Jacking

The jack supplied with the vehicle should only be used for raising the vehicle when changing a tire or placing jackstands under the frame. **Warning:** *Never work under the vehicle or start the engine while this jack is being used as the only means of support.*

The vehicle should be on level ground with the wheels blocked and the transaxle in Park (automatic) or Reverse (manual). If the tire is to be changed, remove the hub cap **(see illustration)**. If the wheel is being replaced, loosen the lug nuts one-half turn and leave them in place until the wheel is raised off the ground.

Place the jack under the side of the vehicle in the indicated position **(see illustration)**. Operate the jack with a slow, smooth motion until the wheel is raised off the ground. Remove the tire and install the spare. Tighten the lug nuts until they're snug, but wait until the vehicle is lowered to use the wrench.

Lower the vehicle, remove the jack and tighten the nuts in a criss-cross sequence by turning the wrench clockwise.

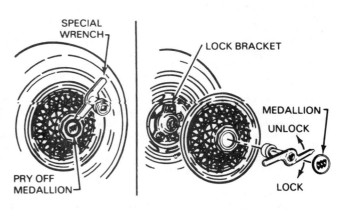

The wire-type hub cap requires a special tool for removal

Jacking points and procedure

Towing

Vehicles can be towed with all four wheels on the ground, provided that speeds do not exceed 35 mph and the distance is not over 50 miles, otherwise transaxle damage can result.

Towing equipment specifically designed for this purpose should be used and should be attached to the main structural members of the vehicle, not the bumper or brackets.

Safety is a major consideration when towing and all applicable state and local laws must be obeyed. A safety chain must be used for all towing.

While towing, the parking brake should be released and the transaxle must be in Neutral. The steering must be unlocked (ignition switch in the Off position). Remember that power steering and power brakes will not work with the engine off.

Automotive chemicals and lubricants

A number of automotive chemicals and lubricants are available for use during vehicle maintenance and repair. They include a wide variety of products ranging from cleaning solvents and degreasers to lubricants and protective sprays for rubber, plastic and vinyl.

Cleaners

Carburetor cleaner and choke cleaner is a strong solvent for gum, varnish and carbon. Most carburetor cleaners leave a dry-type lubricant film which will not harden or gum up. Because of this film it is not recommended for use on electrical components.

Brake system cleaner is used to remove grease and brake fluid from the brake system where clean surfaces are absolutely necessary. It leaves no residue and often eliminates brake squeal caused by contaminants.

Electrical cleaner removes oxidation, corrosion and carbon deposits from electrical contacts, restoring full current flow. It can also be used to clean spark plugs, carburetor jets, voltage regulators and other parts where an oil-free surface is desired.

Demoisturants remove water and moisture from electrical components such as alternators, voltage regulators, electrical connectors and fuse blocks. It is non-conductive, non-corrosive and non-flammable.

Degreasers are heavy-duty solvents used to remove grease from the outside of the engine and from chassis components. They can be sprayed or brushed on, and, depending on the type, are rinsed off either with water or solvent.

Lubricants

Motor oil is the lubricant formulated for use in engines. It normally contains a wide variety of additives to prevent corrosion and reduce foaming and wear. Motor oil comes in various weights (viscosity ratings) from 5 to 80. The recommended weight of the oil depends on the season, temperature and the demands on the engine. Light oil is used in cold climates and under light load conditions. Heavy oil is used in hot climates and where high loads are encountered. Multi-viscosity oils are designed to have characteristics of both light and heavy oils and are available in a number of weights from 5W-20 to 20W-50.

Gear oil is designed to be used in differentials, manual transaxles and other areas where high-temperature lubrication is required.

Chassis and wheel bearing grease is a heavy grease used where increased loads and friction are encountered, such as for wheel bearings, balljoints, tie rod ends and universal joints.

High temperature wheel bearing grease is designed to withstand the extreme temperatures encountered by wheel bearings in disc brake equipped vehicles. It usually contains molybdenun disulfide (moly), which is a dry-type lubricant.

White grease is a heavy grease for metal to metal applications where water is a problem. White grease stays soft under both low and high temperatures (usually from -100°F to +190°F), and will not wash off or dilute in the presence of water.

Assembly lube is a special extreme pressure lubricant, usually containing moly, used to lubricate high-load parts such as main and rod bearings and cam lobes for initial start-up of a new engine. The assembly lube lubricates the parts without being squeezed out or washed away until the engine oiling system begins to function.

Silicone lubricants are used to protect rubber, plastic, vinyl and nylon parts.

Graphite lubricants are used where oils cannot be used due to contamination problems, such as in locks. The dry graphite will lubricate metal parts while remaining uncontaminated by dirt, water, oil or acids. It is electrically conductive and will not foul electrical contacts in locks such as the ignition switch.

Moly penetrants loosen and lubricate frozen, rusted and corroded fasteners and prevent future rusting or freezing.

Heat-sink grease is a special electrically non-conductive grease that is used for mounting HEI ignition modules where it is essential that heat be transferred away from the module.

Sealants

RTV sealant is one of the most widely used gasket compounds. Made from silicone, RTV is air curing, it seals, bonds, waterproofs, fills surface irregularities, remains flexible, doesn't shrink, is relatively easy to remove, and is used as a supplementary sealer with almost all low and medium temperature gaskets.

Anaerobic sealant is much like RTV in that it can be used either to seal gaskets or to form gaskets by itself. It remains flexible, is solvent resistant and fills surface imperfections. The difference between an anaerobic sealant and an RTV-type sealant is in the curing. RTV cures when exposed to air, while an anaerobic sealant cures only in the absence of air. This means that an anaerobic sealant cures only after the assembly of parts, sealing them together.

Thread and pipe sealant is used for sealing hydraulic and pneumatic fittings and vacuum lines. It is usually made from a teflon compound, and comes in a spray, a paint-on liquid and as a wrap-around tape.

Chemicals

Anti-seize compound prevents seizing, galling, cold welding, rust and corrosion in fasteners. High temperature anti-seize, usually made with copper and graphite lubricants, is used for exhaust system and manifold bolts.

Anaerobic locking compounds are used to keep fasteners from vibrating or working loose, and cure only after installation, in the absence of air. Medium strength locking compound is used for small nuts, bolts and screws that you expect to be removing later. High strength locking compound is for large nuts, bolts and studs which you don't intend to be removing on a regular basis.

Oil additives range from viscosity index improvers to chemical treatments that claim to reduce internal engine friction. It should be noted that most oil manufacturers caution against using additives with their oils.

Gas additives perform several functions, depending on their chemical makeup. They usually contain solvents that help dissolve gum and varnish that build up on carburetor and intake parts. They also serve to break down carbon deposits that form on the inside surfaces of the combustion chambers. Some additives contain upper cylinder lubricants for valves and piston rings, and others chemicals to remove condensation from the gas tank.

Miscellaneous

Brake fluid is specially formulated hydraulic fluid that can withstand the heat and pressure encountered in brake systems. Care must be taken that this fluid does not come in contact with painted surfaces or plastics. An opened container should always be resealed to prevent contamination by water or dirt.

Weatherstrip adhesive is used to bond weatherstripping around doors, windows and trunk lids. It is sometimes used to attach trim pieces.

Undercoating is a petroleum-based tar-like substance that is designed to protect metal surfaces on the underside of the vehicle from corrosion. It also acts as a sound-deadening agent by insulating the bottom of the vehicle.

Waxes and polishes are used to help protect painted and plated surfaces from the weather. Different types of paint may require the use of different types of wax and polish. Some polishes utilize a chemical or abrasive cleaner to help remove the top layer of oxidized (dull) paint on older vehicles. In recent years many non-wax polishes that contain a wide variety of chemicals such as polymers and silicones have been introduced. These non-wax polishes are usually easier to apply and last longer than conventional waxes and polishes.

Safety first!

Regardless of how enthusiastic you may be about getting on with the job at hand, take the time to ensure that your safety is not jeopardized. A moment's lack of attention can result in an accident, as can failure to observe certain simple safety precautions. The possibility of an accident will always exist, and the following points should not be considered a comprehensive list of all dangers. Rather, they are intended to make you aware of the risks and to encourage a safety conscious approach to all work you carry out on your vehicle.

Essential DOs and DON'Ts

DON'T rely on a jack when working under the vehicle. Always use approved jackstands to support the weight of the vehicle and place them under the recommended lift or support points.

DON'T attempt to loosen extremely tight fasteners (i.e. wheel lug nuts) while the vehicle is on a jack — it may fall.

DON'T start the engine without first making sure that the transmission is in Neutral (or Park where applicable) and the parking brake is set.

DON'T remove the radiator cap from a hot cooling system — let it cool or cover it with a cloth and release the pressure gradually.

DON'T attempt to drain the engine oil until you are sure it has cooled to the point that it will not burn you.

DON'T touch any part of the engine or exhaust system until it has cooled sufficiently to avoid burns.

DON'T siphon toxic liquids such as gasoline, antifreeze and brake fluid by mouth, or allow them to remain on your skin.

DON'T inhale brake lining dust — it is potentially hazardous (see *Asbestos* below)

DON'T allow spilled oil or grease to remain on the floor — wipe it up before someone slips on it.

DON'T use loose fitting wrenches or other tools which may slip and cause injury.

DON'T push on wrenches when loosening or tightening nuts or bolts. Always try to pull the wrench toward you. If the situation calls for pushing the wrench away, push with an open hand to avoid scraped knuckles if the wrench should slip.

DON'T attempt to lift a heavy component alone — get someone to help you.

DON'T rush or take unsafe shortcuts to finish a job.

DON'T allow children or animals in or around the vehicle while you are working on it.

DO wear eye protection when using power tools such as a drill, sander, bench grinder, etc. and when working under a vehicle.

DO keep loose clothing and long hair well out of the way of moving parts.

DO make sure that any hoist used has a safe working load rating adequate for the job.

DO get someone to check on you periodically when working alone on a vehicle.

DO carry out work in a logical sequence and make sure that everything is correctly assembled and tightened.

DO keep chemicals and fluids tightly capped and out of the reach of children and pets.

DO remember that your vehicle's safety affects that of yourself and others. If in doubt on any point, get professional advice.

Asbestos

Certain friction, insulating, sealing, and other products — such as brake linings, brake bands, clutch linings, torque converters, gaskets, etc. — contain asbestos. *Extreme care must be taken to avoid inhalation of dust from such products since it is hazardous to health.* If in doubt, assume that they *do* contain asbestos.

Fire

Remember at all times that gasoline is highly flammable. Never smoke or have any kind of open flame around when working on a vehicle. But the risk does not end there. A spark caused by an electrical short circuit, by two metal surfaces contacting each other, or even by static electricity built up in your body under certain conditions, can ignite gasoline vapors, which in a confined space are highly explosive. Do not, under any circumstances, use gasoline for cleaning parts. Use an approved safety solvent.

Always disconnect the battery ground (–) cable *at the battery* before working on any part of the fuel system or electrical system. Never risk spilling fuel on a hot engine or exhaust component.

It is strongly recommended that a fire extinguisher suitable for use on fuel and electrical fires be kept handy in the garage or workshop at all times. Never try to extinguish a fuel or electrical fire with water.

Fumes

Certain fumes are highly toxic and can quickly cause unconsciousness and even death if inhaled to any extent. Gasoline vapor falls into this category, as do the vapors from some cleaning solvents. Any draining or pouring of such volatile fluids should be done in a well ventilated area.

When using cleaning fluids and solvents, read the instructions on the container carefully. Never use materials from unmarked containers.

Never run the engine in an enclosed space, such as a garage. Exhaust fumes contain carbon monoxide, which is extremely poisonous. If you need to run the engine, always do so in the open air, or at least have the rear of the vehicle outside the work area.

If you are fortunate enough to have the use of an inspection pit, never drain or pour gasoline and never run the engine while the vehicle is over the pit. The fumes, being heavier than air, will concentrate in the pit with possibly lethal results.

The battery

Never create a spark or allow a bare light bulb near a battery. They normally give off a certain amount of hydrogen gas, which is highly explosive.

Always disconnect the battery ground (–) cable *at the battery* before working on the fuel or electrical systems.

If possible, loosen the filler caps or cover when charging the battery from an external source (this does not apply to sealed or maintenance-free batteries). Do not charge at an excessive rate or the battery may burst.

Take care when adding water to a non maintenance-free battery and when carrying a battery. The electrolyte, even when diluted, is very corrosive and should not be allowed to contact clothing or skin.

Always wear eye protection when cleaning the battery to prevent the caustic deposits from entering your eyes.

Household current

When using an electric power tool, inspection light, etc., which operates on household current, always make sure that the tool is correctly connected to its plug and that, where necessary, it is properly grounded. Do not use such items in damp conditions and, again, do not create a spark or apply excessive heat in the vicinity of fuel or fuel vapor.

Secondary ignition system voltage

A severe electric shock can result from touching certain parts of the ignition system (such as the spark plug wires) when the engine is running or being cranked, particularly if components are damp or the insulation is defective. In the case of an electronic ignition system, the secondary system voltage is much higher and could prove fatal.

Conversion factors

Length (distance)

Inches (in)	X	25.4	= Millimetres (mm)	X 0.0394	= Inches (in)
Feet (ft)	X	0.305	= Metres (m)	X 3.281	= Feet (ft)
Miles	X	1.609	= Kilometres (km)	X 0.621	= Miles

Volume (capacity)

Cubic inches (cu in; in³)	X	16.387	= Cubic centimetres (cc; cm³)	X 0.061	= Cubic inches (cu in; in³)
Imperial pints (Imp pt)	X	0.568	= Litres (l)	X 1.76	= Imperial pints (Imp pt)
Imperial quarts (Imp qt)	X	1.137	= Litres (l)	X 0.88	= Imperial quarts (Imp qt)
Imperial quarts (Imp qt)	X	1.201	= US quarts (US qt)	X 0.833	= Imperial quarts (Imp qt)
US quarts (US qt)	X	0.946	= Litres (l)	X 1.057	= US quarts (US qt)
Imperial gallons (Imp gal)	X	4.546	= Litres (l)	X 0.22	= Imperial gallons (Imp gal)
Imperial gallons (Imp gal)	X	1.201	= US gallons (US gal)	X 0.833	= Imperial gallons (Imp gal)
US gallons (US gal)	X	3.785	= Litres (l)	X 0.264	= US gallons (US gal)

Mass (weight)

Ounces (oz)	X	28.35	= Grams (g)	X 0.035	= Ounces (oz)
Pounds (lb)	X	0.454	= Kilograms (kg)	X 2.205	= Pounds (lb)

Force

Ounces-force (ozf; oz)	X	0.278	= Newtons (N)	X 3.6	= Ounces-force (ozf; oz)
Pounds-force (lbf; lb)	X	4.448	= Newtons (N)	X 0.225	= Pounds-force (lbf; lb)
Newtons (N)	X	0.1	= Kilograms-force (kgf; kg)	X 9.81	= Newtons (N)

Pressure

Pounds-force per square inch (psi; lbf/in²; lb/in²)	X	0.070	= Kilograms-force per square centimetre (kgf/cm²; kg/cm²)	X 14.223	= Pounds-force per square inch (psi; lbf/in²; lb/in²)
Pounds-force per square inch (psi; lbf/in²; lb/in²)	X	0.068	= Atmospheres (atm)	X 14.696	= Pounds-force per square inch (psi; lbf/in²; lb/in²)
Pounds-force per square inch (psi; lbf/in²; lb/in²)	X	0.069	= Bars	X 14.5	= Pounds-force per square inch (psi; lbf/in²; lb/in²)
Pounds-force per square inch (psi; lbf/in²; lb/in²)	X	6.895	= Kilopascals (kPa)	X 0.145	= Pounds-force per square inch (psi; lbf/in²; lb/in²)
Kilopascals (kPa)	X	0.01	= Kilograms-force per square centimetre (kgf/cm²; kg/cm²)	X 98.1	= Kilopascals (kPa)

Torque (moment of force)

Pounds-force inches (lbf in; lb in)	X	1.152	= Kilograms-force centimetre (kgf cm; kg cm)	X 0.868	= Pounds-force inches (lbf in; lb in)
Pounds-force inches (lbf in; lb in)	X	0.113	= Newton metres (Nm)	X 8.85	= Pounds-force inches (lbf in; lb in)
Pounds-force inches (lbf in; lb in)	X	0.083	= Pounds-force feet (lbf ft; lb ft)	X 12	= Pounds-force inches (lbf in; lb in)
Pounds-force feet (lbf ft; lb ft)	X	0.138	= Kilograms-force metres (kgf m; kg m)	X 7.233	= Pounds-force feet (lbf ft; lb ft)
Pounds-force feet (lbf ft; lb ft)	X	1.356	= Newton metres (Nm)	X 0.738	= Pounds-force feet (lbf ft; lb ft)
Newton metres (Nm)	X	0.102	= Kilograms-force metres (kgf m; kg m)	X 9.804	= Newton metres (Nm)

Power

Horsepower (hp)	X	745.7	= Watts (W)	X 0.0013	= Horsepower (hp)

Velocity (speed)

Miles per hour (miles/hr; mph)	X	1.609	= Kilometres per hour (km/hr; kph)	X 0.621	= Miles per hour (miles/hr; mph)

Fuel consumption*

Miles per gallon, Imperial (mpg)	X	0.354	= Kilometres per litre (km/l)	X 2.825	= Miles per gallon, Imperial (mpg)
Miles per gallon, US (mpg)	X	0.425	= Kilometres per litre (km/l)	X 2.352	= Miles per gallon, US (mpg)

Temperature

Degrees Fahrenheit = (°C x 1.8) + 32   Degrees Celsius (Degrees Centigrade; °C) = (°F - 32) x 0.56

It is common practice to convert from miles per gallon (mpg) to litres/100 kilometres (l/100km), where mpg (Imperial) x l/100 km = 282 and mpg (US) x l/100 km = 235

Troubleshooting

Contents

This section provides an easy reference guide to the more common problems which may occur during the operation of your vehicle. These problems and their possible causes are grouped under headings denoting various components or systems, such as Engine, Cooling system, etc. They also refer you to the Chapter and/or Section which deals with the problem.

Remember that successful troubleshooting is not a mysterious black art practiced only by professional mechanics. It is simply the result of the right knowledge combined with an intelligent, systematic approach to the problem. Always work by a process of elimination, starting with the simplest solution and working through to the most complex — and never overlook the obvious. Anyone can run the gas tank dry or leave the lights on overnight, so don't assume that you are exempt from such oversights.

Finally, always establish a clear idea of why a problem has occurred and take steps to ensure that it doesn't happen again. If the electrical system fails because of a poor connection, check all other connections in the system to make sure that they don't fail as well. If a particular fuse continues to blow, find out why - don't just replace one fuse after another. Remember, failure of a small component can often be indicative of potential failure or incorrect functioning of a more important component or system.

Engine

1   Engine will not rotate when attempting to start

1   Battery terminal connections loose or corroded (Chapter 1).
2   Battery discharged or faulty (Chapter 1).
3   Automatic transaxle not completely engaged in Park (Chapter 7) or clutch not completely depressed (Chapter 8).
4   Broken, loose or disconnected wiring in the starting circuit (Chapters 5 and 12).
5   Starter motor pinion jammed in flywheel ring gear (Chapter 5).
6   Starter solenoid faulty (Chapter 5).
7   Starter motor faulty (Chapter 5).
8   Ignition switch faulty (Chapter 12).
9   Starter pinion or flywheel teeth worn or broken (Chapter 5).

2   Engine rotates but will not start

1   Fuel tank empty.
2   Battery discharged (engine rotates slowly) (Chapter 5).
3   Battery terminal connections loose or corroded (Chapter 1).
4   Leaking fuel injector(s), fuel pump, pressure regulator, etc. (Chapter 4).
5   Fuel not reaching fuel injection system (Chapter 4).
6   Ignition components damp or damaged (Chapter 5).
7   Worn, faulty or incorrectly gapped spark plugs (Chapter 1).
8   Broken, loose or disconnected wiring in the starting circuit (Chapter 5).
9   Loose distributor is changing ignition timing (Chapter 5).
10 Broken, loose or disconnected wires at the ignition coil or faulty coil (Chapter 5).

3   Engine hard to start when cold

1   Battery discharged or low (Chapter 1).
2   Fuel system malfunctioning (Chapter 4).
3   Injector(s) leaking (Chapter 4).
4   Distributor rotor carbon tracked (Chapter 1).

4   Engine hard to start when hot

1   Air filter clogged (Chapter 1).
2   Fuel not reaching the fuel injection system (Chapter 4).
3   Corroded battery connections, especially ground (Chapter 1).

5   Starter motor noisy or excessively rough in engagement

1   Pinion or flywheel gear teeth worn or broken (Chapter 5).
2   Starter motor mounting bolts loose or missing (Chapter 5).

6   Engine starts but stops immediately

1   Loose or faulty electrical connections at distributor, coil or alternator (Chapter 5).
2   Insufficient fuel reaching the fuel injectors (Chapter 4).
3   Vacuum leak at the gasket between the intake manifold/plenum and throttle body (Chapters 1 and 4).

7   Oil puddle under engine

1   Oil pan gasket and/or oil pan drain bolt seal leaking (Chapter 2).
2   Oil pressure sending unit leaking (Chapter 2).
3   Rocker cover gaskets leaking (Chapter 2).
4   Engine oil seals leaking (Chapter 2).
5   Timing cover sealant or sealing flange leaking (Chapter 2).

8   Engine lopes while idling or idles erratically

1   Vacuum leakage (Chapter 4).
2   Leaking EGR valve or plugged PCV valve (Chapters 1 and 6).
3   Air filter clogged (Chapter 1).
4   Fuel pump not delivering sufficient fuel to the fuel injection system (Chapter 4).
5   Leaking head gasket (Chapter 2).
6   Timing chain and/or gears worn (Chapter 2).
7   Camshaft lobes worn (Chapter 2).

9   Engine misses at idle speed

1   Spark plugs worn or not gapped properly (Chapter 1).
2   Faulty spark plug wires (Chapter 1).
3   Vacuum leaks (Chapters 1 and 4).
4   Incorrect ignition timing (Chapter 5).
5   Uneven or low compression (Chapter 2).

10   Engine misses throughout driving speed range

1   Fuel filter clogged and/or impurities in the fuel system (Chapters 1 and 4).
2   Low fuel output at the injector (Chapter 4).
3   Faulty or incorrectly gapped spark plugs (Chapter 1).
4   Incorrect ignition timing (Chapter 5).
5   Cracked distributor cap, disconnected distributor wires or damaged distributor components (Chapter 1).
6   Leaking spark plug wires (Chapter 1).
7   Faulty emission system components (Chapter 6).
8   Low or uneven cylinder compression pressures (Chapter 2).
9   Weak or faulty ignition system (Chapter 5).
10 Vacuum leak in fuel injection system, intake manifold or vacuum hoses (Chapter 4).

11   Engine stumbles on acceleration

1   Spark plugs fouled (Chapter 1).
2   Fuel injection system needs adjustment or repair (Chapter 4).
3   Fuel filter clogged (Chapter 1).
4   Incorrect ignition timing (Chapter 5).
5   Intake manifold air leak (Chapter 4).

12 Engine surges while holding accelerator steady

1 Intake air leak (Chapter 4).
2 Fuel pump faulty (Chapter 4).
3 Loose fuel injector harness connections (Chapter 4).
4 Defective ECM (Chapter 6).

13 Engine hard to start and surges when cold (1986 Oldsmobile Calais with 3.0L V6 engine only)

A General Motors dealer technical service bulletin concerning this problem has been issued. Take the vehicle to your dealer and inform him of the problem.

14 Engine stalls

1 Idle speed incorrect (Chapters 1 and 4).
2 Fuel filter clogged and/or water and impurities in the fuel system (Chapters 1 and 4).
3 Distributor components damp or damaged (Chapter 5).
4 Faulty emissions system components (Chapter 6).
5 Faulty or incorrectly gapped spark plugs (Chapter 1).
6 Faulty spark plug wires (Chapter 1).
7 Vacuum leak in the fuel injection system, intake manifold or vacuum hoses (Chapter 4).

15 Engine lacks power

1 Incorrect ignition timing (Chapter 5).
2 Excessive play in distributor shaft (Chapter 5).
3 Worn rotor, distributor cap or wires (Chapter 1).
4 Faulty or incorrectly gapped spark plugs (Chapter 1).
5 Fuel injection system out of adjustment or malfunctioning (Chapter 4).
6 Faulty coil (Chapter 5).
7 Brakes binding (Chapter 1).
8 Automatic transaxle fluid level incorrect (Chapter 1).
9 Clutch slipping (Chapter 8).
10 Fuel filter clogged and/or impurities in the fuel system (Chapter 1).
11 Emission control system not functioning properly (Chapter 6).
12 Low or uneven cylinder compression pressures (Chapter 2).

16 Engine backfires

1 Emissions system not functioning properly (Chapter 6).
2 Ignition timing incorrect (Chapter 5).
3 Faulty secondary ignition system (cracked spark plug insulator, faulty plug wires, distributor cap and/or rotor) (Chapter 1).
4 Fuel injection system in need of adjustment or worn excessively (Chapter 4).
5 Vacuum leak at fuel injectors, intake manifold or vacuum hoses (Chapter 4).
6 Valves sticking (Chapter 2).

17 Pinging or knocking engine sounds during acceleration or uphill

1 Incorrect grade of fuel.
2 Ignition timing incorrect (Chapter 5).
3 Fuel injection system in need of adjustment (Chapter 4).
4 Improper or damaged spark plugs or wires (Chapter 1).
5 Worn or damaged distributor components (Chapter 5).
6 Faulty emissions system (Chapter 6).
7 Vacuum leak (Chapter 4).

18 Engine runs with oil pressure light on

1 Low oil level (Chapter 1).
2 Idle rpm below specification (Chapter 1).
3 Short in wiring circuit (Chapter 12).
4 Faulty oil pressure sender (Chapter 2).
5 Worn engine bearings and/or oil pump (Chapter 2).

19 Engine diesels (continues to run) after switching off

1 Idle speed too high (Chapters 1 and 4).
2 Thermo-controlled air cleaner heat valve not operating properly (TBI equipped engines only) (Chapter 6).
3 Excessive engine operating temperature (Chapter 3).

Engine electrical system

20 Battery will not hold a charge

1 Alternator drivebelt defective or not adjusted properly (Chapter 1).
2 Battery terminals loose or corroded (Chapter 1).
3 Alternator not charging properly (Chapter 5).
4 Loose, broken or faulty wiring in the charging circuit (Chapter 5).
5 Short in vehicle wiring (Chapters 5 and 12).
6 Internally defective battery (Chapters 1 and 5).

21 Voltage warning light fails to go out

1 Faulty alternator or charging circuit (Chapter 5).
2 Alternator drivebelt defective or out of adjustment (Chapter 1).
3 Alternator voltage regulator inoperative (Chapter 5).

22 Voltage warning light fails to come on when key is turned on

1 Warning light bulb defective (Chapter 12).
2 Fault in the printed circuit, dash wiring or bulb holder (Chapter 12).

Fuel system

23 Excessive fuel consumption

1 Dirty or clogged air filter element (Chapter 1).
2 Incorrectly set ignition timing (Chapter 5).
3 Emissions system not functioning properly (Chapter 6).
4 Fuel injection internal parts excessively worn or damaged (Chapter 4).
5 Low tire pressure or incorrect tire size (Chapter 1).

24 Fuel leakage and/or fuel odor

1 Leak in a fuel feed or vent line (Chapter 4).
2 Tank overfilled.
3 Evaporative canister filter clogged (Chapters 1 and 6).
4 Fuel injector internal parts excessively worn (Chapter 4).

Cooling system

25 Overheating

1 Insufficient coolant in system (Chapter 1).
2 Water pump drivebelt defective or out of adjustment (Chapter 1).
3 Radiator core blocked or grille restricted (Chapter 3).

4   Thermostat faulty (Chapter 3).
5   Electric cooling fan blades broken or cracked (Chapter 3).
6   Radiator cap not maintaining proper pressure (Chapter 3).
7   Ignition timing incorrect (Chapter 5).

26   Overcooling

Faulty thermostat (Chapter 3).

27   External coolant leakage

1   Deteriorated/damaged hoses or loose clamps (Chapters 1 and 3).
2   Water pump seal defective (Chapters 1 and 3).
3   Leakage from radiator core or header tank (Chapter 3).
4   Engine drain or water jacket core plugs leaking (Chapter 2).

28   Internal coolant leakage

1   Leaking cylinder head gasket (Chapter 2).
2   Cracked cylinder bore or cylinder head (Chapter 2).

29   Coolant loss

1   Too much coolant in system (Chapter 1).
2   Coolant boiling away because of overheating (Chapter 3).
3   Internal or external leakage (Chapter 3).
4   Faulty radiator cap (Chapter 3).

30   Poor coolant circulation

1   Inoperative water pump (Chapter 3).
2   Restriction in cooling system (Chapters 1 and 3).
3   Water pump drivebelt defective or out of adjustment (Chapter 1).
4   Thermostat sticking (Chapter 3).

31   Drivebelt squeals or chirps (1986 Pontiac Grand Am with 3.0L V6 engine only)

A General Motors dealer technical service bulletin concerning this problem has been issued. Take the vehicle to your dealer and inform him of the problem.

Clutch

32   Pedal travels to floor — no pressure or very little resistance

1   Master or slave cylinder faulty (Chapter 8).
2   Hose/pipe burst or leaking (Chapter 8).
3   Connections leaking (Chapter 8).
4   No fluid in reservoir (Chapter 8).
5   If fluid is present in master cylinder dust cover, rear master cylinder seal has failed (Chapter 8).
6   If fluid level in reservoir rises as pedal is depressed, master cylinder center valve seal is faulty (Chapter 8).
7   Broken release bearing or fork (Chapter 8).

33   Fluid in area of master cylinder dust cover and on pedal

Rear seal failure in master cylinder (Chapter 8).

34   Fluid on slave cylinder

Slave cylinder seal faulty (Chapter 8).

35   Pedal feels spongy when depressed

Air in system (Chapter 8).

36   Unable to select gears

1   Faulty transaxle (Chapter 7).
2   Faulty clutch disc (Chapter 8).
3   Fork and bearing not assembled properly (Chapter 8).
4   Faulty pressure plate (Chapter 8).
5   Pressure plate-to-flywheel bolts loose (Chapter 8).

37   Clutch slips (engine speed increases with no increase in vehicle speed)

1   Clutch plate worn (Chapter 8).
2   Clutch plate is oil soaked by leaking rear main seal (Chapter 8).
3   Clutch plate not seated. It may take 30 or 40 normal starts for a new one to seat.
4   Warped pressure plate or flywheel (Chapter 8).
5   Weak diaphragm spring (Chapter 8).
6   Clutch plate overheated. Allow to cool.

38   Grabbing (chattering) as clutch is engaged

1   Oil soaked, burned or glazed linings (Chapter 8).
2   Worn or loose engine or transaxle mounts (Chapters 2 and 7).
3   Worn splines on clutch plate hub (Chapter 8).
4   Warped pressure plate or flywheel (Chapter 8).

39   Noise in clutch area

1   Fork shaft improperly installed (Chapter 8).
2   Faulty release bearing (Chapter 8).

40   Clutch pedal stays on floor

1   Fork shaft binding in housing (Chapter 8).
2   Broken release bearing or fork (Chapter 8).

41   High pedal effort

1   Fork shaft binding in housing (Chapter 8).
2   Pressure plate faulty (Chapter 8).

Manual transaxle

42   Vibration

1   Rough wheel bearing (Chapter 10).
2   Damaged driveaxle (Chapter 8).
3   Out-of-round tires (Chapter 1).
4   Tire out-of-balance (Chapter 10).
5   Worn or damaged CV joint (Chapter 8).

43 Noisy in Neutral with engine running

Damaged clutch release bearing (Chapter 8).

44 Noisy in one particular gear

1   Damaged or worn constant mesh gears (Chapter 7).
2   Damaged or worn synchronizers (Chapter 7).

45 Noisy in all gears

1   Insufficient lubricant (Chapter 1).
2   Damaged or worn bearings (Chapter 7).
3   Worn or damaged input gear shaft and/or output gear shaft (Chapter 7).

46 Slips out of gear

1   Worn or improperly adjusted linkage (Chapter 7).
2   Transaxle loose on engine (Chapter 7).
3   Shift linkage does not work freely, binds (Chapter 7).
4   Input shaft bearing retainer broken or loose (Chapter 7).
5   Dirt between clutch cover and engine housing (Chapter 7).
6   Worn shift fork (Chapter 7).

47 Leaks lubricant

1   Excessive amount of lubricant in transaxle (Chapter 1).
2   Loose or broken input shaft bearing retainer (Chapter 7).
3   Input shaft bearing retainer O-ring and/or lip seal damaged (Chapter 7).

Automatic transaxle

Note: *Due to the complexity of the automatic transaxle, it is difficult for the home mechanic to properly diagnose and service this component. For problems other than the following, the vehicle should be taken to a dealer or transmission shop.*

48 Fluid leakage

1   Automatic transmission fluid is a deep red color. Fluid leaks should not be confused with engine oil, which can easily be blown by air flow to the transaxle.
2   To pinpoint a leak, first remove all built-up dirt and grime from the transaxle housing with degreasing agents and/or steam cleaning. Drive the vehicle at low speeds so air flow will not blow the leak far from its source. Raise the vehicle and determine where the leak is coming from. Common areas of leakage are:

   a) Pan (Chapters 1 and 7)
   b) Filler pipe (Chapter 7)
   c) Transaxle oil lines (Chapter 7)
   d) Speedometer gear or sensor (Chapter 7)
   e) Modulator

49 Transaxle fluid brown or has a burned smell

Transaxle overheated. Change fluid (Chapter 1).

50 General shift mechanism problems

1   Chapter 7 Part B deals with checking and adjusting the shift linkage on automatic transaxles. Common problems which may be attributed to poorly adjusted linkage are:

   a) Engine starting in gears other than Park or Neutral.
   b) Indicator on shifter pointing to a gear other than the one actually being used.
   c) Vehicle moves when in Park.
2   Refer to Chapter 7 Part B for the shift linkage adjustment procedure.

51 Transaxle will not downshift with accelerator pedal pressed to the floor

Throttle valve (TV) cable out of adjustment (Chapter 7).

52 Engine will start in gears other than Park or Neutral

Starter safety switch malfunctioning (Chapter 7).

53 Transaxle slips, shifts roughly, is noisy or has no drive in forward or reverse gears

There are many probable causes for the above problems, but the home mechanic should be concerned with only one possibility — fluid level. Before taking the vehicle to a repair shop, check the level and condition of the fluid as described in Chapter 1.
Correct the fluid level as necessary or change the fluid and filter if needed. If the problem persists, have a professional diagnose the probable cause.

Driveaxles

54 Clicking noise in turns

Worn or damaged outer CV joint. Check for cut or damaged boots (Chapter 1). Repair as necessary (Chapter 8).

55 Knock or clunk when accelerating after coasting

Worn or damaged outer CV joint. Check for cut or damaged boots (Chapter 1). Repair as necessary (Chapter 8).

56 Shudder or vibration during acceleration

1   Excessive inner CV joint angle. Check and correct as necessary (Chapter 8).
2   Worn or damaged CV joints. Repair or replace as necessary (Chapter 8).
3   Sticking inboard joint assembly. Correct or replace as necessary (Chapter 8).

Brakes

Note: *Before assuming that a brake problem exists, make sure that:*
   a) The tires are in good condition and properly inflated (Chapter 1).
   b) The front end alignment is correct (Chapter 10).
   c) The vehicle is not loaded with weight in an unequal manner.

57 Vehicle pulls to one side during braking

1   Incorrect tire pressures (Chapter 1).
2   Front end out of line (have the front end aligned).
3   Unmatched tires on same axle.
4   Restricted brake lines or hoses (Chapter 9).
5   Malfunctioning brake assembly (Chapter 9).
6   Loose suspension parts (Chapter 10).
7   Loose brake calipers (Chapter 9).

58 Noise (high-pitched squeal when the brakes are applied)

Front disc brake pads worn out. The noise comes from the wear sensor rubbing against the disc. Replace pads with new ones immediately (Chapter 9).

59 Brake roughness or chatter (pedal pulsates)

1   Excessive front brake disc lateral runout (Chapter 9).
2   Parallelism not within specifications (Chapter 9).
3   Uneven pad wear caused by caliper not sliding due to improper clearance or dirt (Chapter 9).
4   Defective brake disc (Chapter 9).
5   Rear brake drum out-of-round.

60 Excessive pedal effort required to stop vehicle

1   Malfunctioning power brake booster (Chapter 9).
2   Partial system failure (Chapter 9).
3   Excessively worn pads or shoes (Chapter 9).
4   One or more caliper pistons or wheel cylinders seized or sticking (Chapter 9).
5   Brake pads or shoes contaminated with oil or grease (Chapter 9).
6   New pads or shoes installed and not yet seated. It will take a while for the new material to seat.

61 Excessive brake pedal travel

1   Partial brake system failure (Chapter 9).
2   Insufficient fluid in master cylinder (Chapters 1 and 9).
3   Air trapped in system (Chapters 1 and 9).

62 Dragging brakes

1   Master cylinder pistons not returning correctly (Chapter 9).
2   Restricted brakes lines or hoses (Chapters 1 and 9).
3   Incorrect parking brake adjustment (Chapter 9).

63 Grabbing or uneven braking action

1   Malfunction of proportioner valves (Chapter 9).
2   Malfunction of power brake booster unit (Chapter 9).
3   Binding brake pedal mechanism (Chapter 9).

64 Brake pedal feels spongy when depressed

1   Air in hydraulic lines (Chapter 9).
2   Master cylinder mounting bolts loose (Chapter 9).
3   Master cylinder defective (Chapter 9).

65 Brake pedal travels to the floor with little resistance

Little or no fluid in the master cylinder reservoir caused by leaking caliper or wheel cylinder pistons, loose, damaged or disconnected brake lines (Chapter 9).

66 Parking brake does not hold

Parking brake linkage improperly adjusted (Chapter 9).

Suspension and steering systems

Note: Before attempting to diagnose the suspension and steering systems, perform the following preliminary checks:
   a) Tires for wrong pressure and uneven wear.
   b) Steering universal joints or coupling from the column to the steering gear for loose fasteners or wear.
   c) Front and rear suspension and the steering gear assembly for loose or damaged parts.
   d) Out-of-round or out-of-balance tires, bent rims and loose and/or rough wheel bearings.

67 Vehicle pulls to one side

1   Mismatched or uneven tires (Chapter 10).
2   Broken or sagging springs (Chapter 10).
3   Front wheel alignment incorrect (Chapter 10).
4   Front brakes dragging (Chapter 9).

68 Abnormal or excessive tire wear

1   Front wheel alignment incorrect (Chapter 10).
2   Sagging or broken springs (Chapter 10).
3   Tire out-of-balance (Chapter 10).
4   Worn shock absorber (Chapter 10).
5   Overloaded vehicle.
6   Tires not rotated regularly.

69 Wheel makes a 'thumping' noise

1   Blister or bump on tire (Chapter 1).
2   Improper shock absorber action (Chapter 10).

70 Shimmy, shake or vibration

1   Tire or wheel out-of-balance or out-of-round (Chapter 10).
2   Loose or worn wheel bearings (Chapter 10).
3   Worn tie-rod ends (Chapter 10).
4   Worn balljoints (Chapter 10).
5   Excessive wheel runout (Chapter 10).
6   Blister or bump on tire (Chapter 1).

71 Hard steering

1   Lack of lubrication at balljoints, tie-rod ends and steering gear assembly (Chapter 10).
2   Front wheel alignment incorrect (Chapter 10).
3   Low tire pressure (Chapter 1).

72 Steering wheel does not return to center position correctly

1   Lack of lubrication at balljoints and tie-rod ends (Chapter 10).
2   Binding in steering column (Chapter 10).
3   Lack of lubricant in steering gear assembly (Chapter 10).
4   Front wheel alignment (Chapter 10).

73 Squeaking or squawking noise from the front stabilizer bar bushings (1985 and 1986 Oldsmobile Calais, 1985 and 1986 Pontiac Grand Am and 1986 Buick Somerset only)

A General Motors dealer technical service bulletin concerning this problem has been issued. Take the vehicle to your dealer and inform him of the problem.

74 Abnormal noise at the front end

1   Lack of lubrication at balljoints and tie-rod ends (Chapter 1).
2   Loose upper strut mounting (Chapter 10).
3   Worn tie-rod ends (Chapter 10).
4   Loose stabilizer bar (Chapter 10).
5   Loose wheel lug nuts (Chapters 1 and 10).
6   Loose suspension bolts (Chapter 10).

75 Wander or poor steering stability

1   Mismatched or uneven tires (Chapter 10).
2   Lack of lubrication at balljoints or tie-rod ends (Chapters 1 and 10).
3   Worn shock absorbers (Chapter 10).
4   Loose stabilizer bar (Chapter 10).
5   Broken or sagging springs (Chapter 10).
6   Front wheel alignment incorrect (Chapter 10).
7   Worn steering gear clamp bushings (Chapter 10).

76 Erratic steering when braking

1   Wheel bearings worn (Chapters 8 and 10).
2   Broken or sagging springs (Chapter 10).
3   Leaking wheel cylinder or caliper (Chapter 10).
4   Warped rotors or brake drums (Chapter 10).
5   Worn steering gear clamp bushings (Chapter 10).

77 Excessive pitching and/or rolling around corners or during braking

1   Loose stabilizer bar (Chapter 10).
2   Worn shock absorbers or mounts (Chapter 10).
3   Broken or sagging springs (Chapter 10).
4   Overloaded vehicle.

78 Suspension bottoms

1   Overloaded vehicle.
2   Worn shock absorbers (Chapter 10).
3   Incorrect, broken or sagging springs (Chapter 10).

79 Cupped tires

1   Front wheel alignment incorrect (Chapter 10).
2   Worn shock absorbers (Chapter 10).
3   Wheel bearings worn (Chapters 8 and 10).
4   Excessive tire or wheel runout (Chapter 10).
5   Worn balljoints (Chapter 10).

80 Excessive tire wear on outside edge

1   Inflation pressures incorrect (Chapter 1).
2   Excessive speed in turns.
3   Front end alignment incorrect (excessive toe-in or positive camber).
Have professionally aligned.
4   Suspension arm bent or twisted (Chapter 10).

81 Excessive tire wear on inside edge

1   Inflation pressures incorrect (Chapter 1).
2   Front end alignment incorrect (toe-out or excessive negative camber). Have professionally aligned.
3   Loose or damaged steering components (Chapter 10).

82 Tire tread worn in one place

1   Tires out-of-balance.
2   Damaged or buckled wheel. Inspect and replace if necessary.
3   Defective tire (Chapter 1).

83 Excessive play or looseness in steering system

1   Wheel bearings worn (Chapter 10).
2   Tie-rod end loose or worn (Chapter 10).
3   Steering gear loose (Chapter 10).

84 Rattling or clicking noise in rack and pinion

Steering gear clamps loose (Chapter 10).

Chapter 1 Tune up and routine maintenance

Contents

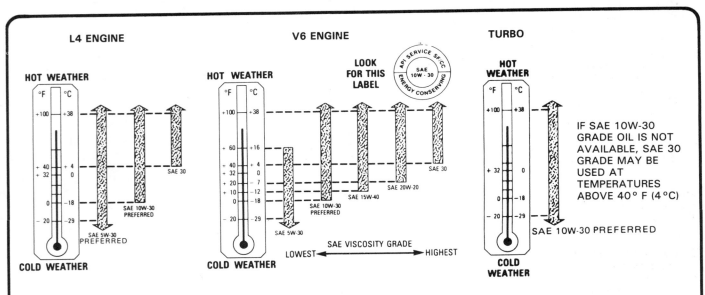

For best fuel economy and cold starting, select the lowest SAE viscosity grade oil for the expected temperature range.

ENGINE OIL VISCOSITY RECOMMENDATIONS

Specifications

Recommended lubricants and fluids

Engine oil type	SF, SF/CC or SF/CD
Engine oil viscosity	See accompanying charts
Automatic transaxle fluid	Dexron II Automatic Transmission Fluid (ATF)
Manual transaxle lubricant	
RPO MG1/MG2 (Muncie)	SAE 5W30 oil (GM part number 10036600)
RPO MK7/MT2 (Isuzu)	Dexron II Automatic Transmission Fluid (ATF)
Engine coolant	Mixture of water and good quality ethylene glycol-base antifreeze
Brake fluid	Delco Supreme II or DOT 3 fluid
Clutch fluid	Delco Supreme II or DOT 3 fluid
Power steering fluid	GM power steering fluid or equivalent
Chassis lubrication	Multi-purpose lithium-base chassis grease meeting the specifications of GM-6031M

General

Spark plug type and gap	Refer to *Vehicle Emission Control Information label* located in the engine compartment
Ignition timing	Refer to *Vehicle Emission Control Information label* located in the engine compartment
Firing order	
2.5L four-cylinder engine	1-3-4-2
2.0L four-cylinder engine	1-3-4-2
3.0L V6 engine	1-6-5-4-3-2
Engine idle speed	Not owner adjustable (see Section 26)
Drivebelt tension	
conventional drivebelt (V-belt)	
alternator and air conditioning compressor	
new belt	155 lbs
used belt	75 lbs
power steering pump	
new belt	200 lbs
used belt	150 lbs
serpentine drivebelt	67 lbs
Radiator cap pressure rating	15 psi

Filters

Oil filter type	
2.0 and 2.5L four-cylinder (engine block mounted)	AC type PF47
2.5L four-cylinder (oil pan mounted)	AC type PF1072
3.0L V6 engine	AC type PF47
Air filter type	
2.5L four-cylinder engine	AC type 785C
2.0L four-cylinder engine	AC type GF481
3.0L V6 engine	
1984 through 1986 models	AC type 861C
1987 models	AC type A875C or A913C
PCV valve	
2.5L four-cylinder engine	
1984 through 1986 models	AC type CV881C
1987 models	AC type CV895C
2.0L four-cylinder engine	AC type CV873C
3.0L V6 engine	
1984 through 1986 models	AC type CV878C
1987 models	AC type CV781C
PCV filter	AC type FB86
Fuel filter	AC type GF481

Brakes

Brake pad wear limit	1/8 in
Brake shoe wear limit	1/16 in

Torque specifications

	Ft-lbs
Throttle body nuts	12
Spark plugs	
2.5L four-cylinder engine	10 to 15
2.0L four-cylinder turbocharged engine	7 to 10
3.0L V6 engine	20
Engine oil drain plug	15 to 20
Automatic transaxle oil pan bolts	8 to 10

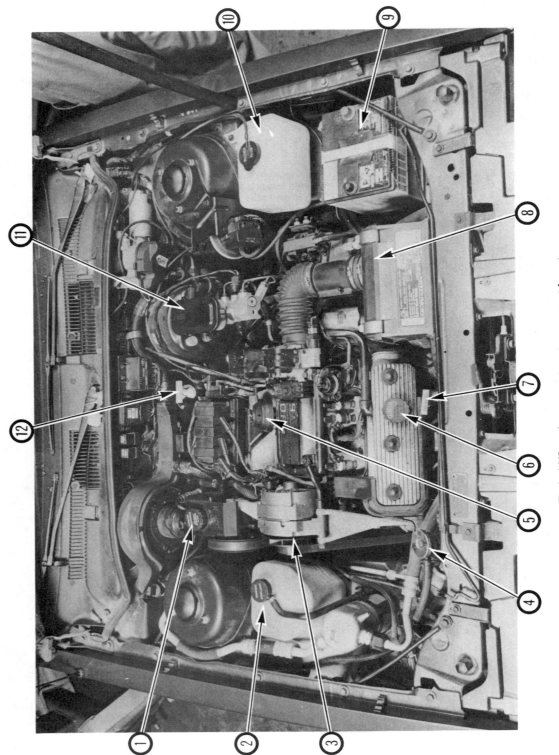

Typical V6 engine compartment component layout

1 Power steering dipstick
2 Coolant reservoir
3 Alternator
4 Radiator cap
5 EGR valve
6 Engine oil filler cap
7 Engine oil dipstick
8 Air cleaner assembly
9 Battery
10 Windshield washer fluid reservoir
11 Brake fluid reservoir
12 Automatic transaxle dipstick

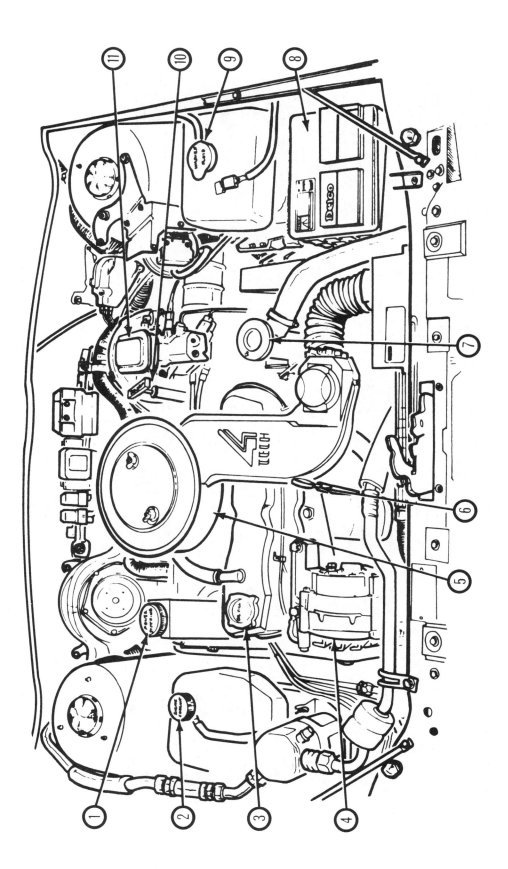

Typical 2.5L four-cylinder engine compartment component layout

1 Power steering fluid dipstick
2 Coolant reservoir
3 Engine oil filler cap
4 Alternator

5 Air cleaner assembly
6 Engine oil dipstick
7 Thermostat housing cap
8 Battery

9 Windshield washer
  fluid reservoir
10 Automatic transaxle dipstick
11 Brake fluid reservoir

1

Underside view of engine/transaxle (V6 shown)

1 CV joint boot
2 Automatic transaxle
3 Exhaust pipe
4 Engine oil filter
5 Engine oil drain plug
6 Disc brake caliper

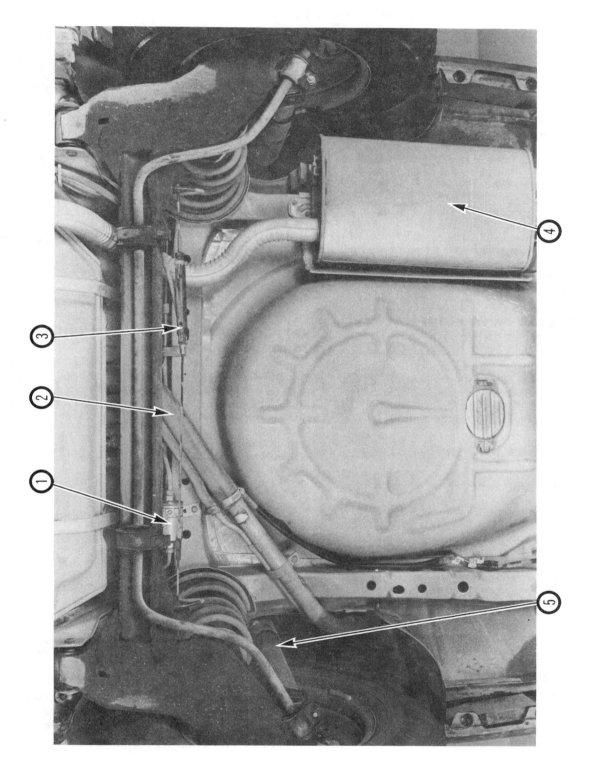

Typical rear underside component layout

1 Fuel filter   3 Parking brake cable   5 Shock absorber
2 Fuel tank filler hose and pipe   4 Muffler

1

1 GM N-car Maintenance schedule

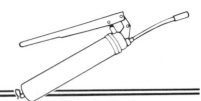

The following maintenance intervals are based on the assumption that the vehicle owner will be doing the maintenance or service work, as opposed to having a dealer service department do the work. Although the time/mileage intervals are loosely based on factory recommendations, most have been shortened to ensure, for example, that such items as lubricants and fluids are checked/changed at intervals that promote maximum engine/driveline service life. Also, subject to the preference of the individual owner interested in keeping his or her vehicle in peak condition at all times, and with the vehicle's ultimate resale in mind, many of the maintenance procedures may be performed more often than recommended in the following schedule. We encourage such owner initiative.

When the vehicle is new it should be serviced initially by a factory authorized dealer service department to protect the factory warranty. In many cases the initial maintenance check is done at no cost to the owner (check with your dealer service department for more information).

Every 250 miles or weekly, whichever comes first

Check the engine oil level (Section 4)
Check the engine coolant level (Section 4)
Check the windshield washer fluid level (Section 4)
Check the brake and clutch fluid levels (Section 4)
Check the tires and tire pressures (Section 5)

Every 3000 miles or 3 months, whichever comes first

All items listed above plus:
Change the engine oil and filter (turbocharged engines) (Section 13)
Check the automatic transaxle fluid level (Section 6)*
Check the power steering fluid level (Section 7)*
Check and service the battery (Section 8)
Check the cooling system (Section 9)
Inspect and replace if necessary all underhood hoses (Section 10)
Inspect and replace if necessary the windshield wiper blades (Section 11)

Every 5000 miles or 5 months, whichever comes first

Adjust the clutch pedal (1984 and 1985 models) (Section 12)

Every 7500 miles or 12 months, whichever comes first

All items listed above plus:
Change the engine oil and filter (Section 13)*

Lubricate the chassis components (Section 14)
Check the driveaxle boots (Section 15)
Inspect the suspension and steering components (Section 16)*
Inspect the exhaust system (Section 17)*
Check the manual transaxle lubricant level (Section 18)*
Rotate the tires (Section 19)
Check the brakes (Section 20)*
Inspect the fuel system (Section 21)
Replace the air filter and PCV filter (Section 22)
Check the throttle body mounting nut torque (Section 23)
Check the throttle linkage (Section 24)
Check the thermostatically-controlled air cleaner (2.5L engine) (Section 25)
Check the engine idle speed (Section 26)
Check the engine drivebelts (Section 27)
Check the seat belts (Section 28)
Check the starter safety switch (Section 29)
Check the seatback latch (Section 30)
Check the spare tire and jack (Section 31)

Every 30,000 miles or 24 months, whichever comes first

All items listed above plus:
Replace the fuel filter (Section 32)
Change the automatic transaxle fluid (Section 33)**
Change the manual transaxle lubricant (Section 34)
Service the cooling system (drain, flush and refill) (Section 35)
Inspect and replace if necessary the PCV valve (Section 36)
Inspect the evaporative emissions control system (Section 37)
Check the EGR system (Section 38)
Replace the spark plugs (Section 39)
Inspect the spark plug wires, distributor cap and rotor (Section 40)
Check and adjust if necessary the ignition timing (see Chapter 4)

* This item is affected by ''severe'' operating conditions as described below. If your vehicle is operated under severe conditions, perform all maintenance indicated with an asterisk (*) at 3000 mile/3 month intervals.

Severe conditions are indicated if you mainly operate your vehicle under one or more of the following:

Operating in dusty areas
Towing a trailer
Idling for extended periods and/or low speed operation
Operating when outside temperatures remain below freezing and when most trips are less than 4 miles

** If operated under one or more of the following conditions, change the automatic transaxle fluid every 15,000 miles:

In heavy city traffic where the outside temperature regularly reaches 90°F (32°C) or higher
In hilly or mountainous terrain
Frequent trailer pulling

2 Introduction

This Chapter is designed to help the home mechanic maintain the GM N-car with the goals of maximum performance, economy, safety and reliability in mind.

Included is a master maintenance schedule (page 34), followed by procedures dealing specifically with each item on the schedule. Visual checks, adjustments, component replacement and other helpful items are included. Refer to the accompanying illustrations of the engine compartment and the underside of the vehicle for the locations of various components.

Servicing your vehicle in accordance with the mileage/time maintenance schedule and the step-by-step procedures will result in a planned maintenance program that should produce a long and reliable service life. Keep in mind that it is a comprehensive plan, so maintaining some items but not others at the specified intervals will not produce the same results.

As you service your vehicle, you will discover that many of the procedures can — and should — be grouped together because of the nature of the particular procedure you're performing or because of the close proximity of two otherwise unrelated omponents to one another.

For example, if the vehicle is raised for chassis lubrication, you should inspect the exhaust, suspension, steering and fuel systems while you're under the vehicle. When you're rotating the tires, it makes good sense to check the brakes since the wheels are already removed. Finally, let's suppose you have to borrow or rent a torque wrench. Even if you only need it to tighten the spark plugs, you might as well check the torque of as many critical fasteners as time allows.

The first step in this maintenance program is to prepare yourself before the actual work begins. Read through all the procedures you're planning to do, then gather up all the parts and tools needed. If it looks like you might run into problems during a particular job, seek advice from a mechanic or an experienced do-it-yourselfer.

3 Tune-up general information

The term *tune-up* is used in this manual to represent a combination of individual operations rather than one specific procedure.

If, from the time the vehicle is new, the routine maintenance schedule is followed closely and frequent checks are made of fluid levels and high wear items, as suggested throughout this manual, the engine will be kept in relatively good running condition and the need for additional work will be minimized.

More likely than not, however, there will be times when the engine is running poorly due to lack of regular maintenance. This is even more likely if a used vehicle, which has not received regular and frequent maintenance checks, is purchased. In such cases, an engine tune-up will be needed outside of the regular routine maintenance intervals.

The first step in any tune-up or diagnostic procedure to help correct a poor running engine is a cylinder compression check. A compression check (see Chapter 2 Part D) will help determine the condition of internal engine components and should be used as a guide for tune-up and repair procedures. If, for instance, a compression check indicates serious internal engine wear, a conventional tune-up will not improve the performance of the engine and would be a waste of time and money. Because of its importance, the compression check should be done by someone with the right equipment and the knowledge to use it properly.

The following procedures are those most often needed to bring a generally poor running engine back into a proper state of tune.

Minor tune-up

Clean, inspect and test the battery (Section 8)
Check all engine related fluids (Section 4)
Check and adjust the drivebelts (Section 27)
Replace the spark plugs (Section 39)
Inspect the distributor cap and rotor (Section 40)
Inspect the spark plug and coil wires (Section 40)
Check and adjust the ignition timing (Chapter 5)
Check the PCV valve (Section 36)
Check the air and PCV filters (Section 22)
Check the cooling system (Section 9)
Check all underhood hoses (Section 10)

Major tune-up

All items listed under Minor tune-up plus . . .
Check the EGR system (Chapter 6)
Check the ignition system (Chapter 5)
Check the charging system (Chapter 5)
Check the fuel system (Section 21)
Replace the air and PCV filters (Section 22)
Replace the distributor cap and rotor (Section 40)
Replace the spark plug wires (Section 40)

4 Fluid level checks

Refer to illustrations 4.2, 4.4, 4.9, 4.14 and 4.18
Note: *The following are fluid level checks to be done on a 250 mile or weekly basis. Additional fluid level checks can be found in specific maintenance procedures which follow. Regardless of intervals, be alert to fluid leaks under the vehicle which would indicate a problem to be corrected immediately.*

1   Fluids are an essential part of the lubrication, cooling, brake and windshield washer systems. Because the fluids gradually become depleted and/or contaminated during normal operation of the vehicle, they must be periodically replenished. See *Recommended lubricants, fluids and capacities* at the beginning of this Chapter before adding fluid to any of the following components. **Note:** *The vehicle must be on level ground when fluid levels are checked.*

Engine oil

2   The engine oil level is checked with a dipstick **(see illustration)**. The dipstick extends through a metal tube down into the oil pan.
3   The oil level should be checked before the vehicle has been driven, or about 15 minutes after the engine has been shut off. If the oil is checked immediately after driving the vehicle, some of the oil will remain in the upper part of the engine, resulting in an inaccurate reading on the dipstick.

4.2   If you have a V6 engine, the oil dipstick T-handle is clearly marked ''engine oil'' (arrow), as is the oil filler cap which threads into the rocker arm cover (arrow)

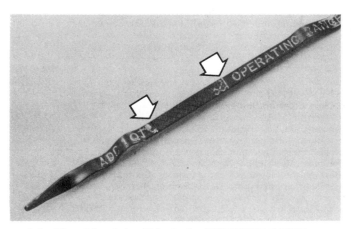

**4.4   The oil level should be in the OPERATING RANGE —
if it's below the ADD line, add enough oil to bring the level
into the OPERATING RANGE (cross-hatched area)**

**4.9   The coolant level must be maintained between the
FULL HOT and FULL COLD marks on the reservoir**

4   Pull the dipstick from the tube and wipe all the oil from the end with a clean rag or paper towel. Insert the clean dipstick all the way back into the tube and pull it out again. Note the oil at the end of the dipstick. Add oil as necessary to keep the level above the ADD mark in the OPERATING RANGE of the dipstick **(see illustration)**.

5   Do not overfill the engine by adding too much oil since this may result in oil fouled spark plugs, oil leaks or oil seal failures.

6   Oil is added to the engine after removing a twist off cap located on the rocker arm or camshaft cover **(see illustration 4.2)**. An oil can spout or funnel may help to reduce spills.

7   Checking the oil level is an important preventive maintenance step. A consistently low oil level indicates oil leakage through damaged seals, defective gaskets or past worn rings or valve guides. If the oil looks milky in color or has water droplets in it, the cylinder head gasket may be blown or the head or block may be cracked. The engine should be checked immediately. The condition of the oil should also be checked. Whenever you check the oil level, slide your thumb and index finger up the dipstick before wiping off the oil. If you see small dirt or metal particles clinging to the dipstick, the oil should be changed (Section 13).

Engine coolant

Warning: *Do not allow antifreeze to come in contact with your skin or painted surfaces of the vehicle. Flush contaminated areas immediately with plenty of water. Do not store new coolant or leave old coolant lying around where it's accessible to children or pets — they are attracted by its sweet taste. Ingestion of even a small amount of coolant can be fatal! Wipe up garage floor and drip pan coolant spills immediately. Keep antifreeze containers covered and repair leaks in your cooling system immediately.*

8   All vehicles covered by this manual are equipped with a pressurized coolant recovery system. A white plastic coolant reservoir located in the right front corner of the engine compartment is connected by a hose to the radiator filler neck. If the engine overheats, coolant escapes through a valve in the radiator cap and travels through the hose into the reservoir. As the engine cools, the coolant is automatically drawn back into the cooling system to maintain the correct level.

9   The coolant level in the reservoir should be checked regularly. **Warning:** *Do not remove the radiator cap to check the coolant level when the engine is warm.* The level in the reservoir varies with the temperature of the engine. When the engine is cold, the coolant level should be at or slightly above the FULL COLD mark on the reservoir. Once the engine has warmed up, the level should be at or near the FULL HOT mark **(see illustration)**. If it isn't, allow the engine to cool, then remove the cap from the reservoir and add a 50/50 mixture of ethylene glycol based antifreeze and water.

10   Drive the vehicle and recheck the coolant level. If only a small amount of coolant is required to bring the system up to the proper level, water can be used. However, repeated additions of water will dilute the antifreeze and water solution. In order to maintain the proper ratio of antifreeze and water, always top up the coolant level with the correct mixture. An empty plastic milk jug or bleach bottle makes an excellent container for mixing coolant. Do not use rust inhibitors or additives.

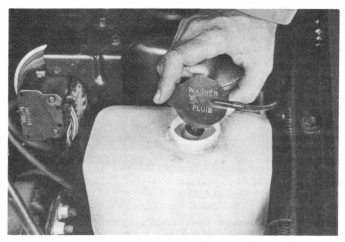

**4.14   The reservoir for the windshield washer is located in
the left corner of the engine compartment and fluid is
added after pulling the top up and out — how often you
use the washers will dictate how often you need to
check the reservoir**

11   If the coolant level drops consistently, there may be a leak in the system. Inspect the radiator, hoses, filler cap, drain plugs and water pump (see Section 9). If no leaks are noted, have the radiator cap pressure tested by a service station.

12   If you have to remove the radiator cap, wait until the engine has cooled completely, then wrap a thick cloth around the cap and turn it to the first stop. If coolant or steam escapes, let the engine cool down longer, then remove the cap.

13   Check the condition of the coolant as well. It should be relatively clear. If it is brown or rust colored, the system should be drained, flushed and refilled. Even if the coolant appears to be normal, the corrosion inhibitors wear out, so it must be replaced at the specified intervals.

Windshield washer fluid

14   Fluid for the windshield washer system is located in a plastic reservoir on the left side of the engine compartment **(see illustration)**. In milder climates, plain water can be used in the reservoir, but it should be kept no more than 2/3 full to allow for expansion if the water freezes. In colder climates, use windshield washer system antifreeze, available at any auto parts store, to lower the freezing point of the fluid. Mix the antifreeze with water in accordance with the manufacturer's directions on the container. **Caution:** *Do not use cooling system antifreeze — it will damage the vehicle's paint.*

15   To help prevent icing in cold weather, warm the windshield with the defroster before using the washer.

4.18   The fluid level inside the brake reservoirs is easily checked through the inspection windows (when adding fluid, grasp the tabs and rotate the cover up as shown)

Battery electrolyte

16   All vehicles with which this manual is concerned are equipped with a battery which is permanently sealed (except for vent holes) and has no filler caps. Water does not have to be added to these batteries at any time.

Brake and clutch fluid

17   The brake master cylinder is mounted on the front of the power booster unit in the engine compartment. The clutch cylinder used on manual transaxles is mounted adjacent to it on the firewall.
18   The fluid inside is readily visible. The level should be above the MIN marks on the reservoirs **(see illustration)**. If a low level is indicated, be sure to wipe the top of the reservoir cover with a clean rag to prevent contamination of the brake and/or clutch system before removing the cover.
19   When adding fluid, pour it carefully into the reservoir to avoid spilling it onto surrounding painted surfaces. Be sure the specified fluid is used, since mixing different types of brake fluid can cause damage to the system. See *Recommended lubricants and fluids* at the front of this Chapter or your owner's manual. **Warning:** *Brake fluid can harm your eyes and damage painted surfaces, so use extreme caution when handling or pouring it. Do not use brake fluid that has been standing open or is more than one year old. Brake fluid absorbs moisture from the air. Excess moisture can cause a dangerous loss of braking effectiveness.*
20   At this time the fluid and cylinder can be inspected for contamination. The system should be drained and refilled if deposits, dirt particles or water droplets are seen in the fluid.
21   After filling the reservoir to the proper level, make sure the lid is on tight to prevent fluid leakage.
22   The brake fluid level in the master cylinder will drop slightly as the pads and the brake shoes at each wheel wear down during normal operation. If the master cylinder requires repeated replenishing to keep it at the proper level, this is an indication of leakage in the brake system, which should be corrected immediately. Check all brake lines and connections (see Section 20 for more information).
23   If, upon checking the master cylinder fluid level, you discover one or both reservoirs empty or nearly empty, the brake system should be bled (Chapter 9).

---

5   Tire and tire pressure checks

Refer to illustrations 5.6a and 5.6b

1   Periodic inspection of the tires may spare you the inconvenience of being stranded with a flat tire. It can also provide you with vital information regarding possible problems in the steering and suspension systems before major damage occurs.

2   The original tires on most vehicles are equipped with wear bands that will appear when tread depth reaches 1/16-inch, but they don't appear until the tires are worn out. Tread wear can be monitored with a simple, inexpensive device known as a tread depth indicator.
3   Note any abnormal tread wear. Tread pattern irregularities such as cupping, flat spots and more wear on one side than the other are indications of front end alignment and/or balance problems. If any of these conditions are noted, take the vehicle to a tire shop or service station to correct the problem.
4   Look closely for cuts, punctures and embedded nails or tacks. Sometimes a tire will hold air pressure for a short time or leak down very slowly after a nail has embedded itself in the tread. If a slow leak persists, check the valve stem core to make sure it is tight. Examine the tread for an object that may have embedded itself in the tire or for a ''plug'' that may have begun to leak (radial tire punctures are repaired with a plug that is installed in a puncture). If a puncture is suspected, it can be easily verified by spraying a solution of soapy water onto the puncture area. The soapy solution will bubble if there is a leak. Unless the puncture is unusually large, a tire shop or service station can usually repair the tire.
5   Carefully inspect the inner sidewall of each tire for evidence of brake fluid leakage. If you see any, inspect the brakes immediately.
6   Correct air pressure adds miles to the lifespan of the tires, improves mileage and enhances overall ride quality. Tire pressure cannot be accurately estimated by looking at a tire, especially if it's a radial **(see illustration)**. A tire pressure gauge is essential. Keep an accurate gauge in the glovebox **(see illustration)**. The pressure gauges attached to the nozzles of air hoses at gas stations are often inaccurate.
7   Always check tire pressure when the tires are cold. Cold, in this case, means the vehicle has not been driven over a mile in the three

 1

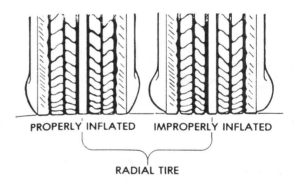

PROPERLY INFLATED   IMPROPERLY INFLATED

RADIAL TIRE

5.6a   It's difficult to judge the air pressure inside radial tires simply by looking at them; use a reliable tire pressure gauge

5.6b   Tire pressure gauges are available in a variety of styles — because service station gauges are often inaccurate, keep a gauge in your glove compartment

hours preceding a tire pressure check. A pressure rise of four to eight pounds is not uncommon once the tires are warm.

8   Unscrew the valve cap protruding from the wheel or hubcap and push the gauge firmly onto the valve stem. Note the reading on the gauge and compare the figure to the recommended tire pressure shown on the tire placard on the driver's side door. Be sure to reinstall the valve cap to keep dirt and moisture out of the valve stem mechanism. Check all four tires and, if necessary, add enough air to bring them up to the recommended pressure.

9   Don't forget to keep the spare tire inflated to the specified pressure (refer to your owner's manual or the tire sidewall). Note that the pressure recommended for the compact spare is higher than for the tires on the vehicle.

6   Automatic transaxle fluid level check

Refer to illustrations 6.3 and 6.6

1   The automatic transaxle fluid level should be carefully maintained. Low fluid level can lead to slipping or loss of drive, while overfilling can cause foaming and loss of fluid.

2   With the parking brake set, start the engine, then move the shift lever through all the gear ranges, ending in Park. The fluid level must be checked with the vehicle level and the engine running at idle. **Note:** *Incorrect fluid level readings will result if the vehicle has just been driven at high speeds for an extended period, in hot weather in city traffic, or if it has been pulling a trailer. If any of these conditions apply, wait until the fluid has cooled (about 30 minutes).*

3   With the transaxle at normal operating temperature, remove the dipstick from the filler tube. The dipstick is located at the rear of the engine compartment **(see illustration)**.

4   Carefully touch the fluid at the end of the dipstick to determine if the fluid is cool, warm or hot. Wipe the fluid from the dipstick with

6.3   The automatic transaxle fluid dipstick is clearly marked and is located at the rear of the engine compartment (V6 engine shown)

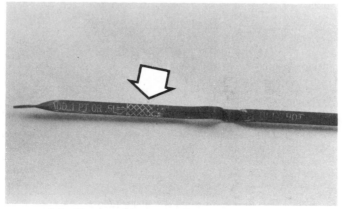

6.6   The automatic transaxle fluid level must be maintained within the cross-hatched area on the dipstick

a clean rag and push it back into the filler tube until the cap seats.

5   Pull the dipstick out again and note the fluid level.

6   If the fluid felt cool, the level should be about 1/8-to-3/8 inch below the ADD mark **(see illustration)**. If it felt warm, the level should be close to the ADD mark. If the fluid was hot, the level should be at the FULL mark. If additional fluid is required, pour it directly into the tube using a funnel. It takes about one pint to raise the level from the ADD mark to the FULL mark with a hot transaxle, so add the fluid a little at a time and keep checking the level until it's correct.

7   The condition of the fluid should also be checked along with the level. If the fluid at the end of the dipstick is a dark reddish-brown color, or if the fluid has a burned smell, the fluid should be changed. If you are in doubt about the condition of the fluid, purchase some new fluid and compare the two for color and smell.

7   Power steering fluid level check

Refer to illustrations 7.2 and 7.6

1   Unlike manual steering, the power steering system relies on fluid which may, over a period of time, require replenishing.

2   The fluid reservoir for the power steering pump is located behind the radiator near the front of the engine **(see illustration)**.

7.2   The power steering fluid reservoir is located near the front of the engine; turn the cap clockwise for removal

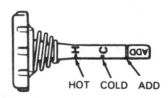

HOT   COLD   ADD

7.6   The markings on the power steering fluid dipstick indicate the safe range

3   For the check, the front wheels should be pointed straight ahead and the engine should be off.

4   Use a clean rag to wipe off the reservoir cap and the area around the cap. This will help prevent any foreign matter from entering the reservoir during the check.

5   Twist off the cap and check the temperature of the fluid at the end of the dipstick with your finger.

6   Wipe off the fluid with a clean rag, reinsert it, then withdraw it and read the fluid level. The level should be at the HOT mark if the fluid was hot to the touch **(see illustration)**. It should be at the COLD mark if the fluid was cool to the touch. Note that on some models the marks (Full Hot and Cold) are on opposite sides of the dipstick. At no time should the fluid level drop below the ADD mark.

7   If additional fluid is required, pour the specified type directly into the reservoir, using a funnel to prevent spills.

8   If the reservoir requires frequent fluid additions, all power steering hoses, hose connections, the power steering pump and the rack and pinion assembly should be carefully checked for leaks.

8 Battery check and maintenance

Refer to illustrations 8.1 and 8.3

Warning: *Certain precautions must be followed when checking and servicing the battery. Hydrogen gas, which is highly flammable, is always present in the battery cells, so keep lighted tobacco and all other open flames and sparks away from the battery. The electrolyte inside the battery is actually dilute sulfuric acid, which will cause injury if splashed on your skin or in your eyes. It will also ruin clothes and painted surfaces. When removing the battery cables, always detach the negative cable first and hook it up last!*

1   Battery maintenance is an important procedure which will help ensure that you are not stranded because of a dead battery. Several tools are required for this procedure **(see illustration)**.

2   A sealed battery is standard equipment on all vehicles with which this manual is concerned. Although this type of battery has many advantages over the older, capped cell type, and never requires the addition of water, it should nevertheless be routinely maintained according to the procedures which follow.

3   The battery is located on the left side of the engine compartment **(see illustration)**. The exterior of the battery should be inspected periodically for damage such as a cracked case or cover.

4   Check the tightness of the battery cable bolts to ensure good electrical connections and check the entire length of each cable for cracks and frayed conductors.

5   If corrosion (visible as white, fluffy deposits) is evident, remove the cables from the terminals, clean them with a battery brush and reinstall the cables. Corrosion can be kept to a minimum by using special treated fiber washers available at auto parts stores or by applying a layer of petroleum jelly to the terminals and cables after they are assembled.

6   Make sure that the battery tray is in good condition and that the hold-down clamp bolt is tight. If the battery is removed from the tray, make sure that no parts remain in the bottom of the tray when the battery is reinstalled. When reinstalling the hold-down clamp bolt, do not overtighten it.

7   Corrosion on the hold-down components, battery case and surrounding areas may be removed with a solution of water and baking soda. Thoroughly wash all cleaned areas with plain water.

8   Any metal parts of the vehicle damaged by corrosion should be covered with a zinc-based primer then painted.

9   Further information on the battery, charging and jump starting can be found in Chapter 5 and at the front of this manual.

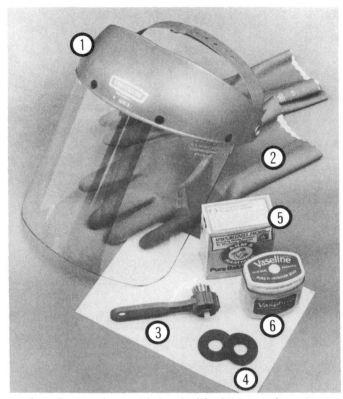

8.1   Tools and materials required for battery maintenance

1   *Face shield/safety goggles* — *When removing corrosion with a brush, the acidic particles can easily fly up into your eyes*

2   *Rubber gloves* — *Another safety item to consider when servicing the battery; remember that's acid inside the battery!*

3   *Battery terminal/ cable cleaner* — *This wire brush cleaning tool will remove all traces of corrosion from the battery and cable*

4   *Treated felt washers* — *Placing one of these on each terminal, directly under the cable end, will help prevent corrosion (be sure to get the correct type for side terminal batteries)*

5   *Baking soda* — *A solution of baking soda and water can be used to neutralize corrosion*

6   *Petroleum jelly* — *A layer of this on the battery terminal bolts will help prevent corrosion*

9 Cooling system check

Refer to illustration 9.4

1   Many major engine failures can be attributed to a faulty cooling system. If the vehicle is equipped with an automatic transaxle, the cooling system also cools the transaxle fluid and thus plays an important role in prolonging transaxle life.

2   The cooling system should be checked with the engine cold. Do this before the vehicle is driven for the day or after it has been shut off for at least three hours.

3   Remove the radiator cap by turning it to the left until it reaches a stop. If you hear any hissing sound (indicating there is still pressure in the system), wait until it stops. Now press down on the cap with the palm of your hand and continue turning to the left until the cap can be removed. Thoroughly clean the cap, inside and out, with clean water. Also clean the filler neck on the radiator. All traces of corrosion should be removed. The coolant inside the radiator should be relatively transparent. If it is rust colored, the system should be drained and refilled (Section 35). If the coolant level is not up to the top, add addi-

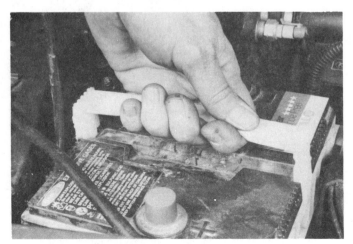

8.3   The battery is located just ahead of the left front tire and is a ''side post'' design (some models have a pull-up handle which makes removal and installation easier)

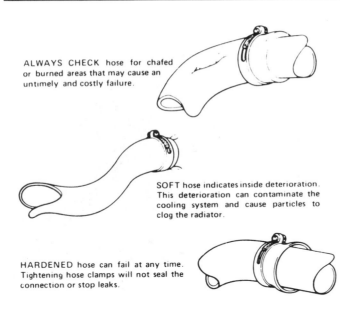

ALWAYS CHECK hose for chafed or burned areas that may cause an untimely and costly failure.

SOFT hose indicates inside deterioration. This deterioration can contaminate the cooling system and cause particles to clog the radiator.

HARDENED hose can fail at any time. Tightening hose clamps will not seal the connection or stop leaks.

SWOLLEN hose or oil soaked ends indicate danger and possible failure from oil or grease contamination. Squeeze the hose to locate cracks and breaks that cause leaks.

9.4 Hoses, like drivebelts, have a habit of failing at the worst possible time — to prevent the inconvenience of a blown radiator or heater hose, inspect them carefully as shown here

tional antifreeze/coolant mixture (see Section 4).
4   Carefully check the large upper and lower radiator hoses along with any smaller diameter heater hoses which run from the engine to the firewall. Inspect each hose along its entire length, replacing any hose which is cracked, swollen or shows signs of deterioration. Cracks may become more apparent if the hose is squeezed **(see illustration)**.
5   Make sure that all hose connections are tight. A leak in the cooling system will usually show up as white or rust colored deposits on the areas adjoining the leak. If wire-type clamps are used at the ends of the hoses, it may be wise to replace them with more secure screw-type clamps.
6   Use compressed air or a soft brush to remove bugs, leaves, etc. from the front of the radiator or air conditioning condenser. Be careful not to damage the delicate cooling fins or cut yourself on them.
7   Every other inspection, or at the first indication of cooling system problems, have the cap and system pressure tested. If you do not have a pressure tester, most gas stations and repair shops will do this for a minimal charge.

10   Underhood hose check and replacement

Refer to illustration 10.1
General

1   **Caution:** *Replacement of air conditioning hoses must be left to a dealer service department or air conditioning shop that has the equipment to depressurize the system safely. Never remove air conditioning components or hoses* **(see illustration)** *until the system has been depressurized.*
2   High temperatures under the hood can cause the deterioration of the rubber and plastic hoses used for engine, accessory and emission

systems operation. Periodic inspection should be made for cracks, loose clamps, material hardening and leaks. Information specific to the cooling system hoses can be found in Section 9.
3   Some, but not all, hoses are secured to the fittings with clamps. Where clamps are used, check to be sure they haven't lost their tension, allowing the hose to leak. If clamps aren't used, make sure the hose has not expanded and/or hardened where it slips over the fitting, allowing it to leak.

Vacuum hoses

4   It is quite common for vacuum hoses, especially those in the emissions system, to be color coded or identified by colored stripes molded into each hose. Various systems require hoses with different wall thicknesses, collapse resistance and temperature resistance. When replacing hoses, be sure the new ones are made of the same material.
5   Often the only effective way to check a hose is to remove it completely from the vehicle. If more than one hose is removed, be sure to label the hoses and fittings to ensure correct installation.
6   When checking vacuum hoses, be sure to include any plastic T-fittings in the check. Inspect the fittings for cracks and the hose where it fits over the fitting for distortion, which could cause leakage.
7   A small piece of vacuum hose (1/4-inch inside diameter) can be used as a stethoscope to detect vacuum leaks. Hold one end of the hose to your ear and probe around vacuum hoses and fittings, listening for the ''hissing'' sound characteristic of a vacuum leak. **Warning:** *When probing with the vacuum hose stethoscope, be careful not to allow your body or the hose to come into contact with moving engine components such as the drivebelt, cooling fan, etc.*

Fuel hose

Warning: *There are certain precautions which must be taken when inspecting or servicing fuel system components. Work in a well ventilated area and do not allow open flames (cigarettes, appliance pilot lights, etc.) or bare light bulbs near the work area. Mop up any spills immediately and do not store fuel soaked rags where they could ignite. The fuel system is under pressure, so if any fuel lines are to be disconnected, the pressure in the system must be relieved first (see Chapter 4 for more information).*

8   Check all rubber fuel lines for deterioration and chafing. Check especially for cracks in areas where the hose bends and just before fittings, such as where a hose attaches to the fuel filter and fuel injection unit.
9   High quality fuel line, usually identified by the word *Fluroelastomer* printed on the hose, should be used for fuel line replacement. Never, under any circumstances, use unreinforced vacuum line, clear plastic tubing or water hose for fuel lines.
10   Spring-type clamps are commonly used on fuel lines. These clamps

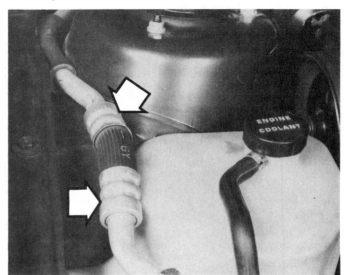

10.1 Air conditioning hoses are best identified by the metal tubes used at all bends (arrows) — DO NOT disconnect or accidentally damage the air conditioning hoses as the system is under high pressure

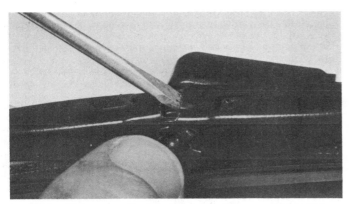

11.5a Using a small screwdriver, gently pry on the spring
at the center of the windshield wiper arm . . .

often lose their tension over a period of time, and can be "sprung"
during the removal process. As a result it is recommended that all
spring-type clamps be replaced with screw clamps whenever a hose
is replaced.

Metal lines

11 Sections of metal line are often used for fuel line between the fuel
pump and fuel injection unit. Check carefully to be sure the line has
not been bent and crimped and that cracks have not started in the line.
12 If a section of metal fuel line must be replaced, only seamless steel
tubing should be used, since copper and aluminum tubing do not have
the strength necessary to withstand normal engine vibration.
13 Check the metal brake lines where they enter the master cylinder
and brake proportioning unit (if used) for cracks in the lines and loose
fittings. Any sign of brake fluid leakage calls for an immediate thorough
inspection of the brake system.

11 Wiper blade inspection and replacement

Refer to illustrations 11.5a, 11.5b and 11.7

1 The windshield wiper and blade assembly should be inspected
periodically for damage, loose components and cracked or worn blade
elements.
2 Road film can build up on the wiper blades and affect their efficiency, so they should be washed regularly with a mild detergent
solution.
3 The action of the wiping mechanism can loosen the bolts, nuts
and fasteners, so they should be checked and tightened, as necessary,
at the same time the wiper blades are checked.
4 If the wiper blade elements (sometimes called inserts) are cracked,
worn or warped, they should be replaced with new ones.
5 Remove the wiper blade assembly from the wiper arm by inserting
a small screwdriver into the opening and gently prying on the spring
while pulling on the blade to release it **(see illustrations)**.
6 With the blade removed from the vehicle, you can remove the rubber element from the blade.
7 Using pliers, pinch the metal backing of the element **(see illustration)** and then slide the element out of the blade assembly.
8 Compare the new element with the old for length, design, etc.
9 Slide the new element into place. It will automatically lock at the
correct location.
10 Reinstall the blade assembly on the arm, wet the windshield glass
and test for proper operation.

12 Clutch pedal adjustment (1984 and 1985 models)

Refer to illustration 12.2

1 At the specified interval the clutch pedal must be adjusted to maintain a constant tension on the clutch self-adjusting mechanism cable.
2 Grasp the pedal and pull it up to the rubber stop, then depress the
pedal slowly **(see illustration)**.

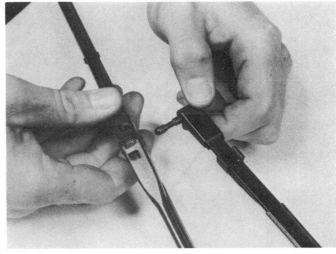

11.5b . . . while pulling the blade assembly away from
the arm

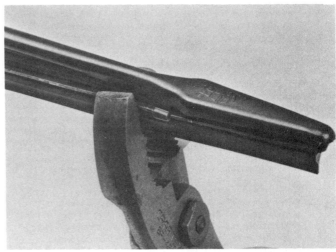

11.7 The rubber element is retained in the blade by little
clips — at one end, the metal backing of the rubber
element can be compressed with pliers, allowing the
element to slide out of the clips

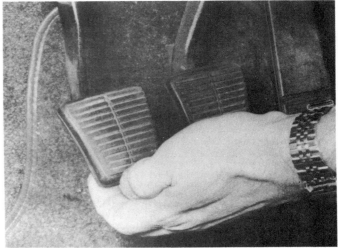

12.2 Pull the clutch pedal back to the stop, then depress
it slowly to adjust the free play

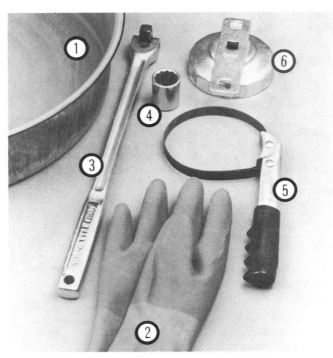

13.3   These tools are required when changing the engine oil and filter

1   **Drain pan** — *It should be fairly shallow in depth, but wide in order to prevent spills*
2   **Rubber gloves** — *When removing the drain plug and filter it is inevitable that you will get oil on your hands (the gloves will prevent burns)*
3   **Breaker bar** — *Sometimes the oil drain plug is pretty tight and a long breaker bar is needed to loosen it*
4   **Socket** — *To be used with the breaker bar or a ratchet (must be the correct size to fit the drain plug)*
5   **Filter wrench** — *This is a metal band-type wrench, which requires clearance around the filter to be effective*
6   **Filter wrench** — *This type fits on the bottom of the filter and can be turned with a ratchet or breaker bar (different size wrenches are available for different types of filters)*

---

13   Engine oil and filter change

Refer to illustrations 13.3, 13.10, 13.15 and 13.21

1   Frequent oil changes are the most important preventive maintenance procedures that can be done by the home mechanic. As engine oil ages, it becomes diluted and contaminated, which leads to premature engine wear.
2   Although some sources recommend oil filter changes every other oil change, we feel that the minimal cost of an oil filter and the relative ease with which it is installed dictate that a new filter be used every time the oil is changed.
3   Gather together all necessary tools and materials before beginning the procedure **(see illustration)**.
4   In addition, you should have plenty of clean rags and newspapers handy to mop up any spills. Access to the underside of the vehicle is greatly improved if the vehicle can be lifted on a hoist, driven onto ramps or supported by jackstands. **Warning:** *Do not work under a vehicle which is supported only by a bumper, hydraulic or scissors-type jack.*
5   If this is your first oil change, get under the vehicle and familiarize yourself with the locations of the oil drain plug and the oil filter. The engine and exhaust components will be warm during the actual work, so note how they are situated to avoid touching them when working under the vehicle.

6   Warm the engine to normal operating temperature. If the new oil or any tools are needed, use this warm-up time to gather everything necessary for the job. The correct type of oil for your application can be found in *Recommended lubricants and fluids* at the beginning of this Chapter.
7   With the engine oil warm (warm engine oil will drain better and more built-up sludge will be removed with the oil), raise and support the vehicle. Make sure it's safely supported.
8   Move all necessary tools, rags and newspapers under the vehicle. Position the drain pan under the drain plug. Keep in mind that the oil will initially flow from the pan with some force, so place the pan accordingly.
9   Two different oil change procedures are used on these models, depending on whether the oil filter is mounted on the engine block or in the oil pan. All V6 engines and most four-cylinder models are equipped with a block-mounted filter, while some later four-cylinder models have an oil pan-mounted filter.
10   Being careful not to touch any of the hot exhaust components, remove the drain plug at the bottom of the oil pan **(see illustration)**. Depending on how hot the oil has become, you may want to wear gloves while unscrewing the plug the final few turns.
11   Allow the old oil to drain into the pan. It may be necessary to move the pan farther under the engine as the oil flow slows to a trickle.
12   After all the oil has drained, wipe off the drain plug with a clean rag. Small metal particles may cling to the plug which would immediately contaminate the new oil.
13   Clean the area around the drain plug opening and reinstall the plug. Tighten the plug securely with the wrench. If a torque wrench is available, use it to tighten the plug.
14   Move the drain pan into position under the oil filter.

13.10   The oil drain plug is located at the rear of the pan (V6 shown) — it's usually in very tight, so use a six-point socket to avoid rounding off the hex

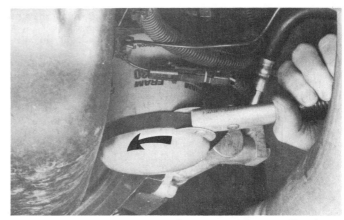

13.15   The oil filter is usually on very tight as well and will require a special wrench for removal — DO NOT use the wrench to tighten the new filter!

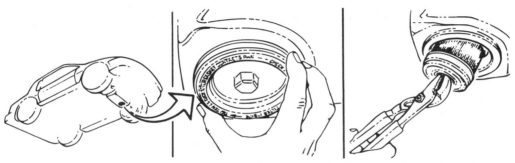

13.21   On four-cylinder engines with the oil filter mounted in the pan, the drain plug (center) is much larger than normal and the filter is a replaceable element that must be removed with a pair of pliers (right)

Engine block-mounted oil filter

15   Use the filter wrench to loosen the oil filter **(see illustration)**. Chain or metal band filter wrenches may distort the filter canister, but this is of no concern as the filter will be discarded anyway.
16   Completely unscrew the old filter. Be careful, as it is full of oil. Empty the oil inside the filter into the drain pan.
17   Compare the old filter with the new one to make sure they are the same type.
18   Use a clean rag to remove all oil, dirt and sludge from the area where the oil filter mounts to the engine. Check the old filter to make sure the rubber gasket is not stuck to the engine mounting surface. If the gasket is stuck to the engine (use a flashlight if necessary), remove it.
19   Apply a light coat of oil around the full circumference of the rubber gasket of the new oil filter. Open a can of oil and partially fill the oil filter with fresh oil. Oil pressure will not build in the engine until the oil pump has filled the filter with oil, so partially filling the filter at this time will reduce the amount of time the engine runs with no oil pressure.
20   Attach the new filter to the engine, following the tightening directions printed on the filter canister or packing box. Most filter manufacturers recommend against using a filter wrench due to the possibility of overtightening and damage to the seal.

Oil pan-mounted oil filter

21   Reach up inside the oil drain plug hole with a pair of pliers, grasp the filter securely, pull it down using a twisting motion and remove it from the oil pan **(see illustration)**.
22   Check the filter to make sure the rubber O-ring has come out with it. If it hasn't, reach up inside the pan opening and remove it.
23   Coat the new O-ring (included with the new filter) with clean engine oil and then slide it into position, all the way up in the filter opening.
24   Coat the inside of the grommet on the top of the new filter with clean engine oil.
25   Slide the new oil filter up into the oil pan opening as far as possible without forcing it.
26   Wipe off the drain plug with a clean cloth. Inspect the gasket, replacing it with a new one if necessary, and coat it with clean engine oil.
27   Clean the area around the drain plug opening. Reinstall the plug, tighten it by hand until the gasket contacts the oil pan, then tighten it an additional 1/4-turn with a wrench.

All models

28   Remove all tools, rags, etc. from under the vehicle, being careful not to spill the oil in the drain pan, then lower the vehicle.
29   Move to the engine compartment and locate the oil filler cap.
30   If an oil can spout is used, push the spout into the top of the oil can and pour the fresh oil through the filler opening. A funnel may also be used.
31   Pour three quarts of fresh oil into the engine. Wait a few minutes to allow the oil to drain into the pan, then check the level on the dipstick (see Section 4 if necessary). If the oil level is above the ADD mark, start the engine and allow the new oil to circulate.
32   Run the engine for only about a minute and then shut it off. Immediately look under the vehicle and check for leaks at the oil pan drain plug and around the oil filter. If either is leaking, tighten with a bit more force.
33   With the new oil circulated and the filter now completely full, recheck the level on the dipstick and add more oil as necessary.

34   During the first few trips after an oil change, make it a point to check frequently for leaks and proper oil level.
35   The old oil drained from the engine cannot be reused in its present state and should be disposed of. Oil reclamation centers, auto repair shops and gas stations will normally accept the oil, which can be refined and used again. After the oil has cooled it can be drained into a suitable container (capped plastic jugs, topped bottles, milk cartons, etc.) for transport to one of these disposal sites.

---

14   Chassis lubrication

Refer to illustrations 14.1, 14.2 and 14.6

1   Refer to *Recommended lubricants and fluids* at the front of this Chapter to obtain the necessary grease, etc. You will also need a grease gun **(see illustration)**. Occasionally plugs will be installed rather than grease fittings. If so, grease fittings will have to be purchased and installed.

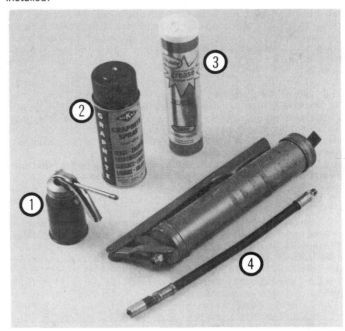

14.1   Materials required for chassis and body lubrication

1   **Engine oil** — *Light engine oil in a can like this can be used for door and hood hinges*
2   **Graphite spray** — *Used to lubricate lock cylinders*
3   **Grease** — *Grease, in a variety of types and weights, is available for use in a grease gun. Check the Specifications for your requirements*
4   **Grease gun** — *A common grease gun, shown here with a detachable hose and nozzle, is needed for chassis lubrication. After use, clean it thoroughly!*

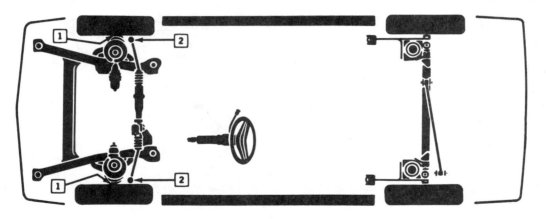

14.2 This diagram shows where balljoint (1) and steering system (2) lubrication points are located

2   Look under the vehicle and see if grease fittings or plugs are installed in the indicated locations **(see illustration)**. If there are plugs, remove them and buy grease fittings, which will thread into the component. A dealer or auto parts store will be able to supply the correct fittings. Straight, as well as angled, fittings are available.

3   For easier access under the vehicle, raise it with a jack and place jackstands under the frame. Make sure it is securely supported by the stands. If the wheels are to be removed at this interval for rotation or brake inspection, loosen the lug nuts slightly while the vehicle is still on the ground.

4   Before beginning, force a little grease out of the nozzle to remove any dirt from the end of the gun. Wipe the nozzle clean with a rag.

5   With the grease gun and plenty of clean rags, crawl under the vehicle and begin lubricating the components.

6   Wipe the grease fitting nipple clean and push the nozzle firmly over it **(see illustration)**. Squeeze the trigger on the grease gun to force grease into the component. The balljoints and tie-rod ends should be lubricated until each rubber seal is firm to the touch. Do not pump too much grease into the fitting or it could rupture the seal. If the grease escapes around the grease gun nozzle, the nipple is clogged or the nozzle is not completely seated on the fitting. Resecure the gun nozzle to the fitting and try again. If necessary, replace the fitting with a new one.

7   Wipe the excess grease from the components and the grease fitting. Repeat the procedure for the remaining fittings.

8   If equipped with a manual transaxle, lubricate the shift linkage with a little multi-purpose grease. While you are under the vehicle, clean and lubricate the parking brake cable along with the cable guides and levers. This can be done by smearing some of the chassis grease onto the cable and its related parts with your fingers.

9   Open the hood and smear a little chassis grease on the hood latch mechanism. Have an assistant pull the hood release lever from inside the vehicle as you lubricate the cable at the latch.

10   Lubricate all the hinges (door, hood, etc.) with engine oil to keep them in proper working order.

11   The key lock cylinders can be lubricated with spray-on graphite or silicone lubricant, which is available at auto parts stores. **Caution:** *The manufacturer does not recommend using oil in black plastic lock cylinders as it could damage them by washing out the factory applied lubricant.*

12   Lubricate the door weatherstripping with silicone spray. This will reduce chafing and retard wear.

15   Driveaxle boot check

Refer to illustration 15.2

1   The driveaxle boots are very important because they prevent dirt, water and foreign material from entering and damaging the constant velocity (CV) joints. Oil and grease can cause the boot material to deteriorate prematurely so it's a good idea to wash the boots with soap and water.

2   Inspect the boots for tears and cracks as well as loose clamps **(see illustration)**. If there is any evidence of cracks or leaking lubricant, they must be replaced as described in Chapter 8.

14.6   After wiping the grease fitting clean, push the nozzle firmly into place and pump the grease into the component (usually about two pumps of the gun will be sufficient)

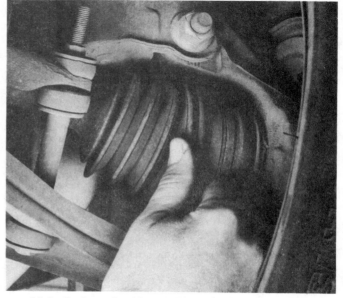

15.2   Push on the driveaxle boots to check for cracks

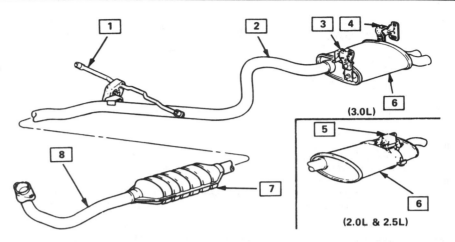

17.2   The exhaust system should be carefully inspected from the engine all the way back to the rear of the vehicle

1 Intermediate pipe hanger
2 Intermediate pipe
3 Front muffler hanger
4 Rear muffler hanger
5 Muffler hanger
6 Muffler
7 Catalytic converter
8 Front exhaust pipe

(3.0L)

(2.0L & 2.5L)

16   Suspension and steering check

1   Raise the front of the vehicle periodically and visually check the suspension and steering components for wear.
2   Indications of a fault in these systems are excessive play in the steering wheel before the front wheels react, excessive sway around corners, body movement over rough roads or binding at some point as the steering wheel is turned.
3   Raise the front end of the vehicle and support it securely on jackstands placed under the frame rails. Because of the work to be done, make sure the vehicle cannot fall from the stands.
4   Check the front wheel hub nuts for looseness and make sure they are securely locked in place.
5   From under the vehicle check for loose bolts, broken or disconnected parts and deteriorated rubber bushings on all suspension and steering components. Look for grease or fluid leaking from the steering assembly. Check the power steering hoses and connections for leaks.
6   Have an assistant turn the steering wheel from side-to-side and check the steering components for free movement, chafing and binding. If the steering does not react with the movement of the steering wheel, try to determine where the slack is located.

17   Exhaust system check

Refer to illustration 17.2

1   With the engine cold (at least three hours after the vehicle has been driven), check the complete exhaust system from the engine to the end of the tailpipe. Ideally, the inspection should be done with the vehicle on a hoist to permit unrestricted access. If a hoist is not available, raise the vehicle and support it securely on jackstands.
2   Check the exhaust pipes and connections for evidence of leaks, severe corrosion and damage. Make sure that all brackets and hangers are in good condition and tight **(see illustration).**
3   At the same time, inspect the underside of the body for holes, corrosion, open seams, etc. which may allow exhaust gases to enter the passenger compartment. Seal all body openings with silicone or body putty.
4   Rattles and other noises can often be traced to the exhaust system, especially the mounts and hangers. Try to move the pipes, muffler and catalytic converter. If the components can come in contact with the body or suspension parts, secure the exhaust system with new mounts.
5   Check the running condition of the engine by inspecting inside the end of the tailpipe. The exhaust deposits here are an indication of engine state-of-tune. If the pipe is black and sooty or coated with white deposits, the engine is in need of a tune-up, including a thorough fuel system inspection and adjustment.

18   Manual transaxle lubricant level check

Refer to illustrations 18.2 and 18.3

1   A dipstick is used for checking the lubricant level in the manual

18.2   The manual transaxle dipstick (arrow) is located adjacent to the master cylinder

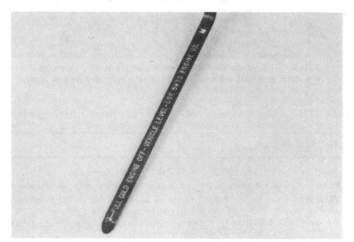

18.3   Follow the manual transaxle oil level checking procedure printed on the dipstick

transaxles used on these models.
2   With the transaxle cold (cool to the touch) and the vehicle parked on a level surface, remove the dipstick from the filler tube located at the rear left side of the engine compartment, adjacent to the brake master cylinder **(see illustration).**
3   The level must be even with our slightly above the FULL COLD mark on the dipstick **(see illustration).** Make sure the level is at the FULL COLD mark because lubricant may appear on the end of the dipstick even when the transaxle is several pints low.
4   If the level is low, add the specified lubricant through the filler tube,

using a funnel.

5   Insert the dipstick into the filler tube and seat it securely.

19   Tire rotation

Refer to illustration 19.2

1   The tires should be rotated at the specified intervals and whenever uneven wear is noticed.

2   Front wheel drive vehicles use a special tire rotation pattern **(see illustration)**.

3   Refer to the information in *Jacking and towing* at the front of this manual for the proper procedures to follow when raising the vehicle and changing a tire. If the brakes are to be checked, do not apply the parking brake as stated. Make sure the tires are blocked to prevent the vehicle from rolling as it is raised.

4   Preferably, the entire vehicle should be raised at the same time. This can be done on a hoist or by jacking up each corner and then lowering the vehicle onto jackstands placed under the frame rails. Always use four jackstands and make sure the vehicle is safely supported.

5   After rotation, check and adjust the tire pressures as necessary and be sure to check the lug nut tightness.

6   For further information on the wheels and tires, refer to Chapter 10.

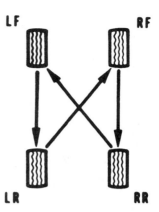

DO NOT INCLUDE "TEMPORARY USE ONLY" SPARE TIRE IN ROTATION

19.2   Tire rotation diagram

20.3   The brake pad wear indicator (arrow) will contact the disc and make a squealing noise when the pad is worn

20.5   Looking through the opening in the front of the caliper, the brake pads (arrows) can be inspected — the pad lining, which rubs against the disc, can also be inspected by looking through each end of the caliper

20   Brake check

Refer to illustrations 20.3, 20.5, 20.10 and 20.12

Note: *For detailed photographs of the brake system, refer to Chapter 9.*

Warning: *Brake system dust contains asbestos, which is hazardous to your health. DO NOT blow it out with compressed air and DO NOT inhale it. DO NOT use gasoline or solvents to remove the dust. Use brake system cleaner or denatured alcohol only.*

1   In addition to the specified intervals, the brakes should be inspected every time the wheels are removed or whenever a defect is suspected. Raise the vehicle and place it securely on jackstands. Remove the wheels (see *Jacking and towing* at the front of the manual, if necessary).

Disc brakes

2   Disc brakes are used on the front of this vehicle. Extensive rotor damage can occur if the pads are not replaced when needed.

3   The disc brake pads have built-in wear indicators which make a high-pitched squealing or cricket-like warning sound when the pads are worn **(see illustration)**. **Caution:** *Expensive rotor damage can result if the pads are not replaced soon after the wear indicators start*

squealing.

4   The disc brake calipers, which contain the pads, are now visible. There is an outer pad and an inner pad in each caliper. All pads should be inspected.

5   Each caliper has a "window" to inspect the pads **(see illustration)**. If the pad material has worn to about 1/8-inch thick or less, the pads should be replaced.

6   If you are unsure about the exact thickness of the remaining lining material, remove the pads for further inspection or replacement (refer to Chapter 9).

7   Before installing the wheels, check for leakage and/or damage at the brake hoses and connections. Replace the hose or fittings as necessary, referring to Chapter 9.

8   Check the condition of the brake rotor. Look for score marks, deep scratches and overheated areas (they will appear blue or discolored). If damage or wear is noted, the rotor can be removed and resurfaced by an automotive machine shop or replaced with a new one. Refer to Chapter 9 for more detailed inspection and repair procedures.

Drum brakes

9   Using a scribe or chalk, mark the drum and hub so the drum can be reinstalled in the same position on the hub.

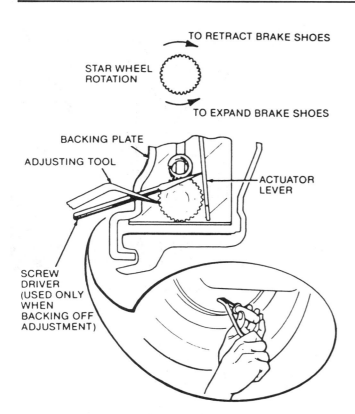

20.10 Use a screwdriver and adjusting tool to back off the rear brake shoes if necessary so the brake drum can be removed

20.12 Measure the depth of the rivet hole (arrow) to determine the thickness of remaining brake shoe material

10 Remove and discard any retaining clip and pull the brake drum off the hub and brake assembly. If this proves difficult, make sure the parking brake is released, then squirt some penetrating oil around the center hub area. Allow the oil to soak in and try to pull the drum off again. If the drum still cannot be pulled off, the brake shoes will have to be adjusted in. This is done by first removing the plug in the backing plate. With the plug removed, pull the self-adjusting lever off the star wheel and use a small screwdriver to turn the wheel, which will move the shoes away from the drum **(see illustration)**.

11 With the drum removed, carefully brush away any accumulations of dirt and dust. **Warning:** *Brake system dust contains asbestos, which is hazardous to your health. DO NOT blow it out with compressed air and DO NOT inhale it. DO NOT use gasoline or solvents to remove the dust. Brake system solvent should be used to flush the dust into a drain pan. After the brake components are wiped clean with a rag, dispose of the contaminated rags and solvent in a covered container.*

12 Note the thickness of the lining material on the brake shoes. If the material is worn to within 1/16-inch of the recessed rivets or metal backing the shoes should be replaced **(see illustration)**. If the linings look worn, but you are unable to determine their exact thickness, compare them with a new set at an auto parts store. The shoes should also be replaced if they are cracked, glazed, (shiny surface) or contaminated with brake fluid.

13 Check to make sure that all the brake assembly springs are connected and in good condition.

14 Check the brake components for signs of fluid leakage. Carefully pry back the rubber cups on the wheel cylinder, located at the top of the backing plate. Any leakage is an indication that the wheel cylinders should be replaced or overhauled immediately (Chapter 9). Also check the hoses and connections for signs of leakage.

15 Wipe the inside of the drum with a clean rag and brake cleaner or denatured alcohol.

16 Check the inside of the drum for cracks, scoring, deep scratches and hard spots, which will appear as small discolored areas. If imperfections cannot be removed with fine emery cloth, the drum must be taken to a machine shop for resurfacing.

17 After the inspection process is complete, and if all the components are found to be in good condition, reinstall the brake drums. Install the wheels and lower the vehicle to the ground.

Parking brake

18 The parking brake is operated by a hand lever and locks the rear drum brake system. The easiest, and perhaps most obvious method of periodically checking the operation of the parking brake assembly is to park the vehicle on a steep hill with the parking brake set and the transaxle in Neutral. If the parking brake cannot prevent the vehicle from rolling, it is in need of adjustment (see Chapter 9).

21 Fuel system check

Warning: *There are certain precautions to take when inspecting or servicing the fuel system components. Work in a well ventilated area and do not allow open flames (cigarettes, appliance pilot lights, etc.) near the work area. Mop up spills immediately and do not store fuel soaked rags where they could ignite. The fuel system is under pressure — no component should be disconnected until the pressure is relieved (see Chapter 4).*

1 The fuel system is most easily checked with the vehicle raised on a hoist so the components underneath the vehicle are readily visible and accessible.

2 If the smell of gasoline is noticed while driving or after the vehicle has been in the sun, the system should be thoroughly inspected immediately.

3 Remove the gas filler cap and check for damage, corrosion and an unbroken sealing imprint on the gasket. Replace the cap with a new one if necessary.

4 With the vehicle raised, inspect the gas tank and filler neck for punctures, cracks and other damage. The connection between the filler neck and the tank is especially critical. Sometimes a rubber filler neck will leak due to loose clamps or deteriorated rubber, problems a home mechanic can usually rectify. **Warning:** *Do not, under any circumstances, try to repair a fuel tank yourself (except rubber components). A welding torch or any open flame can easily cause the fuel vapors to explode if the proper precautions are not taken.*

5 Carefully check all rubber hoses and metal lines leading away from the fuel tank. Check for loose connections, deteriorated hoses, crimped lines and other damage. Follow the lines to the front of the vehicle, carefully inspecting them all the way. Repair or replace damaged sections as necessary.

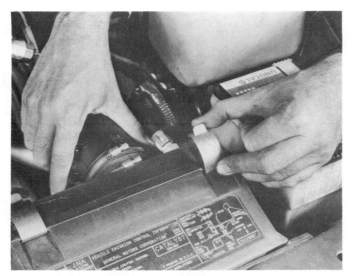

22.2a   On V6 models, disengage the air cleaner clips, . . .

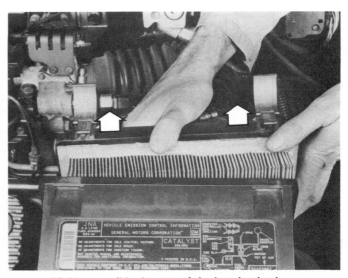

22.2b   . . . slide the rear of the housing back . . .

22.2c   . . . and pull the air filter element from the housing

22   Air filter and PCV filter replacement

Refer to illustrations 22.2a, 22.2b, 22.2c, 22.3, 22.5, 22.8 and 22.9

1   At the specified intervals, the air filter and PCV filter (if equipped) should be replaced with new ones. A thorough program of preventive maintenance would call for the two filters to be inspected between changes. **Note:** *Because of its advanced design, the fuel injection system used on the V6 and turbocharged engines does not have an individual PCV filter. The engine air cleaner supplies filtered air to the PCV system.*

Multi-Port Fuel Injection (MFI) models

2   The air filter is located inside the air cleaner housing located at the front of the engine on V6 models and is replaced by releasing the two clips on the top of the assembly and pulling the housing back **(see illustrations)**.

3   On turbocharged four-cylinder models, the air cleaner assembly is mounted in the corner of the engine compartment and the filter is replaced after removing the wing nut and lifting the top plate off **(see illustration)**.

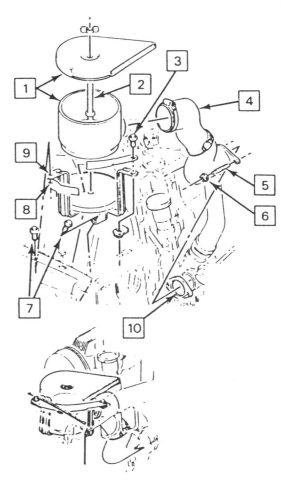

22.2d   Turbocharged four-cylinder engine air cleaner details

1	Air cleaner assembly	6	Nut
2	Stud	7	Bolt
3	Bolt	8	Bracket
4	Duct	9	Support
5	Stud	10	Gasket

22.5 On Throttle Body Injection (TBI) models, the air filter element can be lifted out of the housing after removing the cover

22.8 Remove the clip and withdraw the PCV filter housing from the air cleaner (TBI equipped engine)

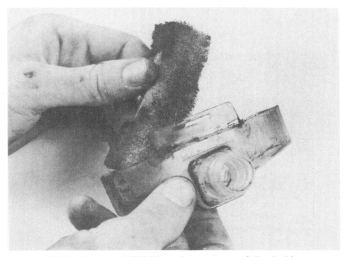

22.9 Pull the PCV filter element out of the holder (TBI equipped engine)

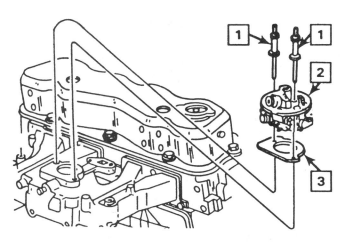

23.4 Throttle body installation details

1 Stud and nut   3 Gasket
2 TBI assembly

Throttle Body Injection (TBI) models

4 The air filter element is located on top of the throttle body and is replaced by unscrewing the wing nuts from the top of the filter housing and lifting off the cover. While the filter housing cover is off, be careful not to drop anything down into the throttle body or air cleaner assembly.

5 Remove the air filter element from the housing **(see illustration)**.

6 Wipe out the inside of the air cleaner housing with a clean rag.

7 Place the new filter in the air cleaner housing. Make sure it seats properly in the bottom of the housing.

8 The PCV filter is located in a holder in the side of the filter housing and can be removed after disconnecting the hose and removing a clip **(see illustration)**.

9 Pull the PCV filter from the holder **(see illustration)**.

10 Install a new PCV filter in the holder and install it in the air cleaner housing.

11 Install the air filter.

12 Install the top plate.

---

23 Throttle Body Injection (TBI) mounting nut torque check (2.5L engine only)

Refer to illustration 23.4

1 The TBI throttle body is attached to the top of the intake manifold by two studs and nuts. These fasteners can sometimes work loose from vibration and temperature changes during normal engine operation and cause a vacuum leak.

2 If you suspect that a vacuum leak exists at the bottom of the throttle body, obtain a length of fuel hose. Start the engine and place one end of the hose next to your ear as you probe around the base with the other end. You will hear a hissing sound if a leak exists (be careful of hot or moving engine components).

3 Remove the air cleaner assembly, tagging each hose to be disconnected with a piece of numbered tape to make reassembly easier.

4 Locate the mounting studs on the throttle body **(see illustration)**. Decide what special tools or adapters will be necessary, if any, to tighten the fasteners.

5 Tighten the stud nuts securely and evenly. Do not overtighten them, as the threads could strip.

6 If, after the stud nuts are properly tightened, a vacuum leak still exists, the throttle body must be removed and a new gasket installed. See Chapter 4 for more information.

7 After tightening the fasteners, reinstall the air cleaner and return all hoses to their original positions.

24.1   The throttle linkage should be periodically checked for free movement

---

24   Throttle linkage inspection

Refer to illustration 24.1

1   Inspect the throttle linkage for damaged or missing parts and for binding and interference when the accelerator pedal is operated **(see illustration)**
2   Lubricate the various linkage pivot points with a drop of engine oil.

---

25   Thermostatic air cleaner check (2.5L engine only)

Refer to illustrations 25.2, 25.7 and 25.8

1   On models equipped with throttle body fuel injection, a heated air system is used to give good driveability under a variety of climatic conditions. By having a relatively constant inlet air temperature, the fuel system can be calibrated to reduce exhaust emissions and eliminate throttle plate icing.
2   The thermostatic air cleaner, THERMAC as the system is sometimes called, operates on intake manifold vacuum and heated air. Air can enter from outside the engine compartment or through a heat stove built around the exhaust manifold **(see illustration)**.
3   A vacuum diaphragm motor, built into the air cleaner snorkel, operates a damper door to admit hot air from the stove, air from outside, or a combination of both. A temperature sensor inside the air cleaner housing that is sensitive to intake air temperature controls how much vacuum goes to the motor.
4   This is a visual check. If access is limited, a small mirror can be used.
5   Open the hood and locate the damper door inside the air cleaner assembly. It will be located inside the long snorkel of the metal air cleaner housing.
6   If there is a flexible air duct attached to the end of the snorkel, leading to an area behind the grill, disconnect it at the snorkel. This will enable you to look through the end of the snorkel and see the damper door inside.
7   The check should be done when the engine is cold. Start the engine and look through the snorkel at the damper door, which should move to a closed position. With the damper closed, air cannot enter through the end of the snorkel, and instead enters the air cleaner though the flexible duct attached to the exhaust manifold and the heat stove passage **(see illustration)**.
8   As the engine warms up to operating temperature, the damper door should open to allow air through the snorkel end **(see illustration)**. Depending on ambient temperature, this make take 10 to 15 minutes. To speed up this check you can reconnect the snorkel air duct, drive

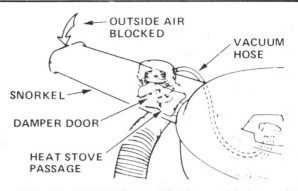

25.2   The THERMAC assembly shown with the snorkel passage (damper door) closed

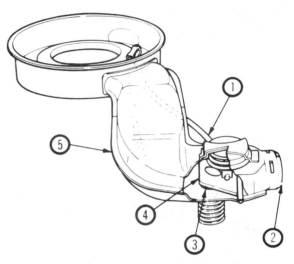

25.7   Thermac assembly shown with the snorkel closed

1 Vacuum hose
2 Outside air passage (blocked)
3 Heat stove passage
4 Damper door
5 Snorkel

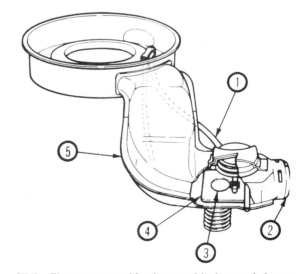

25.8   Thermac assembly shown with the snorkel open

1 Vacuum hose
2 Outside air passage (open)
3 Heat stove passage
4 Damper door
5 Snorkel

the vehicle, then check to see if the snorkel passage is open.
9   If the thermo-controlled air cleaner is not operating properly see Chapter 6 for more information.

26   Idle speed check and adjustment

The engine idle speed on these models is controlled by the ECM and is not a regular maintenance item. In fact, most models are equipped with tamper-proof plugs to discourage changing the factory pre-set idle speeds. For more information, refer to Chapter 4 and Chapter 6.

27   Drivebelt check, adjustment and replacement

1   The number of drivebelts used on a particular model depends on the accessories installed. Drivebelts are used to turn the alternator, power steering pump, water pump and air conditioning compressor. Some models use a single serpentine drivebelt to drive all of these components.

Conventional drivebelts

Refer to illustration 27.3

2   With the engine off, open the hood and locate the various belts at the front of the engine. Using your fingers (and a flashlight, if necessary), move along the belts checking for cracks and separation of the belt plies. Also check for fraying and glazing, which gives the belt a shiny appearance. Both sides of the belt should be inspected, which means you will have to twist each belt to check the underside.
3   Check the tension of each belt by pushing on it at a distance half-way between the pulleys. Push firmly with your thumb and see how much the belt deflects. Measure this deflection with a ruler **(see illustration)**. As a general rule, the belt should deflect 1/4-inch if the distance between pulley centers is between 7 and 11 inches and 1/2-inch is the distance is between 12 and 16 inches.

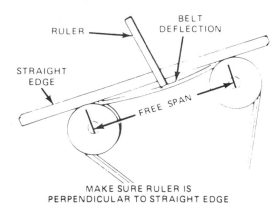

27.3   On conventional drivebelts, the tension can be checked with a straightedge and a ruler

4   Another, more precise method of measuring and adjusting belt deflection is accomplished with a special belt tension tool such as GM tool J-23600 or equivalent.
5   If it is necessary to adjust tension to either make the drivebelt looser or tighter, it is done by moving the belt-driven accessory on the bracket.
6   For each component there will be an adjusting bolt and a pivot bolt. Both bolts must be loosened slightly to enable you to move the component.
7   After the two bolts have been loosened, move the component away from the engine to tighten the belt or toward the engine to loosen the belt. Hold the accessory in position and check the belt tension. If it is correct, tighten the two bolts until just snug, then recheck the tension. If the tension is correct, tighten the bolts.
8   It will often be necessary to use some sort of pry bar to move the accessory while the belt is adjusted. If this must be done to gain the proper leverage, be very careful not to damage the component being

moved or the part being pried against. **Note:** *Some components are equipped with a square hole which will accept a 3/8-inch breaker bar, which can be used to lever the component and tension the belt.*
9   To replace a belt, follow the instructions above for adjustment. However, completely remove the belt from the pulleys.
10 In some cases you will have to remove more than one belt because of their arrangement on the front of the engine. Since belts tend to fail at the same time, it is a good idea to replace all belts. Mark each belt and its appropriate pulley groove so all replacement belts can be installed in their proper positions.
11 When replacing belts, it is a good idea to take the old belts with you to the parts store in order to make a direct comparison for length, width and design.

Serpentine drivebelt

Refer to illustrations 27.16, 27.20a and 27.20b

12 A single drivebelt, or serpentine belt as it is more often called, is located at the front of the engine and plays an important role in the overall operation of the engine and its components. Due to its function and material make up, the belt is prone to failure as it wears and should be periodically inspected.
13 A single belt is be used to drive the alternator, power steering pump, water pump and air conditioning compressor.
14 With the engine off, open the hood and use your fingers (and a flashlight, if necessary), to move along the belt checking for cracks and separation of the belt plies. Also check for fraying and glazing, which gives the belt a shiny appearance. Both sides of the belt should be inspected, which means you will have to twist the belt to check the underside.
15 Check the ribs on the underside of the belt. They should all be the same depth, with none of the surface uneven.
16 The tension of the belt is checked visually. Locate the belt tensioner at the front of the engine under the air conditioning compressor on the right (passenger) side, and then locate the tensioner operating marks **(see illustration)** located on the side of the tensioner. If the indicator mark is outside of the operating range, the belt should be replaced.
17 If available, a belt tension gauge (GM tool J-23600-B or equivalent) can be placed between the alternator and the air conditioning compressor to check the belt tension. Refer to the Specifications for the exact tension.
18 To replace the belt, rotate the tensioner clockwise to release belt tension. The tensioner will swing down once the tension of the belt is released.
19 Remove the belt from the auxiliary components and carefully release the tensioner.

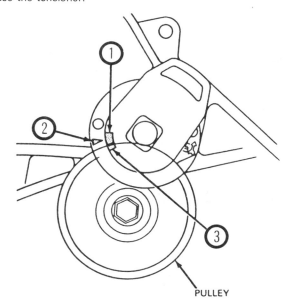

27.16   On the serpentine drivebelt, the drivebelt tensioner automatically keeps proper tension on the drivebelt, but does have limits — the indicator pointer (2) should remain between the minimum (1) and maximum (3) marks

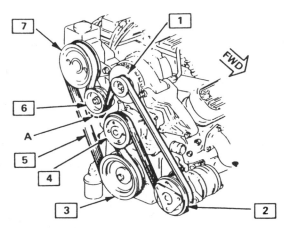

27.20a   Typical serpentine drivebelt routing details

1 Alternator	A Rotate the drivebelt
2 Air conditioning compressor	tensioner in the direction
3 Crankshaft pulley	of the arrow during
4 Water pump	removal or installation
5 Serpentine drivebelt	
6 Tensioner	
7 Power steering pump	

20   Route the new belt over the various pulleys **(see illustration)**, again rotating the tensioner to allow the belt to be installed, then release the belt tensioner. **Note:** *Most models have a drivebelt routing decal on the power steering pump reservoir to help in the proper placement of the drivebelt* **(see illustration)**.

28   Seat belt check

1   Check the seat belts, buckles, latch plates and guide loops for any obvious damage or signs of wear.
2   Check that the seat belt reminder light comes on when the key is turned to the Run or Start positions. A chime should also sound.
3   The seat belts are designed to lock up during a sudden stop or impact, yet allow free movement during normal driving. Check that the retractors return the belt against your chest while driving and rewind the belt fully when the buckle is unlatched.
4   If any of the above checks reveal problems with the seat belt system, replace parts as necessary.

29   Starter safety switch check

Warning: *During the following checks there is a chance that the vehicle could lunge forward, possibly causing damage or injuries. Allow plenty of room around the vehicle, apply the parking brake and hold down the regular brake pedal during the following checks.*

1   On automatic transaxle vehicles, try to start the vehicle in each gear. The engine should crank only in Park or Neutral.
2   If equipped with a manual transaxle, place the shift lever in Neutral and push the clutch pedal down about halfway. The engine should crank only with the clutch pedal fully depressed.
3   Check that the steering column lock allows the key to go into the Lock position only when the shift lever is in Park (automatic transaxle) or Reverse (manual transaxle).
4   The ignition key should come out only in the Lock position.

30   Seatback latch check

1   It is important to periodically check the seatback latch mechanism to prevent to seatback from moving forward during a sudden stop or an accident.
2   Grasping the top of the seat, attempt to tilt the seatback forward.

27.20b   The serpentine drivebelt routing diagram is located on the power steering pump reservoir (arrow)

It should tilt only when the latch on the rear of the seat is pulled up. Note that there is a certain amount of free play built into the latch mechanism.
3   When returned to the upright position, the seatback should latch securely.

31   Spare tire and jack check

1   Periodically checking the security and condition of the spare tire and jack will help to familiarize you with the procedures necessary for emergency tire replacement and also help to insure that no components work loose during normal vehicle operation.
2   Following the instructions in your owner's manual or under *Jacking and towing* near the front of this manual, remove the spare tire and jack.
3   Using a reliable air pressure gauge, check the pressure in the spare tire. It should be kept at the pressure marked on the tire sidewall.
4   Check that the jack operates freely and all components are undamaged.
5   When finished, make sure that the wing nuts hold the jack and tire securely in place.

32   Fuel filter replacement

Refer to illustration 32.3
Warning: *Gasoline is extremely flammable, so extra safety precautions must be observed when working on any part of the fuel system. Do not smoke and do not allow open flames or bare light bulbs near the vehicle. Also, do not perform fuel system maintenance procedures in a garage where a natural gas type appliance, such as a water heater or clothes dryer, with a pilot light is present.*

1   Relieve the fuel system pressure (Chapter 4).
2   Raise the vehicle and support it securely on jackstands.
3   Using a backup wrench, disconnect the fuel line-to-fuel filter fittings **(see illustration)**.
4   Grasp the filter securely, pull it from the clip and remove it from the vehicle.

32.3   To remove the fuel filter, detach the fuel line fittings from both ends and pull the filter from the clip

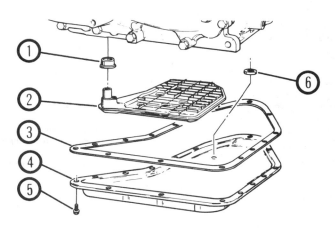

33.11 Automatic transaxle filter installation details

1 Seal	*4 Oil pan*
2 Filter	*5 Bolt*
3 Oil pan gasket	*6 Magnet*

5   Snap the new filter securely into the clip. Make sure the arrow on the filter points toward the engine.
6   The remaining steps of the installation procedure are the reverse of removal.

33   Automatic transaxle fluid and filter change

Refer to illustration 33.11

1   At the specified time intervals, the transaxle fluid should be drained and replaced. Since the fluid will remain hot long after driving, perform this procedure only after sufficient cooling.
2   Before beginning work, purchase the specified transaxle fluid (see *Recommended lubricants and fluids* at the front of this Chapter) and a new filter.
3   Other tools necessary for this job include jackstands to support the vehicle in a raised position, a drain pan capable of holding at least 8 pints, newspapers and clean rags.
4   Raise and support the vehicle on jackstands.
5   With a drain pan in place, remove the front and side oil pan mounting bolts.
6   Loosen the rear pan bolts approximately four turns.
7   Carefully pry the transaxle oil pan loose with a screwdriver, allowing the fluid to drain.
8   Remove the remaining bolts, pan and gasket. Carefully clean the gasket surface of the transaxle to remove all traces of the old gasket and sealant.
9   Drain the fluid from the transaxle oil pan, clean the pan with solvent and dry it with compressed air. Be careful not to lose the magnet.
10   Remove the filter screen from the mount inside the transaxle.
11   Install a new filter screen and seal **(see illustration)**.
12   Make sure the gasket surface on the transaxle oil pan is clean, then install a new gasket. Put the pan in place against the transaxle and, working around the pan, tighten each pan bolt a little at a time until the final torque figure is reached.
13   Lower the vehicle and add the specified amount of automatic transaxle fluid through the filler tube (Section 6).
14   With the selector in Park and the parking brake set, run the engine at a fast idle, but do not race the engine.
15   Move the gear selector through each range and back to Park. Check the fluid level.
16   Check under the vehicle for leaks during the first few trips.

34   Manual transaxle lubricant change

Refer to illustration 34.3

1   Raise the vehicle and support it securely on jackstands.

34.3 Manual transaxle drain plug location (arrow)

2   Move a drain pan, rags, newspapers and wrenches under the transaxle.
3   Remove the transaxle drain plug and allow the oil to drain into the pan **(see illustration)**.
4   After the oil has drained completely, reinstall the plug and tighten it securely.
5   Remove the transaxle dipstick. Using a hand pump, syringe or funnel, fill the transaxle with the correct amount of the specified lubricant.
6   Lower the vehicle. With the vehicle on a level surface, check the oil level as described in Section 4, adding more oil as necessary.

35   Cooling system servicing (draining, flushing and refilling)

1   Periodically, the cooling system should be drained, flushed and refilled to replenish the antifreeze mixture and prevent formation of rust and corrosion, which can impair the performance of the cooling system and cause engine damage.
2   At the same time the cooling system is serviced, all hoses and the radiator cap should be inspected and replaced if defective (see Section 9).
3   Since antifreeze is a corrosive and poisonous solution, be careful not to spill any of the coolant mixture on the vehicle's paint or your skin. If this happens, rinse immediately with plenty of clean water. Consult your local authorities about the dumping of antifreeze before draining the cooling system. In many areas, reclamation centers have been set up to collect automobile oil and drained antifreeze/water mixtures, rather than allowing them to be added to the sewage system.
4   With the engine cold, remove the radiator cap. On four-cylinder models which have the thermostat in a housing with a removable cap, remove the cap and lift out the thermostat (Chapter 3).
5   Move a large container under the radiator to catch the coolant as it is drained.
6   Drain the radiator by removing the drain plug at the bottom. If this drain has excessive corrosion and cannot be turned easily, or if the radiator is not equipped with a drain, disconnect the lower radiator hose to allow the coolant to drain. Be careful that none of the solution is splashed on your skin or into your eyes.
7   Disconnect the hose from the coolant reservoir and remove the reservoir. Flush it out with clean water.
8   Place a garden hose in the radiator filler neck and flush the system until the water runs clear at all drain points.
9   In severe cases of contamination or clogging of the radiator, remove it (see Chapter 3) and reverse flush it. This involves inserting the hose in the bottom radiator outlet to allow the water to run against the normal flow, draining through the top. A radiator repair shop should be consulted if further cleaning or repair is necessary.
10   When the coolant is regularly drained and the system refilled with the correct antifreeze/water mixture, there should be no need to use chemical cleaners or descalers.
11   To refill the system, reconnect the radiator hoses and install the

reservoir and the overflow hose.

12 Fill the radiator with the proper mixture of antifreeze and water (see Section 4) to the base of the filler neck and then add more coolant to the reservoir until it reaches the lower mark. On four-cylinder models, add coolant to the thermostat housing until it reaches the cap seat and install the thermostat and cap.

13 With the radiator cap still removed, start the engine and run until normal operating temperature is reached. With the engine idling, add additional coolant to the radiator and the reservoir to bring up to the proper levels. Install the radiator and reservoir caps.

14 Keep a close watch on the coolant level and the cooling system hoses during the first few miles of driving. Tighten the hose clamps and/or add more coolant as necessary.

36   Positive Crankcase Ventilation (PCV) valve check and replacement

Refer to illustration 36.1

1 With the engine idling at normal operating temperature, pull the valve (with hose attached) from the rubber grommet in the rocker arm cover **(see illustration)**.

2 Place your finger over the end of the valve. If there is no vacuum at the valve, check for a plugged hose, manifold port, or the valve itself. Replace any plugged or deteriorated hoses.

3 Turn off the engine and shake the PCV valve, listening for a rattle. If the valve does not rattle, replace it with a new one.

4 To replace the valve, pull it from the end of the hose, noting its installed position and direction.

5 When purchasing a replacement PCV valve, make sure it is for your particular vehicle, model year and engine size. Compare the old valve with the new one to make sure they are the same.

6 Push the valve into the end of the hose until it is seated.

7 Inspect the rubber grommet for damage and replace it with a new one if necessary.

8 Push the PCV valve and hose securely into position in the rocker arm cover or manifold.

37   Evaporative emissions control system check

Refer to illustration 37.2

1 The function of the evaporative emissions control system is to draw fuel vapors from the gas tank and fuel system, store them in a charcoal

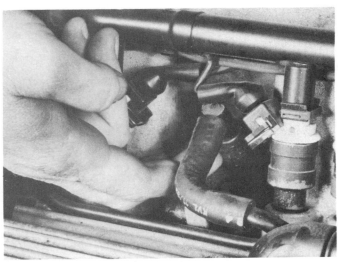

36.1   The PCV valve plugs into the rocker arm cover or manifold; place your finger under the valve and pull it out, then feel for suction at the end of the valve and shake it, listening for a clicking sound

37.2   The evaporative system canister is located at the right front corner of the engine compartment (arrow) — inspect the various hoses attached to it and the canister itself for damage

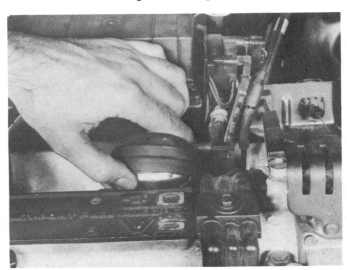

38.2a   Some EGR valves have plastic covers, which can be pried off with your fingers

38.2b   The diaphragm, reached from under the EGR valve, should move easily with finger pressure

canister and then burn them during normal engine operation.

2   The most common symptom of a fault in the evaporative emissions system is a strong fuel odor in the engine compartment. If a fuel odor is detected, inspect the charcoal canister, located at the front of the engine compartment **(see illustration)**. Check the canister and all hoses for damage and deterioration.

3   The evaporative emissions control system is explained in more detail in Chapter 6.

38   Exhaust Gas Recirculation (EGR) system check

Refer to illustrations 38.2a and 38.2b

1   The EGR valve is located on the intake manifold. Most of the time, when a problem develops in the emissions system, it is due to a stuck or corroded EGR valve.

2   With the engine cold to prevent burns, remove the cover (if equipped), reach under the valve and manually push on the diaphragm **(see illustration)**. Using moderate pressure, you should be able to move the diaphragm up-and-down within the housing **(see illustration)**.

3   If the diaphragm does not move or moves only with much effort, replace the EGR valve with a new one. If in doubt about the quality of the valve, compare the free movement of your EGR valve with a new valve.

4   Refer to Chapter 6 for more information on the EGR system.

39   Spark plug replacement

Refer to illustrations 39.2, 39.5a, 39.5b and 39.6

1   The spark plugs are located on the front (radiator) side of the engine on four-cylinder models. On the V6 engine, three plugs are located at the front and three at the rear (firewall) side of the engine.

2   In most cases, the tools necessary for spark plug replacement include a spark plug socket which fits onto a ratchet (spark plug sockets are padded inside to prevent damage to the porcelain insulators on the new plugs), various extensions and a gap gauge to check and adjust the gaps on the new plugs **(see illustration)**. A special plug wire removal tool is available for separating the wire boots from the spark plugs, but it isn't absolutely necessary. A torque wrench should be used to tighten the new plugs.

3   The best approach when replacing the spark plugs is to purchase the new ones in advance, adjust them to the proper gap and replace the plugs one at a time. When buying the new spark plugs, be sure to obtain the correct plug type for your particular engine. This information can be found on the *Emission Control Information label* located under the hood and in the factory owner's manual. If differences exist between the plug specified on the emissions label and in the owner's manual, assume that the emissions label is correct.

4   Allow the engine to cool completely before attempting to remove

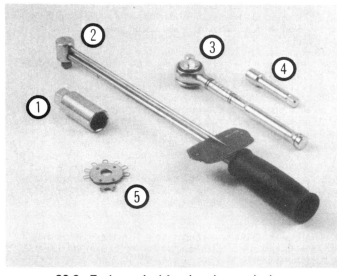

39.2   Tools required for changing spark plugs

1   **Spark plug socket** — *This will have special padding inside to protect the spark plug porcelain insulator*

2   **Torque wrench** — *Although not mandatory, use of this tool is the best way to ensure that the plugs are tightened properly*

3   **Ratchet** — *Standard hand tool to fit the plug socket*

4   **Extension** — *Depending on model and accessories, you may need special extensions and universal joints to reach one or more of the plugs*

5   **Spark plug gap gauge** — *This gauge for checking the gap comes in a variety of styles. Make sure the gap for your engine is included*

any of the plugs. While you are waiting for the engine to cool, check the new plugs for defects and adjust the gaps.

5   The gap is checked by inserting the proper thickness gauge between the electrodes at the tip of the plug **(see illustration)**. The gap between the electrodes should be the same as the one specified on the *Emissions Control Information label*. The wire should just slide between the electrodes with a slight amount of drag. If the gap is incorrect, use the adjuster on the gauge body to bend the curved side electrode slightly until the proper gap is obtained **(see illustration)**. If the side electrode is not exactly over the center electrode, bend it with the adjuster until it is. Check for cracks in the porcelain insulator (if any are found, the plug should not be used).

39.5a   Spark plug manufacturers recommend using a wire-type gauge when checking the gap — if the wire does not slide between the electrodes with a slight drag, adjustment is required

39.5b   To change the gap, bend the *side* electrode only, as indicated by the arrows, and be very careful not to crack or chip the porcelain insulator surrounding the center electrode

6   With the engine cool, remove the spark plug wire from one spark plug. Pull only on the boot at the end of the wire — do not pull on the wire. A plug wire removal tool should be used if available **(see illustration)**.

7   If compressed air is available, use it to blow any dirt or foreign material away from the spark plug hole. A common bicycle pump will also work. The idea here is to eliminate the possibility of debris falling into the cylinder as the spark plug is removed.

8   Place the spark plug socket over the plug and remove it from the engine by turning it in a counterclockwise direction.

9   Compare the spark plug to those shown in the accompanying color photos to get an indication of the general running condition of the engine.

10   Thread one of the new plugs into the hole until you can no longer turn it with your fingers, then tighten it with a torque wrench (if available) or the ratchet. It might be a good idea to slip a short length of rubber hose over the end of the plug to use as a tool to thread it into place. The hose will grip the plug well enough to turn it, but will start to slip if the plug begins to cross-thread in the hole — this will prevent damaged threads and the accompanying repair costs.

11   Before pushing the spark plug wire onto the end of the plug, inspect it following the procedures outlined in Section 40.

12   Attach the plug wire to the new spark plug, again using a twisting motion on the boot until it is seated on the spark plug.

13   Repeat the procedure for the remaining spark plugs, replacing them one at a time to prevent mixing up the spark plug wires.

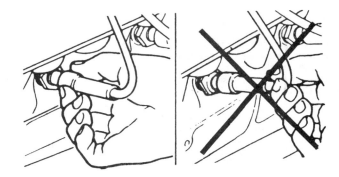

39.6   When removing a spark plug wire from a spark plug, pull on the end of the boot (as shown on the left) and not on the wire itself (as shown at the right); a slight twisting motion will also help

---

40   Spark plug wire, distributor cap and rotor check and replacement

---

Refer to illustrations 40.10, 40.13, 40.14 and 40.16

Note: *Some later models are equipped with distributorless ignition. On these models, the spark plugs are connected directly to the ignition coils or module and distributor cap inspection is, of course, not necessary.*

Spark plug wires

1   The spark plug wires should be checked at the recommended intervals and whenever new spark plugs are installed in the engine.

2   The wires should be inspected one at a time to prevent mixing up the order, which is essential for proper engine operation.

3   Disconnect the plug wire from the spark plug. To do this, grab the rubber boot, twist slightly and pull the wire free. Do not pull on the wire itself, only on the rubber boot.

4   Inspect inside the boot for corrosion, which will look like a white crusty powder. Push the wire and boot back onto the end of the spark plug. It should be a tight fit on the plug. If it is not, remove the wire and use pliers to carefully crimp the metal connector inside the boot until it fits securely on the end of the spark plug.

5   Using a clean rag, wipe the entire length of the wire to remove any built-up dirt and grease. Once the wire is clean, check for burns, cracks and other damage. Do not bend the wire excessively or pull the wire since the conductor inside might break.

6   Disconnect the wire from the distributor cap. Again, pull only on the rubber boot. Check for corrosion and a tight fit in the same manner as the spark plug end. Replace the wire into the distributor cap.

7   Check the remaining spark plug wires one at a time, making sure they are securely fastened at the distributor or ignition coil and the spark plug when the check is complete.

8   If new spark plug wires are required, purchase a new set for your specific engine model. Wire sets are available pre-cut, with the rubber boots already installed. Remove and replace the wires one at a time to avoid mix-ups in the firing order.

Distributor cap and rotor

9   It is common practice to install a new cap and rotor whenever new spark plug wires are installed. Although the breakerless distributor used on this vehicle requires much less maintenance than conventional distributors, periodic inspections should be performed when the plug wires are inspected.

10   On models so equipped, begin distributor cap removal by removing the retaining ring on the top of the distributor **(see illustration)**. This ring may have to be pried from the top of each plug wire, and more

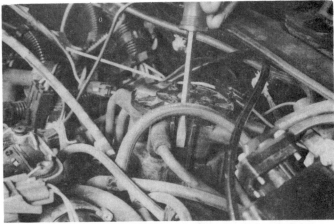

40.10   Use a screwdriver to pry the plug wire retaining ring (if equipped) from the top of the distributor cap

40.13   Visible with the distributor cap removed are the internal components (the rotor is held in place with screws — be careful not to drop anything down into the distributor)

than likely some of the spark plug wires will come off the cap at this time.

11   Loosen the screws which hold the distributor cap to the distributor body.

12   Release the clips on the side of the distributor cap, if necessary, and remove the cap.

13   The rotor is now visible at the center of the distributor. It is held in place by two screws **(see illustration)**.

CARBON DEPOSITS

Symptoms: Dry sooty deposits indicate a rich mixture or weak ignition. Causes misfiring, hard starting and hesitation.

Recommendation: Check for a clogged air cleaner, high float level, sticky choke and worn ignition points. Use a spark plug with a longer core nose for greater anti-fouling protection.

OIL DEPOSITS

Symptoms: Oily coating caused by poor oil control. Oil is leaking past worn valve guides or piston rings into the combustion chamber. Causes hard starting, misfiring and hesition.

Recommendation: Correct the mechanical condition with necessary repairs and install new plugs.

TOO HOT

Symptoms: Blistered, white insulator, eroded electrode and absence of deposits. Results in shortened plug life.

Recommendation: Check for the correct plug heat range, over-advanced ignition timing, lean fuel mixture, intake manifold vacuum leaks and sticking valves. Check the coolant level and make sure the radiator is not clogged.

PREIGNITION

Symptoms: Melted electrodes. Insulators are white, but may be dirty due to misfiring or flying debris in the combustion chamber. Can lead to engine damage.

Recommendation: Check for the correct plug heat range, over-advanced ignition timing, lean fuel mixture, clogged cooling system and lack of lubrication.

HIGH SPEED GLAZING

Symptoms: Insulator has yellowish, glazed appearance. Indicates that combustion chamber temperatures have risen suddenly during hard acceleration. Normal deposits melt to form a conductive coating. Causes misfiring at high speeds.

Recommendation: Install new plugs. Consider using a colder plug if driving habits warrant.

GAP BRIDGING

Symptoms: Combustion deposits lodge between the electrodes. Heavy deposits accumulate and bridge the electrode gap. The plug ceases to fire, resulting in a dead cylinder.

Recommendation: Locate the faulty plug and remove the deposits from between the electrodes.

NORMAL

Symptoms: Brown to grayish-tan color and slight electrode wear. Correct heat range for engine and operating conditions.

Recommendation: When new spark plugs are installed, replace with plugs of the same heat range.

ASH DEPOSITS

Symptoms: Light brown deposits encrusted on the side or center electrodes or both. Derived from oil and/or fuel additives. Excessive amounts may mask the spark, causing misfiring and hesitation during acceleration.

Recommendation: If excessive deposits accumulate over a short time or low mileage, install new valve guide seals to prevent seepage of oil into the combustion chambers. Also try changing gasoline brands.

WORN

Symptoms: Rounded electrodes with a small amount of deposits on the firing end. Normal color. Causes hard starting in damp or cold weather and poor fuel economy.

Recommendation: Replace with new plugs of the same heat range.

DETONATION

Symptoms: Insulators may be cracked or chipped. Improper gap setting techniques can also result in a fractured insulator tip. Can lead to piston damage.

Recommendation: Make sure the fuel anti-knock values meet engine requirements. Use care when setting the gaps on new plugs. Avoid lugging the engine.

SPLASHED DEPOSITS

Symptoms: After long periods of misfiring, deposits can loosen when normal combustion temperature is restored by an overdue tune-up. At high speeds, deposits flake off the piston and are thrown against the hot insulator, causing misfiring.

Recommendation: Replace the plugs with new ones or clean and reinstall the originals.

MECHANICAL DAMAGE

Symptoms: May be caused by a foreign object in the combustion chamber or the piston striking an incorrect reach (too long) plug. Causes a dead cylinder and could result in piston damage.

Recommendation: Remove the foreign object from the engine and/or install the correct reach plug.

1

40.14   Check the distributor rotor contact (arrow) for
corrosion and burn marks

40.16   Inspect the inside of the cap, especially the metal
contacts (arrow) for corrosion and wear. If in doubt,
replace it with a new one

14   Visually inspect the rotor for cracks or damage. Carefully check the condition of the metal contact at the top of the rotor for excessive corrosion and burned areas **(see illustration)**. If in doubt as to its condition, replace it with a new one.

15   Install the rotor on the distributor shaft. It's keyed to fit properly only one way.

16   Before installing the distributor cap, inspect the cap for cracks or other damage. Closely examine the contacts on the inside of the cap for excessive corrosion or damage **(see illustration)**. Slight scoring is normal. Again, if in doubt as to the condition of the cap, replace it with a new one.

17   Replace the cap and secure it with the screws or clips.

18   Install the spark plug wires on the cap in their proper positions and secure (if equipped) with the retaining ring at the top.

Chapter 2 Part A
2.0L overhead cam (OHC) 4-cylinder engine

Contents

Specifications

General
Cylinder numbers (timing belt end-to-transaxle end) 1-2-3-4
Firing order 1-3-4-2

Camshaft
Lobe lift (intake and exhaust) . . . . 0.2409 in
End play . . . . 0.016 to 0.064 in
Journal diameters
  no. 1 . . . . 1.672 to 1.6714 in
  no. 2 . . . . 1.6816 to 1.6812 in
  no. 3 . . . . 1.6917 to 1.6911 in
  no. 4 . . . . 1.7015 to 1.7009 in
  no. 5 . . . . 1.7114 to 1.7108 in
Bearing oil clearance . . . . 0.0008 in

Oil pump
Idler gear-to-body clearance . . . . 0.004 to 0.007 in
Drive gear-to-body clearance . . . . 0.014 to 0.018 in
Gear-to-cover clearance . . . . 0.001 to 0.004 in

Torque specifications

	Ft-lbs
Camshaft cover bolts	6
Camshaft carrier/cylinder head bolts*	18 plus 180° additional rotation in 3 equal steps
Camshaft sprocket retaining bolt	34
Camshaft retainer bolts	6
Crankshaft pulley-to-sprocket bolts	20
Crankshaft sprocket retaining bolt	107
Exhaust manifold bolts	16
Intake manifold nuts	16
Oil pan bolts	4
Oil pump mounting bolts	5
Oil pump plug	15
Pick-up tube-to-block bolts	5
Pick-up tube-to-oil pump bolts	5
Timing belt cover bolts	5
Flywheel-to-crankshaft bolts*	48 plus 30° additional rotation
Driveplate-to-crankshaft bolts	48

* Discard the bolts each time they're removed and use new ones for installation — be sure to follow the detailed tightening procedure in the text

1   General information

This Part of Chapter 2 is devoted to in-vehicle repair procedures for the 2.0L OHC turbocharged four-cylinder engine.

Information concerning engine removal and installation, as well as engine block and cylinder head overhaul, is in Part D of this Chapter.

The following repair procedures are based on the assumption that the engine is installed in the vehicle. If the engine has been removed from the vehicle and mounted on a stand, many of the steps included in this Part of Chapter 2 will not apply.

The Specifications included in this Part of Chapter 2 apply only to the engine and procedures in this Part. The Specifications necessary for rebuilding the block and cylinder head are found in Part D.

2   Repair operations possible with the engine in the vehicle

Many major repair operations can be accomplished without removing the engine from the vehicle.

Clean the engine compartment and the exterior of the engine with some type of pressure washer before any work is done. A clean engine will make the job easier and will help keep dirt out of the internal areas of the engine.

Depending on the components involved, it may be a good idea to remove the hood to improve access to the engine as repairs are performed (refer to Chapter 11 if necessary).

If vacuum, exhaust, oil or coolant leaks develop, indicating a need for gasket or seal replacement, the repairs can generally be made with the engine in the vehicle. The intake and exhaust manifold gaskets,

oil pan gasket and cylinder head gasket are all accessible with the engine in place.

Exterior engine components such as the intake and exhaust manifolds, the oil pan, the oil pump, the water pump, the starter motor, the alternator, the distributor, the turbocharger and the fuel injection system can be removed for repair with the engine in place.

Since the cylinder head can be removed without pulling the engine, camshaft and valve component servicing can also be accomplished with the engine in the vehicle.

In extreme cases caused by a lack of necessary equipment, repair or replacement of piston rings, pistons, connecting rods and rod bearings is possible with the engine in the vehicle. However, this practice is not recommended because of the cleaning and preparation work that must be done to the components involved.

3   Camshaft cover — removal and installation

Refer to illustrations 3.3, 3.4 and 3.5

1   Detach the induction tube.

2   Remove the crankcase breather hoses.

3   Remove the bolts and separate the cover from the engine. It may be necessary to break the gasket seal by tapping the cover with a soft-face hammer. If it's really stuck, use a knife, gasket scraper or chisel to remove it, but be very careful not to damage the gasket sealing surfaces of the cover or housing **(see illustration)**.

4   Place clean rags in the camshaft gallery to keep foreign material out of the engine **(see illustration)**.

5   Remove all traces of gasket material from the cover and housing.

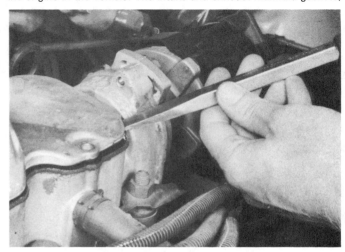

3.3   Breaking the camshaft cover gasket seal with a chisel and hammer — be careful not to damage the sealing surfaces!

3.4   Rags placed in the camshaft gallery will keep foreign material out

Be careful not to nick or gouge the soft aluminum (see illustration). Clean the mating surfaces with lacquer thinner or acetone.

6   Reinstall the cover with a new gasket — no sealant is required. Install the bolts and tighten them to the specified torque in a criss-cross pattern.

7   Reinstall the induction tube and breather hoses.

4   Timing belt front cover — removal and installation

Refer to illustration 4.3

1   Detach the negative battery cable from the battery.
2   Remove the serpentine drivebelt (Chapter 1).
3   Unsnap the retaining clips and detach the upper cover from the engine (see illustration).
4   Unsnap the retaining clips and remove the lower cover.
5   Installation is the reverse of removal.

5   Timing belt rear cover — removal and installation

1   Remove the timing belt front cover (Section 4) and the timing belt (Section 6).
2   Remove the bolts and separate the rear cover from the engine (see illustration 4.3).
3   Installation is the reverse of removal.
4   Install the timing belt and front cover.

6   Timing belt — removal, installation and adjustment

Refer to illustrations 6.7a, 6.7b, 6.10, 6.11, 6.15, 6.16a and 6.16b
Caution: *Incorrect installation or adjustment of the timing belt could result in engine damage. Although a skilled mechanic may be able to set timing belt tension without them, we recommend the use of factory tools (GM no. J26486A and J33039). DO NOT turn the camshaft with*

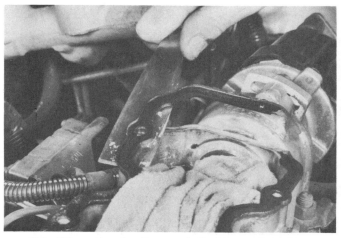

3.5   When removing the camshaft cover gasket with a scraper, be careful not to nick or gouge the carrier (it's made of aluminum and is very soft)

a wrench on the sprocket bolt — damage to the cam bearings may result. When neccessary, turn the camshaft with an open end wrench on the machined hex above cylinder number four (inside the camshaft cover).

Removal

1   Remove the timing belt front cover (Section 4).
2   Drain the coolant (Chapter 1).
3   Remove the coolant reservoir.
4   Disconnect the negative battery cable from the battery.
5   Raise the vehicle and support it securely on jackstands.
6   Remove the right front wheel. Remove the bolts and detach the inner splash panel from the wheel well.

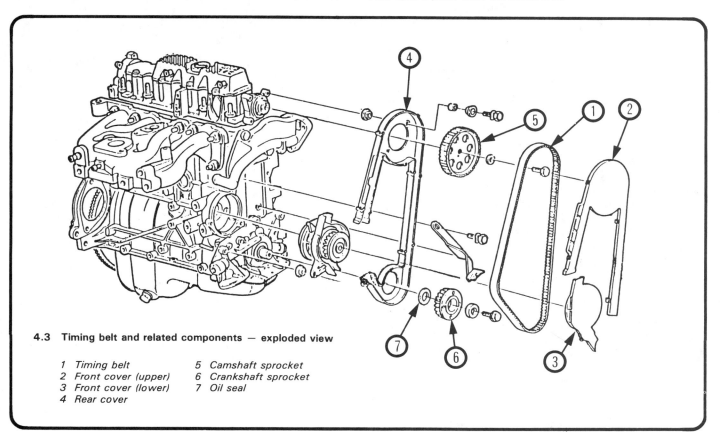

4.3   Timing belt and related components — exploded view

    1 Timing belt   *5 Camshaft sprocket*
    2 Front cover (upper) *6 Crankshaft sprocket*
    3 Front cover (lower) *7 Oil seal*
    4 Rear cover

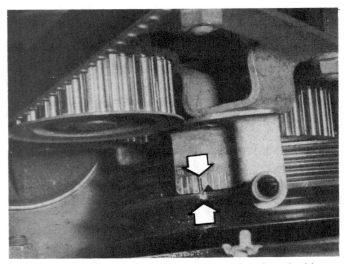

6.7a   The crankshaft pulley notch must be aligned with the 10 degree BTDC mark (arrows) before the timing belt is removed

6.7b   The valve timing marks are easy to see grooves cast into the camshaft sprocket and carrier (arrows)

6.10   Carefully pry out on the water pump to break the gasket seal, . . .

6.11   . . . then rotate the water pump in the direction shown (arrow) to release the timing belt tension

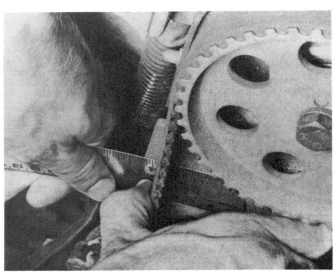

6.15   Using a ruler to check the timing belt tension

7   Rotate the crankshaft until the timing mark on the crankshaft pulley is aligned with the ten degree BTDC mark on the indicator scale and the camshaft sprocket mark lines up with the mark on the camshaft carrier (**see illustrations**).

8   Remove the bolts and detach the pulley from the crankshaft.

9   Remove the timing probe for access and loosen the water pump bolts.

10   Use a large screwdriver to break the water pump gasket seal (**see illustration**).

11   Grasp the water pump with a pair of pliers and release the tension from the timing belt by rotating the pump toward the engine (**see illustration**).

12   Slip the belt off the sprockets. **Caution:** *Don't rotate the crankshaft or camshaft while the belt is off.*

Installation

13   Slip the new belt onto the sprockets, install the crankshaft pulley and make sure the crankshaft and camshaft marks are aligned.

Adjustment without factory tool

14   Rotate the water pump to apply tension to the timing belt and tighten the water pump bolts.

15   Measure the belt deflection midway between the water pump and the camshaft pulley with a straightedge and ruler (**see illustration**). Ad-

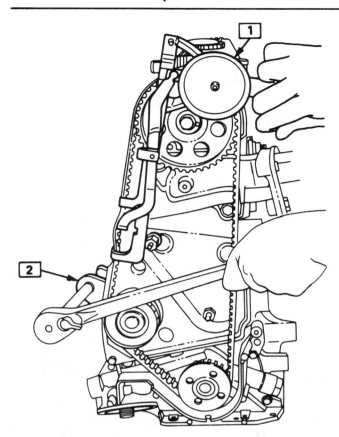

6.16a The factory recommends two special tools for timing belt adjustment — a tension gauge (1) and an adjustment tool (2)

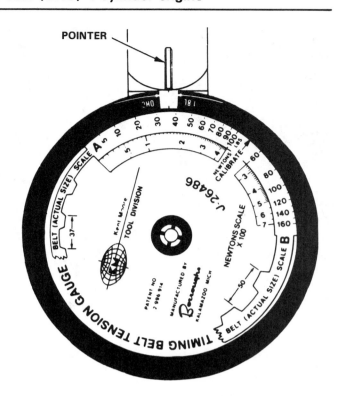

6.16b The pointer must fall within the band on the outer edge of the gauge before the timing belt tension can be considered correct

7.4 Hold the camshaft with a large wrench at the flats provided and remove the sprocket bolt

just the belt tension until the deflection is 1/4-inch. **Caution:** *Be sure to have the belt checked and adjusted by a dealer service department or a repair shop before driving the vehicle extensively.*

Adjustment with factory tool

16 Install the adjusting tool and gauge as described in the instructions accompanying the tools. Adjust the tension until it's within the range on the gauge **(see illustrations)**.

17 After adjusting the tension, remove the gauge, then carefully turn the crankshaft clockwise (viewed from the timing belt end) with a socket and breaker bar on the crankshaft sprocket bolt. While slowly rotating the crankshaft two full turns (720 degrees), feel and listen for valve-to-piston contact. Don't force the engine — if binding is felt, back up and recheck your work. When you reach 720 degrees, check the timing marks again (they should be aligned). **Note:** *New belts should be run in several minutes and then retensioned.*

18 Reinstall all components, then refill the cooling system and run the engine. After normal operating temperature is reached, check carefully for leaks.

7 Camshaft sprocket — removal and installation

Refer to illustration 7.4

Removal

1 Remove the timing belt front cover (Section 4).

2 Remove the timing belt (make sure the mark on the sprocket is aligned with the one on the cover) (Section 6).

3 Remove the camshaft cover (Section 3).

4 Hold the camshaft with a wrench on the flats located between the lobes and remove the sprocket bolt **(see illustration)**. The camshaft must not be allowed to turn.

5 Detach the sprocket and washer.

Installation

6 Align the hole in the sprocket with the pin in the end of the camshaft, then install the sprocket on the camshaft (make sure the mark on the sprocket is aligned with the mark on the cover).

7 Hold the camshaft with the wrench and install the washer and bolt. Tighten the bolt to the specified torque.

8 Install the timing belt, cover and any other components that were removed.

2A

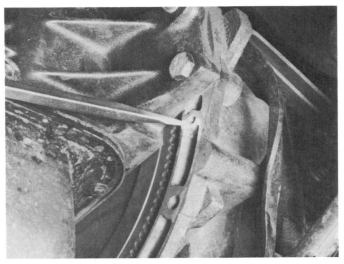

8.2 A screwdriver wedged in the starter ring gear teeth will lock the engine so the crankshaft sprocket bolt can be loosened

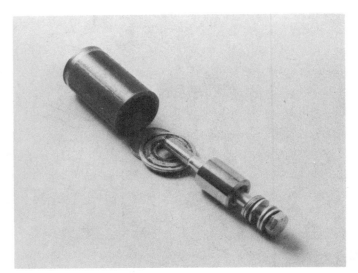

9.6a A tool for installing the front crankshaft oil seal can be made from pieces of pipe, washers and a bolt

8   Crankshaft sprocket — removal and installation

Refer to illustration 8.2

Removal

1   Remove the serpentine drivebelt (Chapter 1), timing belt front cover (Section 4) and timing belt (Section 6).
2   Remove the flywheel cover and lock the flywheel by wedging a screwdriver in the starter ring gear teeth. The screwdriver must be held against the engine block, not the transaxle case **(see illustration)**.
3   Remove the bolt and washer and detach the sprocket. The bolt is usually very tight, so a 1/2-inch drive breaker bar and a six-point socket should be used.

Installation

4   Align the keyway in the sprocket with the key in the end of the crankshaft, then slide the sprocket into place. Install the washer and bolt and tighten the bolt to the specified torque.
5   Remove the screwdriver and install the flywheel cover.
6   Install the timing belt, front cover and serpentine drivebelt.

9   Crankshaft front oil seal — replacement

Refer to illustrations 9.6a and 9.6b

1   Drain the engine oil and install a new oil filter (Chapter 1).
2   Remove the crankshaft sprocket and Woodruff key from the crankshaft nose (Section 8). If access to the seal is restricted, you may have to remove the rear timing belt cover as well (Section 5).
3   Pry the old oil seal out with a seal removal tool or a screwdriver. Be very careful not to nick or otherwise damage the crankshaft in the process.
4   Apply a thin coat of RTV-type sealant to the outer edge of the new seal. Lubricate the seal lip with moly-base grease or clean engine oil.
5   Place the seal squarely in position in the bore.
6   Push the seal into the bore with a hammer and the factory special tool (no. J330831) or a tool made up of a long metric coarse thread bolt, a piece of pipe and washers **(see illustrations)**. Be sure the bolt diameter and thread pitch match the sprocket bolt and the pipe diameter matches the seal to prevent distortion. Make sure the seal is seated completely in the bore.
7   Install the rear timing belt cover (if removed), the Woodruff key and the crankshaft sprocket.
8   Refill the engine with oil (see Chapter 1), start it and check for oil leaks at the seal.

9.6b Tighten the tool bolt slowly to push the seal squarely into place in the oil pump bore

10   Camshaft — removal and installation

Refer to illustrations 10.3 and 10.4

Note: *GM recommends special tools for this procedure (no. J22794 and J33302-25). If they aren't used, the camshaft carrier must be removed first, then the camshaft can be withdrawn from the carrier. When the carrier is removed, the head gasket seal is broken, which means the cylinder head must be completely removed in order to install a new head gasket and bolts. The cost of the special tools is quite high, so, in spite of the extra work and time involved, the procedure outlined here was devised to avoid using them. Before removing the camshaft, refer to Chapter 2, Part D, and check the lobe lift.*

Removal

1   Refer to Section 11 and remove the camshaft carrier.
2   Remove the retainer mounting bolts (at the distributor end of the carrier). If the bolts have Allen heads, a special driver will be required for removal and installation.

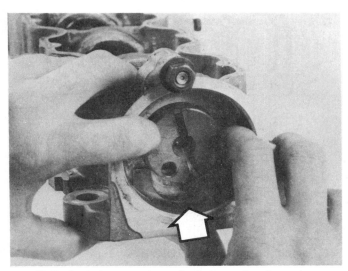

10.3 Push down on the ends of the retainer (arrow) to release it from the groove in the camshaft

3 Remove the retainer (see illustration).
4 Support the camshaft at both ends and carefully withdraw it from the distributor end of the carrier (don't damage the bearing surfaces with the lobes) (see illustration). Refer to Part D of this Chapter for the camshaft inspection procedure and Section 11 for the retainer and carrier inspection procedures.

Installation

Note: *If a new camshaft is installed, replace all rocker arms as well — don't install used rocker arms with a new camshaft.*

5 Apply moly-base grease or engine assembly lube to the lip of the front camshaft seal, the camshaft lobes and the bearing surfaces, then carefully insert the camshaft into the carrier.
6 Install the retainer and bolts. Tighten the bolts to the specified torque.
7 Check the camshaft end play with a dial indicator and compare it to the Specifications.
8 Install the camshaft and carrier assembly as described in Section 11.

---

11 Camshaft carrier — removal, inspection and installation

Refer to illustrations 11.4, 11.9, 11.10, 11.14, 11.16 and 11.17

Caution: *Each time the camshaft carrier/cylinder head bolts are loosened or removed, the cylinder head bolts and head gasket must be replaced with new parts. Also, the engine must be allowed to cool down completely before this procedure is done.*

Removal

1 Disconnect the PCV hose from the camshaft cover.
2 Drain the engine oil and coolant (Chapter 1), then remove the distributor (Chapter 5). Save the oil to temporarily refill the crankcase near the end of the procedure.
3 Remove the camshaft sprocket (Section 7).
4 Loosen the camshaft carrier/cylinder head bolts 1/4-turn at a time in the prescribed order (see illustration). As the bolts are loosened, the force exerted by the valve springs will tend to separate the carrier from the head. Remove the bolts and discard them — new ones must be used when installing the head!
5 Detach the camshaft carrier assembly from the head.
6 Refer to Section 3 and separate the cover from the carrier, then remove the camshaft from the carrier (Section 10).

Inspection

7 Carefully pry the oil seal out of the front of the carrier.
8 Clean all parts with solvent and dry them with compressed air (if available).

10.4 Carefully slide the camshaft out of the carrier to prevent damage to the bearing surfaces

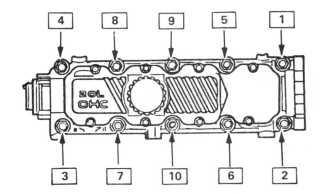

11.4 Camshaft carrier/cylinder head bolt LOOSENING sequence

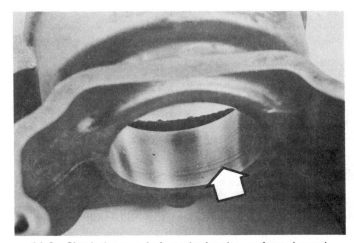

11.9 Check the camshaft carrier bearing surfaces (arrow) for wear and damage

9 Check the bearing surfaces in the carrier for score marks and other damage (see illustration). Use a telescoping gauge and micrometer to measure the camshaft bearing bores in the carrier. Measure the camshaft journal diameters with a micrometer, then subtract each journal diameter from the corresponding bore diameter to determine the oil clearances. If they're excessive, a new carrier may be required. Refer to Part D of this Chapter for additional camshaft inspection procedures.

11.10   Check the camshaft retainer contact surface
(arrow) for wear

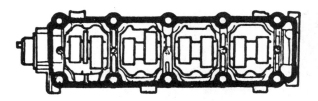

11.14   Apply anaerobic sealant to the camshaft carrier-to-
cylinder head surface as shown here (dark area)

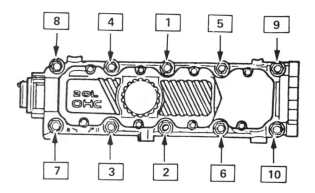

11.16   Camshaft carrier/cylinder head bolt
TIGHTENING sequence

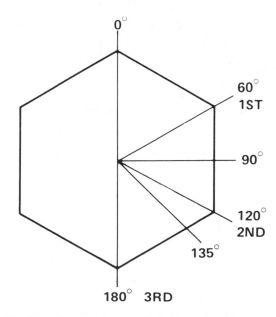

11.17   After the camshaft carrier/cylinder head bolt initial
torque is reached, the bolts must be turned an additional
180-degrees in three increments

10 Check the camshaft retainer surface for wear, score marks and other damage. Replace it with a new one if necessary (see illustration).

Installation

11 Use a hammer and a large socket or block of wood to drive the new seal into the front of the carrier. Make sure the seal is seated completely in the bore.

12 Install the camshaft in the carrier as described in Section 10.

13 Install a new cylinder head gasket (Section 16).

14 Clean the mating surfaces of the camshaft carrier and the cylinder head with lacquer thinner or acetone, then apply a thin (3 mm) bead of anaerobic sealant to the carrier-to-head mating surfaces (see illustration).

15 Make sure the valve lash compensators and rocker arms are in place. Position the carrier on the cylinder head and install the new bolts.

16 Tighten the bolts to 18 ft-lbs in 1/4-turn increments. Work from the center of the head to the ends in the prescribed order (see illustration). Caution: *If the bolts are tightened in increments greater than 1/4-turn, the carrier may be distorted.*

17 Tighten each bolt another 60-degrees, following the same sequence. This must be done three times, until each bolt has been turned an additional 180-degrees (1/2-turn) total (see illustration).

18 Reinstall all components that were removed.

19 Refill the crankcase with the original oil (Chapter 1).

20 Refill the cooling system (Chapter 1).

21 Start the engine and run it until normal operating temperature is reached, then check for oil and coolant leaks.

22 Shut the engine off and tighten all of the head bolts, in sequence, an additional 30-to-50 degrees.

23 Change the engine oil and install a new filter (Chapter 1).

**12   Rocker arms and valve lash compensators — removal
and installation**

Refer to illustrations 12.5a and 12.5b

Removal

1 Disconnect the negative cable from the battery.

2 Disconnect the PCV valve hose from the camshaft cover.

3 Remove the camshaft cover (Section 3).

4 Remove the camshaft carrier assembly (Section 11).

5 Remove the rocker arms, rocker arm guides and valve lash compensators and store them in order in a numbered container (see illustrations). Inspection procedures are included in Part D of this Chapter.

Installation

6 Install a new cylinder head gasket (Section 16).

7 Install the valve lash compensators, followed by the rocker arms, in their original locations. Valve adjustment is not required on these models.

8 Install the camshaft carrier and cover.

9 Connect the PCV hose.

10 Connect the negative battery cable.

13   Valve springs, retainers and seals — replacement

The design of the OHC engine doesn't allow for replacement of the valve stem oil seals or valve springs with the cylinder head in place. To service valve train components, the cylinder head must be removed

12.5a Lift the rocker arms off and keep them in order — they must be reinstalled in their original locations!

12.5b The rocker arm guides and lash compensators (arrow) can be removed with a magnet (keep them in order as well)

2A

from the engine and disassembled on a workbench. Refer to the cylinder head removal and installation procedure in Section 16 and the cylinder head overhaul procedures in Chapter 2, Part D.

14 Intake manifold — removal and installation

Refer to illustration 14.12

Removal

1 Disconnect the negative cable from the battery.
2 Remove the induction, vacuum and PCV hoses connected to the intake system.
3 Drain the coolant (Chapter 1).
4 Remove the alternator and brackets (Chapter 5).
5 Remove the power steering pump and brackets (Chapter 10). Remove the cruise control cable (if equipped) from the intake manifold bracket.
6 Disconnect the throttle cable, downshift cable and TV cable from the EFI assembly. To remove the cable from the bracket, pull up while using a screwdriver to push the snap in.
7 Disconnect and label the wiring to the throttle body, MAP sensor, wastegate and ignition coil.
8 Relieve the fuel system pressure (Chapter 4).
9 Remove the fuel lines at the fuel rail inlet and regulator outlet.
10 Detach the wires at the fuel injectors.
11 Remove the manifold support bracket.
12 Remove the manifold retaining nuts and washers (**see illustration**).
13 Detach the intake manifold and gasket.

Installation

Note: *The mating surfaces of the head and manifold must be perfectly clean when the manifold is installed. Gasket removal solvents in aerosol cans are available at most auto parts stores and may be helpful when removing old gasket material that's stuck to the head and manifold (since the components are made of aluminum, aggressive scraping can cause damage). Be sure to follow the directions printed on the container.*

14 Use a gasket scraper to remove all traces of sealant and gasket material, then clean the mating surfaces with lacquer thinner or acetone. If pieces of gasket, sealant or oil are left on the mating surfaces when the manifold is installed, vacuum leaks may develop.
15 Install a new gasket (no sealant is required), place the manifold in position on the studs and install the retaining nuts. Tighten the nuts to the specified torque. Work from the center of the manifold out, in

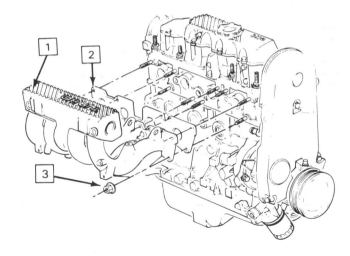

14.12 Intake manifold mounting details

1 Manifold	3 Nut
2 Gasket	

a criss-cross pattern to avoid distorting the manifold.
16 Reinstall the components that were removed to gain access to the intake manifold.
17 Start and run the engine and check for fuel and vacuum leaks.

15 Exhaust manifold — removal and installation

Refer to illustration 15.7

Removal

1 Disconnect the negative cable from the battery.
2 Remove the air induction tube.
3 Disconnect the spark plug wires from the spark plugs and label them.
4 Unplug the oxygen sensor wire.
5 Remove the oil dipstick tube.
6 Remove the bolts and nuts holding the turbo to the manifold.

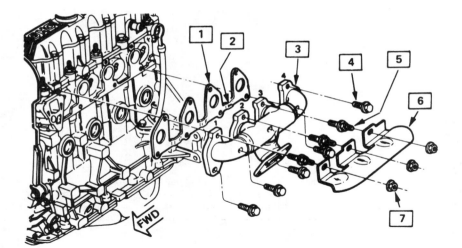

15.7   Exhaust manifold mounting details

1 Gasket
2 Expansion joints
*   (must face out)*
3 Manifold
4 Bolt/lock washer
5 Stud bolt/lock washer
6 Heat shield
7 Nut

7   Remove the exhaust manifold mounting bolts and detach the heat shield **(see illustration)**.
8   Separate the manifold from the engine.

Installation

9   Use a gasket scraper to remove all traces of carbon and old gasket material from the manifold and head mating surfaces, then clean them with lacquer thinner or acetone. Be careful not to nick or gouge the head surface.
10   It may be difficult to hold the manifold in place, position the gasket behind it and install the bolts without assistance, but it can be done. An alternative would be to attach the gasket to the manifold with sewing thread (which will hold it in place as the bolts are installed). Don't use sealant to hold the gasket in place. **Note:** *The expansion joints on the gasket must face out, away from the cylinder head.*
11   When tightening the bolts, work from the center of the manifold to the ends and use a torque wrench. Tighten the bolts in three or four equal steps until the specified torque is reached.
12   Install the components that were removed for access and connect the battery cable.
13   Start the engine and check for exhaust leaks.

---

16   Cylinder head — removal and installation

Refer to illustrations 16.16 and 16.18

Removal

1   Disconnect the negative cable from the battery.
2   Remove the air induction and PCV hoses/tubes. Drain the cooling system, disconnect the upper radiator hose, unplug the connectors and remove the thermostat housing (Chapters 1 and 3).
3   Remove the alternator and bracket (Chapter 5).
4   Remove the power steering pump and bracket assembly and lay it to one side (Chapter 10).
5   Disconnect the spark plug wires and distributor cap and remove them as an assembly.
6   Remove the ignition coil, distributor and wiring (Chapter 5).
7   Disconnect the throttle cable from the intake manifold bracket.
8   Disconnect the throttle, downshift and TV cables from the EFI assembly.
9   Disconnect the ECM connectors from the EFI components.
10   Remove the vacuum hose going to the brake booster.
11   Remove the heater hose from the intake manifold fitting.
12   Disconnect the exhaust manifold from the turbo.
13   Remove the timing belt (Section 6).
14   Refer to Section 11 and remove the camshaft carrier/cylinder head mounting bolts, then detach the carrier from the head.
15   Remove the rocker arms and valve lash compensators (Section 12).
16   Break the gasket seal by tapping the cylinder head with a soft-face hammer or a hammer and wood block **(see illustration)**.
17   Separate the cylinder head from the engine.
18   Remove the gasket from the engine **(see illustration)**.

16.16   Use a block of wood and a hammer to break the cylinder head gasket seal — don't strike the head directly with a metal hammer!

16.18   Use a scraper to remove the old head gasket

Installation

19   The mating surfaces of the camshaft carrier, cylinder head and block must be perfectly clean when the head is installed.
20   Use a gasket scraper to remove all traces of carbon and old gasket material, then clean the mating surfaces with lacquer thinner or acetone. If there's oil on the mating surfaces when the head is installed, the gasket may not seal correctly and leaks may develop. Use a vacuum

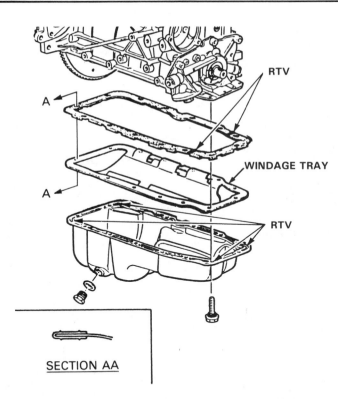

17.12 Oil pan gasket/sealant application details

cleaner to remove any debris that falls into the cylinders.
21 Check the carrier, block and head mating surfaces for nicks, deep scratches and other damage. If damage is slight, it can be removed with a file; if it's excessive, machining may be the only alternative.
22 Use a tap of the correct size to chase the threads of the head bolt holes in the block. Dirt, corrosion, sealant and damaged threads will affect torque readings. The bolts should be discarded — new ones must be used when the head is installed.
23 Position the new gasket over the dowel pins in the block. The top of the gasket should be stamped TOP or THIS SIDE UP to ensure correct installation. Don't use sealant on the gasket.
24 Carefully position the head on the block without disturbing the gasket. Make sure it slips over the dowel pins and rests on the gasket.
25 Refer to Section 11 and install the camshaft carrier and cylinder head bolts.
26 The remaining installation steps are the reverse of removal.

---

17 Oil pan — removal and installation

Refer to illustration 17.12

Removal

1 Disconnect the negative cable from the battery.
2 Loosen the lug nuts on the right front wheel.
3 Raise the front of the vehicle and support it securely on jackstands.
4 Remove the right front wheel.
5 Remove the right front fender liner (Chapter 11).
6 Disconnect the exhaust pipe at the wastegate.
7 Remove the bellhousing dust cover.
8 Drain the engine oil and replace the filter (Chapter 1).
9 Remove the oil pan bolts and separate the oil pan from the engine. Use a hammer and block of wood to dislodge it if it's stuck — don't pry between the sealing surfaces as damage that could lead to oil leaks may occur.

Installation

10 Use a gasket scraper to remove all traces of old gasket material and sealant from the windage tray, oil pan and block, then clean the

mating surfaces with lacquer thinner or acetone.
11 Make sure the bolt holes in the block are clean. Check the oil pan and windage tray flanges for distortion, particularly around the bolt holes. If necessary, place them on a block of wood and use a hammer to flatten and restore the gasket mating surfaces.
12 Attach the new gasket to the windage tray, then apply RTV-sealant to the oil pan flange and the upper side of the gasket **(see illustration)**.
13 Attach the oil pan, windage tray and gasket to the engine and install the bolts. Tighten the bolts to the specified torque in three or four steps. Start at the center of the pan and work out toward the ends in a spiral pattern.
14 The remaining steps are the reverse of removal. **Caution:** *Don't forget to refill the engine with oil before starting it (see Chapter 1).*
15 Start the engine and check carefully for oil leaks at the oil pan-to-block junction.

---

18 Oil pump screen and pick-up tube — removal and installation

Refer to illustration 18.2

1 Remove the oil pan (Section 17).
2 Remove the bolts and detach the pick-up tube from the block **(see illustration)**.

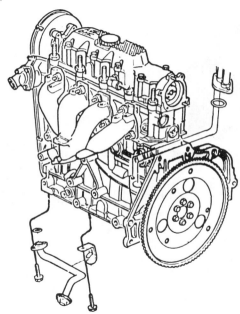

18.2 Oil pump pick-up tube mounting details

3 Remove the O-ring from the tube and discard it. Clean the tube and screen assembly with solvent and dry it with compressed air (if available).
4 Attach a new O-ring to the tube and position the tube on the block. Install the bolts and tighten them to the specified torque.
5 Install the oil pan.

---

19 Oil pump — removal and installation

Removal

1 The oil pump is mounted low on the timing belt end of the engine and is driven directly off the end of the crankshaft. Remove the timing belt, the rear timing belt cover and the crankshaft sprocket (Sections 5, 6 and 8).
2 Unplug the wiring harness from the oil pressure switch, located near the oil filter.
3 Remove the oil pan (Section 17) and the oil filter.
4 Remove the pick-up tube assembly (Section 18).
5 Pry out the crankshaft oil seal — be careful not to damage the shaft or bore in the process!

2A

6 Remove the six bolts and separate the oil pump from the block. Refer to Section 20 for the disassembly, inspection and reassembly procedure.

Installation

7 Use a gasket scraper to remove all old gasket material from the oil pump and block, then clean them with lacquer thinner or acetone.
8 Place the pump and new gasket in position and install the bolts. Tighten the bolts to the specified torque.
9 Install the pick-up tube assembly (Section 18).
10 Install the oil pan (Section 17).
11 Install a new oil filter and connect the oil pressure switch harness.
12 Install the crankshaft sprocket, timing belt and covers.
13 Refill the engine with the specified oil (Chapter 1).
14 Start the engine and check for oil leaks.

---

20 Oil pump — disassembly, inspection and reassembly

Refer to illustrations 20.3a, 20.3b, 20.6, 20.7, 20.8 and 20.11

Disassembly

1 Remove the screws and detach the cover from the rear of the pump.

2 Remove the gears from the pump body. It may be necessary to turn the body over to remove the gears by allowing them to fall out.
3 Mount the pump body in a vise equipped with soft jaws and remove the oil pressure sending unit, plug, pressure regulator valve plunger and spring (**see illustrations**).

Inspection

4 Clean the parts with solvent and dry them with compressed air, if available.
5 Inspect the components for wear, cracks and other damage. Replace any damaged or worn parts with new ones.
6 Check the outer (idler) gear-to-body clearance (**see illustration**).
7 Check the inner (drive) gear-to-body clearance (**see illustration**).
8 Check the gear-to-cover clearance (**see illustration**).

Reassembly

9 Install the valve plunger and spring assembly.
10 Coat the plug threads with Locktite, then install and tighten it to the specified torque.
11 Install the gears, noting that the outer gear is identified by a mark. This mark must face the cover (**see illustration**).
12 Completely pack the pump with petroleum jelly to ensure pump priming. Install the cover and tighten the screws securely.
13 Install the oil pressure sending unit.

20.3a The oil pump will be easier to work on if it's mounted in a vise (be sure to pad the jaws)

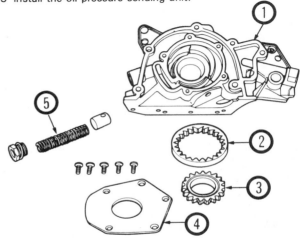

20.3b Oil pump components

1 Pump body
2 Idler gear
3 Drive gear
4 Cover
5 Valve plunger and spring assembly

20.6 Checking the idler gear-to-body clearance with a feeler gauge

20.7 Checking the drive gear-to-body clearance

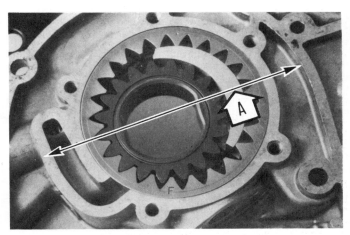

20.8   The gear-to-cover clearance is checked by inserting a feeler gauge between the gear and a straightedge laid across the pump body at point A

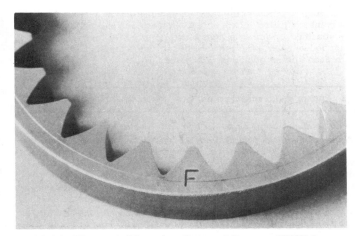

20.11   The mark (F) on the oil pump idler gear MUST face the cover

21   Rear main oil seal — replacement

Refer to illustrations 21.3 and 21.6

Note: *The rear main bearing oil seal is a one piece unit that can be replaced without removing the oil pan or crankshaft. However, the transaxle must be removed and the engine must be supported as this procedure is done. GM special tool no. J36227 is available for seal installation, but the procedure outlined here was devised to avoid having to use the tool.*

Warning: *A special tool (GM no. J28467) is available to support the engine during repair operations. Similar fixtures are available from rental yards. Improper lifting methods or devices are hazardous and could result in severe injury or death. DO NOT place any part of your body under the engine/transaxle when it's supported only by a jack. Failure of the lifting device could result in serious injury or death.*

Removal

1   Remove the transaxle (Chapter 7).
2   Remove the driveplate (automatic transaxle) or pressure plate, clutch disc and flywheel (manual transaxle).
3   Pry the old seal out very carefully with a seal removal tool or a screwdriver **(see illustration)**. If the crankshaft is nicked or scratched as this is done, the new seal will be damaged when the engine is started and oil leaks will result.

Installation

4   Remove all traces of oil from the engine block seal bore and check the seal contact surface on the crankshaft for scratches and burrs that could damage the new seal. If the crankshaft is damaged, a new or different crankshaft may have to be installed.
5   Apply a thin coat of engine oil to the outer edge of the new seal and coat the seal lip with moly-base grease.
6   Insert the new seal squarely into the bore and tap it into place until it's completely seated **(see illustration)**. Be very careful not to damage the seal in the process and make sure it's driven in squarely.
7   Install the clutch and flywheel or driveplate.
8   Reinstall the transaxle.

21.3   Pry out the rear main oil seal very carefully — don't damage the surface of the crankshaft or the new seal will leak

21.6   Tap around the outer edge of the new oil seal with a hammer and a blunt punch to seat it squarely in the bore

22   Flywheel/driveplate — removal and installation

1   Refer to Chapter 7 and remove the transaxle. If your vehicle has a manual transaxle, the pressure plate and clutch will also have to be removed (Chapter 8).
2   Jam a large screwdriver in the starter ring gear to keep the crankshaft from turning, then remove the mounting bolts. Since it's fairly heavy, support the flywheel as the last bolt is removed. The flywheel mounting bolts (manual transaxle only) must be discarded and new ones must be used for installation. The driveplate bolts (automatic trans-

axle) can be reused.
3   Pull straight back on the flywheel/driveplate to detach it from the crankshaft.
4   Installation is the reverse of removal. When installing the flywheel on manual transaxle equipped vehicles, be sure to use new mounting

bolts. Align the hole in the flywheel/driveplate with the dowel pin in the crankshaft. Use Locktite on the bolt threads and tighten them to the specified torque in a criss-cross pattern. On manual transaxle equipped vehicles, after the specified torque is reached, go back and turn each bolt an additional 30-degrees.

23 Engine and transaxle mounts — replacement

Refer to illustrations 23.5, 23.15a and 23.15b

Warning: *A special tool (GM no. J28467) is available to support the engine during repair operations. Similar fixtures are available from rental yards. Improper lifting methods or devices are hazardous and could result in severe injury or death. DO NOT place any part of your body under the engine/transaxle when it's supported only by a jack. Failure of the lifting device could result in serious injury or death.*

1   If the rubber mounts have hardened, cracked or separated from the metal backing plates, they must be replaced. This operation may be carried out with the engine/transaxle still in the vehicle.
2   Disconnect the negative cable from the battery.
3   Raise the front of the vehicle and support it securely on jackstands.
4   Support the engine with a jack.

Front mount

5   Remove the two mount-to-bracket bolts **(see illustration)**.
6   Remove the two top mount bolts.
7   Whenever the mount is removed, a bolt must be inserted to keep the driveaxles properly aligned.
8   Remove the lower mount bolt.
9   Place the new mount in position and install the bolts. If excessive effort is required to remove the alignment bolt, loosen the transaxle mount bolts and adjust the mount position until the bolt can be easily removed.
10   Remove the alignment bolt and tighten the mount bolts.

Rear mount

11   Remove the two mount-to-bracket bolts.
12   Remove the lower mount nuts and reinforcement.
13   Remove the mount from the vehicle.
14   Installation is the reverse of removal.

Transaxle mount

15   Loosen the lower mount bolt **(see illustrations)**.
16   Remove the long bracket-to-mount bolt.
17   Remove the upper mount nuts.

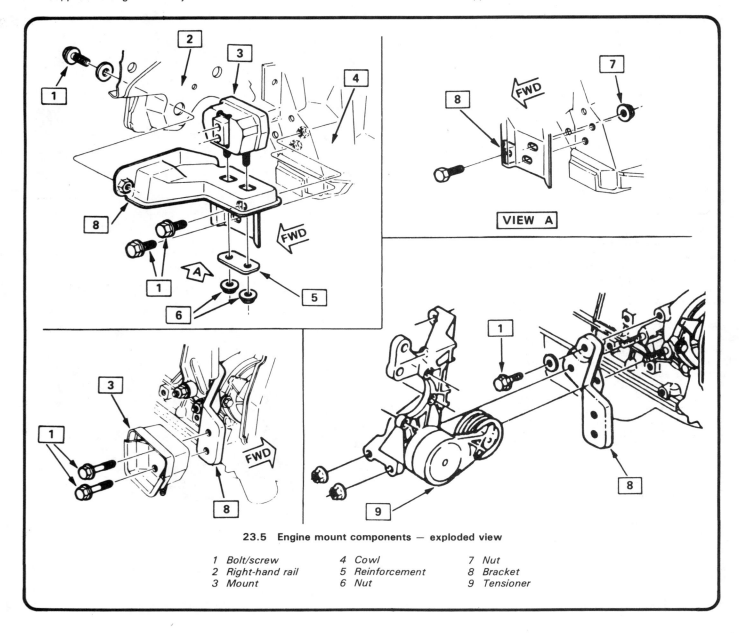

23.5   Engine mount components — exploded view

1 Bolt/screw	4 Cowl	7 Nut
2 Right-hand rail	5 Reinforcement	8 Bracket
3 Mount	6 Nut	9 Tensioner

18 Remove the transaxle mount.
19 Position the transaxle mount over the lower bolt.
20 Loosely attach the upper mount bolts.
21 Insert the long bracket-to-mount bolt.

All mounts

22 Gently lower the lifting device.
23 Tighten the bolts securely.
24 Reconnect the negative battery cable.

2A

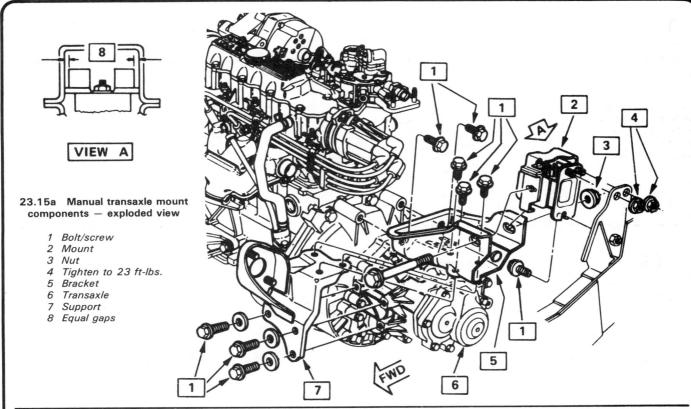

VIEW A

23.15a Manual transaxle mount components — exploded view

1 Bolt/screw
2 Mount
3 Nut
4 Tighten to 23 ft-lbs.
5 Bracket
6 Transaxle
7 Support
8 Equal gaps

FWD

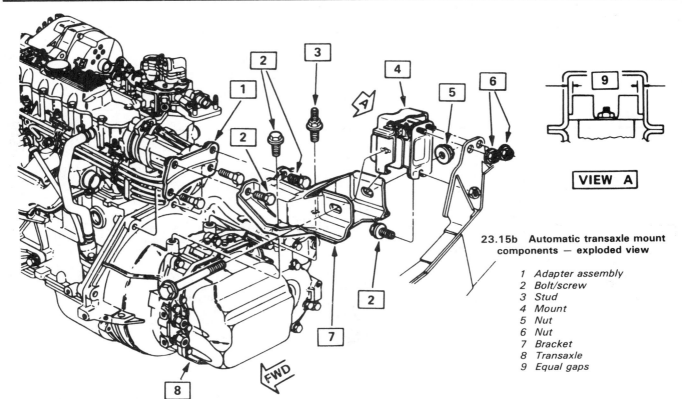

VIEW A

23.15b Automatic transaxle mount components — exploded view

1 Adapter assembly
2 Bolt/screw
3 Stud
4 Mount
5 Nut
6 Nut
7 Bracket
8 Transaxle
9 Equal gaps

FWD

24　Transaxle strut — removal and installation

Refer to illustrations 24.2a, 24.2b and 24.2c

1　The automatic transaxle is equipped with two struts. One, called a lateral strut, and a second to control fore-and-aft movement. Manual transaxles are equipped with only one strut. Disconnect the negative battery cable from the battery.

2　Remove the strut-to-bracket bolt (**see illustrations**).
3　Remove the strut-to-transaxle bolt.
4　Remove the strut from the vehicle.
5　Bolt the strut to the transaxle.
6　Install the strut-to-bracket bolt.
7　Tighten the fasteners securely. **Note:** *Some fasteners must be discarded and replaced with new ones during installation — refer to the appropriate illustration.*
8　Reconnect the battery cable.

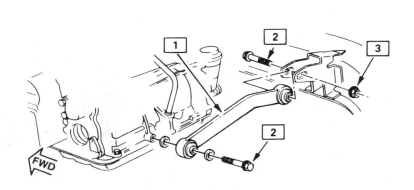

24.2a　Transaxle lateral strut components — exploded view (automatic only)

1　*Strut*
2　*Bolt/screw*
3　*Nut*

24.2b　Transaxle strut components — exploded view (manual)

1　*Bolt/screw*
2　*Transaxle*
3　*Bolt/screw*
4　*Bracket*
5　*Strut*

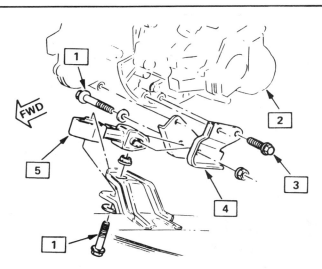

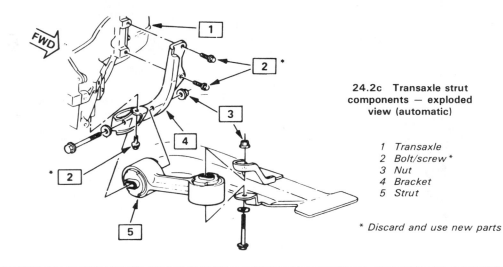

24.2c　Transaxle strut components — exploded view (automatic)

1　*Transaxle*
2　*Bolt/screw ** *
3　*Nut*
4　*Bracket*
5　*Strut*

* *Discard and use new parts*

Chapter 2 Part B
2.5L overhead valve (OHV) 4-cylinder engine

Contents

Specifications

2B

General

Cylinder numbers (drivebelt end-to-transaxle end)	1–2–3–4
Firing order	1–3–4–2

Torque specifications

	Ft-lbs
Cylinder head bolts	
1985	92
1986 on **(see illustration 10.25)**	
step 1 — all bolts, in sequence	18
step 2 — all bolts, except 9, in sequence	22
step 2 — bolt 9	30
step 3 — all bolts, except 9, in sequence	Turn an additional 120°
step 3 — bolt 9	Turn an additional 90°
Exhaust manifold bolts	
1985	44
1986 on **(see illustration 9.12)**	
Bolts 1, 2, 6 and 7	32
Bolts 3, 4 and 5	37
Flywheel-to-crankshaft bolts	
1985	44
1986	55
1987	69
Driveplate-to-crankshaft bolts	
1985	44
1986 on	55
Force balancer-to-engine block bolt	
short bolt	9 plus 75° additional rotation
long bolt	9 plus 90° additional rotation
Crankshaft pulley hub-to-crankshaft bolt	200
Intake manifold-to-cylinder head bolts	
1985	29
1986 **(see illustration 8.15)**	
Bolt A	25
Bolt B	37
Bolt C	28
1987	25
Lifter guide retainer-to-block stud	7.4
Oil pan bolts	7.4
Oil pan drain plug	25
Oil pick-up tube bracket nut	37
Oil pump-to-block bolts	22
Pushrod cover nuts	7.4
Rocker arm bolts	
1985	20
1986 on	24
Rocker arm cover bolts	3.6
Timing gear cover bolts	7.4

1 General information

This Part of Chapter 2 is devoted to in-vehicle repair procedures for the 2.5 liter four-cylinder engine. Information concerning engine removal and installation, as well as engine block and cylinder head overhaul, is in Part D of this Chapter.

The following repair procedures are based on the assumption that the engine is installed in the vehicle. If the engine has been removed from the vehicle and mounted on a stand, many of the steps included in this Part of Chapter 2 will not apply.

The Specifications included in this Part of Chapter 2 apply only to the engine and procedures in this Part. The Specifications necessary for rebuilding the block and cylinder head are found in Part D.

2 Repair operations possible with the engine in the vehicle

Many major repair operations can be accomplished without removing the engine from the vehicle.

Clean the engine compartment and the exterior of the engine with some type of pressure washer before any work is done. A clean engine will make the job easier and will help keep dirt out of the internal areas of the engine.

Depending on the components involved, it may be a good idea to remove the hood to improve access to the engine as repairs are performed (refer to Chapter 11 if necessary).

If vacuum, exhaust, oil or coolant leaks develop, indicating a need for gasket or seal replacement, the repairs can generally be made with the engine in the vehicle. The intake and exhaust manifold gaskets, oil pan gasket and cylinder head gasket are all accessible with the engine in place.

Exterior engine components such as the intake and exhaust manifolds, the oil pan (and the oil pump), the water pump, the starter motor, the alternator, the distributor and the fuel injection system can be removed for repair with the engine in place.

Since the cylinder head can be removed without pulling the engine, valve component servicing can also be accomplished with the engine in the vehicle.

In extreme cases caused by a lack of necessary equipment, repair or replacement of piston rings, pistons, connecting rods and rod bearings is possible with the engine in the vehicle.

However, this practice is not recommended because of the cleaning and preparation work that must be done to the components involved.

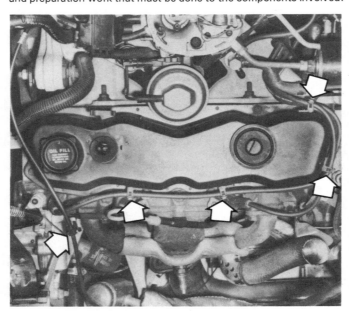

3.4   Disconnect all four spark plug wire harness retainer clips and detach the throttle cable from the exhaust manifold bracket (arrows)

3 Rocker arm cover — removal and installation

Refer to illustrations 3.3, 3.4, 3.8, 3.9 and 3.10

1   Remove the air cleaner assembly.
2   Disconnect the throttle cable from the fuel injection assembly. Make careful note of the exact locations of the cable components and hardware to ensure correct reinstallation.
3   Remove the PCV valve from the rocker arm cover **(see illustration)**.
4   Label each spark plug wire before removal to ensure that all wires are reinstalled correctly, then remove the wires from the plugs (refer to Chapter 1). Detach the wires and retaining clips from the rocker arm cover **(see illustration)**.
5   Remove the EGR valve (Chapter 6).
6   Remove the rocker arm cover bolts.
7   Starting with 1987 models, a special tool is recommended for cover removal (GM no. J34144-A).
8   Remove the rocker arm cover. If it sticks to the head, use a soft-face hammer or a block of wood and a hammer to dislodge it. If the cover still won't come loose, pry on it carefully at several points until the seal is broken, but don't distort the cover flange **(see illustration)**. **Note:** *If you bend the cover, straighten it with a block of wood and a hammer.*

3.3   The PCV valve can be pulled out of the rubber grommet in the rocker arm cover (leave the hose attached to the valve)

3.8   The rocker arm cover is sealed with RTV — if you have to pry it off the head, try to avoid bending the flange

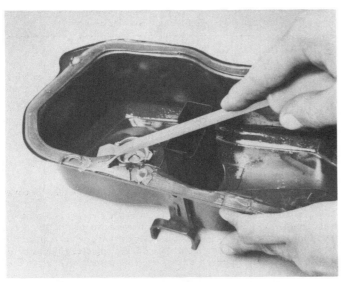

3.9   Remove the old sealant from the rocker arm cover flange and the cylinder head with a gasket scraper, then clean the mating surfaces with lacquer thinner or acetone

3.10   Apply a continuous 3/16-in diameter bead of RTV sealant (arrow) to the rocker arm cover flange

9   Prior to reinstallation, remove all dirt, oil and old gasket material from the cover and cylinder head with a scraper (**see illustration**). Clean the mating surfaces with lacquer thinner or acetone.
10   Apply a continuous 3/16-inch (5 mm) diameter bead of RTV sealant to the flange on the cover. Be sure the sealant is applied to the inside of the bolt holes (**see illustration**). **Note:** *Don't get the sealant in the bolt holes in the head or damage to the head may occur.*
11   Place the rocker arm cover on the cylinder head while the sealant is still wet and install the mounting bolts. Tighten the bolts a little at a time until the specified torque is reached.
12   Complete the installation by reversing the removal procedure.
13   Start the engine and check for oil leaks at the rocker arm cover-to-head joint.

2B

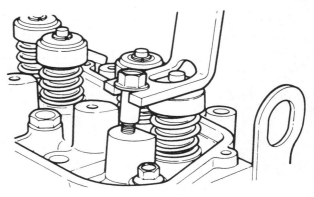

4.8a   A lever-type valve spring compressor is used to compress the spring and remove the keepers to replace valve seals or springs with the head installed

---

4   Valve springs, retainers and seals — replacement

Refer to illustrations 4.8a, 4.8b, 4.16 and 4.17
Note: *Broken valve springs and defective valve stem seals can be replaced without removing the cylinder head. Two special tools and a compressed air source are normally required to perform this operation, so read through this Section carefully and rent or buy the tools before beginning the job. If compressed air isn't available, a length of nylon rope can be used to keep the valves from falling into the cylinder during this procedure.*

1   Refer to Section 3 and remove the rocker arm cover.
2   Remove the spark plug from the cylinder which has the defective component. If all of the valve stem seals are being replaced, all of the spark plugs should be removed.
3   Turn the crankshaft until the piston in the affected cylinder is at top dead center on the compression stroke (refer to Part D for instructions). If you're replacing all of the valve stem seals, begin with cylinder number one and work on the valves for one cylinder at a time. Move from cylinder-to-cylinder following the firing order sequence (1-3-4-2).
4   Thread an adapter into the spark plug hole and connect an air hose from a compressed air source to it. Most auto parts stores can supply the air hose adapter. **Note:** *Many cylinder compression gauges utilize a screw-in fitting that may work with your air hose quick-disconnect fitting.*
5   Remove the bolt, pivot ball and rocker arm for the valve with the defective part and pull out the pushrod. If all of the valve stem seals are being replaced, all of the rocker arms and pushrods should be removed (refer to Section 6).
6   Apply compressed air to the cylinder. The valves should be held in place by the air pressure. If the valve faces or seats are in poor condition, leaks may prevent the air pressure from retaining the valves

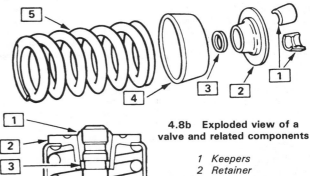

4.8b   Exploded view of a valve and related components

1   *Keepers*
2   *Retainer*
3   *O-ring seal*
4   *Shield*
5   *Spring*

— refer to the alternative procedure below.
7   If you don't have access to compressed air, an alternative method can be used. Position the piston at a point just before TDC on the compression stroke, then feed a long piece of nylon rope through the spark plug hole until it fills the combustion chamber. Be sure to leave the end of the rope hanging out of the engine so it can be removed easily. Use a large breaker bar and socket to rotate the crankshaft in the normal direction of rotation until slight resistance is felt.
8   Stuff shop rags into the cylinder head holes above and below the valves to prevent parts and tools from falling into the engine, then use a valve spring compressor to compress the spring (**see illustration**). Remove the keepers with small needle-nose pliers or a magnet (**see illustration**). **Note:** *A couple of different types of tools are available for compressing the valve springs with the head in place. One type grips the lower spring coils and presses on the retainer as the knob is turned, while the other type, shown here, utilizes the rocker arm bolt for leverage. Both types work very well, although the lever type is usually less expensive.*
9   Remove the valve stem O-ring seal, spring retainer, shield and valve

4.16   Make sure the O-ring seal under the retainer is seated in the groove and not twisted before installing the keepers

4.17   Keepers don't always stay in place, so apply a small dab of grease to each one as shown here before installation — it'll hold them in place on the valve stem as the spring is released

spring, then remove the umbrella type guide seal, if equipped (the O-ring seal will most likely be hardened and will probably break when removed, so plan on installing a new one each time the original is removed). **Note:** *If air pressure fails to hold the valve in the closed position during this operation, the valve face or seat is probably damaged. If so, the cylinder head will have to be removed for additional repair operations.*

10 Wrap a rubber band or tape around the top of the valve stem so the valve will not fall into the combustion chamber, then release the air pressure. **Note:** *If a rope was used instead of air pressure, turn the crankshaft slightly in the direction opposite normal rotation.*

11 Inspect the valve stem for damage. Rotate the valve in the guide and check the end for eccentric movement, which would indicate that the valve is bent.

12 Move the valve up-and-down in the guide and make sure it doesn't bind. If the valve stem binds, either the valve is bent or the guide is damaged. In either case, the head will have to be removed for repair.

13 Reapply air pressure to the cylinder to retain the valve in the closed position, then remove the tape or rubber band from the valve stem. If a rope was used instead of air pressure, rotate the crankshaft in the normal direction of rotation until slight resistance is felt.

14 Lubricate the valve stem with engine oil and install a new umbrella type guide seal, if used.

15 Install the spring and shield in position over the valve.

16 Install the valve spring retainer. Compress the valve spring and carefully install the new O-ring seal in the lower groove of the valve stem. Make sure the seal isn't twisted — it must lie perfectly flat in the groove **(see illustration).**

17 Position the keepers in the upper groove. Apply a small dab of grease to the inside of each keeper to hold it in place if necessary **(see illustration).** Remove the pressure from the spring tool and make sure the keepers are seated. Refer to Chapter 2, Part D, and check the seals with a vacuum pump.

18 Disconnect the air hose and remove the adapter from the spark plug hole. If a rope was used in place of air pressure, pull it out of the cylinder.

19 Refer to Section 6 and install the rocker arm(s) and pushrod(s).

20 Install the spark plug(s) and hook up the wire(s).

21 Refer to Section 3 and install the rocker arm cover.

22 Start and run the engine, then check for oil leaks and unusual sounds coming from the rocker arm cover area.

5.3   The pushrod cover is held in place with four nuts (arrows)

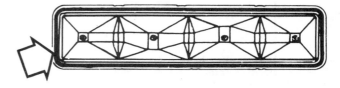

5.7   The pushrod cover is sealed with RTV — no gasket is required

5.8 Don't forget to install new rubber sealing washers around the pushrod cover mounting studs or oil will leak past the studs

5.9 Install the pushrod cover while the sealant is still tacky — be sure the semi-circular cutout (arrow) is facing down

5 Pushrod cover — removal and installation

Refer to illustrations 5.3, 5.7, 5.8 and 5.9

1 Remove the air intake assembly. Tag each hose with a piece of numbered or colored tape to ensure correct installation.

2 Remove the intake manifold (Section 8).

3 Loosen the four pushrod cover nuts **(see illustration)**.

4 Flip one nut over so the washer faces out and reinstall it on the long inner stud. Put a second nut on the stud with the washer facing in. Put two 6 mm nuts on the shorter stud. Jam them together with two wrenches. Unscrew the studs by turning the inner nuts until the cover breaks free.

5 Remove the pushrod cover. **Caution:** *Careless prying may damage the sealing surface of the cover. If you bend the cover during removal, place it on a flat surface and straighten it with a soft-face hammer.*

6 Remove all traces of old gasket material with a scraper, then clean the mating surfaces with lacquer thinner or acetone.

7 Apply a continuous 3/16-inch diameter bead of RTV sealant to the mating surface of the pushrod cover **(see illustration)**.

8 Install new rubber pushrod cover seals **(see illustration)**.

9 Install the cover while the sealant is still wet. Make sure the semi-circular cutout in the edge of the pushrod cover is facing down **(see illustration)**.

10 Tighten the nuts gradually until they're snug, then tighten them to the specified torque.

11 Reattach the wire harness to the pushrod cover.

12 Install the intake manifold.

13 Install the air intake duct.

6 Rocker arms and pushrods — removal, inspection and installation

Refer to illustrations 6.3, 6.4a, 6.4b and 6.5

Removal

1 Refer to Section 3 and detach the rocker arm cover from the cylinder head.

2 Beginning at the front of the cylinder head, loosen the rocker arm bolts. **Note:** *If the pushrods are the only items being removed, rotate the rocker arms to one side so the pushrods can be lifted out.*

3 Remove the bolts, the rocker arms and the pivot balls **(see illustration)** and store them in marked containers (they must be reinstalled in their original locations).

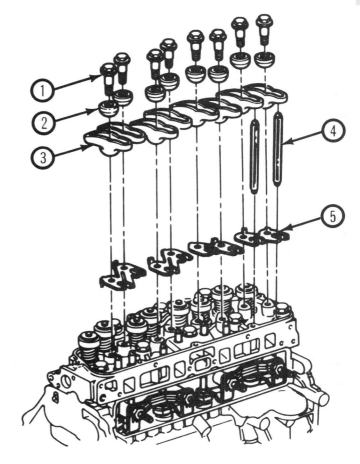

6.3 Rocker arms, pushrods and related components — exploded view

1 Rocker arm bolt	*4 Pushrod*
2 Pivot ball	*5 Pushrod guide*
3 Rocker arm	

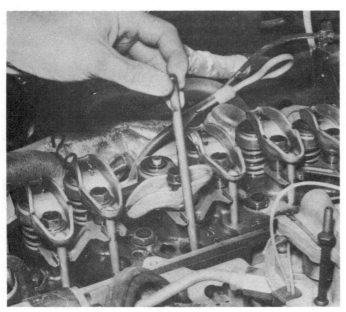

6.4a   Loosen the rocker arm bolt, rotate the rocker arm to one side and lift out the pushrod

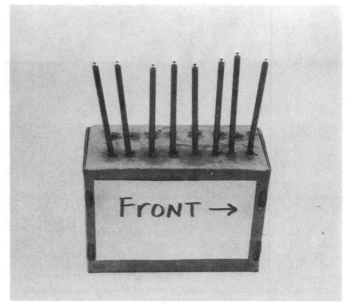

6.4b   If more than one pushrod is being removed, store them in a perforated cardboard box to prevent mixups during installation — note the label indicating the front of the engine

4   Remove the pushrods and store them separately to make sure they don't get mixed up during installation (**see illustrations**).
5   If the pushrod guides must be removed for any reason, make sure they're marked so they can be reinstalled in their original locations (**see illustration**).

Inspection

6   Check each rocker arm for wear, cracks and other damage, especially where the pushrods and valve stems contact the rocker arm faces.
7   Make sure the hole at the pushrod end of each rocker arm is open.
8   Check each rocker arm pivot area for wear, cracks and galling. If the rocker arms are worn or damaged, replace them with new ones and use new pivot balls as well.
9   Inspect the pushrods for cracks and excessive wear at the ends. Roll each pushrod across a piece of plate glass to see if it's bent (if it wobbles, it's bent).

Installation

10   Lubricate the lower ends of the pushrods with clean engine oil or moly-base grease and install them in their original locations. Make sure each pushrod seats completely in the lifter socket.
11   Apply moly-base grease to the ends of the valve stems and the upper ends of the pushrods before positioning the rocker arms and installing the bolts.
12   Set the rocker arms in place, then install the pivot balls and bolts. Apply moly-base grease to the pivot balls to prevent damage to the mating surfaces before engine oil pressure builds up. Tighten the bolts to the specified torque.

7   Hydraulic lifters — removal, inspection and installation

Refer to illustrations 7.7, 7.8 and 7.9

Removal

1   A noisy valve lifter can be isolated when the engine is idling. Place a length of hose or tubing near the position of each valve while listening at the other end. Or remove the rocker arm cover and, with the engine idling, place a finger on each of the valve spring retainers, one at a time. If a valve lifter is defective, it'll be evident from the shock felt at the retainer as the valve seats.
2   The most likely cause of a noisy valve lifter is a piece of dirt trapped between the plunger and the lifter body.

6.5   If they're removed, make sure the pushrod guides (arrows) are kept in order also

3   Remove the rocker arm cover (Section 3).
4   Loosen both rocker arm bolts at the cylinder with the noisy lifter and rotate the rocker arms away from the pushrods. Remove the pushrod guides and pushrods (Section 6).
5   Remove the intake manifold (Section 8).
6   Remove the pushrod cover (Section 5).
7   Remove the lifter guide retainer by unscrewing the locknuts on the pushrod cover studs. Remove the lifter guide (**see illustration**).
8   There are several ways to extract a lifter from its bore. A special removal tool is available, but isn't always necessary. On newer engines without a lot of varnish buildup, lifters can often be removed with a small magnet or even with your fingers (**see illustration**). A scribe can also be used to pull the lifter out of the bore. **Caution:** *Don't use pliers of any type to remove a lifter unless you intend to replace it with a new one — they will damage the precision machined and hardened surface of the lifter, rendering it useless.*
9   Store the lifters in a clearly labelled box to insure their reinstallation in the same lifter bores (**see illustration**).

Inspection

10   Refer to Part D for the inspection procedure. It's much easier to simply replace a worn lifter with a new one than attempt to repair a

7.7 Remove the lifter guide — if you're removing more than one guide, keep them in order to prevent mixups during installation

7.8 On engines that haven't become sticky with sludge and varnish, the lifters can usually be removed by hand

2B

7.9 If you're removing more than one lifter, keep them in order in a clearly labelled box

defective lifter. The internal components are not available separately — you must buy a lifter as a complete assembly.

Installation

11 The used lifters must be installed in their original bores. Coat them with moly-base grease or engine assembly lube.
12 Lubricate the bearing surfaces of the lifter bores with engine oil.
13 Install the lifter(s) in the lifter bore(s). **Note:** *Make sure that the oil orifice is facing toward the front of the engine.*
14 Install the lifter guide(s) and retainer(s).
15 Install the pushrods, pushrod guides, rocker arms and rocker arm retaining bolts (Section 6). **Caution:** *Make sure that each pair of lifters is on the base circle of the camshaft; that is, with both valves closed, before tightening the rocker arm bolts.*
16 Tighten the rocker arm bolts to the specified torque.
17 Install the pushrod cover (Section 5).
18 Install the intake manifold (Section 8).
19 Install the rocker arm cover (Section 3).

8   Intake manifold — removal and installation

Refer to illustrations 8.9, 8.10 and 8.15

1   Disconnect the cable from the negative battery terminal.
2   Remove the air cleaner assembly (Chapter 4).
3   Remove the PCV valve and hose.
4   Drain the cooling system (Chapter 1).
5   Refer to Chapter 4 and detach the fuel lines, vacuum lines and wire leads from the fuel injection assembly. When disconnecting the fuel line be prepared to catch some fuel, then plug the line to prevent contamination.
6   After noting how it's installed, disconnect the fuel injection throttle linkage.
7   Disconnect the cruise control linkage (if so equipped).
8   Remove the coolant hoses from the manifold.
9   Remove the mounting bolts and separate the manifold from the cylinder head **(see illustration)**. Don't pry between the manifold and head, as damage to the gasket sealing surfaces may result.

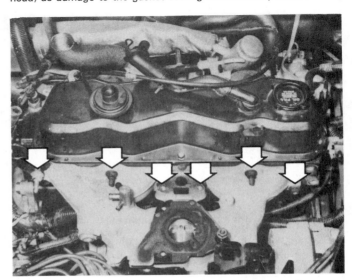

8.9 Location of the intake manifold mounting bolts (arrows)

8.10   Remove the old intake manifold gasket with a scraper — don't leave any material on the mating surfaces

10   Remove the old gasket (see illustration).
11   If a new manifold is being installed, transfer all components still attached to the old manifold to the new one.
12   Before installing the manifold, clean the cylinder head and manifold gasket surfaces with lacquer thinner or acetone. All gasket material and sealing compound must be removed prior to installation.
13   Apply a thin coat of RTV sealant to the intake manifold and cylinder head mating surfaces. Make certain that the sealant will not spread into the air or coolant passages when the manifold is installed.
14   Place a new gasket on the manifold, hold the manifold in position against the cylinder head and install the mounting bolts finger tight.
15   Tighten the mounting bolts a little at a time in the correct sequence (see illustration) until they're all at the specified torque.
16   Install the remaining components in the reverse order of removal.
17   Fill the radiator with coolant, start the engine and check for leaks.

9   Exhaust manifold — removal and installation

Refer to illustration 9.12
1   Remove the cable from the negative battery terminal.

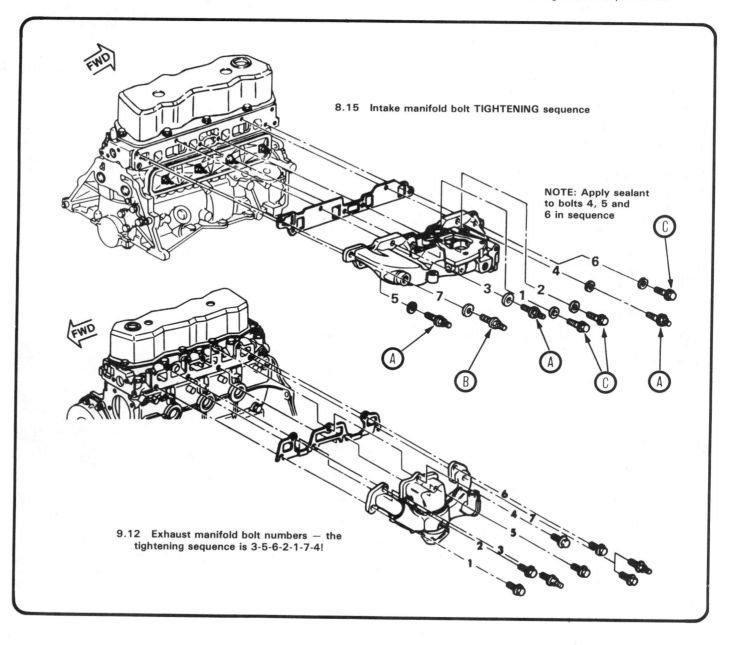

8.15   Intake manifold bolt TIGHTENING sequence

NOTE: Apply sealant to bolts 4, 5 and 6 in sequence

9.12   Exhaust manifold bolt numbers — the tightening sequence is 3-5-6-2-1-7-4!

2   Remove the air cleaner assembly (Chapter 4).
3   Remove the alternator support bracket and tip the alternator out of the way.
4   Raise the vehicle and support it securely on jackstands.
5   Disconnect the oxygen sensor.
6   Label the four spark plug wires, then disconnect them and secure them out of the way.
7   Disconnect the exhaust pipe from the exhaust manifold. You may have to apply penetrating oil to the fastener threads, as they are usually corroded. The exhaust pipe can be hung from the frame with a piece of wire.
8   Remove the exhaust manifold end bolts first, then remove the center bolts and separate the exhaust manifold from the engine.
9   Remove the exhaust manifold gasket.
10 Before installing the manifold, clean the gasket mating surfaces on the cylinder head and manifold. All old gasket material and carbon deposits must be removed.
11 Place a new exhaust manifold gasket in position on the cylinder head, then place the manifold in position and install the mounting bolts finger tight.
12 Tighten the mounting bolts a little at a time in the correct sequence **(see illustration)** until all of the bolts are at the specified torque.
13 Reconnect the exhaust pipe.
14 Lower the vehicle.
15 Install the remaining components in the reverse order of removal.
16 Start the engine and check for exhaust leaks between the manifold and cylinder head and between the manifold and exhaust pipe.

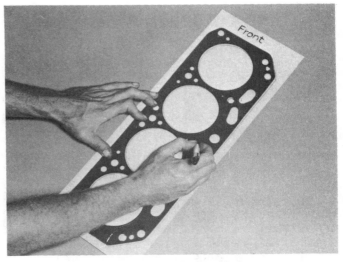

10.14   To avoid mixing up the head bolts, use a new gasket to transfer the bolt hole pattern to a piece of cardboard, then punch holes to accept the bolts . . .

---

10   Cylinder head — removal and installation

Refer to illustrations 10.14, 10.15, 10.16, 10.20, 10.22, 10.25 and 10.28

Removal

1   Disconnect the negative cable from the battery.
2   Drain the cooling system (Chapter 1).
3   Remove the air cleaner assembly Chapter 4).
4   Remove the intake manifold as described in Section 8.
5   Remove the exhaust manifold as described in Section 9.
6   Remove the bolts that secure the alternator bracket to the cylinder head.
7   If top mounted, unbolt the air conditioner compressor and swing it out of the way for clearance. **Caution:** *Don't disconnect any of the air-conditioning lines unless the system has been depressurized by a dealer service department or a repair shop.*
8   Disconnect all wires and vacuum hoses from the cylinder head. Be sure to label them to simplify reinstallation.
9   Remove the upper radiator and heater hoses.
10 Disconnect the spark plug wires and remove the spark plugs. Be sure to label the plug wires to simplify reinstallation.
11 Remove the rocker arm cover (Section 3).
12 Remove the pushrods (Section 6).
13 If the ignition coil is mounted separately from the distributor, disconnect the wires and remove the coil.
14 Using a new head gasket, outline the cylinders and bolt pattern on a piece of cardboard **(see illustration)**. Be sure to indicate the front of the engine for reference. Punch holes at the bolt locations.
15 Loosen the cylinder head mounting bolts in 1/4-turn increments until they can be removed by hand. Store the bolts in the cardboard holder as they're removed — this will ensure that they are reinstalled in their original locations **(see illustration)**.
16 Lift the head off the engine. If it's stuck, pry on it only at the overhang on the thermostat end of the head **(see illustration)**. **Caution:** *If you pry on the head anywhere else, damage to the gasket surface may result.*
17 Place the head on a block of wood to prevent damage to the gasket surface. Refer to Part D for cylinder head disassembly and valve service procedures.

Installation

18 If a new cylinder head is being installed, transfer all external parts from the old cylinder head to the new one.
19 The mating surfaces of the cylinder head and block must be perfectly clean when the head is installed.

10.15   . . . and push each head bolt through the matching hole in the cardboard

10.16   If the head is stuck, pry it up at the overhang just behind and below the thermostat housing

2B

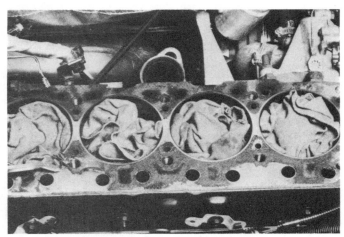

10.20   Once the head is off, stuff the cylinders with clean shop rags to prevent debris from falling into them and scrape off the old gasket material with a gasket scraper

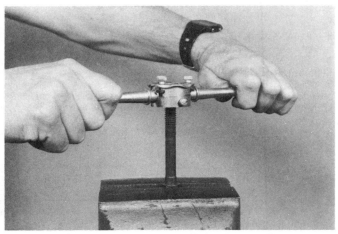

10.22   A die should be used to remove sealant and corrosion from the head bolt threads prior to installation

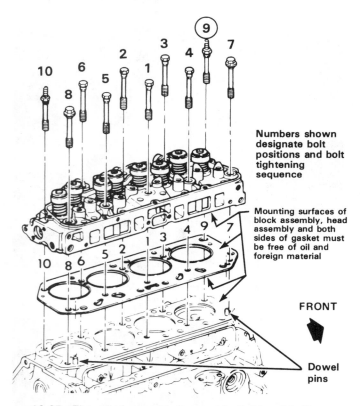

Numbers shown designate bolt positions and bolt tightening sequence

Mounting surfaces of block assembly, head assembly and both sides of gasket must be free of oil and foreign material

FRONT

Dowel pins

10.25   The cylinder head bolts must be tightened in three stages to the specified torque in the numerical sequence shown here

BOLT 9 ONLY

90°

120°

10.28   The final step in tightening the cylinder head bolts is known as ''angle torquing'' — all bolts except number 9 should be turned an additional 120-degrees, while bolt 9 should be turned an additional 90-degrees

20   Use a gasket scraper to remove all traces of carbon and old gasket material, then clean the mating surfaces with lacquer thinner or acetone **(see illustration)**. If there's oil on the mating surfaces when the head is installed, the gasket may not seal correctly and leaks may develop. Use a vacuum cleaner to remove any debris that falls into the cylinders.
21   Check the block and head mating surfaces for nicks, deep scratches and other damage. If damage is slight, it can be removed with a file; if it's excessive, machining may be the only alternative.
22   Use a tap of the correct size to chase the threads in the head bolt holes. Mount each bolt in a vise and run a die down the threads to remove corrosion and restore the threads **(see illustration)**. Dirt, corrosion, sealant and damaged threads will affect critical head bolt torque readings.

23   Position the new gasket over the dowel pins in the block.
24   Carefully position the head on the block without disturbing the gasket.
25   Coat the threads and the undersides of the heads of cylinder head bolt numbers 9 and 10 with GM sealing compound (no. 1052080 or equivalent) and install the bolts finger tight **(see illustration)**.
26   Tighten each of the bolts a little at a time in the sequence shown in illustration 10.25 until all bolts are at 18 ft-lbs.
27   On 1985 models only, continue tightening the bolts, in sequence, to 40, then to 70 and finally to 92 ft-lbs.
28   On 1986 and later models, tighten all bolts EXCEPT the left front bolt (number 9 in the sequence) to 22 ft-lbs. Tighten number 9 to 30 ft-lbs. Following the sequence one more time, tighten all bolts EXCEPT number 9 an additional 120-degrees (1/3-turn). Tighten number 9 an additional 90-degrees (1/4-turn) **(see illustration)**.
29   The remaining installation steps are the reverse of removal.
30   Change the oil and filter, run the engine and check for leaks.

---

11   Crankshaft pulley and hub — removal and installation

Refer to illustrations 11.8 and 11.11
1   Remove the cable from the negative battery terminal.
2   Remove the drivebelts (Chapter 1). Tag each belt as it's removed to simplify reinstallation.
3   Raise the vehicle and place it securely on jackstands.
4   Remove the right front wheel.
5   Remove the right front fender liner (Chapter 11).

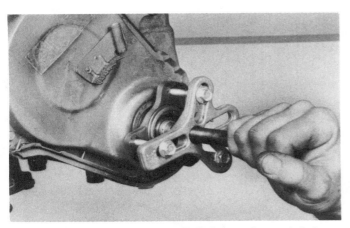

11.8 Use a puller to remove the hub from the crankshaft

11.11 Use the pulley hub bolt to press the hub onto the crankshaft

6   If your vehicle is equipped with a manual transaxle, apply the parking brake and put the transaxle in gear to prevent the engine from turning over, then remove the crank pulley bolts. If your vehicle is equipped with an automatic transaxle, remove the starter motor (Chapter 5) and immobilize the starter ring gear with a large screwdriver while an assistant loosens the pulley bolts.

7   To loosen the crankshaft hub retaining bolt, install a bolt in one of the pulley bolt holes. Attach a breaker bar, extension and socket to the hub retaining bolt and immobilize the hub by wedging a large screwdriver between the bolt and the socket. Remove the hub retaining bolt.

8   Remove the crankshaft hub. Use a puller if necessary (see illustration).

9   Refer to Section 12 for the front oil seal replacement procedure.

10   Apply a thin layer of moly-base grease to the seal contact surface of the hub.

11   Slide the pulley hub onto the crankshaft until it bottoms against the crankshaft timing gear. Note that the slot in the hub must be aligned with the Woodruff key in the end of the crankshaft. The hub retaining bolt can also be used to press the hub into position (see illustration).

12   Tighten the hub-to-crankshaft bolt to the specified torque.

13   Install the crank pulley on the hub. Use Locktite on the bolt threads.

14   Install the drivebelts (Chapter 1).

15   Install the right front fender liner.

12   Front crankshaft oil seal — replacement

12.2 The front crankshaft seal can be removed in the vehicle with a seal removal tool or a large screwdriver, providing there's enough room to work (V6 engine shown — 2.5L 4-cylinder similar)

Note: *The front crankshaft oil seal can be replaced with the timing gear cover in place. However, due to the limited amount of room available, you may conclude that the procedure would be easier if the cover were removed from the engine first. If so, refer to Section 13 for the cover removal and installation procedure.*

Timing gear cover in place

Refer to illustration 12.2

1   Remove the crankshaft pulley hub (Section 11).

2   Note how the seal is installed — the new one must face the same direction! Carefully pry the oil seal out of the cover with a seal puller or a large screwdriver (see illustration). Be very careful not to distort the cover or scratch the crankshaft!

3   Apply clean engine oil or multi-purpose grease to the outer edge of the new seal, then install it in the cover with the lip (open end) facing IN. Drive the seal into place with a large socket and a hammer (if a large socket isn't available, a piece of pipe will also work). Make sure the seal enters the bore squarely and stop when the front face is flush with the cover.

4   Install the pulley hub (Section 11).

Timing gear cover removed

Refer to illustrations 12.6 and 12.8

5   Remove the timing gear cover as described in Section 13.

6   Using a large screwdriver, pry the old seal out of the cover (see illustration). Be careful not to distort the cover or scratch the wall of

12.6 Once the timing gear cover is removed, place it on a flat surface and gently pry the old seal out with a large screwdriver

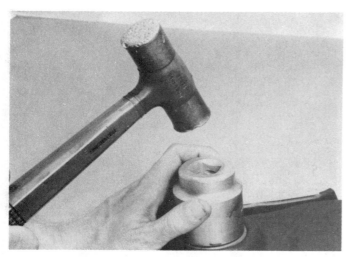

12.8   Clean the bore, then apply a small amount of oil to the outer edge of the new seal and drive it squarely into the opening with a large socket and a hammer — don't damage the seal in the process!

the seal bore. If the engine has accumulated a lot of miles, apply penetrating oil to the seal-to-cover joint and allow it to soak in before attempting to remove the seal.

7   Clean the bore to remove any old seal material and corrosion. Support the cover on a block of wood and position the new seal in the bore with the lip (open end) of the seal facing IN. A small amount of oil applied to the outer edge of the new seal will make installation easier — don't overdo it!

8   Drive the seal into the bore with a large socket and hammer until it's completely seated **(see illustration)**. Select a socket that's the same outside diameter as the seal (a section of pipe can be used if a socket isn't available).

9   Reinstall the timing gear cover.

13   Timing gear cover — removal and installation

Refer to illustrations 13.8 and 13.9

1   Detach the cable from the negative terminal of the battery.

2   Raise the front of the vehicle and support it on jackstands. Apply the parking brake.

3   Remove the crankshaft pulley and hub (Section 11).

4   Remove the timing gear cover-to-block bolts.

5   Remove the cover by carefully prying it off. The cover is sealed with RTV, so it may be stuck to the block. The flange between the cover and oil pan may be bent during removal. Try to minimize damage to the flange or it may be too distorted to be straightened.

6   Use a scraper to remove all old sealant from the cover, oil pan and block, then clean the mating surfaces with lacquer thinner or acetone.

7   Check the cover flanges for distortion, particularly around the bolt holes. If necessary, place the cover on a block of wood and use a hammer to flatten and restore the mating surfaces.

8   Apply a 3/8-inch wide by 3/16-inch thick bead of RTV sealant to the timing gear cover flange that mates with the oil pan. Apply a 1/4-inch wide by 1/8-inch thick bead to the cover-to-block flange **(see illustration)**.

9   Apply a dab of sealant to the joints between the oil pan and the engine block **(see illustration)**.

10   Place the cover in position and loosely install a couple of mounting bolts.

11   Install the crankshaft hub to center the cover (Section 11). Be sure to lubricate the seal contact surface of the hub.

12   Install the remaining mounting bolts and tighten them to the specified torque.

13   Install the crankshaft pulley.

14   Lower the vehicle.

15   Reattach the cable to the negative terminal of the battery.

16   Start the engine and check for oil leaks at the seal.

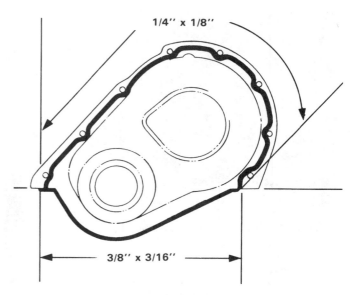

13.8   Apply a 1/4-inch wide by 1/8-inch thick bead of RTV sealant to the timing gear cover flange that contacts the block and a 3/8-inch wide by 3/16-inch thick bead to the cover-to-oil pan flange

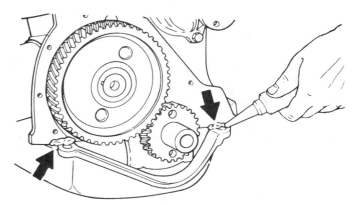

13.9   Put a dab of sealant at the junction between the oil pan and the bottom edge of the block (arrows)

14   Oil pump driveshaft — removal and installation

Refer to illustrations 14.3, 14.7 and 14.8

Note: *This procedure applies only to engines with the oil filter mounted on the side of the engine. It does not apply to engines with the filter mounted in the oil pan.*

1   Disconnect the cable from the negative terminal of the battery.

2   Raise the vehicle and support it on jackstands.

3   Remove the oil pump driveshaft retainer plate bolts **(see illustration)**.

4   Remove the oil pump driveshaft and bushing with a magnet.

5   Clean the mating surfaces of the block and retainer plate with lacquer thinner or acetone.

6   Check the bushing and driveshaft for wear. Replace them if they're worn or damaged.

7   Install the bushing and oil pump driveshaft in the block. The shaft driven gear must mesh with the camshaft drive gear and the slot in the lower end of the shaft must mate with the oil pump gear tang **(see illustration)**.

8   Apply a 1/16-inch bead of RTV sealant to the retainer plate so it completely seals around the oil pump driveshaft hole in the block **(see illustration)**.

9   Install the retainer plate and tighten the mounting bolts securely.

14.3   The oil pump driveshaft retainer plate is located on the engine block, just below the pushrod cover and just above the oil filter

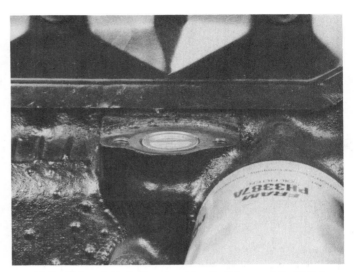

14.7   If the slotted oil pump driveshaft is properly mated with the oil pump gear tang, the top of the bushing will be flush with the retainer plate mounting surface

2B

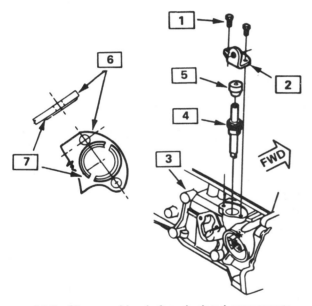

14.8   Oil pump driveshaft and related components

1 *Bolts*	5 *Bushing*
2 *Retainer plate*	6 *Retainer plate*
3 *Engine block*	7 *RTV sealant*
4 *Driveshaft and gear assembly*	

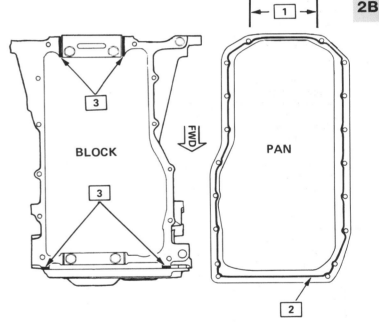

15.8   Oil pan sealant application details

1 *3/8-inch wide by* *3/16-inch thick*	2 *3/16-inch wide by* *1/8-inch thick*
	3 *1/8-inch bead*

15 Oil pan — removal and installation

Refer to illustration 15.8

1   Disconnect the cable from the negative battery terminal.
2   Raise the vehicle and support it securely on jackstands.
3   Drain the engine oil and remove the oil filter (Chapter 1).
4   Disconnect the exhaust pipe at the manifold and hangers and tie the system aside.
5   Remove the starter (Chapter 5) and the bellhousing dust cover.
6   Remove the bolts and detach the oil pan. Don't pry between the block and pan or damage to the sealing surfaces may result and oil leaks could develop. If the pan is stuck, dislodge it with a block of wood and a hammer.
7   Use a scraper to remove all traces of sealant from the pan and

block, then clean the mating surfaces with lacquer thinner or acetone.
8   Apply a 3/16-inch wide by 1/8-inch thick bead of RTV sealant to the oil pan flange. Make the bead 3/8-inch wide by 3/16-inch thick between the bolt holes at the rear end of the pan. Apply a 1/8-inch bead of sealant to the block at the rear main bearing cap joints and the timing gear cover joints **(see illustration)**.
9   Install the oil pan and tighten the mounting bolts to the specified torque. Start at the center of the pan and work out toward the ends in a spiral pattern.
10   Install the bellhousing dust cover and the starter.
11   Lower the vehicle.
12   Install a new filter and add oil to the engine.
13   Reattach the negative battery cable.
14   Start the engine and check for leaks.

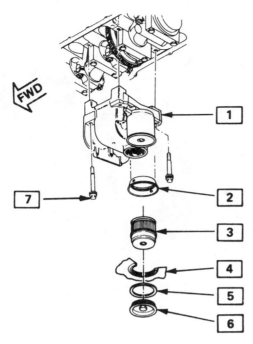

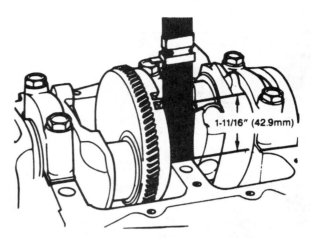

16.4   Position the crankshaft as shown here, . . .

1-11/16" (42.9mm)

16.3   Balancer assembly and related components — exploded view

1 Balancer assembly	5 Gasket
2 Restrictor	6 Plug
3 Oil filter	7 Bolt
4 Oil pan	

COUNTERWEIGHTS

16.5a   . . . then position the counterweights like this and install the balancer assembly — they must be in phase or vibration and damage could occur!

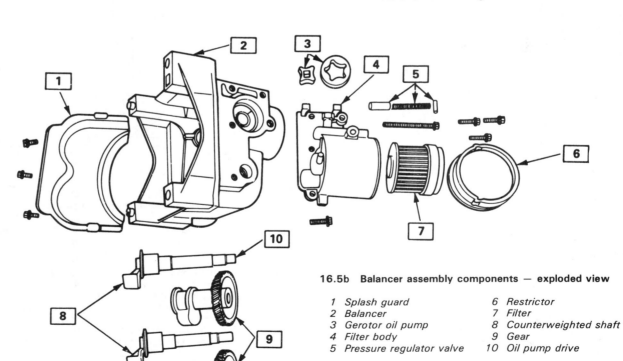

16.5b   Balancer assembly components — exploded view

1 Splash guard	6 Restrictor
2 Balancer	7 Filter
3 Gerotor oil pump	8 Counterweighted shaft
4 Filter body	9 Gear
5 Pressure regulator valve	10 Oil pump drive

16 Engine force balancer/oil pump assembly — removal and installation

Refer to illustrations 16.3, 16.4, 16.5a and 16.5b

Note: *This component is used on some 1987 and later models and is easily identified by the oil filter mounted in the oil pan. The oil pump is incorporated into the balancer assembly.*

Removal

1 Remove the oil pan (Section 15).
2 Position the number 1 piston at TDC on the compression stroke (see Part D of this Chapter).
3 Unbolt the balancer assembly **(see illustration)**.

Installation

4 Position the crankshaft by measuring from the engine block to the first cut of the double notch on the reluctor ring. The distance should be 1-11/16 inches **(see illustration)**. If it isn't, turn the crankshaft until it is.
5 Mount the balancer with the counterweights parallel and pointing AWAY from the crankshaft. Tighten the bolts to the specified torque **(see illustrations)**.
6 Install the oil pan.
7 Install a new filter and add oil (Chapter 1). Run the engine and check for leaks.

17 Oil pump — removal and installation

Refer to illustrations 17.2 and 17.3

Note: *This procedure applies only to engines not equipped with force balancers (see Section 16).*

1 Remove the oil pan (Section 15).
2 Remove the two oil pump mounting bolts and the pick-up tube bracket nut from the main bearing cap bolt **(see illustration)**.
3 Detach the oil pump and pick-up assembly from the block **(see illustration)**.
4 If the pump is defective, replace it with a new one. If the engine is being completely overhauled, install a new oil pump — don't reuse the original or attempt to rebuild it.
5 To install the pump, turn the shaft so the gear tang mates with the slot on the lower end of the oil pump driveshaft. The oil pump should slide easily into place over the oil pump driveshaft lower bushing. If

17.2 Remove the oil pump flange mounting bolts and the pick-up tube bracket nut

it doesn't, pull it off and turn the tang until it's aligned with the pump driveshaft slot.
6 Install the pump mounting bolts and the tube bracket nut. Tighten them to the specified torque.
7 Reinstall the oil pan (Section 15).
8 Add oil, run the engine and check for leaks.

18 Flywheel/driveplate — removal and installation

Refer to illustration 18.3

1 Refer to Chapter 7 and remove the transaxle. If your vehicle has a manual transaxle, the pressure plate and clutch will also have to be removed (Chapter 8).
2 Jam a large screwdriver in the starter ring gear to keep the crankshaft from turning, then remove the mounting bolts. Since it's fairly heavy, support the flywheel as the last bolt is removed.
3 Pull straight back on the flywheel/driveplate to detach it from the crankshaft. Note the shim installed between the driveplate and crankshaft on vehicles equipped with an automatic transaxle **(see illustration)**.

2B

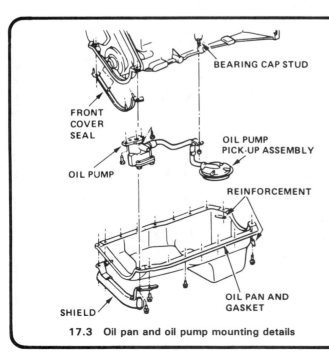

17.3 Oil pan and oil pump mounting details

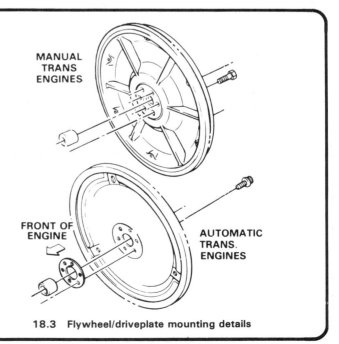

18.3 Flywheel/driveplate mounting details

19.5   Carefully pry the oil seal out with a screwdriver — don't nick or scratch the crankshaft or the new seal will be damaged and leaks will develop

19.8   Tap around the outer edge of the new seal with a hammer and a punch to seat it squarely in the bore

4   Installation is the reverse of removal. Be sure to align the hole in the flywheel/driveplate with the dowel pin in the crankshaft. Use Locktite on the bolt threads and tighten them to the specified torque in a criss-cross pattern.

19   Rear main oil seal — replacement

Refer to illustrations 19.5 and 19.8

1   The rear main bearing oil seal can be replaced without removing the oil pan or crankshaft.
2   Remove the transaxle (Chapter 7).
3   If equipped with a manual transaxle, remove the pressure plate and clutch disc (Chapter 8).
4   Remove the flywheel or driveplate (Section 18).
5   Using a seal removal tool or a large screwdriver, carefully pry the seal out of the block **(see illustration)**. Don't scratch or nick the crankshaft in the process.
6   Clean the bore in the block and the seal contact surface on the crankshaft. Check the crankshaft surface for scratches and nicks that could damage the new seal lip and cause oil leaks. If the crankshaft is damaged, the only alternative is a new or different crankshaft.
7   Apply a light coat of engine oil or multi-purpose grease to the outer edge of the new seal. Lubricate the seal lip with moly-base grease.

8   Press the new seal into place with GM tool no. J34924 (if available). The seal lip must face toward the front of the engine. If the special tool isn't available, carefully work the seal lip over the end of the crankshaft and tap the seal in with a hammer and punch until it's seated in the bore **(see illustration)**.
9   Install the flywheel or driveplate.
10   If equipped with a manual transaxle, reinstall the clutch disc and pressure plate.
11   Reinstall the transaxle as described in Chapter 7.

20   Engine and transaxle mounts — replacement

Refer to illustrations 20.5, 20.13 and 20.19

Warning: *A special tool (GM no. J28467) is available to support the engine during repair operations. Similar fixtures are available from rental yards. Improper lifting methods or devices are hazardous and could result in severe injury or death. DO NOT place any part of your body under the engine/transaxle when it's supported only by a jack. Failure of the lifting device could result in serious injury or death.*

1   If the rubber mounts have hardened, cracked or separated from the metal backing plates, they must be replaced. This operation may be carried out with the engine/transaxle still in the vehicle.

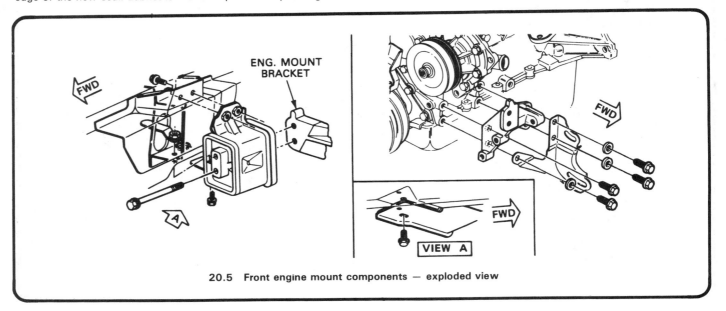

20.5   Front engine mount components — exploded view

2 Disconnect the negative cable from the battery.
3 Raise the front of the vehicle and support it securely on jackstands.
4 Support the engine with a jack.

Front engine mount

5 Remove the engine mount-to-chassis bolts **(see illustration)**.
6 Remove the mount-to-engine support bracket bolts. It's not necessary to detach the support bracket from the engine.
7 Remove the engine mount.
8 Place the new mount in position.
9 Install the mount-to-engine support bracket bolts and tighten them securely.
10 Tighten the mount-to-chassis bolts securely.
11 Remove the jack or engine support fixture.
12 Remove the jackstands and lower the vehicle.

Rear engine mount

13 Remove the nuts from the engine mount-to-chassis bracket **(see illustration)**.
14 Remove the bolts holding the mount to the engine bracket and withdraw the mount.
15 Installation is the reverse of removal.
16 Tighten all fasteners securely.
17 Remove the jack or engine support fixture.
18 Remove the jackstands and lower the vehicle.

Transaxle mount

19 Remove the bolt holding the transaxle bracket to the mount **(see illustration)**.
20 Remove the bolts holding the upper mount to the side frame support.

2B

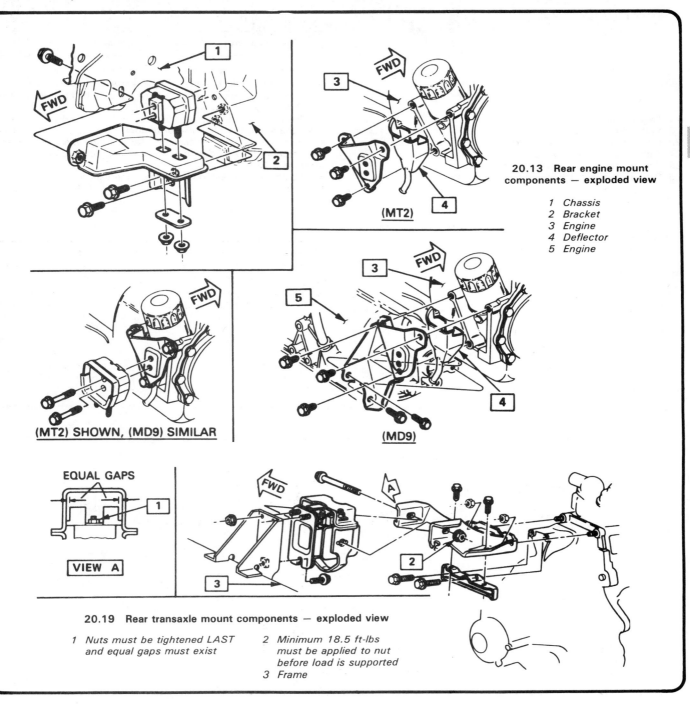

20.13 **Rear engine mount components — exploded view**

1 Chassis
2 Bracket
3 Engine
4 Deflector
5 Engine

(MT2)

(MT2) SHOWN, (MD9) SIMILAR

(MD9)

EQUAL GAPS

VIEW A

20.19 **Rear transaxle mount components — exploded view**

1 Nuts must be tightened LAST and equal gaps must exist
2 Minimum 18.5 ft-lbs must be applied to nut before load is supported
3 Frame

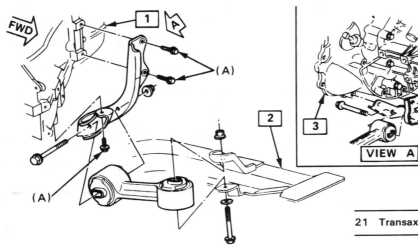

21.2 Transaxle strut and related components — exploded view

1 *Transaxle — MD9*
2 *Crossmember*
3 *Transaxle — MT2*

A *Discard and use new parts each time bolts are removed*

21 Loosen the lower mount-to-side frame bolt.
22 Remove the mount.
23 Installation is the reverse of removal.
24 Tighten all fasteners securely.
25 Remove the jack or engine support fixture.
26 Remove the jackstands and lower the vehicle.

21 Transaxle strut — removal and installation

Refer to illustration 21.2

1 Raise the vehicle and support it securely on jackstands.
2 Remove the crossmember-to-transaxle strut bolt **(see illustration)**.
3 Remove the transaxle strut-to-bracket bolt.
4 Remove the transaxle strut.
5 Installation is the reverse of removal.
6 Tighten all fasteners securely. **Note:** *Some fasteners must be discarded and replaced with new ones during installation — refer to illustration 21.2.*
7 Remove the jackstands and lower the vehicle.

Chapter 2 Part C V6 engine

Contents

Specifications

General

Cylinder numbers (drivebelt end-to-transaxle end)	
front bank	1-3-5
rear bank	2-4-6
Firing order	1-6-5-4-3-2

Oil pump

Gear length	1.5075 to 1.5095 in
Outer gear diameter	3.497 to 3.500 in
Outer gear-to-housing clearance	0.008 to 0.015 in
Inner gear diameter	2.839 in
Inner gear-to-outer gear clearance	0.006 in
Gear pocket depth	1.500 to 1.509 in
Gear pocket diameter	1.534 to 1.539 in
Gear lash	0.0004 to 0.007 in
Gear end clearance	0.001 to 0.0035 in

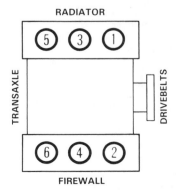

Cylinder number locations

Torque specifications

	Ft-lbs
Main bearing cap bolts	100
Crankshaft balancer bolt	200
Cylinder head bolts	See text
Exhaust crossover pipe bolt	14
Driveplate-to-crankshaft bolts	60
Oil pan bolts	7.3
Oil pump	
Cover-to-timing chain cover bolts	10
Pipe and screen assembly-to-engine block	7
Oil filter adapter-to-front cover bolts	30
Timing chain cover bolts	22
Water pump cover-to-timing chain cover bolts	7
Intake manifold-to-cylinder head bolts/nuts	32
Exhaust manifold-to-cylinder head bolts	37
Engine mount-to-engine bolts	60 to 70
Timing chain sprocket-to-camshaft bolts	31
Rocker arm cover-to-cylinder head bolts	5 to 10
Rocker arm pedestal bolts	45

1   General information

This Part of Chapter 2 is devoted to in-vehicle repair procedures for the 3.0 liter V6 engine.

Information concerning engine removal and installation, as well as engine block and cylinder head overhaul, is in Part D of this Chapter.

The following repair procedures are based on the assumption that the engine is installed in the vehicle. If the engine has been removed from the vehicle and mounted on a stand, many of the steps included in this Part of Chapter 2 will not apply.

The Specifications included in this Part of Chapter 2 apply only to the engine and procedures in this Part. The Specifications necessary for rebuilding the block and cylinder heads are found in Part D.

2   Repair operations possible with the engine in the vehicle

Many major repair operations can be accomplished without removing the engine from the vehicle.

Clean the engine compartment and the exterior of the engine with some type of pressure washer before any work is done. A clean engine will make the job easier and will help keep dirt out of the internal areas of the engine.

Depending on the components involved, it may be a good idea to remove the hood to improve access to the engine as repairs are performed (refer to Chapter 11 if necessary).

If vacuum, exhaust, oil or coolant leaks develop, indicating a need for gasket or seal replacement, the repairs can generally be made with the engine in the vehicle. The intake and exhaust manifold gaskets, oil pan gasket and cylinder head gaskets are all accessible with the engine in place.

Exterior engine components such as the intake and exhaust manifolds, the oil pan, the oil pump, the water pump, the starter motor, the alternator, the distributor and the fuel injection system can be removed for repair with the engine in place. The timing chain and sprockets can also be replaced with the engine in the vehicle, but the camshaft cannot be removed.

Since the cylinder heads can be removed without pulling the engine, valve component servicing can also be accomplished with the engine in the vehicle.

In extreme cases caused by a lack of necessary equipment, repair or replacement of piston rings, pistons, connecting rods and rod bearings is possible with the engine in the vehicle. However, this practice is not recommended because of the cleaning and preparation work that must be done to the components involved.

3   Rocker arm covers — removal and installation

Refer to illustrations 3.6 and 3.17

Removal — right side (rear) cover

1   Disconnect the negative battery cable from the battery.

2   Remove the throttle cables and bracket (Chapter 4).

3   Remove the spark plug wires from the spark plugs (Chapter 1). Be sure to label each wire before removal to ensure correct reinstallation.

4   Remove the ignition coil module and wiring (Chapter 5) and the EGR solenoid, wiring and vacuum hoses (Chapter 6).

5   Drain at least three quarts of coolant from the radiator (Chapter 1).

6   Disconnect the coolant hoses at the throttle body (see illustration). **Note:** *You may have to remove the throttle body to gain access to the hose clamp screws (see Chapter 4).*

7   Remove the rocker arm cover mounting nuts.

8   Detach the rocker arm cover. **Note:** *If the cover sticks to the cylinder head, use a block of wood and a hammer to dislodge it. If the cover still won't come loose, pry on it carefully, but don't distort the sealing flange.*

Removal — left side (front) cover

9   Disconnect the negative battery cable from the battery.

10 Remove the spark plug wire harness cover.

11 Remove the spark plug wires from the spark plugs (Chapter 1). Be sure to label each wire before removal to ensure correct reinstallation.

12 Remove the PCV tube from the cover.

13 Remove the rocker arm cover mounting nuts.

14 Detach the rocker arm cover. **Note:** *If the cover sticks to the cylinder head, use a block of wood and a hammer to dislodge it. If the cover still won't come loose, pry on it carefully, but don't distort the sealing flange.*

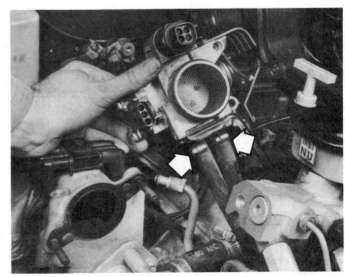

3.6   You may have to remove the throttle body to gain access to the hose clamp screws (arrows)

Installation — both covers

15 The mating surfaces of each cylinder head and rocker arm cover must be perfectly clean when the covers are installed. Use a gasket scraper to remove all traces of sealant or old gasket, then clean the mating surfaces with lacquer thinner or acetone (if there's sealant or oil on the mating surfaces when the cover is installed, oil leaks may develop). The rocker arm covers are made of aluminum, so be extra careful not to nick or gouge the mating surfaces with the scraper.

16 Clean the mounting nut stud threads with a die to remove any corrosion and restore damaged threads.

17 Place the rocker arm cover and new gasket in position, then install new rubber grommets, the washers and mounting nuts **(see illustration)**. Tighten the nuts in several steps to the specified torque.

18 Reinstall the coolant hoses and refill the engine with coolant (rear cover only).

19 Complete the installation by reversing the removal procedure. Start the engine and check carefully for oil leaks at the rocker arm cover-to-head joints.

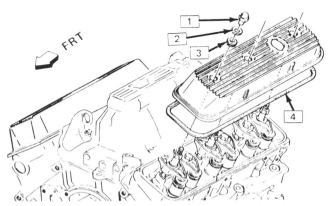

3.17   Rocker arm cover and related components — exploded view

1	Nut	3	Rubber grommet
2	Washer	4	Formed rubber gasket

4   Valve springs, retainers and seals — replacement

Refer to illustrations 4.8, 4.9 and 4.17

Note: *Broken valve springs and defective valve stem seals can be replaced without removing the cylinder heads. Two special tools and a compressed air source are normally required to perform this operation, so read through this Section carefully and rent or buy the tools before beginning the job. If compressed air is not available, a length of nylon rope can be used to keep the valves from falling into the cylinder during this procedure.*

1 Refer to Section 3 and remove the rocker arm cover from the affected cylinder head. If all of the valve stem seals are being replaced, remove both rocker arm covers.

2 Remove the spark plug from the cylinder which has the defective component. If all of the valve stem seals are being replaced, all of the spark plugs should be removed.

3 Turn the crankshaft until the piston in the affected cylinder is at top dead center on the compression stroke (refer to Part D for instructions). If you're replacing all of the valve stem seals, begin with cylinder number one and work on the valves for one cylinder at a time. Move from cylinder-to-cylinder following the firing order sequence (1-6-5-4-3-2).

4 Thread an adapter into the spark plug hole and connect an air hose from a compressed air source to it. Most auto parts stores can supply the air hose adapter. **Note:** *Many cylinder compression gauges utilize a screw-in fitting that may work with your air hose quick-disconnect fitting.*

5 Remove the bolt, pedestal and rocker arm for the valve with the defective part and pull out the pushrod. If all of the valve stem seals are being replaced, all of the rocker arms and pushrods should be removed.

6 Apply compressed air to the cylinder. The valves should be held in place by the air pressure. If the valve faces or seats are in poor condition, leaks may prevent the air pressure from retaining the valves — refer to the alternative procedure below.

7 If you don't have access to compressed air, an alternative method can be used. Position the piston at a point just before TDC on the compression stroke, then feed a long piece of nylon rope through the spark plug hole until it fills the combustion chamber. Be sure to leave the end of the rope hanging out of the engine so it can be removed easily. Use a large breaker bar and socket to rotate the crankshaft in the normal direction of rotation until slight resistance is felt.

8 Stuff shop rags into the cylinder head holes above and below the valves to prevent parts and tools from falling into the engine, then use a valve spring compressor to compress the spring. Remove the keepers with small needle-nose pliers or a magnet **(see illustration)**. **Note:** *A couple of different types of tools are available for compressing the valve springs with the head in place. One type grips the lower spring coils and presses on the retainer as the knob is turned, while the other type, shown here, utilizes the rocker arm bolt for leverage. Both types work very well, although the lever type is usually less expensive.*

9 Remove the spring retainer, oil shield and valve spring, then remove the valve stem O-ring seal (if so equipped) and the umbrella-type guide seal (intake valve only) **(see illustration)**. The O-ring seal will most likely be hardened and will probably break when removed, so plan on installing a new one each time the original is removed. **Note:** *If air pressure fails to hold the valve in the closed position during this operation, the valve face or seat is probably damaged. If so, the cylinder head will have to be removed for additional repair operations.*

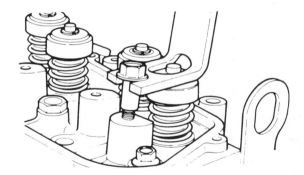

4.8   A lever-type valve spring compressor is used to compress the spring and remove the keepers to replace seals or springs while the head is installed

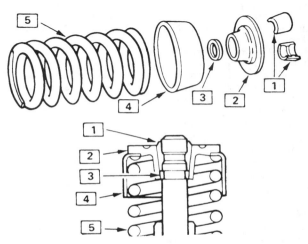

4.9   Typical valve spring assembly components

1	Keepers	4	Shield
2	Retainer	5	Spring
3	O-ring seal		

4.17 Keepers don't always want to stay in place, so apply a small dab of grease to each one as shown here before installation — it'll hold them in place on the valve stem as the spring is released

10 Wrap a rubber band or tape around the top of the valve stem so the valve won't fall into the combustion chamber, then release the air pressure. **Note:** *If a rope was used instead of air pressure, turn the crankshaft slightly in the direction opposite normal rotation.*
11 Inspect the valve stem for damage. Rotate the valve in the guide and check the end for eccentric movement, which would indicate that the valve is bent.
12 Move the valve up-and-down in the guide and make sure it doesn't bind. If the valve stem binds, either the valve is bent or the guide is damaged. In either case, the head will have to be removed for repair.
13 Reapply air pressure to the cylinder to retain the valve in the closed position, then remove the tape or rubber band from the valve stem. If a rope was used instead of air pressure, rotate the crankshaft in the normal direction of rotation until slight resistance is felt.
14 Lubricate the valve stem with engine oil and install a new umbrella-type guide seal (intake valves only).
15 Install the spring and shield in position over the valve.
16 Install the valve spring retainer. Compress the valve spring and carefully install the new O-ring seal (if so equipped) in the lower groove of the valve stem. Make sure the seal isn't twisted — it must lie perfectly flat in the groove.
17 Position the keepers in the upper groove. Apply a small dab of grease to the inside of each keeper to hold it in place if necessary **(see illustration)**. Remove the pressure from the spring tool and make sure the keepers are seated. Refer to Part D and check the O-ring seals with a vacuum pump.
18 Disconnect the air hose and remove the adapter from the spark plug hole. If a rope was used in place of air pressure, pull it out of the cylinder.
19 Install the rocker arm(s) and pushrod(s).
20 Install the spark plug(s) and hook up the wire(s).
21 Refer to Section 3 and install the rocker arm cover(s).
22 Start and run the engine, then check for oil leaks and unusual sounds coming from the rocker arm cover area.

---

5   Rocker arms and pushrods — removal, inspection and installation

---

Refer to illustrations 5.2 and 5.3
Removal

1   Refer to Section 3 and detach the rocker arm covers from the cylinder heads.
2   Beginning at the front of one cylinder head, loosen the rocker arm pedestal bolts one at a time and detach the rocker arms, bolts, pedestals and pedestal retainers **(see illustration)**. Store each set of valve components separately in a marked plastic bag to ensure that they're reinstalled in their original locations.
3   Remove the pushrods and store them separately to make sure they don't get mixed up during installation **(see illustration)**.

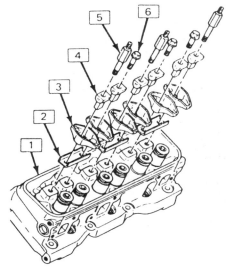

5.2   Rocker arms and related components — exploded view

1 Cylinder head   *4 Pedestal*
2 Pedestal retainer   *5 Stud bolt*
3 Rocker arm   *6 Bolt*

5.3   A perforated cardboard box can be used to store the pushrods to ensure that they're reinstalled in their original locations — note the label indicating the front of the engine

Inspection

4   Check each rocker arm for wear, cracks and other damage, especially where the pushrods and valve stems contact the rocker arm.
5   Check the pedestal seat in each rocker arm and the pedestal faces. Look for galling, stress cracks and unusual wear patterns. If the rocker arms are worn or damaged, replace them with new ones and install new pedestals as well.
6   Make sure the hole at the pushrod end of each rocker arm is open.
7   Inspect the pushrods for cracks and excessive wear at the ends. Roll each pushrod across a piece of plate glass to see if it's bent (if it wobbles, it's bent).

Installation

8   Lubricate the lower end of each pushrod with clean engine oil or moly-base grease and install them in their original locations. Make sure each pushrod seats completely in the lifter socket.
9   Apply moly-base grease to the ends of the valve stems and the

6.12a Some vacuum lines are equipped with fittings that prevent mixing them up during installation

6.12b Removing the vacuum line bracket nut

2C

6.14 Note the locations of the mounting studs prior to manifold removal

6.15 Use a gasket scraper to remove all traces of sealant and old gasket material from the head and manifold mating surfaces

upper ends of the pushrods.

10 Apply moly-base grease to the pedestal faces to prevent damage to the mating surfaces before engine oil pressure builds up. Install the rocker arms, pedestals, pedestal retainers and bolts and tighten the bolts to the specified torque. As the bolts are tightened, make sure the pushrods engage properly in the rocker arms.

11 Install the rocker arm covers.

---

6 Intake manifold — removal and installation

Refer to illustrations 6.12a, 6.12b, 6.14, 6.15, 6.17 and 6.19

Removal

1 Relieve the fuel system pressure (Chapter 4).
2 Disconnect the negative battery cable from the battery.
3 Remove the mass airflow sensor and the air intake duct (Chapter 4).
4 Remove the PCV valve from the intake manifold (Chapter 1).
5 Remove the throttle (and cruise control — when equipped) cable(s) from the manifold bracket.
6 Remove the transaxle TV cable from the manifold bracket (automatic transaxle only) (Chapter 7).
7 Remove the serpentine drivebelt (Chapter 1).
8 Disconnect and remove the alternator and brackets (Chapter 5).
9 Drain the cooling system (Chapter 1).
10 Remove the ignition module assembly and spark plug wires (Chapters 1 and 5).

11 Disconnect the upper radiator and coolant hoses at the manifold and throttle body.

12 Label and disconnect the fuel and vacuum lines **(see illustrations)** and electrical leads at the manifold and throttle body. When disconnecting fuel line fittings, be prepared to catch some fuel, then cap the fittings to prevent contamination.

13 Remove the fuel rail and injectors (Chapter 4).

14 Remove the manifold mounting bolts and separate the manifold from the engine **(see illustration)**. Do not pry between the manifold and heads, as damage to the gasket sealing surfaces may result. If you're installing a new manifold, transfer the EGR valve and all fittings and sensors to the new manifold.

Installation

Note: *The mating surfaces of the cylinder heads, block and manifold must be perfectly clean when the manifold is installed. Gasket removal solvents in aerosol cans are available at most auto parts stores and may be helpful when removing old gasket material that's stuck to the heads and manifold (since the manifold is made of aluminum, aggressive scraping can cause damage). Be sure to follow the directions printed on the container.*

15 Use a gasket scraper to remove all traces of sealant and old gasket material **(see illustration)**, then clean the mating surfaces with lacquer thinner or acetone. If there's old sealant or oil on the mating surfaces when the manifold is installed, oil or vacuum leaks may develop. Use a vacuum cleaner to remove any gasket material that falls into the intake ports or the lifter valley.

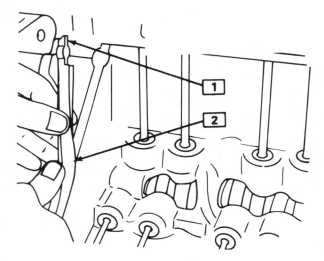

6.17   Installing the intake manifold-to-block seals

1 RTV sealant application area
2 Seal

16   Use a tap of the correct size to chase the threads in the bolt holes, then use compressed air (if available) to remove the debris from the holes. **Warning:** *Wear safety glasses or a face shield to protect your eyes when using compressed air.*
17   If steel manifold gaskets are used, apply GM sealant number 1050026 or equivalent to both sides of the gaskets before positioning them on the heads. Apply RTV sealant to the ends of the new manifold-to-block seals **(see illustration)**, then install them. Make sure the pointed end of the seal fits snugly against both the head and block.
18   Carefully lower the manifold into place and install the mounting bolts finger tight.
19   Tighten the mounting bolts in three stages, following the recommended sequence **(see illustration)**, until they're all at the specified torque.
20   Install the remaining components in the reverse order of removal.
21   Change the oil and filter (Chapter 1).
22   Fill the cooling system (Chapter 1), start the engine and check for leaks.

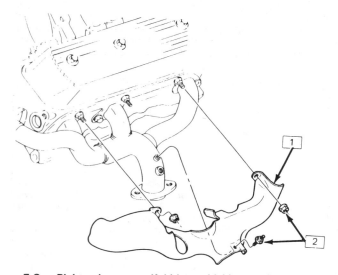

7.8a   Right exhaust manifold heat shield mounting details

1 Heat shield
2 Tighten to 11 ft-lbs

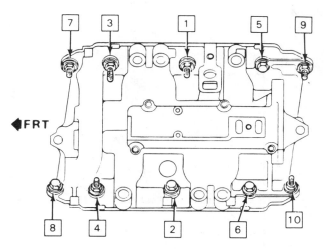

6.19   Intake manifold bolt tightening sequence

7   Exhaust manifolds — removal and installation

Right (rear) manifold
Refer to illustrations 7.8a, 7.8b and 7.12
1   Disconnect the negative battery cable.
2   Allow the engine to cool completely, then drain the coolant and remove the heater hoses and tubing above the exhaust manifold.
3   Remove the two nuts attaching the crossover pipe to the rear exhaust manifold.
4   Disconnect the spark plug wires from the rear plugs (Chapter 1).
5   Remove the serpentine drivebelt (Chapter 1).
6   Unbolt the power steering pump without removing the hoses and hold it to one side with wire (Chapter 10).
7   Remove the ignition module bracket nuts.
8   Remove the manifold heat shield and coolant tube brackets **(see illustrations)**.
9   Set the parking brake, block the rear wheels and raise the front of the vehicle, supporting it securely on jackstands.
10   Working under the vehicle, remove the two exhaust pipe-to-manifold bolts. You may have to apply penetrating oil to the fastener threads — they're usually corroded.
11   Disconnect the oxygen sensor wire (the sensor is threaded into the manifold), then lower the vehicle.

7.8b   Manifold mounting details (shown here with engine removed for clarity) — note the oxygen sensor wire connector (arrow)

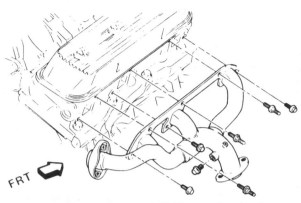

7.12   Right exhaust manifold mounting details

12   Remove the six bolts and detach the manifold from the head **(see illustration)**.
13   Clean the mating surfaces to remove all traces of old sealant, then check for warpage and cracks. Warpage can be checked with a precision staightedge held against the mating flange. If a feeler gauge thicker than 0.030-inch can be inserted between the straightedge and flange surface, take the manifold to an automotive machine shop for resurfacing.
14   Place the manifold in position and install the bolts finger tight.
15   Starting in the middle and working out toward the ends, tighten the mounting bolts a little at a time until all of them are at the specified torque.

16   Install the remaining components in the reverse order of removal.
17   Start the engine and check for exhaust leaks between the manifold and cylinder head and between the manifold and exhaust pipe.

Left (front) manifold
Refer to illustrations 7.24a, 7.24b, 7.24c and 7.25
18   Disconnect the negative battery cable.
19   Remove the cooling fan (Chapter 3).
20   Unbolt the crossover pipe from the manifold.
21   Remove the dipstick tube hold-down nut and wiggle the dipstick tube out of the block.
22   Remove the spark plug wire cover and wires (Chapter 1).
23   Remove the spark plugs to prevent breaking them.
24   Unbolt the heat shield. If turning the nuts causes the studs to turn and bend the shield **(see illustration)**, keep the stud from turning with a thin 14 mm open end wrench or a pair of vise-grip pliers **(see illustrations)**.
25   Unbolt and remove the exhaust manifold **(see illustration)**.
26   Clean the mating surfaces to remove all traces of old sealant, then check for warpage and cracks. Warpage can be checked with a precision staightedge held against the mating flange. If a feeler gauge thicker than 0.030-inch can be inserted between the straightedge and flange surface, take the manifold to an automotive machine shop for resurfacing.
27   Place the manifold in position and install the bolts finger tight.
28   Starting in the middle and working out toward the ends, tighten the mounting bolts a little at a time until all of them are at the specified torque.
29   Install the remaining components in the reverse order of removal.
30   Start the engine and check for exhaust leaks between the manifold and cylinder head and between the manifold and exhaust pipe.

2C

7.24a   When removing the nut, the stud may turn and distort the heat shield, so . . .

7.24b   . . . hold the stud with a pair of pliers while loosening the nut

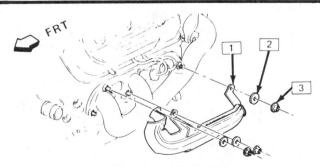

7.24c   Left exhaust manifold heat shield mounting details

1   Heat shield
2   Washer
3   Tighten to 11 ft-lbs

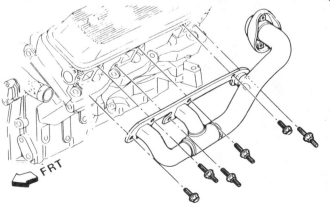

7.25   Left exhaust manifold mounting details

8.3   Remove the bolts holding the brackets to the cylinder head (arrows)

---

8   Cylinder heads — removal and installation

Refer to illustrations 8.3, 8.11, 8.14, 8.19, 8.20 and 8.22

Removal

1   Disconnect the negative battery cable at the battery.

2   Remove the intake manifold as described in Section 6.

3   When removing the left (front) cylinder head, remove the dipstick tube retaining nut and wiggle the tube out of the block. Remove the bolts holding the brackets to the head **(see illustration)**.

4   When removing the right cylinder head, remove the power steering pump and brackets (Chapter 10).

5   Disconnect all wires and vacuum hoses from the cylinder head(s). Be sure to label them to simplify reinstallation.

6   Disconnect the spark plug wires and remove the spark plugs (Chapter 1). Be sure to label the plug wires to simplify reinstallation.

7   Detach the exhaust manifold from the cylinder head being removed (Section 7).

8   Remove the rocker arm cover(s) (Section 3).

9   Remove the rocker arms and pushrods (Section 5).

10   Loosen the head bolts in 1/4-turn increments until they can be removed by hand. Work from bolt-to-bolt in a pattern that's the reverse

of the tightening sequence shown in illustration 8.20. Remove the bolts and discard them — NEW ONES MUST BE USED when installing the head(s)!

11   Lift the head(s) off the engine. If resistance is felt, don't pry between the head(s) and block as damage to the mating surfaces will result. Recheck for head bolts that may have been overlooked, then use a hammer and block of wood to tap the head(s) and break the gasket seal. Be careful because there are locating dowels in the block which position each head. As a last resort, pry each head up at the rear corner only and be careful not to damage anything **(see illustration)**. After removal, place the head(s) on blocks of wood to prevent damage to the gasket surfaces.

12   Refer to Chapter 2, Part D, for cylinder head disassembly, inspection and valve service procedures.

Installation

13   The mating surfaces of the cylinder heads and block must be perfectly clean when the heads are installed.

14   Use a gasket scraper to remove all traces of carbon and old gasket material, then clean the mating surfaces with lacquer thinner or acetone. If there's oil on the mating surfaces when the heads are installed, the gaskets may not seal correctly and leaks may develop. When working on the block, it's a real good idea to cover the lifter valley with shop rags to keep debris out of the engine. Use a shop rag or vacuum cleaner to remove any debris that falls into the cylinders **(see illustration)**.

15   Check the block and head mating surfaces for nicks, deep scratches and other damage. If damage is slight, it can be removed with a file; if it's excessive, machining may be the only alternative.

16   Use a tap of the correct size to chase the threads in the head bolt holes. Dirt, corrosion, sealant and damaged threads will affect torque readings.

17   Position the new gaskets over the dowel pins in the block. If steel gaskets are used, apply GM sealant no. 1050026 or equivalent. Install "non-retorquing" type gaskets dry (no sealant), unless the manufacturer states otherwise. Some gaskets are marked TOP or THIS SIDE UP because they must be installed a certain way.

18   Carefully position the heads on the block without disturbing the gaskets.

19   Remember to use NEW head bolts — don't reinstall the old ones — and apply GM sealant (no. 1052080) to the threads and the undersides of the bolt heads. Install the bolts in the correct locations — three different lengths are used **(see illustration)**.

20   Tighten the bolts to 25 ft-lbs in the sequence shown **(see illustration)**. **Caution:** *If you reach 60 ft-lbs. at any time during the following two steps, stop immediately — DO NOT complete the balance of the 90-degree turn. Go on to the next bolt in the sequence.*

21   Tighten each bolt an additional 90-degrees (1/4-turn) following the

8.11   Pry the cylinder head loose at the rear corner to avoid damage to the gasket sealing surfaces

8.14   The cylinder head and block mating surfaces must be perfectly clean to ensure a good gasket seal

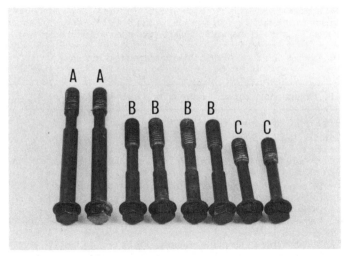

8.19 Head bolt locations (refer to illustration 8.20)

A: 1 and 3
B: 5, 6, 7 and 8
C: 2 and 4

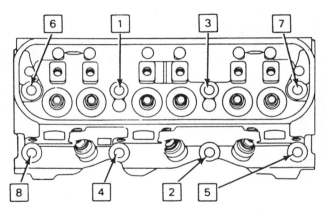

8.20 Cylinder head bolt tightening sequence

recommended sequence.

22 Tighten each bolt, one last time, yet another 90-degrees (1/4-turn) in the recommended sequence **(see illustration)**.

23 The remaining installation steps are the reverse of removal.

24 Change the oil and filter (Chapter 1).

---

9 Hydraulic lifters — removal, inspection and installation

Refer to illustration 9.8

1 A noisy valve lifter can be isolated when the engine is idling. Hold a mechanic's stethoscope or a length of hose near the position of each valve while listening at the other end. Another method is to remove the rocker arm cover and, with the engine idling, place a finger on each of the valve spring retainers, one at a time. If a valve lifter is defective, it will be evident from the shock felt at the retainer as the valve seats.

2 The most likely causes of noisy valve lifters are dirt trapped between the plunger and the lifter body or lack of oil flow, viscosity or pressure. Before condemning the lifters, we recommend checking the oil for fuel contamination, correct level, cleanliness and correct viscosity.

Removal

3 Remove the rocker arm cover(s) as described in Section 3.

4 Remove the intake manifold as described in Section 6.

5 Remove the rocker arms and pushrods (Section 5).

6 Early models have conventional lifters. Later production engines have roller lifters. Roller lifters are kept from turning by guide plates, which must be removed to access the lifters.

7 There are several ways to extract the lifters from the bores. A special tool designed to grip and remove lifters is manufactured by many tool companies and is widely available, but it may not be required in every case. On newer engines without a lot of varnish buildup, the lifters can often be removed with a small magnet or even with your fingers. A machinist's scribe with a bent end can be used to pull the lifters out by positioning the point under the retainer ring in the top of each lifter. **Caution:** *Don't use pliers to remove the lifters unless you intend to replace them with new ones (along with the camshaft). The pliers will damage the precision machined and hardened lifters, rendering them useless.*

8 Before removing the lifters, arrange to store them in a clearly labelled box to ensure that they're reinstalled in their original locations. Remove the lifters and store them where they won't get dirty **(see illustration)**.

Inspection and installation

9 Parts for valve lifters are not available separately. The work required to remove them from the engine again if cleaning is unsuccessful

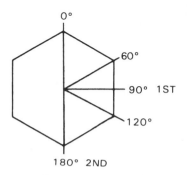

8.22 After the cylinder head bolt initial torque is reached, the bolts must be turned an additional 180° in two stages

outweighs any potential savings from repairing them. Refer to Chapter 2, Part D, for lifter and camshaft inspection procedures. If the lifters are worn, they must be replaced with new ones and the camshaft must be replaced as well — never install used lifters with a new camshaft or new lifters with a used camshaft.

10 When reinstalling used lifters, make sure they're replaced in their original bores. Soak new lifters in oil to remove trapped air. Coat all lifters with moly-base grease or engine assembly lube prior to installation.

11 The remaining installation steps are the reverse of removal.

12 Run the engine and check for oil leaks.

9.8 The lifters on an engine that has accumulated many miles may have to be removed with a special tool — be sure to store the lifters in an organized manner to make sure they're reinstalled in their original locations

2C

9 Installation is the reverse of removal. Be sure to apply moly-base grease to the seal contact surface on the back side of the balancer (if it isn't lubricated, the seal lip could be damaged and oil leakage would result).

10 Tighten the crankshaft bolt to the specified torque.

11 Timing chain cover — removal and installation

Refer to illustrations 11.10 and 11.12

Note: *In 1987 a change was made to the timing chain cover and oil pressure relief valve. If excessive wear in the camshaft thrust area or other related problems are noted, refer to Buick Service Bulletin no. 87-6-5, Dec. 86, reference no. 87-036-6.*

1 Disconnect the negative battery cable from the battery.
2 Drain the coolant (Chapter 1).
3 Drain the oil (Chapter 1).
4 Remove the lower radiator hose and the heater return hose at the timing chain cover.
5 Remove the water pump (Chapter 3).
6 Remove the crankshaft balancer from the front of the crankshaft (Section 10).
7 Remove the crankshaft sensor (Chapter 5).
8 Remove the timing chain cover-to-oil pan bolts.
9 Remove the timing chain cover-to-engine block bolts.
10 Separate the cover from the front of the engine. Inside the cover is a spring and button that controls camshaft end play. If it's missing, look for it in the oil pan **(see illustration)**.
11 Use a gasket scraper to remove all traces of old gasket material and sealant from the cover and engine block. The cover is made of aluminum, so be careful not to nick or gouge it. Clean the gasket sealing surfaces with lacquer thinner or acetone.
12 Check the camshaft thrust surface in the cover for excessive wear **(see illustration)**. If it's worn, a new cover will be required (see the note at the beginning of this Section).
13 The oil pump cover must be removed and the cavity packed with petroleum jelly as described in Section 13 before the cover is installed.
14 Apply a thin layer of RTV sealant to both sides of the new gasket, then position the gasket on the engine block (the dowel pins should keep it in place). Make sure the spring and button are in place in the end of the camshaft, then attach the cover to the engine. The oil pump drive must engage with the distributor gear.
15 Apply GM thread sealant (no. 1052080 or equivalent) to the bolt threads, then install them finger tight. Follow a criss-cross pattern when tightening them and work up to the specified torque in three steps to avoid warping the cover.
16 The remainder of installation is the reverse of removal.
17 Add oil and coolant, start the engine and check for leaks.

10.7　The crankshaft balancer is attached to the end of the crankshaft — the bolt is very tight, so use a large breaker bar and six-point socket to remove it

10 Crankshaft balancer — removal and installation

Refer to illustration 10.7

Note: *The V6 engine balancer, which is essentially the same as a vibration dampener, is serviced as an assembly. Do not attempt to separate the pulley from the balancer hub.*

1 Disconnect the negative cable from the battery.
2 Loosen the lug nuts on the right front wheel.
3 Raise the vehicle and support it securely on jackstands.
4 Remove the right front wheel.
5 Remove the right front fender liner (Chapter 11).
6 Remove the serpentine drivebelt (Chapter 1).
7 Remove the flywheel cover plate and position a large screwdriver in the ring gear teeth to keep the crankshaft from turning while an assistant removes the crankshaft balancer bolt **(see illustration)**. The bolt is normally quite tight, so use a large breaker bar and a six-point socket.
8 Pull the balancer off the crankshaft by hand. Leave the Woodruff key in place in the end of the crankshaft.

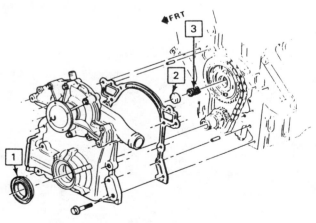

11.10　Timing chain cover and related components — exploded view

1 Front crankshaft oil seal
2 Camshaft button
3 Spring

11.12　The camshaft thrust surface on this cover is worn away (arrow), which means that a new cover must be installed

12.6 Use a cold chisel and hammer to separate the seal from the cover — drive the chisel into the joint, but don't distort the cover

12 Front crankshaft oil seal — replacement

Note: *The front crankshaft oil seal can be replaced with the timing chain cover in place. However, due to the limited amount of room available, you may conclude that the procedure would be easier if the cover were removed from the engine first. If so, refer to Section 11 for the cover removal and installation procedure.*

Timing chain cover in place

1   Remove the crankshaft balancer (Section 10).
2   Use a small cold chisel and a hammer to remove the seal from the cover. Carefully drive the chisel under the outer flange of the seal at several points until the seal can be pried out. Be very careful not to distort the cover!
3   Apply clean engine oil or multi-purpose grease to the outer edge of the new seal, then install it in the cover. Drive the seal into place with a large socket and a hammer (if a large socket isn't available, a piece of pipe will also work). Make sure the seal enters the bore squarely and seats completely.
4   Install the crankshaft balancer (Section 10).

Timing chain cover removed

Refer to illustrations 12.6, 12.7a and 12.7b

5   Remove the timing chain cover as described in Section 11.
6   Use a small cold chisel and a hammer to remove the seal from the cover. Carefully drive the chisel under the outer flange of the seal at several points until the seal can be pried out **(see illustration)**. Be very careful not to distort the cover!
7   Apply clean engine oil or multi-purpose grease to the outer edge of the new seal, then install it in the cover. Drive the seal into place with a large socket and a hammer (if a large socket isn't available, a piece of pipe or even a large block of wood will also work) **(see illustrations)**. Make sure the seal enters the bore squarely and seats completely.
8   Reinstall the timing chain cover.

13 Oil pump — removal, inspection and installation

Refer to illustrations 13.4, 13.5, 13.10, 13.11 and 13.12

Removal

1   Remove the oil filter (Chapter 1).
2   Remove the oil filter adapter, pressure regulator valve and spring (Section 14).
3   Remove the timing chain cover (Section 11).
4   Remove the oil pump cover-to-timing chain cover bolts with a T-30 Torx bit **(see illustration)**.

12.7a   Clean the bore, then apply grease or oil to the outer edge of the new seal and drive it squarely into the cover with a large socket . . .

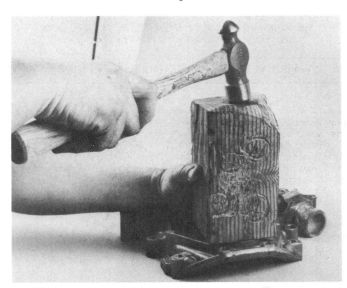

12.7b   . . . or a block of wood and hammer — DO NOT damage the seal in the process!

13.4   The oil pump cover is attached to the inside of the timing chain cover — a T-30 Torx driver is required for removal of the screws

2C

5 Lift out the cover and oil pump gears as an assembly (**see illustration**).

Inspection

6 Clean the parts with solvent and dry them with compressed air (if available).
7 Inspect all components for wear and score marks. Replace any worn out or damaged parts.
8 Refer to Section 14 for bypass valve information.
9 Reinstall the gears in the timing chain cover.
10 Measure the outer gear-to-cover clearance with a feeler gauge (**see illustration**).
11 Measure the inner gear-to-outer gear clearance at several points (**see illustration**).
12 Use a dial indicator or straightedge and feeler gauges to measure the gear end clearance (distance from the gear to the gasket surface of the cover) (**see illustration**).
13 Check for pump cover warpage by laying a precision straightedge across the cover and trying to slip a feeler gauge between the cover and straightedge.
14 Compare the measurements to the Specifications. Replace all worn or damaged components with new ones.

Installation

15 Remove the gears and pack the pump cavity with petroleum jelly.
16 Install the gears — make sure petroleum jelly is forced into every cavity. Failure to do so could cause the pump to lose its prime when the engine is started, causing damage from lack of oil pressure.
17 Install the pump cover, using a new GM gasket only — its thickness is critical for maintaining the correct clearances.
18 Install the pressure regulator spring and valve.
19 Install the timing chain cover.
20 Install the oil filter and check the oil level. Start and run the engine and check for correct oil pressure, then look carefully for oil leaks at the timing chain cover.

---

14 Oil filter adapter and pressure regulator valve — removal and installation

Refer to illustrations 14.3, 14.4 and 14.6
Note: *The oil pressure regulator valve and timing chain cover were changed in 1987. Refer to Buick Service Bulletin no. 87-6-5, Dec. 86, reference no. 87-036-6.*

1 Remove the oil filter (Chapter 1).
2 Remove the timing chain cover (Section 11).
3 Remove the four bolts holding the oil filter adapter to the timing chain cover (**see illustration**). The cover is spring loaded, so remove the bolts while keeping pressure on the cover, then release the spring

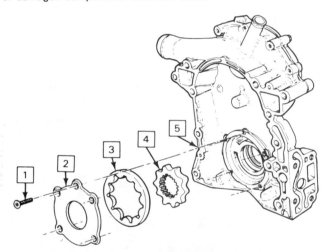

13.5 Oil pump components — exploded view

1 *Screw*	4 *Inner gear*
2 *Oil pump cover*	5 *Timing chain cover*
3 *Outer gear*	

13.10 Measuring the outer gear-to-housing clearance with a feeler gauge

13.11 Measuring the inner gear-to-outer gear clearance with a feeler gauge

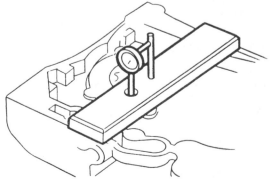

13.12 Measuring gear end clearance with the special fixture and a dial indicator

pressure carefully.

4   Remove the pressure regulator valve and spring **(see illustration)**. Use a gasket scraper to remove all traces of the old gasket.

5   Clean all parts with solvent and dry them with compressed air (if available). Check for wear, score marks and valve binding.

6   Installation is the reverse of removal. Be sure to use a new gasket.

Caution: *If a new timing chain cover is being installed on the engine, make sure the oil pressure relief valve supplied with the new cover is used. If the old style relief valve is installed in a new cover, oil pressure problems will result* **(see illustration)**.

7   Tighten the bolts to the specified torque.

8   Run the engine and check for oil leaks.

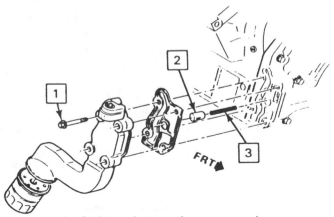

14.3   Oil filter adapter and pressure regulator valve — exploded view

1 *Bolt (4)*
2 *Pressure regulator valve*
3 *Spring*

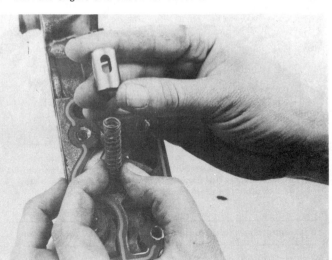

14.4   Remove the pressure regulator valve and spring, then check the valve for wear and damage

2C

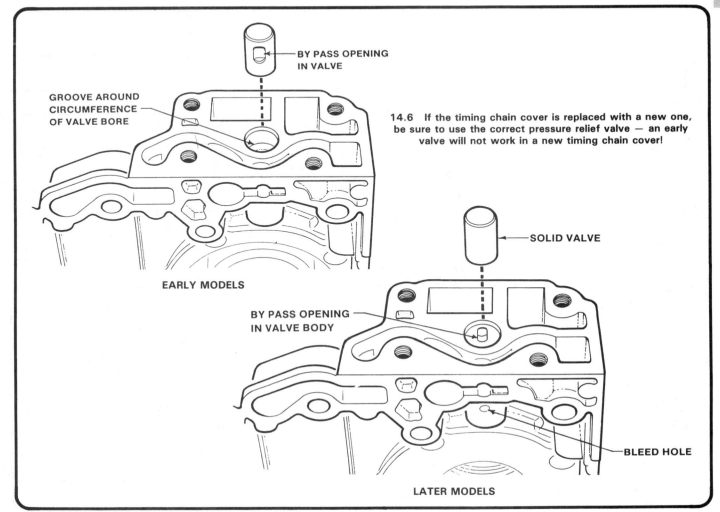

14.6   If the timing chain cover is replaced with a new one, be sure to use the correct pressure relief valve — an early valve will not work in a new timing chain cover!

15.1   The marks on the crankshaft and camshaft sprockets must be aligned opposite each other as shown here (the mark on the camshaft sprocket is a dimple — the one on the crankshaft sprocket is a circle)

15   Timing chain and sprockets — removal and installation

Refer to illustrations 15.1 and 15.4

Removal

1   Remove the timing chain cover (Section 11), then slide the shim off the nose of the crankshaft **(see illustration)**.
2   The timing chain should be replaced with a new one if the total free play midway between the sprockets exceeds one inch. Failure to replace the timing chain may result in erratic engine performance, loss of power and lowered gas mileage.
3   Temporarily install the crankshaft balancer bolt and turn the bolt to align the timing marks on the crankshaft and camshaft sprockets directly opposite each other **(see illustration 15.1)**.
4   Remove the camshaft sprocket bolts **(see illustration)**. Try not to turn the camshaft in the process (if you do, realign the timing marks after the bolts are out).
5   Use two large screwdrivers to alternately pry the camshaft sprocket and then the crankshaft sprocket forward and remove the camshaft sprocket and timing chain.
6   Remove the crankshaft sprocket.
7   Detach the spring, then remove the bolt and separate the timing chain dampener from the block.
8   Clean the timing chain and sprockets with solvent and dry them with compressed air (if available).
9   Inspect the components for wear and damage. Look for teeth that are deformed, chipped, pitted, polished or discolored.

Installation

Note: *If the crankshaft has been disturbed, turn it until the O stamped*

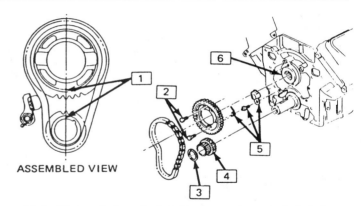

15.4   Timing chain and related components — exploded view

1 Timing marks (aligned)	*4 Crankshaft sprocket*
2 Camshaft sprocket bolts	*5 Chain dampener assembly*
3 Shim	*6 Camshaft*

on the crank sprocket is exactly at the top. If the camshaft was turned, install the sprocket temporarily and turn the camshaft until the timing mark is at the bottom, opposite the mark on the crank sprocket **(see illustration 15.1)**.

10   Attach the dampener assembly to the block and install the spring. Assemble the timing chain on the sprockets, then slide the sprocket and chain assembly onto the shafts with the timing marks aligned as shown in illustration 15.1. Hold the dampener out of the way, against spring pressure, as the chain/sprocket assembly is installed.
11   Install the camshaft sprocket bolts and tighten them to the specified torque.
12   Install the camshaft thrust button and spring. Hold it in place with grease.
13   Lubricate the chain and sprocket with clean engine oil. Install the timing chain cover (Section 11).

16   Oil pan — removal and installation

Refer to illustrations 16.6a and 16.6b

1   Disconnect the cable from the negative battery terminal.
2   Raise the vehicle, place it securely on jackstands and drain the engine oil (refer to Chapter 1 if necessary).
3   Remove the flywheel inspection cover.
4   Remove the bolts and stiffener plates and carefully separate the oil pan from the block. Don't pry between the block and the pan or damage to the sealing surfaces may result and oil leaks may develop. Instead, tap the pan with a soft-face hammer to break the gasket seal.
5   Clean the pan with solvent and remove all old sealant and gasket material from the block and pan mating surfaces. Clean the mating surfaces with lacquer thinner or acetone and make sure the bolt holes in the block are clear. Check the oil pan flange for distortion, particularly

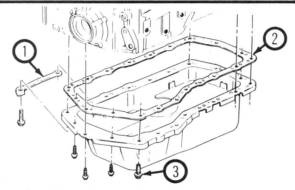

16.6a   Oil pan and related components

1   Stiffener plates   2   Gasket   3   Bolts

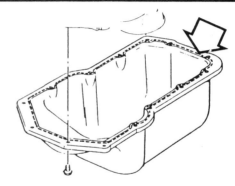

16.6b   Make sure the RTV sealant is applied to the inside of the bolt holes on the oil pan

around the bolt holes. If necessary, place the pan on a block of wood and use a hammer to flatten and restore the gasket surface.

6   Some models have a gasket, while others use RTV sealant to seal the oil pan. On models that have a gasket, always use a new gasket whenever the oil pan is installed **(see illustration)**. On models that use RTV sealant, apply a 1/8-inch diameter bead of sealant to the oil pan flange, inboard of the bolt holes **(see illustration)**.

7   Place the oil pan in position on the block and install the bolts. Don't forget the stiffener plates (if used).

8   After the bolts are installed, tighten them to the specified torque. Starting at the center, follow a criss-cross pattern and work up to the final torque in three steps.

9   The remaining steps are the reverse of the removal procedure.

10   Refill the engine with oil, run it until normal operating temperature is reached and check for leaks.

17   Oil pump pipe and screen assembly — removal and installation

Refer to illustration 17.2

1   Remove the oil pan (Section 16).

2   Unbolt the oil pump pipe and screen assembly and detach it from the engine **(see illustration)**.

3   Clean the screen and housing assembly with solvent and dry it with compressed air, if available. **Note:** *If the oil screen is damaged or has metal chips in it, replace it. An abundance of metal chips indicates a major engine problem which must be corrected.*

4   Make sure the mating surfaces of the pipe flange and the engine block are clean and free of nicks and install the pump and screen assembly with a new gasket.

5   Install the oil pan (Section 16).

6   Refill the engine with oil before running it.

18   Rear main bearing oil seal — replacement

Refer to illustrations 18.3, 18.6, 18.7, 18.10 and 18.13

Note: *Braided fabric seals inserted into grooves in the engine block and main bearing cap are used to seal against oil leakage around the crankshaft. The upper rear main bearing oil seal can be replaced only with the crankshaft removed (Chapter 2, Part D) but it can be repaired with the crankshaft in place. Two piece rubber seals are available from aftermarket suppliers. Several special tools are required for this procedure.*

1   Remove the oil pan (Section 16).

2   Remove the rear main bearing cap.

3   Using the special GM tool (no. J-21156-2), drive the upper seal gently back into the groove in the engine block, packing it tight. It will pack in to a depth of between 1/4-inch and 3/4-inch **(see illustration)**.

4   Repeat the procedure on the other end of the seal.

5   Measure how far the seal was driven up in the groove on each side and add 1/16-inch. Remove the old seal from the main bearing cap. Use the main bearing cap as a fixture and cut two pieces of the old seal to the predetermined lengths.

6   Install the special GM tool (no. J-21526-1) on the engine block **(see illustration)**.

7   Using the packing tool (no. J-21256-2), work the short pieces of the previously cut seal into the guide tool (J-21256-1) and pack them into the engine block groove. The guide and packing tools have been machined to provide a built-in stop. Lubricate the seal with oil to ease installation **(see illustration)**.

2C

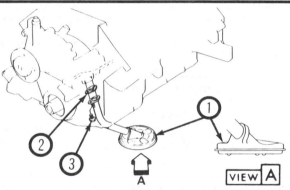

17.2   Oil pump pipe and screen assembly

1 Oil pump pipe and screen   *2 Gasket*   *3 Bolt*

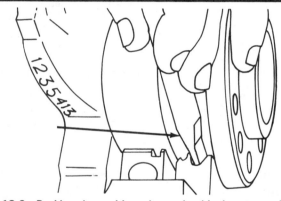

18.3   Packing the seal into the engine block groove with the special tool (arrow)

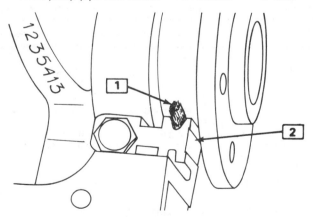

18.6   Seal installation requires a special tool that bolts to the block

1 Short piece of seal   *2 Guide tool (J-21526-1)*

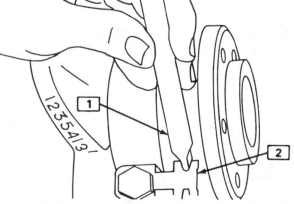

18.7   Packing the short pieces of rope seal into the guide tool and engine block

1 Packing tool   *2 Guide tool*

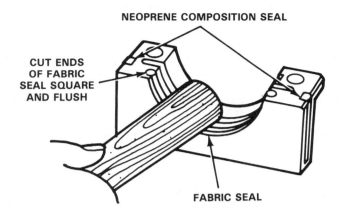

18.10   Rear main bearing cap oil seal installation details

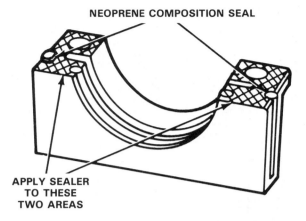

18.13   Sealant applied to the parting line of the main bearing cap

8   Remove the guide tool.
9   Place a new seal in the main bearing cap groove with both ends projecting above the parting surface of the cap.
10 Use the handle of a hammer or similar tool to force the seal into the groove until it projects no more than 1/16-inch. Cut the ends of the seal flush with the surface of the cap with a single-edge razor blade **(see illustration)**.
11 Soak the neoprene seals which fit into the side grooves in the bearing cap in light oil or kerosene for one or two minutes.
12 Install the neoprene seals in the groove between the bearing cap and the block. The seals are slightly undersize and swell in the presence of heat and oil. They are slightly longer than the groove in the bearing cap and must be cut to fit.
13 Apply a small amount of RTV sealant to the joint where the bearing cap meets the block to help eliminate oil leakage. A very thin coat is all that's necessary **(see illustration)**.
14 Install the main bearing cap on the block. Force the seals up into the bearing cap with a blunt instrument to be sure of a good seal at the upper parting line. Install the bolts and tighten them to the specified torque.
15 Install the oil pan.

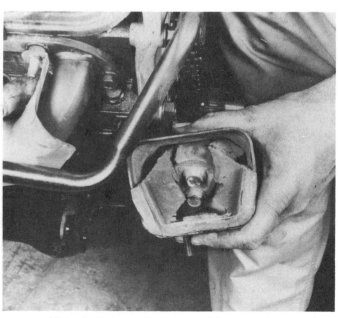

20.1   Broken rear engine mount (removed from vehicle for clarity)

19   Driveplate — removal and installation

1   Refer to Chapter 7 and remove the automatic transaxle.
2   Jam a large screwdriver in the starter ring gear to keep the crankshaft from turning, then remove the mounting bolts.
3   Pull straight back on the driveplate to detach it from the crankshaft.
4   Installation is the reverse of removal. Be sure to align the hole in the driveplate with the dowel pin in the crankshaft. Use Locktite on the bolt threads and tighten them to the specified torque in a criss-cross pattern.
5   Mount a dial indicator on the engine block and check the driveplate runout at the three torque converter mounting bolt bosses. Make sure the crankshaft end play doesn't affect the runout check.
6   If the runout exceeds 0.015-inch, tap the high spot with a soft-face hammer to try to correct it. If the driveplate can't be trued in this manner, replace it with a new one.

20   Engine and transaxle mounts and strut — replacement

Refer to illustrations 20.1, 20.4, 20.9 and 20.14
Warning: *A special tool (GM no. J28467) is available to support the engine during repair operations. Similar fixtures are available from rental yards. Improper lifting methods or devices are hazardous and could result in severe injury or death. DO NOT place any part of your body under the engine/transaxle when it's supported only by a jack. Failure of the lifting device could result in serious injury or death.*

1   If the rubber mounts have hardened, cracked or separated from the metal backing plates, they must be replaced **(see illustration)**. This operation may be carried out with the engine/transaxle still in the vehicle.

Front engine mount
2   Raise the front of the vehicle and support it securely on jackstands.
3   Support the engine.
4   Remove the mount-to-engine bracket nuts **(see illustration)**.
5   Raise the engine slightly, remove the mount-to-frame nuts and detach the mount.
6   Installation is the reverse of removal.

Rear engine mount
7   Raise the vehicle and support it securely on jackstands.
8   Support the engine.
9   Remove the mount-to-cradle nuts **(see illustration)**.
10 Remove the mount-to-engine support bracket nut and detach the mount from the vehicle.
11 Installation is the reverse of removal.

20.4 Front engine mount (rocker arm cover removed for clarity) — arrows point to spacers

20.9 Rear engine mounting nuts viewed from right wheel well

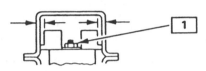

20.14 Rear transaxle mount (typical)

1 *Nuts must be tightened last and provide equal gaps, as marked*
2 *Minimum torque of 18 ft-lbs must be applied to nut before load is supported*
3 *Frame*

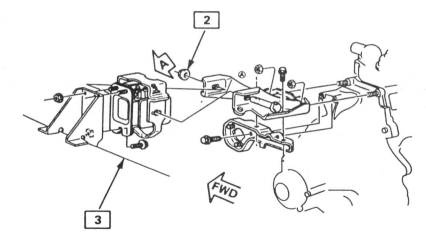

Transaxle mount

12 Raise the vehicle and support it securely on jackstands.
13 Support the transaxle.
14 Remove the large bolt holding the transaxle bracket to the mount **(see illustration)**.
15 Remove the bottom bolt holding the mount to the chassis bracket.
16 Remove the two top nuts holding the mount to the chassis bracket.

17 Raise the engine with a jack enough to allow removal of the mount.
18 Installation is the reverse of removal.

Transaxle strut

19 Remove the through-bolt at the chassis bracket.
20 Remove the through-bolt at the engine bracket.
21 Detach the strut.
22 Installation is the reverse of removal. Tighten the nuts securely.

Chapter 2 Part D
General engine overhaul procedures

Contents

Specifications

2.0L OHC four-cylinder engine

General

RPO sales code	LT2 and LT3
VIN engine code	K and M
Displacement	122 cubic inches (2.0L)
Cylinder compression pressure	Lowest reading cylinder must be 75% of highest reading cylinder (100 psi minimum)
Oil pressure	65 psi at 2500 rpm

Cylinder head

Warpage limit	Consult dealer service department or automotive machine shop

Valves and related components

Valve face angle	46°
Valve seat angle	45°
Stem-to-guide clearance	
Intake	0.0006 to 0.002 in
Exhaust	0.001 to 0.0024 in
Valve seat runout limit	
Intake	0.002 in
Exhaust	0.002 in

Crankshaft and connecting rods

Crankshaft end play	0.003 to 0.012 in
Connecting rod side clearance (end play)	0.0027 to 0.0095 in
Main bearing journal	
Diameter	
Coded brown	2.2830 to 2.2833 in
Coded green	2.2827 to 2.2830 in
Taper limit	0.0002 in
Out-of-round limit	0.0002 in
Main bearing oil clearance	0.0006 to 0.0016 in
Connecting rod bearing journal	
Diameter	1.9278 to 1.9286 in
Taper limit	0.0002 in
Out-of-round limit	0.0002 in
Connecting rod bearing oil clearance	0.0007 to 0.0024 in

Engine block

Cylinder bore	
Diameter	3.385 to 3.387 in
Out-of-round limit	0.005 in
Taper limit (thrust side)	0.005 in

Pistons and rings
Piston-to-bore clearance
  VIN K . . . . 0.0004 to 0.0012 in
  VIN M . . . . 0.0012 to 0.0020 in
Piston ring end gap
  Top compresssion ring . . . . 0.012 to 0.020 in
  2nd compression ring . . . . 0.012 to 0.020 in
  Oil control ring . . . . 0.016 to 0.055 in
Piston ring side clearance
  Top compression ring . . . . 0.002 to 0.003 in
  2nd compression ring . . . . 0.001 to 0.0024 in

Camshaft
Lobe lift (intake and exhaust) . . . . 0.2409 in
End play . . . . 0.016 to 0.064 in
Journal diameters
  No. 1 . . . . 1.672 to 1.6714 in
  No. 2 . . . . 1.6816 to 1.6812 in
  No. 3 . . . . 1.6917 to 1.6911 in
  No. 4 . . . . 1.7015 to 1.7009 in
  No. 5 . . . . 1.7114 to 1.7108 in
Bearing oil clearance . . . . 0.0008 in

Torque specifications*
Ft-lbs
Main bearing cap bolts . . . . 44 plus 40° to 50° additional rotation
Connecting rod cap nuts** . . . . 26 plus 40° to 45° additional rotation

  * **Note:** *Refer to Part A for additional torque specifications.*

  ** *Discard the bolts each time the nuts are removed and use new ones for installation*

2.5L OHV four-cylinder engine

2D

General
RPO sales code L4
Displacement . . . . 151 cubic inches (2.5L)
Cylinder compression pressure . . . . Lowest reading cylinder must be 75% of
  highest reading cylinder (100 psi minimum)
Oil pressure . . . . 36 to 41 psi

Cylinder head
Warpage limit . . . . 0.006 in

Valves and related components
Valve face angle . . . . 45°
Valve seat angle
  1985 and 1986 . . . . 45°
  1987 . . . . 46°
Stem-to-guide clearance . . . . 0.001 to 0.0027 in
Valve seat width
  Intake . . . . 0.035 to 0.075 in
  Exhaust
    1985 and 1986 . . . . 0.058 to 0.097 in
    1987 . . . . 0.058 to 0.105 in
Valve spring free length . . . . 1.780 in
Valve spring installed height
  1985 and 1986 . . . . 1.690 in
  1987 . . . . 1.440 in
Valve spring pressure and length (intake and exhaust)
  Valve closed
    1985 and 1986 . . . . 78 to 86 lbs at 1.660 in
    1987 . . . . 71 to 78 lbs at 1.440 in
  Valve open
    1985 and 1986 . . . . 170 to 180 lbs at 1.260 in
    1987 . . . . 158 to 170 lbs at 1.040 in
Pushrod length . . . . 8.299 in
Lifter
  Diameter . . . . 0.8420 to 0.8427 in
  Bore diameter . . . . 0.8435 to 0.8445 in
  Lifter-to-bore clearance limit . . . . 0.0025 in

Crankshaft and connecting rods
Crankshaft end play . . . . 0.0035 to 0.0085 in
Connecting rod side clearance (end play) . . . . 0.006 to 0.022 in

2.5L OHV four-cylinder engine (continued)

Main bearing journal
Diameter . . . .   2.300 in
Taper/out-of-round limit . . . .   0.0005 in
Bearing oil clearance . . . .   0.0005 to 0.0022 in
Connecting rod journal
Diameter . . . .   2.000 in
Taper/out-of-round limit . . . .   0.0005 in
Bearing oil clearance . . . .   0.0005 to 0.0026 in

Engine block

Cylinder bore diameter . . . .   4.000 in
Out-of-round limit . . . .   0.001 in
Taper limit . . . .   0.005 in

Pistons and rings

Piston-to-bore clearance . . . .   0.0014 to 0.0022 in
Piston ring side clearance
Top compression ring . . . .   0.002 to 0.003 in
2nd compression ring . . . .   0.001 to 0.003 in
Oil ring . . . .   0.015 to 0.055 in
Piston ring end gap
Compression rings . . . .   0.010 to 0.020 in
Oil ring . . . .   0.020 to 0.060 in

Camshaft

Lobe lift (intake and exhaust) . . . .   0.398 in
Bearing journal diameter . . . .   1.869 in
Bearing oil clearance. . . . .   0.0007 to 0.0027 in
Gear/thrust plate end clearance . . . .   0.0015 to 0.0050 in

Torque specifications*   Ft-lbs

Connecting rod nuts   32
Main bearing cap bolts   70
Camshaft thrust plate-to-block bolts 7.5

* **Note:** *Refer to Part B for additional torque specifications.*

3.0L V6 engine

General

RPO sales code LN7
VIN code   7
Displacement . . . .   181 cubic inches (3.0L)
Cylinder compression pressure . . . .   Lowest reading cylinder must be 75% of
                                                                                highest reading cylinder (100 psi minimum)
Oil pressure . . . .   35 to 42 psi

Cylinder head

Warpage limit . . . .   0.006 in

Valves and related components

Face angle . . . .   45 degrees
Minimum recommended valve margin . . . .   0.025 in
Intake valve
Seat angle . . . .   45 degrees
Stem diameter . . . .   0.3412 to 0.3401 in
Valve-to-guide clearance . . . .   0.0015 to 0.0035 in
Exhaust valve
Seat angle . . . .   45 degrees
Stem diameter . . . .   0.3412 to 0.3405 in
Valve-to-guide clearance . . . .   0.0015 to 0.0032 in
Valve spring pressure (not including dampener)
Closed . . . .   88 to 98 lbs at 1.727 in
Open . . . .   210 to 230 lbs at 1.340 in
Valve spring free length . . . .   2.03 in
Valve spring installed height . . . .   1.720 ± 0.030 in
Valve lifter
Diameter . . . .   0.8420 to 0.8427 in
Lifter-to-bore clearance . . . .   0.0008 to 0.0025 in

Cylinder bore

Diameter 3.80
Out-of-round 0.00039
Taper 0.005

Crankshaft and connecting rods

Connecting rod journal	
Diameter	2.2487 to 2.2495 in
Bearing oil clearance	0.0005 to 0.0026 in
Connecting rod side clearance (end play)	0.003 to 0.015 in
Connecting rod/main bearing journal taper/out-of-round limit .	0.0003 in
Main bearing journal	
Diameter	2.4995 in
Bearing oil clearance	0.0003 to 0.0018 in
Crankshaft end play (at thrust bearing)	0.003 to 0.011 in

Pistons and rings

Piston-to-bore clearance limits	
Top land	0.046 to 0.056 in
Skirt top	0.0008 to 0.0020 in
Skirt bottom	0.0013 to 0.0035 in
Piston ring end gap	
Compression rings	0.010 to 0.020 in
Oil ring	0.015 to 0.055 in
Piston ring side clearance	
Compression rings	0.003 to 0.005 in
Oil ring	0.0035 in

Camshaft

Lobe lift	
Intake	0.210 in
Exhaust	0.240 in
Bearing journal diameter (all)	1.785 to 1.786 in
Bearing oil clearance	
No. 1	0.0005 to 0.0025 in
All others	0.0005 to 0.0035 in

Torque specifications*

	Ft-lbs
Main bearing cap bolts	100
Connecting rod cap nuts	
1985	41
1986 and 1987	45

Note: Refer to Part C for additional torque specifications.

2D

1   General information

Included in this portion of Chapter 2 are the general overhaul procedures for the cylinder head(s) and internal engine components. The information ranges from advice concerning preparation for an overhaul and the purchase of replacement parts to detailed, step-by-step procedures covering removal and installation of internal engine components and the inspection of parts. Engine removal and installation procedures are also included.

The following Sections have been written based on the assumption that the engine has been removed from the vehicle. For information concerning in-vehicle engine repair, as well as removal and installation of the external components necessary for the overhaul, see Part A, B or C of this Chapter and Section 7 of this Part.

The Specifications included here in Part B are only those necessary for the inspection and overhaul procedures which follow. Refer to Part A, B or C for additional Specifications.

2   Engine removal — methods and precautions

If you've decided that the engine must be removed for overhaul or major repair work, several preliminary steps should be taken.

Deciding on a work area is the first step. A shop, obviously, is the most desirable place to work. Adequate work space, along with storage space for the vehicle, will be needed. If a shop or garage isn't available, try to find a flat, level, clean work surface made of concrete or asphalt. **Warning:** *Jackstands used on asphalt may sink into the surface and cause the vehicle to fall! Place pieces of thick plywood under the jackstands.*

Cleaning the engine compartment and engine before beginning the removal procedure will help keep you and your tools clean.

An engine hoist or A-frame will also be needed. Make sure the equip-

ment is load rated in excess of the combined weight of the engine and transaxle. Safety is the most important item, considering the potential hazards involved in lifting the engine out of the vehicle.

If the engine is being removed by a novice, a helper should be available. Advice and aid from someone more experienced would also be helpful. There are many times when one person can't do everything required at one time when lifting the engine out of the vehicle.

Plan the operation ahead of time. Arrange for or obtain all the tools and equipment you'll need before beginning the job. Some of the equipment necessary to perform engine removal and installation safely and easily are an engine hoist, a heavy duty floor jack, complete sets of wrenches and sockets as described in the front of this manual, drain pans for coolant and oil, wooden blocks and plenty of rags and cleaning solvent for mopping up spills. If the hoist must be rented, make sure that you arrange for it in advance and perform beforehand all of the operations possible without it. This will save you money and time.

Plan for the vehicle to be out of use for quite a while. A machine shop will be required to perform some of the work which the do-it-yourselfer cannot accomplish due to a lack of special equipment. These shops often have a busy schedule, so it would be a good idea to consult them before removing the engine in order to accurately estimate the amount of time required to rebuild or repair components that may need work.

Always be very careful when removing and installing the engine. Serious injury can result from careless actions. Plan ahead, take your time and a job of this nature, although major, can be accomplished successfully.

3   Engine overhaul — general information

It's not always easy to determine when, or if, an engine should be completely overhauled, as a number of factors must be considered.

High mileage isn't necessarily an indication that an overhaul is needed, while low mileage doesn't preclude the need for an overhaul. Frequency of servicing is probably the most important consideration. An engine that's had regular and frequent oil and filter changes, as well as other required maintenance, will most likely give many thousands of miles of reliable service. Conversely, a neglected engine may require an overhaul very early in its life.

Excessive oil consumption is an indication that cylinder walls, pistons, rings and/or valve guides are in need of attention. Make sure that oil leaks aren't responsible before deciding that the rings and/or guides are bad. Have a cylinder compression or leakdown test performed by an experienced tune-up mechanic to determine the extent of the work required.

If the engine is making obvious knocking or rumbling noises, the connecting rod and/or main bearings may be at fault. Check the oil pressure with a gauge installed in place of the oil pressure sending unit and compare it to the Specifications. **Note:** *The oil pressure sending unit is located near the oil filter on all engines.* If it's extremely low, the bearings and/or oil pump are probably worn out.

Loss of power, rough running, excessive valve train noise and high fuel consumption rates may also point to the need for an overhaul, especially if they're all present at the same time. If a complete tune-up doesn't remedy the situation, major mechanical work is the only solution.

An engine overhaul involves restoring the internal parts to the specifications of a new engine. During an overhaul, the piston rings are replaced and the cylinder walls are reconditioned (rebored and/or honed). If a rebore is done, new pistons are required. The main bearings, connecting rod bearings and camshaft bearings are generally replaced with new ones and, if necessary, the crankshaft may be reground to restore the journals. Generally, the valves are serviced as well, since they're usually in less-than-perfect condition at this point. While the engine is being overhauled, other components, such as the distributor, starter and alternator, can be rebuilt as well. The end result should be a like new engine that will give many trouble free miles. **Note:** *Critical cooling system components such as the hoses, drivebelts, thermostat and water pump MUST be replaced with new parts when an engine is overhauled. The radiator should be checked carefully to ensure that it isn't clogged or leaking; if in doubt, replace it with a new one. Also, we don't recommend overhauling the oil pump — always install a new one when an engine is rebuilt.*

Before beginning an engine overhaul, read through the entire procedure to familiarize yourself with the scope and requirements of the job. Overhauling an engine is not extremely difficult, but it is time consuming. Plan on the vehicle being tied up for a minimum of two weeks, especially if parts must be taken to an automotive machine shop for repair or reconditioning. Check on availability of parts and make sure that any necessary special tools and equipment are obtained in advance. Most work can be done with typical hand tools, although a number of precision measuring tools are required for inspecting parts to determine if they must be replaced. Often an automotive machine shop will handle the inspection of parts and offer advice concerning reconditioning and replacement. **Note:** *Always wait until the engine has been completely disassembled and all components, especially the engine block, have been inspected before deciding what service and repair operations must be performed by an automotive machine shop.* Since the block's condition will be the major factor to consider when determining whether to overhaul the original engine or buy a rebuilt one, never purchase parts or have machine work done on other components until the block has been thoroughly inspected. Since an overhaul requires so much labor, it doesn't pay to cut corners or install worn or substandard parts.

To ensure maximum life and minimum trouble from a rebuilt engine, everything must be assembled with care in a spotlessly clean environment.

4   Cylinder compression check

1   A compression check will tell you what mechanical condition the upper end (pistons, rings, valves, head gasket[s]) of your engine is in. Specifically, it can tell you if the compression is down due to leakage caused by worn piston rings, defective valves and seats or a blown head gasket. **Note:** *The engine must be at normal operating temperature for this check and the battery must be fully charged.*
2   Begin by cleaning the area around the spark plugs before you remove them (compressed air should be used, if available, otherwise

a small brush or even a bicycle tire pump will work). This will prevent dirt from getting into the cylinders as the compression check is being done. Remove all of the spark plugs from the engine. Be careful not to burn yourself.
3   Block the throttle wide open and remove the ECM fuse to disable the ignition.
4   With the compression gauge in the number one spark plug hole, crank the engine over at least four compression strokes while watching the gauge. The compression should build up quickly in a healthy engine. Low compression on the first stroke, followed by gradually increasing pressure on successive strokes, indicates worn piston rings. A low compression reading on the first stroke, which doesn't build up during successive strokes, indicates leaking valves or a blown head gasket (a cracked head could also be the cause). Record the highest gauge reading obtained.
5   Repeat the procedure for the remaining cylinders and compare the results to the Specifications.
6   Add some engine oil (about three squirts from a plunger-type oil can) to each cylinder, through the spark plug hole, and repeat the test.
7   If the compression increases significantly after the oil is added, the piston rings are definitely worn. If the compression doesn't increase significantly, the leakage is occurring at the valves or head gasket. Leakage past the valves may be caused by burned valve seats and/or faces or warped, cracked or bent valves.
8   If two adjacent cylinders have equally low compression, there's a strong possibility that the head gasket between them is blown. The appearance of coolant in the combustion chambers or the crankcase would verify this condition.
9   If the compression is unusually high, the combustion chambers are probably coated with carbon deposits. If that's the case, the cylinder head(s) should be removed and decarbonized.
10   If compression is way down or varies greatly between cylinders, it would be a good idea to have a leak-down test performed by an automotive repair shop. This test will pinpoint exactly where the leakage is occurring and how severe it is.

5   Engine rebuilding alternatives

The do-it-yourselfer is faced with a number of options when performing an engine overhaul. The decision to replace the engine block, piston/connecting rod assemblies and crankshaft depends on a number of factors, with the number one consideration being the condition of the block. Other considerations are cost, access to machine shop facilities, parts availability, time required to complete the project and the extent of prior mechanical experience on the part of the do-it-yourselfer.

Some of the rebuilding alternatives include:
Individual parts — If the inspection procedures reveal that the engine block and most engine components are in reusable condition, purchasing individual parts may be the most economical alternative. The block, crankshaft and piston/connecting rod assemblies should all be inspected carefully. Even if the block shows little wear, the cylinder bores should be surface honed.

Crankshaft kit — This rebuild package consists of a reground crankshaft and a matched set of pistons and connecting rods. The pistons will already be installed on the connecting rods. Piston rings and the necessary bearings will be included in the kit. These kits are commonly available for standard cylinder bores, as well as for engine blocks that have been bored to a regular oversize.

Short block — A short block consists of an engine block with a crankshaft and piston/connecting rod assemblies already installed. All new bearings are incorporated and all clearances will be correct. The existing camshaft, valve train components, cylinder head(s) and external parts can be bolted to the short block with little or no machine shop work necessary.

Long block — A long block consists of a short block plus an oil pump, oil pan, cylinder head(s), rocker arm cover(s), camshaft and valve train components, timing sprockets and chain or gears and timing cover. All components are installed with new bearings, seals and gaskets incorporated throughout. The installation of manifolds and external parts is all that's necessary.

Give careful thought to which alternative is best for you and discuss the situation with local automotive machine shops, auto parts dealers and experienced rebuilders before ordering or purchasing replacement parts.

6.36   Use a large screwdriver or pry bar to separate the engine from the transaxle

6.37   Make sure all wires and hoses are disconnected before lifting the engine out (lifting brackets are provided on the engine for attaching a chain or cable)

2D

6   Engine — removal and installation

Refer to illustrations 6.36 and 6.37

Warning: *The engine and transaxle are very heavy. Use proper lifting equipment. Never place any part of your body under the engine/transaxle when it's supported only by lifting equipment. It could shift or fall, causing serious injury or death!*

Note: *On 2.0L OHC and 2.5L OHV engines with a low mount A/C compressor, have the A/C system discharged by a professional before proceeding with engine removal.*

Removal

All models

1   Disconnect the battery and remove the ground straps. Refer to Chapter 11 and remove the hood.
2   Drain the coolant (Chapter 1).
3   Drain the engine oil (Chapter 1).
4   Remove the air cleaner assembly (Chapter 4).
5   Relieve the fuel pressure and disconnect the fuel lines at the engine (Chapter 4).
6   Disconnect the engine wiring harness at the bulkhead connector and lay it on the engine.
7   Tag and disconnect all other wires and vacuum hoses attached to the engine.
8   Detach the radiator and heater hoses connected to the engine.
9   Disconnect the shift, throttle, TV and cruise control cables as applicable.
10   Unbolt the power steering pump and tie it aside. On 2.0L turbocharged engines you have to disconnect the hoses and drain the pump.
11   Disconnect the exhaust pipe and tie it out of the way.
12   Remove the cooling fan (Chapter 3).
13   Remove the front fender liners (Chapter 11).
14   The following items apply to specific models. On manual transaxle equipped vehicles only, remove the clutch slave cylinder (Chapter 8).
15   If your vehicle has a four-cylinder engine and an automatic transaxle, disconnect the transmission oil cooler lines. Catch the fluid in a drain pan.
16   On 2.5L OHV four-cylinder engines, remove the multi-relay bracket and power steering line bracket.
17   To remove the A/C compressor on four-cylinder engines with a low mount compressor, disconnect the refrigerant hoses from the compressor and cap the ends (after system discharge). On 2.5L four-cylinder engines with a top mounted compressor and all V6 engines, leave the hoses connected and unbolt the compressor from the engine, then tie it aside.
18   Recheck to be sure all wires, hoses and linkages are disconnected.

Four-cylinder models

19   Remove the front wheels (Chapter 10).
20   Remove the front brake calipers and rotors (Chapter 9).
21   Remove the two steering knuckle-to-strut bolts on each side of the vehicle. Be sure to mark their positions before disassembly (Chapter 10).
22   Unbolt the two body-to-cradle bolts at the lower control arm on each side.
23   Loosen the eight remaining body-to-cradle bolts at the ends.
24   Remove one bolt at each end of each side, leaving one bolt per corner.
25   Support the body using a floor jack and a six foot long 4x4 timber placed crosswise under the firewall. Keep jackstands under the vehicle for safety.
26   Place a strong four wheel dolly under the engine/transaxle assembly. Use wooden blocks to position the engine/transaxle on the dolly.
27   Lower the vehicle gently until the engine rests on the dolly.
28   Disconnect the engine/transaxle and strut mounting bolts.
29   Remove the four remaining cradle-to-body bolts.
30   Lift the body up, leaving the engine/transaxle on the dolly.

V6 models

31   Remove the mass air flow sensor (Chapter 4).
32   Remove the radiator (Chapter 3).
33   Attach an engine hoist to the engine. Make sure the cables or chains are securely bolted to the engine.
34   Unbolt the torque converter from the driveplate (Chapter 7).
35   Unbolt the engine mounts.
36   Unbolt and separate the transaxle from the engine **(see illustration)**.
37   Lift the engine out through the top of the engine compartment **(see illustration)**.

Installation

38   Installation is the reverse of removal.
39   On automatic transaxle equipped models, be sure the torque converter is completely seated in the transaxle before installation of the engine.
40   Keep the hoist hooked up until all mounts are connected.
41   Add coolant, transaxle oil and engine oil as needed.
42   Adjust the drivebelt(s).
43   Check all cables and linkages for proper adjustment.
44   Run the engine, check for leaks and proper operation of all systems.
45   Recheck all fluid levels.
46   Where applicable, have the A/C system evacuated, charged and leak tested by a professional.
47   On four-cylinder models, have the front end alignment checked.

7　Engine overhaul — disassembly sequence

1　It's much easier to disassemble and work on the engine if it's mounted on a portable engine stand. These stands can often be rented quite cheaply from an equipment rental yard. Before the engine is mounted on a stand, the flywheel/driveplate should be removed from the crankshaft.

2　If a stand isn't available, it's possible to disassemble the engine with it blocked up on a sturdy workbench or on the floor. Be extra careful not to tip or drop the engine when working without a stand.

3　If you're going to buy a rebuilt engine, all external components must come off first, to be transferred to the replacement engine, just as they will if you're doing a complete engine overhaul yourself. They include:

Alternator and brackets
Emissions control components
Distributor, spark plug wires and spark plugs
Thermostat and housing cover
Water pump
EFI components
Intake/exhaust manifolds
Oil filter
Engine mounts
Clutch and flywheel or driveplate

Note: *When removing the external components from the engine, pay close attention to details that may be helpful or important during reassembly. Note the installed position of gaskets, seals, spacers, pins, washers, bolts and other small items.*

4　If you're installing a short block, which consists of the engine block, crankshaft, pistons and connecting rods all assembled, then the cylinder head(s), oil pan and oil pump will have to be removed as well. See *Engine rebuilding alternatives* for additional information regarding the different possibilities to be considered.

5　If you're planning a complete overhaul, the engine must be disassembled and the internal components removed in the following general order:

2.0L OHC four-cylinder engine
Clutch and flywheel or driveplate
Camshaft cover
Intake and exhaust manifolds
Timing belt/sprockets
Camshaft carrier
Cylinder head
Camshaft
Oil pan
Oil pump
Piston/connecting rod assemblies
Crankshaft and main bearings

2.5L OHV four-cylinder and V6 engines
Clutch and flywheel or driveplate
Rocker arm cover(s)
Intake and exhaust manifolds
Rocker arms and pushrods
Valve lifters
Cylinder head(s)
Timing cover
Timing chain and sprockets or timing gears
Camshaft
Oil pan
Oil pump (2.5L four-cylinder only)
Engine force balancer assembly (not all models)
Piston/connecting rod assemblies
Crankshaft and main bearings

6　Critical cooling system components such as the hoses, drivebelts, thermostat and water pump MUST be replaced with new parts when an engine is overhauled. Also, we don't recommend overhauling the oil pump — always install a new one when an engine is rebuilt.

7　Before beginning the disassembly and overhaul procedures, make sure the following items are available:

Common hand tools
Small cardboard boxes or plastic bags for storing parts
Gasket scraper
Ridge reamer
Vibration damper puller
Micrometers
Telescoping gauges
Dial indicator set
Valve spring compressor
Cylinder surfacing hone
Piston ring groove cleaning tool
Electric drill motor
Tap and die set
Wire brushes
Oil gallery brushes
Cleaning solvent

8　Cylinder head — disassembly

Refer to illustrations 8.1, 8.2, 8.3a and 8.3b

Note: *New and rebuilt cylinder heads are commonly available for most engines at dealerships, automotive machine shops and auto parts stores. Due to the fact that some specialized tools are necessary for the disassembly and inspection procedures, and replacement parts may not be readily available, it may be more practical and economical for the home mechanic to purchase exchange replacement head(s) rather than taking the time to disassemble, inspect and recondition the original(s).*

1　Cylinder head disassembly involves removal of the intake and exhaust valves and related components. If they're still in place, remove the rocker arms before proceeding (2.5L four-cylinder and V6 engines). Before the valves are removed, arrange to label and store them, along with their related components, so they can be kept separate and reinstalled in their original locations **(see illustration)**.

2　If you're working on a 2.5L four-cylinder engine, measure the valve spring installed height for each valve and compare it to the Specifications. The measurement is taken from the bottom of the spring to the underside of the retainer **(see illustration)**.

3　Compress the springs on the first valve with a spring compressor and remove the keepers **(see illustration)**. Carefully release the valve spring compressor and remove the retainer, the springs and the spring seat. Next, remove the O-ring seal from the upper end of the valve stem and the umbrella-type seal (if used) from the guide, then pull the valve out of the head. If the valve binds in the guide (won't pull through), push it back into the head and deburr the area around the keeper groove with a fine file or whetstone **(see illustration)**.

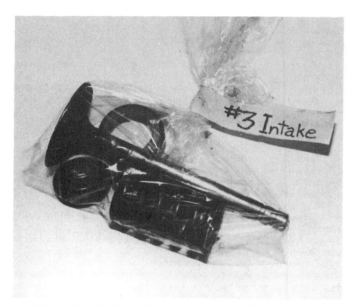

8.1　A small plastic bag, with an appropriate label, can be used to store the valve train components so they can be kept together and reinstalled in the correct guide

8.2   Be sure to check the valve spring installed height (the distance from the top of the seat/shims to the underside of the retainer)

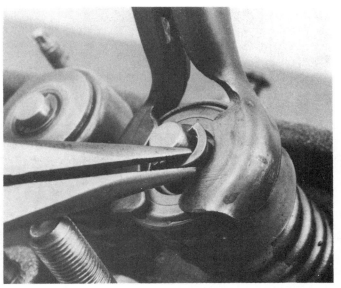

8.3a   Use a valve spring compressor to compress the spring, then remove the keepers from the valve stem

4   Repeat the procedure for the remaining valves. Remember to keep all the parts for each valve together so they can be reinstalled in the same locations.
5   Once the valves and related components have been removed and stored in an organized manner, the head should be thoroughly cleaned and inspected. If a complete engine overhaul is being done, finish the engine disassembly procedures before beginning the cylinder head cleaning and inspection process.

9   Cylinder head — cleaning and inspection

Refer to illustrations 9.11a, 9.11b, 9.13, 9.15, 9.16, 9.17 and 9.18
1   Thorough cleaning of the cylinder head(s) and related valve train components, followed by a detailed inspection, will enable you to decide how much valve service work must be done during the engine overhaul.

Cleaning

2   Remove all traces of old gasket material and sealing compound from the head gasket, intake manifold and exhaust manifold sealing surfaces with a gasket scraper. Be very careful not to gouge the cylinder head, particularly if it's made of aluminum. Special gasket removal solvents, which soften gaskets and make removal much easier, are available at auto parts stores.
3   Remove any built up scale from the coolant passages.
4   Run a stiff wire brush through the various holes to remove any deposits that may have formed in them.
5   Run an appropriate size tap into each of the threaded holes to remove corrosion and thread sealant that may be present. If compressed air is available, use it to clear the holes of debris produced by this operation.
6   On overhead valve models, clean the rocker arm pivot bolt threads with a wire brush.
7   Clean the cylinder head with solvent and dry it thoroughly. Compressed air will speed the drying process and ensure that all holes and recessed areas are clean. **Note:** *Decarbonizing chemicals are available and may prove very useful when cleaning cylinder heads and valve train components. They are very caustic and should be used with caution. Wear eye protection and solvent proof gloves. Be sure to follow the instructions on the container.*

8.3b   If the valve won't pull through the guide, deburr the edge of the stem end and the area around the top of the keeper groove with a file or whetstone

8   Clean the valve train parts with solvent and dry them thoroughly. Do the components from one valve at a time to avoid mixing up the parts.
9   Scrape off any heavy deposits that may have formed on the valves. Use a motorized wire brush to remove deposits from the valve heads and stems (be sure to wear eye protection). Again, make sure the valves don't get mixed up.

Inspection

10   Inspect the head very carefully for cracks, evidence of coolant leakage and other damage. If cracks are found, a replacement cylinder head should be obtained.

9.11a   Check the cylinder head gasket surface for warpage by trying to slip a feeler gauge under the straightedge (see the Specifications for the maximum warpage allowed and use a feeler gauge of that thickness)

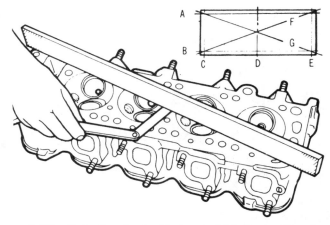

9.11b   Make the check with the straightedge positioned diagonally, lengthwise and across the head as shown in the inset (upper right corner)

11   Using a straightedge and feeler gauge, check the head gasket mating surface for warpage **(see illustrations)**. If the warpage exceeds the specified limit, it can be resurfaced at an automotive machine shop. **Note:** *On V6 engines, if the heads are resurfaced, the intake manifold flanges will also require machining. If more than 0.010-inch must be removed, a new head will be required.*

12   Examine the valve seats in each of the combustion chambers. If they're pitted, cracked or burned, the head will require valve service that's beyond the scope of the home mechanic.

13   Check the valve stem-to-guide clearance by measuring the lateral movement of the valve stem with a dial indicator attached securely to the head **(see illustration)**. The valve must be in the guide and approximately 1/16-inch off the seat. The total valve stem movement indicated by the gauge needle must be divided by two to obtain the

actual clearance. After this is done, if there is still some doubt regarding the condition of the valve guides they should be checked by an automotive machine shop (the cost should be minimal).

Valves

14   Carefully inspect each valve face for uneven wear, deformation, cracks, pits and burned spots. Check the valve stem for scuffing and galling and the neck for cracks. Rotate the valve and check for any obvious indication that it's bent. Look for pits and excessive wear on the end of the stem. The presence of any of these conditions indicates the need for valve service by an automotive machine shop.

15   Measure the margin width on each valve **(see illustration)**. Any valve with a margin narrower than 1/32-inch (0.025-inch on V6 engines) will have to be replaced with a new one.

Valve components

16   Check each valve spring for wear (on the ends) and pits. Measure the free length and compare it to the Specifications **(see illustration)**. Any springs that are shorter than specified have sagged and should not be reused. The tension of all springs should be checked with a special fixture before deciding that they're suitable for use in a rebuilt engine (take the springs to an automotive machine shop for this check).

17   Stand each spring on a flat surface and check it for squareness **(see illustration)**. If any of the springs are distorted or sagged, replace all of them with new parts.

18   Check the spring retainers and keepers for obvious wear and cracks. Any questionable parts should be replaced with new ones, as extensive damage will occur if they fail during engine operation. Make sure the exhaust valve rotators (if used) operate smoothly with no binding or excessive play **(see illustration)**.

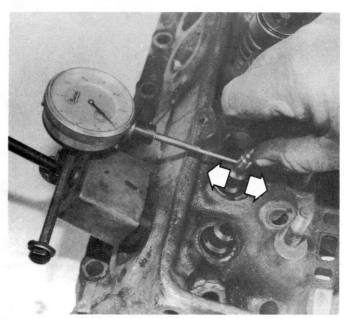

9.13   A dial indicator can be used to determine the valve stem-to-guide clearance (move the valve stem as indicated by the arrows)

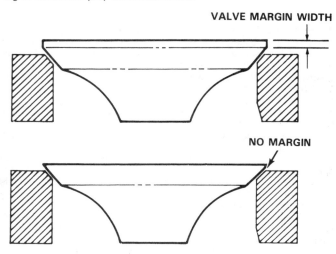

VALVE MARGIN WIDTH

NO MARGIN

9.15   The margin width on each valve must be as specified (if no margin exists, the valve cannnot be reused)

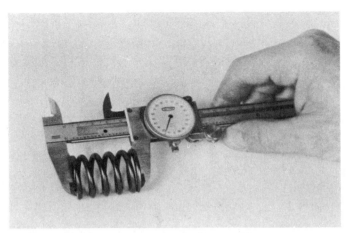

9.16   Measure the free length of each valve spring with a dial or vernier caliper

9.17   Check each valve spring for squareness

Rocker arm components

19   Check the rocker arm faces (the areas that contact the pushrod ends and valve stems or, in the case of the OHC four-cylinder engine, the areas that contact the lash compensators, rocker arm guides and camshaft lobes) for pits, wear, galling, score marks and rough spots.

20   Check the rocker arm pivot contact areas and pedestals/pivot balls as well. Look for cracks in each rocker arm. Check the rocker arm bolts to make sure they're in good condition.

21   On overhead valve models, check the pushrod ends for scuffing and excessive wear. Roll each pushrod on a flat surface, such as a piece of plate glass, to determine if it's bent.

22   If you're working on an OHC four-cylinder engine, check the valve lash compensators and bores for wear and damage. Look for score marks, galling and pits.

23   Any damaged or excessively worn parts must be replaced with new ones.

24   If the inspection process indicates that the valve components are in generally poor condition and worn beyond the limits specified, which is usually the case in an engine that's being overhauled, reassemble the valves in the cylinder head and refer to Section 10 for valve servicing recommendations.

25   If the inspection turns up no excessively worn parts, and if the valve faces and seats are in good condition, the valve train components can be reinstalled in the cylinder head without major servicing. However, most engines will need at least minor refacing of the valves and seats. Refer to the appropriate Section for the cylinder head reassembly procedure.

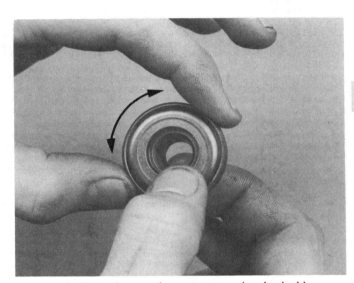

9.18   The exhaust valve rotators can be checked by turning the inner and outer sections in opposite directions, feeling for smooth movement and excessive play

2D

---

10   Valves — servicing

1   Because of the complex nature of the job and the special tools and equipment needed, servicing of the valves, the valve seats and the valve guides, commonly known as a valve job, is best left to a professional.

2   The home mechanic can remove and disassemble the head(s), do the initial cleaning and inspection, then reassemble and deliver the head(s) to a dealer service department or an automotive machine shop for the actual valve servicing.

3   The dealer service department, or automotive machine shop, will remove the valves and springs, recondition or replace the valves and valve seats, recondition the valve guides, check and replace the valve springs, spring retainers or rotators and keepers (as necessary), replace the valve seals with new ones, reassemble the valve components and make sure the installed spring and stem height is correct. The cylinder head gasket surface will also be resurfaced if it's warped.

4   After the valve job has been performed by a professional, the head will be in like new condition. When the head is returned, be sure to clean it again before installation on the engine to remove any metal particles and abrasive grit that may still be present from the valve service or head resurfacing operations. Use compressed air, if available, to blow out all the oil holes and passages.

---

11   Cylinder head reassembly

Refer to illustrations 11.6a, 11.6b and 11.8

1   Regardless of whether or not a cylinder head is sent to an automotive repair shop for valve servicing, it must be clean before beginning reassembly.

2   If the head was sent out for valve servicing, the valves and related components will already be in place. Begin the reassembly procedure with Step 8.

3   Install new seals on each of the intake valve guides. Using a hammer and deep socket, gently tap each seal into place until it's completely seated on the guide. Don't twist or cock the seals during installation or they won't seal properly on the valve stems. The umbrella-type seals are installed over the exhaust valves after the valves are in place.

4   Beginning at one end of the head, lubricate and install the first valve. Apply moly-base grease or clean engine oil to the valve stem.

5   Drop the spring seat or shim(s) over the valve guide and set the valve springs, shield and retainer (or rotator) in place.

11.6a   Make sure the O-ring seal under the retainer is seated in the groove and not twisted before installing the keepers

11.6b   Apply a small dab of grease to each keeper as shown here before installation — it will hold them in place on the valve stem as the spring is released

6   Compress the springs with a valve spring compressor and carefully install the O-ring oil seal in the lower groove of the valve stem (not used on all engines). Make sure the seal is not twisted — it must lie perfectly flat in the groove **(see illustration)**. Position the keepers in the upper groove, then slowly release the compressor and make sure the keepers seat properly. Apply a small dab of grease to each keeper to hold it in place if necessary **(see illustration)**.

7   Repeat the procedure for the remaining valves. Be sure to return the components to their original locations — don't mix them up!

8   Once all the valves are in place, the valve stem O-ring seals must be checked to make sure they don't leak. This procedure requires a vacuum pump and special adapter (GM tool no. J-23994), so it may be a good idea to have it done by a dealer service department, repair shop or automotive machine shop. The adapter is positioned on each valve retainer or rotator and vacuum is applied with the hand pump **(see illustration)**. If the vacuum cannot be maintained, the seal is leaking and must be checked/replaced before the head is installed on the engine.

9   Check the installed valve spring height with a ruler graduated in 1/32-inch increments or a dial caliper. If the head was sent out for service work, the installed height should be correct (but don't automatically assume that it is). The measurement is taken from the top of each spring seat or shim(s) to the top of the oil shield (or the bottom of the retainer/rotator, the two points are the same) **(see illustration 8.2)**. If the height is greater than specified, shims can be added under the springs to correct it. **Caution:** *Do not, under any circumstances, shim the springs to the point where the installed height is less than specified.*

10   On overhead valve models, apply moly-base grease to the rocker arm faces and the pivot balls or pedestals, then install the rocker arms, but don't tighten the bolts completely.

---

12   Camshaft, bearings and lifters — removal, inspection and installation

---

Removal

2.0L OHC four-cylinder engine

1   The camshaft and valve lash compensators (roughly equivalent to lifters) on this engine can be removed with the engine in the vehicle (refer to Chapter 2, Part A).

2.5L OHV four-cylinder engine

Refer to illustrations 12.4 and 12.10

Note: *It's assumed that the engine is already out of the vehicle and the rocker arm cover has been removed. This procedure is not possible with the engine in the vehicle.*

2   In order to determine the extent of cam lobe wear, the lobe lift should be checked prior to camshaft removal.

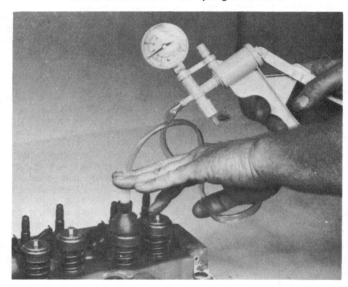

11.8   A special adapter and vacuum pump are required to check the O-ring valve stem seals for leaks (not all engines)

3   Position the number one piston at TDC on the compression stroke (see Section 22).

4   Beginning with the number one cylinder valves, mount a dial indicator on the engine and position the plunger against the top surface of the first rocker arm. The plunger should be directly above and in-line with the pushrod **(see illustration)**.

5   Zero the dial indicator, then very slowly turn the crankshaft in the normal direction of rotation until the indicator needle stops and begins to move in the opposite direction. The point at which it stops indicates maximum cam lobe lift.

6   Record this figure for future reference, then reposition the piston at TDC on the compression stroke.

7   Move the dial indicator to the remaining number one cylinder rocker arm and repeat the check. Be sure to record the results for each valve.

8   Repeat the check for the remaining valves. Since each piston must be at TDC on the compression stroke for this procedure, work from cylinder-to-cylinder following the firing order sequence.

9   After the check is complete, compare the results to the Specifications. If camshaft lobe lift is less than specified, cam lobe wear has occurred and a new camshaft should be installed. Once lobe lift has

12.4   When checking the camshaft lobe lift (OHV engines only), the dial indicator plunger must be positioned directly above the pushrod

12.10   On the 2.5L OHV four-cylinder engine, turn the camshaft until the holes in the gear are aligned with the thrust plate bolts, then remove them with a ratchet and socket

12.12   Support the camshaft near the block to prevent damage to the bearings (V6 engine)

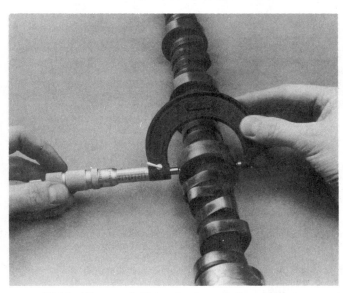

12.14   The camshaft bearing journal diameters are checked to pinpoint excessive wear and out-of-round conditions

2D

been determined, the pushrods, pushrod cover, hydraulic lifters, distributor, oil pump driveshaft, crankshaft pulley and hub and timing gear cover must be removed (see Part B) before the camshaft can be removed from the block.

10   Turn the crankshaft until the holes in the camshaft gear are aligned with the thrust plate bolts, then remove the bolts (see illustration).

11   Carefully pull the camshaft and gear assembly out of the block. **Caution:** *To avoid damage to the camshaft bearings as the lobes pass over them, support the camshaft near the block as it's withdrawn.*

V6 engine

Refer to illustration 12.12

Note: *It's assumed that the engine is already out of the vehicle and the rocker arm covers have been removed. This procedure is not possible with the engine in the vehicle. The pushrods, intake manifold, hydraulic lifters, crankshaft balancer, timing chain cover, timing chain and camshaft sprocket must be removed (see Part C) before the camshaft can be removed from the block.*

12   Carefully pull the camshaft out of the block. **Caution:** *To avoid damage to the camshaft bearings as the lobes pass over them, support the camshaft near the block as it's withdrawn* (see **illustration**).

Inspection

Refer to illustrations 12.14, 12.17, 12.19a, 12.19b, 12.19c and 12.21

Camshaft

13   After the camshaft has been removed from the engine, cleaned with solvent and dried, inspect the bearing journals for uneven wear, pitting and evidence of seizure. If the journals are damaged, the bearing inserts in the block (or the bearing surfaces in the camshaft carrier on the OHC four-cylinder engine) are probably damaged as well. Both the camshaft and bearings will have to be replaced. If the bearing surfaces in the camshaft carrier on the OHC engine are worn or damaged, a new carrier will be required.

14   If the journals are in good condition, measure the bearing journals with a micrometer (see **illustration**) to determine their sizes and whether

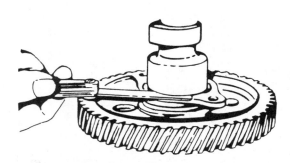

12.17   Use a feeler gauge to check the thrust plate (gear) end clearance (2.5L OHV four-cylinder engine)

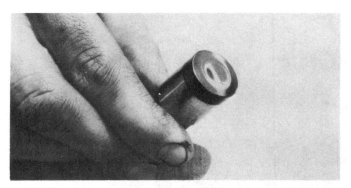

12.19a   If the bottom (foot) of any lifter is worn concave, scratched or pitted, replace the entire set with new lifters

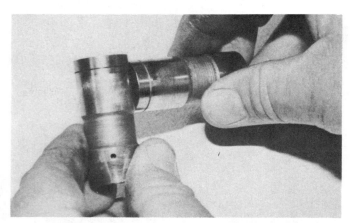

12.19b   The bottom (foot) of each lifter should be slightly convex — the side of another lifter can be used as a straightedge to check it (if it appears flat, it's worn and should be discarded)

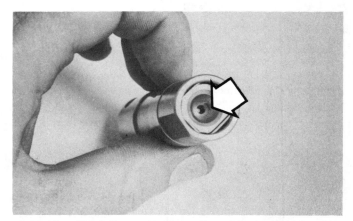

12.19c   Check the pushrod seat (arrow) in the top of each lifter for wear

or not they're out-of-round. The inside diameter of each bearing can be measured with a telescoping gauge and micrometer. Subtract each cam journal diameter from the corresponding bearing inside diameter to obtain the bearing oil clearance. Compare the clearance for each bearing to the Specifications. If it's excessive for any of the bearings, have new bearings installed by an automotive machine shop.

15   Check the camshaft lobes for heat discoloration, score marks, chipped areas, pitting and uneven wear. If the lobes are in good condition and if the lobe lift measurements are as specified, the camshaft can be reused.

Gears (2.5L OHV four-cylinder engine only)

16   Check the camshaft drive and driven gears for cracks, missing teeth and excessive wear. If the teeth are highly polished, pitted and galled, or if the outer hardened surface of the teeth is flaking off, new parts will be required. If one gear is worn or damaged, replace both gears as a set. Never install one new and one used gear.

17   Check the gear end clearance with a feeler gauge and compare it to the Specifications **(see illustration)**. If it's less than the minimum specified, the spacer ring should be replaced. If it's excessive, the thrust plate must be replaced. In either case, the gear will have to be pressed off the camshaft, so take the parts to an automotive machine shop.

Conventional lifters

18   Clean the lifters with solvent and dry them thoroughly without mixing them up.

19   Check each lifter wall, pushrod seat and foot for scuffing, score marks and uneven wear. Each lifter foot (the surface that rides on the cam lobe) must be slightly convex, although this can be difficult to determine by eye. If the base of the lifter is concave **(see illustrations)**, the lifters and camshaft must be replaced. If the lifter walls are damaged or worn (which isn't very likely), inspect the lifter bores in the engine block as well. If the pushrod seats **(see illustration)** are worn, check the pushrod ends.

20   If new lifters are being installed, a new camshaft must also be in-

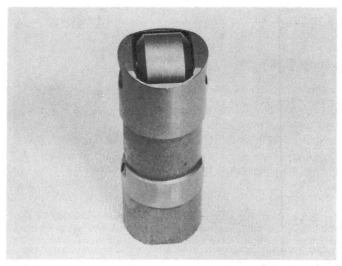

12.21   The roller on roller lifters must turn freely — check for wear and excessive play as well

stalled. If a new camshaft is installed, then use new lifters as well. **Never install used lifters unless the original camshaft is used and the lifters can be installed in their original locations!**

Roller lifters

21   Check the rollers carefully for wear and damage and make sure they turn freely without excessive play **(see illustration)**. The inspection procedure for conventional lifters also applies to roller lifters.

22   Used roller lifters can be reinstalled with a new camshaft and the original camshaft can be used if new lifters are installed.

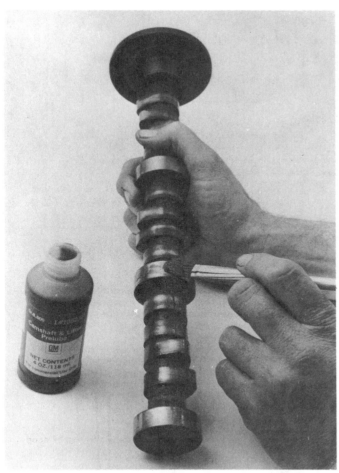

12.25   Be sure to prelube the camshaft bearing journals and lobes before installation

Bearing replacement

23   Camshaft bearing replacement requires special tools and expertise that place it outside the scope of the home mechanic. Take the block to an automotive machine shop to ensure that the job is done correctly. The OHC four-cylinder engine doesn't have bearing inserts — if the bearing surfaces are damaged or excessively worn, a new camshaft carrier will have to be installed.

Installation

2.0L OHC four-cylinder engine

24   Since it's part of the cylinder head installation procedure and can be done with the engine in the vehicle, camshaft installation is covered in Part A.

2.5L OHV four-cylinder engine

Refer to illustrations 12.25 and 12.27

25   Lubricate the camshaft bearing journals and cam lobes with moly-base grease, engine assembly lube or GM camshaft and lifter prelube **(see illustration)**.

26   Slide the camshaft into the engine. Support the cam near the block and be careful not to scrape or nick the bearings.

27   Install the gear on the end of the crankshaft (if not already done). Don't forget the Woodruff key and don't hammer the gear onto the shaft. Align the timing marks on the gears as the gears mesh **(see illustration)**.

28   Line up the access holes in the gear with the thrust plate holes and the bolt holes in the block. Apply Locktite to the threads, then install the thrust plate bolts and tighten them to the specified torque.

V6 engine

29   Lubricate the camshaft bearing journals and cam lobes with moly-base grease, engine assembly lube or GM camshaft and lifter prelube

12.27   Align the timing marks as shown here when installing the camshaft on the 2.5L OHV four-cylinder engine

13.1   A ridge reamer is required to remove the ridge from the top of the cylinder — do this before removing the pistons!

(see illustration 12.25).

30   Slide the camshaft into the engine. Support the cam near the block and be careful not to scrape or nick the bearings.

---

13   Piston/connecting rod assembly — removal

Refer to illustrations 13.1, 13.3 and 13.5

Note: *Prior to removing the piston/connecting rod assemblies, remove the cylinder head(s), the oil pan and the oil pump (2.5L four-cylinder engine) by referring to the appropriate Parts of Chapter 2. If your engine is a later model with the force balancer assembly, remove it as well.*

1   Completely remove the ridge at the top of each cylinder with a ridge reaming tool **(see illustration)**. Follow the manufacturer's instructions provided with the tool. Failure to remove the ridge before attempting to remove the piston/connecting rod assemblies may result in piston breakage.

13.3   Check the connecting rod side clearance with a feeler gauge as shown

13.5   To prevent damage to the crankshaft journals and cylinder walls, slip sections of hose over the rod bolts before removing the pistons

2   After the cylinder ridges have been removed, turn the engine upside-down so the crankshaft is facing up.

3   Before the connecting rods are removed, check the side clearance with feeler gauges. Slide them between the first connecting rod and the crankshaft throw until the play is removed **(see illustration)**. The clearance is equal to the thickness of the feeler gauge(s). If it exceeds the service limit, new connecting rods will be required. If new rods (or a new crankshaft) are installed, the clearance may fall under the specified minimum (if it does, the rods will have to be machined to restore it — consult an automotive machine shop for advice if necessary). Repeat the procedure for the remaining connecting rods.

4   Check the connecting rods and caps for identification marks. If they're not plainly marked, use a small center punch to make the appropriate number of indentations on each rod and cap to match the cylinder they're associated with. **Note:** *If you're working on a 2.0L OHC four-cylinder engine, refer to Section 26, Steps 11 through 13, and check the connecting rod bearing oil clearance with Plastigage before removing the piston/connecting rod assemblies from the engine. This should be done now since the rod cap nuts can't be tightened more than once during engine reassembly without ruining the new rod cap bolts (which means the bearing oil clearance can't be checked with Plastigage during reassembly).*

5   Loosen each of the connecting rod cap nuts 1/2-turn at a time until they can be removed by hand. Remove the number one connecting rod cap and bearing insert. Don't drop the bearing insert out of the cap. Slip a short length of plastic or rubber hose over each connecting rod cap bolt to protect the crankshaft journal and cylinder wall when the piston is removed **(see illustration)**. Push the connecting rod/piston assembly out through the top of the engine. Use a wooden hammer handle to push on the upper bearing insert in the connecting rod. If resistance is felt, double-check to make sure all of the ridge was removed from the cylinder.

6   Repeat the procedure for the remaining cylinders. After removal, reassemble the connecting rod caps and bearing inserts in their respective connecting rods and install the cap nuts finger tight. Leaving the old bearing inserts in place until reassembly will help prevent the connecting rod bearing surfaces from being accidentally nicked or gouged. **Caution:** *If you're working on a 2.0L OHC four-cylinder engine, take the piston/connecting rod assemblies to an automotive machine shop and have new rod bolts installed. DO NOT reinstall the connecting rod caps with the original bolts in place!*

14   Crankshaft — removal

Refer to illustrations 14.1, 14.3, 14.4a, 14.4b and 14.4c
Note: *The crankshaft can be removed only after the engine has been*

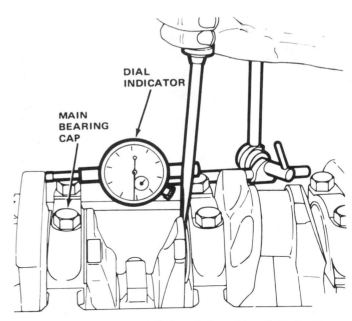

14.1   Checking crankshaft end play with a dial indicator

removed from the vehicle. It's assumed that the flywheel or driveplate, crankshaft balancer/pulley hub, timing chain or gears, oil pan, oil pump and piston/connecting rod assemblies have already been removed. If your engine is equipped with a one-piece rear main oil seal (four-cylinder engines), the seal (and housing on the OHC engine) must be removed from the block before proceeding with crankshaft removal.

1   Before the crankshaft is removed, check the end play. Mount a dial indicator with the stem in-line with the crankshaft and just touching one of the crank throws **(see illustration)**.

2   Push the crankshaft all the way to the rear and zero the dial indicator. Next, pry the crankshaft to the front as far as possible and check the reading on the dial indicator. The distance that it moves is the end play. If it's greater than specified, check the crankshaft thrust surfaces for wear. If no wear is evident, new main bearings should correct the end play.

14.3 Checking crankshaft end play with a feeler gauge (this must be done at the thrust bearing)

14.4a Use a center punch or number stamping dies to mark the main bearing caps to ensure that they're reinstalled in their original locations on the block (make the punch marks near one of the bolt heads)

14.4b Mark the caps in order from the front of the engine to the rear (one mark for the front cap, two for the second one and so on) — the rear cap doesn't have to be marked since it usually can't be installed in any other location

14.4c The arrow on the main bearing cap indicates the front of the engine

3   If a dial indicator isn't available, feeler gauges can be used. Gently pry or push the crankshaft all the way to the front of the engine. Slip feeler gauges between the crankshaft and the front face of the thrust main bearing to determine the clearance (see illustration).

4   Check the main bearing caps to see if they're marked to indicate their locations. They should be numbered consecutively from the front of the engine to the rear. If they aren't, mark them with number stamping dies or a center punch (see illustrations). Main bearing caps generally have a cast-in arrow, which points to the front of the engine (see illustration). Loosen each of the main bearing cap bolts 1/4-turn at a time each, until they can be removed by hand.

5   Gently tap the caps with a soft-face hammer, then separate them from the engine block. If necessary, use the bolts as levers to remove the caps. Try not to drop the bearing inserts if they come out with the caps.

6   Carefully lift the crankshaft out of the engine. Keep the bearing inserts in place in the engine block and main bearing caps, return the caps to their respective locations on the engine block and tighten the bolts finger tight.

15 Engine block — cleaning

Refer to illustrations 15.8 and 15.10

Note: *The core plugs (also known as freeze or soft plugs) may be difficult or impossible to retrieve if they're driven into the block coolant passages.*

1   Drill a small hole in each core plug and pull them out with an auto body type dent puller.

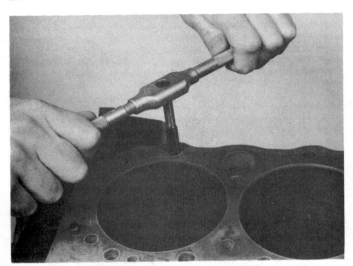

15.8   All bolt holes in the block — particularly the main bearing cap and head bolt holes — should be cleaned and restored with a tap (be sure to remove debris from the holes after this is done)

15.10   A large socket on an extension can be used to drive the new soft plugs into the block holes

2   Using a gasket scraper, remove all traces of gasket material from the engine block. Be very careful not to nick or gouge the gasket sealing surfaces.

3   Remove the main bearing caps and separate the bearing inserts from the caps and the engine block. Tag the bearings, indicating which cylinder they were removed from and whether they were in the cap or the block, then set them aside.

4   Unscrew and remove all of the threaded oil gallery plugs from the rear of the block. Use new plugs when the engine is reassembled.

5   If the engine is extremely dirty it should be taken to an automotive machine shop to be steam cleaned or hot tanked.

6   After the block is returned, clean all oil holes and oil galleries one more time. Brushes specifically designed for this purpose are available at most auto parts stores. Flush the passages with warm water until the water runs clear, dry the block thoroughly and wipe all machined surfaces with a light, rust preventative oil. If you have access to compressed air, use it to speed the drying process and to blow out all the oil holes and galleries.

7   If the block isn't extremely dirty or sludged up, you can do an adequate cleaning job with hot soapy water and a stiff brush. Take plenty of time and do a thorough job. Regardless of the cleaning method used, be sure to clean all oil holes and galleries very thoroughly, dry the block completely and coat all machined surfaces with light oil.

8   The threaded holes in the block must be clean to ensure accurate torque readings during reassembly. Run the proper size tap into each of the holes to remove any rust, corrosion, thread sealant or sludge and to restore any damaged threads **(see illustration)**. If possible, use compressed air to clear the holes of debris produced by this operation. Now is a good time to clean the threads on the head bolts and the main bearing cap bolts as well.

9   Reinstall the main bearing caps and tighten the bolts finger tight.

10   After coating the sealing surfaces of the new core plugs with RTV sealant, install them in the engine block **(see illustration)**. Make sure they're driven in straight and seated properly or leakage could result. Special tools are available for this purpose, but equally good results can be obtained using a large socket, with an outside diameter that will just slip into the core plug, a 1/2-inch drive extension and a hammer.

11   Apply non-hardening sealant (such as Permatex number 2 or Teflon tape) to the new oil gallery plugs and thread them into the holes at the rear of the block. Make sure they're tightened securely.

12   If the engine isn't going to be reassembled right away, cover it with a large plastic trash bag to keep it clean.

---

16   Engine block — inspection

Refer to illustrations 16.4a, 16.4b and 16.4c

1   Before the block is inspected, it should be cleaned as described

in Section 15. Make sure the ridge at the top of each cylinder has been completely removed.

2   Visually check the block for cracks, rust and corrosion. Look for stripped threads in the bolt holes. It's also a good idea to have the block checked for hidden cracks by an automotive machine shop that has the special equipment to do this type of work. If defects are found, have the block repaired, if possible, or replaced.

3   Check the cylinder bores for scuffing and scoring.

4   Measure the diameter of each cylinder at the top (just under the ridge area), center and bottom of the cylinder bore, parallel to the crankshaft axis **(see illustrations)**. Next, measure each cylinder's diameter at the same three locations *across* the crankshaft axis. Compare the results to the Specifications. If the cylinder walls are badly scuffed or scored, or if they're out-of-round or tapered beyond the limits given in the Specifications, have the engine block rebored and honed at an automotive machine shop. If you don't have the necessary measuring tools, the machine shop will also check the cylinder bores. If a rebore is done, oversize pistons and rings will be required.

5   If the cylinders are in good condition and not worn beyond specified limits, and if the piston-to-cylinder clearances can be maintained properly, then they don't have to be rebored. Honing is all that's necessary (Section 17).

---

17   Cylinder honing

Refer to illustrations 17.3a and 17.3b

1   Prior to engine reassembly, the cylinder bores must be honed so the new piston rings will seat correctly and provide the best possible combustion chamber seal. **Note:** *If you don't have the tools or don't want to tackle the honing operation, most automotive machine shops will do it for a reasonable fee.*

2   Before honing the cylinders, install the main bearing caps and tighten the bolts to the specified torque.

3   Two types of cylinder hones are commonly available — the flex hone or "bottle brush" type and the more traditional surfacing hone with spring-loaded stones. Both will do the job, but for the less experienced mechanic the "bottle brush" hone will probably be easier to use. You'll also need plenty of light oil or honing oil, some rags and an electric drill motor. Proceed as follows:

a)   Mount the hone in the drill motor, compress the stones and slip it into the first cylinder **(see illustration)**. Be sure to wear eye protection!

b)   Lubricate the cylinder with plenty of oil, turn on the drill and move the hone up-and-down in the cylinder at a pace that will produce a fine crosshatch pattern on the cylinder walls. Ideally, the crosshatch lines should intersect at approximately a 60° angle **(see illustration)**. Be sure to use plenty of lubricant and don't take off

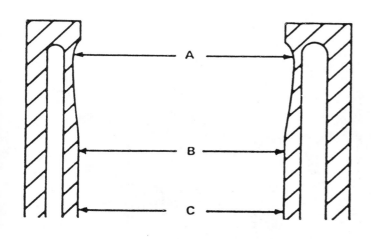

16.4a   Measure the diameter of each cylinder just under the wear ridge (A), at the center (B) and at the bottom (C)

16.4b   The ability to ''feel'' when the telescoping gauge is at the correct point will be developed over time, so work slowly and repeat the check until you're satisfied the bore measurement is accurate

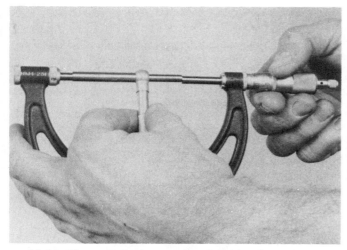

16.4c   The gauge is then measured with a micrometer to determine the bore size

17.3a   A ''bottle brush'' hone will produce better results if you've never done cylinder honing before

2D

any more material than is absolutely necessary to produce the desired finish. **Note:** *Piston ring manufacturers may specify a smaller crosshatch angle than the traditional 60° — read and follow any instructions printed on the piston ring packages.*

c) Don't withdraw the hone from the cylinder while it's running. Instead, shut off the drill and continue moving the hone up-and-down in the cylinder until it comes to a complete stop, then compress the stones and withdraw the hone. If you're using a ''bottle brush'' type hone, stop the drill motor, then turn the chuck in the normal direction of rotation while withdrawing the hone from the cylinder.

d) Wipe the oil out of the cylinder and repeat the procedure for the remaining cylinders.

4   After the honing job is complete, chamfer the top edges of the cylinder bores with a small file so the rings won't catch when the pistons are installed. **Be very careful not to nick the cylinder walls with the end of the file.**

5   The entire engine block must be washed again very thoroughly with warm, soapy water to remove all traces of the abrasive grit produced during the honing operation. **Note:** *The bores can be considered clean when a white cloth — dampened with clean engine oil — used to wipe down the bores doesn't pick up any more honing residue, which will show up as gray areas on the cloth.* Be sure to run a brush through all oil holes and galleries and flush them with running water.

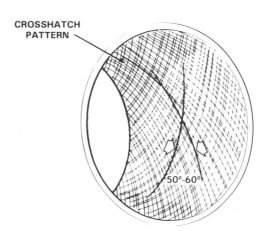

CROSSHATCH PATTERN

50°-60°

17.3b   The cylinder hone should leave a smooth, crosshatch pattern with the lines intersecting at approximately a 60-degree angle

18.4a   The piston ring grooves can be cleaned with a special tool, as shown here, . . .

18.4b   . . . or a section of a broken ring

6   After rinsing, dry the block and apply a coat of light rust preventive oil to all machined surfaces. Wrap the block in a plastic trash bag to keep it clean and set it aside until reassembly.

18   Piston/connecting rod assembly — inspection

Refer to illustrations 18.4a, 18.4b, 18.10 and 18.11
Caution: *On 2.0L OHC four-cylinder engines, the connecting rod bolts must be discarded each time the nuts are removed. After you have completed the following inspection procedure for all piston/connecting rod assemblies, take them to an automotive machine shop to have new bolts installed — DO NOT reinstall them with the original bolts in place!*

1   Before the inspection process can be carried out, the piston/connecting rod assemblies must be cleaned and the original piston rings removed from the pistons. **Note:** *Always use new piston rings when the engine is reassembled.*
2   Using a piston ring installation tool, remove the rings from the pistons. Be careful not to nick or gouge the pistons in the process.
3   Scrape all traces of carbon from the tops of the pistons. A hand-held wire brush or a piece of fine emery cloth can be used once the majority of the deposits have been scraped away. Do not, under any circumstances, use a wire brush mounted in a drill motor to remove deposits from the pistons. The piston material is soft and may be eroded away by the wire brush.
4   Use a piston ring groove cleaning tool to remove carbon deposits from the ring grooves. If the tool isn't available, a piece broken off the old ring will do the job. Be very careful to remove only the carbon deposits — don't remove any metal and don't nick or scratch the sides of the ring grooves **(see illustrations)**.
5   Once the deposits have been removed, clean the piston/rod assemblies with solvent and dry them with compressed air (if available). Make sure the oil return holes in the back sides of the ring grooves are clear.
6   If the pistons aren't damaged or worn excessively, and if the engine block isn't rebored, new pistons won't be necessary. Normal piston wear appears as even vertical wear on the piston thrust surfaces and slight looseness of the top ring in its groove.
7   Carefully inspect each piston for cracks, especially around the skirt, at the pin bosses and the ring lands.
8   Look for scoring and scuffing on the thrust faces of the skirt, holes in the piston crown and burned areas at the edge of the crown. If the skirt is scored or scuffed, the engine may have been suffering from overheating and/or abnormal combustion, which caused excessively

high operating temperatures. The cooling and lubrication systems should be checked thoroughly. A hole in the top of the piston is an indication that abnormal combustion (preignition) was occurring. Burned areas at the edge of the piston crown are usually evidence of spark knock (detonation). If any of the above problems exist, the causes must be corrected or the damage will occur again.
9   Corrosion of the piston, in the form of small pits, indicates that coolant is leaking into the combustion chamber and/or the crankcase. Again, the cause must be corrected or the problem may persist in the rebuilt engine.
10   Measure the piston ring side clearance by laying a new piston ring in each ring groove and slipping a feeler gauge in beside it **(see illustration)**. Check the clearance at three or four locations around each groove. Be sure to use the correct ring for each groove; they are different. If the side clearance is greater than specified, new pistons will have to be used.
11   Check the piston-to-bore clearance by measuring the bore (see Section 16) and the piston diameter. Make sure the pistons and bores are correctly matched. Measure the piston across the skirt, at a 90° angle

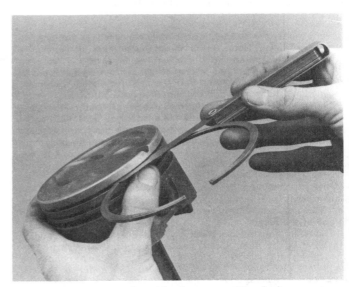

18.10   Check the ring side clearance with a feeler gauge at several points around the groove

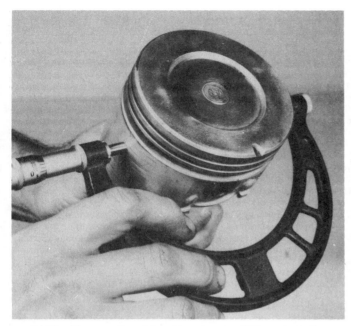

18.11 Measure the piston diameter at a 90° angle to the piston pin and in line with it

to and in-line with the piston pin **(see illustration)**. Subtract the piston diameter from the bore diameter to obtain the clearance. If it's greater than specified, the block will have to be rebored and new pistons and rings installed.

12 Check the piston-to-rod clearance by twisting the piston and rod in opposite directions. Any noticeable play indicates that there's excessive wear, which must be corrected. The piston/connecting rod assemblies should be taken to an automotive machine shop to have the pistons and rods rebored and new pins installed. Usually when the wrist pins are loose the pistons are worn out also.

13 If the pistons must be removed from the connecting rods for any reason, they should be taken to an automotive machine shop. While they are there have the connecting rods checked for bend and twist, since automotive machine shops have special equipment for this purpose. **Note:** *Unless new pistons and/or connecting rods must be installed, don't disassemble the pistons and connecting rods.*

14 Check the connecting rods for cracks and other damage. Temporarily remove the rod caps, lift out the old bearing inserts, wipe the rod and cap bearing surfaces clean and inspect them for nicks, gouges and scratches. After checking the rods, replace the old bearings, slip the caps into place and tighten the nuts finger tight.

19 Crankshaft — inspection

Refer to illustration 19.2

1 Clean the crankshaft with solvent and dry it with compressed air (if available). Be sure to clean the oil holes with a stiff brush and flush them with solvent. Check the main and connecting rod bearing journals for uneven wear, scoring, pits and cracks. Check the rest of the crankshaft for cracks and other damage.

2 Using a micrometer, measure the diameter of the main and connecting rod journals and compare the results to the Specifications **(see illustration)**. By measuring the diameter at a number of points around each journal's circumference, you'll be able to determine whether or not the journal is out-of-round. Take the measurement at each end of the journal, near the crank throws, to determine if the journal is tapered.

3 If the crankshaft journals are damaged, tapered, out-of-round or worn beyond the limits given in the Specifications, have the crankshaft reground by an automotive machine shop. Be sure to use the correct size bearing inserts if the crankshaft is reconditioned.

4 Crankshafts damaged by spun bearings, etc., can sometimes be repaired by shops specializing in crankshaft welding.

5 Refer to Section 20 and examine the main and rod bearing inserts.

20 Main and connecting rod bearings — inspection

1 Even though the main and connecting rod bearings should be replaced with new ones during the engine overhaul, the old bearings should be retained for close examination, as they may reveal valuable information about the condition of the engine.

2 Bearing failure occurs because of lack of lubrication, the presence of dirt or other foreign particles, fuel and coolant contamination, overstressing the engine and corrosion. Regardless of the cause of bearing failure, it must be corrected before the engine is reassembled to prevent it from reoccuring.

3 When examining the bearings, remove them from the engine block, the main bearing caps, the connecting rods and the rod caps and lay them out on a clean surface in the same general position as their location in the engine. This will enable you to match any bearing problems with the corresponding crankshaft journal. Be sure to note the position of the thrust bearing!

4 Dirt and other foreign particles get into the engine in a variety of ways. If may be left in the engine during assembly, or it may pass through filters or the PCV system. It may get into the oil, and from there into the bearings. Metal chips from machining operations and normal engine wear are often present. Abrasives are sometimes left in engine components after reconditioning, especially when parts are not thoroughly cleaned using the proper cleaning methods. Whatever the source, these foreign objects often end up embedded in the soft bearing material and are easily recognized. Large particles will not embed in the bearing and will score or gouge the bearing and journal. The best prevention for this cause of bearing failure is to clean all parts thoroughly and keep everything spotlessly clean during engine assembly. Frequent and regular engine oil and filter changes are also recommended.

5 Lack of lubrication (or lubrication breakdown) has a number of interrelated causes. Excessive heat (which thins the oil), overloading (which squeezes the oil from the bearing face) and oil leakage or throw off (from excessive bearing clearances, worn oil pump or high engine speeds) all contribute to lubrication breakdown. Blocked oil passages, which usually are the result of misaligned oil holes in a bearing shell or foreign matter, will also oil starve a bearing and destroy it. When lack of lubrication is the cause of bearing failure, the bearing material is wiped or extruded from the steel backing of the bearing. Temperatures may increase to the point where the steel backing turns blue from overheating.

6 Driving habits can have a definite effect on bearing life. Full throttle,

2D

19.2 Measure the diameter of each crankshaft journal at several points to detect taper and out-of-round conditions

low speed operation (lugging the engine) puts very high loads on bearings, which tends to squeeze out the oil film. These loads cause the bearings to flex, which produces fine cracks in the bearing face (fatigue failure). Eventually the bearing material will loosen in pieces and tear away from the steel backing. Short trip driving leads to corrosion of bearings because insufficient engine heat is produced to drive off the condensed water and corrosive gases. These products collect in the engine oil, forming acid and sludge. As the oil is carried to the engine bearings, the acid attacks and corrodes the bearing material.

7   Incorrect bearing installation during engine assembly will lead to bearing failure as well. Tight fitting bearings leave insufficient bearing oil clearance and will result in oil starvation. Dirt or foreign particles trapped behind a bearing insert result in high spots on the bearing which lead to failure.

8   Determine the cause of any unusual wear before reassembling the engine. Any good automotive machine shop should be able to assist in determining the reason for bearing damage.

21   Engine overhaul — reassembly sequence

1   Before beginning engine reassembly, make sure you have all the necessary new parts, gaskets and seals as well as the following items on hand:

Common hand tools
1/2-inch drive torque wrench
Piston ring installation tool
Piston ring compressor
Short lengths of rubber or plastic hose to fit over connecting rod bolts
Plastigage
Feeler gauges
A fine-tooth file
New engine oil
Engine assembly lube or moly-base grease
RTV gasket sealant
Anaerobic-type gasket sealant
Thread locking compound (Locktite)

2   In order to save time and avoid problems, engine reassembly should be done in the following general order:

2.0L OHC four-cylinder engine

Crankshaft and main bearings
Piston rings
Piston/connecting rod assemblies
Oil pump/front crankshaft oil seal
Rear main oil seal
Oil pan
Cylinder head
Camshaft/camshaft carrier
Timing belt/sprockets and covers
Intake and exhaust manifolds
Camshaft cover
Flywheel or driveplate

2.5L OHV four-cylinder and V6 engines

New camshaft bearings (must be done by automotive machine shop)
Crankshaft, main bearings and rear main oil seal
Piston rings
Piston/connecting rod assemblies
Oil pump (2.5L four-cylinder only)
Engine force balancer assembly (not all models)
Camshaft
Timing chain and sprockets (V6 only)
Timing cover/front crankshaft oil seal
Oil pan
Valve lifters
Cylinder head(s)
Rocker arms and pushrods
Pushrod cover (2.5L four-cylinder only)
Intake and exhaust manifolds
Rocker arm cover(s)
Flywheel or driveplate

22   Top Dead Center (TDC) for number 1 piston — locating

Note: *Since 2.5L four-cylinder and V6 engines with distributorless ignition have no timing marks or distributor, this procedure does not apply to them.*

1   Top Dead Center (TDC) is the highest point in the cylinder that each piston reaches as it travels up-and-down when the crankshaft turns. Each piston reaches TDC on the compression stroke and again on the exhaust stroke, but TDC generally refers to piston position on the compression stroke. The timing marks are referenced to the number one piston at TDC on the compression stroke. Refer to the *Vehicle Emission Control Information label* for the location of the timing marks on your engine.

2   Positioning the piston(s) at TDC is an essential part of many procedures such as in-vehicle valve train service, timing chain and sprocket replacement and distributor removal.

3   In order to bring any piston to TDC, the crankshaft must be turned using one of the methods outlined below. When looking at the front of the engine, normal crankshaft rotation is clockwise. **Warning:** *Before beginning this procedure, be sure to place the transmission in Neutral and disable the ignition system.*

   a) The preferred method is to turn the crankshaft with a large socket and breaker bar attached to the large bolt that's threaded into the front of the crankshaft.

   b) A remote starter switch, which may save some time, can also be used. Attach the switch leads to the S (switch) and B (battery) terminals on the starter motor. Once the piston is close to TDC, use a socket and breaker bar as described in the previous paragraph.

   c) If an assistant is available to turn the ignition switch to the Start position in short bursts, you can get the piston close to TDC without a remote starter switch. Use a socket and breaker bar as described in Paragraph a) to complete the procedure.

4   Locate the number one spark plug wire terminal in the distributor cap, then mark the distributor base directly under the terminal or make a mark on the engine directly opposite the terminal.

5   Remove the distributor cap as described in Chapter 1.

6   Turn the crankshaft (see Paragraph 3 above) until the ignition timing mark for TDC (usually a zero or a T) is aligned with the pointer.

7   The rotor should now be pointing directly at the mark you made earlier. If it isn't, the piston is at TDC on the exhaust stroke.

8   To get the piston to TDC on the compression stroke, turn the crankshaft one complete turn (360°) clockwise. The rotor should now be pointing at the mark. When the rotor is pointing at the number one spark plug wire terminal in the distributor cap (which is indicated by the mark on the distributor base or engine) and the ignition timing marks are aligned, the number one piston is at TDC on the compression stroke.

9   After the number one piston has been positioned at TDC on the compression stroke, TDC for any of the remaining cylinders can be located by turning the crankshaft and following the firing order (refer to the Specifications in the appropriate Part of Chapter 2).

23   Piston rings — installation

Refer to illustrations 23.3, 23.4, 23.5, 23.9a, 23.9b and 23.12

1   Before installing the new piston rings, the ring end gaps must be checked. It's assumed that the piston ring side clearance has been checked and verified correct (Section 18).

2   Lay out the piston/connecting rod assemblies and the new ring sets so the ring sets will be matched with the same piston and cylinder during the end gap measurement and engine assembly.

3   Insert the top (number one) ring into the first cylinder and square it up with the cylinder walls by pushing it in with the top of the piston **(see illustration)**. The ring should be near the bottom of the cylinder, at the lower limit of ring travel.

4   To measure the end gap, slip feeler gauges between the ends of the ring until a gauge equal to the gap width is found **(see illustration)**. The feeler gauge should slide between the ring ends with a slight amount of drag. Compare the measurement to the Specifications. If the gap is larger or smaller than specified, double check to make sure you have the correct rings before proceeding.

5   If the gap is too small, it must be enlarged or the ring ends may

23.3 When checking piston ring end gap, the ring must be square in the cylinder bore (this is done by pushing the ring down with the top of a piston as shown)

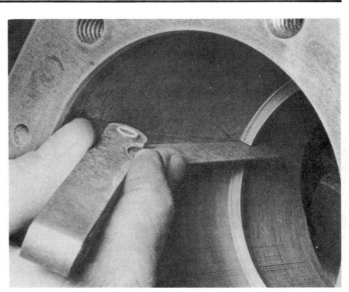

23.4 With the ring square in the cylinder, measure the end gap with a feeler gauge

23.5 If the end gap is too small, clamp a file in a vise and file the ring ends (from the outside in only) to enlarge the gap slightly

23.9a Installing the spacer/expander in the oil control ring groove

come in contact with each other during engine operation, which can cause serious damage to the engine. The end gap can be increased by filing the ring ends very carefully with a fine file. Mount the file in a vise equipped with soft jaws, slip the ring over the file with the ends contacting the file face and slowly move the ring to remove material from the ends. When performing this operation, file only from the outside in (see illustration).

6   Excess end gap is not critical unless it's greater than 0.040-inch. Again, double check to make sure you have the correct rings for your engine.

7   Repeat the procedure for every ring in the engine. Remember to keep rings, pistons and cylinders matched up.

8   Once the ring end gaps have been checked/corrected, the rings can be installed on the pistons.

9   The oil control ring (lowest one on the piston) is installed first. It's composed of three separate components. Slip the spacer/expander into the groove (see illustration). If an anti-rotation tang is used, make sure it's inserted into the drilled hole in the ring groove. Next, install the lower side rail. Don't use a piston ring installation tool on the oil ring side rails, as they may be damaged. Instead, place one end of the side rail into the groove between the spacer/expander and the ring land, hold it firmly in place and slide a finger around the piston while pushing the rail into the groove (see illustration). Next, install the upper side rail in the same manner.

23.9b DO NOT use a piston ring installation tool when installing the oil ring side rails

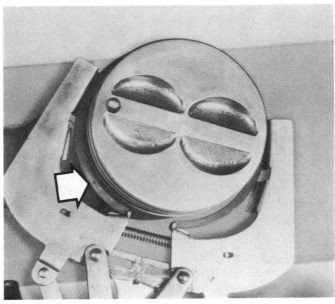

23.12 Installing the compression rings with a ring expander — the mark (arrow) must face up

24.4 When correctly installed, the ends of the rope-type seal should extend out of the block slightly

10 After the three oil ring components have been installed, check to make sure both the upper and lower side rails can be turned smoothly in the ring groove.

11 The number two (middle) ring is installed next. It may be stamped with a mark which must face up, toward the top of the piston. **Note:** *Always follow the instructions printed on the ring package or box — different manufacturers may require different approaches. Don't mix up the top and middle rings, as they have different cross sections.*

12 Use a piston ring installation tool and make sure the identification mark is facing the top of the piston, then slip the ring into the middle groove on the piston **(see illustration)**. Don't expand the ring any more than necessary to slide it over the piston.

13 Install the number one (top) ring in the same manner. Make sure the mark, if any, is facing up. Be careful not to confuse the number one and number two rings.

14 Repeat the procedure for the remaining pistons and rings.

---

24 Rear main oil seal — installation

Four-cylinder engines

1 The rear main oil seal is installed after the crankshaft is in place and the main bearing caps have been installed.

2 Clean and inspect the block and crankshaft seal mating surfaces. Lubricate the new seal with oil and press it into place with GM tool no. J36227 (2.0L OHC engine) or J34924 (2.5L OHV engine).

3 As an alternative, the seal can be installed by tapping it with a soft-face hammer. Using the old seal as a driver, gently tap on it until the new seal bottoms in the bore.

V6 engine

Refer to illustrations 24.4, 24.5, 24.6a, 24.6b, 24.7 and 24.10

Note: *The rear main oil seal must be in place prior to crankshaft installation. An aftermarket neoprene lip type seal is available for V6 engines (manufactured by Fel-Pro). Follow the instructions included with the new seal if you decide to install one.*

4 Lay one seal section on edge in the seal groove in the block and push it into place with your thumbs. Both ends of the seal should extend out of the block slightly **(see illustration)**.

5 Seat it in the groove by rolling a large socket or piece of bar stock along the entire length of the seal **(see illustration)**. As an alternative, roll the seal very carefully into place with a wooden hammer handle.

6 Once the seal is completely seated in the groove, trim off the excess

24.5 Seat the seal in the groove, but don't depress it below the bearing surface (the seal must contact the crankshaft journal)

on the ends with a single-edge razor blade or razor knife **(see illustrations)**. The seal ends must be flush with the block-to-cap mating surfaces. Make sure the cut is clean so no seal fibers get caught between the block and cap.

7 Repeat the entire procedure to install the other half of the seal in the bearing cap. Apply a thin film of assembly lube or moly-base grease to the edge of the seal where it contacts the crankshaft **(see illustration)**.

8 Soak the bearing cap side seals in kerosene or light oil prior to installation. They swell in the presence of oil and heat. The seals are slightly longer than the bearing cap grooves and must be cut to length.

9 Lightly coat the crankshaft journal with assembly lube or moly-base grease, then refer to Section 25 and install the crankshaft.

10 During final installation of the crankshaft (after the main bearing oil clearances have been checked with Plastigage), apply a thin, even coat of anerobic gasket sealant to the parting surfaces of the bearing cap or block **(see illustration)**. Don't get any sealant on the bearing

24.6a   Trim the seal ends flush with the block, . . .

24.6b   . . . but leave the inner edge (arrow) protruding slightly

24.7   Lubricate the seal with assembly lube or moly-base grease

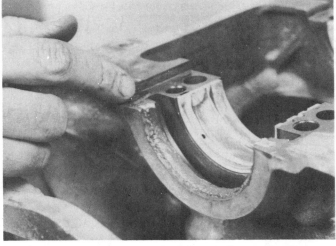

24.10   When applying sealant, be sure it gets into each corner and onto the vertical cap-to-block mating surfaces or oil leaks will result

2D

or seal faces.

11 Install the cap, bearing and oil seal assembly and tighten the cap bolts to the specified torque (see Section 25). After the cap is bolted in place, insert the side seals into the grooves and make sure they're seated. As an alternative, you can inject RTV sealant into the grooves.

25 Crankshaft — installation and main bearing oil clearance check

Refer to illustrations 25.10 and 25.14

1 Crankshaft installation is the first step in engine reassembly. It's assumed at this point that the engine block and crankshaft have been cleaned, inspected and repaired or reconditioned.

2 Position the engine with the bottom facing up.

3 Remove the main bearing cap bolts and lift out the caps. Lay them out in the proper order to ensure correct installation.

4 Wipe the main bearing surfaces of the block and caps with a clean, lint free cloth. They must be kept spotlessly clean.

5 Clean the back sides of the new main bearing inserts and lay one bearing half in each main bearing saddle in the block. Install the other bearing half from each bearing set in the corresponding main bearing cap. Make sure the tab on the bearing insert fits into the recess in the block or cap. Also, the oil holes in the block must line up with the oil holes in the bearing insert. Do not hammer the bearing into place and don't nick or gouge the bearing faces. No lubrication should be used at this time.

6 The flanged thrust bearing is the center (number 3) bearing on the OHC four-cylinder engine, the rear (number 5) bearing on the OHV four-cylinder engine and the number 2 bearing on the V6 engine (number 1 is the front).

7 Clean the faces of the bearings in the block and the crankshaft main bearing journals with a clean, lint free cloth. Check or clean the oil holes in the crankshaft, as any dirt here will go straight through the new bearings.

8 Once you're certain the crankshaft is clean, carefully lay it in position in the main bearings.

9 Before the crankshaft can be permanently installed, the main bearing oil clearance must be checked.

25.10 Lay the Plastigage strips (arrow) on the main bearing journals, parallel to the crankshaft centerline

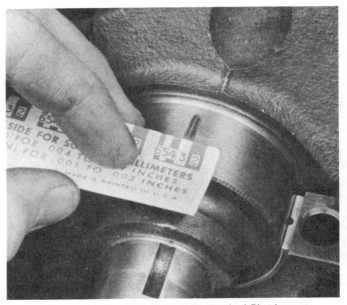

25.14 Compare the width of the crushed Plastigage to the scale on the container to determine the main bearing oil clearance (always take the measurement at the widest point of the Plastigage); be sure to use the correct scale — standard and metric scales are included

10 Trim several pieces of the appropriate size Plastigage (they must be slightly shorter than the width of the main bearings) and place one piece on each crankshaft main bearing journal, parallel with the journal axis **(see illustration)**.

11 Clean the faces of the bearings in the caps and install the caps in their respective positions (don't mix them up) with the arrows pointing toward the front of the engine. Don't disturb the Plastigage.

12 Starting with the center main and working out toward the ends, tighten the main bearing cap bolts, in three steps, to the specified torque. Don't rotate the crankshaft at any time during this operation.

13 Remove the bolts and carefully lift off the main bearing caps. Keep them in order. Don't disturb the Plastigage or rotate the crankshaft. If any of the main bearing caps are difficult to remove, tap them gently from side-to-side with a soft-face hammer to loosen them.

14 Compare the width of the crushed Plastigage on each journal to the scale printed on the Plastigage container to obtain the main bearing oil clearance **(see illustration)**. Check the Specifications to make sure it's correct.

15 If the clearance isn't as specified, the bearing inserts may be the wrong size (which means different ones will be required). Before deciding that different inserts are needed, make sure that no dirt or oil was between the bearing inserts and the caps or block when the clearance was measured. If the Plastigage was wider at one end than the other, the journal may be tapered (refer to Section 19).

16 Carefully scrape all traces of the Plastigage material off the main bearing journals and/or the bearing faces with your fingernails or a piece of wood. Don't nick or scratch the bearing faces.

17 Carefully lift the crankshaft out of the engine. Clean the bearing faces in the block, then apply a thin, uniform layer of clean moly-base grease or engine assembly lube to each of the bearing surfaces. Be sure to coat the thrust faces as well as the journal face of the thrust bearing.

18 If you're working on a V6 engine, refer to Section 24 and install the rear main oil seal sections in the block and bearing cap. Lubricate the seal faces with moly-base grease or engine assembly lube.

19 Make sure the crankshaft journals are clean, then lay the crankshaft back in place in the block. Clean the faces of the bearings in the caps, then apply lubricant to them. Install the caps in their respective positions with the arrows pointing toward the front of the engine. Install the bolts finger tight.

20 Tighten all except the thrust bearing cap bolts to the specified torque (work from the center out and approach the final torque in three steps). Tighten the thrust bearing cap bolts to 10-to-12 ft-lbs. Tap the ends of the crankshaft forward and backward with a block of wood and a hammer to line up the main bearing and crankshaft thrust surfaces. Retighten all main bearing cap bolts to the specified torque, start-

ing with the center main and working out toward the ends.

21 Rotate the crankshaft a number of times by hand to check for any obvious binding (if the crankshaft binds, correct it before proceeding).

22 The final step is to check the crankshaft end play as described in Section 14. The end play should be correct if the crankshaft thrust faces are not worn or damaged and new bearings have been installed.

23 On manual transaxle equipped models, install a new pilot bearing in the end of the crankshaft (see Chapter 8).

24 If your engine has a one-piece rear main oil seal (four-cylinder), refer to Section 24 and install a new seal.

25 If you're working on a 2.0L OHC four-cylinder engine, inject RTV sealant into the rear main bearing cap-to-block parting line holes until it runs out of the joint at the base of the cap (where it meets the block horizontally).

26 If you're working on a V6 engine, don't forget to install the rear main bearing cap side seals (Section 24).

26 Piston/connecting rod assembly — installation and rod bearing oil clearance check

Refer to illustrations 26.8, 26.9, 26.11 and 26.13

Note: *On 2.0L OHC four-cylinder engines, the connecting rod bolts must be discarded each time the nuts are removed, so don't use the following procedure to check the rod bearing oil clearance. If the clearances were correct when the engine was disassembled, they should still be correct if the original bearings or new standard size bearings are being installed. If the crankshaft was reground and oversize bearings are being installed, you'll have to trust the machine shop's work! Begin the procedure with Step 15.*

1 Before installing the piston/connecting rod assemblies, the cylinder walls must be perfectly clean, the top edge of each cylinder must be chamfered, and the crankshaft must be in place.

2 Remove the connecting rod cap from the end of the number one connecting rod. Remove the old bearing inserts and wipe the bearing surfaces of the connecting rod and cap with a clean, lint free cloth. They must be kept spotlessly clean.

3 Clean the back side of the new upper bearing half, then lay it in place in the connecting rod. Make sure the tab on the bearing fits into the recess in the rod. Don't hammer the bearing insert into place and be very careful not to nick or gouge the bearing face. Don't lubricate the bearing at this time.

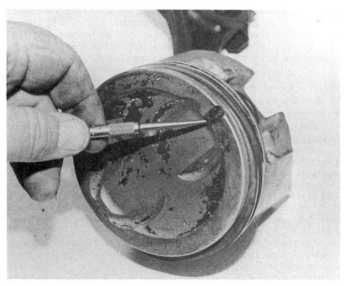

26.8   The notch in each piston must face the FRONT of the engine as the pistons are installed

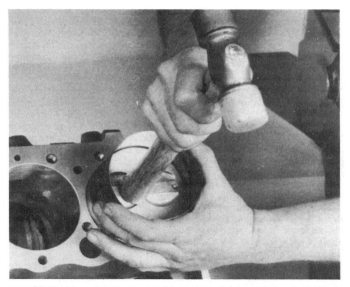

26.9   The piston can be driven (gently) into the cylinder bore with the end of a wooden hammer handle

4   Clean the back side of the other bearing insert and install it in the rod cap. Again, make sure the tab on the bearing fits into the recess in the cap and don't apply any lubricant. It's critically important that the mating surfaces of the bearing and connecting rod are perfectly clean and oil free when they're assembled.

5   Position the piston ring gaps at 120-degree intervals around the piston, then slip a section of plastic or rubber hose over each connecting rod cap bolt.

6   Lubricate the piston and rings with clean engine oil and attach a piston ring compressor to the piston. Leave the skirt protruding about 1/4-inch to guide the piston into the cylinder. The rings must be compressed until they're flush with the piston.

7   Rotate the crankshaft until the number one connecting rod journal is at BDC (bottom dead center) and apply a coat of engine oil to the cylinder walls.

8   With the notch on top of the piston **(see illustration)** facing the front of the engine, gently insert the piston/connecting rod assembly into the number one cylinder bore and rest the bottom edge of the ring compressor on the engine block. Tap the top edge of the ring compressor to make sure it's contacting the block around its entire circumference.

9   Carefully tap on the top of the piston with the end of a wooden hammer handle **(see illustration)** while guiding the end of the connecting rod into place on the crankshaft journal. The piston rings may try to pop out of the ring compressor just before entering the cylinder bore, so keep some downward pressure on the ring compressor. Work slowly, and if any resistance is felt as the piston enters the cylinder, stop immediately. Find out what's hanging up and fix it before proceeding. Do not, for any reason, force the piston into the cylinder — you'll break a ring and/or the piston.

10   Once the piston/connecting rod assembly is installed, the connecting rod bearing oil clearance must be checked before the rod cap is permanently bolted in place.

11   Cut a piece of the appropriate size Plastigage slightly shorter than the width of the connecting rod bearing and lay it in place on the number one connecting rod journal, parallel with the journal axis **(see illustration)**.

12   Clean the connecting rod cap bearing face, remove the protective hoses from the connecting rod bolts and install the rod cap. Make sure the mating mark on the cap is on the same side as the mark on the connecting rod. Install the nuts and tighten them to the specified torque, working up to it in three steps. **Note:** *Use a thin-wall socket to avoid erroneous torque readings that can result if the socket becomes wedged between the rod cap and nut.* Don't rotate the crankshaft at any time during this operation.

13   Remove the rod cap, being very careful not to disturb the Plastigage. Compare the width of the crushed Plastigage to the scale printed on the Plastigage container to obtain the oil clearance **(see illustration)**. Compare it to the Specifications to make sure the clearance is correct.

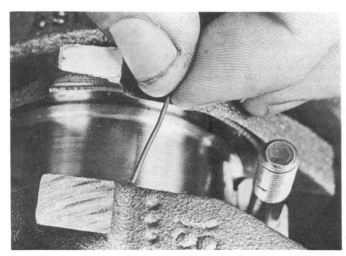

26.11   Lay the Plastigage strips on each rod bearing journal, parallel to the crankshaft centerline

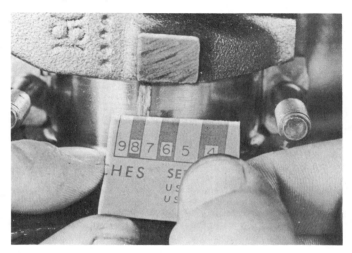

26.13   Measuring the width of the crushed Plastigage to determine the rod bearing oil clearance (be sure to use the correct scale — standard and metric scales are included)

2D

If the clearance isn't as specified, the bearing inserts may be the wrong size (which means different ones will be required). Before deciding that different inserts are needed, make sure that no dirt or oil was between the bearing inserts and the connecting rod or cap when the clearance was measured. Also, recheck the journal diameter. If the Plastigage was wider at one end than the other, the journal may be tapered (refer to Section 19).

14 Carefully scrape all traces of the Plastigage material off the rod journal and/or bearing face. Be very careful not to scratch the bearing — use your fingernail or a piece of wood. Make sure the bearing faces are perfectly clean, then apply a uniform layer of clean moly-base grease or engine assembly lube to both of them. You'll have to push the piston into the cylinder to expose the face of the bearing insert in the connecting rod — be sure to slip the protective hoses over the rod bolts first.

15 Slide the connecting rod back into place on the journal, remove the protective hoses from the rod cap bolts, install the rod cap with the marks properly aligned and tighten the nuts to the specified torque. Again, work up to the torque in three steps. **Note:** *2.0L OHC engines have special "torque-to-yield" connecting rod cap bolts that require additional rotation of the nut after the final torque figure is reached. Be sure to refer to the Specifications at the front of this Chapter.*

16 Repeat the entire procedure for the remaining piston/connecting rod assemblies. Keep the back sides of the bearing inserts and the inside of the connecting rod and cap perfectly clean when assembling them. Make sure you have the correct piston for the cylinder and that the notch on the piston faces to the front of the engine when the piston is installed. Remember, use plenty of oil to lubricate the piston before installing the ring compressor. Also, when installing the rod caps for the final time, be sure to lubricate the bearing faces adequately.

17 After all the piston/connecting rod assemblies have been properly installed, rotate the crankshaft a number of times by hand to check for any obvious binding.

18 As a final step, the connecting rod side clearance must be checked. Refer to Section 12 for this procedure. Compare the measured clearance to the Specifications to make sure it's correct. If it was correct before disassembly and the original crankshaft and rods were reinstalled,

it should still be right. If new rods or a new crankshaft were installed, the clearance may be too small. If so, the rods will have to be removed and taken to an automotive machine shop for resizing.

19 If you're working on a later model 2.5L OHV four-cylinder engine, be sure to install the engine force balancer.

27 Initial start-up and break-in after overhaul

1 Once the engine has been installed in the vehicle, double check the engine oil and coolant levels.

2 With the spark plugs out of the engine and the ECM fuse removed, crank the engine until oil pressure registers on the gauge or the oil light goes out.

3 Install the spark plugs, hook up the plug wires and reconnect the ECM fuse.

4 Start the engine. It may take a few moments for the gasoline to reach the injectors, but the engine should start without a great deal of effort.

5 After the engine starts, it should be allowed to warm up to normal operating temperature. While the engine is warming up, make a thorough check for oil and coolant leaks.

6 Shut the engine off and recheck the engine oil and coolant levels.

7 Drive the vehicle to an area with minimum traffic, accelerate at full throttle from 30 to 50 mph, then allow the vehicle to slow to 30 mph with the throttle closed. Repeat the procedure 10 or 12 times. This will load the piston rings and cause them to seat properly against the cylinder walls. Check again for oil and coolant leaks.

8 Drive the vehicle gently for the first 500 miles (no sustained high speeds) and keep a constant check on the oil level. It isn't unusual for an engine to use oil during the break-in period.

9 At approximately 500 to 600 miles, change the oil and filter.

10 For the next few hundred miles, drive the vehicle normally. Don't pamper it or abuse it.

11 After 2000 miles, change the oil and filter again and consider the engine fully broken in.

Chapter 3
Cooling, heating and air conditioning systems

Contents

Specifications

Coolant capacity	see Chapter 1
Radiator cap pressure rating	15 psi
Thermostat rating	195°F
Torque specifications	**Ft-lbs**
Fan assembly-to-radiator support bolts	7
Transaxle oil cooler fittings	20
Radiator shroud bolts	7
Radiator-to-support bolts	7
Coolant recovery reservoir bolts	7
Thermostat housing bolts	
four-cylinder engine	20
V6 engine	13
Water pump-to-block bolts	
2.0L four-cylinder engine	19
2.5L four-cylinder engine	20
V6 engine	22
Water pump-to-timing chain cover bolts (V6 engine)	7
Water pump pulley bolts	
2.5L four-cylinder engine	18
V6 engine	12

1 General information

Refer to illustrations 1.2 and 1.4

Engine cooling system

All vehicles covered by this manual employ a pressurized engine cooling system with thermostatically controlled coolant circulation. An impeller type water pump mounted on the front of the block pumps coolant through the engine. The coolant flows around each cylinder and toward the rear of the engine. Cast-in coolant passages direct coolant around the intake and exhaust ports, near the spark plug areas and in close proximity to the exhaust valve guide inserts.

A wax pellet type thermostat is located in the intake manifold near the throttle body. During warm up, the closed thermostat prevents coolant from circulating through the radiator. When the engine reaches normal operating temperature, the thermostat opens and allows hot coolant to travel through the radiator, where it is cooled before returning to the engine **(see illustration)**.

The aluminum radiator is the crossflow type, with tanks on either side of the core.

The cooling system is sealed by a pressure type radiator cap. This raises the boiling point of the coolant and the higher boiling point of the coolant increases the cooling efficiency of the radiator. If the system pressure exceeds the cap pressure relief value, the excess pressure in the system forces the spring-loaded valve inside the cap off its seat and allows the coolant to escape through the overflow tube into a coolant reservoir. When the system cools the excess coolant is automatically drawn from the reservoir back into the radiator **(see illustration)**.

The coolant reservoir does double duty as both the point at which fresh coolant is added to the cooling system to maintain the proper fluid level and as a holding tank for overheated coolant.

This type of cooling system is known as a closed design because coolant that escapes past the pressure cap is saved and reused.

Heating system

The heating system consists of a blower fan and heater core located under the dashboard, the inlet and outlet hoses connecting the heater core to the engine cooling system and the heater/air conditioning control head on the dashboard. Hot engine coolant is circulated through the heater core at all times. When the heater mode is activated, a flap door opens to expose the heater box to the passenger compartment. A fan switch on the control head activates the blower motor, which forces air through the core, heating the air.

Air conditioning system

The air conditioning system consists of a condenser mounted in front of the radiator, an evaporator mounted under the dash, a compressor mounted on the engine, a filter-drier (accumulator) which contains a high pressure relief valve and the plumbing connecting all of the above.

A blower fan forces the warmer air of the passenger compartment through the evaporator core (sort of a radiator-in-reverse), transferring the heat from the air to the refrigerant. The liquid refrigerant boils off into low pressure vapor, taking the heat with it when it leaves the evaporator.

2 Antifreeze — general information

Warning: *Do not allow antifreeze to come in contact with your skin or painted surfaces of the vehicle. Flush contacted areas immediately with plenty of water. Antifreeze can be fatal to children and pets. They like it because it is sweet. Just a few drops can cause death. Wipe up garage floor and drip pan coolant spills immediately. Keep antifreeze containers covered and repair leaks in your cooling system immediately.*

The cooling system should be filled with a water/ethylene glycol based antifreeze solution, which will prevent freezing down to at least −20°F, or lower if local climate requires it. It also provides protection against corrosion and increases the coolant boiling point.

The cooling system should be drained, flushed and refilled at least every other year (see Chapter 1). The use of antifreeze solutions for periods of longer than two years is likely to cause damage and encourage the formation of rust and scale in the system. If your tap water

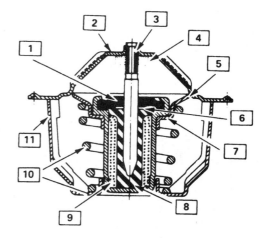

1.2   Pellet type thermostat

1	*Flange seal*	5	*Valve seat*	8	*Rubber diaphragm*
2	*Flange*	6	*Teflon seal*	9	*Wax pellet*
3	*Piston*	7	*Valve*	10	*Coil spring*
4	*Nut*			11	*Frame*

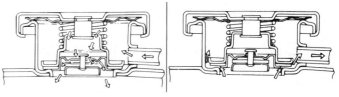

VACUUM RELIEF   **PRESSURE RELIEF**

1.4   Pressure-type radiator cap

is ''hard'', use distilled water with the antifreeze.

Before adding antifreeze to the system, check all hose connections, because antifreeze tends to search out and leak through very minute openings. Engines do not normally consume coolant. Therefore, if the level goes down find the cause and correct it.

The exact mixture of antifreeze-to-water which you should use depends on the relative weather conditions. The mixture should contain at least 50 percent antifreeze, but should never contain more than 70 percent antifreeze. Consult the mixture ratio chart on the antifreeze container before adding coolant. Hydrometers are available at most auto parts stores to test the ratio of antifreeze to water. Use antifreeze which meets GM Specification 1825-M (Part No. 1052753) or equivalent.

3 Thermostat — check

Caution: *Do not drive the vehicle without a thermostat. The computer may stay in open loop and emissions and fuel economy will suffer.*

1   Before condemning the thermostat, check coolant level, belt tension, and temperature gauge (or light) operation.

2   If the engine takes a long time to warm up, the thermostat is probably stuck open. Replace the thermostat.

3   If the engine runs too hot, check the temperature of the upper radiator hose. If the hose is not hot, the thermostat is probably stuck shut. Replace the thermostat (see Section 4).

4   If the upper radiator hose is hot, it means the coolant is flowing through the system and the thermostat is probably open, and the overheating problem lies elsewhere.

5   If an engine has been overheated, you may find damage such as leaking head gaskets, scuffed pistons and warped or cracked heads.

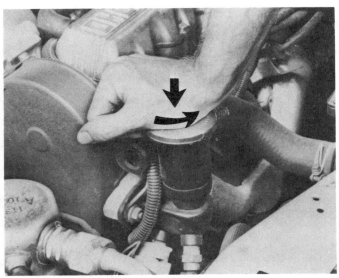

4.3   Push down while rotating (arrows) to remove the
thermostat cap

4.4   Removing the thermostat

4.5   Whenever the thermostat is removed, make sure the
O-ring (arrow) is not damaged

4.8   V6 engine thermostat housing bolts (arrows)

4   Thermostat — removal and installation

Refer to illustrations 4.3, 4.4, 4.5 and 4.8
Warning: *The engine must be completely cool before beginning this procedure.*
1   Disconnect the cable from the negative battery terminal.
2   Drain the cooling system until the level is below the thermostat by opening the petcock at the bottom right side of the radiator.

Thermostat-in-cap models
3   Remove the thermostat housing cap by pushing it down and turning in a counterclockwise direction **(see illustration)**.
4   Grasp the handle and pull the thermostat from the housing **(see illustration)**.
5   If the old thermostat is to be reinstalled, inspect the rubber O-ring for cuts or damage **(see illustration)**.
6   To install, insert the thermostat fully into the housing until it is seated.

Thermostat-in-housing models
7   Remove the upper radiator and heater hoses from the water outlet housing.
8   Remove the two housing bolts **(see illustration)** and separate the housing from the engine.
9   Remove the thermostat from the thermostat housing.
10   Before installing the thermostat, clean the gasket sealing surfaces on the water outlet and thermostat housing.
11   Apply a 1/8-inch bead of RTV-type sealant to the sealing surface on the engine and place the thermostat in the housing. Install the water outlet and tighten the bolts to the specified torque.
12   Install the upper radiator hose.

All models
13   Fill the cooling system with the proper antifreeze/water mixture (see Chapter 1).
14   Reconnect the negative battery cable and start the engine.
15   Run the engine with the radiator cap removed until the upper radiator hose is warm (thermostat open).

3

5.3 Coolant fan relay location (arrow) — V6 shown, others similar

5.6a The resistor block location on the fan brace (arrow)

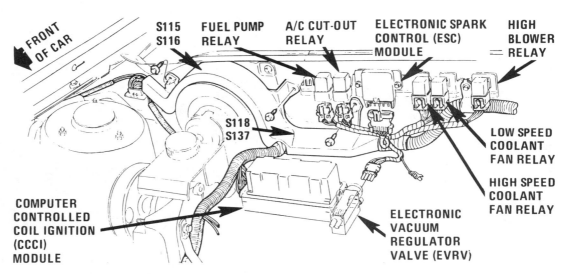

5.6b Location of the fan relays on V6 models — others similar

16 With the engine idling, add coolant to the radiator until the level reaches the bottom of the filler neck.

17 Install the radiator cap, making sure it seats properly.

18 Run the engine until the fan comes on to verify its operation.

5 Engine cooling fan — troubleshooting

Refer to illustrations 5.3, 5.6a and 5.6b

1 Current is available to the fan circuit when the ignition switch is ON. The fan should come on when the coolant temperature reaches 230°F and shut off below 210°F.

2 The circuit is protected by a 20 amp fuse marked C/H and a fusible link by the battery junction block (Chapter 12). Check these first if the fan does not work.

3 The fan switch activates the fan by grounding the fan relay when coolant temperature reaches 230°F **(see illustration)**.

4 The fan switch is located between the exhaust port of the number four cylinder and the thermostat housing on 4-cylinder engines. On V6 models the switch is in the intake manifold above the water pump. It is the rearmost of the three switches mounted there.

5 If the fan runs when the A/C is off and the engine is cool, unplug the fan switch at the engine. If the fan stops, replace the switch. If the fan still runs, replace the relay.

6 V6 equipped vehicles have two speed blower circuits with a double relay and a resistor on the fan bracket **(see illustrations)**. The fan should run whenever the A/C is on. Vehicles with 4-cylinder engines have the relay mounted in the same location, but there is no double relay and the fan will not necessarily be on when the A/C is on.

7 If the fan won't run, ground the wire at the fan switch on the engine. If the fan runs, replace the fan switch. If the relay clicks but the fan doesn't run, check for power at the fan with a test light.

8 Leave the switch grounded as above. Using a test light, check for power before the fan resistor. If there is, check after the resistor at the fan motor.

9 If there is power at the fan motor, check the ground connection. If that is OK, replace the fan motor.

10 If the fuse, fusible link, resistor, fan and switch are OK check the relay(s).

11 On non-A/C vehicles, perform the same test as above. The fan should run on low speed. If not, replace relay. Ground the light green/white wire at the relay. If the fan doesn't run at high speed, replace the relay.

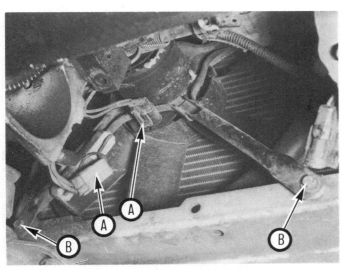

6.4 Fan motor (from under the vehicle) showing electrical plug and mounting bolt locations (arrows)

A Electrical connectors   *B Mounting bolts*

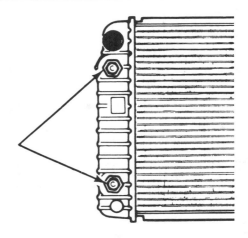

7.5 Automatic transaxle cooling line fittings (arrows)

6 Engine cooling fan — removal and installation

Refer to illustration 6.4

Warning: *The engine must be completely cool before beginning this procedure. Also, when working in the vicinity of the electric fan, disconnect the negative battery cable from the battery to prevent the fan from coming on accidentally.*

1 Raise the vehicle and place it securely on jackstands.
2 Drain the coolant (Chapter 1).
3 Remove the upper radiator hose.
4 From beneath the vehicle, unplug the fan connectors **(see illustration)**.
5 Remove the lower fan mounting bolts.
6 Remove the upper fan mounting bolts.
7 Lift the fan assembly from the engine compartment.
8 To install, place the fan assembly in position and install the retaining bolts.
9 Reconnect the electrical plugs.
10 Remove the jackstands.
11 Replace the upper radiator hose and coolant.
12 Connect the negative battery cable.
13 Run the engine and check for proper fan operation as the engine reaches operating temperature.

7.7 Radiator mounting points (arrows) — two bolts have already been removed in this photo

7 Radiator — removal and installation

Refer to illustrations 7.5, 7.7 and 7.8

Warning: *The engine must be completely cool before beginning this procedure. Also, do not let antifreeze come in contact with your skin or painted surfaces of the vehicle. Flush contacted areas immediately with plenty of water. Antifreeze can be fatal to children and pets. They like it because it is sweet, and just a few drops can cause death. Wipe up garage floor and drip pan coolant spills immediately. Keep antifreeze containers covered and repair leaks in your cooling system immediately.*

1 Disconnect the cable from the negative battery terminal.
2 Drain the radiator (see Chapter 1).
3 On some models, it may be necessary to remove the portion of the air cleaner assembly which is adjacent to the radiator.
4 Remove the radiator hoses from the radiator.
5 Disconnect the coolant recovery hose and, on automatic transaxle

7.8 Remove the radiator by tilting it to the rear then sliding it to the right

models, disconnect and plug the cooler lines **(see illustration)**.
6 Remove the fan and shroud assembly (Section 6).
7 Remove the radiator hold down bolts **(see illustration)**.
8 Lean the top of the radiator rearward, then slide the radiator toward the right and lift it from the engine compartment **(see illustration)**.
9 Carefully examine the radiator for evidence of leaks or damage. It is recommended that any necessary repairs be performed by a radiator repair shop.

3

10 With the radiator removed, brush accumulations of insects and leaves from the fins.

11 Examine and replace, if necessary, any hoses or clamps which have deteriorated.

12 The radiator can be flushed as described in Chapter 1.

13 Replace the radiator cap with a new one of the recommended rating, or if the cap is comparatively new, have it tested by a service station.

14 If you are installing a new radiator, transfer the fittings from the old unit to the new one.

15 Installation is the reverse of removal. When setting the radiator in the chassis, make sure that it seats securely in the lower rubber mounting pads.

16 After installing the radiator, refill it with the proper coolant mixture (see Chapter 1), then start the engine and check for leaks.

17 On automatic transaxle equipped models, check the fluid level and fill as needed (Chapter 1).

8   Coolant reservoir — removal and installation

Refer to illustration 8.1

1 Disconnect the radiator overflow hose from the reservoir (**see illustration**).

2 Remove the three bolts holding the reservoir to the inner fender.

3 Lift out the reservoir and pour the contents into a drain pan.

4 Installation is the reverse of removal.

9   Water pump — check

Refer to illustration 9.4

1 A failure of the water pump can cause overheating and serious engine damage because the pump may not circulate coolant through the engine.

2 There are three ways to check the operation of the water pump while it is still installed on the engine. If the pump is defective, it should be replaced with a new or rebuilt unit.

3 With the engine running at normal operating temperature, squeeze the upper radiator hose. If the water pump is pumping properly, a pressure surge will be felt as the hose is released.

4 Water pumps are equipped with ''weep'' or vent holes. If a pump seal failure occurs, coolant will leak from the weep holes (**see illustration**). In most cases it will be necessary to use a flashlight from under the vehicle to see evidence of leakage from this point on the pump body. Sometimes this leakage will be intermittent.

5 If the water pump shaft bearings fail, there may be a rumbling or squealing sound emitted from the front of the engine while it is running.

8.1   Disconnect the coolant reservoir hose (arrow)

Bearing failure may be felt by removing the drive belt and turning and rocking the water pump pulley by hand. Do not mistake drivebelt slippage (which also causes a squealing sound) for water pump failure.

10   Water pump — removal and installation

Warning: *The engine must be completely cool before beginning this procedure.*

1 Disconnect the negative battery cable from the battery.

2 Drain the cooling system (Chapter 1) and place a large drain pan under the pump.

2.0L OHC engine

Refer to illustration 10.5

3 Remove the timing belt and rear cover (Chapter 2).

4 Remove the lower radiator and heater hose from the pump.

5 Remove the three pump mounting bolts (**see illustration**).

6 Remove the pump and seal ring.

7 Clean the sealing surfaces and put a 2 mm (3/32-inch) bead of GM sealer No. 1050026 (or equivalent) on the sealing surface.

8 Installation is the reverse of removal.

9 Go to Step 28.

9.4   The water pump weep hole (arrow) will drip coolant when the seal for the pump shaft bearing fails

10.5   OHC engine water pump retaining bolts (arrows)

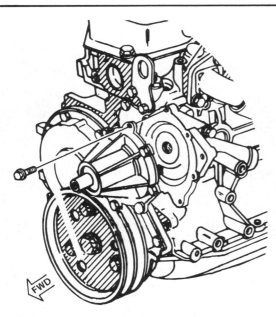

10.12 Water pump front cover assembly mounting for the 2.5L engine

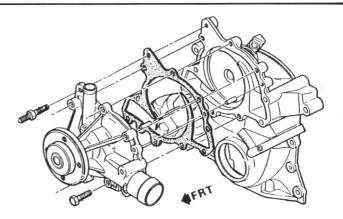

10.20 V6 water pump mounting details

2.5L OHV engine

Refer to illustration 10.12

Caution: *The water pump pulley may separate on some 2.5L engines. Inspect the spot welds attaching the pulleys and hubs. Refer to Pontiac service bulletin 85-6 (Gasoline)-10.*

10 Remove the accessory drivebelt (Chapter 1).

11 Remove the lower radiator hose from the pump.

12 Remove the water pump attaching bolts and lift the pump out. The water pump can be removed as a unit from the housing for replacement **(see illustration)**, or the entire assembly can be unbolted from the block.

13 Clean the pump mating surfaces.

14 If the pump is being replaced, remove the pulley with GM tool No. J-25034-B or J-29785-A or equivalent. Install the pulley with GM tool No. J-25033-B or equivalent. **Caution:** *Do not hammer the pulley onto the pump as damage may occur. If these special tools are not available, take the pump to a GM dealer or repair shop to have the pulley pressed on and off.*

15 Apply a 3 mm (1/8-inch) bead of sealer to the mating surface.

16 Coat the mounting bolts with GM sealer No. 1050026 or equivalent.

17 Install the pump and tighten the bolts to the specified torque.

18 Reinstall the hoses and drivebelt.

19 Go to Step 28.

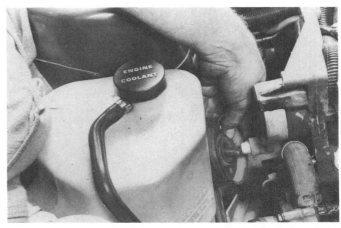

10.21 Removing drivebelt tensioner pulley (left-hand thread)

V6 engine

Refer to illustrations 10.20, 10.21, 10.23 and 10.24

20 Loosen the four water pump pulley bolts **(see illustration)**.

21 Remove the serpentine drivebelt (Chapter 1) and tensioner **(see illustration)**.

22 Remove the alternator (Chapter 5).

23 Remove the four water pump pulley bolts and move the pulley aside. It won't clear the frame for removal until the pump is removed **(see illustration)**.

24 Remove the water pump bolts and lift the pump out **(see illustration)**.

10.23 The V6 water pump pulley (arrow) won't clear the frame until the pump is removed

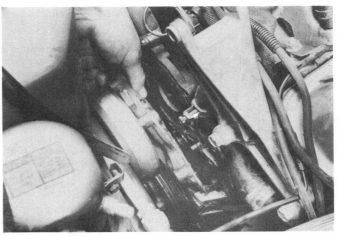

10.24 Removing the V6 water pump

3

11.7   Typical temperature sending unit location (V6 shown)

12.2   Heater fan electrical connectors (arrows)

12.4   Heater blower motor and cage removal

13.5   Remove the console air ducts (right side shown)

25 Clean the gasket surfaces on the engine (and pump if old one is being reused).

26 Installation is the reverse of removal. Coat the bolt threads with thread sealant (GM No. 1052080 or equivalent).

27 Tighten the mounting bolts to the specified torque.

All models

28 Refill the cooling system with the proper solution of water and anti-freeze (Chapter 1).

29 Connect the negative battery cable.

30 Start the engine and run it until normal operating temperature is reached, checking for leaks, thermostat opening and fan operation.

31 Shut off the engine, allow it to cool, then recheck the coolant level.

---

11   Coolant temperature sending unit — check and replacement

Refer to illustration 11.7

1   The coolant temperature indicator system is composed of a light or temperature gauge mounted in the instrument panel and a coolant temperature sending unit mounted on the engine.

2   **Warning:** *Be especially careful to stay clear of the electric fan blades, which can come on at any time.*

3   If an overheating indication occurs, check the coolant level in the system and then make sure that the wiring between the light or gauge and the sending unit is secure and all fuses are intact.

4   When the ignition switch is turned on and the starter motor is turning, the indicator light should be on (overheated engine indication).

5   If the light is not on, the bulb may be burned out, the ignition switch may be faulty or the circuit may be open. Test the circuit by grounding the wire to the sending unit while the ignition is ON (engine not running for safety). If the gauge deflects or the light comes on, replace the sending unit.

6   As soon as the engine starts, the light should go out and remain out unless the engine overheats. Failure of the light to go out may be due to grounded wiring between the light and the sending unit, a defective sending unit or a faulty ignition switch. Check the coolant to make sure it is of the proper type, as plain water has too low a boiling point to activate the sending unit.

7   If the sending unit is to be replaced, it is simply unscrewed from the cylinder head or thermostat housing and the replacement installed (**see illustration**). Use GM sealer No. 1052080 (or equivalent) on the threads. Make sure that the engine is cool before removing the defective sending unit. There will be some coolant loss as the unit is removed, so be prepared to catch the coolant in a pan and to check the level after the replacement has been installed.

8   Sending unit locations:
   a) 2.0L Turbos have two possible locations. Either in the cylinder head under the distributor or in the thermostat housing next to the ECM sensor. The ECM sensor can be identified because it has a two wire connector.
   b) On 2.5L OHV engines the sending unit is installed in the top of the cylinder head next to the thermostat housing.
   c) On 3.0L V6 engines the sending unit is located in the intake manifold above the water pump. Three sending units are mounted there. The temperature sending unit is nearest to the front of the vehicle.

13.7   Heater core and air conditioning condenser assembly — exploded view

1 Blower air inlet case
2 Blower gasket
3 Blower air inlet flange mount
4 Mode valve
5 Defroster valve seat
6 Evaporator case seal
7 Defroster valve
8 Core mounting strap
9 Evaporator case seal
10 Evaporator to case seal
11 Rear core cover
12 Heater core
13 Front core cover
14 Evaporator core seal
15 Tube mounting bracket
16 Orifice
17 Tube clamp
18 Evaporator mounting bracket
19 Heater core shroud
20 Vacuum reservoir retaining clip
21 Evaporator case
22 Defroster duct
23 Mode valve shaft
24 Mode slave lever
25 Retainer
26 Water core filter
27 Evaporator
28 Temperature valve
29 Mode vacuum actuator
30 Defroster vacuum actuator
31 Vacuum actuator mounting bracket
32 Mode valve adjusting slave link
33 Mode valve actuator bracket
34 Blower motor cooling tube
35 Blower motor ground terminal
36 Blower motor
37 Blower fan

12   Heater and air conditioning blower motor — removal and installation

Refer to illustrations 12.2 and 12.4

1   Disconnect the cable from the negative battery terminal.
2   Working in the engine compartment at the firewall, disconnect the wires at the blower motor (see illustration).
3   On V6 engines, remove the power steering pump for access (Chapter 10).
4   Remove the blower motor mounting bolts and separate the motor/cage assembly from the housing (see illustration).
5   Remove the cage retaining nut and slide the cage off the motor shaft.
6   Installation is the reverse of the removal procedure.

13   Heater core — removal and installation

Refer to illustrations 13.5, 13.7, 13.8 and 13.9

1   Disconnect the battery, negative cable first.
2   Raise the front of the vehicle and support it securely on jackstands.
3   Drain the cooling system (Chapter 1).
4   Remove the console extensions (see Chapter 11).
5   Remove the console air ducts (see illustration).
6   Remove the sound insulation panels above the footwells (see Chapter 11).
7   Remove the air plenum assembly (see illustration).

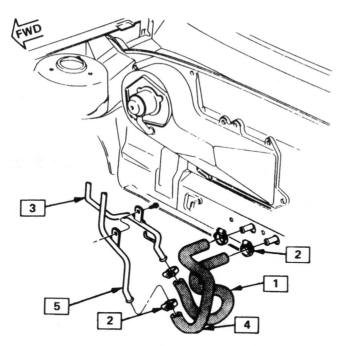

13.8　Heater hose connections to the heater core

1　Heater outlet hose
2　Clamp
3　Heater outlet pipe
4　Heater inlet hose
5　Heater inlet pipe

8　From under the vehicle, disconnect the heater hoses at the firewall **(see illustration)**.
9　Remove the heater core housing **(see illustration)**.
10　Remove the heater core.
11　Installation is the reverse of removal.

14　Air conditioning system — servicing

Refer to illustration 14.2

Warning: *The air conditioning system is under high pressure. Sudden discharge can freeze skin and eyes, causing blindness. Allowing the refrigerant to be burned, such as when drawn into an engine, creates a deadly poisonous gas. Do not disassemble any portion of the system (hoses, compressor, line fittings, etc.) without having the system depressurized by a dealer or A/C repair facility.*

1　Regularly inspect the condenser fins (located ahead of the radiator) and brush away leaves and bugs.
2　Clean the evaporator drain tube by slipping a wire into the opening. This is located on the firewall **(see illustration)**.
3　Check the condition of the refrigerant hoses. If there is any sign of deterioration or hardening, have them replaced by a dealer or air conditioning repair facility.
4　At the recommended intervals, check and adjust the compressor drivebelt as described in Chapter 1.

15　Air conditioning accumulator — removal and installation

Refer to illustrations 15.2, 15.3a, 15.3b and 15.3c

Caution: *The accumulator (also called receiver/dryer) removes moisture and foreign particles from the refrigerant. If the system is left discharged or the compressor fails, the accumulator should be replaced.*

1　Have the system discharged by a professional.
2　Disconnect the refrigerant lines from the accumulator **(see illustration)**. Be sure to hold the accumulator fittings with a wrench while loosening the hose fittings to prevent twisting the housing.

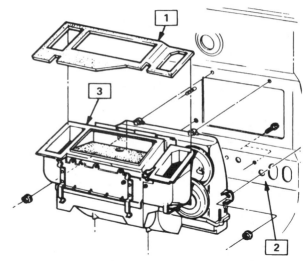

13.9　Heater and A/C evaporator housing

1　Seal
2　Dash panel
3　Housing assembly

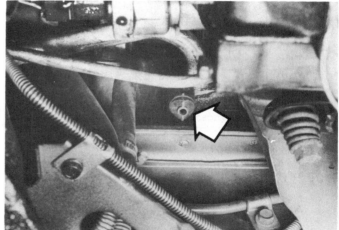

14.2　Evaporator housing drain tube on firewall (arrow)

15.2　A/C accumulator refrigerant line fittings (arrows)

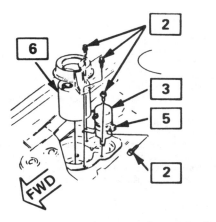

15.3a 2.0L Turbo accumulator mounting

2 Bolt/screw
3 Accumulator
5 Bracket
6 Canister and retainer

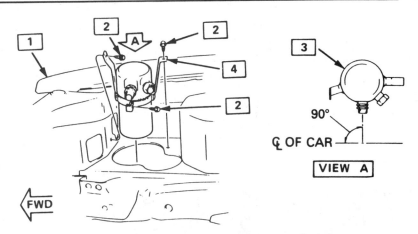

15.3b 2.5L OHV accumulator mounting

1 Right fender
2 Bolt/screw
3 Accumulator
4 Bracket

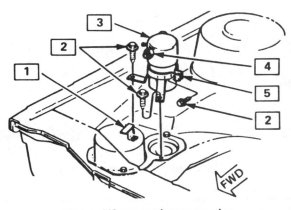

15.3c V6 accumulator mounting

1 Bracket
2 Bolt/screw
3 Accumulator
4 Position outlet parallel to centerline of vehicle
5 Bracket

3 Remove the clamp bolt from the accumulator bracket (see illustrations).
4 Slide the accumulator out of its bracket and cap all the fittings.
5 Installation is the reverse of removal.
6 Have the system evacuated, charged and leak tested by a professional.

16 Air conditioning compressor — removal and installation

Refer to illustrations 16.9, 16.10, 16.11a, 16.11b and 16.11c

Caution: *If the compressor fails, particles may be released into the refrigerant. This contamination may plug the expansion valve and/or the accumulator. Failure to remove these particles may result in another compressor failure. If contamination is suspected have the system flushed by a professional.*

1 Have the system discharged by a professional.
2 The compressor clutch, seal and bearings may be serviced separately. Expensive special tools are required. Take this work to an A/C shop.
3 Four-cylinder vehicles use a variable displacement (V-5) compressor. Six-cylinder vehicles use a fixed displacement (R-4 or DA-6) compressor.
4 It is normal for compressors on 6-cylinder vehicles to cycle on and

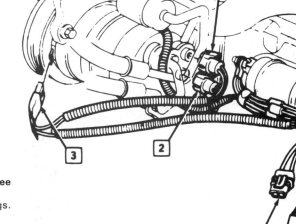

16.9 Typical A/C compressor switch wiring

1 Coolant fan leads
2 High pressure switch
3 Compressor clutch switch
4 Compressor pulley
5 Low pressure switch

off when operating. A hissing noise lasting up to 60 seconds is also normal following shutdown.
5 An engine idle shake on some 3.0L V6 models which changes when the A/C is off may need a different bracket. Refer to Pontiac service bulletin no. 85-6 (Gasoline)-10.
6 Disconnect the battery, negative cable first, before removing the compressor.
7 Raise the vehicle and support it securely on jackstands.
8 Remove the drivebelt (Chapter 1).
9 Unplug the wiring connectors (see illustration).

10 Disconnect the refrigerant lines at the compressor **(see illustration)**.
11 Unbolt the compressor from its mounting brackets and remove it from the engine compartment **(see illustrations)**.
12 Measure the amount of oil in the compressor and note it.
13 Installation is the reverse of removal.
14 Have the system professionally evacuated, charged and leak tested.

17 Air conditioning condenser — removal and installation

Refer to illustrations 17.5, 17.8, 17.10a, 17.10b and 17.11
1 Have the air conditioning system discharged by a professional.

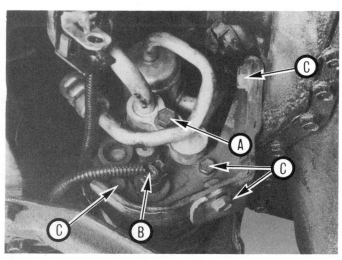

**16.10   Rear view of A/C compressor
(V6 shown — others similar)**

A *Refrigerant line
    hold-down bolt*
B *Electrical plug*
C *Mounting bolts*

2 Remove the grille (Chapter 11).
3 Remove the headlight bezels (Chapter 11).
4 Remove the side marker lights (Chapter 11).
5 Unbolt the front panel **(see illustration)**.
6 Unbolt the plastic panel which holds the headlights.
7 Raise the vehicle and place it securely on jackstands.
8 From beneath the vehicle, unbolt the lower spoiler to gain access to the two bolts holding the vertical hood latch brace and remove them **(see illustration)**.
9 Lift the hood latch brackets out and pull the headlight panel away from the radiator support.
10 Disconnect the refrigerant lines to the condenser **(see illustration)**, then unbolt the condenser hold down brackets and carefully lift out the condenser **(see illustration)**. Tilt the condenser to pour any oil remaining in it into a measuring cup. Note the quantity.

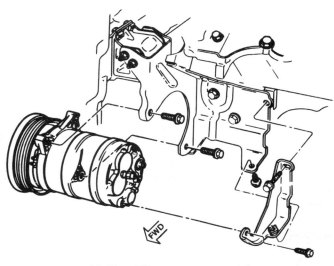

16.11a   V6 compressor mounting

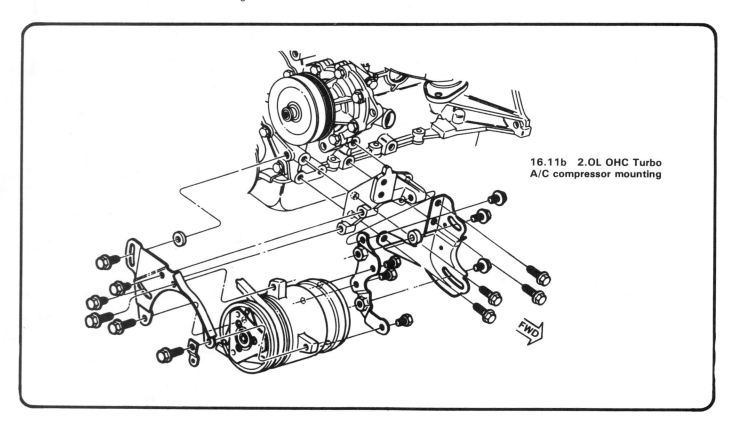

**16.11b   2.0L OHC Turbo
A/C compressor mounting**

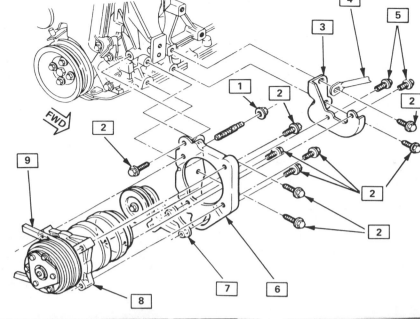

16.11c   2.5L OHV compressor mounting

1 Nut
2 Bolts
3 Rear bracket
4 Brace
5 Bolts
6 Front bracket
7 Idler pulley assembly
8 Compressor
9 Drivebelt

17.5   Front panel mounting bolt locations (arrows)

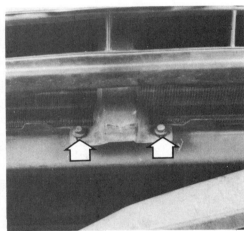

17.8   Bolt locations for the vertical hood latch brace (arrows)

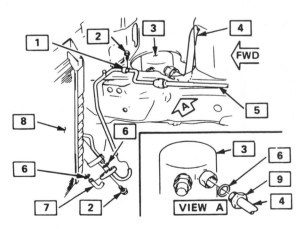

17.10a   Condenser refrigerant line connection locations

1 Clip	4 Outlet hose	7 Compressor to condenser hose
2 Bolt/screw	5 Inlet tube	8 Condenser
3 Accumulator	6 O-ring	9 Accumulator fitting

17.10b   The condenser lifts out ahead of the radiator support

3

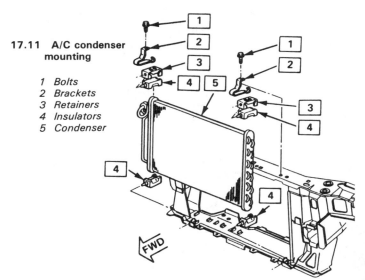

17.11   A/C condenser mounting

1 *Bolts*
2 *Brackets*
3 *Retainers*
4 *Insulators*
5 *Condenser*

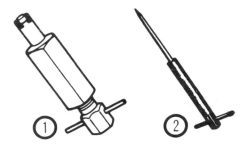

18.3   Removal of the orifice tube requires these special GM tools

1 *Tool No. J-26549-C orifice tube remover*
2 *Tool No. J-26459-10 orifice tube extractor*

19.3   Unplug the electrical and vacuum connectors from the back of the control panel. Be sure to unplug the entire vacuum connector — not the individual hoses

19.2   Remove the A/C and heater control panel screws (arrows)

11 Installation is the reverse of removal **(see illustration)**.
12 Have the system recharged by a professional. Advise the technician of what was done and how much oil was recovered.

18   Orifice tube screen (V6 only) — removal and installation

Refer to illustration 18.3

1 Have the system discharged by a professional.
2 Disconnect the high pressure refrigerant line at the orifice tube adjacent to the accumulator.
3 Remove the orifice tube using GM tools No. J-26549-C and J-26549-10 **(see illustration)** and inspect the filter screens. Replace any contaminated or damaged parts.
4 Replace the O-ring and lubricate it with refrigerant oil.
5 Reinsert the screens and tube.
6 Reconnect the line fitting.
7 Have the system professionally evacuated, charged and leak tested.

19   Air conditioning and heater control assembly — removal and installation

Refer to illustrations 19.2, 19.3 and 19.4

1 Remove the trim panel around the A/C and heater control (Chapter 12).

19.4   Two mounting clips (arrows) attach the temperature control cable and cable housing to the A/C and heater control assembly

2 Remove the two screws on each side of the A/C and heater control **(see illustration)**.
3 Pull the control out of the dash then label and unplug the vacuum and electrical connectors **(see illustration)**. **Note:** *Do not disconnect the individual vacuum lines — disconnect the vacuum connector as a unit.*
4 Carefully pry the cable housing and cable retaining clips off with a small screwdriver **(see illustration)**.
5 Installation is the reverse of removal.

Chapter 4 Fuel and Exhaust Systems

Contents

Specifications

4

Fuel pressure
2.5L four with TBI	9 to 13 psi
3.0L V6 or 2.0L Turbo four with MFI	26 to 46 psi

Torque specifications　　　　　　　　　　　　　　　　　　**Ft-lbs**
Turbocharger assembly
turbocharger-to-exhaust manifold mounting nuts	18
turbocharger outlet elbow-to-turbocharger mounting nuts . .	18
support bracket	
retaining nut	18
lower bolt	37
exhaust pipe-to-elbow	18
oil feed pipe-to-turbocharger	12
oil feed pipe union	12
oil feed pipe-to-block	12
oil drain hose (both ends)	35

Fuel injection throttle body assemblies
2.5L TBI	
bolts	10 to 15
stud	3 to 6
nuts	10 to 15
3.0L MFI bolts	10 to 15
2.0L Turbo bolts	10 to 15

---

1 General information

The fuel system consists of a fuel tank, an electric fuel pump, a fuel pump relay, an air cleaner assembly and either a Throttle Body Injection (TBI) system or a Multi-port Fuel Injection (MFI) system. The TBI system is used on 2.5L four-cylinder models; the MFI system is used on 3.0L V6 and 2.0L OHC 4-cylinder engines.

The basic difference between throttle body and port fuel injection systems is the number and location of the fuel injectors.

Throttle Body Injection (TBI) system

The throttle body system utilizes one injector, centrally mounted in a carburetor-like housing. The injector is an electrical solenoid, with fuel delivered to the injector at a constant pressure level. To maintain the fuel pressure at a constant level, excess fuel is returned to the fuel tank.

A signal from the ECM opens the solenoid, allowing fuel to spray through the injector into the throttle body. The amount of time the injector is held open by the ECM determines the fuel/air mixture ratio.

Multi-port Fuel Injection (MFI) system

The port system utilizes six injectors of the same type as the throttle body injector and the fuel/air ratio is controlled in the same manner. Instead of a single injector mounted in a centrally located throttle body, one injector is installed above each intake port. The throttle body serves only to control the amount of air passing into the system. Because each cylinder is equipped with an injector mounted immediately adjacent to the intake valve, much better control of the fuel/air mixture ratio is possible.

Fuel pump and lines

Fuel is circulated from the fuel tank to the fuel injection system, and back to the fuel tank, through a pair of metal lines running along the underside of the vehicle. An electric fuel pump is attached to the fuel sending unit inside the fuel tank. To reduce the likelihood of vapor lock, a vapor return system routes all vapors and hot fuel back to the fuel tank through a separate return line.

Exhaust system

The exhaust system, which is similar for both four-cylinder and V6 powered vehicles, includes an exhaust manifold fitted with an exhaust oxygen sensor, a catalytic converter, an exhaust pipe, and a tri-flow muffler design.

The catalytic converter is an emission control device added to the exhaust system to reduce pollutants. A single-bed converter design is used in combination with a three-way (reduction) catalyst. Refer to Chapter 6 for more information regarding the catalytic converter.

---

2   Fuel pressure relief procedure

1   Before servicing any component on a fuel injected vehicle, it is necessary to relieve the fuel pressure to minimize the risk of fire or personal injury.
2   Remove the fuse marked *FP* (fuel pump) from the fuse block under the left side of the dash.
3   Crank the engine over. It will start and run until the fuel supply remaining in the fuel lines is used. When the engine stops, engage the starter again for another three seconds to assure that any remaining pressure is dissipated.
4   With the ignition turned to Off, replace the fuel pump fuse. Unless this procedure is followed before servicing fuel lines or connections, fuel spray (and possible injury) may occur.

---

3   Fuel pump — testing

Warning: *Gasoline is extremely flammable, so extra precautions must be taken when working on any part of the fuel system. Do not smoke or allow open flames or bare light bulbs near the work area. Also, do not work in a garage if a natural gas-type appliance with a pilot light is present.*

Preliminary inspection (all vehicles)

1   Should the fuel system fail to deliver the proper amount of fuel, or any fuel at all, to the fuel injection system, inspect it as follows.
2   Always make certain that there is fuel in the tank.
3   With the engine running, inspect for leaks at the threaded fittings at both ends of the fuel line (see Chapter 1). Tighten any loose connections. Inspect all hoses for flattening or kinks which would restrict the flow of fuel.

2.5L four-cylinder engine with TBI
Refer to illustrations 3.7, 3.13, 3.20, 3.24 and 3.29
Fuel pump flow test
4   Relieve fuel pressure (see Section 2).
5   Disconnect the fuel feed line threaded fitting at the throttle body.
6   Place the fuel feed line inside a suitable container.
7   Apply battery voltage to terminal ''G'' of the ALCL pump test terminal **(see illustration)**.
8   The fuel pump should supply 1/2-pint or more in 15 seconds.
9   If the flow is below the minimum, check for a restriction in the fuel line (see Section 4).
Fuel system pressure test
10   In order to perform the following procedure, you will need to obtain a fuel pressure gauge and adapter set for GM TBI-equipped vehicles.
11   Relieve fuel pressure (see Section 2).
12   Disconnect the fuel line from the throttle body.
13   Attach the fuel pressure gauge **(see illustration)**.
14   Start the engine and check for leaks.
15   Note the fuel pressure reading. It should be within the specified fuel pressure range. If it isn't, proceed to the following fuel system diagnosis.
16   The fuel pump test terminal is located on the left side of the engine compartment. When the engine is stopped, the pump can be turned

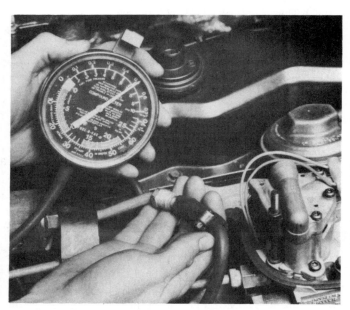

3.7   To activate the fuel pump, apply battery voltage to terminal ''G'' (arrow) on the Assembly Line Communications Link (ALCL) under the left side of the dashboard

3.13   On a TBI equipped vehicle, install a fuel pressure gauge between the fuel feed hose and the throttle body

on by applying battery voltage to the test terminal.

17 If there is fuel pressure, but it is less than specified, proceed to Step 29.

18 If the fuel pressure is higher than specified, proceed to Step 31.

19 If there is no pressure, check the fuel pump fuse, then refer to the accompanying diagnostic flow charts as you test fuel system pressure. The test numbers indicated in the following Steps correspond with the test numbers on the diagnostic charts.

20 If the fuse is okay, Test #1 **(see illustration)** determines if the pump circuit is ECM controlled. The ECM will turn on the pump relay. Since the engine is not cranking or running, the ECM will turn off the relay within two seconds after the ignition is turned on.

21 If the fuse is blown, Test #2 **(see illustration 3.20)** will confirm a short to ground on circuit 120 (see Wiring Diagrams at the end of this book). To prevent misdiagnosis, make sure that the fuel pump is disconnected.

22 Test #3 **(see illustration 3.20)** will turn on the fuel pump if the wiring in circuit 120 is okay. If the pump runs, the problem is in the fuel delivery system.

23 Test #4 **(see illustration 3.20)**, checks for battery voltage at the

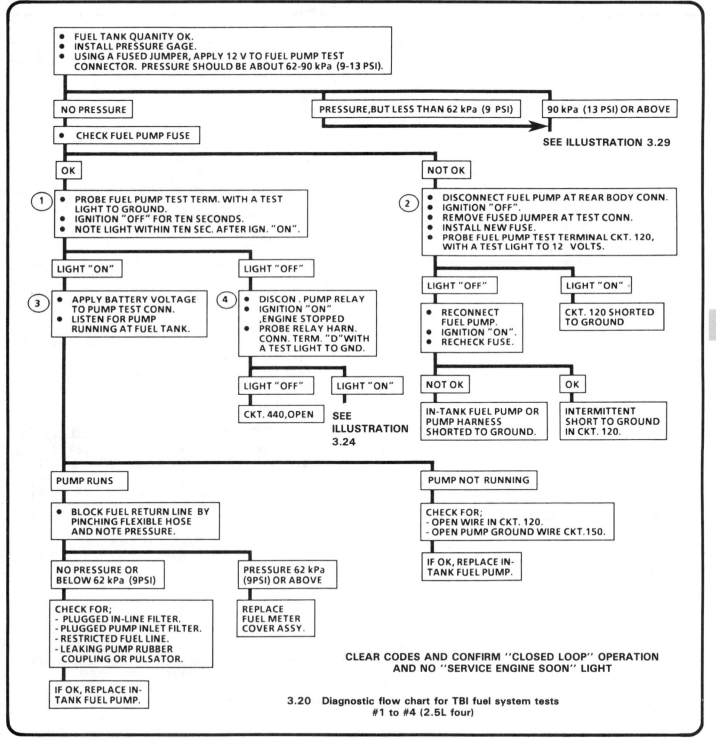

3.20 **Diagnostic flow chart for TBI fuel system tests**
#1 to #4 (2.5L four)

FROM
ILLUSTRATION 3.20

(5) • CONNECT A TEST LIGHT BETWEEN HARN. TERMS. "C" AND "D".

LIGHT "ON"

LIGHT "OFF"

REPAIR OPEN GROUND CKT 450.

(6) • CONNECT TEST LIGHT BETWEEN HARN. TERMS. "A" AND "C".
• IGNITION "OFF" FOR TEN SECONDS.
• NOTE TEST LIGHT WITHIN 2 SECONDS AFTER IGNITION "ON".

LIGHT "ON"

LIGHT "OFF"

(7) • REPLACE RELAY. IF ORIGINAL PROBLEM WAS "CRANKS BUT WILL NOT RUN", MAKE FOLLOWING ADDITIONAL CHECKS:

• DISCONNECT WHITE ECM CONNECTOR AND CHECK FOR OPEN OR SHORT TO GROUND IN CKT 465.

CKT. 465 NOT OK

CKT. 465 OK

(8) • ENGINE RUNNING AT NORMAL OPERATING TEMPERATURE.
• DISCONNECT FUEL PUMP RELAY, (ENGINE SHOULD CONTINUE TO RUN)

REPAIR CKT. 465. IF CKT WAS SHORTED TO GROUND., RECHECK FOR "LIGHT ON" BETWEEN HARNESS CONNECTOR TERMINAL "A" AND GROUND WITHIN 2 SECONDS AFTER IGNITION "ON".

CHECK RESISTANCE ACROSS PUMP RELAY PINS OPPOSITE HARN. CONN. TERMS. "A" AND "C". (SHOULD MEASURE 20 OHMS OR MORE)

OK

NOT OK

LIGHT "OFF"

LIGHT "ON"

NOT OK

OK

(9) • RECONNECT FUEL PUMP RELAY.
• IGNITION "OFF".
• PROBE FUEL PUMP TEST CONNECTOR WITH A TEST LIGHT TO GROUND.

FAULTY OIL PRESSURE SWITCH.

POOR CONN. AT ECM TERM. "18", OR FAULTY ECM.

RECONNECT RELAY

REPLACE RELAY AND ECM.

REPLACE ECM.

LIGHT "OFF"

LIGHT "ON"

NO TROUBLE FOUND.

FAULTY OIL PRESSURE SWITCH.

CLEAR CODES AND CONFIRM "CLOSED LOOP" OPERATION
AND NO "SERVICE ENGINE SOON" LIGHT

3.24 Diagnostic flow chart for TBI fuel system tests #5 to #9 (2.5L four)

pump relay.

24   Test #5 **(see illustration)** checks circuit 450 (see the Wiring Diagrams at the end of this book), the ground for the fuel pump relay.

25   Test #6 **(see illustration 3.24)** checks for ECM control of the relay through circuit 465 (see the Wiring Diagrams at the end of this book).

26   Test # **(see illustration 3.24)**: The fuel pump voltage control circuit includes an engine oil pressure switch with a separate set of normally open contacts. The switch closes at about 4 lbs of oil pressure and provides a second battery feed path to the fuel pump. If the relay fails, the pump will continue to run using the battery feed supplied by the closed oil pressure switch. A failed pump relay will result in extended engine crank time because of the time required to build enough oil pressure to close the oil pressure switch and turn on the fuel pump. There may be instances when the relay has failed but the engine will not crank quickly enough to build sufficient pressure to close the switch. This or a faulty oil pressure switch can result in a "Engine cranks but will not run" condition.

27   Test #8 **(see illustration 3.24)** checks the oil pressure switch to be sure it provides battery feed to the fuel pump should the relay fail.

28   Test #9 checks for an open oil pressure switch with the ignition off. Should the switch stick closed, the fuel pump will continue to run and discharge the battery.

29   If the indicated fuel pressure is below the specified pressure, one of two conditions exists:

   a)   The oil pressure is regulated but low. The amount of fuel to the injector is okay but the pressure is too low. The system will run lean and may set a Code 44 (see Chapter 6). Hard starting when the engine is cold and poor overall performance may also result.

   b)   The flow is restricted, causing the pressure to drop.

Normally, a vehicle with a fuel pressure lower than specified at idle

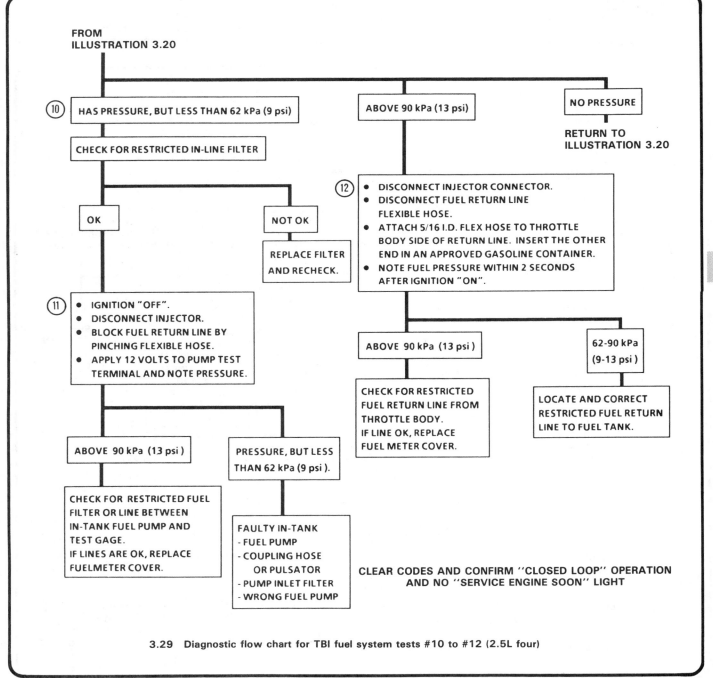

3.29   Diagnostic flow chart for TBI fuel system tests #10 to #12 (2.5L four)

3.34   On a vehicle equipped with MFI, install the fuel pressure gauge at the Schrader valve on the fuel rail

will not be drivable. Test #10 (see illustration) will determine which of the above situations applies.

30 Test #11 (see illustration 3.29) restricts the fuel return line to allow the fuel pump to develop its maximum pressure. When battery voltage is applied to the pump test terminal, pressure should be between 13 and 18 psi.

31 If the fuel pressure is too high, Test #12 (see illustration 3.29) determines if the high fuel pressure is due to a restricted fuel return line (see Section 4) or a pressure regulator problem (see Section 9).

3.0L V6 engine with MFI — fuel system pressure test
Refer to illustrations 3.34, 3.35, 3.39, 3.43 and 3.49

32 Using the accompanying diagnostic flow charts, perform the following test procedures to diagnose fuel system pressure. The test numbers indicated in the following Steps correspond with the test numbers on the diagnostic charts.

33 Relieve the fuel pressure (see Section 2).

34 Attach a GM port fuel injection pressure gauge (Kent-Moore J-34730-1), or equivalent (see illustration). Note: *It's a good idea to*

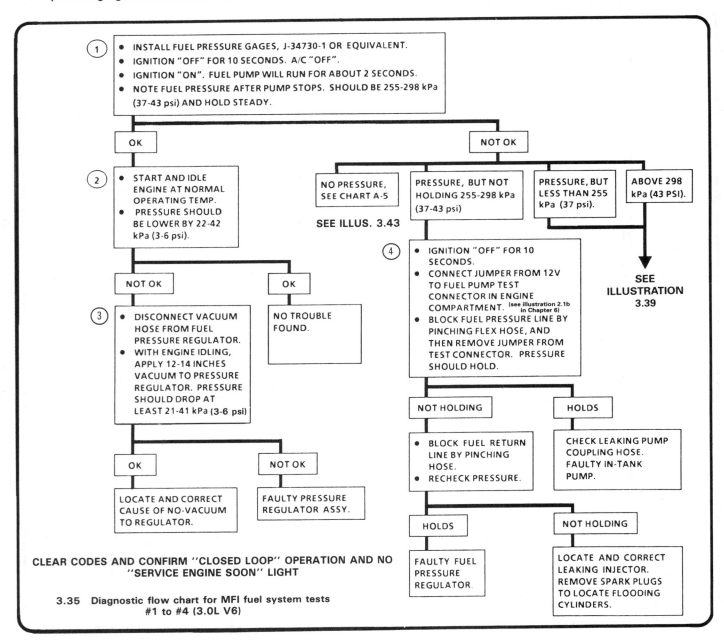

3.35   Diagnostic flow chart for MFI fuel system tests #1 to #4 (3.0L V6)

use a shop towel around the Schrader valve on the fuel rail to absorb any residual fuel that may spray when the valve is opened.

35 Check the fuel pressure in accordance with the steps outlined in Test #1 (see illustration). Pressure should not leak down after the fuel pump is shut off. If it does, proceed to Step 38. If there is no pressure at all, proceed to Step 42.

36 When the engine is idling, the throttle body vacuum is high and is applied to the fuel regulator diaphragm. This will offset the spring and result in a lower fuel pressure. Test #2 (see illustration 3.35) will determine whether this is the case.

37 Test #3 (see illustration 3.35): The application of 12 to 14 inches of vacuum to the pressure regulator should result in a fuel pressure drop.

38 Test #4 (see illustration 3.35): Pressure that leaks down may be caused by one of the following:

    a) In–tank fuel pump check valve not holding (see Section 7).

    b) Pump coupling hose leaking (see Sections 4 and 7).

    c) Fuel pressure regulator valve leaking (see Sections 9 and 10).

    d) Injector sticking open (see Sections 9 and 10).

39 If there is fuel pressure, but it is less than specified, one of the following causes is the problem:

    a) The pressure is regulated but it's less than 34 psi. The amount of fuel to the injectors is okay but the pressure is too low. The system will be running lean and may set a Code 44 (see Chapter 6). Hard starting in cold weather and overall poor performance may also result.

    b) The flow is restricted, causing a pressure drop.

Normally, a vehicle with a fuel pressure of less than 24 psi at idle will not be drivable. However, if the pressure drop occurs only while driving, the engine will normally surge, then stop, as pressure begins to drop rapidly. Test #5 (see illustration 3.39) will determine which one of the above is causing the problem.

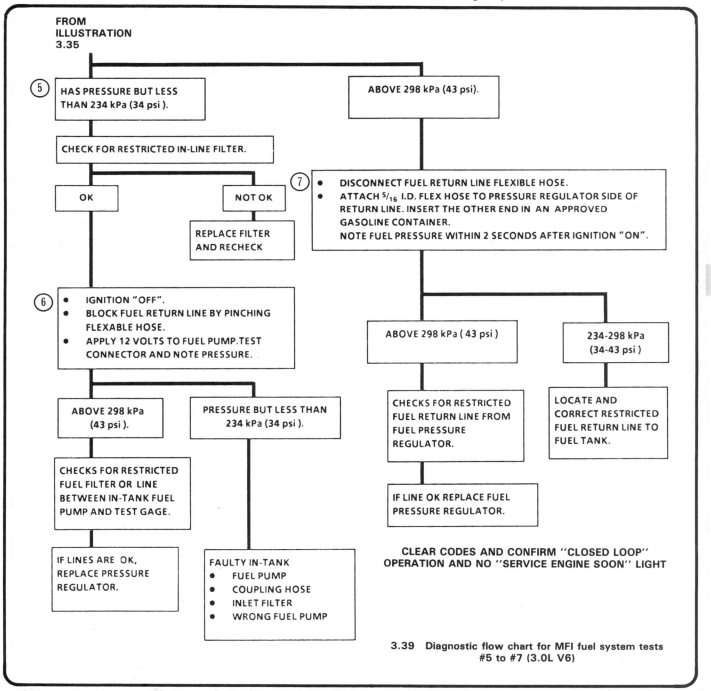

3.39 Diagnostic flow chart for MFI fuel system tests #5 to #7 (3.0L V6)

40 Test #6 (**see illustration 3.39**): Restricting the fuel return line allows the fuel pump to develop its maximum pressure. When battery voltage is applied to the pump test terminal, pressure should be above 75 psi.
41 Test #7: This test determines whether the incorrect fuel pressure is due to a restricted fuel return line or a pressure regulator problem.
42 If there is no pressure at all, check the fuel pump fuse to make sure that it's not blown.
43 If the fuse is blown, test #8 (**see illustration**) will verify a short to ground on circuit 939.
44 If the fuse is blown, test #9 (**see illustration 3.43**) will verify a short to ground on circuit 120. To prevent misdiagnosis, be sure that the fuel pump is disconnected before the test.

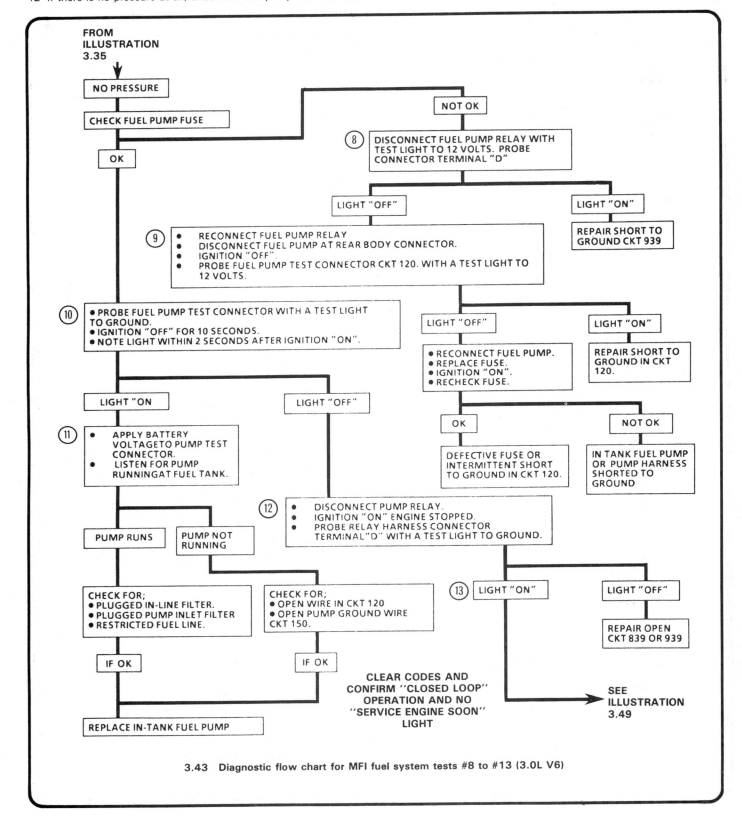

3.43   Diagnostic flow chart for MFI fuel system tests #8 to #13 (3.0L V6)

45 Test #10 (**see illustration 3.43**) determines if the fuel pump circuit is ECM controlled. The ECM will turn on the pump relay. The engine is not cranking or running, so the ECM will turn off the relay within two seconds after the ignition is turned on.

46 Test #11 (**see illustration 3.43**) turns on the the fuel pump if circuit 120 wiring is okay. If the pump runs, the problem is somewhere in fuel delivery.

47 Test #12 (**see illustration 3.43**) checks for battery voltage at the pump relay.

48 Test #13 (**see illustration 3.43**) checks the relay ground, circuit 450.

49 Test #14 (**see illustration**) checks the relay ground, circuit 450.

50 Test #15 (**see illustration 3.49**) checks for ECM control of the relay through circuit 465.

51 Test #16 (**see illustration 3.49**): The fuel pump control circuit includes an engine oil pressure switch with a separate set of normally

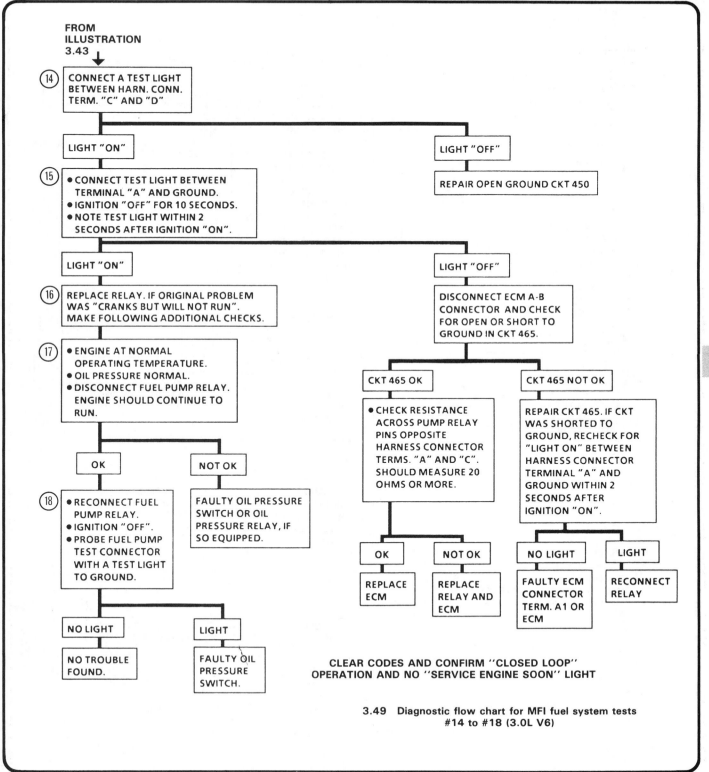

4

3.49 Diagnostic flow chart for MFI fuel system tests
#14 to #18 (3.0L V6)

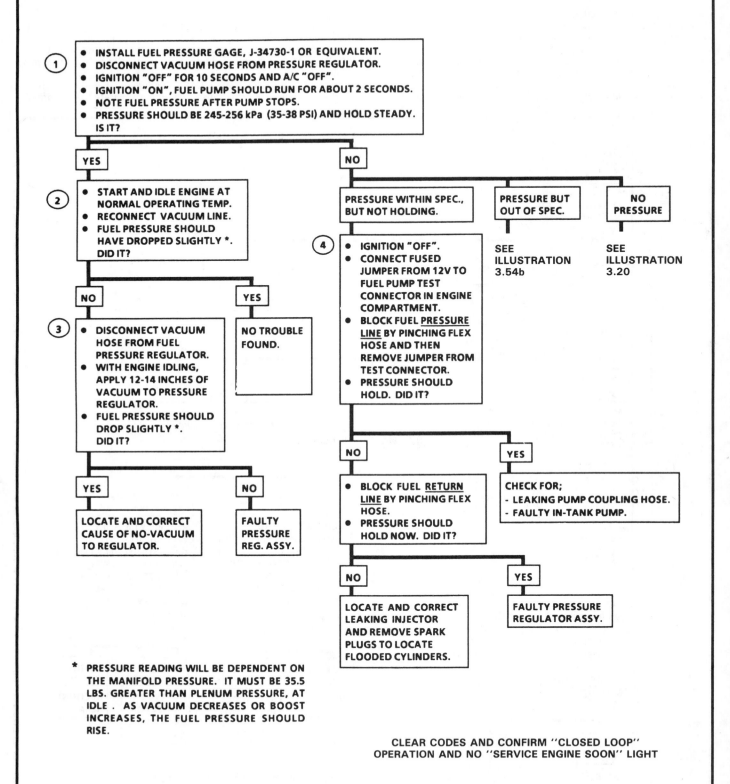

① • INSTALL FUEL PRESSURE GAGE, J-34730-1 OR EQUIVALENT.
• DISCONNECT VACUUM HOSE FROM PRESSURE REGULATOR.
• IGNITION "OFF" FOR 10 SECONDS AND A/C "OFF".
• IGNITION "ON", FUEL PUMP SHOULD RUN FOR ABOUT 2 SECONDS.
• NOTE FUEL PRESSURE AFTER PUMP STOPS.
• PRESSURE SHOULD BE 245-256 kPa (35-38 PSI) AND HOLD STEADY. IS IT?

YES

NO

② • START AND IDLE ENGINE AT NORMAL OPERATING TEMP.
• RECONNECT VACUUM LINE.
• FUEL PRESSURE SHOULD HAVE DROPPED SLIGHTLY *. DID IT?

PRESSURE WITHIN SPEC., BUT NOT HOLDING.

PRESSURE BUT OUT OF SPEC.

SEE ILLUSTRATION 3.54b

NO PRESSURE

SEE ILLUSTRATION 3.20

NO

YES

④ • IGNITION "OFF".
• CONNECT FUSED JUMPER FROM 12V TO FUEL PUMP TEST CONNECTOR IN ENGINE COMPARTMENT.
• BLOCK FUEL PRESSURE LINE BY PINCHING FLEX HOSE AND THEN REMOVE JUMPER FROM TEST CONNECTOR.
• PRESSURE SHOULD HOLD. DID IT?

③ • DISCONNECT VACUUM HOSE FROM FUEL PRESSURE REGULATOR.
• WITH ENGINE IDLING, APPLY 12-14 INCHES OF VACUUM TO PRESSURE REGULATOR.
• FUEL PRESSURE SHOULD DROP SLIGHTLY *. DID IT?

NO TROUBLE FOUND.

NO

YES

YES

NO

BLOCK FUEL RETURN LINE BY PINCHING FLEX HOSE.
• PRESSURE SHOULD HOLD NOW. DID IT?

CHECK FOR;
- LEAKING PUMP COUPLING HOSE.
- FAULTY IN-TANK PUMP.

LOCATE AND CORRECT CAUSE OF NO-VACUUM TO REGULATOR.

FAULTY PRESSURE REG. ASSY.

NO

YES

LOCATE AND CORRECT LEAKING INJECTOR AND REMOVE SPARK PLUGS TO LOCATE FLOODED CYLINDERS.

FAULTY PRESSURE REGULATOR ASSY.

* PRESSURE READING WILL BE DEPENDENT ON THE MANIFOLD PRESSURE. IT MUST BE 35.5 LBS. GREATER THAN PLENUM PRESSURE, AT IDLE . AS VACUUM DECREASES OR BOOST INCREASES, THE FUEL PRESSURE SHOULD RISE.

CLEAR CODES AND CONFIRM "CLOSED LOOP" OPERATION AND NO "SERVICE ENGINE SOON" LIGHT

3.54a   Diagnostic flow chart for MFI fuel system tests #1 to #4 (2.0L Turbo four)

open contacts. The switch closes at about 4 lbs of oil pressure and provides a second battery feed path to the fuel pump. If the relay fails, the pump will continue to run using the battery feed supplied by the closed oil pressure switch. A failed pump relay will result in extended engine crank time because of the time required to build enough oil pressure to close the oil pressure switch and turn on the fuel pump. There may be instances when the relay has failed but the engine will not crank quickly enough to build sufficient oil pressure to close the switch. The result of this, or a faulty oil pressure switch, is an engine that will crank but won't start.

52 Test #17 **(see illustration 3.49)** checks the oil pressure switch to be sure that it provides battery feed to the fuel pump should the pump relay fail.

53 Test #18 **(see illustration 3.49)** checks for an open in the oil

pressure switch with the ignition off. Should the switch stick closed, the fuel pump will continue to run and discharge the battery.

2.0L Turbo four-cylinder OHC engine with MFI — fuel system pressure test

Refer to illustrations 3.54a, 3.54b, 3.56 and 3.60

54 Using the accompanying diagnostic flow charts, perform the same test procedures as outlined above in Steps 32 through 41 to diagnose fuel system pressure. The test numbers (#1 through #7) described in the above Steps for the MFI fuel pressure system in 3.0L V6-equipped vehicles correspond with the test numbers on the accompanying diagnostic charts for the 2.0L Turbo four OHC engine **(see illustrations).**

55 If, after performing a fuel pressure check (Test #1 above), there

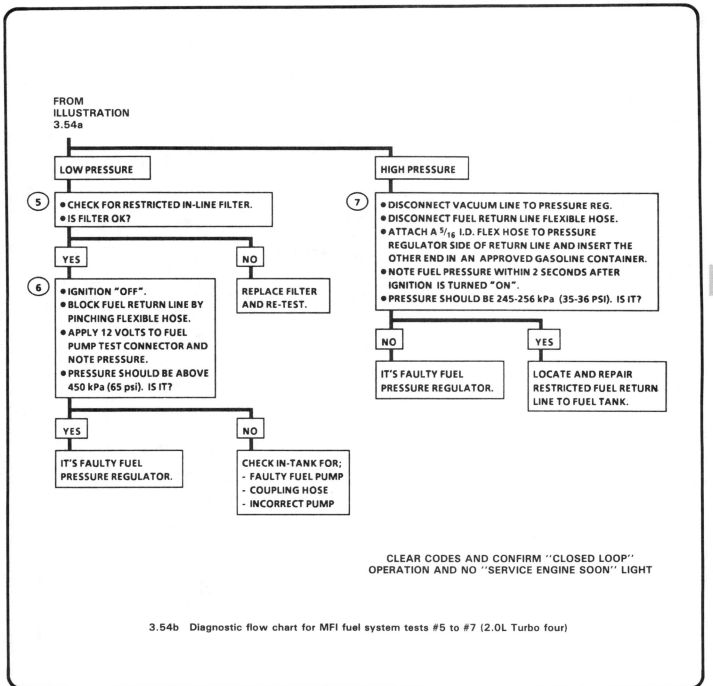

3.54b Diagnostic flow chart for MFI fuel system tests #5 to #7 (2.0L Turbo four)

is pressure but it is not within specification, diagnose the fuel pump relay circuit in accordance with the following additional tests.

56 Test #8 (see illustration) determines if the pump circuit is ECM controlled. The ECM will turn on the pump relay. The engine is not cranking or running, so the ECM will turn off the relay two seconds after the ignition is turned on.

57 Test #9 (see illustration 3.56) turns on the fuel pump if circuit 120 wiring is okay. If the pump runs, it is a fuel delivery problem.

58 Test #10 (see illustration 3.56) checks circuit 450, the relay ground.

59 If the fuse is blown, Test #11 will confirm a short to ground on circuit 120. To prevent misdiagnosis, be sure that the fuel pump is disconnected before doing the test.

60 Test #12 (see illustration) checks for ECM control of the relay through circuit 465.

61 Test #13 (see illustration 3.60): The fuel pump control circuit includes an engine oil pressure switch with a separate set of normally open contacts. The switch closes at about 4 lbs of oil pressure and provides a second battery feed path to the fuel pump. If the relay fails, the pump will continue to run using the battery feed supplied by the closed oil pressure switch. A failed pump relay will result in extended engine crank time because of the time required to build enough oil pressure to close the oil pressure switch and turn on the the fuel pump. There may be instances when the relay has failed but the engine will not crank quickly enough to build enough oil pressure to close the switch. This or a faulty oil pressure switch can result in an engine that will crank but won't run if the fuel pump relay is inoperative.

62 Test #14 (see illustration 3.60) checks the oil pressure switch to be sure it provides battery feed to the fuel pump should the fuel pump relay fail.

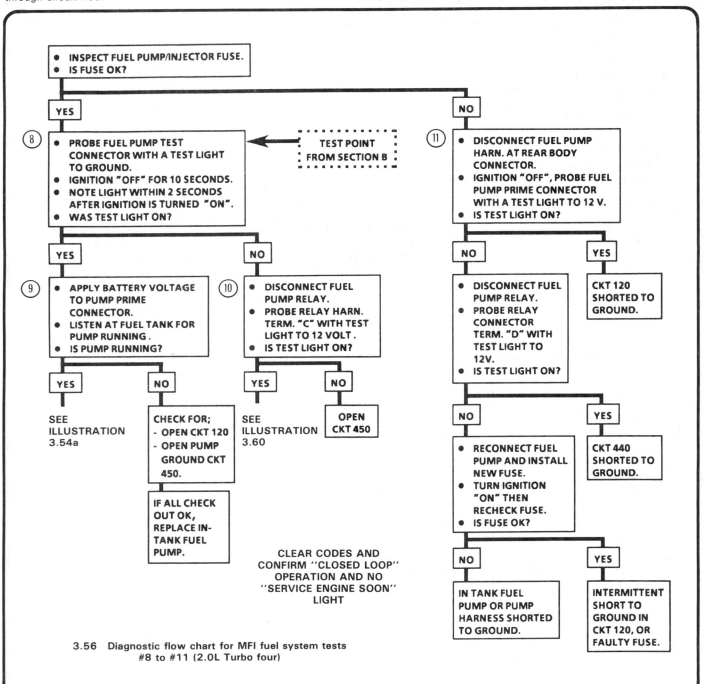

3.56 Diagnostic flow chart for MFI fuel system tests
#8 to #11 (2.0L Turbo four)

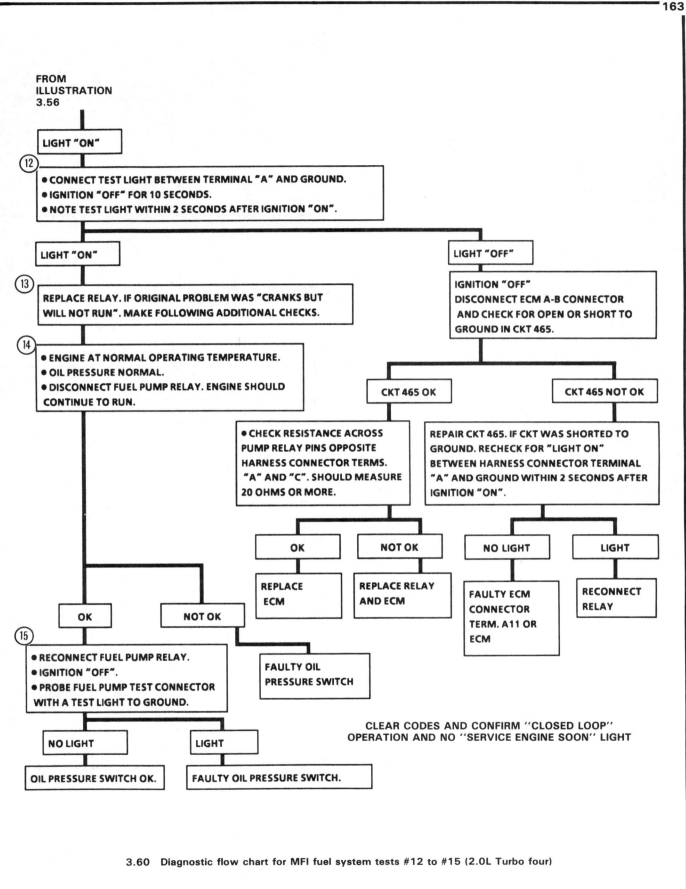

FROM ILLUSTRATION 3.56

LIGHT "ON"

(12)
- CONNECT TEST LIGHT BETWEEN TERMINAL "A" AND GROUND.
- IGNITION "OFF" FOR 10 SECONDS.
- NOTE TEST LIGHT WITHIN 2 SECONDS AFTER IGNITION "ON".

LIGHT "ON"

(13) REPLACE RELAY. IF ORIGINAL PROBLEM WAS "CRANKS BUT WILL NOT RUN". MAKE FOLLOWING ADDITIONAL CHECKS.

(14)
- ENGINE AT NORMAL OPERATING TEMPERATURE.
- OIL PRESSURE NORMAL.
- DISCONNECT FUEL PUMP RELAY. ENGINE SHOULD CONTINUE TO RUN.

LIGHT "OFF"

IGNITION "OFF" DISCONNECT ECM A-B CONNECTOR AND CHECK FOR OPEN OR SHORT TO GROUND IN CKT 465.

CKT 465 OK

CKT 465 NOT OK

- CHECK RESISTANCE ACROSS PUMP RELAY PINS OPPOSITE HARNESS CONNECTOR TERMS. "A" AND "C". SHOULD MEASURE 20 OHMS OR MORE.

REPAIR CKT 465. IF CKT WAS SHORTED TO GROUND. RECHECK FOR "LIGHT ON" BETWEEN HARNESS CONNECTOR TERMINAL "A" AND GROUND WITHIN 2 SECONDS AFTER IGNITION "ON".

OK

NOT OK

NO LIGHT

LIGHT

REPLACE ECM

REPLACE RELAY AND ECM

FAULTY ECM CONNECTOR TERM. A11 OR ECM

RECONNECT RELAY

OK

NOT OK

(15)
- RECONNECT FUEL PUMP RELAY.
- IGNITION "OFF".
- PROBE FUEL PUMP TEST CONNECTOR WITH A TEST LIGHT TO GROUND.

FAULTY OIL PRESSURE SWITCH

CLEAR CODES AND CONFIRM ''CLOSED LOOP'' OPERATION AND NO ''SERVICE ENGINE SOON'' LIGHT

NO LIGHT

LIGHT

OIL PRESSURE SWITCH OK.

FAULTY OIL PRESSURE SWITCH.

4

3.60 Diagnostic flow chart for MFI fuel system tests #12 to #15 (2.0L Turbo four)

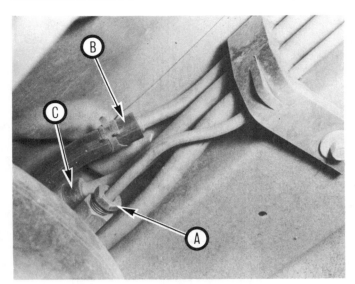

4.12 The fuel feed (A), fuel return (B) and vapor return (C) lines at the fuel tank

4.18 Typical fuel feed and return line threaded fittings in the left side of the engine compartment

63 Test #15 (see illustration 3.60) checks for a faulty oil pressure switch with the ignition off. Should the switch stick closed, the fuel pump will continue to run and discharge the battery.

4 Fuel lines and fittings — repair and replacement

Refer to illustrations 4.12, 4.18, 4.19a and 4.19b

Warning: *Gasoline is extremely flammable, so extra precautions must be taken when working on any part of the fuel system. Do not smoke or allow open flames or bare light bulbs near the work area. Finally, do not work in an enclosed space where a natural gas-type appliance with a pilot light is present.*

1   Always relieve the fuel pressure before servicing fuel lines or fittings (Section 2).
2   The fuel feed and return lines extend from the in-tank fuel pump to the engine compartment. The lines are secured to the underbody with clip and screw assemblies. Both fuel feed lines must be occasionally inspected for leaks, kinks or dents.
3   If evidence of dirt is found in the system or fuel filter during disassembly, the line should be disconnected and blown out. Check the fuel strainer on the fuel gauge sending unit (see Section 7) for damage or deterioration.

Steel tubing

4   If replacement of a fuel line or emission line is called for, use welded steel tubing meeting GM specification 124-M or its equivalent.
5   Do not use copper or aluminum tubing to replace steel tubing. These materials do not have satisfactory durability to withstand normal vehicle vibration.
6   Because fuel lines used on fuel injected vehicles are under high pressure, these systems require special consideration when they are serviced.
7   Most feed and return pipes use screw couplings with O-rings. Any time these fittings are loosened to service or replace components, ensure that:
    a) A backup wrench is used while loosening and tightening the fittings.
    b) Check all O-rings for cuts, cracking or deterioration. Replace any that appear worn or damaged.
    c) If the lines are replaced, always use original equipment parts, or parts that meet the GM standards specified in this Section.

Rubber hose

8   When rubber hose is used to replace a metal line, you must use reinforced, fuel resistant hose (GM Specification 6163-M) with the

word "Fluoroelastomer" imprinted on it. Hose(s) not clearly marked like this could cause premature failure or could fail to meet Federal emission standards. Hose inside diameter must match pipe outside diameter.
9   Do not use rubber hose within four inches of any part of the exhaust system or within ten inches of the catalytic converter. Metal lines and rubber hoses must never be allowed to chafe against the frame. A minimum of 1/4-inch clearance must be maintained around a line or hose to prevent contact with the frame.

Removal and installation

10   The following procedure and accompanying illustrations are typical for vehicles covered by this manual.
11   Relieve fuel pressure (see Section 2).
12   Disconnect the fuel feed, return or vapor line at the fuel tank **(see illustration)**.
13   Detach the bracket from the rear crossmember.
14   Detach the bracket from the rear end of the left frame member, just in front of the left rear wheel.
15   Detach the three brackets from the left frame member.
16   Detach the bracket from the left front end of the left frame member, just behind the left front wheel.
17   Detach the bracket from the lower left rear corner of the engine compartment.
18   Detach the threaded fitting(s) that attach the metal lines to the engine compartment fuel hoses **(see illustration)**.
19   Installation is the reverse of removal. Be sure to use new O-rings at the threaded fittings **(see illustrations)**.

Repair

20   In repairable areas, cut a piece of fuel hose four inches longer than the portion of the line removed. If more than a six inch length of line is removed, use a combination of steel line and hose so that hose lengths will not be more than ten inches. Always follow the same routing as the original line.
21   Cut the ends of the line with a tube cutter. Using the first step of a double flaring tool, form a bead on the end of both line sections. If the line is too corroded to withstand bead operation without damage, the line should be replaced.
22   Use a screw type hose clamp. Slide the clamp onto the line and push the hose on. Tighten the clamps on each side of the repair.
23   Secure the lines properly to the frame to prevent chafing.

5 Fuel tank — removal and installation

Refer to illustrations 5.5, 5.6 and 5.9
Warning: *Gasoline is extremely flammable, so extra precautions must*

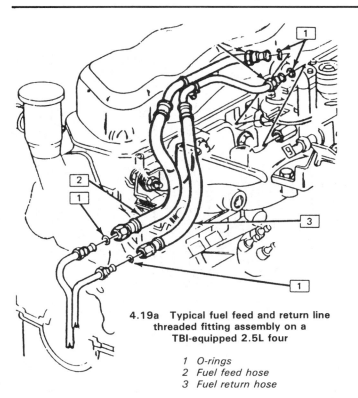

4.19a Typical fuel feed and return line threaded fitting assembly on a TBI-equipped 2.5L four

1 O-rings
2 Fuel feed hose
3 Fuel return hose

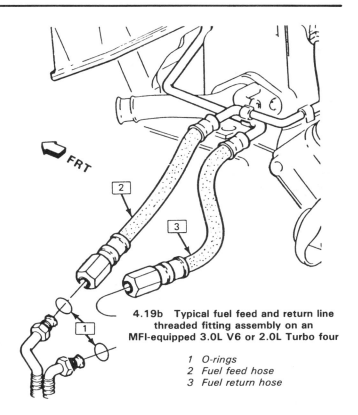

4.19b Typical fuel feed and return line threaded fitting assembly on an MFI-equipped 3.0L V6 or 2.0L Turbo four

1 O-rings
2 Fuel feed hose
3 Fuel return hose

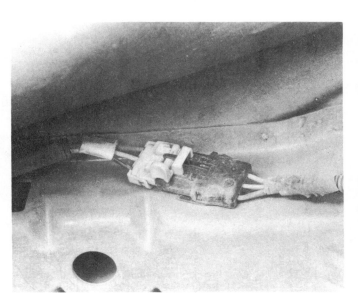

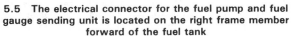

5.5 The electrical connector for the fuel pump and fuel gauge sending unit is located on the right frame member forward of the fuel tank

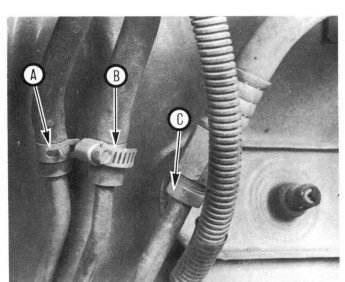

5.6 The fuel vapor (A), return (B) and feed (C) lines

be taken when working on any part of the fuel system. Do not smoke or allow open flames or bare light bulbs near the work area. Also, do not work in a garage if a natural gas-type appliance with a pilot light is present. While performing any work on the fuel tank it is advisable to wear safety glasses and to have a dry chemical (Class B) fire extinguisher on hand.

1   Relieve the fuel pressure (see Section 2).
2   Detach the cable from the negative terminal of the battery.
3   If the tank is full or nearly full, use a hand-operated pump to remove as much fuel through the filler tube as possible (if no such pump is available, you can drain the tank at the fuel feed line after raising the

vehicle).
4   Raise the vehicle and place it securely on jackstands.
5   Locate the electrical connector for the electric fuel pump and fuel gauge sending unit **(see illustration)** on the right frame member just in front of the tank, and unplug it. If your vehicle does not have a connector, see Step 10 below.
6   Disconnect the fuel feed and return lines and the vapor return line **(see illustration)**.
7   If you didn't have a hand pump, siphon the fuel from the tank at the fuel feed — not the return — line.
8   Support the fuel tank with a floor jack or some other suitable means

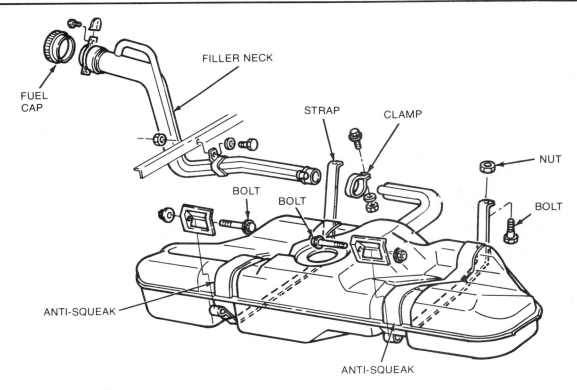

FILLER NECK

FUEL CAP

STRAP

CLAMP

NUT

BOLT

BOLT

BOLT

BOLT

ANTI-SQUEAK

ANTI-SQUEAK

5.9   Typical fuel tank assembly components

of support.

9   Disconnect both fuel tank retaining straps **(see illustration)**.

10   Lower the tank enough to disconnect the electrical wires and ground strap from the fuel pump/fuel gauge sending unit, if you have not already done so.

11   Remove the tank from the vehicle.

12   Installation is the reverse of removal.

---

6   Fuel tank — cleaning and repair

1   Any repairs to the fuel tank or filler neck should be carried out by a professional who has experience in this critical and potentially dangerous work. Even after cleaning and flushing of the fuel system, explosive fumes can remain and ignite during repair of the tank.

2   If the fuel tank is removed from the vehicle, it should not be placed in an area where sparks or open flames could ignite the fumes coming out of the tank. Be especially careful inside garages where a natural gas-type appliance is located, because the pilot light could cause an explosion.

---

7   Fuel pump — removal and installation

Refer to illustrations 7.5 and 7.8

Warning: *Gasoline is extremely flammable, so extra precautions must be taken when working on any part of the fuel system. Do not smoke or allow open flames or bare light bulbs near the work area. Also, do not work in a garage if a natural gas type appliance with a pilot light is present.*

Removal

1   Relieve the fuel pressure (Section 2).

2   Remove the cable from the negative battery terminal.

3   Remove the fuel tank (Section 5).

4   The fuel pump/sending unit assembly is located inside the fuel tank. It is held in place by a cam lock ring mechanism consisting of an inner ring with three locking cams and an outer ring with three retaining tangs.

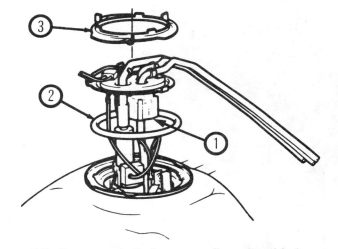

7.5   To remove the fuel gauge sending unit and fuel pump assembly (1), turn the inner cam lockring (3) counterclockwise and pull the pump and O-ring gasket (2) out of the tank — be extremely careful not to bang the float mechanism on the sides of the hole

5   To unlock the fuel pump/sending unit assembly, turn the inner ring clockwise until the locking cams are free of the retaining tangs **(see illustration)**. **Note:** *If the rings are locked together too tightly to release them by hand, gently knock them loose with a soft-face mallet of rubber or brass.* **Warning:** *Do not use a steel headed mallet or hammer to knock the lockrings loose. A spark could cause an explosion.*

6   Extract the fuel pump/sending unit assembly from the fuel tank. **Caution:** *The fuel level float and sending unit are delicate. Do not bump them into the lockring during removal or the accuracy of the sending unit may be affected.*

7   Inspect the condition of the rubber gasket around the mouth of the lockring mechanism. If it is dried, cracked or deteriorated, replace it.

8   Inspect the strainer on the lower end of the fuel pump **(see illustration)**. If it is dirty, remove it, clean it with a suitable solvent and blow it out with compressed air. If it is too dirty to be cleaned, replace it.
9   If it is necessary to separate the fuel pump and sending unit, remove the pump from the sending unit by pulling the fuel pump assembly into the rubber connector and sliding the pump away from the bottom support. Care should be taken to prevent damage to the rubber insulator and fuel strainer during removal. After the pump assembly is clear of the bottom support, pull the pump assembly out of the rubber connector.

Installation

10   Insert the fuel pump/sending unit assembly into the fuel tank.
11   Turn the inner lockring counterclockwise until the locking cams are fully engaged by the retaining tangs. **Note:** *If you have installed a new O-ring type rubber gasket, it may be necessary to push down on the inner lockring until the locking cams slide under the retaining tangs.*
12   Install the fuel tank (Section 5).

8   Air cleaner housing assembly — removal and installation

2.5L four

Refer to illustration 8.2

1   Detach the cable from the negative terminal of the battery.
2   Unclip and remove the upper half of the air cleaner cover **(see illustration)**.
3   Remove the filter element cover nuts, the filter cover and the filter itself.
4   Remove the two studs which attach the lower half of the air cleaner housing cover to the TBI.
5   Remove the lower half of the air cleaner housing cover.
6   Installation is the reverse of removal.

3.0L V6

Refer to illustrations 8.8 and 8.11

7   Detach the cable from the negative terminal of the battery.

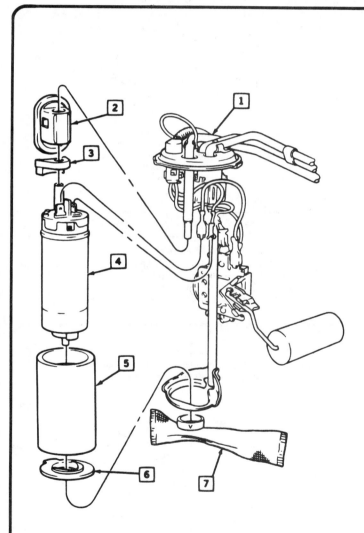

7.8   **Exploded view of a typical fuel gauge sending unit and pump assembly**

1 *Fuel tank meter assembly*
2 *Pulsator (MFI equipped vehicles only)*
3 *Bumper*
4 *Fuel pump*
5 *Sound isolator sleeve*
6 *Sound insulator*
7 *Filter*

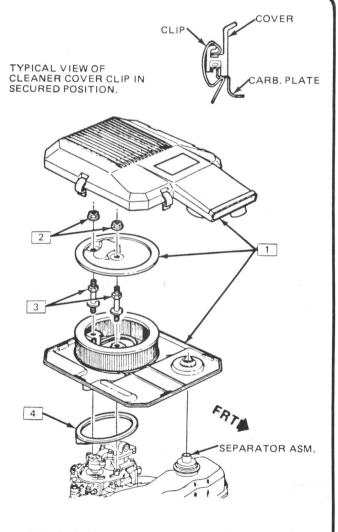

8.2   **Exploded view of a typical air cleaner housing assembly for a 2.5L four-cylinder engine**

1 *Air cleaner housing assembly*
2 *Filter element retaining nuts*
3 *Air cleaner housing assembly retaining studs*
4 *Air cleaner housing assembly seal*

4

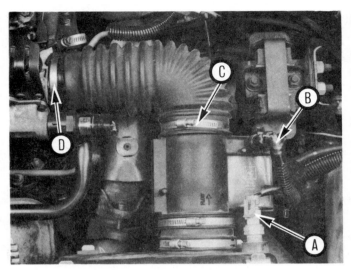

8.8   To remove the duct and Mass Air Flow (MAF) sensor from a 3.0L V6 engine, unplug the Air Temperature Sensor (A) and the MAF sensor (B) electrical connectors, then loosen the hose clamps (C) and (D) and remove the duct and MAF sensor assembly

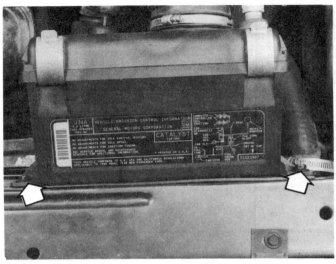

8.11   To remove the air cleaner housing assembly, remove the two upper bolts (arrows) and loosen the lower bolt (not shown) — it is not necessary to remove the lower bolt because the lower housing tab is slotted to fit over it

8   Unplug the electrical connectors from the Mass Air Flow (MAF) sensor and the air cleaner housing (**see illustration**).
9   Loosen the hose clamps at either end of the intake duct.
10 Remove the intake duct.
11 Remove the two upper air cleaner housing bolts (**see illustration**).
12 Loosen the lower air cleaner housing bolt and remove the air cleaner housing.
13 Installation is the reverse of removal.

2.0L Turbo four
Refer to illustration 8.15

14 Detach the cable from the negative terminal of the battery.
15 Loosen the hose clamp at the air cleaner housing end of the duct between the housing and the turbocharger assembly and detach the duct from the air cleaner housing (**see illustration**).
16 Remove the wing nut from the stud protruding through the upper

half of the air cleaner housing.
17 Remove the air cleaner housing cover.
18 Remove the filter element from the housing.
19 Remove the air cleaner housing retaining stud.
20 Remove the air cleaner housing assembly.
21 Installation is the reverse of removal.

9   Fuel injection system — general information

Refer to illustrations 9.4, 9.6 and 9.7

Electronic fuel injection provides optimum mixture ratios at all stages of combustion and offers immediate throttle response characteristics. It also enables the engine to run at the leanest possible air/fuel mixture ratio, reducing exhaust gas emissions.

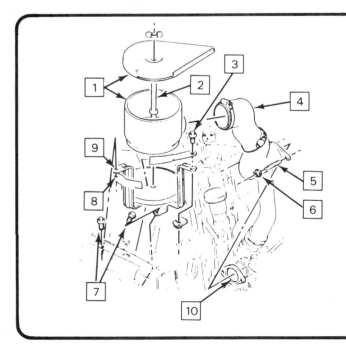

8.15   Exploded view of the air cleaner housing assembly on a 2.0L Turbo four-cylinder engine

1 Air cleaner assembly	6 Nut
2 Stud	7 Bolt
3 Bolt	8 Bracket
4 Duct	9 Support
5 Stud	10 Gasket

ASSEMBLED VIEW

On 2.5L four-cylinder models, a Throttle Body Injection (TBI) unit replaces a conventional carburetor atop the intake manifold. The 3.0L V6 and 2.0L Turbo powered vehicles are fitted with a Multi-port Fuel Injection (MFI) system. Both TBI and MFI systems are controlled by an Electronic Control Module (ECM), which monitors engine performance and adjusts the air/fuel mixture accordingly (see Chapter 6 for a complete description of the fuel control system).

An electric fuel pump located in the fuel tank with the fuel gauge sending unit pumps fuel to the fuel injection system through the fuel feed line and an in-line fuel filter. A pressure regulator keeps fuel available at a constant pressure. Fuel in excess of injector needs is returned to the fuel tank by a separate line.

The basic TBI unit is made up of two major casting assemblies — a throttle body with an Idle Air Control (IAC) valve controls air flow and a throttle position sensor monitors throttle angle. A fuel body consists of a fuel meter cover with a built-in pressure regulator and a fuel injector to supply fuel to the engine (see illustration).

The fuel injector is a solenoid operated device controlled by the ECM. The ECM turns on the solenoid, which lifts a normally closed ball valve off its seat. The fuel, which is under pressure, is injected in a conical spray pattern at the walls of the throttle body bore above the throttle valve. The fuel which is not used by the injector passes through the pressure regulator before being returned to the fuel tank.

On Multi-port Fuel Injection (MFI) systems, the throttle body (see illustration) has a throttle valve to control the amount of air delivered to the engine. The Throttle Position Sensor (TPS) and Idle Air Control (IAC) valves are located on the throttle body.

9.4 Typical TBI throttle body assembly

A Fuel injector
B Fuel pressure regulator
C Idle Air Control (IAC) valve
D Throttle Position Sensor (TPS)
E Fuel meter cover

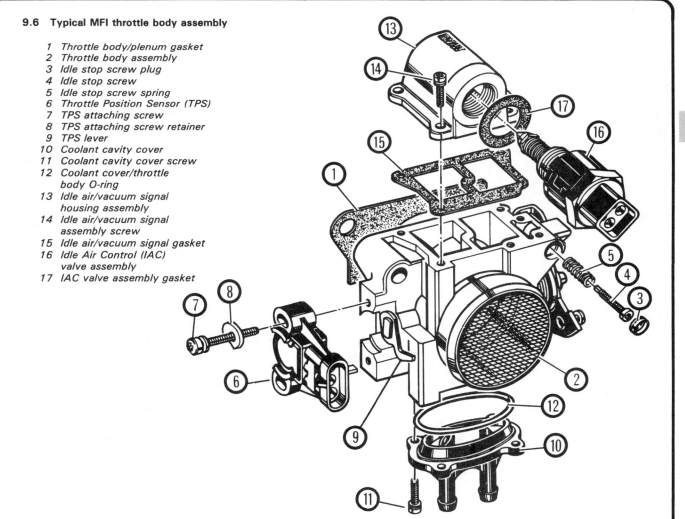

9.6 Typical MFI throttle body assembly

1 Throttle body/plenum gasket
2 Throttle body assembly
3 Idle stop screw plug
4 Idle stop screw
5 Idle stop screw spring
6 Throttle Position Sensor (TPS)
7 TPS attaching screw
8 TPS attaching screw retainer
9 TPS lever
10 Coolant cavity cover
11 Coolant cavity cover screw
12 Coolant cover/throttle body O-ring
13 Idle air/vacuum signal housing assembly
14 Idle air/vacuum signal assembly screw
15 Idle air/vacuum signal gasket
16 Idle Air Control (IAC) valve assembly
17 IAC valve assembly gasket

4

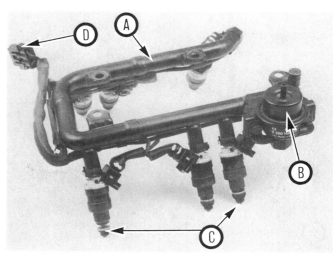

9.7 Typical MFI fuel rail assembly

A *Fuel rail*
B *Fuel pressure regulator*
C *Fuel injectors*
D *Fuel injector harness electrical connector*

10.8a The best way to remove the fuel injector is to pry on it with a screwdriver, using a second screwdriver as a fulcrum

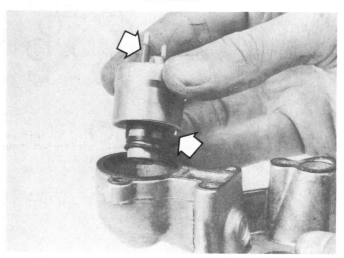

10.8b Note the position of the terminals on top and the dowel pin on bottom of the injector in relation to the fuel meter cover when you lift the injector out of the cover

10.7 The fuel pressure regulator is installed in the fuel meter cover and pre-adjusted by the factory — do not remove the four retaining screws (arrows) or you may damage the regulator

The fuel rail is mounted to the top of the engine. It distributes fuel to the individual injectors (**see illustration**).

Fuel is delivered to the input end of the rail by the fuel lines, goes through the rail and then to the pressure regulator. The regulator keeps the pressure to the injectors at a constant level.

The remaining fuel is returned to the fuel tank.

10 Throttle Body Injection (TBI) — removal, overhaul and installation

Refer to illustrations 10.7, 10.8a, 10.8b, 10.8c, 10.10, 10.11, 10.17, 10.18, 10.19, 10.25, 10.26, 10.35 and 10.36

Note: *Because of its relative simplicity, a throttle body assembly need be neither removed from the intake manifold nor completely disassembled during component replacement. However, for the sake of clarity, the following procedures are shown with the TBI assembly removed from the vehicle.*

1   Relieve the fuel pressure (Section 2).
2   Detach the cable from the negative terminal of the battery.
3   Remove the air cleaner housing assembly (see Section 14).

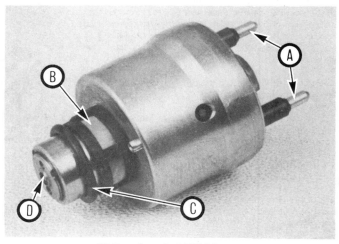

10.8c A typical TBI injector

A *Electrical terminals*
B *Injector fuel filter*
C *O-ring*
D *Nozzle*

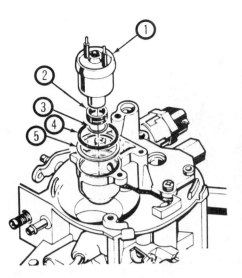

10.10 Remove the large O-ring and steel back up washer from the injector cavity of the fuel meter body

1 *Fuel injector*   4 *Large O-ring*
2 *Filter*   5 *Steel back-up washer*
3 *Small O-ring*

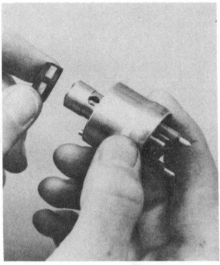

10.11 Gently rotate the fuel injector filter back and forth and carefully pull it off the nozzle

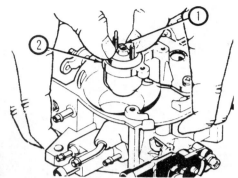

10.17 Push straight down with both thumbs to install the injector in the fuel meter body cavity

1 *Fuel injector*   2 *Fuel meter body*

Fuel meter cover and fuel injector

Disassembly

4   Remove the injector electrical connector (on top of the TBI) by squeezing the two tabs together and pulling straight up.

5   Unscrew the five fuel meter cover retaining screws and lockwashers securing the fuel meter cover to the fuel meter body. Note the location of the two short screws.

6   Remove the fuel meter cover. **Caution:** *Do not immerse the fuel meter cover in solvent. It might damage the pressure regulator diaphragm and gasket.*

7   The fuel meter cover contains the fuel pressure regulator, which is pre-set and plugged at the factory. If a malfunction occurs, it cannot be serviced, and must be replaced as a complete assembly. **Warning:** *Do not remove the screws securing the pressure regulator to the fuel meter cover* **(see illustration)**. *It has a large spring inside under heavy compression.*

8   With the old fuel meter cover gasket in place to prevent damage to the casting, carefully pry the injector from the fuel meter body with a screwdriver until it can be lifted free **(see illustrations)**. **Caution:** *Use care in removing the injector to prevent damage to the electrical connector terminals, the injector fuel filter, the O-ring and the nozzle* **(see illustration)**.

9   The fuel meter body should be removed from the throttle body if it needs to be cleaned. To remove it, remove the fuel feed and return line fittings and the Torx screws that attach the fuel meter body to the throttle body.

10 Remove the old gasket from the fuel meter cover and discard it. Remove the large O-ring and steel back-up washer from the upper counterbore of the fuel meter body injector cavity **(see illustration)**. Clean the fuel meter body thoroughly in solvent and blow dry.

11 Remove the small O-ring from the nozzle end of the injector. Carefully rotate the injector fuel filter back and forth and remove the filter from the base of the injector **(see illustration)**. Gently clean the filter in solvent and allow it to drip dry. It is too small and delicate to dry with compressed air. **Caution:** *The fuel injector itself is an electrical component. Do not immerse it in any type of cleaning solvent.*

12 The fuel injector is not serviceable. If it is malfunctioning, replace it as an assembly.

Reassembly

13 Install the clean fuel injector nozzle filter on the end of the fuel injector with the larger end of the filter facing the injector so that the

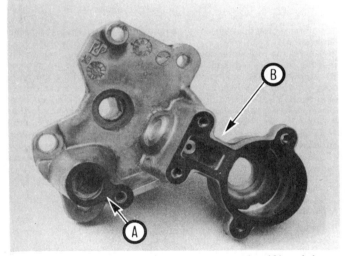

10.18 Position the fuel outlet passage gasket (A) and the fuel meter cover gasket (B) properly

filter covers the raised rib at the base of the injector. Use a twisting motion to position the filter against the base of the injector.

14 Lubricate a new small O-ring with automatic transmission fluid. Push the O-ring onto the nozzle end of the injector until it presses against the injector fuel filter.

15 Insert the steel backup washer in the top counterbore of the fuel meter body injector cavity.

16 Lubricate a new large O-ring with automatic transmission fluid and install it directly over the backup washer. Be sure that the O-ring is seated properly in the cavity and is flush with the top of the fuel meter body casting surface. **Caution:** *The back-up washer and large O-ring must be installed before the injector or improper seating of the large O-ring could cause fuel to leak.*

17 Install the injector in the cavity in the fuel meter body, aligning the raised lug on the injector base with the cast-in notch in the fuel meter body cavity. Push straight down on the injector with both thumbs **(see illustration)** until it is fully seated in the cavity. **Note:** *The electrical terminals of the injector should be approximately parallel to the throttle shaft.*

18 Install a new fuel outlet passage gasket on the fuel meter cover and a new fuel meter cover gasket on the fuel meter body **(see illustration)**.

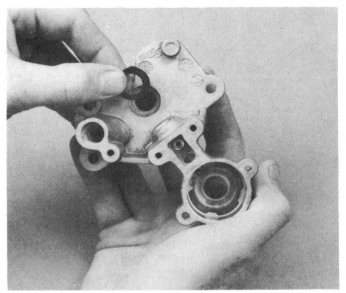

10.19   Install a new dust seal into the recess of the fuel meter body

10.25   Remove the IAC valve with a large wrench, but be careful — it's a delicate device

19   Install a new dust seal into the recess on the fuel meter body **(see illustration)**.
20   Install the fuel meter cover onto the fuel meter body, making sure that the pressure regulator dust seal and cover gaskets are in place.
21   Apply a thread locking compound to the threads of the fuel meter cover attaching screws. Install the screws (the two short screws go next to the injector) and tighten them securely. **Note:** *Service repair kits include a small vial of thread compound with directions for use. If this material is not available, use Loctite 262, GM part number 1052624, or equivalent. Do not use a higher strength locking compound than recommended, as this may prevent subsequent removal of the attaching screws or cause breakage of the screwhead if removal becomes necessary.*
22   Plug in the electrical connector to the injector.
23   Install the air cleaner.

Idle Air Control (IAC) valve

Removal
24   Unplug the electrical connector at the IAC valve.
25   Remove the IAC valve with a wrench on the hex surface only **(see illustration)**.

Adjustment
26   Before installing a new IAC valve, measure the distance the valve is extended **(see illustration)**. The measurement should be made from the motor housing to the end of the cone. The distance should be no greater than 1-1/8 inch. If the cone is extended too far, damage may occur to the valve when it is installed.
27   Identify the replacement IAC valve as either a Type I (with a collar at the electric terminal end) or a Type II (without a collar) **(see illustration 10.26)**. If the measured dimension ''A'' is greater than 1-1/8 inch, the distance must be reduced as follows:
   Type I — Exert firm pressure on the valve to retract it (a slight side-to-side movement may be helpful).
   Type II — Compress the retaining spring of the valve while turning the valve in a clockwise direction. Return the spring to its original position with the straight portion of the spring aligned with the flat surface of the valve.

Installation
28   Install the new IAC valve to the throttle body. Use the new gasket supplied with the assembly.
29   Plug in the electrical connector.
30   Install the air cleaner.
31   Start the engine and allow it to reach normal operating temperature. The Electronic Control Module (ECM) will reset the idle speed when the vehicle is driven above 35 mph.

Throttle Position Sensor (TPS)

32   The Throttle Position Sensor (TPS) is connected to the throttle shaft on the TBI unit. As the throttle valve angle is changed (as the accelerator pedal is moved), the output of the TPS also changes. At a closed throttle position, the output of the TPS is below 1.25 volts. As the throttle valve opens, the output increases so that, at wide-open throttle, the output voltage is approximately 5 volts.
33   A broken or loose TPS can cause intermittent bursts of fuel from the injector and an unstable idle, because the ECM thinks the throttle is moving. A problem in any of the TPS circuits will set either a Code 21 or 22 (see ''Trouble Codes,'' Chapter 6).
34   The TPS is not adjustable. The ECM uses the reading at idle for the zero reading. If the TPS malfunctions, it is replaced as a unit.

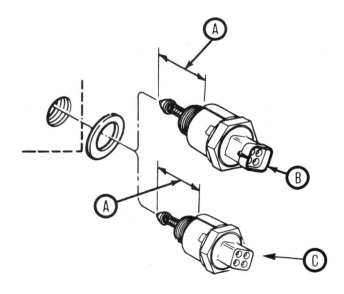

10.26   Distance ''A'' should be less than 1-1/8 inch for either type of Idle Air Control valve — if it isn't, determine what kind of IAC valve you have and adjust it accordingly

B   Type I with collar   *C   Type II without collar*

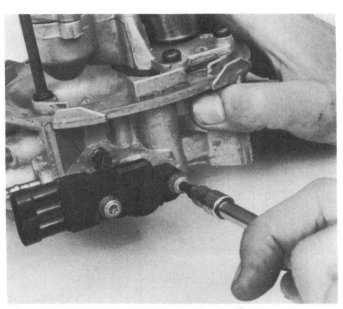

10.35   The throttle position sensor is mounted on the side of the TBI with two Torx screws

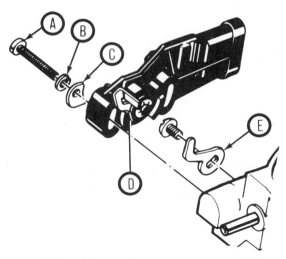

10.36   Make sure that you use the new TPS switch attaching screws (A), lockwashers (B) and retainers (C) that are included in the TPS service kit — also make sure that the TPS lever (D) is located above the tang on the throttle actuator (E)

35   Unscrew the two Torx screws (**see illustration**) and remove the TPS.

36   Install the new TPS. **Note:** *Make sure that the tang on the lever is properly engaged with the stop on the TBI* (**see illustration**).

---

11   Multi-port Fuel Injection (MFI) — component removal and installation

---

Warning: *Before servicing an injector, fuel rail or pressure regulator, always relieve the fuel pressure in the fuel system to minimize the risk of fire and injury. After servicing the system, always cycle the ignition on and off several times (wait 10 seconds between cycles) and check the system for leaks.*

Idle Air Control (IAC) valve
Refer to illustrations 11.2, 11.3 and 11.7

1   Detach the cable from the negative terminal of the battery.
2   Unplug the electrical connector from the IAC valve assembly (**see illustration**).
3   Remove the IAC valve assembly from the idle air/vacuum signal housing assembly (**see illustration**). **Caution:** *Do not remove any thread locking compound from the threads.*
4   Remove the IAC valve assembly gasket and discard it.
5   Clean the gasket mounting surface of the idle air/vacuum signal housing assembly to ensure a good seal. **Caution:** *The IAC valve assembly itself is an electrical component, and must not be soaked in any liquid cleaner or solvent, as damage may result.*
6   Before installing the IAC valve assembly, the position of the pintle must be checked. If the pintle is extended too far, damage to the assembly may occur.

4

11.2   There are two electrical connectors plugged into the MFI type throttle body — the IAC valve (A) and the TPS switch (B). The connector below the throttle body is for the knock sensor (C)

11.3   To remove the IAC valve from the throttle body, use a large adjustable wrench — if there is thread locking compound on the threads and you are going to install the same IAC, don't remove the thread compound

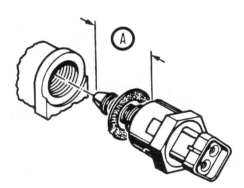

11.7　Before installing the IAC valve, make sure that dimension A is 1-1/8 inches

11.15　You can't see the two coolant hoses attached to the throttle body until you unbolt the throttle body from the plenum and turn it over

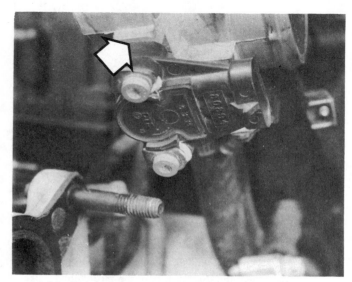

11.21　If you plan to install the same TPS switch, be sure to make an alignment mark between the plastic TPS switch body and the aluminum throttle body casting

11.14　To detach the throttle body from the plenum/intake manifold assembly, remove these two nuts (arrows)

7　Measure the distance from the gasket mounting surface of the IAC valve assembly to the tip of the pintle **(see illustration)**.
8　If the distance is greater than 1-1/8 inch, reduce it as follows:
  a)　If the IAC valve assembly has a collar around its electrical connector end, use firm hand pressure on the pintle to retract it (a slight side-to-side motion may help).
  b)　If the IAC valve assembly has no collar, compress the pintle retaining spring toward the body of the IAC and try to turn the pintle clockwise. If the pintle will turn, continue turning it until the 1-1/8 inch dimension is reached. Return the spring to its original position with the straight part of the spring end lined up with the flat surface under the pintle head. If the pintle will not turn, use firm hand pressure to retract it.
9　Installation is the reverse of removal. Be sure to use a new gasket and tighten the IAC securely. **Note:** *No adjustment is made to the IAC assembly after reinstallation. IAC resetting is controlled by the ECM when the vehicle is operated.*

Throttle Body
Refer to illustrations 11.14 and 11.15
10　Detach the cable from the negative terminal of the battery.
11　Remove the duct between the air cleaner housing and the throttle body (see Section 8).
12　Unplug the IAC, the TPS and the knock sensor electrical connectors **(see illustration 11.2)**.
13　Detach the throttle cable and, if equipped, the cruise control cables. Detach the cables from the bracket (see Section 13).
14　Remove the throttle body mounting nuts **(see illustration)** and separate the throttle body from the plenum/intake manifold assembly.
15　Turn the throttle body until its underside is exposed, loosen both hose clamps and detach the coolant hoses **(see illustration)**.
16　Remove all old gasket material from the mating surfaces of the throttle body and the plenum.
17　Installation is the reverse of removal. Be sure to use a new gasket and tighten the throttle body mounting nuts to the specified torque.

Throttle position sensor (TPS)
Refer to illustrations 11.21, 11.22, 11.23 and 11.26
18　Detach the cable from the negative terminal of the battery.
19　Unplug the connector from the TPS switch **(see illustration 11.2)**.
20　If the TPS switch on your vehicle is located on the side of the throttle body, proceed to the next Step. If the switch is attached to the underside of the throttle body (like the one shown in this book), remove the throttle body (see Steps 10 through 16), then proceed to the next Step.
21　If you intend to install the same TPS switch scribe or paint an alignment mark between the TPS and the throttle body **(see illustration)**. If you are installing a new switch, you will have to set it with a voltmeter.

11.22 You'll need a Torx bit or screwdriver to remove the TPS retaining screws

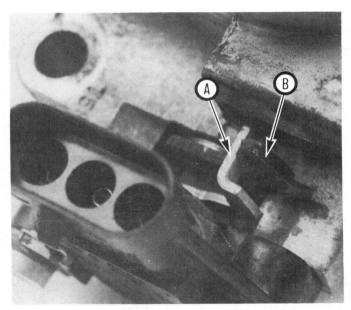

11.23 The TPS lever (A) must mate with the TPS drive lever (B) when you attach the TPS switch to the throttle body

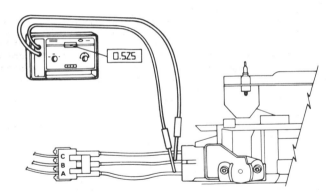

11.26 Typical connections for adjusting the TPS switch. Detach the TPS harness connector from the switch, bridge the two halves of the plug with jumper wires and, with the ignition on and the engine off, take a reading from the indicated wires

22 Using a Torx screwdriver or bit **(see illustration)**, remove the TPS switch.

23 Installation is the reverse of removal. Be sure to install the TPS switch onto the throttle body with the throttle valve in the closed position. Make sure that the TPS lever lines up with the TPS drive lever on the throttle shaft **(see illustration)**.

24 Install the TPS screw retainers with the TPS retaining screws. Finger tighten the screws.

25 If you had to remove the throttle body to get at the TPS, install the throttle body at this time (see Steps 10 through 17).

26 Install three jumper wires between the TPS and the wire harness electrical connector **(see illustration)**.

27 With the ignition turned to On and a digital voltmeter connected to the top and middle, or left and center, terminals (marked A and B on some connectors), adjust the TPS to obtain a reading of 0.55 ± 0.05 volts (3.0L V6) or under 1.25 volts (2.0L Turbo four).

28 Tighten the TPS mounting screws and recheck your reading to ensure that the adjustment has not changed.

29 Turn the ignition off, remove the jumper wires and connect the wiring harness electrical connector to the TPS switch.

11.33 To remove the fuel pressure regulator from the fuel rail, detach the vacuum hose (A), unscrew the fuel return line threaded fitting (B) and remove the bracket mounting bolts (C)

30 If you removed the throttle body to get at the TPS, install the air intake duct between the air cleaner housing and the throttle body and plug in the MAF and air temperature sensors (see Section 8).

Fuel pressure regulator

Refer to illustrations 11.33, 11.34a and 11.34b

Note: *The pressure regulator is factory adjusted and is not serviceable. Do not attempt to remove the regulator from the fuel rail unless you intend to replace it with a new unit.*

31 Relieve the fuel pressure (see Section 2).

32 Detach the cable from the negative terminal of the battery.

33 Detach the vacuum line from the top of the pressure regulator **(see illustration)**.

34 Unscrew the fuel line from the fuel pressure regulator. Be sure to use a backup wrench **(see illustration)**. **Note:** *If your vehicle is equipped with a 2.0L Turbo four, the fuel pressure regulator is located underneath the intake runners instead of atop the fuel rail* **(see illustration)**.
35 Remove the pressure regulator bracket mounting bolts and remove the regulator.
36 Installation is the reverse of removal.

Fuel rail assembly

Refer to illustrations 11.38a, 11.38b, 11.40, 11.41 and 11.43

Note: *If you are removing the fuel rail assembly to service or replace an injector, it is not necessary to remove the throttle body. Follow Steps 10 through 13, then continue with the Steps below. If, however, you intend to replace the fuel rail assembly itself, follow Steps 10 through 16, then proceed to the Steps below. Note also that the procedure for removing the fuel rail assembly on the 2.0L Turbo four is slightly different than the procedure outlined below (Refer to illustration 11.34b for the location of the fuel rail bolts, the electrical connector, the injectors, etc.).*

11.34a Use a backup wrench when disconnecting the fuel line threaded fittings at the pressure regulator

11.38a To detach the fuel injector wiring harness from the engine compartment wiring harness, slide the locking tab sideways with a small screwdriver, ...

37 Detach the vacuum hose from the pressure regulator **(see illustration 11.33)**.
38 Unplug the fuel rail wiring harness electrical connector **(see illustrations)**.
39 Unscrew the fuel line from the fuel pressure regulator. Be sure to use a backup wrench **(see illustration 11.34)**.

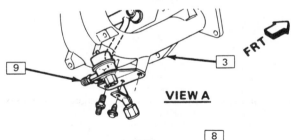

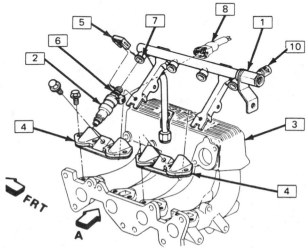

11.34b Exploded view of the fuel rail, pressure regulator and fuel injector assembly on the 2.0L Turbo four

1 Fuel rail assembly
2 Fuel injector
3 Intake manifold
4 Injector housing assembly
5 Injector retaining clip
6 Injector retaining groove
7 Injector cup flange
8 Injector wire harness electrical connector
9 Fuel pressure regulator assembly
10 Fuel pressure gauge test point

11.38b ... then release the locking tab on top of the plug and pull the two halves of the connector apart

40 Unscrew the fuel return line threaded fittings. Be sure to use a backup wrench **(see illustration)**.
41 Remove the alternator support bracket nut **(see illustration)**. Unscrew the alternator through bolt and remove the bracket (see Chapter 5 for further illustrations if necessary).
42 Remove the four fuel rail assembly mounting bolts **(see illustration 11.41)**.
43 Using a gentle rocking motion, remove the fuel rail and fuel injector assembly **(see illustration)**.
44 Installation is the reverse of removal.

Fuel injectors
Refer to illustrations 11.47, 11.48, 11.49, 11.50 and 11.51
45 Relieve the fuel pressure (see Section 2).
46 Detach the cable from the negative terminal of the battery.
47 If you intend to service/replace more than one injector on a cylinder bank, it's a good idea to label the injectors to prevent mixups of the electrical leads at reassembly **(see illustration)**.
48 To unplug the electrical connectors from the injectors you are going to service/replace, push in the connector wire retaining clip with your index finger **(see illustration)** and pull on the plug.

11.40 Use a backup wrench when detaching the fuel feed line from the fuel rail assembly

11.41 To detach the fuel rail assembly from the plenum, remove the nut (A) that attaches the alternator bracket to the right front fuel rail mounting bolt, then remove the four fuel rail bolts (B)

11.43 Use a gentle side-to-side rocking motion while pulling straight up to release the injectors from their bores in the intake manifold

11.47 If you plan to remove more than one injector it's a good idea to clearly label them to prevent mixups during reassembly

11.48 To unplug the electrical connectors from the injectors, push the wire retaining clip in and pull the connector straight up

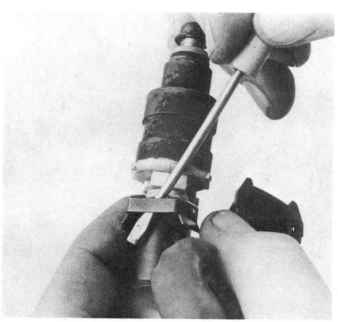

11.49   To detach an injector from the fuel rail assembly, pop off the spring clip with a small screwdriver . . .

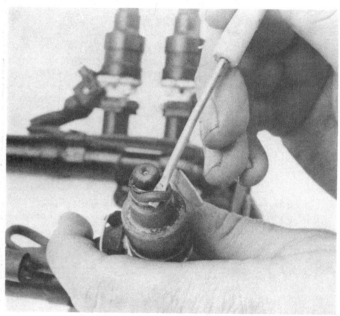

11.51   If you plan to reuse the same injector, always remove the old O-rings with a small screwdriver

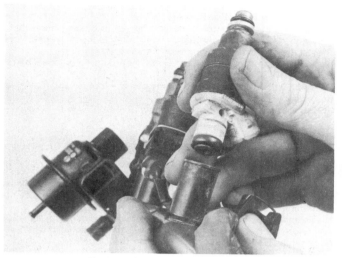

11.50   . . . then pull on the injector while rocking it until the upper O-ring breaks loose from the fuel rail

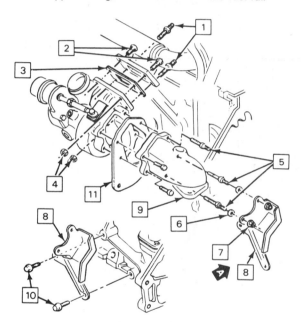

12.6   Exploded view of the turbocharger assembly on the 2.0L OHC engine

1 *Stud*	7 *Nut*
2 *Bolt*	8 *Support bracket*
3 *Gasket*	9 *Exhaust outlet elbow*
4 *Nut*	10 *Bolt*
5 *Stud*	11 *Adapter plate*
6 *Washer*	

49   Pop off the fuel injector spring clip(s) with a small screwdriver **(see illustration)**.

50   Using a gentle side-to-side wiggling motion, pull the injector from the fuel rail **(see illustration)**. Use care when removing injectors to prevent damage to the electrical connector pins on the injector and the nozzle. Repeat the above Steps for each injector you wish to service or replace.

51   Even if you intend to reinstall the old injectors, be sure to remove the O-rings from both ends of each injector with a small screwdriver **(see illustration)** and install new ones. Coat the O-rings with a little engine oil and install them on the new injectors. If you are installing new injectors, they must also be fitted with new O-rings lubricated with a little engine oil.

52   Installation is the reverse of removal.

12   Turbocharger — removal and installation

Refer to illustrations 12.6, 12.7, 12.8, 12.11 and 12.14

1   Detach the cable from the negative terminal of the battery.

2   Raise the vehicle and support it securely on jackstands.

3   Remove the lower fan retaining screw.

4   Remove the exhaust pipe (refer to Section 14).

5   Remove the rear A/C compressor support bracket bolt and loosen the remaining bolts (see Chapter 3).

6   Remove the turbocharger support bracket-to-engine bolt **(see illustration)**.

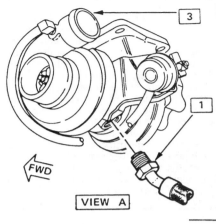

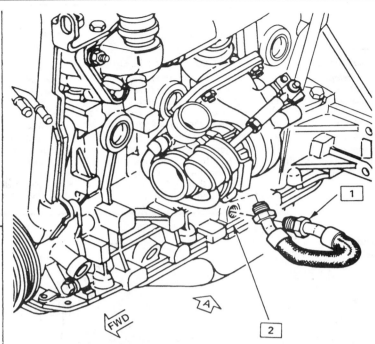

12.7   The turbocharger oil drain hose assembly

1   Turbocharger oil drain hose fitting
2   Cylinder block
3   Turbocharger assembly

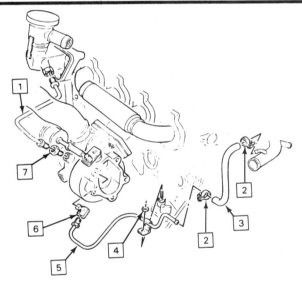

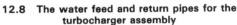

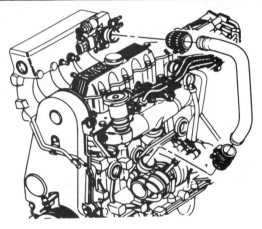

12.11   The turbocharger induction tube and hoses

**12.8   The water feed and return pipes for the
          turbocharger assembly**

1   Pipe   5   Pipe
2   Clamp   6   Fitting
3   Hose   7   Fitting
4   Nut

7   Remove the oil drain hose (**see illustration**) from the turbocharger.
8   Remove the water return pipe (**see illustration**).
9   Lower the vehicle.
10 Remove the coolant recovery pipe and move it to one side.
11 Remove the turbocharger induction tube (**see illustration**).
12 Remove the coolant fan.
13 Remove the oxygen sensor.
14 Disconnect the oil feed and return pipes (**see illustration**).
15 Remove the water feed pipe.
16 Remove the air intake duct and vacuum hose at the actuator.
17 Remove the exhaust manifold and turbocharger.
18 Installation is the reverse of removal.

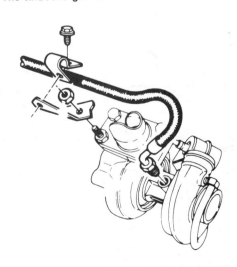

12.14   Turbocharger oil feed pipe hose assembly

13   Throttle cable — removal, installation and adjustment

Refer to illustrations 13.2a, 13.2b, 13.2c, 13.3, 13.4, 13.6a and 13.6b
Note: *The accelerator control system is the cable type. There are no linkage adjustments. Because there are no adjustments, the specific cable for your vehicle must be used. No other replacement part will work. When servicing throttle cables, always check to make sure that all components are installed as removed and that no linkages or cables are rubbing or binding in any manner.*

1   Disconnect the cable from the negative terminal of the battery.
2   If your vehicle is equipped with a 2.5L four, disconnect the cable from the TBI throttle lever arm by removing the retainer clip (**see illustration**). If your vehicle is equipped with a 3.0L V6 or a 2.0L Turbo four, slide the cable forward and lift up (**see illustrations**).

3   If your vehicle is equipped with a cruise control system, pop the retaining clip off the post on the throttle lever arm with a small screwdriver and remove the cable end (**see illustration**).
4   To detach the throttle and, if equipped, cruise control cables from the cable support bracket, use a pair of needle nose pliers to squeeze the locking tabs on the top and bottom of the cable retainer (**see illustration**), then pull the cable assembly through the bracket.
5   Carefully study the routing of the cable before proceeding.
6   From inside the vehicle, pull the cable toward you and detach it from the accelerator pedal (**see illustrations**).
7   Follow the cable with your hand until you locate the locking cable retainer on the passenger compartment side of the firewall. Again, with a pair of needle nose pliers, squeeze the locking tabs of the retainer together and push the retainer through the firewall.
8   Remove the accelerator cable assembly.
9   Installation is the reverse of removal.

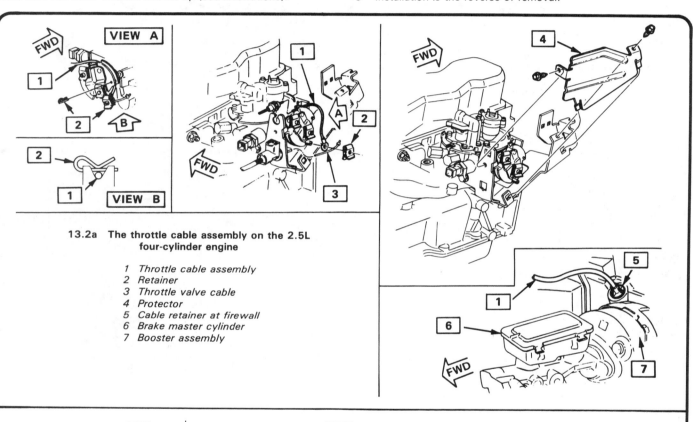

**13.2a   The throttle cable assembly on the 2.5L
four-cylinder engine**

1   *Throttle cable assembly*
2   *Retainer*
3   *Throttle valve cable*
4   *Protector*
5   *Cable retainer at firewall*
6   *Brake master cylinder*
7   *Booster assembly*

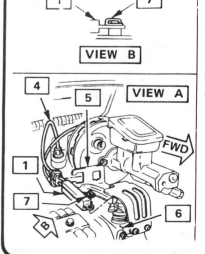

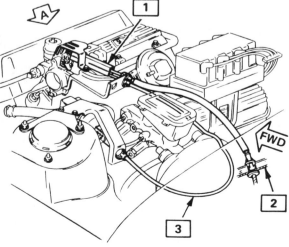

**13.2b   The throttle cable assembly
on the 3.0L V6 engine
(2.0L Turbo four similar)**

1   *Throttle cable assembly*
2   *Cable retainer at firewall*
3   *Cruise control cable*
4   *Make sure that cable is
    routed below engine harness*
5   *Throttle/cruise control
    cable bracket*
6   *Throttle body*
7   *Cable retainer*

13.2c   On MFI-equipped vehicles, push the cable end
forward and lift up to detach the cable from the post on
the throttle lever arm

13.3   On MFI-equipped vehicles, you'll need to pop off the
retaining clip to detach the cruise control cable from the
throttle lever arm

13.4   On MFI-equipped vehicles, the throttle and cruise
control cable retainers can be detached from the cable
bracket by squeezing the locking tabs on the top and
bottom of the retainer with a pair of needle nose pliers

13.6a   The throttle cable at the pedal — once the cable is
detached at the throttle body end, pull this end toward you
and slide it out of the slot in the pedal lever assembly

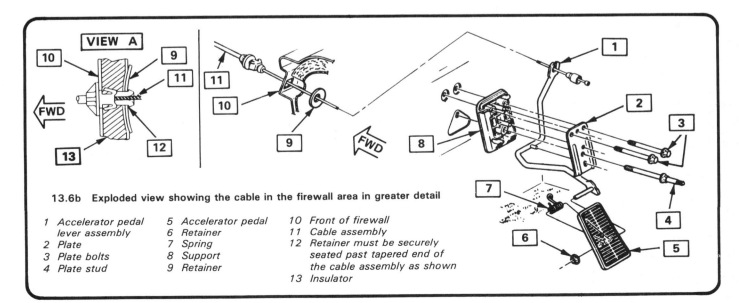

13.6b   Exploded view showing the cable in the firewall area in greater detail

1 Accelerator pedal lever assembly	5 Accelerator pedal	10 Front of firewall
2 Plate	6 Retainer	11 Cable assembly
3 Plate bolts	7 Spring	12 Retainer must be securely seated past tapered end of the cable assembly as shown
4 Plate stud	8 Support	
	9 Retainer	13 Insulator

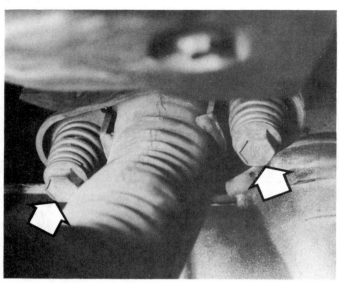

14.3   The exhaust pipe to exhaust manifold flange bolts — make sure you don't lose the springs when removing these bolts

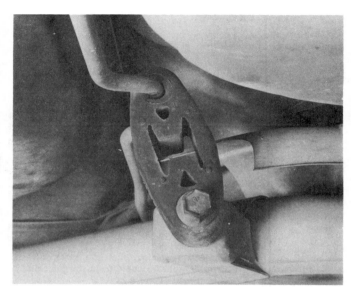

14.4   To detach this rubber block type hanger from the exhaust pipe, remove the large bolt

14   Exhaust system — removal and installation

Refer to illustrations 14.3 and 14.4

Caution: *The exhaust system generates high temperatures. No part of the exhaust should be touched until the entire system has completely cooled. Be especially careful around the catalytic converter, where the highest temperatures are generated.*

1   Disconnect the cable from the negative terminal of the battery.
2   Raise the vehicle and support it securely on jackstands.
3   Disconnect the exhaust pipe from the exhaust manifold flange by removing the two flange bolts **(see illustration)**.
4   Remove the bolt from the rubber exhaust pipe hanger just in front of the fuel tank **(see illustration)**.
5   Remove the bolt and detach the hanger from the forward end of the muffler.
6   Remove the bolt and detach the hanger from the rear end of the muffler.
7   Remove the exhaust pipe, catalytic converter and muffler as an assembly. **Note:** *These components cannot be separated without a cutting torch. If you need to replace any of these parts, take the entire assembly to a dealer or a muffler shop for further service.*

Chapter 5   Engine electrical systems

Contents

Specifications

Cylinder numbers	
four-cylinder engines (drivebelt end-to-transaxle end)	1-2-3-4
V6 engine	
front bank	1-3-5
rear bank	2-4-6
Firing order	
four-cylinder engines	1-3-4-2
V6 engine	1-6-5-4-3-2
Distributor rotation	clockwise
Alternator charging output	12 to 14 volts

5

1   Ignition system — general information

The 3.0L V6 engines in the early Pontiac Grand Am, the 2.5L fours in all 1985 through 1986 vehicles covered in this manual and the 2.0L OHC Turbo fours used in the Grand Am are equipped with High Energy Ignition (HEI) systems consisting of an ignition switch, battery, coil, primary (low tension) and secondary (high tension) wiring circuits, a distributor and spark plugs. All other vehicles covered by this manual are equipped with a distributorless ignition system consisting of a coil pack, an ignition module, a crankshaft reluctor ring, a magnetic sensor and the ECM.

High Energy Ignition (HEI) distributor

HEI equipped vehicles use a special HEI distributor with Electronic Spark Timing (EST). Some HEI distributors combine all the ignition components into one unit with the ignition coil in the distributor cap. On other HEI distributors, the coil is mounted separately.

All spark timing changes in the HEI/EST distributor are carried out by the Electronic Control Module (ECM), which monitors data from various engine sensors, computes the desired spark timing and signals the distributor to change the timing accordingly. No vacuum or mechanical advance is used.

Electronic Spark Control (ESC)

Some engines are equipped with an Electronic Spark Control (ESC), which uses a knock sensor in connection with the ECM to control spark timing to allow the engine to have maximum spark advance without spark knock. This improves drivability and fuel economy.

Secondary (spark plug) wiring

The secondary (spark plug) wire used with the HEI system is a carbon impregnated cord conductor encased in an 8 mm diameter rubber jacket with an outer silicone jacket. This type of wire will withstand very high temperatures and provides an excellent insulator for the HEI's high voltage. **Warning:** *Because of the very high voltage generated by the HEI system, extreme care should be taken whenever an operation involving ignition components is performed. This not only includes the distributor, coil, control module and spark plug wires, but related items that are connected to the systems as well, such as the plug connections, tachometer and testing equipment.*

Direct Ignition System (DIS)

Many of the 2.5L four and 3.0L V6 engines covered in this manual are equipped with "distributorless ignitions," which use a "waste spark" method of spark distribution. Each cylinder is paired with its opposing cylinder in the firing order (1-4, 2-3 on a four, 1-4, 2-5, 3-6 on a V6) so that one cylinder on compression fires simultaneously with its opposing cylinder on exhaust. Since the cylinder on exhaust requires very little of the available voltage to fire its plug, most of the voltage is used to fire the cylinder on compression.

The DIS system includes a coil pack, an ignition module, a crankshaft reluctor ring, a magnetic sensor and the ECM. The ignition module is located under the coil pack and is connected to the ECM.

The magnetic crankshaft sensor mounted to the bottom of the DIS module protrudes through the engine block, just above the oil pan rail, within about 0.050-inch of the crankshaft reluctor ring.

The reluctor ring is a special disc cast into the crankshaft, which acts as a signal generator for the ignition timing.

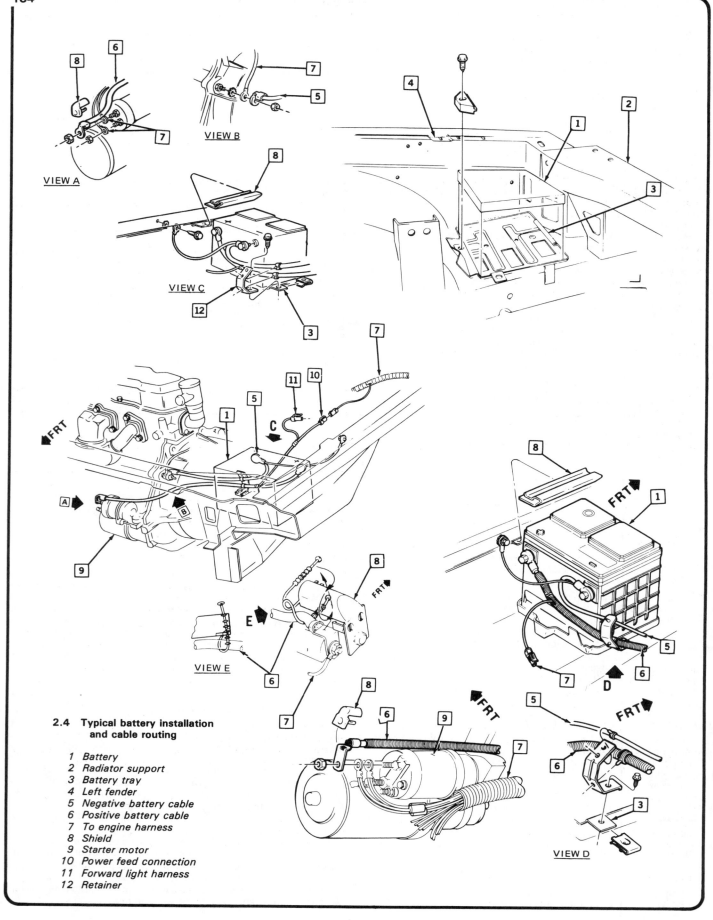

184

VIEW A

VIEW B

VIEW C

VIEW E

VIEW D

FRT

2.4 Typical battery installation and cable routing

1 Battery
2 Radiator support
3 Battery tray
4 Left fender
5 Negative battery cable
6 Positive battery cable
7 To engine harness
8 Shield
9 Starter motor
10 Power feed connection
11 Forward light harness
12 Retainer

The system uses Electronic Spark Timing (EST) and control wires from the ECM, just like conventional distributor systems. The ECM controls timing using crankshaft position, engine rpm, engine temperature and manifold absolute pressure (MAP) sensing.

Computer controlled coil ignition (C3I) system

The computer controlled coil ignition (C3I) system consists of the ECM, ignition module, ignition coils, a "Hall effect" cam, the crank sensors and the connecting wires. On 3.0L V6 applications, the crank and cam sensor functions are combined into one dual sensor called a combination sensor which is mounted on the harmonic balancer.

Two types of module/coil assemblies are commonly used. They can be distinguished by the configuration of their coil towers: Type I module/coil assemblies have evenly spaced towers, with three on either side; Type IIs have all six towers (two per coil) placed on one side. The wiring harness and sensors, however, are interchangeable between either type.

The C3I system uses a waste spark method spark distribution. Each cylinder is paired with its opposite cylinder, i.e. 1-4, 5-2, 3-6. The spark occurs simultaneously in the cylinder coming up on compression and the cylinder coming up on exhaust.

The cylinder, on exhaust, requires very little of the available voltage to fire the spark plug. The remaining high voltage can then be used, as required, by the cylinder on compression.

The spark distribution is accomplished by a signal from the crank sensor, which is used by the ignition module to determine the proper time to trigger the next ignition coil. This signal is also processed by the C3I module into the reference signal used by the ECM.

The C3I system uses the electronic spark timing (EST) signal from the crankshaft, just like a HEI distributor ignition system equipped with EST, to control spark timing.

Timing is controlled by the ECM using the following inputs:
Crankshaft position
Engine speed (rpm)
Engine temperature
Amount of air entering the intake (mass air flow sensor)

2 Battery — removal and installation

Refer to illustration 2.4
Warning: *Hydrogen gas is produced by the battery, so keep open flames and lighted cigarettes away from it at all times. Always wear eye protection when working around a battery. Rinse off spilled electrolyte immediately with large amounts of water.*

1   The battery is located at the right front of the engine compartment, underneath the right louvered cover panel.

Removal

2   Remove the two wing screws securing the cover panel, if so equipped, and remove the cover panel.
3   Detach the cables from the negative and positive terminals of the battery. **Caution:** *To prevent arcing, disconnect the negative (–) cable first, then remove the the positive (+) cable.*
4   Remove the hold-down clamp bolt **(see illustration)** and the clamp from the battery carrier.
5   Carefully lift the battery from the carrier. **Warning:** *Always keep the battery in an upright position to reduce the likelihood of electrolyte spillage. If you spill electrolyte on your skin, rinse it off immediately with large amounts of water.*

Installation

Note: *The battery carrier and hold-down clamp should be clean and free from corrosion before installing the battery. Make certain that there are no parts in the carrier before installing the battery.*

6   Set the battery in position in its carrier. Don't tilt it.
7   Install the hold-down clamp and bolt. The bolt should be snug, but overtightening it may damage the battery case.
8   Install both battery cables, positive first, then the negative. **Note:** *The battery terminals and cable ends should be cleaned prior to connection (see Chapter 1).*
9   Install the cover panel and tighten both wing screws securely.

3 Battery — emergency jump starting

Refer to the *Booster battery (jump) starting* procedure at the front of this manual.

4 Battery cables — check and replacement

1   Periodically inspect the entire length of each battery cable for damage, cracked or burned insulation and corrosion. Poor battery cable connections can cause starting problems and decreased engine performance.
2   Check the cable-to-terminal connections at the ends of the cables for cracks, loose wire strands and corrosion. The presence of white, fluffy deposits under the insulation at the cable terminal connection is a sign the cable is corroded and should be replaced. Check the terminals for distortion, missing mounting bolts or nuts and corrosion.
3   If only the positive cable is to be replaced, be sure to disconnect the negative cable from the battery first.
4   Disconnect and remove the cable **(see illustration 2.4)**. Make sure the replacement cable is the same length and diameter.
5   Clean the threads of the starter or ground connection with a wire brush to remove rust and corrosion. Apply a light coat of petroleum jelly to the threads to ease installation and prevent future corrosion.
6   Attach the cable to the starter or ground connection and tighten the mounting nut securely.
7   Before connecting the new cable to the battery, make sure it reaches the terminals without having to be stretched.
8   Connect the positive cable first, followed by the negative cable. Tighten the nuts and apply a thin coat of petroleum jelly to the terminal and cable connection.

5 Ignition system — check

Refer to illustrations 5.1, 5.8, 5.13, 5.17, 5.23, 5.25, 5.30 and 5.34
Warning: *Because of the very high voltage generated by the ignition system, extreme care should be taken whenever an operation is performed involving ignition components. This not only includes the distributor, coil(s), control module and spark plug wires, but related items that are connected to the system as well, such as the plug connections, tachometer and any test equipment.*

HEI

1   Test #1 **(see illustration)**: Two wires are checked to ensure that an open is not present in a spark plug wire. Test #1A: If spark occurs with the four-terminal distributor connector disconnected, pickup coil output is too low for EST operation.
2   Test #2 **(see illustration 5.1)**: A spark indicates that the problem must be the distributor cap or rotor. **Note:** *A few sparks followed by no spark is the same condition as no spark at all.*
3   Test #3 **(see illustration 5.1)**: Normally, there should be battery voltage at the "C" and "+" terminals. Low voltage indicates an open or high resistance circuit from the distributor to the coil or ignition switch. If the "C" terminal voltage is low, but the "+" terminal voltage is 10 volts or more, the circuit from "C" terminal to the ignition coil or ignition coil primary winding is open.
4   Test #4 **(see illustration 5.1)** checks for a shorted module or grounded circuit from the ignition coil to the module. The distributor module should be turned off, so normal voltage should be about 12 volts. If the module is turned on, the voltage will be low, but above one volt. This could cause the ignition coil to fail from excessive heat. With an open ignition coil primary winding, a small amount of voltage will leak through the module from the "Bat" to the tach terminal.
5   Applying a voltage (1.5 to 8V) to module terminal "P" should turn the module on and the tach terminal voltage should drop to about 7 to 9 volts. Test #5 **(see illustration 5.1)** will determine whether the module or coil is faulty or if the pickup coil is not generating the proper signal to turn the module on. This test can be performed by using a DC battery with a rating of 1.5 to 8 volts. The use of the test light is to allow the "P" terminal to be probed more easily. Some digital multimeters can also be used to trigger the module by selecting *ohms*,

5

① • Check spark at plug with spark tester J-26792 or equivalent (ST-125) while cranking (if no spark on one wire, check a second wire) A few sparks and then nothing is considered no spark.

No Spark	Spark

①A • Disconnect 4 term. distributor connector and check for spark.

Check fuel, spark plugs, etc.

No spark	Spark

② • Check for spark at coil wire with tester while cranking. (Leave spark tester connected to coil wire for Steps 3-6).

Replace pick-up coil

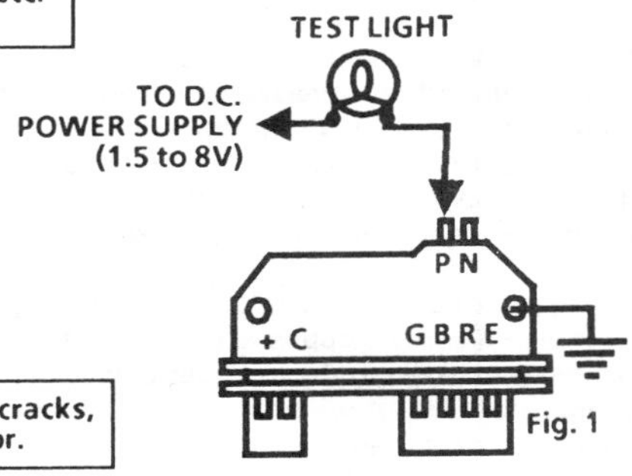

TEST LIGHT

TO D.C. POWER SUPPLY (1.5 to 8V)

P N
+ C   G B R E

Fig. 1

No Spark	Spark

③ • Disconnect distributor 2 term. "C / + " connector.
• Ignition switch "on", Engine stopped.
• Check volts at " + " and "C" term's. of dist. harn. conn.

Inspect cap for water, cracks, etc. If OK, replace rotor.

Both term's. 10 volts or more	Both term's. under 10 volts	Under 10 volts "C" term. only

④ • Reconnect dist. 2 term. conn.
• With ign. "ON", check voltage from tach. term. to gnd. (term. may be taped back in harness).

Repair wire from module " + " term. to "B" term. of black Ign. coil connector or primary ckt. to ign. sw.

Check for open or gnd. in ckt. from "C" term. to ign. coil. If Ckt. is OK, fault is. ign. coil or conn..

Over10 volts	Under 1 volt	1 to 10 volts

• Connect test light from tach. term. to ground.
• Crank engine and observe light.

Repair open tach. lead or conn and repeat test #4.

Replace module and check for spark from coil as in Step 6.

Light on steady	Light blinks	Spark	No Spark

⑤ • Disconnect distributor 4 term. connector.
• Remove dist. cap.
• Disconnect pick-up coil connector from module.
• Connect voltmeter from tach. term. to ground.
• Ignition on.
• Insulate a test light probe to 1/4" from tip and note voltage, as test light is momentarily connected from a voltage source (1.5 to 8V) to module term. "P".

System OK

Replace ign. coil, it too is faulty

Replace ignition coil and recheck for spark with spark tester. If still no spark, re-install original coil and replace dist. module..

Voltage drops	No drop in voltage

⑥ • Check for spark from coil wire with spark tester as test light is removed from module term.

Check module ground. If OK, replace module.

No Spark	Spark

• If no module tester (J24642) is available; Replace ign. coil and repeat Step 5.

• If module tester (J24642) is available: test module

Check pick-up coil or conns. (Coil resistance should be 500-1500 ohms and not grounded).

No Spark	Spark	OK	Bad

Ign. coil removed is OK, reinstall coil and check coil wire from dist. cap. if OK, replace dist. module.

System OK

Check coil wire from cap to coil. If OK, replace coil.

Replace module

5.1   Diagnostic flow chart for HEI ignition system check, tests #1 to #6

usually the diode position. In this position, the meter may have a voltage across its terminals which can be used to trigger the module. The voltage in the *ohms* position can be checked by using a second meter or by checking the manufacturer's specifications for the tool being used.

6   Test #6 **(see illustration 5.1)** should turn off the module and cause a spark. If no spark occurs, the fault is most likely in the ignition coil because most module problems would have been found before this point in the procedure. A GM HEI module tester (Kent Moore J-24642-F) can determine which is at fault.

7   If you cannot obtain the module tester, take the vehicle to a dealer at this point.

Direct Ignition System (DIS)

8   If the engine misfires at idle, perform the first test indicated in the accompanying diagnostic flow chart **(see illustration)**. If the engine misfires under a load, proceed to Step 13.

9   Test #2 **(see illustration 5.8)**: Use a spark tester to verify adequate available secondary voltage (25,000 volts) at the spark plug.

10   Test #3 **(see illustration 5.8)**: If the spark jumps the test gap after grounding the opposite plug wire, it indicates excessive resistance in the plug which was bypassed. A faulty or poor connection at that plug could also result in a miss condition. Also check for carbon deposits inside the spark plug boot.

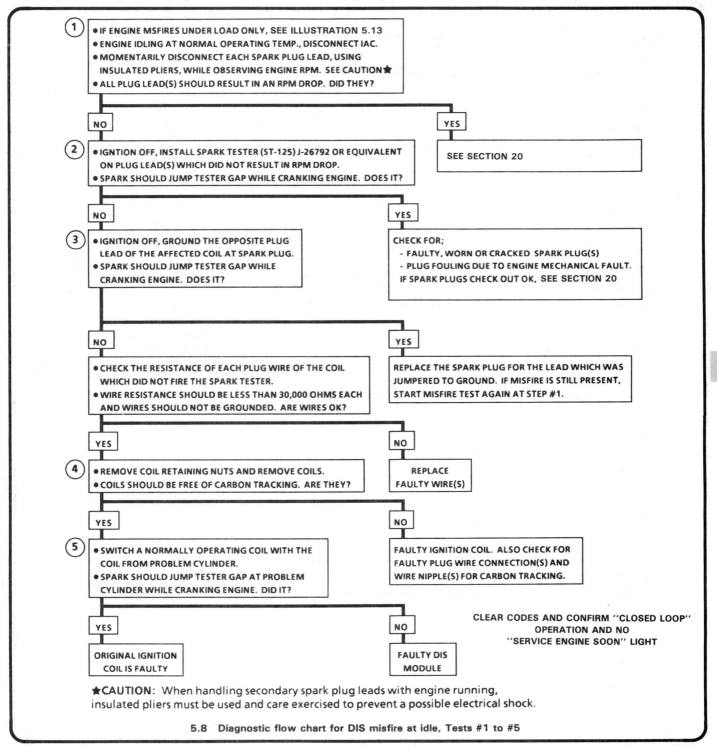

5.8   Diagnostic flow chart for DIS misfire at idle, Tests #1 to #5

11 Test #4 (see illustration 5.8): If carbon tracking is evident, replace the coil and be sure that the plug wires relating to that coil are clean and tight. Excessive wire resistance or faulty connections could cause damage to the coil.

12 Test #5 (see illustration 5.8): If a no spark condition disappears when the coil is switched for another coil, the original coil is faulty. If not, the ignition module is the cause of the no spark condition. This test can also be performed by substituting a known good coil for the one causing the no spark condition.

13 If the engine misfires under a load, perform test #6 on the accom-

panying diagnostic flow chart (see illustration). Use a spark tester to verify adequate available secondary voltage (25,000 volts) at the spark plug. The spark should jump the test gap on all four leads. This simulates a ''load'' condition.

14 Test #7 (see illustration 5.13): If the spark jumps the tester gap after grounding the opposite plug wire, it indicates excessive resistance in the plug which was bypassed. A faulty or poor connection at that plug could also result in the miss condition. Also check for carbon deposits inside the spark plug boot.

15 Test #8 (see illustration 5.13): If carbon tracking is evident, replace

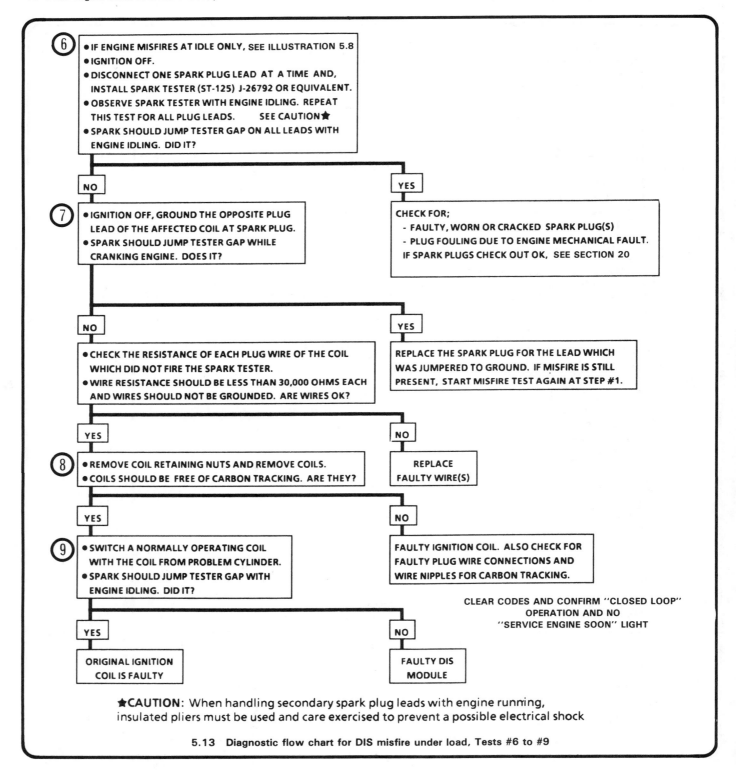

5.13   Diagnostic flow chart for DIS misfire under load, Tests #6 to #9

the coil and be sure that the plug wires attached to that coil are clean and tight. Excessive wire resistance or faulty connections could damage the coil.

16 Test #9 **(see illustration 5.13)**: If the no spark condition vanishes when the suspected coil is replaced by one of the other coils, that coil is faulty. If not, the ignition module is the reason there is no spark.

This test could also be performed by substituting a known good coil for the one causing the no spark condition.

C3I

Type I module/coil assembly

17 **Note:** *Determining whether the module/coil assembly in your ve-*

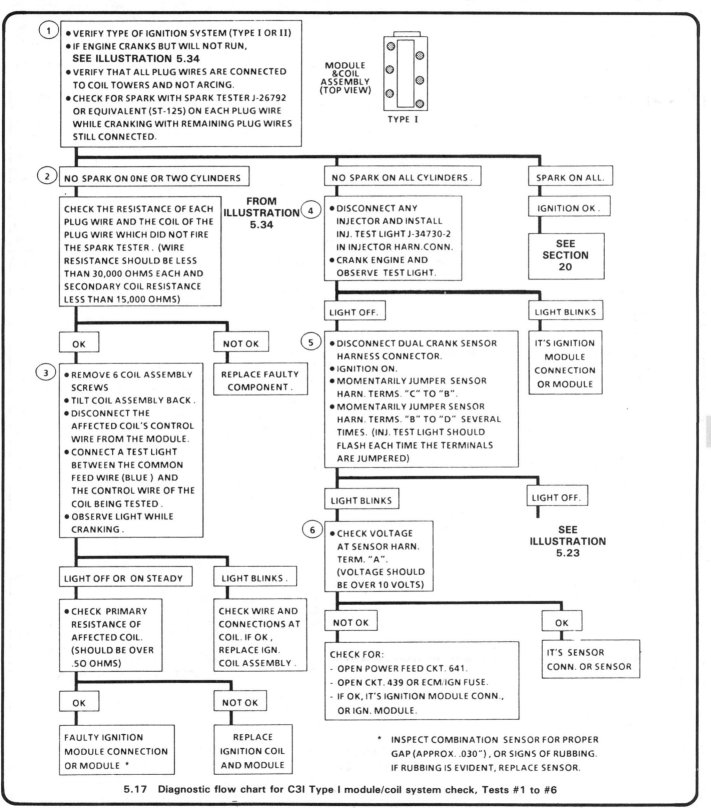

5.17   **Diagnostic flow chart for C3I Type I module/coil system check, Tests #1 to #6**

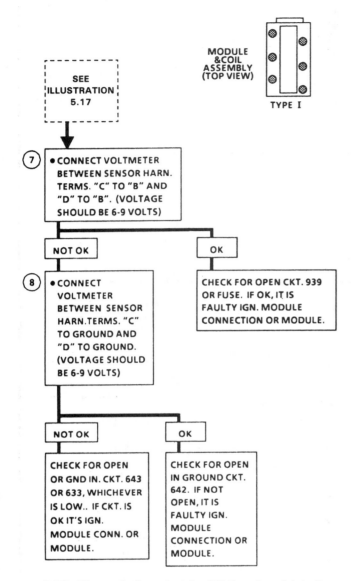

MODULE
&COIL
ASSEMBLY
(TOP VIEW)

TYPE I

7 • CONNECT VOLTMETER BETWEEN SENSOR HARN. TERMS. "C" TO "B" AND "D" TO "B". (VOLTAGE SHOULD BE 6-9 VOLTS)

NOT OK / OK

8 • CONNECT VOLTMETER BETWEEN SENSOR HARN. TERMS. "C" TO GROUND AND "D" TO GROUND. (VOLTAGE SHOULD BE 6-9 VOLTS)

CHECK FOR OPEN CKT. 939 OR FUSE. IF OK, IT IS FAULTY IGN. MODULE CONNECTION OR MODULE.

NOT OK / OK

CHECK FOR OPEN OR GND IN. CKT. 643 OR 633, WHICHEVER IS LOW.. IF CKT. IS OK IT'S IGN. MODULE CONN. OR MODULE.

CHECK FOR OPEN IN GROUND CKT. 642. IF NOT OPEN, IT IS FAULTY IGN. MODULE CONNECTION OR MODULE.

5.23 Diagnostic flow chart for C3I Type I module/coil system check, Tests #7 and #8

hicle is Type I or II is very important because Type I diagnostics will not work on a Type II system, or vice versa. If you determine that it is a Type I, proceed with the following series of tests. If it's a Type II, go to Step 25. If the engine cranks but will not run, perform the sequence of checks beginning with Step 34, then return to Step 20 (Test #4) of this procedure. If a plug wire is open, the other plug on that coil may still fire at idle. Test #1 **(see illustration)** verifies the ability of the system to produce at least 25,000 volts.

18 Test #2 **(see illustration 5.17)**: No spark on one cylinder may be caused by an open plug wire or secondary winding. Therefore, both wires related to a coil and the secondary winding resistance should be checked. Resistance readings over the upper limit but not infinite will probably not cause a no start condition but may cause an engine miss under certain conditions.

19 Test #3 **(see illustration 5.17)** tests the triggering circuit in the ignition module. A blinking light indicates the module is triggering. The wiring diagrams at the end of this book show the control wire color for each coil. For example, if you are testing why the #1 plug did not fire, connect the test light between the blue feed wire and the yellow/black control wire.

20 Test #4 **(see illustration 5.17)** determines whether the ECM is see-

ing the cam and crank sensor signals. If the test light blinks, the ECM is receiving good cam and crank signals, so the problem is a faulty module connection or module.

21 Test #5 **(see illustration 5.17)** provides the ECM with substitute cam and crank signals. The ECM must see a cam signal first before it will recognize the crank signal. Momentarily jumping the cam signal first is therefore very important in making an accurate test at this point.

22 Test #6 **(see illustration 5.17)** determines whether the problem is in the cam or the crank sensor, the ignition module or the power circuits.

23 Test #7 **(see illustration)** is supplied by the module and is pulled low each time the crank signal occurs.

24 Test #8 **(see illustration 5.23)** checks to see if the problem is the ground (circuit 643), the cam signal (circuit 633) or the ignition module.

Type II module/coil assembly

25 **Note:** *Determining whether the module/coil assembly in your vehicle is Type I or II is very important because Type I diagnostics will not work on a Type II system, or vice versa.* If you determine that it is a Type I, see Steps 17 to 24 above. If it's a Type II, perform the following series of tests. If the engine cranks but will not run, perform the sequence of checks beginning with Step 34, then return to Step 28 (Test #4) of this procedure. If a plug wire is open, the other plug on that coil may still fire at idle. Test #1 **(see illustration)** verifies the ability of the system to produce at least 25,000 volts.

26 Test #2 **(see illustration 5.25)**: No spark on one cylinder may be caused by an open plug wire or secondary winding. Both wires related to a coil and the secondary winding resistance should therefore be checked. Resistance readings over the upper limit, but not infinite, will probably not cause a no start but may cause an engine miss under certain conditions.

27 Test #3 **(see illustration 5.25)** tests the triggering circuit in the ignition module. A blinking light indicates the module is triggering.

28 Test #4 **(see illustration 5.25)**: A slowly blinking light, at this point, indicates the ECM is not seeing a crank sensor signal.

29 Test #5 **(see illustration 5.25)**: At this point, the cam sensor and its control circuits have proved to be good. The problem is in the combination sensor, sensor circuits or the ignition module.

30 Test #6 **(see illustration)**: Turn the ignition on and listen for the fuel pump within the first two seconds. If the fuel pump runs, the fuse is okay.

31 Test #7 **(see illustration 5.30)** checks to see if a problem is a grounded crank signal circuit or a cam signal circuit fault.

32 The ignition module supplies the power to operate the sensor. Test #8 **(see illustration 5.30)** checks to see if the problem is the module or the harness.

33 Test #6 checked the fuse. Test #9 determines whether the problem is in circuit 939 (see Wiring Diagrams at the end of this book) between the fuse and the ignition module or is in the module itself.

Engine cranks but won't run

34 Test #1 **(see illustration)**: A ''service engine soon'' light is a basic check for ignition and battery supply to the ECM.

35 Test #2 **(see illustration 5.34)** checks to see if the ECM is controlling the fuel injectors. A blinking test light at this point indicates that the ECM is controlling the injectors and that ignition reference signal to the ECM is good.

36 Test #3 **(see illustration 5.34)** checks to see if the problem is fuel or ignition related.

37 Test #4 **(see illustration 5.34)** checks to see if the fuel pump and relay are operating correctly. The fuel pump should run for only two seconds after the ignition is turned on.

38 Test #5 **(see illustration 5.34)** checks to see if the ECM is receiving a reference signal from the ignition system.

---

6 HEI distributor — removal and installation

2.5L four-cylinder engine
Refer to illustrations 6.4 and 6.5
Removal
1   Disconnect the cable from the negative battery terminal.
2   Remove the coil wire from the distributor cap.
3   Remove the distributor cap.

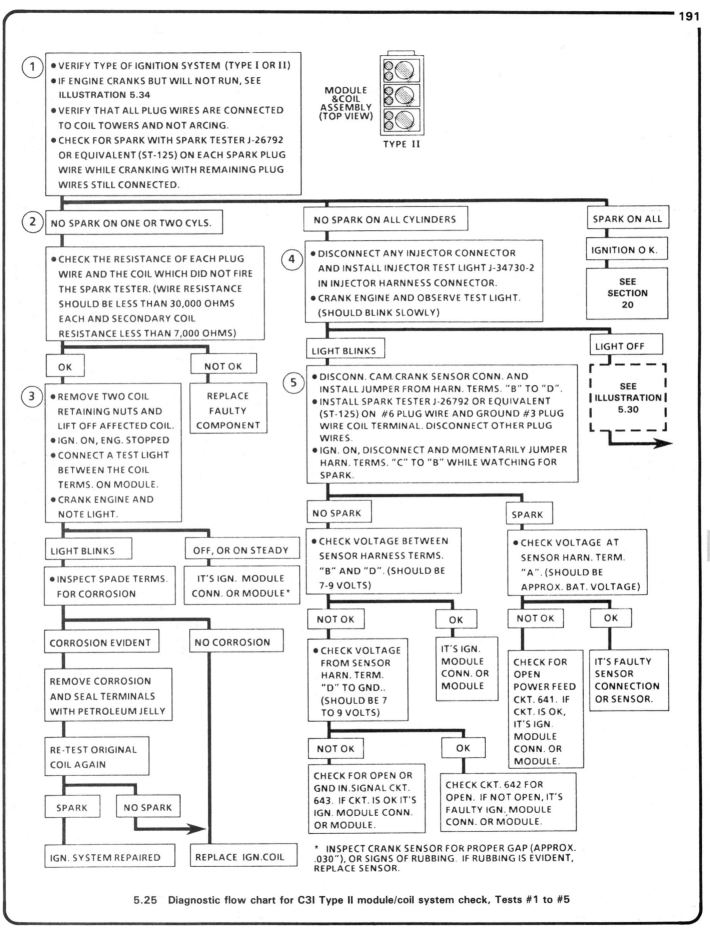

1
- VERIFY TYPE OF IGNITION SYSTEM (TYPE I OR II)
- IF ENGINE CRANKS BUT WILL NOT RUN, SEE ILLUSTRATION 5.34
- VERIFY THAT ALL PLUG WIRES ARE CONNECTED TO COIL TOWERS AND NOT ARCING.
- CHECK FOR SPARK WITH SPARK TESTER J-26792 OR EQUIVALENT (ST-125) ON EACH SPARK PLUG WIRE WHILE CRANKING WITH REMAINING PLUG WIRES STILL CONNECTED.

MODULE &COIL ASSEMBLY (TOP VIEW)

TYPE II

2 NO SPARK ON ONE OR TWO CYLS.

- CHECK THE RESISTANCE OF EACH PLUG WIRE AND THE COIL WHICH DID NOT FIRE THE SPARK TESTER. (WIRE RESISTANCE SHOULD BE LESS THAN 30,000 OHMS EACH AND SECONDARY COIL RESISTANCE LESS THAN 7,000 OHMS)

OK | NOT OK

3
- REMOVE TWO COIL RETAINING NUTS AND LIFT OFF AFFECTED COIL.
- IGN. ON, ENG. STOPPED
- CONNECT A TEST LIGHT BETWEEN THE COIL TERMS. ON MODULE.
- CRANK ENGINE AND NOTE LIGHT.

REPLACE FAULTY COMPONENT

LIGHT BLINKS | OFF, OR ON STEADY

- INSPECT SPADE TERMS. FOR CORROSION

IT'S IGN. MODULE CONN. OR MODULE *

CORROSION EVIDENT | NO CORROSION

REMOVE CORROSION AND SEAL TERMINALS WITH PETROLEUM JELLY

RE-TEST ORIGINAL COIL AGAIN

SPARK | NO SPARK

IGN. SYSTEM REPAIRED | REPLACE IGN. COIL

NO SPARK ON ALL CYLINDERS

4
- DISCONNECT ANY INJECTOR CONNECTOR AND INSTALL INJECTOR TEST LIGHT J-34730-2 IN INJECTOR HARNNESS CONNECTOR.
- CRANK ENGINE AND OBSERVE TEST LIGHT. (SHOULD BLINK SLOWLY)

LIGHT BLINKS

5
- DISCONN. CAM CRANK SENSOR CONN. AND INSTALL JUMPER FROM HARN. TERMS. "B" TO "D".
- INSTALL SPARK TESTER J-26792 OR EQUIVALENT (ST-125) ON #6 PLUG WIRE AND GROUND #3 PLUG WIRE COIL TERMINAL. DISCONNECT OTHER PLUG WIRES.
- IGN. ON, DISCONNECT AND MOMENTARILY JUMPER HARN. TERMS. "C" TO "B" WHILE WATCHING FOR SPARK.

NO SPARK | SPARK

- CHECK VOLTAGE BETWEEN SENSOR HARNESS TERMS. "B" AND "D". (SHOULD BE 7-9 VOLTS)

- CHECK VOLTAGE AT SENSOR HARN. TERM. "A". (SHOULD BE APPROX. BAT. VOLTAGE)

NOT OK | OK

- CHECK VOLTAGE FROM SENSOR HARN. TERM. "D" TO GND.. (SHOULD BE 7 TO 9 VOLTS)

IT'S IGN. MODULE CONN. OR MODULE

NOT OK | OK

CHECK FOR OPEN POWER FEED CKT. 641. IF CKT. IS OK, IT'S IGN. MODULE CONN. OR MODULE.

IT'S FAULTY SENSOR CONNECTION OR SENSOR.

NOT OK | OK

CHECK FOR OPEN OR GND IN SIGNAL CKT. 643. IF CKT. IS OK IT'S IGN. MODULE CONN. OR MODULE.

CHECK CKT. 642 FOR OPEN. IF NOT OPEN, IT'S FAULTY IGN. MODULE CONN. OR MODULE.

* INSPECT CRANK SENSOR FOR PROPER GAP (APPROX. .030"), OR SIGNS OF RUBBING. IF RUBBING IS EVIDENT, REPLACE SENSOR.

SPARK ON ALL

IGNITION O K.

SEE SECTION 20

LIGHT OFF

SEE ILLUSTRATION 5.30

 5

5.25 Diagnostic flow chart for C3I Type II module/coil system check, Tests #1 to #5

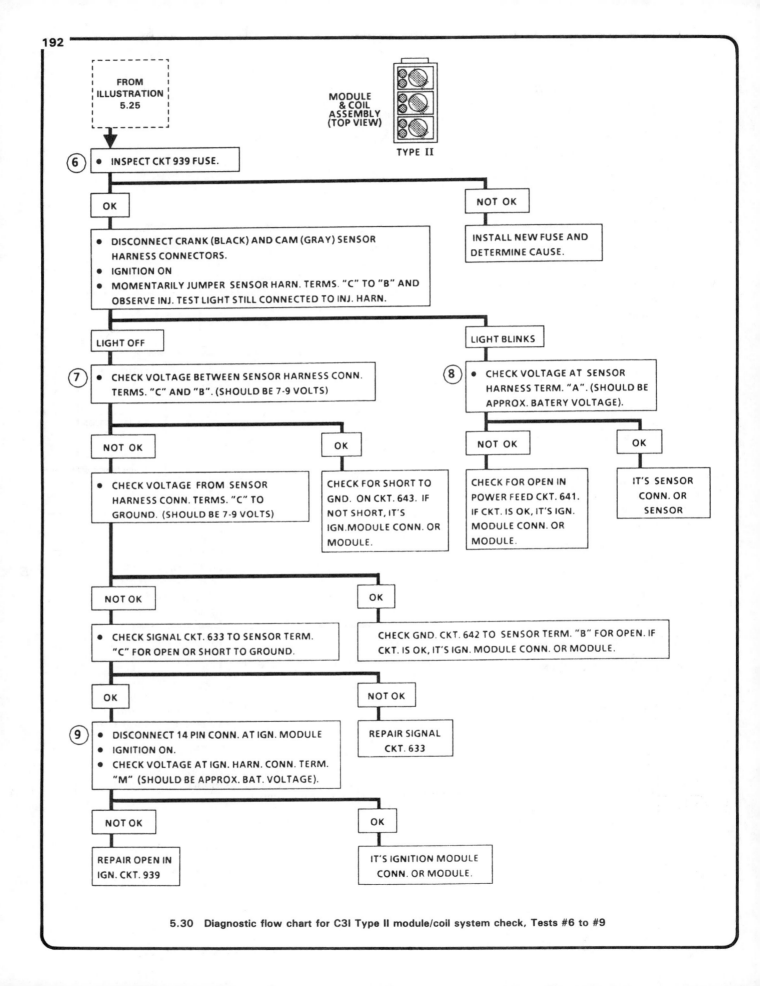

FROM ILLUSTRATION 5.25

MODULE & COIL ASSEMBLY (TOP VIEW)

TYPE II

6 • INSPECT CKT 939 FUSE.

OK

NOT OK

INSTALL NEW FUSE AND DETERMINE CAUSE.

• DISCONNECT CRANK (BLACK) AND CAM (GRAY) SENSOR HARNESS CONNECTORS.
• IGNITION ON
• MOMENTARILY JUMPER SENSOR HARN. TERMS. "C" TO "B" AND OBSERVE INJ. TEST LIGHT STILL CONNECTED TO INJ. HARN.

LIGHT OFF

LIGHT BLINKS

7 • CHECK VOLTAGE BETWEEN SENSOR HARNESS CONN. TERMS. "C" AND "B". (SHOULD BE 7-9 VOLTS)

8 • CHECK VOLTAGE AT SENSOR HARNESS TERM. "A". (SHOULD BE APPROX. BATERY VOLTAGE).

NOT OK

OK

NOT OK

OK

• CHECK VOLTAGE FROM SENSOR HARNESS CONN. TERMS. "C" TO GROUND. (SHOULD BE 7-9 VOLTS)

CHECK FOR SHORT TO GND. ON CKT. 643. IF NOT SHORT, IT'S IGN.MODULE CONN. OR MODULE.

CHECK FOR OPEN IN POWER FEED CKT. 641. IF CKT. IS OK, IT'S IGN. MODULE CONN. OR MODULE.

IT'S SENSOR CONN. OR SENSOR

NOT OK

OK

• CHECK SIGNAL CKT. 633 TO SENSOR TERM. "C" FOR OPEN OR SHORT TO GROUND.

CHECK GND. CKT. 642 TO SENSOR TERM. "B" FOR OPEN. IF CKT. IS OK, IT'S IGN. MODULE CONN. OR MODULE.

OK

NOT OK

9 • DISCONNECT 14 PIN CONN. AT IGN. MODULE
• IGNITION ON.
• CHECK VOLTAGE AT IGN. HARN. CONN. TERM. "M" (SHOULD BE APPROX. BAT. VOLTAGE).

REPAIR SIGNAL CKT. 633

NOT OK

OK

REPAIR OPEN IN IGN. CKT. 939

IT'S IGNITION MODULE CONN. OR MODULE.

5.30   Diagnostic flow chart for C3I Type II module/coil system check, Tests #6 to #9

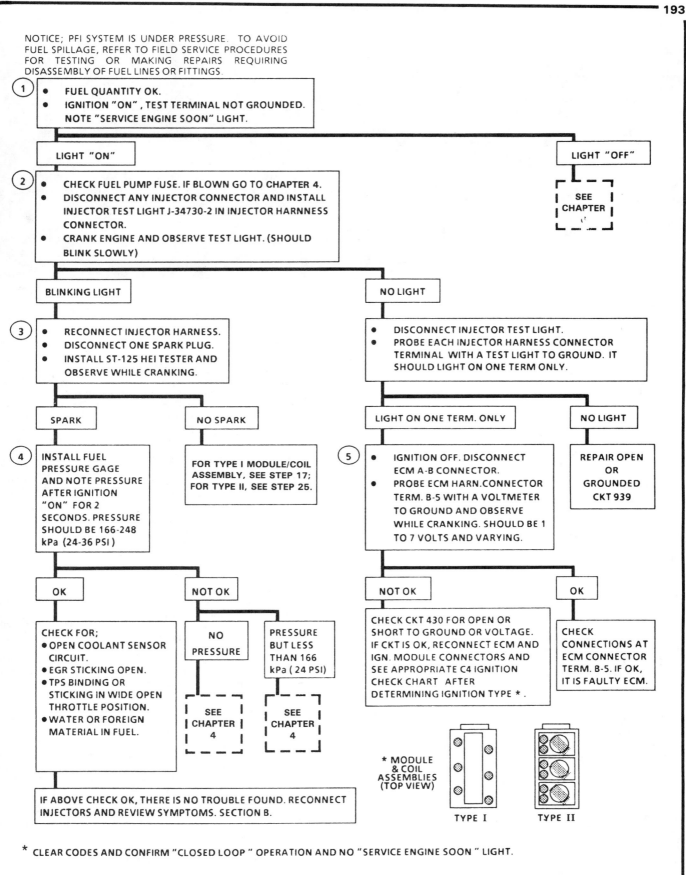

NOTICE; PFI SYSTEM IS UNDER PRESSURE. TO AVOID FUEL SPILLAGE, REFER TO FIELD SERVICE PROCEDURES FOR TESTING OR MAKING REPAIRS REQUIRING DISASSEMBLY OF FUEL LINES OR FITTINGS.

1
- FUEL QUANTITY OK.
- IGNITION "ON", TEST TERMINAL NOT GROUNDED. NOTE "SERVICE ENGINE SOON" LIGHT.

LIGHT "ON"

LIGHT "OFF"

SEE CHAPTER

2
- CHECK FUEL PUMP FUSE. IF BLOWN GO TO CHAPTER 4.
- DISCONNECT ANY INJECTOR CONNECTOR AND INSTALL INJECTOR TEST LIGHT J-34730-2 IN INJECTOR HARNNESS CONNECTOR.
- CRANK ENGINE AND OBSERVE TEST LIGHT. (SHOULD BLINK SLOWLY)

BLINKING LIGHT

NO LIGHT

3
- RECONNECT INJECTOR HARNESS.
- DISCONNECT ONE SPARK PLUG.
- INSTALL ST-125 HEI TESTER AND OBSERVE WHILE CRANKING.

- DISCONNECT INJECTOR TEST LIGHT.
- PROBE EACH INJECTOR HARNESS CONNECTOR TERMINAL WITH A TEST LIGHT TO GROUND. IT SHOULD LIGHT ON ONE TERM ONLY.

SPARK

NO SPARK

LIGHT ON ONE TERM. ONLY

NO LIGHT

4 INSTALL FUEL PRESSURE GAGE AND NOTE PRESSURE AFTER IGNITION "ON" FOR 2 SECONDS. PRESSURE SHOULD BE 166-248 kPa (24-36 PSI)

FOR TYPE I MODULE/COIL ASSEMBLY, SEE STEP 17; FOR TYPE II, SEE STEP 25.

5
- IGNITION OFF. DISCONNECT ECM A-B CONNECTOR.
- PROBE ECM HARN.CONNECTOR TERM. B-5 WITH A VOLTMETER TO GROUND AND OBSERVE WHILE CRANKING. SHOULD BE 1 TO 7 VOLTS AND VARYING.

REPAIR OPEN OR GROUNDED CKT 939

5

OK

NOT OK

NOT OK

OK

CHECK FOR;
- OPEN COOLANT SENSOR CIRCUIT.
- EGR STICKING OPEN.
- TPS BINDING OR STICKING IN WIDE OPEN THROTTLE POSITION.
- WATER OR FOREIGN MATERIAL IN FUEL.

NO PRESSURE

PRESSURE BUT LESS THAN 166 kPa (24 PSI)

SEE CHAPTER 4

SEE CHAPTER 4

CHECK CKT 430 FOR OPEN OR SHORT TO GROUND OR VOLTAGE. IF CKT IS OK, RECONNECT ECM AND IGN. MODULE CONNECTORS AND SEE APPROPRIATE C4 IGNITION CHECK CHART AFTER DETERMINING IGNITION TYPE * .

CHECK CONNECTIONS AT ECM CONNECTOR TERM. B-5. IF OK, IT IS FAULTY ECM.

* MODULE & COIL ASSEMBLIES (TOP VIEW)

TYPE I

TYPE II

IF ABOVE CHECK OK, THERE IS NO TROUBLE FOUND. RECONNECT INJECTORS AND REVIEW SYMPTOMS. SECTION B.

* CLEAR CODES AND CONFIRM "CLOSED LOOP " OPERATION AND NO "SERVICE ENGINE SOON " LIGHT.

5.34 Diagnostic flow chart for a 3.0L V6 or 2.0 Turbo four engine that cranks but will not run, Tests #1 to #5

6.4 Mark the position of the rotor with respect to the distributor before removing the rotor (HEI distributor on 2.5L four)

6.5 The distributor hold-down clamp and bolt must be removed before the distributor can be removed from the engine (HEI distributor on 2.5L four)

4   Note the position of the rotor and the distributor-to-block alignment. Make an alignment mark on the distributor to indicate the position of the rotor (see illustration).

5   Remove the distributor hold-down clamp bolt and clamp (see illustration). Remove the distributor from the engine. Caution: *Do not turn the crankshaft while the distributor is removed from the engine. If the crankshaft is turned, the position of the rotor will be altered and the engine will have to be retimed.*

Installation (crankshaft not turned after distributor removal)

6   Insert the distributor into the engine in exactly the same relation to the block in which it was removed. To mesh the gears, it may be necessary to turn the rotor slightly. At this point the distributor may not seat down against the block completely. This is due to the lower end of the distributor shaft not mating properly with the oil pump shaft. If this is the case, check again to make sure the distributor is aligned with the block in the same position it was in before removal and that the rotor is correctly aligned with the distributor body. The gear on the distributor shaft is engaged with the gear on the camshaft, and this relationship cannot change as long as the distributor is not lifted from the engine. Use a socket and breaker bar on the crankshaft bolt to turn the engine over in the normal direction of rotation. The rotor will turn, but the oil pump shaft will not because the two shafts are not engaged. When the proper alignment is reached the distributor will drop down over the oil pump shaft, and the distributor body will seat properly against the block.

7   Install the hold-down clamp and tighten the bolt securely.

8   Install the distributor cap and coil wire.

9   Connect the cable to the negative terminal of the battery.

Installation (crankshaft turned after distributor removal)

10 Remove the number one spark plug.

11 Place your finger over the spark plug hole while turning the crankshaft in the normal direction of rotation with a wrench on the pulley bolt at the front of the engine.

12 When you feel compression, continue turning the crankshaft slowly until the timing mark on the crankshaft pulley is aligned with the ''0'' on the engine timing indicator.

13 Position the rotor to point to between the number one and number three distributor terminals.

14 Insert the distributor into the engine in exactly the same relation to the block in which it was removed. To mesh the gears, it may be necessary to turn the rotor slightly. If the distributor does not seat fully against the block it is because the oil pump shaft has not seated in the distributor shaft. Make sure the distributor drive gear is fully engaged with the camshaft gear, then use a socket on the crankshaft bolt to turn the engine over in the normal direction of rotation until the two shafts engage and the distributor seats against the block.

15 Install the hold-down clamp and tighten the bolt securely.

16 Install the distributor cap and coil wire.

17 Connect the cable to the negative terminal of the battery.

3.0L V6 engine

Removal

18 Disconnect the cable from the negative battery terminal.

19 Disconnect the ignition switch battery feed wire and the tachometer lead, if so equipped, from the distributor cap.

20 Disconnect the coil connector from the cap. Depress the locking tabs by hand. Caution: *Do not use a screwdriver or other tool to release the locking tabs.*

21 Turn the four distributor cap locking screws counterclockwise, remove the cap and position it out of the way.

22 Disconnect the four-terminal ECM wiring harness connector from the distributor.

23 If necessary for clearance, on distributor caps with a secondary wiring harness attached to the cap, release the wiring harness latches and remove the wiring harness retainer. Note that the spark plug wire numbers are indicated on the retainer.

24 Make matching marks on the base of the distributor and the engine block to insure that you will be able to put the distributor back in the same position.

25 Remove the distributor hold-down clamp bolt and the hold-down clamp.

26 Make a mark on the distributor housing to show the direction the rotor is pointing. Lift the distributor slowly. As you lift it the rotor will turn slightly. When it stops turning make another mark on the distributor body to show where it is pointing when the gear on the distributor is disengaged. This is the position the rotor should be in when you begin reinstallation.

27 Remove the distributor. Caution: *Avoid turning the crankshaft while the distributor is removed. Turning the crankshaft while the distributor is removed will change the timing position of the rotor and require re-timing the engine.*

Installation (crankshaft not turned after distributor removal)

28 Position the rotor in the exact location (second mark on the housing) it was in when the distributor was removed.

29 Lower the distributor into the engine. To mesh the gears at the bottom of the distributor it may be necessary to turn the rotor slightly. It is possible that the distributor may not seat down fully against the block because the lower part of the distributor shaft has not properly engaged the oil pump shaft. Make sure the distributor and rotor are properly aligned with the marks made earlier, then use a large socket and breaker bar on the crankshaft bolt to turn the engine in the normal direction of rotation until the two shafts engage and the distributor drops down against the block.

30 With the base of the distributor seated against the engine block turn the distributor housing to align the marks made on the distributor base and the engine block.

31 With the distributor properly seated, and the marks aligned, the rotor should point to the first mark made on the distributor housing.

32 Place the hold-down clamp in position and loosely install the hold-

down bolt.

33 Reconnect the ignition wiring harness.

34 Install the distributor cap. If the secondary wiring harness was removed from the cap, reinstall it.

35 Reconnect the coil connector.

36 With the distributor in its original position, tighten the hold-down bolt and check the ignition timing (Chapter 1).

Installation (crankshaft turned after distributor removal)

37 Remove the number one spark plug.

38 Place your finger over the spark plug hole while turning the crankshaft with a wrench on the pulley bolt at the front of the engine.

39 When you feel compression, continue turning the crankshaft slowly until the timing mark on the crankshaft pulley is aligned with the ''O'' on the engine timing indicator.

40 Position the rotor between the number one and six spark plug terminals on the cap.

41 Lower the distributor into the engine. To mesh the gears at the bottom of the distributor, it may be necessary to turn the rotor slightly. If the distributor does not drop down flush against the block it is because the distributor shaft has not mated to the oil pump shaft. Place a large socket and breaker bar on the crankshaft bolt and turn the engine over in the normal direction of rotation until the two shafts engage properly, allowing the distributor to seat flush against the block.

42 With the base of the distributor properly seated against the engine block, turn the distributor housing to align the marks made on the distributor base and the engine block.

43 With the distributor all the way down and the marks aligned, the rotor should point to the first mark made on the distributor housing.

44 Place the hold-down clamp in position and loosely install the hold-down bolt.

45 Reconnect the ignition wiring harness.

46 Install the distributor cap. If the secondary wiring harness was removed from the cap, reinstall it.

47 Reconnect the coil connector.

48 With the distributor in its original position, tighten the hold-down bolt and check the ignition timing.

2.0L OHC four-cylinder engine

Refer to illustrations 6.52 and 6.53

Removal

49 Disconnect the negative cable at the battery.

50 Remove the air cleaner assembly.

51 Remove the distributor cap.

52 Connect the battery negative cable temporarily so the engine can be rotated with the starter until the distributor rotor points straight up **(see illustration)**.

53 Scribe a line across the distributor body and base for reference during installation **(see illustration)**.

54 Unplug the electrical connectors from the ignition coil and the distributor.

55 Remove the two retaining nuts and lift the distributor from the engine.

Installation

56 Place the distributor in position, align the drive tabs with the slot in the camshaft and insert, lining up the marks made during removal. Install the retaining nuts and tighten them securely.

57 Plug in the electrical connectors and install the distributor cap.

58 Install the air cleaner assembly.

59 Connect the battery negative cable.

---

7 Ignition module — check and replacement

HEI

Refer to illustrations 7.4, 7.6, 7.11, 7.14, 7.16a, 7.16b, 7.22 and 7.24

Note: *It is not necessary to remove the distributor to check or replace the module.*

Check

1 Disconnect the tachometer (if so equipped) at the distributor.

2 Check for a spark at the coil and spark plug wires (Section 5).

3 If there is no spark, remove the distributor cap. Remove the ignition module from the distributor but leave the connector plugged in.

4 With the ignition switch turned On, check for voltage at the module positive terminal **(see illustration)**.

6.52 The distributor rotor must be pointed straight up (in the direction of the arrow) prior to removal (2.0L OHC Turbo four)

6.53 A line scribed across the distributor and block (arrow) will make installation easier (2.0L OHC Turbo four)

7.4 To check the module for voltage, insert the voltmeter probe into the module positive terminal (arrow)

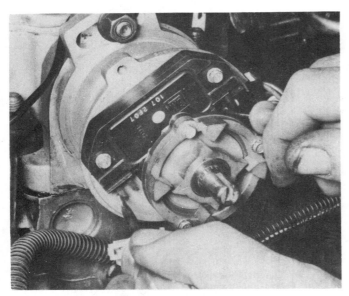

7.6   With a test light connected at terminal "P," check the voltage with the meter probe at the "C" terminal

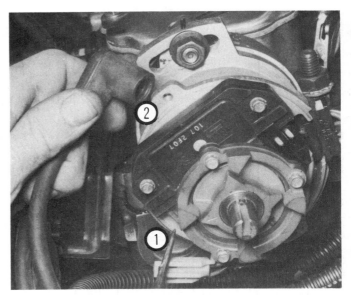

7.11   As the test light probe (1) is removed, check for a spark at the coil wire (2)

7.14   The ignition module is secured by two mounting screws (arrows)

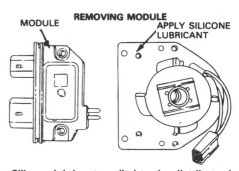

7.16a   Silicone lubricant applied to the distributor base in the area under the ignition module dissipates heat (separate coil distributor)

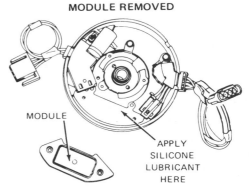

7.16b   Module silicone lubricant application (coil-in-cap models)

5   If the reading is less than ten volts, there is a fault in the wire between the module positive (+) terminal and the ignition coil positive connector or the ignition coil and primary circuit-to-ignition switch.

6   If the reading is ten volts or more, check the "C" terminal on the module **(see illustration)**.

7   If the reading is less than one volt, there is an open or grounded lead in the distributor-to-coil "C" terminal connection or ignition coil or an open primary circuit in the coil itself.

8   If the reading is one to ten volts, replace the module with a new one and check for a spark (Section 5). If there is a spark the module was faulty and the system is now operating properly. If there is no spark, there is a fault in the ignition coil.

9   If the reading in Step 4 is 10 volts or more, unplug the pickup coil connector from the module. Check the "C" terminal voltage with the ignition switch On and watch the voltage reading as a test light is momentarily (five seconds or less) connected between the battery positive (+) terminal and the module "P" terminal **(see illustration 7.6)**.

10   If there is no drop in voltage, check the module ground and, if it is good, replace the module with a new one.

11   If the voltage drops, check for spark at the coil wire as the test light is removed from the module terminal. If there is no spark, the module is faulty and should be replaced with a new one. If there is a spark, the pickup coil or connections are faulty or not grounded **(see illustration)**.

Replacement (2.5L four-cylinder engine)

12   Detach the cable from the negative terminal of the battery.

13   Remove the distributor cap and rotor (see Chapter 1).

14   Remove both module attaching screws and lift the module up and away from the distributor **(see illustration)**.

15   Disconnect both electrical leads from the module. Note that the leads cannot be interchanged.

16   Do not wipe the grease from the module or the distributor base if the same module is to be reinstalled. If a new module is to be installed,

7.22 Remove the ignition module retaining screws (arrows)

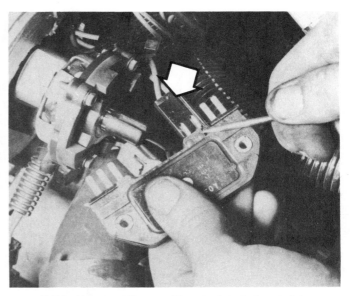

7.24 Use a small screwdriver to detach the module electrical connector (arrow)

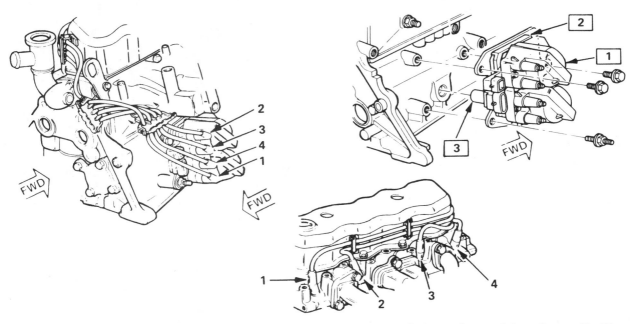

7.32 The coil high tension terminals (2, 3, 4 and 1) and their respective cylinder numbers and the coil assembly (1), ignition module (2) and sensor (3) of a typical DIS system (2.5L four)

a package of silicone grease will be included with it. Wipe the distributor base and the new module clean, then apply the silicone grease on the face of the module and on the distributor base where the module seats **(see illustrations)**. This grease is necessary for heat dissipation.

17 Install the module and attach both electrical leads.
18 Install the distributor rotor and cap (see Chapter 1).
19 Attach the cable to the negative terminal of the battery.

Replacement (2.0L OHC Turbo four-cylinder engine)
20 Detach the cable from the negative terminal of the battery.
21 Remove the distributor cap and rotor (see Chapter 1).
22 Remove the module retaining screws **(see illustration)**.
23 Rotate the module clear of the distributor.
24 Unplug the connectors and remove the module **(see illustration)**.
25 Coat the back of the module with silicone grease.
26 Plug in the electrical connector, rotate the module into position and install the retaining screws, tightening them securely.

27 Install the distributor rotor and cap (see Chapter 1).
28 Attach the cable to the negative terminal of the battery.

Distributorless ignition
See illustrations 7.32, 7.35, 7.39, 7.41, 7.44, 7.45, 7.52, 7.54, 7.55, 7.57 and 7.59
Check
29 See Section 5.
Replacement (2.5L four-cylinder engine)
30 Detach the cable from the negative terminal of the battery.
31 Unplug the electrical connectors from the module.
32 Detach the plug wires at the coil assembly **(see illustration)**.
33 Remove the module/coil assembly attaching bolts.
34 Remove the module/coil assembly. **Caution:** *The sensor is attached below the module. To avoid damage to the sensor, remove the module slowly and carefully.*

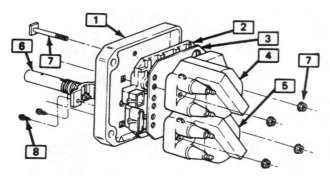

7.35 Exploded view of the DIS assembly

1 *Base plate*
2 *Module*
3 *Shield*
4 *Coil (#2 and #3 cylinders)*
5 *Coil (#1 and #4 cylinders)*
6 *Sensor*
7 *Mounting studs*
8 *Mounting screws*

7.39 Unbolt and unplug the connector from the right end of the C3I ignition coil/module assembly

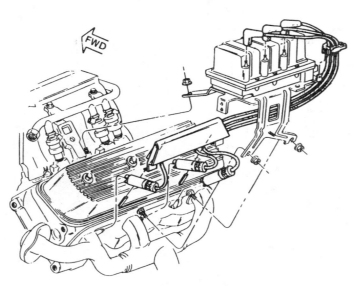

7.41 Exploded view of the C3I ignition coil/module assembly support bracket

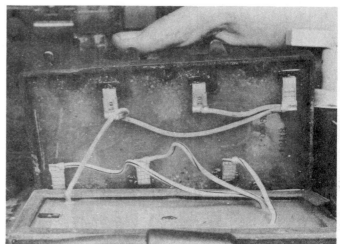

7.44 After removing the Torx screws that hold the coil and module assemblies together, label, then detach, the wire leads from the module

35 Remove the bolts attaching the coils to the module and separate the two assemblies **(see illustration)**.
36 Installation is the reverse of removal. Be careful when inserting the module/coil assembly to avoid damage to the sensor.

Replacement (V6 engine)
37 Detach the cable from the negative terminal of the battery.
38 Clearly label, then disconnect, all six spark plug wires from the coil.
39 Unbolt and unplug the electrical connector at the module **(see illustration)**.
40 Detach the vacuum lines and the electrical connector from the EGR valve solenoid on the left end of the coil/module assembly (see Chapter 6 if necessary).
41 Remove the front bracket leg mounting nut from the stud on the intake manifold (next to the EGR valve) and the two rear bracket nuts from the studs protruding from the exhaust manifold side of the rear cylinder head **(see illustration)**. **Note:** *It is possible to remove the coil/module assembly from the support bracket by removing the three nuts from the underside of the bracket* **(see illustration 7.45)**, *but it's difficult to get a wrench on these nuts.*
42 Remove the coil/module and support bracket assembly.
43 Using a Torx screwdriver or bit, remove the coil-to-module attaching screws and separate the coil and module assemblies.
44 Open the coil and module halves as shown **(see illustration)**. Label, then detach, the wires between the module and the coil assemblies from the spade terminals on the underside of the coils.
45 Unbolt the module **(see illustration)** from the support bracket.

7.45 To detach the C3I module from the support bracket, remove the three nuts

7.52 The electrical connector for the crankshaft sensor is located near the starter motor

7.54 To remove the sensor and pedestal assemblies, rotate the harmonic balancer until the windows (arrows) in the interrupter rings are lined up with the sensor and pedestal (in this photo the balancer has been removed and turned around so you can see the windows in the interrupter rings)

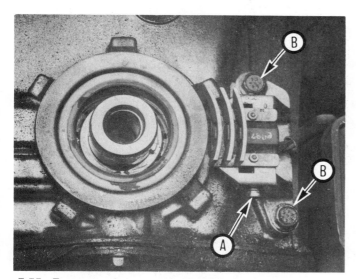

7.55 To remove the sensor, loosen the pinch bolt (A) and the two pedestal bolts (B), then slide the two assemblies sideways through the windows in the interrupter rings (the harmonic balancer has been removed for clarity in this photo)

7.57 Although you can't see this side when the sensor, pedestal and harmonic balancer are installed on the vehicle, this is what they look like when the sensor and pedestal assemblies are being removed

46 Installation is the reverse of removal. Be sure to attach the wires of the new module to the coil assembly spade terminals in exactly the same order in which they were removed.

Combination sensor check and replacement

47 Turn the harmonic balancer until the interrupter ring(s) fills the sensor slots and the edge of the interrupter window is aligned with the edge of the deflector on the pedestal.

48 Insert the special adjustment tool (Kent-Moore J-36179) or equivalent into the gap between the sensor and interrupter on each side of the interrupter ring (see illustration 7.59). If the gauge will not slide past the sensor on either side of the interrupter ring, the sensor is out of adjustment or the interrupter ring is bent. This clearance should be checked at three positions around the the outer interrupter ring, approximately 120° apart.

49 If the sensor is found to be out of adjustment, it should be removed and inspected for potential damage.

50 Detach the cable from the negative terminal of the battery.

51 Raise the vehicle and place it securely on jackstands.

52 Locate the combination sensor electrical connector (see illustration) near the starter motor.

53 Remove the right side lower engine compartment filler panel and the right lower wheel house-to-engine compartment bolt.

54 Turn the crankshaft balancer (see Chapter 2C) until the windows in both interrupter rings (see illustration) are lined up with the sensor.

55 Loosen the sensor pedestal pinch bolt (see illustration) until the sensor is free to slide in the pedestal.

56 Remove the pedestal-to-engine mounting bolts.

57 Carefully slide the sensor and pedestal assemblies sideways through the windows in the interrupter rings (see illustration). Be extremely careful — the size of the space afforded by the two overlapping windows of the interrupter rings is slightly smaller than the sensor itself. The sensor and pedestal assemblies must be worked out with a side to side motion as the harmonic balancer is slowly turned back and forth.

58 Installation is the reverse of removal.

5

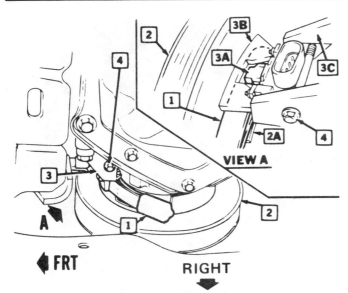

7.59   Study this drawing carefully before attempting to measure the gap between the sensor and the interrupter rings

1	Special tool (Kent-Moore J-36179)	3	Crankshaft position sensor assembly:
2	Crankshaft harmonic balancer assembly	3A	Sensor
		3B	Deflector
2A	Interrupter ring	3C	Pedestal
		4	Pinch bolt

59   To adjust the combination sensor loosen the pinch bolt on the sensor pedestal and insert the special adjustment tool (Kent-Moore J-36179) or equivalent into the gap between the sensor and the interrupter on each side of the interrupter ring **(see illustration)**.

60   Be sure that the interrupter is sandwiched between the blades of the adjustment tool and both blades are properly inserted into the sensor slot.

61   Tighten the sensor retaining pinch bolt securely while maintaining light pressure on the sensor against the gauge and the interrupter ring. This clearance should be checked again, at three positions around the interrupter ring, approximately 120° apart. If the interrupter ring contacts the sensor at any point during rotation of the harmonic balancer, the interrupter ring has excessive runout and must be replaced.

---

8   Ignition pickup coil — check and replacement

2.5L OHV four-cylinder engine
Refer to illustrations 8.5, 8.9 and 8.10

Removal

1   Detach the cable from the negative terminal of the battery.

2   Remove the distributor cap and rotor (see Chapter 1).

3   Remove the distributor from the engine (see Section 6).

4   Detach the pickup coil leads from the module.

Check

5   Connect one lead of an ohmmeter to the terminal of the pickup coil lead and the other to ground as shown **(see illustration)**. Flex the leads by hand to check for intermittent opens. The ohmmeter should indicate infinite resistance at all times. If it doesn't, the pickup coil is defective and must be replaced.

6   Connect the ohmmeter leads to both terminals of the pickup coil lead. Flex the leads by hand to check for intermittent opens. The ohmmeter should read one steady value between 500 and 1500 ohms as the leads are flexed by hand. If it doesn't, the pickup coil is defective and must be replaced.

Installation

7   Remove the spring from the distributor shaft.

8   Mark the distributor tang drive and shaft so that they can be re-

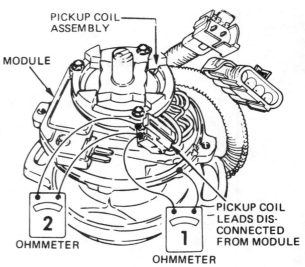

8.5   Pickup coil test connections

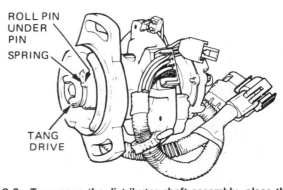

8.9   To remove the distributor shaft assembly, place the distributor assembly in a soft-jawed vise and knock out the roll pin with a punch and hammer

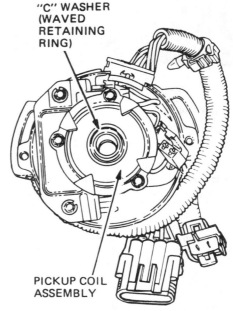

8.10   To remove the pickup coil assembly, you must first remove the "C" washer

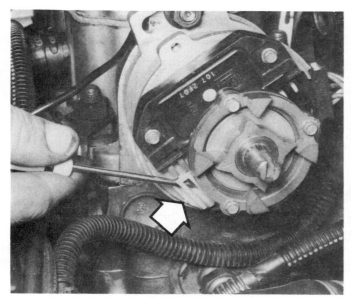

8.14 Use a small screwdriver to release the clip (arrow) on the pickup coil electrical connector

8.15 To check the resistance of the pickup coil, insert the probes of an ohmmeter into the pickup coil electrical connector

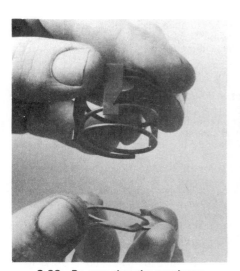

8.23 Be sure that the tensioner assembly is properly assembled

8.25 This is how the tensioner assembly looks when it is properly installed in the distributor body

8.28 Lower the distributor into the drive tang, aligning the shaft slot with the tang pin hole (arrow)

assembled in the same position.

9 Carefully mount the distributor in a soft-jawed vise and, using a hammer and punch, remove the roll pin from the distributor shaft and gear (see illustration).

10 To remove the pick up coil, remove the thin "C" washer (see illustration).

11 Lift the pickup coil assembly straight up and remove it from the distributor.

12 Reassembly is the reverse of disassembly.

13 Installation is the reverse of removal.

2.0L OHC Turbo four-cylinder engine

Refer to illustrations 8.14, 8.15, 8.23, 8.25, 8.28 and 8.30

Check

14 Remove the distributor cap and unplug the pickup coil connector (see illustration).

15 Check the pickup coil resistance with an ohmmeter. The meter should read between 500 and 1500 ohms (see illustration).

Replacement

16 Remove the distributor from the engine (Section 6).

17 Mount the distributor drive tang securely in a vise. Mark the tang and shaft so they can be reassembled in the same position.

18 Use a hammer and suitable size punch to drive out retaining pin. Have an assistant hold the distributor, as the shaft is spring loaded. Remove the shaft, spring and washers from the distributor body.

19 Remove the pole piece and pickup coil from the body.

20 Install the new pickup coil.

21 Install the pole piece with the screws snug.

22 Lubricate the shaft with light oil and insert it into the body.

23 Assemble the shaft tensioner assembly (see illustration).

24 Depress the spring and rotate the retainer counterclockwise to lock it.

25 Install the tensioner spring assembly into the body (see illustration).

26 Lightly oil the washer and install it over the spring assembly.

27 Mount the drive tang in the vise.

28 Align the marks made during disassembly and lower the distributor over the drive tang with the slot aligned with the pin hole (see illustration).

29 Insert the pin and drive it into place until the ends are flush with the shaft.

5

**8.30   This is how the retaining spring (arrow) looks when
it's properly installed over the drive tang**

30 Install the retaining spring over the drive tang (see illustration).
31 Position the pole piece so that it does not make contact when the
rotor is turned and tighten the screws securely.

---

9   Ignition coil — removal, check and installation

1   Disconnect the cable from the negative terminal of the battery.

HEI
Refer to illustration 9.12
Removal
2   On models with a separately mounted coil, unplug the coil high
tension wire and both electrical leads from the coil.
3   Remove both mounting nuts and remove the coil from the engine.
4   On models with the coil in the distributor cap, remove the coil cover
screws and lift off the cover. **Note:** *If you are just checking the coil,
it is not necessary to remove the coil from the cap. Refer to the checking
procedure below.*
5   Push the coil electrical leads through the top of the hood with a
small screwdriver.
6   Remove the coil mounting screws and lift the coil, with the leads,
from the cap.

Check
7   It is not necessary to remove the coil from the distributor cap on
coil-in-cap models to test the coil.
8   Disconnect the negative cable from the battery.
9   Remove the distributor cap and turn it over so the coil electrical
connectors are visible.
10   Connect an ohmmeter to the two outercoil terminals. It should indicate zero resistance. If it doesn't, replace the coil.
11   Connect the ohmmeter between one of the outer terminals and
the central coil-to-rotor contact with the ohmmeter on the high scale.
Repeat the test using the other terminal. If both terminals show infinite resistance, replace the coil.
12   On models with a separately mounted coil, check the coil for opens
and grounds by performing the following three tests with an ohmmeter
(see illustration).
13   Using the ohmmeter's high scale, hook up the ohmmeter leads as
illustrated (see test #1 in illustration 9.12). The ohmmeter should indicate a very high, or infinite, resistance value. If it doesn't, replace
the coil.
14   Using the low scale, hook up the leads as illustrated (see test #2
in illustration 9.12). The ohmmeter should indicate a very low, or zero,

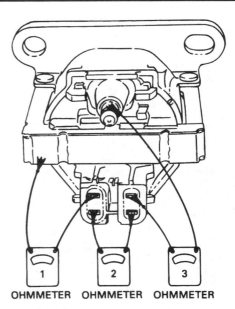

9.12   Test connections for checking the HEI coil

resistance value. If it doesn't, replace the coil.
15   Using the high scale, hook up the leads as illustrated (see test #3
in illustration 9.12). The ohmmeter should not indicate an infinite
resistance. If it does, replace the coil.

Installation
16   Installation of the coil is the reverse of the removal procedure.

Direct Ignition System (DIS) — 2.5L four-cylinder engine
Removal
17   Detach the cable from the negative terminal of the battery.
18   Unplug the electrical connectors from the module.
19   Detach the plug wires at the coil assembly (see illustration in Section 7).
20   Remove the module/coil assembly attaching bolts (see illustration
in Section 7).
21   Remove the module/coil assembly. **Caution:** *The sensor is attached
below the module. To avoid damage to the sensor, remove the module
slowly and carefully.*
22   Remove the bolts that attach the coils to the module and separate
the two assemblies.

Check
23   The three-test checking procedure for the DIS coil is the same as
the one outlined above for the HEI type coil.

Installation
24   Installation is the reverse of removal. Be careful when inserting
the module/coil assembly to avoid damage to the sensor.

Computer controlled coil ignition (C3I) — 3.0L V6 engine
Refer to illustrations 9.34a, 9.34b and 9.34c
Removal
25   Detach the cable from the negative terminal of the battery.
26   Clearly label, then disconnect, all six spark plug wires from the coil.
27   Unbolt and unplug the electrical connector at the module (see illustration in Section 7).
28   Detach the vacuum lines and the electrical connector from the EGR
valve solenoid on the left end of the coil/module assembly (see Chapter 6 if necessary).
29   Remove the front bracket leg mounting nut from the stud on the
intake manifold (next to the EGR valve) and the two rear bracket nuts
from the studs protruding from the exhaust manifold side of the rear
cylinder head (see illustration in Section 7).
30   Remove the coil/module and support bracket assembly.
31   Using a Torx screwdriver or bit, remove the coil-to-module attaching screws and separate the coil and module assemblies.
32   Open the coil and module halves as shown (see illustration in Section 7). Clearly label, then detach, the wires between the module and

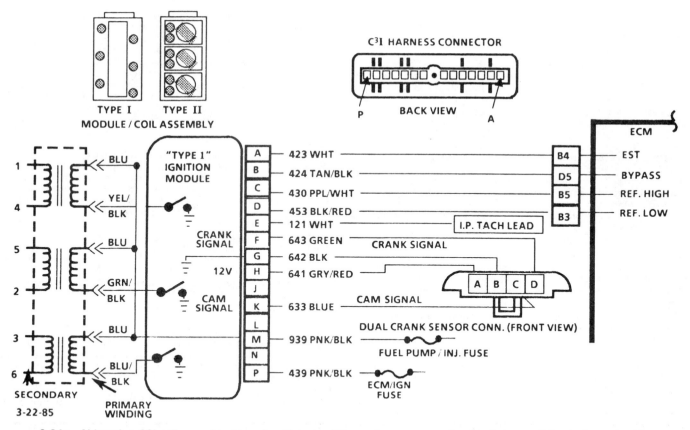

9.34a   Although a C3I coil assembly (Type I or II) looks different from a conventional coil, its condition is determined by performing the same three tests described in the previous illustration — this wiring diagram will help you identify the correct terminals

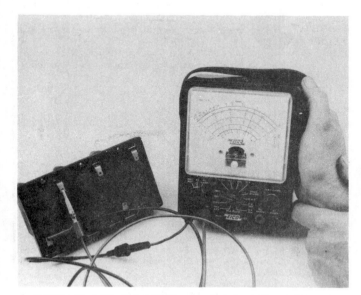

9.34b   Test #2: Using the low scale, check the resistance between the positive terminal and the negative terminal

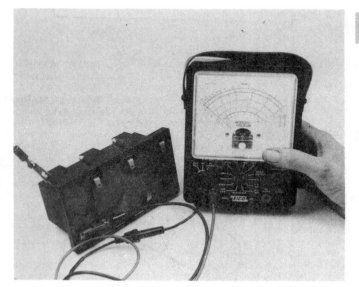

9.34c   Test #3: Using the high scale, check the resistance between the negative terminal of the coil and the high tension tower terminal — it should be infinite

5

the coil assemblies from the spade terminals on the underside of the coil(s).

33   Check the gasket for wear. If it's worn, replace it.

Check

34   The three-part checking procedure for the C3I coil is the same as the procedure outlined above for the HEI type coil. However, the

primary terminals are not marked; study the accompanying photos and wiring diagram before attempting to check the coil (**see illustrations**).

Installation

35   Installation is the reverse of removal. Be sure to attach the wires of the new module to the coil assembly spade terminals in exactly the same order in which they were removed.

10   Hall effect switch — check and replacement

Refer to illustration 10.2

1   Some HEI distributors are equipped with a Hall effect switch which is located above the pickup coil assembly. The Hall effect switch is used in place of the *R* terminal of the HEI distributor to send engine RPM information to the ECM.
2   Test the switch by connecting a 12-volt power supply and voltmeter as shown **(see illustration)**. Check the polarity markings carefully before making any connections.
3   When the knife blade is *not* inserted as shown, the voltmeter should read less than 0.5 volts. If the reading is more, the Hall effect switch is faulty and must be replaced by a new one.
4   With the knife blade inserted, the voltmeter should read within 0.5 volts of battery voltage. Replace the switch with a new one if the reading is more.
5   Remove the Hall effect switch by unplugging the connector and removing the retaining screws.
6   Installation is the reverse of removal.

11   Charging system — general information and precautions

The charging system consists of a belt-driven alternator with an integral voltage regulator and the battery. These components work together to supply electrical power for the ignition system, the lights and all accessories.

There are two types of alternators used. Earlier vehicles use the SI type and later models are equipped with the CS type. There are two types of CS alternators in use, the CS-130 and the CS-144. All types use a conventional pulley and fan.

To determine which type of alternator is fitted to your vehicle, look at the fasteners employed to attach the two halves of the alternator housing. All CS models use rivets instead of screws. CS alternators are rebuildable once the rivets are drilled out. However, we don't recommend this practice. For all intents and purposes, CS types should be considered non-serviceable and, if found to be faulty, should be exchanged as cores for new or rebuilt units.

The purpose of the voltage regulator is to limit the alternator's voltage to a preset value. This prevents power surges, circuit overloads, etc., during peak voltage output. On all models with which this manual is concerned, the voltage regulator is contained within the alternator housing.

The charging system does not ordinarily require periodic maintenance. The drivebelts, electrical wiring and connections should, however, be inspected at the intervals suggested in Chapter 1.

Take extreme care when making circuit connections to a vehicle equipped with an alternator and note the following. When making connections to the alternator from a battery, always match correct polarity. Before using arc welding equipment to repair any part of the vehicle, disconnect the wires from the alternator and the battery terminal. Never start the engine with a battery charger connected. Always disconnect both battery leads before using a battery charger.

The charging indicator lamp on the dash lights when the ignition switch is turned on and goes out when the engine starts. If the lamp stays on or comes on once the engine is running, a charging system problem has occurred. See Section 12 for the proper diagnosis procedure for each type of alternator.

12   Charging system — check

Refer to illustration 12.5

1   If a malfunction occurs in the charging circuit, do not immediately assume that the alternator is causing the problem. First check the

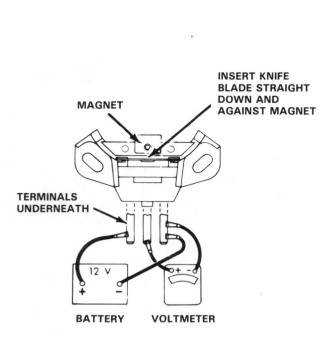

10.2   Hall effect switch test connections

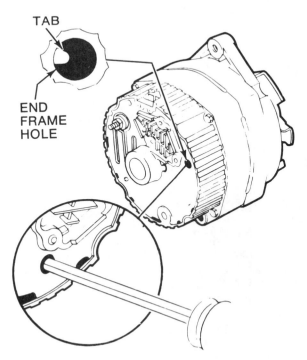

12.5   To full field the alternator, ground the tab located inside the test hole on the end frame (backside) of the alternator by inserting a screwdriver blade into the hole and touching the tab and the case at the same time

following items:

   a) The battery cables where they connect to the battery. Make sure the connections are clean and tight.
   b) The battery electrolyte specific gravity. If it is low, charge the battery.
   c) Check the external alternator wiring and connections. They must be in good condition.
   d) Check the drivebelt condition and tension (Chapter 1).
   e) Make sure the alternator mounting bolts are tight.
   f) Run the engine and check the alternator for abnormal noise (may be caused by a loose drive pulley, loose mounting bolts, worn or dirty bearings, defective diode or defective stator).

2   Using a voltmeter, check the battery voltage with the engine off. It should be approximately 12 volts.
3   Start the engine and check the battery voltage again. It should now be approximately 14 to 15 volts.
4   Locate the test hole in the back of the alternator. **Note:** *If there is no test hole, your vehicle is equipped with a newer CS type alternator. Further testing of this type of alternator must be done by a dealer or automotive electrical shop.*
5   Ground the tab that is located inside the hole by inserting a screwdriver blade into the hole and touching the tab and the case at the same time **(see illustration). Caution:** *Do not run the engine with the tab grounded any longer than necessary to obtain a voltmeter reading. If the alternator is charging, it is running unregulated during the test. This condition may overload the electrical system and cause damage to the components.*
6   The reading on the voltmeter should be 15 volts or higher with the tab grounded in the test hole.
7   If the voltmeter indicates low battery voltage, the alternator is faulty and should be replaced with a new one (Section 15).
8   If the voltage reading is 15 volts or higher and a no charge condition is present, the regulator or field circuit is the problem. Remove the alternator (Section 13) and have it checked further by an auto electric shop.

13 Alternator — removal and installation

Refer to illustration 13.2

1   Detach the cable from the negative terminal of the battery.
2   Clearly label, if necessary, then unplug and unbolt the electrical connectors from the alternator **(see illustration)**.
3   Remove the drivebelt (see Chapter 1).

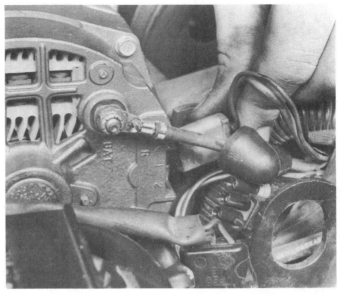

13.2 Remove the alternator electrical connectors

4   Remove the alternator mounting bolts and remove the alternator.
5   Installation is the reverse of removal.

14 Alternator brushes — replacement

Refer to illustrations 14.2, 14.3, 14.4a, 14.4b, 14.5, 14.6, 14.8 and 14.9

Note: *The following procedure applies only to SI type alternators. CS types have riveted housings and cannot be disassembled.*

1   Remove the alternator from the vehicle (Section 15).
2   Scribe or paint marks on the front and rear end frame housings of the alternator to facilitate reassembly **(see illustration)**.
3   From the rear of the alternator, insert a paper clip through the rear end frame to hold the brushes in place **(see illustration)**.

5

14.2 Mark the drive end frame and rectifier end frame assemblies with a scribe or paint before separating the two halves

14.3 To hold the brushes in place during disassembly and reassembly, insert a paper clip through the hole in the end frame nearest to the rotor shaft

14.4a   With the paper clip in place and the through bolts removed, carefully separate the drive end frame and the rectifier end frame

14.4b   Inside a typical SI alternator

A   Brush holder
B   Paper clip retaining brushes
C   Regulator
D   Resistor (not all models)
E   Diode trio
F   Rectifier bridge

14.5   After removing the bolts holding the stator assembly to the end frame, remove the stator

14.6   Remove the nuts attaching the diode trio to the rectifier bridge and remove the trio

4   Remove the four through-bolts holding the front and rear end frames together, then separate the drive end frame from the rectifier end frame with the paper clip still in place (see illustrations).
5   Remove the bolts holding the stator to the rear end frame and separate the stator from the end frame (see illustration).
6   Remove the nuts attaching the diode trio to the rectifier bridge and remove the trio (see illustration).
7   Remove the paper clip from the rear of the end frame while holding your hand over the end of the brush holder to catch the brushes as they are released.
8   Remove the screws attaching the resistor (not used on all models) and regulator to the end frame and remove the regulator (see illustration).
9   Remove the brushes from the regulator by slipping the brush retainer off the regulator (see illustration).
10   Remove the springs from the brush holder.
11   Installation is the reverse of the removal procedure, noting the following:
12   When installing the brushes in the brush holder, install the brush closest to the end frame first. Slip the paper clip through the rear of the end frame to hold the brush, then insert the second brush and push the paper clip in to hold both brushes while reassembly is completed. The paper clip should not be removed until the front and rear end frames have been bolted together.

14.8 After removing the screws that attach the regulator and the resistor (if equipped) to the end frame, remove the regulator

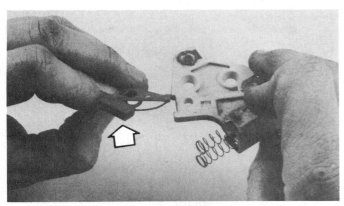

14.9 Slip the brush retainer off the regulator and remove the brushes (arrow)

15 Starting system — general information

The function of the starting system is to crank the engine.

The starting system is composed of a starting motor, solenoid and battery. The battery supplies the electrical energy to the solenoid, which then completes the circuit to the starting motor, which does the actual work of cranking the engine.

The solenoid and starting motor are mounted together at the lower front side of the engine. No periodic lubrication or maintenance is required.

The electrical circuitry of the vehicle is arranged so that the starter motor can only be operated when the clutch pedal is depressed (manual transaxle) or the transaxle selector lever is in Park or Neutral (automatic transaxle).

Never operate the starter motor for more than 30 seconds at a time without pausing to allow it to cool for at least two minutes.

Excessive cranking can cause overheating, which can seriously damage the starter.

16 Starter motor — testing in vehicle

1   If the starter motor does not turn at all when the switch is operated, make sure that the shift lever is in Neutral or Park (automatic transaxle) or that the clutch pedal is depressed (manual transaxle).

2   Make sure that the battery is charged and that all cables, both at the battery and starter solenoid terminals, are secure.

3   If the starter motor spins but the engine is not cranking, the over-running clutch in the starter motor is slipping and the motor must be removed from the engine for replacement.

4   If, when the switch is actuated, the starter motor does not operate at all but the solenoid clicks, then the problem lies with either the battery, the main solenoid contacts or the starter motor itself. **Note:** *Before diagnosing starter problems, make sure that the battery is fully charged.*

5   If the solenoid plunger cannot be heard when the switch is actuated, the solenoid itself is defective or the solenoid circuit is open.

6   To check the solenoid, connect a jumper lead between the battery (+) and the "S" terminal on the solenoid. If the starter motor now operates, the solenoid is OK and the problem is in the ignition switch, neutral start switch or in the wiring.

7   If the starter motor still does not operate, remove the starter/solenoid assembly for disassembly, testing and repair.

8   If the starter motor cranks the engine at an abnormally slow speed, first make sure that the battery is charged and that all terminal connections are tight. If the engine is partially seized, or has the wrong viscosity oil in it, it will crank slowly.

9   Run the engine until normal operating temperature is reached, then disconnect the coil wire from the distributor cap and ground it on the engine.

10   Connect a voltmeter positive lead to the starter motor terminal of the solenoid and then connect the negative lead to ground.

11   Crank the engine and take the voltmeter readings as soon as a steady figure is indicated. Do not allow the starter motor to turn for more than 30 seconds at a time. A reading of 9 volts or more, with the starter motor turning at normal cranking speed, is normal. If the reading is 9 volts or more but the cranking speed is slow, the motor is faulty. If the reading is less than 9 volts and the cranking speed is slow, the solenoid contacts are probably burned.

17 Starter motor — removal and installation

Refer to illustrations 17.3, 17.4a and 17.4b

1   Disconnect the negative battery cable.

2   Raise the front of the vehicle and support it securely on jackstands.

3   From under the vehicle, disconnect the solenoid wire and battery cable from the terminals on the rear of the solenoid (**see illustration**).

5

17.3 There are three terminals on the end of the typical starter solenoid

A Battery terminal	C Motor terminal (M)
B Switch terminal (S)	

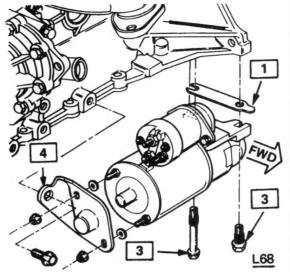
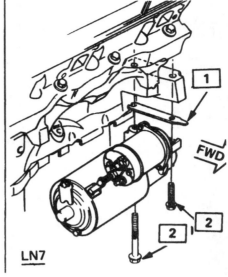

17.4a Exploded view of typical starter motors for 2.5L four (left) and 3.0L V6 (right) applications

1 Shim
2 Bolt
3 Bolt
4 Bracket

L68   LN7

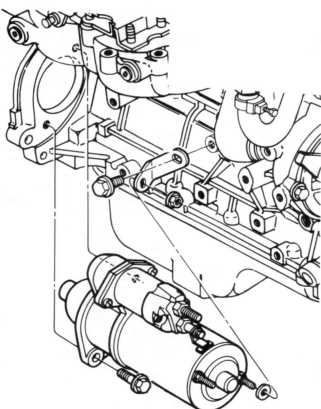

17.4b Typical starter motor installation on the 2.0L OHC Turbo four

4   Remove the starter motor bolts (see illustrations).
5   Remove the starter motor. Note the location of the spacer shim(s).
6   Installation is the reverse of removal. Be sure to install the spacer shim(s) in exactly the same location.

18 Starter solenoid — removal and installation

Refer to illustration 18.5
1   Disconnect the cable from the negative terminal of the battery.
2   Remove the starter motor (Section 17).

18.5 To remove the solenoid housing from the starter motor, remove the screws and turn it clockwise

Removal
3   Disconnect the strap from the solenoid to the starter motor terminal.
4   Remove the two screws which secure the solenoid to the starter motor.
5   Twist the solenoid in a clockwise direction to disengage the flange from the starter body (see illustration).

Installation
6   To install, first make sure the return spring is in position on the plunger, then insert the solenoid body into the starter housing and turn the solenoid counterclockwise to engage the flange.
7   Install the two solenoid screws and connect the motor strap.

19 Symptoms

Throttle Body Injection (TBI) engines
1   Before performing any of the following symptoms procedures, make a careful visual inspection of the following items:

a) Vacuum hoses for splits, kinks and proper connections (see VECI label).
b) Air leaks at the throttle body mounting and intake manifold.
c) Ignition wires for cracking, hardness, proper routing and carbon tracking.
d) Wiring for proper connections, pinches and cuts.

The importance of this step cannot be emphasized too strongly. It can correct a problem without further checks and can save valuable time.

Rough, unstable or incorrect idle, stalling

2 If the engine runs unevenly at idle, the car shakes, the idle varies in rpm, the engine stalls or idles at the wrong speed, check:
a) The ignition timing (see VECI label).
b) The Park/Neutral switch circuit (see Chapter 6 and the Wiring Diagrams at the end of this book).
c) For a leaking injector (see Chapter 4).
d) The injectors for running too rich or too lean (see Chapter 4).

3 If rough idle only occurs when the engine is hot, perform these additional checks:
a) Vacuum leaks: Block the idle air passage using GM tool J-33047 or equivalent. If the closed throttle engine speed is above 650 rpm, locate and correct the vacuum leak (a likely candidate is a disconnected THERMAC or cruise control hose).
b) The Park/Neutral switch (automatic only) (see Chapter 6).
c) A sticking throttle shaft or binding linkage causes a high TPS voltage (open throttle indication), so the ECM will not control idle. Measure the TPS voltage (see Chapter 6). It should be less than 1.2 volts with the throttle closed.
d) If the EGR is on while the engine is idling, it will cause roughness, stoppage and hard starting. Check the EGR (see Chapters 1 and 6).
e) The battery cables and ground straps should be clean and secure. Erratic voltage will cause the IAC to change its position, resulting in poor idle quality.
f) The IAC valve will not move if system voltage is below 9 or greater than 17.8 volts.
g) MAP sensor: With the ignition on and the engine stopped, compare MAP voltage with a known good vehicle. The voltage should be similar ±0.4 volts. Or, start and idle the engine. Detach the sensor electrical connector. If the idle improves, substitute a good sensor and recheck.
h) The A/C compressor or relay: If either is inoperative, replace it (see Chapter 3).
i) The A/C refrigerant pressure is too high. Have the system checked for overcharging or a faulty cycling switch.
j) Check the PCV valve for proper operation by placing a finger over the inlet hole in the valve several times. The valve should snap back. If it doesn't, replace the valve.
k) Perform a cylinder compression check (see Chapter 2).
l) Inspect the oxygen sensor for contamination from fuel or use of improper RTV sealant. The sensor will have a white, powdery coating resulting in a rich exhaust indication.

Cuts out, misses

4 If there is a steady pulsation or jerking that follows engine speed, usually more pronounced as the engine load increases, or if the exhaust has a steady spitting sound at idle or low speed, check for a missing cylinder, by:
a) Unplugging the IAC motor, starting the engine and removing one spark plug wire at a time (use insulated pliers).
b) If there is an rpm drop on all cylinders (equal to within 50 rpm), go to *Rough, unstable or incorrect idle, stalling* symptoms above. Reconnect the IAC motor.
c) If there is no rpm drop on one or more cylinders, or excessive variation in the rpm drop, check for spark on the suspected cylinder(s) with a HEI spark tester. If there is no spark, see Section 5 in this Chapter. If there is spark, remove the spark plug(s) and check for cracks, wear, improper gap, burned electrodes or heavy deposits (see Chapter 1).

5 Check the spark plug wires by connecting an ohmmeter to the ends of each wire in question. If the meter reads over 30,000 ohms, replace the wire(s).

6 Check the ignition coil and secondary voltage using a HEI spark tester (see Section 5).

7 Check for a restricted fuel filter. Also check the fuel tank for water (see Chapter 4).

8 Check for low fuel pressure (see Section 5).

9 Check for proper valve timing (see Chapter 2).

10 Perform a compression check on any questionable cylinders. If compression is low, repair as necessary (see Chapter 2).

11 Visually check the distributor cap and rotor for moisture, dust, cracks, burns, etc. (see Chapter 1). Spray the cap and plug wires with fine water mist to check for shorts.

12 Remove the rocker covers. Check for bent pushrods, worn rocker arms, broken valve springs or worn camshaft lobes. Repair as necessary (see Chapter 2).

Multi-port fuel injection (MFI) engines

13 Before performing any of the following symptoms procedures, make a careful visual inspection of the following items:
a) ECM grounds should be clean and tight.
b) Check the vacuum hoses for splits, kinks and proper connections (see VECI label).
c) Check for air leaks at the throttle body mounting and intake manifold.
d) Check for air leaks between the MAF sensor and the throttle body.
e) Check the ignition wires for cracking, hardness, proper routing and carbon tracking.
f) Check the wiring for proper connections, pinches and cuts.

The importance of this step cannot be emphasized too strongly. It can correct a problem without further checks and can save valuable time.

Rough, unstable or incorrect idle, stalling

14 If the engine runs unevenly at idle, the car shakes, the idle varies in rpm, the engine stalls or idles at the wrong speed, check:
a) The throttle linkage for sticking or binding.
b) The ignition timing (see VECI label).
c) The TPS for sticking or binding (see Chapter 6).
d) The IAC system (see Chapter 6).
e) The alternator output voltage (see Section 12).
f) The Park/Neutral switch circuit (see Chapter 6).
g) The PCV valve for proper operation by placing a finger over the inlet hole in the valve several times. The valve should snap back. If it doesn't, replace the valve (see Chapters 2 and 6).
h) The Evaporative Emission Control System (EVAP) (see Chapters 1 and 6).
i) The EGR valve. There should be no EGR at idle.
j) Perform a cylinder compression check (see Chapter 2).
k) Inspect the oxygen sensor for contamination from fuel or use of improper RTV sealant. The sensor will have a white, powdery coating resulting in a rich exhaust indication.
l) Check for fuel in the pressure regulator hose. If it is present, replace the regulator assembly.
m) Check the ignition system — wires, plugs, rotor, etc.
n) Disconnect the MAF sensor and, if the condition is corrected, replace the sensor.

Cuts out, misses

15 If there is a steady pulsation or jerking that follows engine speed, usually more pronounced as the engine load increases, or if the exhaust has a steady spitting sound at idle or low speed, check for an idle miss.

16 With the engine idling, disconnect the IAC motor. Remove one spark plug wire at a time (use insulated pliers). If there is an rpm drop on all cylinders, go to *Rough, unstable or incorrect idle, stalling* symptoms above. Reconnect the IAC motor.

17 If there is no rpm drop on one or more cylinders, or excessive variation in the rpm drop, check for spark on the suspected cylinder(s) with a HEI spark tester.

18 If there is spark, remove the spark plug(s) and check for cracks, wear, improper gap, burned electrodes or heavy deposits (see Chapter 1). Perform a compression check on the questionable cylinder.

19 If there is no spark and you have a HEI distributor type system (2.0L Turbo four), check the wire resistance. It should not exceed 30,000 ohms. Check the rotor and the distributor cap (see Chapter 1).

20 If you have a distributorless ignition (C3I) system (V6), ground the opposite plug wire of the affected coil pair. If the tester now sparks, replace the spark plug of the wire which was jumped to ground. If the tester still does not spark, see Section 5.

21 If the engine cuts out under load, test for spark on each wire with a HEI spark tester. If there is spark on all cylinders, remove the plugs and check for cracks, wear, improper gap, burned electrodes or heavy deposits.

5

22 If there is no spark at the plug(s), and you have a HEI distributor type system (2.0L Turbo four), check the wire resistance. It should not exceed 30,000 ohms. Check the rotor and the distributor cap (see Chapter 1).

23 If you have a distributorless ignition (C3I) system, ground the opposite plug wire of the affected coil pair. If the tester now sparks, replace the spark plug of the wire which was jumped to ground. If the tester still does not spark, see Section 5.

24 If the above checks do not correct the problem, check the following:

a) Unplug all injector harness connectors. Connect a injector test light or a 6-volt test light between the harness terminals of each injector connector and note the light while cranking. If the test light fails to blink at any connector, it is a faulty injector drive circuit harness, connector or terminal.

b) Have an injector balance test performed (this procedure is beyond the scope of the home mechanic — take the vehicle to a dealer).

c) Visually inspect the distributor cap and rotor for moisture, dust, cracks, burns, etc. (see Chapter 1). Spray the cap and plug wires with fine water mist to check for shorts.

d) Fuel system: Check for a plugged fuel filter, water in the fuel system and low fuel pressure (see Chapter 4).

e) Check the valve timing (see Chapter 2).

f) Remove the rocker covers. Check for bent pushrods, worn rocker arms, broken valve springs or worn camshaft lobes. Repair as necessary (see Chapter 2).

g) Perform a compression check (see Chapter 2).

h) On C3I systems, a misfire may be caused by a misaligned crank sensor or bent vane on the rotating disc. Inspect for proper clearance at each vane (approximately 0.030-inch). The sensor should be replaced if it shows evidence of rubbing.

Chapter 6 Emissions control systems

Contents

---

1 General information

Refer to illustration 1.6

To prevent pollution of the atmosphere from incompletely burned and evaporating gases, and to maintain good driveability and fuel economy, a number of emission control devices are incorporated. They include the:

   Fuel control system
   Electronic Spark Timing (EST)
   Electronic Spark Control (ESC) system
   Exhaust Gas Recirculation (EGR) system
   Evaporative Emission Control System (EECS)
   Positive Crankcase Ventilation (PCV) system
   Transaxle Converter Clutch (TCC)
   Catalytic converter

All of these systems are linked, directly or indirectly, to the Computer Command Control (CCC or C3) system.

The Sections in this Chapter include general descriptions, checking procedures within the scope of the home mechanic and component replacement procedures (when possible) for each of the systems listed above.

Before assuming that an emissions control system is malfunctioning, check the fuel and ignition systems carefully. The diagnosis of some emission control devices requires specialized tools, equipment and training. If checking and servicing become too difficult or if a procedure is beyond the scope of your skills, consult your dealer service department.

This doesn't mean, however, that emission control systems are particularly difficult to maintain and repair. You can quickly and easily perform many checks and do most (if not all) of the regular maintenance at home with common tune-up and hand tools. **Note:** *The most frequent cause of emissions problems is simply a loose or broken vacuum hose or wiring connection, so always check the hose and wiring connections first.*

Pay close attention to any special precautions outlined in this Chapter. It should be noted that the illustrations of the various systems may not exactly match the system installed on your vehicle because of changes made by the manufacturer during production or from year-to-year.

A Vehicle Emissions Control Information label is located in the engine compartment **(see illustration)**. This label contains important emissions specifications and ignition timing procedures, as well as a vacuum hose schematic and emissions components identification guide. When servicing the engine or emissions systems, the VECI label in your particular vehicle should always be checked for up-to-date information.

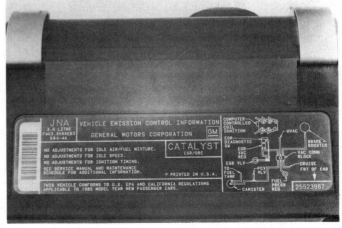

1.6   Look for your vehicle's VECI label under the hood — on the V6, it's located on top of the air cleaner housing as shown

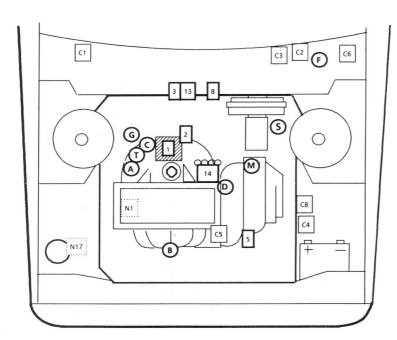

2.1a   Emission control component locations for the 2.5L four

☐ **COMPUTER HARNESS**
C1   Electronic Control Module (ECM)
C2   ALDL diagnostic connector
C3   "Service Engine Soon" light
C4   ECM power
C5   ECM harness ground
C6   Fuse panel
C8   Fuel pump test connector (red)

▢ **NOT ECM CONNECTED**
N1   Crankcase vent valve (PCV)
N17 Fuel vapor canister

☐ **CONTROLLED DEVICES**
1   Fuel injector solenoid
2   Idle air control valve
3   Fuel pump relay
5   Trans. Converter Clutch connector
8   Engine cooling fan relay
13 A/C compressor relay
14 Direct Ignition System Assembly

◯ **INFORMATION SENSORS**
A   Manifold absolute pressure (MAP)
     (Mounted on Air Cleaner)
B   Exhaust oxygen
C   Throttle position
D   Coolant temperature
F   Vehicle speed buffer amplifier (if used)
G   Vehicle Speed PM Generator (if used)
M   P/N switch
S   P/S pressure switch
T   Manifold Air Temperature

⬡   Exhaust Gas Recirculation valve

2.1b   Emission control component locations for the 3.0L V6

☐ **CONTROLLED DEVICES**
1   Fuel injector
2   Idle air control motor (IAC)
3   Fuel pump relay
5   Trans. Converter Clutch connector (TCC)
6   Computer Controlled Coil Ignition(C^3I)
7   Electronic Spark Control module (ESC)
8   Engine coolant fan relay
12 Exh. Gas Recirc. vacuum solenoid
13 A/C compressor relay
15 Fuel vapor canister solenoid

☐ **COMPUTER HARNESS**
C1   Electronic Control Module (ECM)
C2   ALDL diagnostic connector
C3   "SERVICE ENGINE SOON" light
C4   ECM power
C5   ECM harness ground
C6   Fuse panel
C8   Fuel pump test connector   (red)

▢ **NOT ECM CONNECTED**
N 1   Crankcase vent valve (PCV)
N13 Coolant fan temp. override switch

◯ **INFORMATION SENSORS**
B   Exhaust oxygen (0_2)
C   Throttle position (TPS)
D   Coolant temperature
F   Vehicle speed (VSS)
Fa Vehicle speed sensor buffer
H   Crkshft pos. Reference/RPM (C^3I)
J   ESC knock sensor
K   Mass air flow
M   P/N switch
S   P/S switch
T   Air temperature (ATS)

⬡   Exhaust Gas Recirculation valve

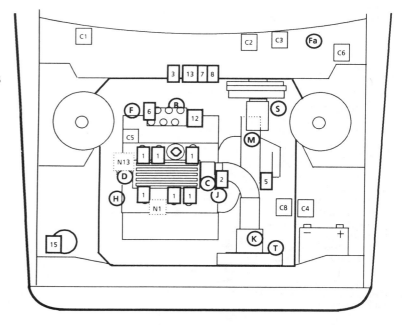

2   Computer Command Control (CCC) system and trouble codes

Refer to illustrations 2.1a, 2.1b, 2.1c and 2.5

The Computer Command Control (CCC) system consists of an Electronic Control Module (ECM) and information sensors which monitor various functions of the engine and send data back to the ECM (see illustrations).

The CCC system is analogous to the central nervous system in the human body. The sensors (nerve endings) constantly relay information to the ECM (brain), which processes the data and, if necessary, sends out a command to change the operating parameters of the engine (body).

Here's a specific example of how one portion of this system operates: An oxygen sensor, located in the exhaust manifold, constantly monitors

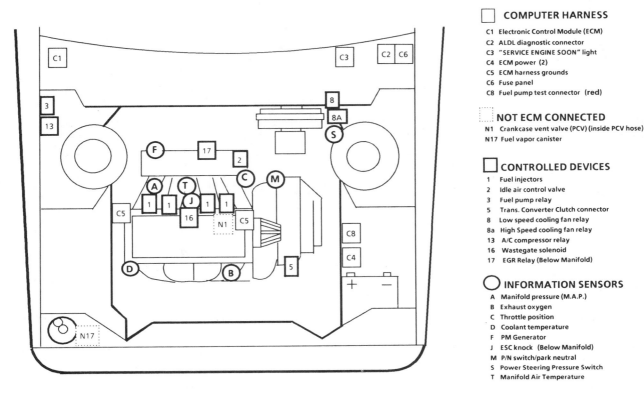

COMPUTER HARNESS

C1   Electronic Control Module (ECM)
C2   ALDL diagnostic connector
C3   "SERVICE ENGINE SOON" light
C4   ECM power (2)
C5   ECM harness grounds
C6   Fuse panel
C8   Fuel pump test connector (red)

NOT ECM CONNECTED

N1   Crankcase vent valve (PCV) (inside PCV hose)
N17 Fuel vapor canister

CONTROLLED DEVICES

1   Fuel injectors
2   Idle air control valve
3   Fuel pump relay
5   Trans. Converter Clutch connector
8   Low speed cooling fan relay
8a   High Speed cooling fan relay
13   A/C compressor relay
16   Wastegate solenoid
17   EGR Relay (Below Manifold)

INFORMATION SENSORS

A   Manifold pressure (M.A.P.)
B   Exhaust oxygen
C   Throttle position
D   Coolant temperature
F   PM Generator
J   ESC knock (Below Manifold)
M   P/N switch/park neutral
S   Power Steering Pressure Switch
T   Manifold Air Temperature

2.1c   Emission control component locations for the 2.0L Turbo

the oxygen content of the exhaust gas. If the percentage of oxygen in the exhaust gas is incorrect, an electrical signal is sent to the ECM. The ECM takes this information, processes it and then sends a command to the fuel injection system, telling it to change the air/fuel mixture. This happens in a fraction of a second and it goes on continuously when the engine is running. The end result is an air/fuel mixture ratio which is constantly maintained at a predetermined ratio, regardless of driving conditions.

One might think that a system which uses an on-board computer and electrical sensors would be difficult to diagnose. This is not necessarily the case. The CCC system has a built-in diagnostic feature which indicates a problem by flashing a *Check Engine* light on the instrument panel. When this light comes on during normal vehicle operation, a fault in one of the information sensor circuits or the ECM itself has been detected. More importantly, the source of the malfunction is stored in the ECM's memory.

To retrieve this information from the ECM memory, you must use a short jumper wire to ground a diagnostic terminal. This terminal is part of a wiring connector known as the Assembly Line Communications Link (ALCL) **(see illustration)**. The ALCL is located underneath the dashboard, just below the instrument panel and to the left of the center console. To use the ALCL, remove the plastic cover by sliding it toward you. With the connector exposed to view, push one end of the jumper wire into the diagnostic terminal and the other end into the ground terminal.

When the diagnostic terminal is grounded with the ignition on and the engine stopped, the system will enter the *Diagnostic Mode*. In this mode the ECM will display a "Code 12" by flashing the *Check Engine* light, indicating that the system is operating. A code 12 is simply one flash, followed by a brief pause, then two flashes in quick succession. This code will be flashed three times. If no other codes are stored, Code 12 will continue to flash until the diagnostic terminal ground is removed.

After flashing Code 12 three times, the ECM will display any stored trouble codes. Each code will be flashed three times, then Code 12

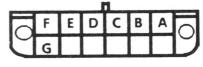

TERMINAL IDENTIFICATION

A	GROUND		E		SERIAL DATA (SEE SPECIAL TOOLS)
B	DIAGNOSTIC TERMINAL		F		T.C.C . (IF USED)
C	A.I.R. (IF USED)		G		FUEL PUMP (NOT USED ON ALL SERIES)
D	SERVICE ENGINE SOON LAMP				

2.5   The Assembly Line Communications Link (ALCL)

will be flashed again, indicating that the display of any stored trouble codes has been completed.

When the ECM sets a trouble code, the *Check Engine* light will come on and a trouble code will be stored in memory. If the problem is intermittent, the light will go out after 10 seconds, when the fault goes away. However, the trouble code will stay in the ECM memory until the battery voltage to the ECM is interrupted. Removing battery voltage for 10 seconds will clear all stored trouble codes. Trouble codes should always be cleared after repairs have been completed. **Caution:** *To prevent damage to the ECM, the ignition switch must be Off when disconnecting power to the ECM.*

Following is a list of the typical trouble codes which may be encountered while diagnosing the Computer Command Control System. Also included are simplified troubleshooting procedures. If the problem persists after these checks have been made, more detailed service procedures will have to be done by a dealer service department.

6

Trouble codes	Circuit or system	Probable cause
Code 12 (1 flash, pause, 2 flashes)	No distributor reference pulses to ECM	This code will flash whenever the diagnostic terminal is grounded with the ignition turned On and the engine not running. If additional trouble codes are stored in the ECM they will appear after this code has flashed three times. If this code appears while the engine is running, no reference pulses from the distributor are reaching the ECM.
Code 13 (1 flash, pause, 3 flashes)	Oxygen sensor circuit	Check for a sticking or misadjusted throttle position sensor. Check the wiring and connectors from the oxygen sensor. Replace the oxygen sensor.
Code 14 (1 flash, pause, 4 flashes)	Coolant sensor circuit	If the engine is experiencing overheating problems the problem must be rectified before continuing. Check all wiring and connectors associated with the coolant temperature sensor. Replace the coolant temperature sensor.*
Code 15 (1 flash, pause, 5 flashes)	Coolant sensor circuit	See above, then check the wiring connections at the ECM.
Code 21 (2 flashes, pause, 1 flash)	Throttle position sensor	Check for a sticking or misadjusted TPS plunger. Check all wiring and connections between the TPS and the ECM. Adjust or replace the TPS (see Chapter 4).*
Code 22 (2 flashes, pause, 2 flashes)	Throttle position sensor	Check the TPS adjustment (Chapter 4). Check the ECM connector. Replace the TPS (Chapter 4).*
Code 23 (2 flashes, pause, 3 flashes)	Manifold air temperature	Check the MAT sensor, wiring and connectors for an open sensor circuit. Replace the MAT sensor.*
Code 24 (2 flashes, pause, 4 flashes)	Vehicle speed sensor	A fault in this circuit should be indicated only when the vehicle is in motion. Disregard Code 24 if it is set when the drive wheels are not turning. Check the connections at the ECM. Check the TPS setting.
Code 25 (V6 only) (2 flashes, pause, 5 flashes)	Manifold air temperature	Check the voltage signal from the MAT sensor to the ECM. It should be above 4 volts.
Code 31 (2.0L Turbo) (3 flashes, pause, 1 flash)	Turbocharger wastegate	Short in circuit 435 (see Wiring Diagrams). Sticking wastegate actuator or wastegate; control valve stuck in closed position; cut or pinched hose; faulty ECM.
Code 32 (V6 only) (3 flashes, pause, 2 flashes)	EGR system	The EGR solenoid should not be energized and vacuum should not pass to the EGR valve. The diagnostic switch should close at about 2 inches of vacuum. With vacuum applied, the switch should close. Replace the EGR valve.*
Code 33 (3 flashes, pause, 3 flashes)	MAP sensor	Check the vacuum hoses from the MAP sensor. Check the electrical connections at the ECM. Replace the MAP sensor.*
Code 34 (3 flashes, pause, 4 flashes)	MAP sensor (4-cyl.) MAF sensor (V6)	Code 34 will set when the signal voltage from the MAP/MAF sensor is too low. Instead the ECM will substitute a fixed MAP/MAF value and use the TPS to control fuel delivery. Replace the MAP/MAF sensor.*
Code 35 (3 flashes, pause, 5 flashes)	Idle Air Control	Code 35 will set when the closed throttle speed is 50 rpm above or below the correct idle speed for 30 seconds. Replace the IAC.*
Code 42 (4 flashes, pause, 2 flashes)	Electronic Spark Timing	If the vehicle will not start and run, check the wire leading to ECM terminal 12. **Note:** *A malfunctioning HEI module can cause this trouble code.* Check the EST wire (terminal 19 at the ECM) leading to the HEI module (E terminal). Check all distributor wires. Check the wire leading from EST terminal A to ECM terminal 12 and the wire from EST terminal A to ECM terminal 3. Replace the HEI module.*
Code 43 (2.0L Turbo) (4 flashes, pause, 3 flashes)	Electronic spark control unit	Coolant temperature is over 90°C; high engine load based on MAP and rpm; voltage on circuit 496 goes above 3.5 volts or below 1.5 volts.
Code 44 (4 flashes, pause, 4 flashes)	Lean exhaust	Check the ECM wiring connections, particularly terminals 15 and 8. Check for vacuum leakage at the TBI base gasket, vacuum hoses or the intake manifold gasket. Replace the oxygen sensor.*
Code 45 (4 flashes, pause, 5 flashes)	Rich exhaust	Check the evaporative charcoal canister and its components for the presence of fuel. Replace the oxygen sensor.*
Code 51 (5 flashes, pause, 1 flash)	PROM or MEM-CAL	Make sure that the PROM or MEM-CAL is properly installed in the ECM. Replace the PROM or MEM-CAL.*
Code 52 (V6 only) (5 flashes, pause, 2 flashes)	CALPAK	Check the CALPAK to insure proper installation. Replace the CALPAK.*
Code 53 (V6 only) (5 flashes, pause, 3 flashes)	System over-voltage	Code 53 will set if the voltage at ECM terminal B2 is greater than 17.1 volts for 2 seconds. Check the charging system.
Code 55 (5 flashes, pause, 5 flashes)	ECM	Be sure that the ECM ground connections are tight. If they are, replace the ECM.*

Component replacement may not cure the problem in all cases. For this reason, you may want to seek professional advice before purchasing replacement parts.

3.4 To remove the Electronic Control Module (ECM) from the vehicle, remove the mounting bolts (arrows) and slide it out far enough to unplug the electrical connectors

---

3 Electronic Control Module (ECM)/Programmable Read Only Memory (PROM)/CALPAK/MEM-CAL

Refer to illustrations 3.4, 3.5, 3.6, 3.8, 3.11, 3.12, 3.13, 3.15, 3.27 and 3.30

1 The Electronic Control Module (ECM) is located under the instrument panel.
2 Disconnect the negative battery cable from the battery.
3 Remove the right sound insulator panel retaining screws and detach the panel (under the right side of the dashboard).
4 Remove the retaining bolts **(see illustration)** and carefully slide the ECM out far enough to unplug the electrical connector.
5 Unplug both electrical connectors **(see illustration)** from the ECM. **Caution:** *The ignition switch must be turned off when pulling out or plugging in the connectors to prevent damage to the ECM.*

PROM

6 To allow one model of ECM to be used for many different vehicles, a device called a PROM (Programmable Read Only Memory) is used **(see illustration)**. The PROM is located inside the ECM and contains information on the vehicle's weight, engine, transaxle, axle ratio, etc. One ECM part number can be used by many GM vehicles but the PROM is very specific and must be used only in the vehicle for which it was designed. For this reason, it is essential to check the latest parts book and Service Bulletin information for the correct part number when replacing a PROM. An ECM purchased at the dealer is purchased without a PROM. The PROM from the old ECM must be carefully removed and installed in the new ECM.

CALPAK

7 A device known as a CALPAK **(see illustration 3.6)** is used to allow fuel delivery if other parts of the ECM are damaged. The CALPAK has an access door in the ECM and replacement is the same as that described for the PROM.

MEM-CAL (2.0L Turbo four and 2.3L Quad-4)

8 The MEM-CAL **(see illustration)** contains the functions of the PROM, CALPAK and ESC module used on other GM applications. Like the PROM, it contains the calibrations needed for a specific vehicle as well as the back-up fuel control circuitry required if the rest of the ECM becomes damaged or faulty.

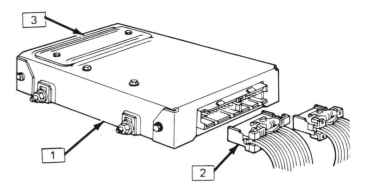

3.5 A typical electronic control module (ECM)

1 ECM assembly	3 PROM access cover
2 ECM harness connectors	

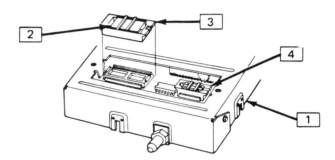

3.6 Once the access cover is removed from the ECM (1), you can replace either the PROM (2), or the CALPAK (4) – don't separate the PROM from the PROM carrier (3)

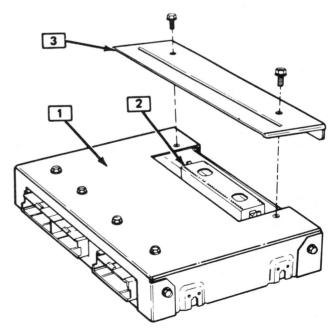

3.8 A typical ECM unit for the 2.0L Turbo four

1 ECM assembly	3 Access cover
2 MEM-CAL unit	

6

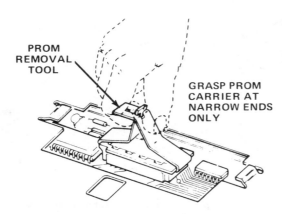

3.11   Grasp the PROM carrier at its narrow ends with the PROM removal tool and gently rock the removal tool until the PROM is unplugged from the socket

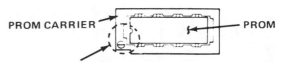

3.12   Note how the notch in the PROM is matched up with the smaller notch in the carrier

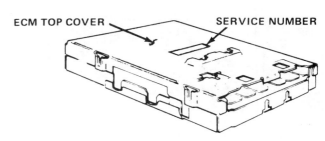

3.13   Make sure that the service numbers on the ECM and the PROM are the same — otherwise, depending on what you are replacing, you could end up with wrong ECM or the wrong PROM

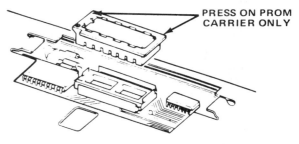

3.15   Press only on the ends of the PROM carrier — pressure on the area in between could result in bent or broken pins or damage to the PROM

PROM/CALPAK replacement

9   Turn the ECM so that the bottom cover is facing up and place it on a clean work surface.

10   Remove the PROM/CALPAK access cover.

11   Using a PROM removal tool (available at your dealer), grasp the PROM carrier at the narrow ends (**see illustration**). Gently rock the carrier from end to end while applying firm upward force. The PROM carrier and PROM should lift off the PROM socket easily. **Caution:** *The PROM carrier should only be removed with a special PROM removal tool. Removal without this tool or with any other type of tool may damage the PROM or the PROM socket.*

12   Note the reference end of the PROM carrier (**see illustration**) before setting it aside.

13   If you are replacing the ECM, remove the new ECM from its container and check the service number to make sure that it is the same as the number on the old ECM (**see illustration**).

14   If you are replacing the PROM, remove the new PROM from its container and check the service number to make sure that it is the same as the number of the old PROM.

15   Position the PROM/PROM carrier assembly squarely over the PROM socket with the small notched end of the carrier aligned with the small notch in the socket at the pin 1 end. Press on the PROM carrier until it seats firmly in the socket (**see illustration**).

16   If the PROM is new, make sure that the notch in the PROM is matched to the small notch in the carrier (**see illustration 3.11**). **Caution:** *If the PROM is installed backwards and the ignition switch is turned on, the PROM will be destroyed.*

17   Using the tool, install the new PROM carrier in the PROM socket of the ECM. The small notch of the carrier should be aligned with the small notch in the socket. Press on the PROM carrier until it is firmly seated in the socket. **Caution:** *Do not press on the PROM — press only on the carrier.*

18   Attach the access cover to the ECM and tighten the two screws.

19   Install the ECM in the support bracket, plug in the electrical connectors to the ECM and install the hush panel.

20   Start the engine.

21   Enter the diagnostic mode by grounding the diagnostic lead of the ALCL (see Section 2). If no trouble codes occur, the PROM is correctly installed.

22   If Trouble Code 51 occurs, or if the *Check Engine* light comes on and remains constantly lit, the PROM is not fully seated, is installed backwards, has bent pins or is defective.

23   If the PROM is not fully seated, pressing firmly on both ends of the carrier should correct the problem.

24   If the pins have been bent, remove the PROM, straighten the pins and reinstall the PROM. If the bent pins break or crack when you attempt to straighten them, discard the PROM and replace it with a new one.

25   If careful inspection indicates that the PROM is fully seated, has not been installed backwards and has no bent pins, but the *Check Engine* light remains lit, the PROM is probably faulty and must be replaced.

MEM-CAL replacement

Note: *With respect to removal of the ECM from the vehicle, MEM-CAL replacement is similar to the procedure described for the PROM or CALPAK. However, the actual removal and installation steps for the MEM-CAL and the functional check to ensure that the MEM-CAL is installed properly differ in detail from the Steps for the PROM and CALPAK.*

26   Remove the MEM-CAL access cover.

27   Using two fingers, push both retaining clips back away from the MEM-CAL (**see illustration**). At the same time, grasp the MEM-CAL at both ends and lift it up out of its socket. Do not remove the MEM-CAL cover itself. **Caution:** *Use of unapproved removal or installation methods may damage the MEM-CAL or socket.*

28   Verify that the numbers on the old ECM and new ECM match up (or that the numbers of the old and new MEM-CALs match up, depending on what component(s) you're replacing) as described in the procedure for removing and installing the PROM and CALPAK.

29   To install the MEM-CAL in the MEM-CAL socket, press only on the ends of the MEM-CAL.

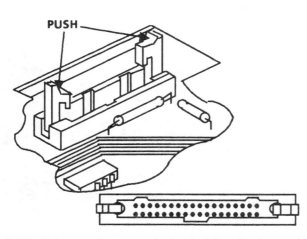

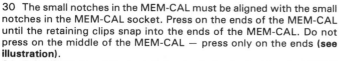

3.27   Using two fingers, push the retaining clips (arrows) back away from the MEM-CAL and simultaneously grasp it at both ends and lift it up out of the socket

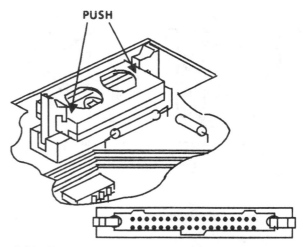

3.30   To install the MEM-CAL, press only on the ends (arrows) until the retaining clips snap into the ends of the MEM-CAL — make sure that the notches in the MEM-CAL are aligned with the small notches in the socket

30   The small notches in the MEM-CAL must be aligned with the small notches in the MEM-CAL socket. Press on the ends of the MEM-CAL until the retaining clips snap into the ends of the MEM-CAL. Do not press on the middle of the MEM-CAL — press only on the ends **(see illustration)**.

31   The remainder of the installation is similar to that for the PROM/ CALPAK.

32   Once the new MEM-CAL is installed in the old ECM (or the old MEM-CAL is installed in the new ECM), check your installation to verify that it has been installed properly by doing the following test:

   a) Turn the ignition switch on.
   b) Enter the diagnostics mode at the ALCL (see Section 2).
   c) Allow Code 12 to flash four times to verify that no other codes are present. This indicates that the MEM-CAL is installed properly and the ECM is functioning properly.

33   If trouble codes 41, 42, 43, 51 or 55 occur, or if the ''Check Engine'' light is on constantly but is flashing no codes, the MEM-CAL is either not fully seated or is defective. If it's not fully seated, press

firmly on the ends of the MEM-CAL. If it is necessary to remove the MEM-CAL, follow the above Steps again.

---

4   Information sensors

Refer to illustrations 4.1a, 4.1b, 4.2, 4.3, 4.5, 4.7, 4.10, 4.12 and 4.24

Note: *See component location illustrations in Section 2 for the location of the following information sensors.*

Engine coolant temperature sensor

1   The coolant sensor **(see illustrations)** is a thermistor (a resistor which varies the value of its voltage output in accordance with temperature changes). A failure in the coolant sensor circuit should set either a Code 14 or a Code 15. These codes indicate a failure in the coolant temperature circuit, so the appropriate solution to the problem will be either repair of a wire or replacement of the sensor.

6

4.1a   The coolant temperature sensor is located in the rear of the thermostat housing on 2.5L fours — to remove it, unplug the connector and unscrew the sensor with a wrench

4.1b   The V6 engine coolant temperature sensor (arrow) is on the right end of the intake manifold — don't confuse it with the other two sensors on either side of it

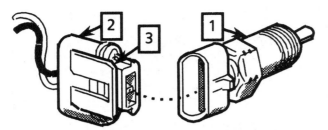

4.2   A typical engine coolant temperature sensor (1) harness connector (2) has a locking tab (3) that must be released to unplug the connector

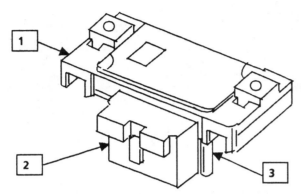

4.5   Typical Manifold Absolute Pressure (MAP) sensor

1   *Sensor assembly*   3   *Manifold vacuum tube*
2   *Electrical connector*

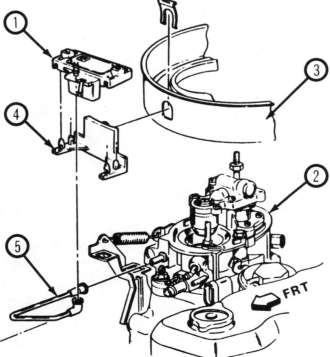

4.7   Typical MAP sensor installation (2.5L four-cylinder engine shown)

1   *MAP sensor assembly*   4   *MAP sensor mounting bracket*
2   *TBI unit*   5   *MAP sensor vacuum line*
3   *Air cleaner assembly*

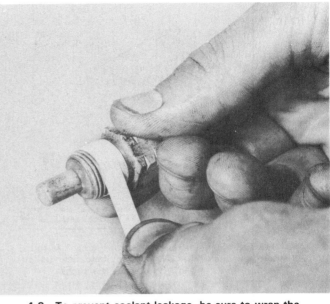

4.3   To prevent coolant leakage, be sure to wrap the temperature sensor threads with Teflon tape before installation

2   To remove the sensor, release the locking tab **(see illustration)**, unplug the electrical connector, then carefully unscrew the sensor. **Caution:** *Handle the coolant sensor with care. Damage to this sensor will affect the operation of the entire fuel injection system.*
3   Before installing the new sensor, wrap the threads with Teflon sealing tape to prevent leakage and thread corrosion **(see illustration)**.
4   Installation is the reverse of removal.

Manifold Absolute Pressure (MAP) sensor (four-cylinder engines only)

5   The Manifold Absolute Pressure (MAP) sensor **(see illustration)** monitors the intake manifold pressure changes resulting from changes in engine load and speed and converts the information into a voltage output. The ECM uses the MAP sensor to control fuel delivery and ignition timing.
6   A failure in the MAP sensor circuit should set a Code 33 or a Code 34.
7   Other than checking for loose hoses and electrical connections, the only service possible is unit replacement should diagnosis show the sensor to be faulty. Study the accompanying exploded view of a typical 2.5L four MAP sensor before attempting to replace it **(see illustration)**.

Manifold Air Temperature (MAT) sensor

8   The Manifold Air Temperature (MAT) sensor, located in the intake manifold on 2.5L fours and 2.0L Turbo fours and in the air cleaner housing on 3.0L V6s, is a thermistor (a resistor which changes the value of its voltage output as the temperature changes). The ECM uses the MAT sensor signal to delay EGR until the manifold air temperature reaches 40°F.
9   A failure in the MAT sensor circuit should set either a Code 23 or a Code 25.
10   To remove a MAT sensor, unplug the electrical connector and remove the sensor with a wrench **(see illustration)**.
11   Installation is the reverse of removal.

Mass Air Flow (MAF) sensor (V6 engine only)

12   The Mass Air Flow (MAF) sensor, which is located in its own housing between the air cleaner housing and the intake duct **(see illustration)**, measures the amount of air entering the engine. The ECM uses this information to control fuel delivery. A large quantity of air indicates acceleration, while a small quantity indicates deceleration or idle.

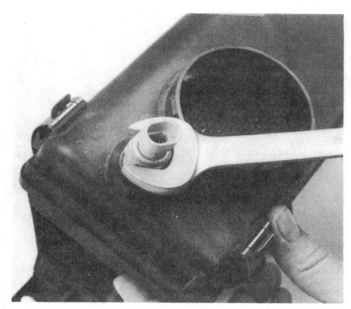

4.10   Removing a MAT sensor from the air cleaner housing on a V6 engine (air cleaner housing removed from engine for clarity)

4.12   Typical Mass Air Flow (MAF) sensor installation (arrow) on a V6 engine

13   If the sensor fails at a high frequency, a Code 33 should set and if it fails at a low frequency or power is lost to the sensor, a Code 34 should set. A code 44 or 45 may also result if the MAF sensor is faulty.
14   To replace the MAF sensor, unplug the electrical connector, loosen the hose clamps and detach the sensor from the ducts.
15   Installation is the reverse of removal.

Oxygen sensor

16   The oxygen sensor is mounted in the exhaust system where it can monitor the oxygen content of the exhaust gas stream.
17   By monitoring the voltage output of the oxygen sensor, the ECM will know what fuel mixture command to give the injector.
18   An open in the oxygen sensor circuit should set a Code 13. A low voltage in the circuit should set a Code 44. A high voltage in the circuit should set a Code 45. Codes 44 and 45 may also be set as a result of fuel system problems.
19   See Section 5 for the oxygen sensor replacement procedure.

Throttle Position Sensor (TPS)

20   The Throttle Position Sensor (TPS) is located on the right end of the throttle shaft on the TBI unit on 2.5L four engines, on the lower end of the throttle shaft on 3.0L V6 engines and on the forward end of the throttle shaft on 2.0L Turbo four engines.
21   By monitoring the output voltage from the TPS, the ECM can determine fuel delivery based on throttle valve angle (driver demand). A broken or loose TPS can cause intermittent bursts of fuel from the injector and an unstable idle because the ECM thinks the throttle is moving.
22   A problem in any of the TPS circuits will set either a Code 21 or 22. Once a trouble code is set, the ECM will use an artificial default value for TPS and some vehicle performance will return.
23   Should the TPS require replacement, the complete procedure is contained in Chapter 4.

Park/Neutral switch (automatic transmission equipped vehicles only)

24   The Park/Neutral (P/N) switch, located on the rear upper part of the automatic transaxle **(see illustration)**, indicates to the ECM when the transaxle is in Park or Neutral. This information is used for Transaxle Converter Clutch (TCC), Exhaust Gas Recirculation (EGR) and Idle Air Control (IAC) valve operation. **Caution:** *The vehicle should not be driven with the Park/Neutral switch disconnected because idle quality*

will be adversely affected and a false Code 24 (failure in the Vehicle Speed Sensor circuit) may be set.
25   For more information regarding the P/N switch, which is part of the Neutral/start and back-up light switch assembly, see Chapter 7.

A/C On signal

26   This signal tells the ECM that the A/C selector switch is turned on the On position and that the high side low pressure switch is closed. The ECM uses this information to turn on the A/C and adjust the idle speed when the air conditioning system is working. If this signal is not available to the ECM, idle may be rough, especially when the A/C compressor cycles.
27   Diagnosis of the circuit between the A/C On signal and the ECM should be left to a dealer service department.

Vehicle Speed Sensor (VSS)

28   The Vehicle Speed Sensor (VSS) sends a pulsing voltage signal to the ECM, which the ECM converts to miles per hour. This sensor controls the operation of the TCC system.

Distributor reference signal

29   The distributor sends a signal to the ECM to tell it both engine rpm and crankshaft position. See Electronic Spark Timing (Section 6), for further information.

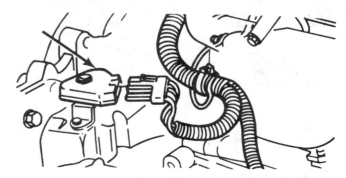

4.24   The Park/Neutral switch (arrow) is located on the upper rear part of the automatic transaxle

6

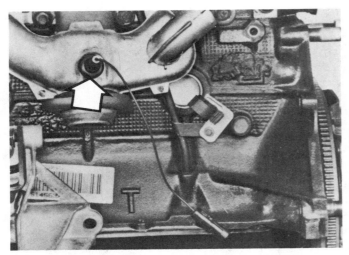

5.1a   The oxygen sensor is located in the center of the exhaust manifold on the 2.5L four cylinder engine (engine removed from vehicle for clarity)

5.1b   The oxygen sensor is located in left side of the exhaust manifold on the 3.0L V6

5   Oxygen sensor

Refer to illustrations 5.1a, 5.1b and 5.10

General description

1   The oxygen sensor, which is located in the exhaust manifold (2.5L four) or the exhaust pipe just below the manifold (3.0L V6) **(see illustrations)**, monitors the oxygen content of the exhaust gas stream. The oxygen content in the exhaust reacts with the oxygen sensor to produce a voltage output which varies from 0.1 volt (high oxygen, lean mixture) to 0.9 volts (low oxygen, rich mixture). The ECM constantly monitors this variable voltage output to determine the ratio of oxygen to fuel in the mixture. The ECM alters the air/fuel mixture ratio by controlling the pulse width (open time) of the fuel injectors. A mixture ratio of 14.7 parts air to 1 part fuel is the ideal mixture ratio for minimizing exhaust emissions, thus allowing the catalytic converter to operate at maximum efficiency. It is this ratio of 14.7 to 1 which the ECM and the oxygen sensor attempt to maintain at all times.

2   The oxygen sensor produces no voltage when it is below its normal operating temperature of about 600°F (315°C). During this initial period before warm-up, the ECM operates in open loop mode.

3   If the engine reaches normal operating temperature and/or has been running for two or more minutes, and if the oxygen sensor is producing a steady signal voltage between 0.35 and 0.55-volts, even though the TPS indicates that the engine is not at idle, the ECM will set a Code 13.

4   A delay of two minutes or more between engine start-up and normal operation of the sensor, followed by a low voltage signal or a short in the sensor circuit, will cause the ECM to set a Code 44. If a high voltage signal occurs, the ECM will set a Code 45.

5   When any of the above codes occur, the ECM operates in the open loop mode — that is it controls fuel delivery in accordance with a programmed default value instead of feedback information from the oxygen sensor.

6   The proper operation of the oxygen sensor depends on four conditions:

   a)   **Electrical** — The low voltages generated by the sensor depend upon good, clean connections which should be checked whenever a malfunction of the sensor is suspected or indicated.

   b)   **Outside air supply** — The sensor is designed to allow air circulation to the internal portion of the sensor. Whenever the sensor is removed and installed or replaced, make sure the air passages are not restricted.

   c)   **Proper operating temperature** — The ECM will not react to the sensor signal until the sensor reaches approximately 600°F (315°C). This factor must be taken into consideration when evaluating the performance of the sensor.

   d)   **Unleaded fuel** — The use of unleaded fuel is essential for proper operation of the sensor. Make sure the fuel you are using is of this type.

7   In addition to observing the above conditions, special care must be taken whenever the sensor is serviced.

   a)   The oxygen sensor has a permanently attached pigtail and connector which should not be removed from the sensor. Damage or removal of the pigtail or connector can adversely affect operation of the sensor.

   b)   Grease, dirt and other contaminants should be kept away from the electrical connector and the louvered end of the sensor.

   c)   Do not use cleaning solvents of any kind on the oxygen sensor.

   d)   Do not drop or roughly handle the sensor.

   e)   The silicone boot must be installed in the correct position to prevent the boot from being melted and to allow the sensor to operate properly.

Replacement

Note: *Because it is installed in the exhaust manifold or pipe, which contracts when cool, the oxygen sensor may be very difficult to loosen when the engine is cold. Rather than risk damage to the sensor (assuming you are planning to reuse it in another manifold or pipe), start and run the engine for a minute or two, then shut it off. Be careful not to burn yourself during the following procedure.*

8   Disconnect the cable from the negative terminal of the battery.

9   Raise the vehicle and place it securely on jackstands.

10   Carefully unsnap the pigtail lead retaining clip **(see illustration)**.

5.10   Typical electrical connector for an oxygen sensor pigtail lead (V6 engine shown) — if you have trouble finding the connector, locate the sensor first, then trace the pigtail lead to its connector

11 Disconnect the electrical connector from the sensor.
12 Note the position of the silicone boot, if equipped, and carefully unscrew the sensor from the exhaust manifold. **Caution:** *Excessive force may damage the threads.*
13 Anti-seize compound must be used on the threads of the sensor to facilitate future removal. The threads of new sensors will already be coated with this compound, but if an old sensor is removed and reinstalled, recoat the threads.
14 Install the sensor and tighten it securely.
15 Reconnect the electrical connector of the pigtail lead to the main engine wiring harness.
16 Snap the pigtail retaining clip closed.
17 Lower the vehicle and reconnect the cable to the negative terminal of the battery.

6 Electronic Spark Timing (EST)

General description

Note: *The following description of the EST system applies to both HEI-equipped and distributorless (C3I and DIS) vehicles. But the check and ignition timing procedures below do not apply to DIS or C3I equipped vehicles because their ignition timing cannot be adjusted. Always consult the VECI label for the exact procedure for your vehicle.*

1   To provide improved engine performance, fuel economy and control of exhaust emissions, the Electronic Control Module (ECM) controls distributor spark advance (ignition timing) with the Electronic Spark Timing (EST) system.
2   The ECM receives a reference pulse from the distributor, which indicates both engine rpm and crankshaft position. The ECM then determines the proper spark advance for the engine operating conditions and sends an EST pulse to the distributor.

Checking

3   The ECM will set spark timing at a specified value when the diagnostic "Test" terminal in the ALCL connector is grounded. To check for EST operation, the timing should be checked at 2000 rpm with the terminal ungrounded. Then ground the test terminal. If the timing changes at 2000 rpm, the EST is operating. A fault in the EST system will usually set Trouble Code 42.

Setting base timing

4   To set the initial base timing, locate, then disconnect the timing connector (the location and wire color of the timing connector is on the VECI label).
5   Set the timing as specified on the VECI label. This will cause a

Code 42 to be stored in the ECM memory. Be sure to clear the memory after setting the timing (see Section 2).
6   For further information regarding the testing and component replacement procedures for either the HEI/EST distributor or the distributorless (DIS or C3I) ignition systems, refer to Chapter 5.

7 Electronic Spark Control (ESC) system (V6 engine)

Refer to illustrations 7.3 and 7.11

General description

1   Irregular octane levels in modern gasoline can cause detonation in an engine. Detonation is sometimes referred to as "spark knock."
2   The Electronic Spark Control (ESC) system is designed to retard spark timing up to 20° to reduce spark knock in the engine. This allows the engine to use maximum spark advance to improve driveability and fuel economy.
3   The ESC knock sensor, which is located on the upper left end of the block under the throttle body **(see illustration)**, sends a voltage signal of 8 to 10-volts to the ECM when no spark knock is occurring and the ECM provides normal advance. When the knock sensor detects abnormal vibration (spark knock), the ESC module turns off the circuit to the ECM and the voltage at ECM terminal B7 drops to zero volts. The ECM then retards the EST distributor until spark knock is eliminated.
4   Failure of the ESC knock sensor signal or loss of ground at the ESC module will cause the signal to the ECM to remain high. This condition will result in the ECM controlling the EST as if no spark knock is occurring. Therefore, no retard will occur and spark knock may become severe under heavy engine load conditions. At this point, the ECM will set a Code 43.
5   Loss of the ESC signal to the ECM will cause the ECM to constantly retard EST. This will result in sluggish performance and cause the ECM to set a Code 43.

Component replacement
ESC sensor
6   Detach the cable from the negative terminal of the battery.
7   Disconnect the wiring harness connector from the ESC sensor.
8   Remove the ESC sensor from the block.
9   Installation is the reverse of the removal procedure.
ESC module
10 Detach the cable from the negative terminal of the battery.
11 Detach the wiring harness electrical connector from the module **(see illustration)**.
12 Remove the module mounting bolts and remove the module.
13 Installation is the reverse of removal.

6

7.3   The Electronic Spark Control (ESC) knock sensor (arrow) is located on the top of the block, underneath the throttle body

7.11   The ESC module is located on the firewall, between the A/C compressor relay and the engine coolant fan relay — to remove it, unplug the connector (A) and remove the two mounting bolts (B)

8 Exhaust Gas Recirculation (EGR) system

Refer to illustrations 8.13, 8.27, 8.31, 8.41 and 8.42

General description

1   The Exhaust Gas Recirculation (EGR) system is used to lower NOx (oxides of nitrogen) emission levels caused by high combustion temperatures. It does this by decreasing combustion temperature. The main element of the system is the EGR valve, which feeds small amounts of exhaust gas back into the combustion chamber.

2   The EGR valve is usually open during warm engine operation and anytime the engine is running above idle speed. The amount of gas recirculated is controlled by variations in vacuum and exhaust backpressure.

3   There are three types of EGR valves. Their names refer to the means by which they are controlled:
Positive backpressure
Negative backpressure (2.5L four-cylinder engine only)
Ported vacuum

Positive backpressure EGR valve

4   The positive backpressure valve has an air bleed, located inside the EGR valve assembly, which acts as a vacuum regulator. This bleed valve controls the amount of vacuum in the vacuum chamber by bleeding vacuum to the atmosphere during the open phase of the cycle. When the bleed valve receives sufficient exhaust backpressure through the hollow shaft, it closes the bleed. At this point, maximum available vacuum is applied to the diaphragm and the EGR valve opens.

5   If there is little or no vacuum in the vacuum chamber, such as at idle or wide open throttle, or if there is little or no pressure in the exhaust manifold, the EGR valve will not open. This type of valve will not open if vacuum is applied to it with the engine stopped or idling.

Negative backpressure EGR valve

6   The negative backpressure EGR valve is similar to the positive backpressure EGR valve except that the bleed valve spring is moved from above the valve to below and the valve is normally closed.

Ported vacuum EGR valve

7   The ported vacuum EGR valve uses ported vacuum connected directly to the EGR valve. The amount of exhaust gas recirculated is controlled by the throttle opening and the amount of manifold vacuum.

Port EGR valve (ECM controlled)

8   This valve is controlled by a flexible diaphragm which is spring loaded to hold the valve closed. Ported vacuum applied to the top side of the diaphragm overcomes the spring pressure and opens the valve in the exhaust gas port.

9   The EGR vacuum control has a vacuum solenoid that uses *pulse width modulation*. This means that the ECM turns the solenoid on and off many times a second and varies the amount of on time (the pulse width) to vary the amount of exhaust gas recirculated.

10   A diagnostic switch is part of the control and monitors vacuum to the EGR valve. This switch will trigger a *Check Engine* light and set a Code 32 in the event of a vacuum circuit failure.

EGR valve identification

11   A series of numbers is stamped into the top of every EGR valve. This identification number indicates the assembly plant code, part number, date built and type of EGR valve.
   a) Positive backpressure EGR valves will have a *P* stamped on the top side of the valve after the part number.
   b) Negative backpressure EGR valves will have an *N* stamped on the top side of the valve after the part number.
   c) Port EGR valves have no identification stamped after the part number.

Checking

Non-ECM controlled EGR valves

12   Hold the top of the EGR valve and try to rotate it back and forth. If looseness is felt, replace the valve.

13   If no looseness is felt, place the transaxle in Neutral (manual) or Park (automatic), run the engine at idle until it warms up to at least 195°F and push up on the underside of the EGR valve diaphragm (**see illustration**). The rpm should drop. If there is no change in rpm, clean the EGR passages. If there is still no change in rpm, replace the valve.

14   If the rpm drops, check for movement of the EGR valve diaphragm as the rpm is changed from approximately 2000 rpm to idle. If the

diaphragm moves, there is no problem.

15   If the diaphragm does not move, check the vacuum signal at the EGR valve as the engine rpm is changed from approximately 2000 rpm to idle.

16   If the vacuum is over six inches, replace the EGR valve. If it is under six inches, check the vacuum hoses for restrictions, leaks or poor connections.

ECM controlled port type EGR valves

17   Disconnect the EGR solenoid vacuum harness. Rotate the harness and reinstall only the EGR valve side. Install a vacuum pump with gauge on the manifold side of the EGR solenoid. Turn the ignition to On (engine stopped). Apply vacuum. Observe the EGR valve. The valve should not move.

18   If the valve moves, disconnect the EGR solenoid electrical connector and repeat the test. If the valve still moves, replace the solenoid.

19   If the valve does not move, ground the diagnostic terminal and repeat the test. If the valve still does not move, replace the EGR valve.

20   If the valve does move, start the engine. Lift up on the EGR valve and note the idle speed.

21   If there is no change in the idle, remove the EGR valve and check the passages for blockage. If the passages are not plugged, replace the EGR valve.

22   If the idle roughens, reconnect the EGR solenoid. Connect a vacuum gauge to the vacuum harness at the EGR valve. Warm up the engine to normal operating temperature. If your transaxle is an automatic, place it in Drive. Hold the brakes and accelerate momentarily up to about 1800 rpm. Observe the gauge. It should indicate over two but less than ten inches of vacuum.

23   If it is zero or less than two inches of vacuum, check for restrictions in the vacuum lines. If there are no restrictions in the vacuum lines, the park/neutral switch is probably faulty (see Chapter 7B).

24   If there is over ten inches of vacuum, replace the EGR filter.

25   If the vacuum is within two to ten inches, the EGR system is okay.

Component replacement

EGR valve

26   Disconnect the vacuum hose from the EGR valve.

27   Remove the nuts or bolts which secure the valve to the intake manifold or adapter (**see illustration**).

28   Separate the EGR valve from the engine.

8.13   To check an EGR valve diaphragm for proper operation, warm up the engine, remove the air cleaner assembly (2.5L four only) and, using a rag to protect your fingers, push up on the diaphragm — the engine should stumble and stall (the EGR valve on a 2.5L four is shown, but the test is the same for all engines)

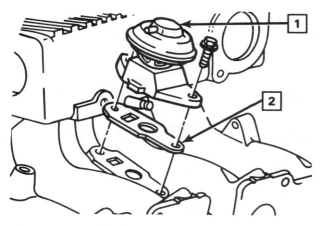

8.27   The EGR valve assembly (1) and gasket (2) on a 2.0L Turbo

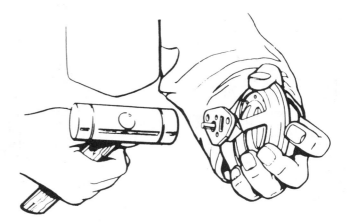

8.31   Deposits can be removed from the EGR pintle seating area by tapping the end of the pintle lightly with a plastic hammer

EGR valve cleaning

29 Inspect the valve pintle for deposits.

30 Depress the valve diaphragm and check for deposits around the valve seating area.

31 Hold the valve securely and tap lightly on the round pintle with a plastic hammer, using a light snapping action, to remove any deposits from the valve seat (**see illustration**). Make sure to empty any loose particles from the valve. Depress the valve diaphragm again and inspect the valve seating area, repeating the cleaning operation as necessary.

32 Use a wire brush to carefully clean deposits from the pintle.

33 Remove any deposits from the valve outlet using a screwdriver.

34 If EGR passages in the intake manifold show an excessive build-up of deposits, the passages should be cleaned. Care should be taken to ensure that all loose particles are completely removed to prevent them from clogging the EGR valve or from being ingested into the engine. **Note:** *It is a good idea to place a rag in the passage opening to keep debris from entering while cleaning the manifold.*

35 With a wire wheel, buff the exhaust deposits from the mounting surface.

36 Look for exhaust deposits in the valve outlet. Remove deposit build-up with a screwdriver.

37 Clean the mounting surfaces of the EGR valve. Remove all traces of old gasket material.

38 Install the new EGR valve, with a new lithium-base grease coated gasket, on the intake manifold or adapter.

39 Connect the vacuum signal hose to the EGR valve.

EGR control solenoid

40 Disconnect the negative battery cable.

41 Unplug the solenoid electrical connector (**see illustration**).

42 Clearly label, then detach, the vacuum hoses (**see illustration**).

43 Remove the mounting nut and the solenoid.

44 Installation is the reverse of removal.

---

9   Evaporative Emission Control System (EECS)

Refer to illustrations 9.2a, 9.2b, 9.2c, 9.16, 9.18, 9.22, 9.23 and 9.24

General description

1   This system is designed to trap and store fuel vapors that evaporate from the fuel tank, throttle body and intake manifold.

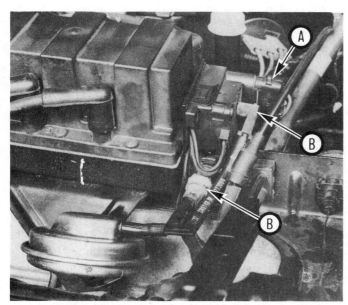

8.41   Typical EGR valve control solenoid on a V6 engine — to remove it, unplug the electrical connector (A) and clearly label and detach the vacuum hoses (B)

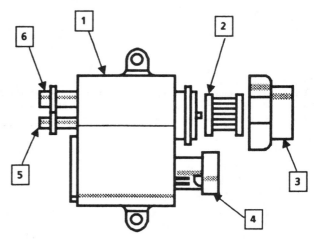

8.42   Typical EGR control solenoid assembly (2.0L Turbo four shown)

1 EGR vacuum control assembly base	5 Vacuum connector from source
2 Filter	6 Vacuum connector to EGR valve
3 Cover	
4 Electrical connector	

6

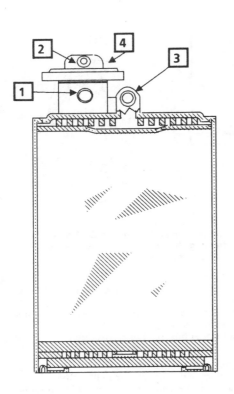

**9.2a   Typical evaporative canister
for the 2.5L four**

1 PCV
2 Control vacuum
3 Fuel tank vapors
4 Purge valve

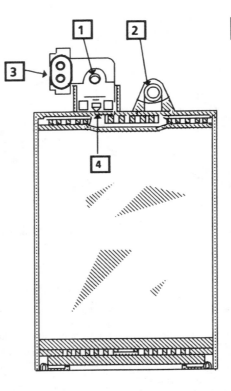

**9.2b   Typical evaporative canister for
the 3.0L V6 with encapsulated solenoid**

1 Purge tube
2 Fuel tank vapors
3 Solenoid
4 Fuel vapor

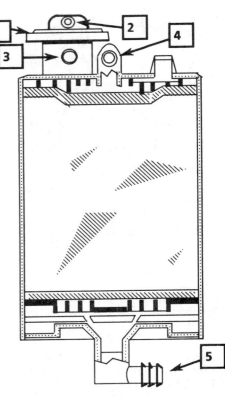

**9.2c   Typical evaporative canister
for the 2.0L Turbo four**

1 Purge valve
2 Control vacuum signal
3 PCV tube
4 Vapor from fuel tank
5 Air inlet/drain tube

2   The Evaporative Emission Control System (EECS) consists of a charcoal-filled canister and the lines connecting the canister to the fuel tank, ported vacuum and intake manifold vacuum **(see illustrations)**.
3   Fuel vapors are transferred from the fuel tank, throttle body and intake manifold to a canister where they are stored when the engine is not operating. When the engine is running, the fuel vapors are purged from the canister by intake air flow and consumed in the normal combustion process.
4   On the 3.0L V6 with MFI, the ECM operates a solenoid valve (located on top of the canister) which controls vacuum to the purge valve in the charcoal canister. Under cold engine or idle conditions, the solenoid is turned on by the ECM, which closes the valve and blocks vacuum to the canister purge valve. The ECM turns off the solenoid valve and allows purge when the engine is warm.

Checking

5   Poor idle, stalling and poor driveability can be caused by an inoperative purge valve, a damaged canister, split or cracked hoses or hoses connected to the wrong tubes.
6   Evidence of fuel loss or fuel odor can be caused by liquid fuel leaking from fuel lines or the TBI, a cracked or damaged canister, an inoperative bowl vent valve, an inoperative purge valve, disconnected, misrouted, kinked, deteriorated or damaged vapor or control hoses or an improperly seated air cleaner or air cleaner gasket.
7   Inspect each hose attached to the canister for kinks, leaks and breaks along its entire length. Repair or replace as necessary.
8   Inspect the canister. It it is cracked or damaged, replace it.
9   Look for fuel leaking from the bottom of the canister. If fuel is leaking, replace the canister and check the hoses and hose routing.
10   Check the filter at the bottom of the canister. If it's dirty, plugged or damaged, replace the filter.
11   Apply a short length of hose to the lower tube of the purge valve

assembly and attempt to blow through it. Little or no air should pass into the canister (a small amount of air will pass because the canister has a constant purge hole).
12   With a hand vacuum pump, apply vacuum through the control vacuum signal tube to the purge valve diaphragm.
13   If the diaphragm does not hold vacuum for at least 20 seconds, the diaphragm is leaking and the canister must be replaced.
14   If the diaphragm holds vacuum, again try to blow through the hose while vacuum is still being applied. An increased flow of air should be noted. If it isn't, replace the canister.

Component replacement

Fuel vapor canister solenoid (3.0L V6 only)
15   Detach the cable from the negative terminal of the battery.
16   Unplug the solenoid electrical connectors **(see illustration)**.
17   Clearly label, then detach, the vacuum hoses from the solenoid.
18   Remove the solenoid from the canister **(see illustration)**.
19   Installation is the reverse of removal.

Fuel vapor canister/filter
20   Detach the electrical connector and vacuum lines from the solenoid, if equipped.
21   Clearly label, then detach, any remaining vacuum lines from the canister.
22   Remove the A/C accumulator bracket bolt and the canister bracket bolt **(see illustration)**.
23   Move the accumulator out of the way and remove the canister by pulling it straight up **(see illustration)**.
24   Check the filter and replace it if it is dirty **(see illustration)** (not applicable to the 2.0L Turbo canister, which has no externally accessible filter on the bottom).
25   Installation is the reverse of removal.

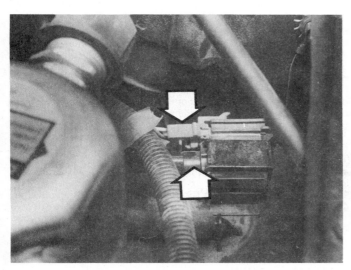

9.16   The evaporative canister solenoid electrical
connectors (arrows) must be unplugged to remove either
the solenoid or the canister

9.18   To remove the solenoid from the canister, pry the
two locking tangs apart with a small screwdriver and lift
up on the solenoid

9.22   To remove the canister, remove the accumulator
bracket bolt (A) and the canister bracket bolt (B) . . .

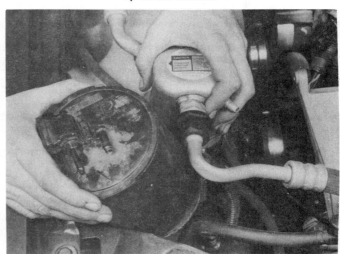

9.23   . . . then push the accumulator aside and lift the
canister out

9.24   To replace the filter on a 2.5L four or a 3.0L V6
canister, simply remove it and install another one (the 2.0L
Turbo four canister does not have a removable filter — the
entire canister must be replaced)

6

10   Positive Crankcase Ventilation (PCV) system

1   The Positive Crankcase Ventilation (PCV) system reduces hydrocarbon emissions by scavenging crankcase vapors. It does this by circulating fresh air from the air cleaner through the crankcase, where it mixes with blow-by gases and is then rerouted through a PCV valve to the intake manifold.
2   The main components of the PCV system are the PCV valve, a fresh air filtered inlet and the vacuum hoses connecting these two components with the engine and the EECS system.
3   To maintain idle quality, the PCV valve restricts the flow when the intake manifold vacuum is high. If abnormal operating conditions arise, the system is designed to allow excessive amounts of blow-by gases to flow back through the crankcase vent tube into the air cleaner to be consumed by normal combustion.
4   Checking and replacement of the PCV valve and filter is covered in Chapter 1.

11   Transaxle Converter Clutch (TCC)

Refer to illustration 11.2
General description
1   The Transaxle Converter Clutch (TCC) uses a solenoid-operated

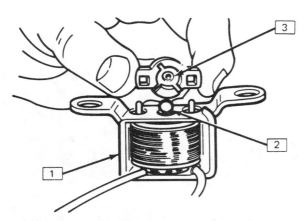

11.2   Typical Transaxle Converter Clutch (TCC) device

1   TCC solenoid   2   Check ball   3   Check ball seat

valve in the automatic transaxle to mechanically couple the engine flywheel to the output shaft of the transmission through the torque converter. This reduces the slippage losses in the converter, reducing emissions because engine rpm at any given speed is reduced. It also increases fuel economy.

2   For the converter clutch to operate properly, two conditions must be met:

a) The engine must be warmed up before the clutch can apply. The engine coolant temperature sensor (see Section 4) tells the ECM when the engine is at operating temperature.

b) The vehicle must be traveling at the necessary minimum speed to raise the pressure to the level necessary to apply the valve. If the hydraulic pressure is correct, the ECM signals the solenoid to apply the converter clutch **(see illustration)**.

3   After the converter clutch applies, the ECM uses the information from the TPS to release the clutch when the car is accelerating or decelerating at a certain rate.

4   Another switch used in the TCC circuit is a brake switch which opens the power supply to the TCC solenoid when the brake is applied.

5   A third gear switch is placed in series on the battery side of the TCC solenoid to prevent TCC application until the transmission is in third gear.

Checking

6   If the converter clutch is applied at all times, the engine will stall immediately, just like a manual transaxle with the clutch applied.

7   If the converter clutch does not apply, fuel economy may be lower than expected. If the Vehicle Speed Sensor (VSS) (see Section 4) fails, the TCC will not apply.

8   A TCC-equipped transaxle has different operating characteristics than an automatic transaxle without TCC. If you detect a "chuggle" or "surge" condition, perform the following check.

9   Install a tachometer.

10   Drive the vehicle until normal operating temperature is reached, then maintain a 50 to 55 mph speed.

11   Lightly touch the the brake pedal and check it for a slight bumpy sensation, indicating that the the TCC is releasing. A slight increase in rpm should also be noted.

12   Release the brake and check for reapplication of the converter clutch and a slight decrease in engine rpm.

13   If the TCC fails to perform satisfactorily during this test, take your vehicle to a dealer to have the TCC serviced.

---

12   Catalytic converter

General description

1   The catalytic converter is an emission control device added to the exhaust system to reduce pollutants from the exhaust gas stream. A single-bed converter design is used in combination with a three-way (reduction) catalyst. The catalytic coating on the three-way catalyst contains platinum and rhodium, which lowers the levels of oxides of nitrogen (NOx) as well as hydrocarbons (HC) and carbon monoxide (CO).

Checking

2   The test equipment for a catalytic converter is expensive and highly sophisticated. If you suspect that the converter on your vehicle is malfunctioning, take it to a dealer or authorized emissions inspection facility for diagnosis and repair.

3   Whenever the vehicle is raised for servicing of underbody components, check the converter for leaks, corrosion and other damage. If damage is discovered, the converter should be replaced.

4   Because the converter is welded to the exhaust system, converter replacement requires removal of the exhaust pipe assembly (see Chapter 4). Take the vehicle, or the exhaust pipe system, to a dealer or a muffler shop.

Chapter 7 Part A Manual transaxle

Contents

Specifications

Torque specifications | Ft-lbs

Clutch housing cover bolts	10
Muncie transaxle shift shaft nut	61
Transaxle mount through-bolt and nut	80
Transaxle mount-to-frame	
bolt	40
nut	29
Transaxle strut	
bracket-to-transaxle bracket bolt	38
bracket nut	40
strut-to-frame bracket through-bolt	50
strut-to-transaxle bracket through-bolt	40
Transaxle-to-engine bolts	55

7A

1 General information

These models are equipped with either a 5-speed manual or a 3-speed automatic transaxle. Information on the manual transaxle is included in this Part of Chapter 7. Information on the automatic transaxle can be found in Part B of this Chapter.

The 5-speed manual transaxle used in these vehicles is essentially a transmission coupled together with a differential in one assembly. Although transaxles on these models are built by two manufacturers, Isuzu and Muncie, they are very similar in design.

Due to the complexity, availability of replacement parts and the special tools necessary, internal repair procedures for the transaxle unit is not recommended for the home mechanic. The information contained within this manual will be limited to general diagnosis, external adjustments and removal and installation.

Depending on the expense involved in having a faulty transaxle overhauled, it may be an advantage to consider replacing the unit with either a new or rebuilt one. Your local dealer or transmission shop should be able to supply you with information concerning cost, availability and exchange policy. Regardless of how you decide to remedy a faulty transaxle problem, however, you can still save considerable expense by removing and installing the unit yourself.

2 Manual transaxle shift cables (Muncie transaxle) — removal and installation

Refer to illustration 2.2

Removal

1 Disconnect the negative cable at the battery. Place the cable out of the way so it cannot accidently come in contact with the negative terminal of the battery, as this would once again allow power into the

electrical system of the vehicle.

2   Remove the nuts retaining the selector and shift cables to the transaxle levers **(see illustration)**.

3   Remove the console (Chapter 11).

4   Use a small screwdriver to pry the cable free of the shift control ball sockets.

5   Remove the screws from the carpeting sill plate in the left front corner of the passenger compartment, remove the plate and then pull the carpet back for access to the cables.

6   Remove the cable retainer and grommet screws at the floor pan and pry the two retaining tabs up.

7   Pull the cables through into the passenger compartment and remove them from the vehicle.

Installation

8   Push the cable assembly through the opening from the passenger compartment into the engine compartment.

9   Install the grommet and cable retainer screws and bend the two

two retaining tabs down.

10   Install the carpet and sill plate.

11   Connect the cable ends to the shifter.

12   Install the console.

13   Connect the cable assembly to the transaxle bracket and shift levers.

---

3   Manual transaxle shifter shaft seal (Muncie transaxle) — removal and installation

Refer to illustration 3.3

1   Disconnect the negative cable at the battery. Place the cable out of the way so it cannot accidently come in contact with the negative terminal of the battery, as this would once again allow power into the electrical system of the vehicle.

2   Disconnect the shift cables from the shift lever.

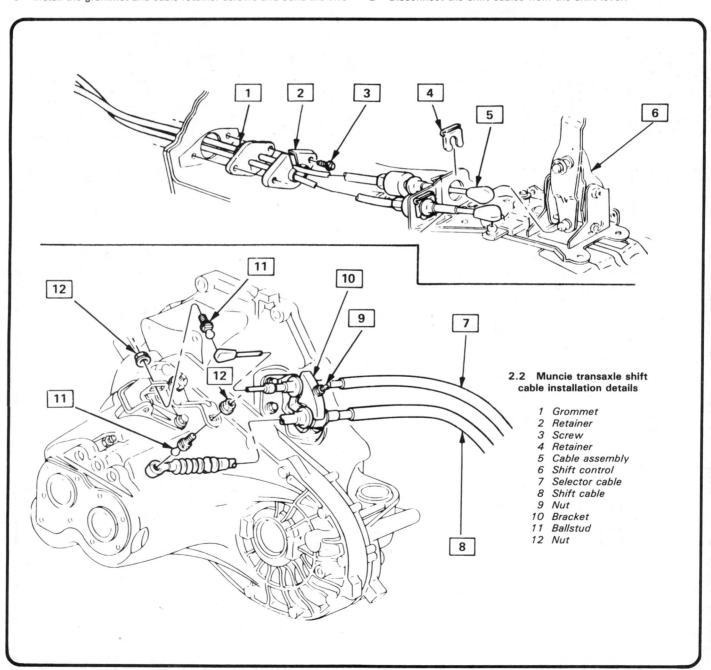

2.2   Muncie transaxle shift cable installation details

1 Grommet
2 Retainer
3 Screw
4 Retainer
5 Cable assembly
6 Shift control
7 Selector cable
8 Shift cable
9 Nut
10 Bracket
11 Ballstud
12 Nut

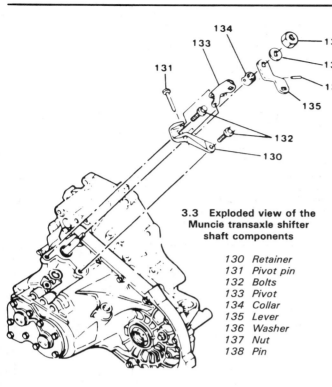

3.3 Exploded view of the Muncie transaxle shifter shaft components

130 Retainer
131 Pivot pin
132 Bolts
133 Pivot
134 Collar
135 Lever
136 Washer
137 Nut
138 Pin

3   Remove the shift lever nut, making sure the shift lever itself does not move while the nut is loosened **(see illustration)**.
4   Remove the shift lever assembly, keeping all of the components in order.
5   Pry out the old seal with a screwdriver or suitably hooked tool.
6   Install the new seal evenly into the bore and tap it fully into place, using a suitable size socket and hammer.
7   Installation of the remaining components is the reverse of removal.

4   Manual transaxle shift cables (Isuzu transaxle) — removal, installation and adjustment

Refer to illustrations 4.2 and 4.14

Removal

1   Disconnect the negative cable at the battery. Place the cable out of the way so it cannot accidentally come in contact with the negative terminal of the battery, as this would once again allow power into the electrical system of the vehicle.
2   In the engine compartment, remove the clamps and nuts retaining the cables to the shift lever **(see illustration)**.
3   In the passenger compartment, remove the shift knob, console and boot (Chapter 11).
4   Disconnect the shift cables from the shifter by prying the cable ends loose from the shifter ballstuds with a screwdriver.
5   Remove the spring clips retaining the cables to the shifter.
6   Remove the right front floor carpet sill and carpet for access to the shift cables.
7   Remove the cable grommet screws, lift off the cover, pull the cable assembly through and remove it from the vehicle.

7A

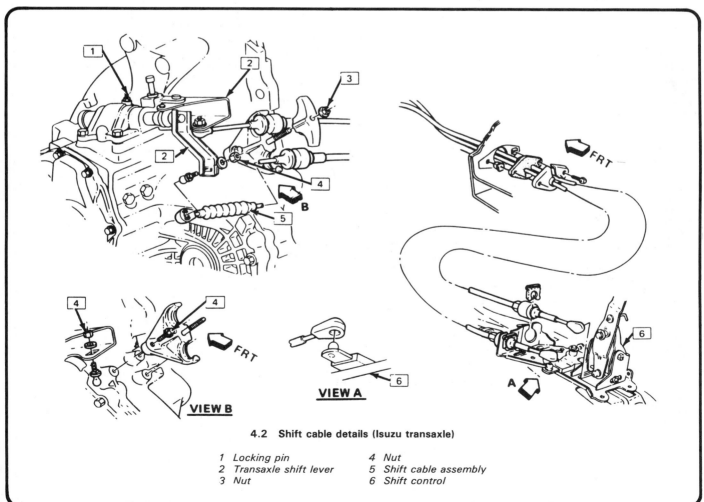

4.2   Shift cable details (Isuzu transaxle)

1 Locking pin
2 Transaxle shift lever
3 Nut
4 Nut
5 Shift cable assembly
6 Shift control

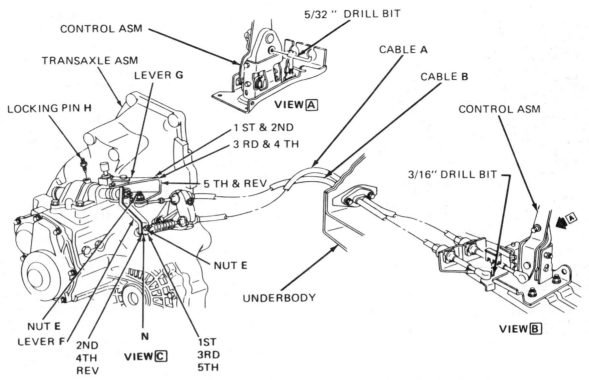

4.14   Isuzu transaxle shift cable adjustment procedure (refer to Section 4 text)

Installation

8   Insert the cable assembly through the floor and install the cable grommet cover.
9   Connect the shift cables to the shifter by placing them in position and popping them onto the ballstuds.
10 Install the cable retainer spring clips.
11 Install the carpet and sill cover.
12 Install the console, shift knob and boot, unless the cables are to be adjusted.
13 In the engine compartment, connect the cables to the shift lever.

Adjustment

14 If adjustment is necessary, shift the transaxle into 3rd gear and lock it in 3rd by removing the locking pin (H) and installing it upside down (**see illustration**).
15 Loosen the shift cable nuts (E) at the shift levers (G and F).
16 Install a 5/32-inch (No. 22) drill bit into the upper shifter alignment hole (View A).
17 Line up the hole in the selector lever with the slot in the shifter plate and insert a 3/16-inch drill bit (View B).
18 Tighten the shift lever nuts (E) at the shift levers (G and F).
19 Remove the drill bits and install the locking pin in the proper direction.
20 Install the console, shift knob and boot.
21 Connect the negative battery cable and test drive the vehicle. Make sure there is sufficient neutral gate feel. It may be necessary to repeat the adjustment procedure to obtain the proper neutral gate and shifting action.

---

5   Manual transaxle shift control (all models) — removal and installation

---

Refer to illustration 5.5

Removal

1   Disconnect the negative cable at the battery. Place the cable out of the way so it cannot accidently come in contact with the negative terminal of the battery, as this would once again allow power into the electrical system of the vehicle.
2   Remove the console, shift boot and knob (Chapter 11).
3   Disconnect the shift cables from the shifter.
4   Remove the shift cable retaining clips.
5   Remove the retaining nuts and lift the shift control assembly from the vehicle (**see illustration**).

Installation

6   Place the shift control assembly in position and install the retaining nuts.
7   Connect the shift cables to the shift control assembly.
8   Install the console.
9   Connect the negative battery cable.

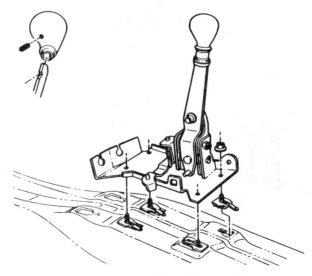

5.5   Shift control installation details

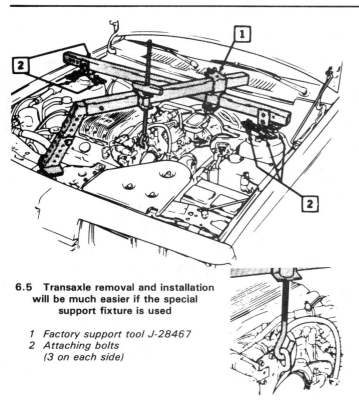

6.5 Transaxle removal and installation will be much easier if the special support fixture is used

1 Factory support tool J-28467
2 Attaching bolts
  (3 on each side)

6 Manual transaxle — removal and installation

Refer to illustrations 6.5, 6.9, 6.10 and 6.18
Removal

1   Disconnect the negative cable at the battery. Place the cable out of the way so that it cannot accidently come into contact with the terminal, which would again allow current flow.
2   Inside the passenger compartment, remove the left hush panel.
3   Disconnect the clutch linkage (Chapter 8). On hydraulic clutch-equipped models, disconnect the master cylinder pushrod from the clutch pedal. Unbolt the slave cylinder from the transaxle bracket and move it out of the way.
4   Disconnect the ground cable, shift cables and clamp from the transaxle.
5   The engine must be supported during transaxle removal and this can be accomplished using factory engine support tool J-28467 or equivalent **(see illustration)**. Install a 1/4-inch by 2-inch bolt in the hole in the right front motor mount to maintain driveline alignment if the support tool is used. If this tool is not available, support the engine with a lifting device which can hold it high enough to allow the transaxle to be lowered from the engine compartment with the vehicle raised.
6   Install the engine support or connect a lifting device and raise the engine sufficiently to take the weight off the engine mounts. Raise the vehicle as necessary to allow the transaxle top be removed (approximately 28 inches), support it securely on jackstands and remove the front wheels.
7   Remove the left front brake caliper, hang it out of the way on a piece of wire and remove the disc (Chapter 9).
8   Drain the transaxle fluid (Chapter 1).
9   Remove the transaxle mount-to-frame bolts **(see illustration)**.

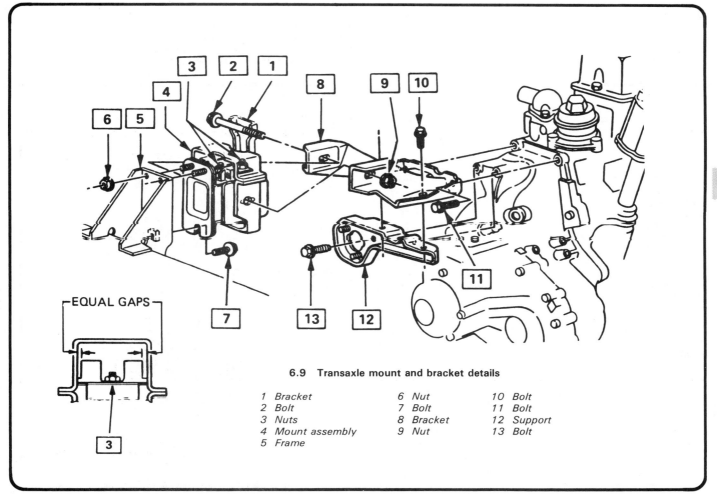

EQUAL GAPS

6.9 Transaxle mount and bracket details

1 Bracket	6 Nut	10 Bolt
2 Bolt	7 Bolt	11 Bolt
3 Nuts	8 Bracket	12 Support
4 Mount assembly	9 Nut	13 Bolt
5 Frame		

7A

10 Remove the front transaxle strut and bracket **(see illustration)**.
11 Remove the clutch housing cover bolts.
12 Disconnect the speedometer cable or sensor at the transaxle.
13 Disconnect the stabilizer bar at the control arm and suspension support.
14 Disconnect the balljoint and remove the left suspension support complete with the lower suspension arm (Chapter 10).
15 Remove the left front fender liner (Chapter 11).
16 Disconnect the right side driveaxle from the transaxle and remove the left driveaxle (Chapter 10).
17 Support the transaxle with a jack, preferably a transmission jack made for this purpose.
18 Remove the bellhousing-to-engine bolts **(see illustration)**.
19 Make a final check that all wiring, cables, etc. are disconnected from the transaxle.
20 Separate the transaxle from the engine by prying the bellhousing away from the engine.
21 Lower the transaxle and remove it from the left side of the engine compartment.
22 The clutch components can now be inspected (Chapter 8). In most cases, new clutch components should be installed as a matter of course if the transaxle is removed.

Installation

23 With the clutch components installed and properly aligned (see Chapter 8), carefully raise the transaxle into place, guide the right side driveaxle into the transaxle and slide the input shaft into place in the clutch splines.
24 Install the transaxle-to-engine bolts **(see illustration 6.18)** Tighten the bolts to the specified torque.
25 Install the left driveaxle.
26 Install the suspension support (Chapter 10).
27 Connect the speedometer cable or sensor.
28 Install the clutch housing cover.
29 Install the front strut bracket and the strut. Tighten the bolts to the specified torque.
30 Install the transaxle mount bolts. Tighten the bolts to the specified torque.
31 Install the front fender liner (Chapter 11).

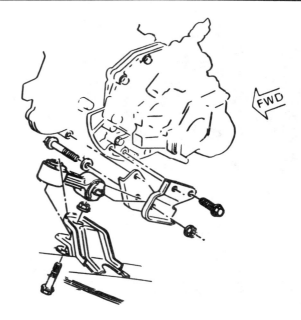

6.10   Transaxle strut and bracket details

32 Install the brake caliper (Chapter 9).
33 Install the wheels and lower the vehicle.
34 Connect the ground cable.
35 Connect the clutch linkage. On hydraulic clutch equipped models, install the slave cylinder and connect the clutch pushrod to the pedal.
36 Connect the shift linkage.
37 Remove the engine support.
38 Fill the transaxle with the specified lubricant (Chapter 1).
39 Connect the battery negative cable.

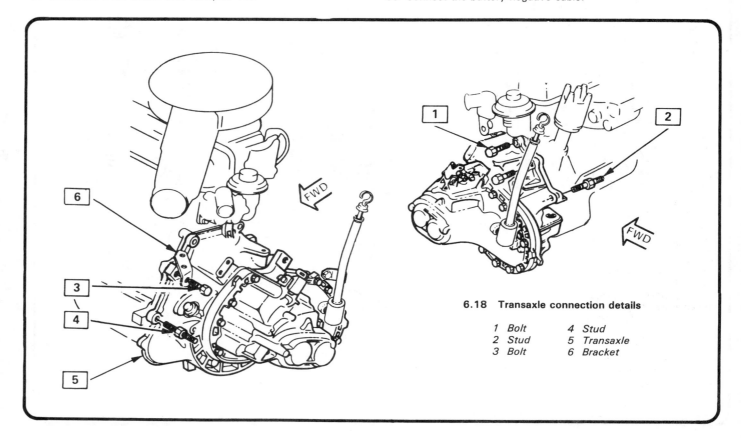

6.18   Transaxle connection details

1 Bolt   *4 Stud*
2 Stud   *5 Transaxle*
3 Bolt   *6 Bracket*

Chapter 7 Part B   Automatic transaxle

Contents

Specifications

Torque specifications

	Ft-lbs
Shift control nuts	17
Transaxle-to-engine bolts	55
Torque converter-to-driveplate	35
Torque converter-to-crankshaft	55
Torque converter shield	10
Transaxle mounting strut through bolt	31
Transaxle mount	
bracket-to-engine bolt	31
bracket-to-transaxle	38
through-bolt	38
TV cable-to-transaxle case bolt	7

---

1   General information

Refer to illustration 1.1

Due to the complexity of the clutches and the hydraulic control system, and because of the special tools and expertise required to perform an automatic transaxle overhaul, it should not be undertaken by the home mechanic. Therefore, the procedures in this Chapter are limited to general diagnosis, routine maintenance, adjustment and transaxle removal and installation.

If the transaxle requires major repair work, it should be left to a dealer service department or an automotive or transmission repair shop. You can, however, remove and install the transaxle yourself and save the expense, even if the repair work is done by a transmission specialist.

Replacement and adjustment procedures that the home mechanic can perform include those involving the throttle valve (TV) cable and

1.1 Underside view of the automatic transaxle

1 Transaxle pan
2 Right driveaxle
3 Driveplate
4 Mounting strut
5 Left driveaxle

the shift linkage. **Caution:** *Never tow a disabled vehicle with an automatic transaxle at speeds greater than 35 mph or distances over 50 miles.*

2 Diagnosis — general

1   Automatic transaxle malfunctions may be caused by a number of conditions, such as poor engine performance, improper adjustments, hydraulic malfunctions and mechanical problems.
2   The first check should be of the transaxle fluid level and condition. Refer to Chapter 1 for more information. Unless the fluid and filter have been recently changed, drain the fluid and replace the filter (also in Chapter 1).
3   Road test the vehicle and drive in all the various selective ranges, noting discrepancies in operation.
4   Verify that the engine is not at fault. If the engine has not received a tune-up recently, refer to Chapter 1 and make sure all engine components are functioning properly.
5   Check the adjustment of the throttle valve (TV) cable (Section 3).
6   Check the condition of all vacuum and electrical lines and fittings at the transaxle, or leading to it.
7   Check for proper adjustment of the shift control cable (Section 5).
8   If at this point a problem remains, there is one final check before the transaxle is removed for overhaul. The vehicle should be taken to a specialist who will connect a special pressure gauge and check the line pressure in the transaxle.

3 Throttle valve (TV) cable — replacement and adjustment

Refer to illustrations 3.2, 3.3, 3.5, 3.6 and 3.9

Replacement

1   Remove the air cleaner assembly.
2   Disconnect the TV cable from the throttle lever by grasping the connector, pulling it forward to disconnect it and then lifting up and off the lever pin **(see illustration)**.
3   Disconnect the TV cable housing from the bracket by compressing the tangs and pushing the housing back through the bracket **(see illustration)**.
4   Disconnect any clips or straps retaining the cable to the transaxle.
5   Remove the bolt retaining the cable to the transaxle **(see illustration)**.
6   Pull up on the cover until the end of the cable can be seen and then disconnect it from the transaxle TV link **(see illustration)**. Remove the cable from the vehicle.
7   To install, connect the cable to the transaxle TV link and install the bolt. Tighten the bolt to the specified torque and push the cover securely over the cable. Route the cable to the top of the engine, push the housing through the bracket until it clicks into place, place the connector over the throttle lever pin and pull back to lock it. Secure the cable with any retaining clips or straps.

Adjustment

8   The engine should not be running during this adjustment.

3.2   Move the TV cable connector forward and then lift up to detach it from the throttle lever pin (arrows)

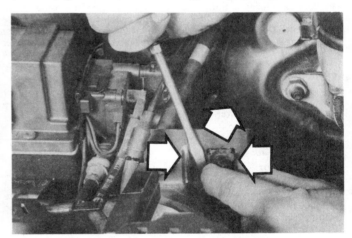

3.3   Use a screwdriver to compress the TV cable tangs (arrows) and then push the housing back through the bracket (arrow)

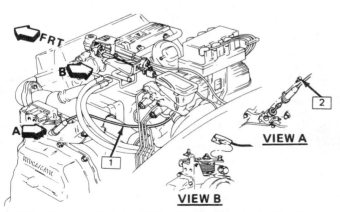

3.5   The throttle valve (TV) cable attaches to the throttle linkage and then travels down to the transmission where it attaches to a link inside the transmission

1   *TV cable*   2   *Cable-to-transaxle bolt*

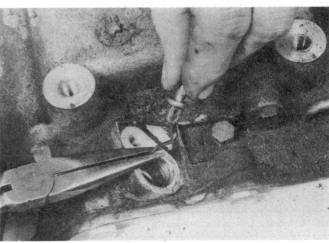

3.6   Hold the transaxle TV link with needle nose pliers and slide the cable link off the pin

7B

3.9   Press down on the TV cable re-adjust tab and then move the adjuster back against the fitting (arrows)

9   Depress the re-adjust tab and move the slider until it stops against the fitting (see illustration).
10   Release the re-adjust tab.
11   Manually turn the throttle lever to the "wide open throttle" position, which will automatically adjust the cable. Release the throttle lever. **Note:** *Do not use excessive force at the throttle lever to adjust the TV cable. If great effort is required to adjust the cable, disconnect the cable at the transaxle end and check for free operation. If it is still difficult, replace the cable. If it is now free, suspect a bent TV link in the transaxle or a problem with the throttle lever.*

4   Starter safety switch (automatic transaxle) — replacement and adjustment

Refer to illustrations 4.4 and 4.5

Replacement

1   Disconnect the negative cable at the battery. Place the cable out of the way so it cannot accidentally come in contact with the negative terminal of the battery, as this would once again allow power into the electrical system of the vehicle.
2   Shift the transaxle into Neutral.
3   Disconnect the shift linkage.
4   Lift the T-latch out of the connector and then unplug the connector (see illustration). It may be necessary to remove the heat shield covering the switch for access.
5   Remove the attaching bolts and lift the switch off the shift shaft (see illustration).
6   To install, line up the flats on the shift shaft with the flats in the switch and lower the switch onto the shaft.
7   Install the bolts. If the switch is new and the shaft has not been moved, tighten the bolts. If the switch requires adjustment, leave the bolts loose and follow the adjustment procedure below. The remainder of replacement is the reverse of removal.

Adjustment

8   Insert a 3/32 inch drill into switch gauge hole (see illustration 4.5).
9   Rotate the switch until the drill bit can be felt dropping into the switch, indicating that it is now in the Neutral position. Tighten the switch bolts.
10   Connect the battery negative cable and verify that the engine will start only in Neutral or Park.

5   Automatic transaxle shift cable — replacement and adjustment

Refer to illustrations 5.2a, 5.2b, 5.2c, 5.6 and 5.8

1   Disconnect the negative cable at the battery. Place the cable out

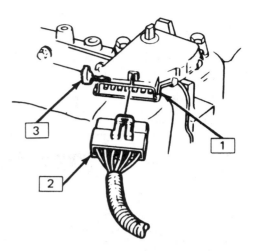

4.4   Starter safety switch connector details

    1   Switch   *3   T-latch*
    2   Connector

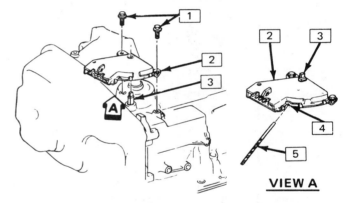

4.5   Starter safety switch installation details

    1   Bolts   *4   Adjustment hole*
    2   Switch   *5   3/32-inch drill bit*
    3   Transaxle shifter shaft   *used for adjustment*

of the way so that it cannot accidently come into contact with the terminal, which would once again allow current flow.

Removal

Console shift

2   Remove the console (Chapter 11) and disconnect the shift cable at the transaxle lever and the shift control lever (see illustrations).
3   Remove the right and left side sound insulators from the under dash portion of the console and then pull back the carpet for access to the cable.
4   Disengage the grommet in the firewall and withdraw the cable assembly.
5   Installation is the reverse of removal. After installation, adjust the cable as described below.

Column shift

6   In the engine compartment, disconnect the cable from the transaxle lever and bracket (see illustration).
7   In the passenger compartment, remove the left sound insulator located under the dash.
8   Disconnect the cable bracket on the steering column and separate the cable from the shift lever (see illustration).
9   Dislodge the grommet in the firewall and withdraw the cable from the vehicle.

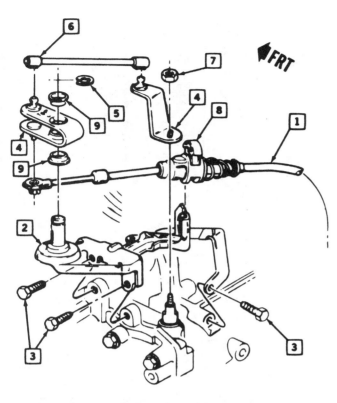

5.2a Floor shift cable engine compartment attachment details

1 Shift cable	4 Shift lever	7 Nut
2 Bracket	5 Retainer	8 Locking tab
3 Bolt	6 Link	9 Bearing

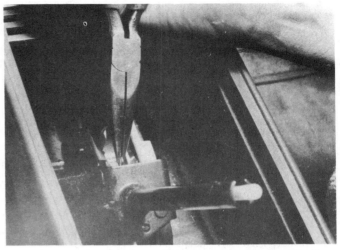

5.2b To disconnect the cable at the shift control, pull off the clip with needle nose pliers . . .

5.2c . . . and pry the cable off the lever pin with a screwdriver

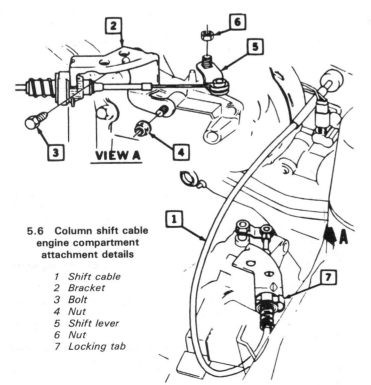

5.6 Column shift cable engine compartment attachment details

1 Shift cable
2 Bracket
3 Bolt
4 Nut
5 Shift lever
6 Nut
7 Locking tab

VIEW A

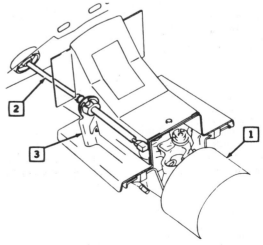

5.8 Column shift cable passenger compartment attachment details

1 Steering column	3 Bracket
2 Shift cable	

7B

10 Installation is the reverse of removal. After installation, adjust the cable as described below.

Adjustment

11 Place the shift control lever and the transaxle shift lever in Neutral, then push the locking tab on the shift cable to automatically adjust the cable **(see illustrations 5.2a and 5.6)**.
12 Connect the negative battery cable.

---

6 Automatic transaxle floor shift control — removal and installation

Refer to illustration 6.4

1   Disconnect the negative cable at the battery. Place the cable out of the way so it cannot accidentally come in contact with the negative terminal of the battery, as this would once again allow power into the electrical system of the vehicle.
2   Remove the console (Chapter 11).
3   Disconnect the shift cable from the shift control (Section 5).
4   Remove the retaining nuts and lift the control from the vehicle **(see illustration)**.
5   Place the shift control in position on the mounting studs and install the nuts. Tighten the nuts to the specified torque.
6   Connect the shift cables.
7   Install the console.
8   Connect the battery negative cable.

---

7 Automatic transaxle park/lock cable — removal and installation

Refer to illustration 7.4

Removal

1   Disconnect the negative cable at the battery. Place the cable out of the way so it cannot accidentally come in contact with the negative terminal of the battery, as this would once again allow power into the electrical system of the vehicle.
2   Remove the console (Chapter 11).
3   Place the transaxle shift lever in Park and the ignition key switch in the Run position.
4   Insert a screwdriver blade into the slot in the ignition switch inhibitor, depress the cable latch and detach the cable **(see illustration)**.
5   Push the cable connector lock button located at the shift control base to the up position and detach the cable from the park lock lever pin. Depress the two cable connector latches and remove the cable from the shift control base.
6   Remove the cable clips.

Installation

7   Make sure the cable lock button is in the up position and the shift lever is in Park. Snap the cable connector into the shift control base.
8   With the ignition key in the Run position (this is very important), snap the cable into the inhibitor housing.
9   Turn the ignition key to the Lock position.
10 Snap the end of the cable onto the shifter park/lock pin.
11 Push the nose of the cable connector forward to remove the slack.
12 With no load on the connector nose, snap the cable connector lock button on.
13 Check the operation of the park/lock cable as follows.
  a) With the shift lever in Park and the key in Lock, make sure the shifter lever cannot be moved to another position and the key can be removed.
  b) With the key in Run and the shift lever in Neutral, make sure the key cannot be turned to Lock.
14 If it operates as described above, the park/lock cable system is properly adjusted. Proceed to Step 16.
15 If the park/lock system does not operate as described, return the cable connector lock to the up position and repeat the adjustment procedure. Push the cable connector down and recheck the operation.
16 If the key cannot be removed in the Park position, snap the lock button to the up position and move the nose of the cable connector rearward until the key can be removed from the ignition switch.
17 Install the cable into the retaining clips.

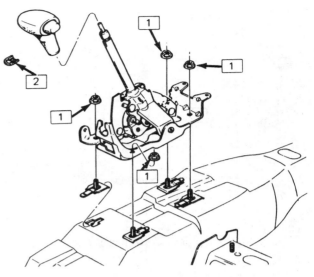

6.4 Floor shift control installation details

1 *Nuts*
2 *Shift handle retaining clip*

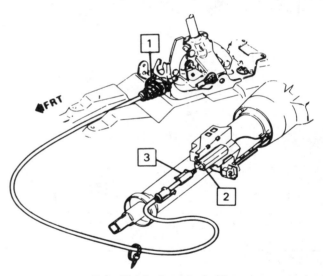

7.4 Park/lock cable details

1 *Lock button*   3 *Cable end fitting*
2 *Inhibitor*

---

8 Transaxle differential seal — replacement

Refer to illustrations 8.3 and 8.4

1   Raise the vehicle and support it securely on jackstands.
2   Remove the driveaxle(s) (Chapter 8).
3   On the rubber-type seal, use a seal remover or a long screwdriver to pry it from the transaxle, taking care not to damage the splines on the output shaft **(see illustration)**.
4   On the metal-type seal, use a hammer and chisel to work around the outer circumference of the seal to dislodge it so it can be pried from the housing **(see illustration)**.
5   Compare the new seal with the old to make sure they are the same.
6   Coat the lips of the new seal with transmission fluid.
7   Place the new seal into position and tap it into the bore using a large socket or a piece of pipe which is the same diameter as the seal.
8   Reinstall the various components in the reverse order of removal, referring to the necessary Chapters as needed.

8.3 The rubber-type differential seal (arrow) can be pried out of the housing with a screwdriver. Be careful not to damage the splines of the axleshaft (transaxle removed for clarity)

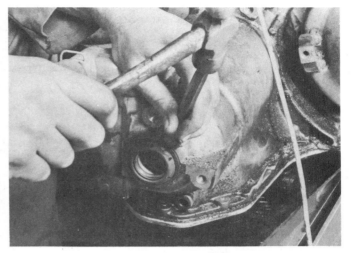

8.4 Dislodge the metal type differential seal by working around the outer circumference with a chisel and hammer (transaxle removed for clarity)

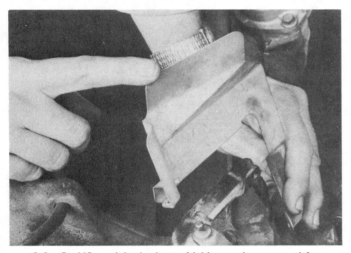

9.3 On V6 models the heat shield must be removed for access to the transaxle lever (transaxle removed for clarity)

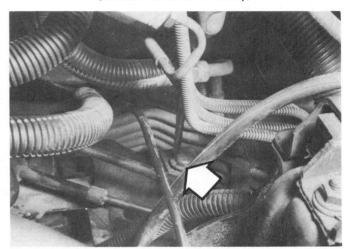

9.5 Pry the shift lever clip (arrow) off the pin with a screwdriver

7B

9 Automatic transaxle — removal and installation

Refer to illustrations 9.3, 9.5, 9.7, 9.8a, 9.8b, 9.8c, 9.9, 9.13, 9.14, 9.15a, 9.15b, 9.19, 9.23, 9.26a, 9.26b, 9.26c, 9.28, 9.30, 9.31a, 9.31b, 9.32 and 9.35

Removal

1   Disconnect the negative cable at the battery. Place the cable out of the way so that it cannot accidently come into contact with the terminal, which would again allow current flow.

2   Remove the hood (Chapter 11).

3   On V6 engine equipped models, remove the air cleaner and mass air flow sensor assembly (Chapter 4). Remove the exhaust crossover pipe followed by the heat shield covering the transaxle shift lever (four bolts, two of which are accessible from underneath) **(see illustration)**.

4   Remove the nut holding the wiring harness to the transaxle and move the harness out of the way.

5   Pry the shift cable from the shift lever, unbolt the cable bracket from the transaxle complete with cables and move the assembly out of the way **(see illustration)**.

6   Disconnect the throttle valve (TV) cable at the throttle lever (Section 3).

7   Remove the transaxle fluid dipstick tube-to-manifold bolt. Disengage the tube from the tab in the transaxle and leave the assembly in place during transaxle removal **(see illustration)**.

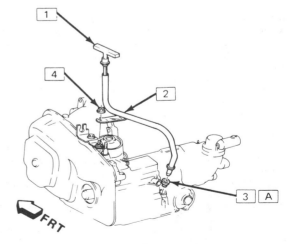

9.7 Typical dipstick installation details

1 *Tube*	3A *The seal must in place before*
2 *Dipstick tube*	*the tube is inserted*
	4 *Nut*

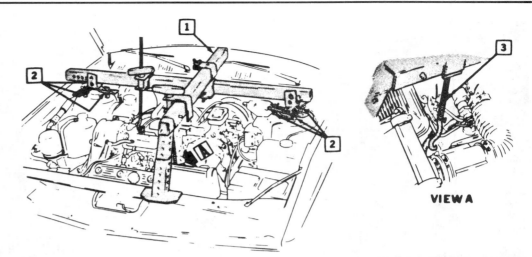

9.8a Typical engine support tool used on four cylinder engine

1 Support tool J-28467
2 Attaching nuts
3 Attachment hook

VIEW A

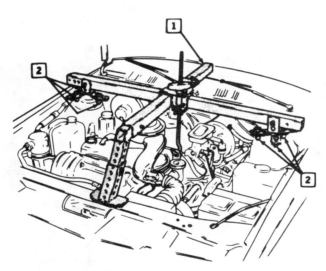

9.8b V6 engine engine support tool installation

1 Support tool J-28467   2 Attaching nuts

9.8c If an engine support tool is not available, connect a chain to the lifting eyes and raise the weight off the engine mounts with a suitable lifting device

9.9 Measure the height of the transaxle and then raise the vehicle sufficiently to allow clearance for the transaxle to be removed under the vehicle

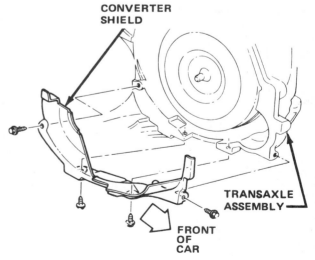

9.13 Torque converter shield details

CONVERTER SHIELD

TRANSAXLE ASSEMBLY

FRONT OF CAR

8   The engine must be supported during transaxle removal and this can be accomplished using factory engine support tool J-28467 or equivalent (see illustrations). Insert a 1/4-inch by 2-inch bolt in the hole in the right front motor mount to maintain driveline alignment if the support tool is used. If the tool is not available, support the engine with a lifting device which can hold it high enough to allow the transaxle to be lowered from the engine compartment with the vehicle raised (see illustration).

9   Install the engine support or connect a lifting device and raise the engine sufficiently to take the weight off the engine mounts. Raise the vehicle as necessary to remove the transaxle (approximately 28 inches), support it securely on jackstands and remove the front wheels (see illustration).

10   Drain the transaxle fluid (Chapter 1).

11   Unplug the speed sensor and Torque Converter Clutch (TCC) connectors and disconnect the ground cable.

12   Unplug the starter safety switch by lifting the pin out of the connector and pulling it off. Do not remove the switch mounting bolts as this will require readjustment of the switch.

13   Remove the torque converter shield (see illustration).

14   Mark the relationship of torque converter and driveplate with paint or a scribe. Lock the driveplate using a screwdriver inserted in the starter gear teeth and remove the driveplate-to-torque converter bolts (see illustration). Turn the engine over with a wrench on the crankshaft pulley bolt for access to each torque converter bolt in turn until they are all removed. Push the torque converter back toward the transaxle on the input shaft to make sure it will be removed along with the transaxle.

15   Remove the two upper transaxle-to-engine bolts (see illustration). It will be necessary to work through the right side wheel well to reach one of the bolts because it is only accessible from this side. A 30-inch long extension with a universal or wobble-type socket will be necessary to reach this bolt (see illustration).

16   Disconnect the transaxle vent hose.

17   Remove the remaining upper transaxle-to-engine bolts.

18   Remove the left driveaxle and disconnect the right driveaxle from the transaxle (Chapter 8).

19   Remove the transaxle mounting strut (see illustration).

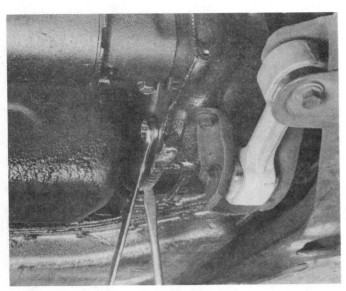

9.14   Lock the driveplate starter ring gear teeth with a screwdriver and remove the torque converter bolts

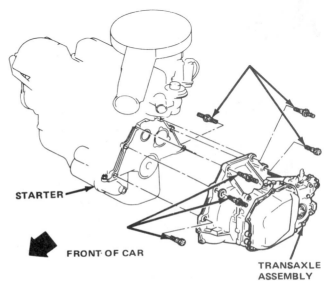

9.15a   Transaxle-to-engine bolt locations

9.15b   One of the upper transaxle bolts can only be reached through the right side wheel well, using a long extension

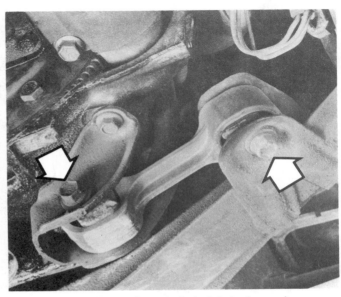

9.19   Transaxle strut through-bolts (arrows)

7B

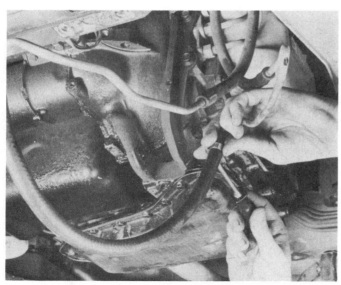

9.23   A simple way to plug the transaxle fluid tubes is to push a piece of rubber tubing on the open ends and secure it with hose clamps

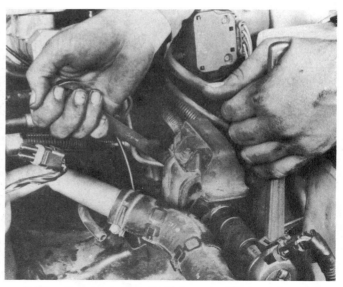

9.26a   Use a wrench to hold the nut while removing the through-bolt with a ratchet and socket

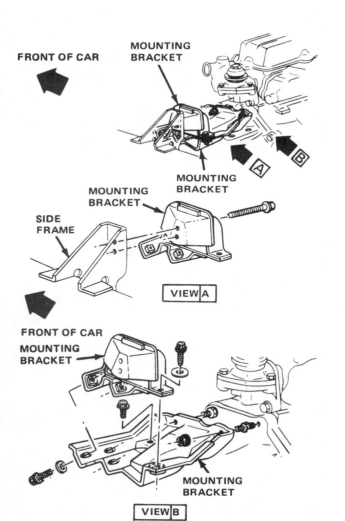

FRONT OF CAR

MOUNTING BRACKET

MOUNTING BRACKET

A   B

MOUNTING BRACKET

SIDE FRAME

VIEW A

FRONT OF CAR

MOUNTING BRACKET

MOUNTING BRACKET

VIEW B

9.26b   Transaxle mount and bracket details

9.26c   Remove the transaxle mount bracket-to-bellhousing bolts. After unbolting it, the bracket can be left in place and removed with the transaxle

20 Remove the brake caliper, hang it out of the way on a piece of wire and remove the disc (Chapter 9).

21 Remove the front suspension support complete with lower suspension arm (Chapter 10).

22 Remove the left front fender liner (Chapter 11).

23 Disconnect the cooler lines at the radiator, push a piece of hose over the connections and secure at both ends with hose clamps so that the residual fluid won't drain out (see illustration).

24 Support the transaxle with a jack, preferably a transmission jack made for this purpose.

25 Remove the remaining transaxle-to-engine bolts.

26 Remove the transaxle mount through-bolt, followed by the mount-to-transaxle bolts (see illustrations). The mount bracket can now be pushed back allowing clearance for the transaxle to moved away from the engine sufficiently to allow removal (see illustration).

9.28 Pry the transaxle bellhousing away from the engine with a large screwdriver

9.30 Pull the hub/strut assembly back for clearance when removing the transaxle from under the vehicle

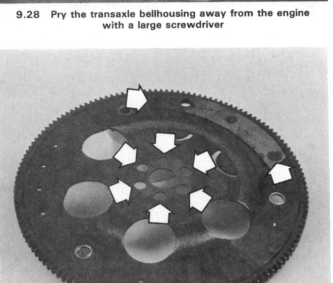

9.31a Check the driveplate for loose weights (arrows) and cracks around the bolt holes (arrows)

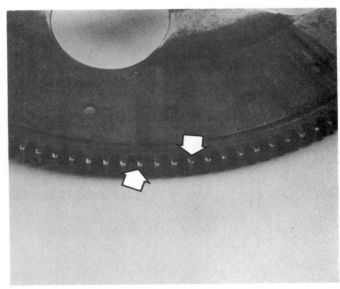

9.31b Inspect the driveplate for broken or worn starter gear teeth (arrows)

7B

27 Make a final check that all wiring, cables, etc. which could interfere with transaxle removal are disconnected or moved out of the way.
28 Separate the transaxle from the engine by prying the bellhousing away from the engine (see illustration). As this is done make sure the torque converter is held back against the transaxle.
29 Disconnect the right side driveaxle from the transaxle.
30 Lower the transaxle and remove it from the left side of the engine compartment (see illustration).
31 Remove the driveplate and inspect it for missing weights, cracks, corrosion and damaged or broken starter gear teeth (see illustrations).
32 Inspect the crankshaft seal area for damage and signs of oil leakage, indicating that the rear seal or oil pan gasket require replacement (see illustration).
33 Inspect the hoses and cables which attach to the transaxle for damage, replacing as necessary.

Installation

34 Remove the rubber gasket from the dipstick tube and install it on the transaxle for ease of installation of the tube as the transaxle is raised into place.

9.32 With the driveplate removed, inspect the sealing joints around the crankshaft for leaks (arrows)

35 Lubricate the torque converter hub with a light coat of chassis grease **(see illustration)**.
36 Move the transaxle under the vehicle and raise it into position.
37 With the help of two assistants, one to guide it into place and the other to move any cables or brackets which would interfere with installation out of the way, raise the transaxle into the engine compartment.
38 Raise the transaxle into position while an assistant guides the right driveaxle into place. Push the dipstick tube into place and install the retaining bolt. Install the mounting bracket, making sure the wiring harness passes under it.
39 Install the transaxle-to-engine bolts **(see illustration 9.15a)**.
40 Install the transaxle mount and through-bolt.
41 Connect the transaxle cooler lines.
42 Move the torque converter to the marked position against the driveplate. Make sure the weld nuts on the converter are flush with the driveplate and the converter rotates freely. Install the bolts and tighten to the specified torque. Install the torque converter shield.
43 Install the transaxle mounting strut.
44 Install the left driveaxle, suspension support and the brake caliper.
45 Install the fender liner.
46 Connect the transaxle vent hose.
47 Plug in the starter safety switch, TCC switch and speed sensor connectors.
48 Remove the jack and engine support.
49 Install the shift cable bracket and connect the shift cable.
50 Install the wiring harness retaining nut.
51 Connect the TV cable.

52 Install the various components which were removed. Refer to the the appropriate Chapters where necessary for additional information.
53 Fill the transaxle with the specified fluid (Chapter 1).
54 After all components are installed, adjust the shift control cable (Section 6) and TV cable (Section 3).

9.35 Lubricate the torque converter hub with grease

Chapter 8   Clutch and driveaxles

Contents

Specifications

Clutch
Fluid type. . . . .   See Chapter 1
Disc runout . . . .   0.020 in maximum
Slave cylinder pushrod travel . . . .   0.433 in minimum

Torque specifications   **Ft-lbs**
Clutch release lever bolt . . . .   30 to 45
Clutch pedal-to-mounting bracket bolt . . . .   20 to 25
Clutch pedal-to-locking pawl bolt . . . .   44 in-lbs
Clutch pressure plate-to-flywheel bolt . . . .   14 to 18
Clutch master cylinder mounting nuts . . . .   15 to 25
Clutch slave cylinder mounting nuts . . . .   14 to 20

Driveaxles
Collapsed CV joint boot dimension . . . .   5-1/16 in

Torque specifications   **Ft-lbs**
Intermediate shaft mounting bolts   35
Hub nut
   initial   70
   final   185
Wheel lug nuts
   steel wheels   80
   aluminum wheels   100

8

1   General information

The information in this Chapter deals with the components from the rear of the engine to the drive wheels, except for the transaxle, which is covered in the previous Chapter. For the purposes of this Chapter, these components are grouped into two categories: clutch and drive-axles. Separate Sections within this Chapter offer general descriptions and checking procedures for each of these groups.

As many of the procedures covered in this Chapter involve working under the vehicle, make sure it is firmly supported on sturdy jackstands or on a hoist where the vehicle can easily be raised and lowered.

2   Clutch — description and check

Refer to illustration 2.1

1   All vehicles with a manual transaxle use a single dry plate, diaphragm spring type clutch **(see illustration)**. The clutch disc has a splined hub which allows it to slide along the splines of the transaxle input shaft. The clutch and pressure plate are held in contact by spring pressure exerted by the diaphragm in the pressure plate.

2   The clutch release system is operated by hydraulic pressure on some models, while on others a mechanical system is used. The hydraulic release system consists of the clutch pedal, a master cylinder, the hydraulic line, a slave cylinder which actuates the clutch release lever and the clutch release (or throwout) bearing. The mechanical release system includes the clutch pedal with adjuster mechanism, a clutch cable which actuates the clutch release lever and the release bearing.

3   When pressure is applied to the clutch pedal to release the clutch, hydraulic or mechanical pressure is exerted against the outer end of the clutch release lever. As the lever pivots the shaft fingers push against the release bearing. The bearing pushes against the fingers of the diaphragm spring of the pressure plate assembly, which in turn releases the clutch plate.

4   Other than to replace components with obvious damage, some preliminary checks should be performed to diagnose a clutch system failure.

a)   The first check should be of the fluid level in the clutch master cylinder. If the fluid level is low, add fluid as necessary and inspect the hydraulic clutch system for leaks. If the master cylinder reservoir has run dry, bleed the system as described in Section 4 and re-test the clutch operation.

b)   To check "clutch spin down time," run the engine at normal idle speed with the transaxle in Neutral (clutch pedal up — engaged). Disengage the clutch (pedal down), wait nine seconds and shift the transaxle into Reverse. No grinding noise should be heard. A grinding noise would most likely indicate a problem in the pressure plate or the clutch disc.

c)   To check for complete clutch release, run the engine (with the parking brake on to prevent movement) and hold the clutch pedal approximately 1/2-inch from the floor. Shift the transaxle between 1st gear and Reverse several times. If the shift is not smooth, component failure is indicated. On vehicles with a hydraulic release system, measure the slave cylinder pushrod travel. With the clutch pedal depressed completely the slave cylinder pushrod should extend 11 mm (0.433 inch) minimum. If the pushrod doesn't meet this requirement, check the fluid level in the clutch master cylinder.

d)   Visually inspect the clutch pedal bushing at the top of the clutch pedal to make sure there is no sticking or excessive wear.

e)   On vehicles with mechanical release systems, a clutch pedal that is difficult to operate is most likely caused by a faulty clutch cable. Check the cable where it enters the casing for fraying, rust or other signs of corrosion. If it looks good, lubricate the cable with penetrating oil. If pedal operation improves, the cable is worn out and should be replaced.

3   Hydraulic clutch components — removal and installation

Refer to illustration 3.4

Note: *The hydraulic clutch release system is serviced as a complete unit and has been bled of air from the factory, as individual components*

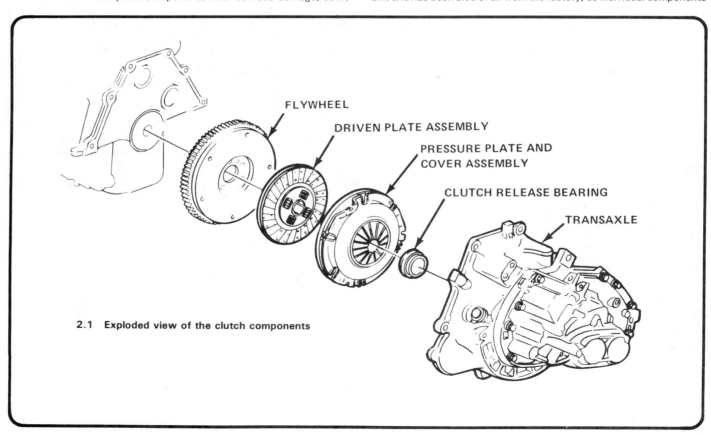

FLYWHEEL

DRIVEN PLATE ASSEMBLY

PRESSURE PLATE AND COVER ASSEMBLY

CLUTCH RELEASE BEARING

TRANSAXLE

2.1   Exploded view of the clutch components

are not available separately. Other than replacing the entire system, bleeding the system of air is the only service procedure that may become necessary. There are no provisions for adjustment of clutch pedal height or free play.

Removal

Four cylinder engine

1 Disconnect the cable from the negative battery terminal.
2 Remove the left side under-dash panel.
3 Remove the clutch master cylinder pushrod retaining clip and slide the pushrod off of the pedal pin.
4 If the system is equipped with a remote fluid reservoir, disconnect the hose at the clutch master cylinder and plug it. Remove the two master cylinder mounting nuts **(see illustration)**.
5 Remove the clutch slave cylinder mounting nuts and detach the slave cylinder, the hydraulic line and the master cylinder from the vehicle as a unit.

V6 engine

6 Remove the air intake duct from the air cleaner.
7 Disconnect the battery cables from the battery, negative cable first.
8 Remove the left fender brace above the battery.
9 Remove the battery from the vehicle (refer to Chapter 5).
10 Using pieces of numbered tape, mark the electrical connectors at the air cleaner and the Mass Air Flow sensor then disconnect the connectors.
11 Remove the PCV pipe clamp from the air intake duct and the air intake duct clamp at the throttle body.
12 Remove the Mass Air Flow sensor mounting bolt and the air cleaner bracket mounting bolts then remove the air cleaner, the Mass Air Flow sensor and the air intake duct as an assembly (refer to Chapter 4).
13 Remove the two bolts retaining the windshield washer bottle to the left inner fender well then remove the bottle.
14 If your vehicle is equipped with cruise control, unbolt the servo bracket nuts from the left strut tower and reposition the servo

assembly.
15 Remove the left side under-dash panel.
16 Remove the clutch master cylinder pushrod retaining clip and slide the pushrod off of the pedal pin.
17 If the system is equipped with a remote fluid reservoir, disconnect the hose at the clutch master cylinder and plug it. Remove the two master cylinder mounting nuts (refer to illustration 3.4).
18 Remove the clutch slave cylinder mounting nuts and detach the slave cylinder, the hydraulic line and the master cylinder from the vehicle as a unit.

Installation (all models)

19 Install the new slave cylinder into the support bracket and insert the pushrod into the cup on the clutch release lever. Tighten the nuts evenly, a little at a time until the specified torque is reached. **Note:** *Do not remove the plastic strap that holds the pushrod in position. It is designed to break off the first time the clutch pedal is depressed.*
20 Mount the clutch master cylinder to the firewall and install the nuts. Tighten the nuts evenly, a little at a time, to the specified torque. If the vehicle is equipped with a remote fluid reservoir, reconnect the hose to the clutch master cylinder.
21 Remove the plastic pedal restrictor from the master cylinder pushrod. Coat the inside of the pushrod bushing with multi-purpose grease, connect the pushrod to the brake pedal pin and install the retaining clip. If the vehicle is equipped with cruise control, check to see that the disengage switch on the clutch pedal bracket is in contact with the clutch pedal when the pedal is at rest. If it is not, adjust it accordingly.
22 Pump the clutch pedal several times to break the slave cylinder retaining strap. Leave the remaining plastic button under the pushrod in place.
23 The remainder of the installation is the reverse of the removal procedure.

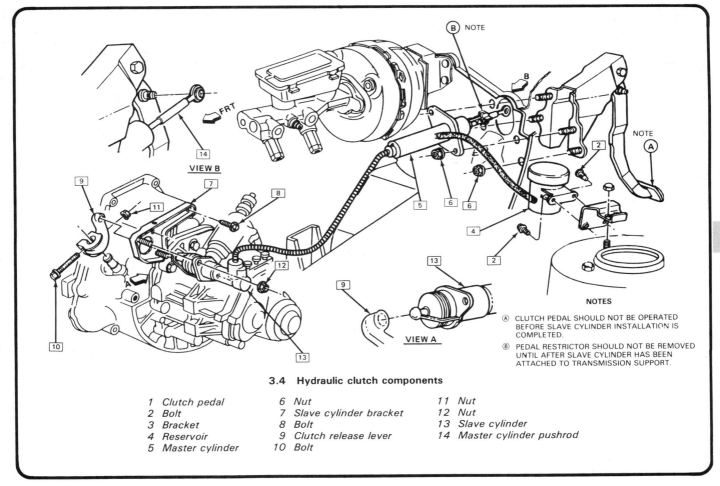

3.4 Hydraulic clutch components

1 Clutch pedal	6 Nut	11 Nut
2 Bolt	7 Slave cylinder bracket	12 Nut
3 Bracket	8 Bolt	13 Slave cylinder
4 Reservoir	9 Clutch release lever	14 Master cylinder pushrod
5 Master cylinder	10 Bolt	

NOTES

Ⓐ CLUTCH PEDAL SHOULD NOT BE OPERATED BEFORE SLAVE CYLINDER INSTALLATION IS COMPLETED.

Ⓑ PEDAL RESTRICTOR SHOULD NOT BE REMOVED UNTIL AFTER SLAVE CYLINDER HAS BEEN ATTACHED TO TRANSMISSION SUPPORT.

8

4   Hydraulic clutch system — bleeding

1   If it becomes necessary to bleed the hydraulic clutch system, clean and remove the reservoir cap and fill the reservoir with the recommended fluid. Open the bleed screw on the slave cylinder body and allow the fluid to drip into a container (do not depress the clutch pedal). When it is apparent that there are no more bubbles at the bleed screw opening and a steady stream of fluid is flowing out, close the bleed screw. Re-check the fluid reservoir, topping it up if necessary. The system should now be free of air.
2   To confirm this, measure the slave cylinder pushrod travel, as described in Section 2.

5   Clutch cable — removal, installation and adjustment

Refer to illustration 5.2

Removal

1   Pull the clutch pedal rearward and support it against the bumper stop so that the adjuster pawl is released.
2   Disconnect the clutch cable from the release lever at the transaxle, taking care not to let it snap rearward, which could damage the adjusting mechanism **(see illustration)**.
3   Remove the left side under-dash panel.
4   Disconnect the clutch cable from the tangs of the detent, lift the locking pawl away from the detent and carefully slide the cable forward between the detent and pawl.
5   Remove the windshield washer reservoir.
6   In the engine compartment, pull the clutch cable out to disengage it from the firewall. Be prepared to retrieve the insulators, dampener and washers, which may separate during removal.
7   Disconnect the cable from the mounting bracket on the transaxle and remove it from the vehicle.
8   Inspect the cable and replace it if it is frayed, worn, damaged or kinked.

Installation

9   Connect the cable into both of the insulators and the damper and washers. Lubricating the rear insulator with a small amount of light oil will ease the installation into the pedal mounting bracket.
10   Inside the passenger compartment, route the cable casing into the rubber isolator on the pedal bracket and then attach the cable end to the detent. Make sure the cable is routed underneath the pawl and into the detent cable groove.
11   Install the under-dash panel.
12   Hold the clutch pedal upward against the bumper stop to release the pawl from the detent and install the other end of the cable to the release lever and transaxle mount bracket.
13   Install the windshield washer reservoir.
14   Lift the clutch pedal up several times to allow the mechanism to adjust the cable length, then depress it several times to mesh the pawl with the detent teeth.

6   Clutch release bearing — removal and installation

Refer to illustrations 6.4, 6.6 and 6.7

Removal

1   Disconnect the negative cable from the battery.
2   On vehicles with hydraulic release systems, remove the under-dash panel and disconnect the clutch master cylinder pushrod from the clutch pedal pin.
3   Remove the transaxle (Chapter 7).
4   Remove the clutch release bearing from the clutch fork. Place a mark on the release bearing pad and the release fork so the bearing can be returned to its original position if it is to be re-used **(see illustration)**. Remove the bearing retaining spring from the release fork holes and remove the bearing.
5   Hold the center of the bearing and spin the outer portion. If the bearing doesn't turn smoothly or if it is noisy, replace it with a new one. Wipe the bearing with a clean rag and inspect it for damage, wear

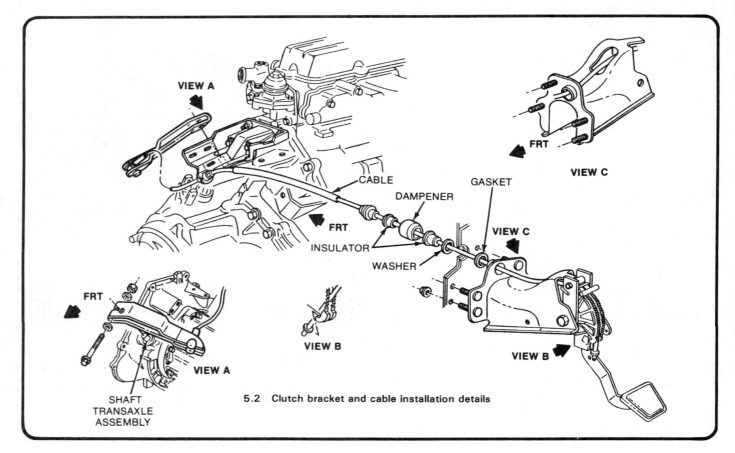

5.2   Clutch bracket and cable installation details

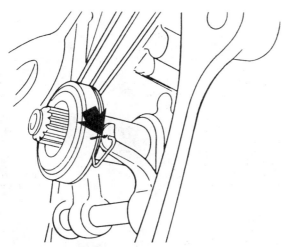

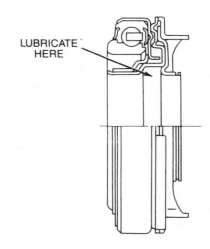

6.4 Before removing the release bearing from the transaxle, index the bearing pad to the clutch release fork (arrow)

6.6 Fill the groove in the inner diameter of the release bearing with lithium base grease

or cracks. Do not immerse the bearing in solvent — it is sealed for life and to do so would ruin it.

Installation

6   Lubricate the clutch fork ends where they contact the bearing lightly with white lithium base grease. Pack the inner diameter of the bearing with this grease **(see illustration)**.

7   Install the release bearing on the transaxle retainer so that both of the fork tangs fit into the outer diameter of the bearing groove. Be sure the bearing pads are resting on the fork ends with the previously inscribed marks aligned, then install the retaining spring. The spring must be fully seated in the retaining groove and both ends secured in the clutch fork holes **(see illustration)**.

8   Install the transaxle, making sure that the clutch lever does not move toward the flywheel until the transaxle is bolted to the engine.

9   On models with hydraulic release systems, reconnect the clutch master cylinder pushrod and install the under-dash cover.

10 Check the clutch operation. Adjust the clutch cable and depress the pedal slowly several times to mesh the pawl with the detent teeth (mechanically actuated systems).

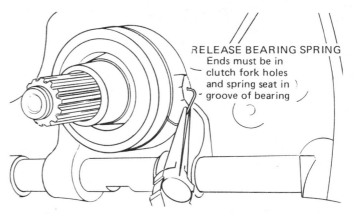

6.7 When installing the release bearing make sure the retaining spring is seated in the bearing groove and the spring ends are located in the clutch release fork holes

---

7 Clutch components — removal, inspection and installation

Refer to illustrations 7.5, 7.9, 7.11 and 7.13

Warning: *Dust produced by clutch wear and deposited on clutch components contains asbestos, which is hazardous to your health. DO NOT blow it out with compressed air and DO NOT inhale it. DO NOT use gasoline or petroleum-based solvents to remove the dust. Brake system cleaner should be used to flush the dust into a drain pan. After the clutch components are wiped clean with a rag, dispose of the contaminated rags and cleaner in a covered container.*

Removal

1   Access to the clutch components is normally accomplished by removing the transaxle, leaving the engine in the vehicle. If, of course, the engine is being removed for major overhaul, then the opportunity should always be taken to check the clutch for wear and replace worn components as necessary. The following procedures assume that the engine will stay in place.

2   Remove the left side under-dash panel and disconnect the clutch master cylinder pushrod from the clutch pedal (hydraulic release systems).

3   Referring to Chapter 7 Part A, remove the transaxle from the vehicle. Remove the release bearing (Section 6).

4   To support the clutch disc during removal, install a clutch alignment tool through the middle of the clutch.

5   If the pressure plate is to be re-used, mark the relationship of the pressure plate-to-flywheel so it can be installed in the same position **(see illustration)**.

6   Turning each bolt a little at a time, loosen the pressure plate-to-

7.5 After removal of the transmission, this will be the view of the clutch components

1 Pressure plate assembly   *2 Flywheel*
   (clutch disc inside)

8

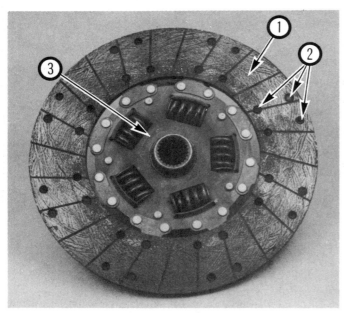

7.9   The clutch disc

1   *Facing — this will wear down in use*
2   *Rivets — these secure the facing and will*
   damage the flywheel or pressure plate if
   allowed to contact the surfaces
3   *Markings — ''Flywheel side'' or similar*

flywheel bolts. Work in a criss-cross pattern, again, loosening only a little at a time until all spring pressure is relieved. Support the pressure plate and completely remove the bolts, followed by the pressure plate and clutch disc.

Inspection

7   Ordinarily, when a fault is found in the clutch system, it can be attributed to wear of the clutch driven plate assembly (clutch disc). However, all components should be inspected at this time.

7.11   The machined face of the pressure plate must be inspected for scoring or any other damage. If damage is slight, a machine shop can make the surface smooth again

8   Inspect the flywheel for cracks, heat checking, grooves or other signs of obvious defects. If the imperfections are slight, a machine shop can machine the surface flat and smooth, which is highly recommended regardless of the surface appearance. Refer to Chapter 2 for the flywheel removal and installation procedure.
9   Inspect the facing on the clutch disc. There should be at least 1/16-inch of lining above the rivet heads. Check for loose rivets, distortion, cracks, broken springs or any other obvious damage **(see illustration)**. As mentioned above, ordinarily the disc is replaced as a matter of course, so if in doubt about the quality, replace it with a new one.
10   Ordinarily, the release bearing is also replaced along with the clutch disc (see Section 6).
11   Check the machined surfaces of the pressure plate **(see illustration)**. If the surface is grooved or otherwise damaged, take it to a machine shop for possible machining or replacement. Also check for

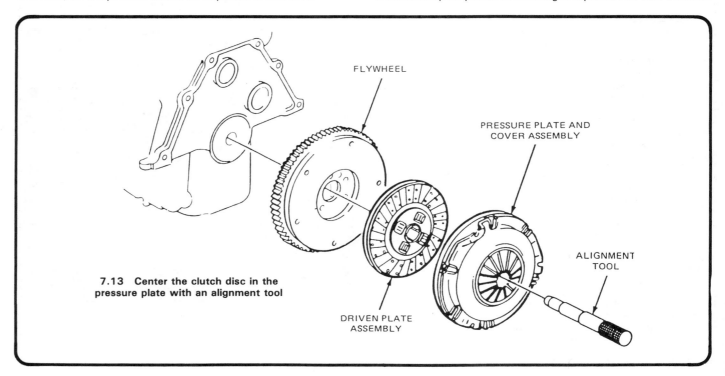

7.13   Center the clutch disc in the pressure plate with an alignment tool

FLYWHEEL

PRESSURE PLATE AND
COVER ASSEMBLY

ALIGNMENT
TOOL

DRIVEN PLATE
ASSEMBLY

obvious damage, distortion, cracking, etc. Light glazing can be removed with medium grit emery cloth. If a new pressure plate is indicated, new or factory-rebuilt units are available.

Installation

12 Before installation, carefully wipe clean the flywheel and pressure plate machined surfaces. It is important that no oil or grease is on these surfaces or the facing of the clutch disc. Handle these parts only with clean hands.

13 Position the clutch disc and pressure plate with the clutch disc held in place with an alignment tool **(see illustration)**. Make sure the disc is installed properly (most replacement discs will be marked ''flywheel side'' or similar. If not marked, install the disc with the damper springs toward the transaxle).

14 Tighten the pressure plate-to-flywheel bolts only finger tight, working around the pressure plate.

15 Center the clutch disc by inserting the alignment tool through the splined hub and into the bore on the crankshaft. Tighten the pressure plate-to-flywheel bolts a little at a time, working in a criss-cross pattern to prevent distorting the cover. After all of the bolts are snug, tighten them to the specified torque. Remove the alignment tool.

16 Using high temperature grease, lubricate the inner groove of the release bearing (refer to Section 6). Also place grease on the fork fingers.

17 Install the clutch release bearing as described in Section 6.

18 Install the transaxle, slave cylinder and all components that were removed previously.

19 Adjust the shift linkage as outlined in Chapter 7 Part A.

---

8 Clutch pedal — removal and installation

Refer to illustrations 8.3 and 8.20

Mechanically actuated clutch

Removal

1 Pull back on the clutch pedal and support it in the raised position. Disconnect the clutch cable from the release lever at the transaxle.

2 Remove the left side under-dash panel then remove the starter safety switch from the pedal and bracket (refer to Section 9).

3 Disconnect the clutch cable from the tangs of the detent, lift the pawl away and slide the cable between the detent and pawl **(see illustration)**.

4 Remove the pivot bolt. Remove the spring, pawl and spacer from the pedal assembly.

5 Remove the detent spacer, bushings, spring and pawl.

6 Clean the parts and inspect for wear or damage. Replace both the pawl and detent if the teeth on either are damaged or worn.

Installation

7 Position the detent spring in the side of the detent and install the detent into the clutch pedal opening, hooking the spring onto the pedal.

8 Install the bushings onto the pedal assembly.

9 Install the pawl, spring, spacer and pivot mounting bolt, tightening to the specified torque.

10 Attach the clutch pedal to the mounting bracket and install the pivot bolt and nut. Both the pivot and pawl bolts must be installed as shown **(see illustration 8.3)**.

11 Check the pawl and detent for proper operation to make sure the pawl disengages when pulled to the upper position and the detent rotates freely in both directions.

12 Attach the cable end to the pawl, making sure to route the cable underneath the pawl and into the detent cable groove.

13 Install the starter safety switch.

14 Hold the clutch pedal up against the bumper stop and release the pawl from the detent.

15 Check the clutch pedal mechanism for proper operation and adjust the cable length by lifting the pedal. Depress the pedal slowly several times so the pawl meshes properly with the detent teeth.

16 Install the under-dash panel.

Hydraulically actuated clutch

Removal

17 Remove the left side under-dash panel.

18 Remove the starter safety switch from the pedal and bracket (refer to Section 9).

19 Remove the clutch master cylinder pushrod retaining clip and slide the pushrod off of the pedal pin.

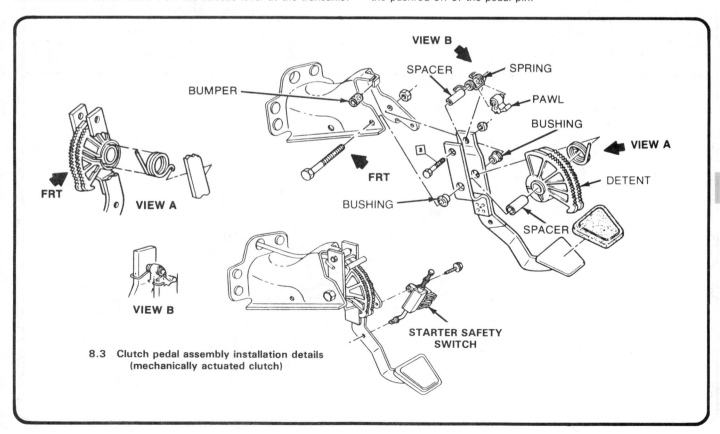

8.3 Clutch pedal assembly installation details (mechanically actuated clutch)

8

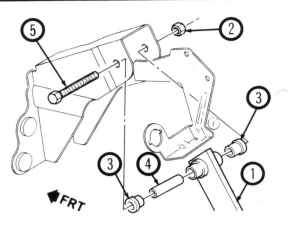

**8.20   Clutch pedal assembly installation details
(hydraulically actuated clutch)**

1 *Clutch pedal*   4 *Spacer*
2 *Pivot bolt nut*   5 *Pivot bolt*
3 *Bushing*

20 Remove the clutch pedal pivot bolt and pull the pedal from the mounting bracket **(see illustration)**. Extract the bushings and spacer and inspect them for wear, replacing them as necessary.

Installation

21 Lubricate the spacer and bushings with multi-purpose grease and install them on the clutch pedal. Position the pedal in the bracket and install the pivot bolt.
22 Lubricate the master cylinder pushrod bushing with multi-purpose grease, slide it onto the pedal pin and install the retaining clip.

23 Install and adjust the neutral start switch (refer to Section 9).
24 If the vehicle is equipped with cruise control, check the adjustment of the clutch switch (refer to Chapter 12).
25 Install the under-dash panel.

9   Starter safety switch — check and replacement

1 The neutral start switch is mounted on the clutch pedal support and allows the vehicle to be started only with the clutch pedal fully depressed. Refer to Chapter 1 for the checking procedure.
2 Disconnect the negative cable at the battery. Place the cable out of the way so it cannot accidentally come in contact with the negative terminal of the battery, as this would once again allow power into the electrical system of the vehicle.
3 Remove the left side under-dash panel to gain access to the top of the clutch pedal.
4 At the top of the clutch pedal is a small rod which passes through the pedal. Remove the clip from the end of this rod **(see illustration 8.3)**.
5 Remove the screw which secures the neutral safety switch to the clutch pedal support bracket.
6 Disconnect the electrical lead to the switch and remove the switch.
7 Install the new switch in the reverse order of removal. Test to be sure that the vehicle can be started only when the clutch pedal is fully depressed. Be sure to perform this test with the transaxle placed in neutral.

10   Driveaxles — general information

Refer to illustrations 10.1a, 10.1b and 10.1c

Power is transmitted from the transaxle to the front wheels by two driveaxles, which consist of splined solid axles with constant velocity

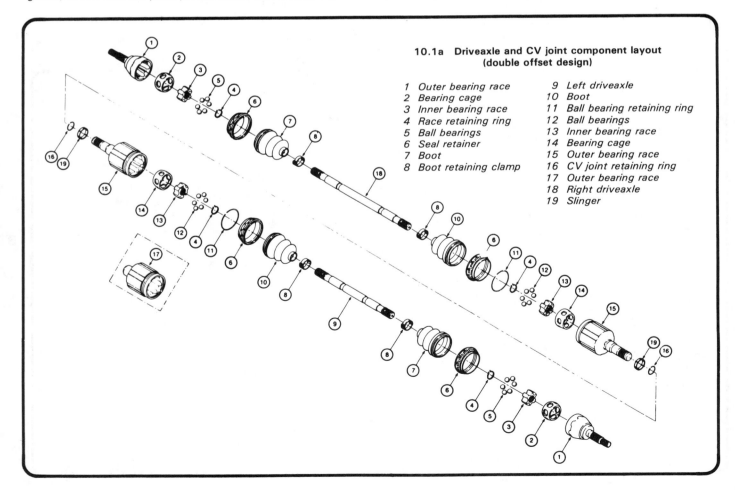

**10.1a   Driveaxle and CV joint component layout
(double offset design)**

1 *Outer bearing race*   9   *Left driveaxle*
2 *Bearing cage*   10   *Boot*
3 *Inner bearing race*   11   *Ball bearing retaining ring*
4 *Race retaining ring*   12   *Ball bearings*
5 *Ball bearings*   13   *Inner bearing race*
6 *Seal retainer*   14   *Bearing cage*
7 *Boot*   15   *Outer bearing race*
8 *Boot retaining clamp*   16   *CV joint retaining ring*
                                17   *Outer bearing race*
                                18   *Right driveaxle*
                                19   *Slinger*

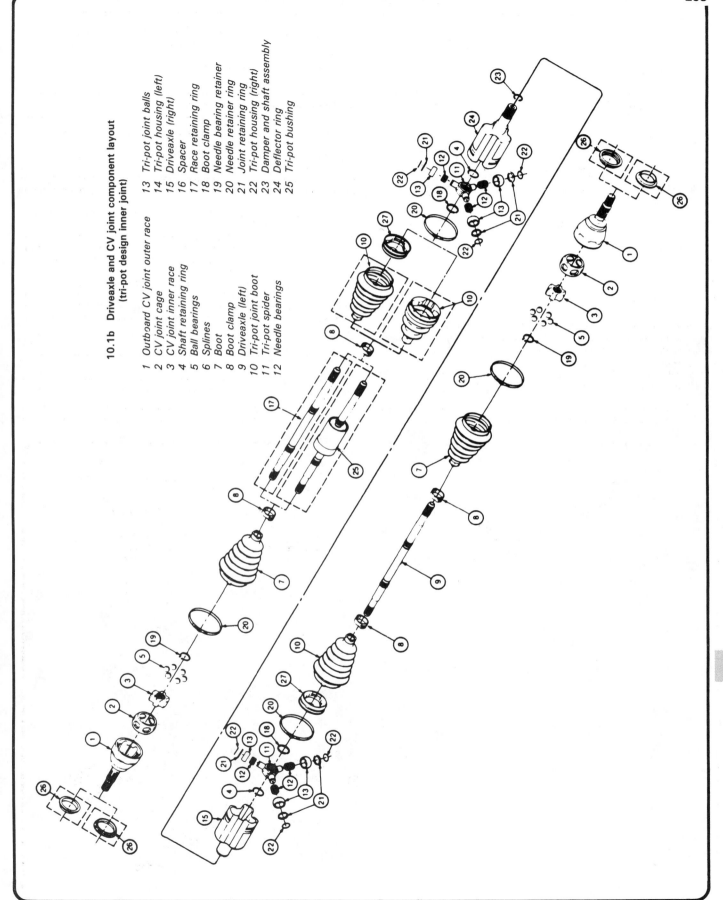

10.1b Driveaxle and CV joint component layout (tri-pot design inner joint)

1 Outboard CV joint outer race
2 CV joint cage
3 CV joint inner race
4 Shaft retaining ring
5 Ball bearings
6 Splines
7 Boot
8 Boot clamp
9 Driveaxle (left)
10 Tri-pot joint boot
11 Tri-pot spider
12 Needle bearings
13 Tri-pot joint balls
14 Tri-pot housing (left)
15 Driveaxle (right)
16 Spacer
17 Race retaining ring
18 Boot clamp
19 Needle bearing retainer
20 Needle retainer ring
21 Joint retaining ring
22 Tri-pot housing (right)
23 Damper and shaft assembly
24 Deflector ring
25 Tri-pot bushing

8

(CV) joints at each end. There are two types of inner CV joints used. On certain models a double-offset design using ball bearings with an inner and outer race is used to allow angular movement. The other CV joint used is a tri-pot design, using a spider bearing assembly and tri-pot housing to allow angular movement **(see illustrations)**. To determine which CV joint is used on your vehicle, look at the housing while it is still installed on the vehicle and compare it to the accompanying illustrations, noting that the tri-pot housing will have three major indentations in it and a very thin retaining clamp holding the boot in position **(see illustration)**. All outer CV joints are the double-offset design.

The CV joints are protected by rubber boots, which are retained by clamps so that the joints are not contaminated by water or dirt. The boots should be inspected periodically (Chapter 1) for damage, eaking lubricant or cuts. The inner boots have very small breather holes which may leak a small amount of lubricant under some circumstances, such as when the joint is compressed during removal. Damaged CV joint boots must be replaced immediately or the joints can be damaged. Boot replacement involves removing the driveaxles (Section 11). It is advisable to disassemble, clean, inspect and repack the CV joint whenever replacing a CV joint boot to ensure that the joint is not contaminated with moisture or dirt, which would cause premature failure of the CV joint.

The most common symptom of worn or damaged CV joints, besides lubricant leaks, are a clicking noise in turns, a clunk when accelerating from a coasting condition or vibration at highway speeds.

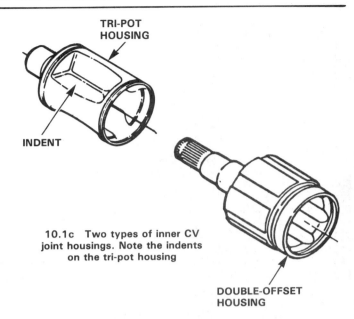

10.1c Two types of inner CV joint housings. Note the indents on the tri-pot housing

11.2 A screwdriver inserted through the caliper and into a disc cooling vane will hold the hub stationary while loosening the hub nut

11.5a A two jaw puller works well for pushing the stub axle from the hub

11 Driveaxles — removal and installation

Refer to illustrations 11.2, 11.5a, 11.5b, 11.6 and 11.8

Removal

1   Remove the wheel cover and break loose the hub nut. Loosen the wheel lug nuts, raise the front of the vehicle and support it securely on jackstands. Remove the front wheel.
2   Remove the driveaxle hub nut. To prevent the hub from turning, insert a screwdriver through the caliper and into a rotor cooling vane, then remove the nut **(see illustration)**.
3   Remove the brake caliper and disc and support the caliper out of the way with a piece of wire (Chapter 9).
4   Remove the control arm-to-steering knuckle balljoint stud nut and separate the lower arm from the steering knuckle (refer to Chapter 10 if necessary).
5   Push the driveaxle from the hub with a puller, then support the outer end of the driveaxle with a piece of wire to prevent damage to the inner CV joint **(see illustrations)**.

11.5b Support the driveaxle with a piece of wire after it has been freed from the hub. Don't let it hang, as this could damage the CV joint

11.6 Use a large pry bar positioned as shown to "pop" the inner CV joint from the transaxle. It may be necessary to tap the pry bar with a hammer if difficulty is encountered

11.8 A large punch or screwdriver, positioned in the groove on the CV joint housing, can be used to seat the joint into the transaxle

6   Carefully pry the inner end of the axle from the transaxle, using a large pry bar positioned between the transaxle housing and the CV joint housing **(see illustration)**. On 2.0L Turbo models, the right drive-axle connects to an intermediate shaft (see Section 13) rather than the transaxle. Removal of the driveaxle is the same except there is no need to pry it from the transaxle.

7   Support the CV joints and carefully remove the driveaxle from the vehicle.

Installation

8   Lubricate the differential seal with multi-purpose grease, raise the driveaxle into position while supporting the CV joints and insert the splined end of the inner CV joint into the the differential side gear. Seat the shaft into the side gear by inserting a screwdriver into the groove in the CV joint and tapping it into position with a hammer **(see illustration)**. On 2.0L Turbo models slide the driveaxle inner CV joint onto the end of the intermediate shaft.

9   Apply a light coat of multi-purpose grease to the outer CV joint splines, pull outward on the strut/steering knuckle assembly and install the stub axle into the hub.

10   Insert the control arm balljoint stud into the steering knuckle and tighten the nut. Be sure to use a new cotter pin (refer to Chapter 10).

11   Install the brake disc and caliper (see Chapter 9 if necessary).

12   Install the hub nut. Lock the disc so that it cannot turn, using a screwdriver or punch inserted through the caliper into a disc cooling vane, and tighten the hub nut to the initial specified torque.

13   Grasp the inner CV joint housing (not the driveaxle) and pull out to make sure that the axle has seated securely in the transaxle.

14   Install the wheel and lower the vehicle.

15   Tighten the hub nut to the final specified torque and install the wheel cover.

12   Driveaxle boot replacement and constant velocity (CV) joint overhaul

Refer to illustrations 12.4, 12.5, 12.10, 12.11, 12.13, 12.14a, 12.14b, 12.15, 12.17, 12.20, 12.21, 12.22, 12.23, 12.24a, 12.24b, 12.27, 12.28 and 12.32

Note: *If the the CV joints exhibit signs of wear indicating need for an overhaul (usually due to torn boots), explore all options before beginning the job. Complete rebuilt driveaxles are available on an exchange basis, which eliminates much time and work. Whichever route you choose to take, check on the cost and availability of parts before disassembling your vehicle.*

12.4 Snap ring pliers should be used to remove both the inner and outer retaining rings

8

1   Remove the driveaxle (Section 11)

2   Place the driveaxle in a vise lined with rags so as not to mar the shaft.

Inner CV joint

Tri-pot design

3   Cut off the boot seal retaining clamps and slide the boot towards the center of the driveaxle. Mark the tri-pot housing to the driveaxle so it can be returned to its original position, then slide the housing off of the spider assembly.

4   Remove the spider assembly from the axle by first removing the inner retaining ring and sliding the spider assembly back to expose the front retaining ring. Remove the front retaining ring and slide the joint off the driveaxle **(see illustration)**.

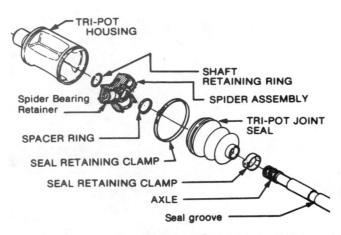

12.5   Boot installation layout of a tri-pot inner CV joint.
Note the tape around the spider assembly to prevent it
from coming apart

12.10   Before installing the CV joint boot, wrap the axle
splines with tape to prevent damage to the boot

12.11   When installing the spider assembly onto the
driveaxle, make sure the recess in the counterbore (arrow)
is facing the end of the driveaxle

5   Use tape or a cloth wrapped around the spider bearing assembly
to retain the bearings during removal and installation (**see illustration**).
6   Remove the spider assembly from the axle.
7   Slide the boot off the axle.
8   Clean old grease from the housing and spider assembly. Carefully
disassemble each section of the spider assembly, one at a time, and
clean the needle bearings with solvent. Inspect the rollers, spider cross,
bearings and housing for scoring, pitting or other signs of abnormal
wear. Apply a coat of CV joint grease to the inner bearing surfaces
to hold the needle bearings in place when reassembling the spider
assembly.
9   Pack the housing with half of the grease furnished with the new
boot and place the remainder in the boot.
10   Wrap the driveaxle splines with tape to avoid damaging the boot,
then slide the boot onto the axle (**see illustration**).
11   Install the spider bearing with the recess in the counterbore facing
the end of the driveaxle (**see illustration**).
12   Install the tri-pot housing.
13   Seat the boot in the housing and axle seal grooves, and adjust the
collapsed dimension of the joint (**see illustration**). Install the retaining
clamps then install the driveaxle as described in Section 11.

Double offset design
14   Refer to the procedure outlined in Steps 15 through 33, but take
note that the cage and inner race assembly is retained in the outer race
by a ball retaining ring, which is removed after the driveaxle is withdrawn from the CV joint (**see illustration**). Also, the inner race and cage
must be marked in relation to each other, as the cage is not symmetrical
(**see illustration**). Refer to Step 13 when adjusting CV joint collapsed
dimension.

Outer CV joint
15   Tap lightly around the outer circumference of the seal retainer with
a hammer and drift to dislodge and remove it. Take care not to deform
the retainer, as this would destroy its ability to seal properly (**see
illustration**).
16   Cut off the band retaining the boot to the shaft.
17   Remove the snap-ring and slide the joint assembly off (**see
illustration**).
18   Slide the old boot off the driveaxle.
19   Place marks on the inner race and cage so that they both face outward when reassembling the joint.
20   Press down on the inner race far enough to allow a ball bearing
to be removed. If it's difficult to tilt, tap the inner race with a brass
drift and a hammer (**see illustration**).
21   Pry the balls from the cage, one at a time, with a blunt screwdriver
or wooden tool (**see illustration**).
22   With all of the balls removed from the cage and the cage/inner race
assembly tilted 90°, align the cage windows with the outer race lands
and remove the assembly from the outer race (**see illustration**).

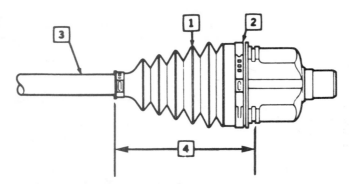

12.13   The collapsed dimension of all inner CV joints must
be adjusted before the large boot clamp is tightened

1   *Boot*   4   *Adjust the collapsed length of the joint,*
2   *Clamp*   *from the small end of the boot to the*
3   *Axleshaft*   *groove on the outer race, to 5-1/6 inches*

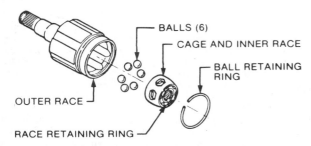

12.14a   After the driveaxle has been removed from the joint assembly, remove the ball retaining ring and slide the inner race and cage from the outer joint

12.14b   The inner race must be assembled as shown, as the cage is not symmetrical. When installing the inner race and cage into the outer race, the large diameter side of the cage goes in first

12.15   Carefully tap around the circumference of the retaining ring to remove it from the housing

12.17   Use snap-ring pliers to remove the inner retaining ring

12.20   Gently tap the inner race with a brass punch to tilt it enough to allow ball bearing removal

12.21   Using a dull bladed screwdriver, carefully pry the balls from the cage

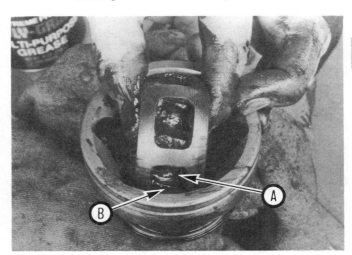

12.22   Tilt the inner race and cage 90°, then align the windows in the cage (A) with the lands (B) and rotate the inner race up and out of the outer race

8

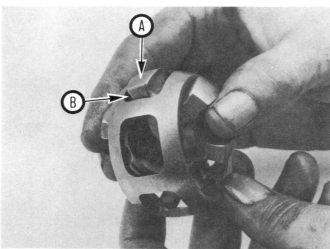

12.23   Align the inner race lands (A) with the cage windows (B) and rotate the inner race out of the cage

23   Remove the inner race from the cage by turning the inner race 90° in the cage, aligning the inner lands with the cage windows and rotating the inner race out of the cage (see illustration).

24   Clean the components with solvent to remove all traces of grease. Inspect the cage and races for pitting, score marks, cracks and other signs of wear and damage. Shiny, polished spots are normal and will not adversely affect CV joint performance (see illustrations).

25   Install the inner race in the cage by reversing the technique described in Step 22.

26   Install the inner race and cage assembly in the outer race by reversing the removal method used in Step 21. The marks that were previously applied to the inner race and cage must both be visible after the assembly is installed in the outer race.

27   Press the balls into the cage windows (see illustration).

28   Pack the CV joint assembly with lubricant through the inner splined hole. Force the grease into the bearing by inserting a wooden dowel through the splined hole and pushing it to the bottom of the joint. Repeat this procedure until the bearing is completely packed (see illustration).

29   Install the boot on the driveaxle as described in Step 10. Apply a liberal amount of grease to the inside of the axle boot.

30   Position the CV joint assembly on the driveaxle, aligning the splines. Using a brass or plastic tipped hammer, drive the CV joint onto the driveaxle until the retaining ring is seated in its groove.

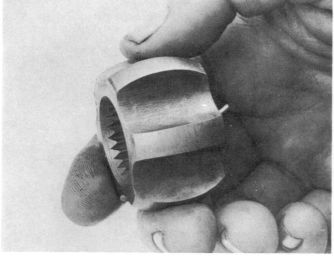

12.24a   Check the inner race lands and grooves for pitting and score marks

12.24b   Check the cage for cracks, pitting and score marks — shiny spots are normal and don't affect operation

12.27   Align the cage windows and the inner and outer race grooves, then tilt the cage and inner race to insert the balls

12.28   Apply grease through the splined hole, then insert a wooden dowel (approximately 15/16-inch diameter) through the splined hole and push down — the dowel will force the grease into the joint

31 Seat the inner end of the boot in the seal groove and install the retaining clamp.
32 Install the seal retainer securely by tapping evenly around the outer circumference with a hammer and punch **(see illustration)**.
33 Install the driveaxle as described in Section 11.

---

13 Intermediate axleshaft (2.0L Turbo models) — removal and installation

Refer to illustration 13.7

Removal

1 Loosen the right front wheel lug nuts, raise the vehicle and support it securely on jackstands. Remove the wheel.
2 Disconnect the stabilizer bar from the right control arm (refer to Chapter 10 if necessary).
3 Remove the balljoint stud nut and separate the control arm from the steering knuckle (refer to Chapter 10).

12.32 Carefully tap around the circumference of the retaining ring to install it on the housing

4 Pull the inboard end of the right driveaxle from the intermediate shaft and support it with a piece of wire. Do not let it hang, or damage to the outer CV joint may occur.
5 Disconnect the detonation (knock) sensor electrical connector and remove the sensor (refer to Chapter 6).
6 Remove the power steering pump brace (see Chapter 10 if necessary).
7 Remove the intermediate shaft bracket bolts and pull the shaft from the transaxle **(see illustration)**.

Installation

8 Lubricate the lips of the differential seal with multi-purpose grease and slide the intermediate shaft into the transaxle. Install the bolts and tighten them to the specified torque.
9 Install the power steering pump brace.
10 Install the detonation sensor and reconnect the electrical connector.
11 Apply multi-purpose grease to the intermediate shaft splines and install the driveaxle to the shaft.
12 Insert the balljoint stud into the steering knuckle and tighten the nut. Be sure to use a new cotter pin.
13 Install the stabilizer bar-to-control arm bolt (refer to Chapter 10 if necessary).
14 Install the wheel and tire and tighten the lug nuts to the specified torque.

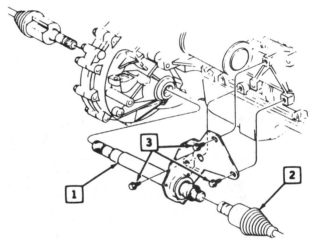

13.7 Intermediate shaft installation details (2.0L Turbo)

1 *Intermediate shaft*
2 *Right driveaxle*
3 *Bracket bolts*

8

Chapter 9   Brakes

Contents

Specifications

Disc brakes
Rotor thickness
   standard . . . . 0.885 in
   minimum thickness after refinishing . . . . 0.830 in
   discard thickness . . . . 0.815 in
Rotor runout . . . . 0.004 in
Rotor thickness variation (parallelism) . . . . 0.0005 in
Caliper-to-bracket stop clearance . . . . 0.005 to 0.012 in

Drum brakes
Drum diameter
   standard . . . . 7.879 in
   service limit . . . . 7.899 in
   discard diameter . . . . 7.929 in
Out-of-round (maximum) . . . . 0.006 in

Torque Specifications   **Ft-lbs**
Caliper mounting bolts 38
Brake hose-to-caliper bolt 33
Master cylinder-to-booster 22
Booster-to-pedal bracket 15
Wheel lug nuts
   steel wheels 80
   aluminum wheels 100

1 General information

All vehicles covered by this manual are equipped with hydraulically operated front and rear brake systems. The front brakes are disc type, and the rear brakes are drum type.

All brakes are self-adjusting. The front disc brakes automatically compensate for pad wear, while the rear drum brakes incorporate an adjustment mechanism which is activated as the brakes are applied when the vehicle is driven in reverse.

The hydraulic system consists of separate front and rear circuits. The master cylinder has separate reservoirs for the two circuits, and in the event of a leak or failure in one hydraulic circuit, the other circuit will remain operative. A visual warning of circuit failure, air in the system, or other pressure differential conditions in the brake system is given by a warning light activated by a failure warning switch in the master cylinder.

The parking brake mechanically operates the rear brakes only. It is activated by a pull-handle in the center console between the front seats.

The power brake booster, located in the engine compartment on the firewall, uses engine manifold vacuum and atmospheric pressure to provide assistance to the hydraulically operated brakes.

After completing any operation involving the disassembly of any part of the brake system, always test drive the vehicle to check for proper braking performance before resuming normal driving. Test the brakes while driving on a clean, dry, flat surface. Conditions other than these can lead to inaccurate test results. Test the brakes at various speeds with both light and heavy pedal pressure. The vehicle should stop evenly without pulling to one side or the other. Avoid locking the brakes because this slides the tires and diminishes braking efficiency and control.

Tires, vehicle load and front end alignment are factors which also affect braking performance.

2 Disc brake pads — replacement

Refer to illustrations 2.5 and 2.6a through 2.6k

Warning: *Disc brake pads must be replaced on both front wheels at the same time — never replace the pads on only one wheel. Also, the dust created by the brake system contains asbestos, which is harmful to your health. Never blow it out with compressed air and do not inhale any of it. An approved filtering mask should be worn whenever servicing the brake system. Do not, under any circumstances, use petroleum-based solvents to clean brake parts. Use brake cleaner or denatured alcohol only.*

Note: *When servicing the disc brakes, use only high quality, nationally recognized brand name pads.*

1   Remove the cover from the brake fluid reservoir, siphon off about two ounces of the fluid into a container and discard it.
2   Loosen the wheel lug nuts, raise the vehicle and support it securely on jackstands.
3   Remove the front wheel, then reinstall two wheel nuts (flat side toward the rotor) to hold the rotor in place. Work on one brake assembly at a time, using the assembled brake for reference if necessary.
4   Inspect the rotor carefully as outlined in Section 4. If machining is necessary, follow the information in that Section to remove the rotor, at which time the pads can be removed from the calipers as well.
5   Push the piston back into its bore. If necessary, a C-clamp can be used, but a flat bar will usually do the job **(see illustration)**. As the piston is depressed to the bottom of the caliper bore, the fluid in the master cylinder will rise. Make sure that it does not overflow. If necessary, siphon off more of the fluid as directed in Step 1.
6   Refer to the accompanying photographs and perform the procedure illustrated. Start with photograph 2.6a.
7   When reinstalling the caliper, be sure to tighten the mounting bolts to the specified torque. After the job has been completed, firmly depress the brake pedal a few times to bring the pads into contact with the rotor.

2.5   A large C-clamp can be used to compress the piston into the caliper for removal

9

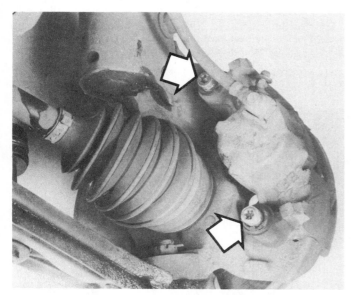

2.6a   A No. 50 Torx bit must be used to remove the two caliper mounting bolts (arrows) — don't attempt to loosen them with an Allen wrench, because the bolt heads could be damaged

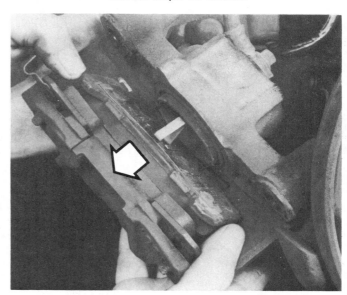

2.6b   Remove the inner pad by snapping it out of the piston in the direction shown (arrow)

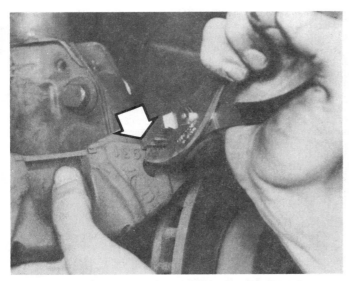

2.6c Remove the outboard pad by bending the tabs (arrow) straight out with a pair of pliers

2.6d After bending the tabs straight, the outboard pad can be removed by using a hammer to dislodge it from the caliper

2.6e Inspect the caliper bolts and bushings (A) for damage and the contact surfaces (B) for corrosion

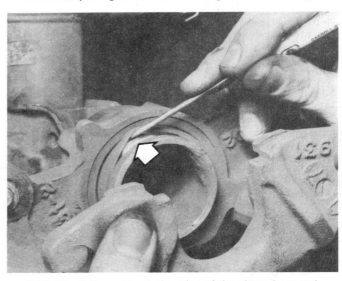

2.6f Carefully peel back the edge of the piston boot and check for corrosion and leaking fluid

2.6g Snap the inner pad retainer spring into the new pad in the direction shown (arrow)

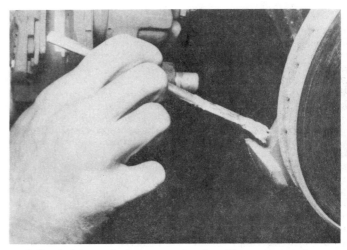

2.6h Lubricate the lower steering knuckle contact surface lightly with white lithium base grease

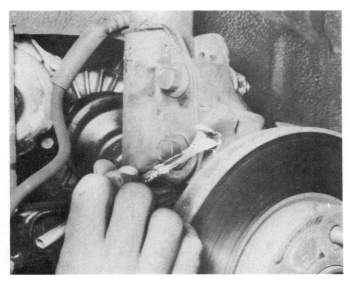

2.6i Apply a light coat of white lithium base grease to the upper steering knuckle-to-caliper contact surface

2.6j Place the pads in position and snap the inner pad into place in the piston

2.6k After installing the caliper, insert a large screwdriver between the outer pad flange and the disc hat to seat the pad and then bend the tabs over with a hammer

3.9 With the caliper padded to catch the piston, use compressed air to force the piston out of its bore — make sure your hands or fingers are not between the piston and caliper!

---

3 Disc brake caliper — removal, overhaul and installation

Refer to illustrations 3.9, 3.10, 3.11, 3.12, 3.15, 3.16, 3.17, 3.18, 3.20 and 3.23

Warning: *Dust created by the brake system contains asbestos, which is harmful to your health. Never blow it out with compressed air and do not inhale any of it. An approved filtering mask should be worn whenever servicing the brake system. Do not, under any circumstances, use petroleum-based solvents to clean brake parts. Use brake cleaner or denatured alcohol only.*

Note: *If an overhaul is indicated (usually because of fluid leakage) explore all options before beginning the job. New and factory rebuilt calipers are available on an exchange basis, which makes this job quite easy. If it is decided to rebuild the calipers, make sure that a rebuild kit is available before proceeding.*

Removal

1   Remove the cover from the brake fluid reservoir, siphon off two-thirds of the fluid into a container and discard it.
2   Loosen the wheel lug nuts, raise the front of the vehicle and support

it securely on jackstands. Remove the front wheels.
3   Reinstall two lug nuts on each rotor, flat side against the rotor, to hold the rotor in place.
4   Bottom the piston in the caliper bore. This is accomplished by pushing on the caliper, although it may be necessary to carefully use a flat pry bar or a C-clamp.
5   Remove the brake hose inlet fitting bolt and disconnect the fitting. Have a rag handy to catch the spilling fluid and wrap a plastic bag tightly around the end of the hose to prevent fluid loss and contamination.
6   Using a #50 Torx bit, remove the two mounting bolts and lift the caliper from the vehicle (refer to Section 2 if necessary).

Overhaul

7   Refer to Section 2 and remove the brake pads from the caliper.
8   Clean the exterior of the caliper with brake cleaner or denatured alcohol. **Never use gasoline, kerosene or any petroleum-based cleaning solvents.** Place the caliper on a clean workbench.
9   Position a wooden block or numerous shop rags in the caliper as a cushion, then use compressed air to remove the piston from the caliper **(see illustration)**. Use only enough air pressure to ease the piston

9

3.10   Carefully pry the dust boot out of the housing,
taking care not to scratch the bore surface

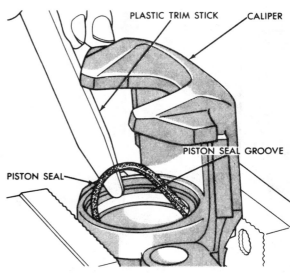

3.11   To avoid damage to the caliper bore or seal groove,
it is best to remove the seal with a plastic or wooden tool

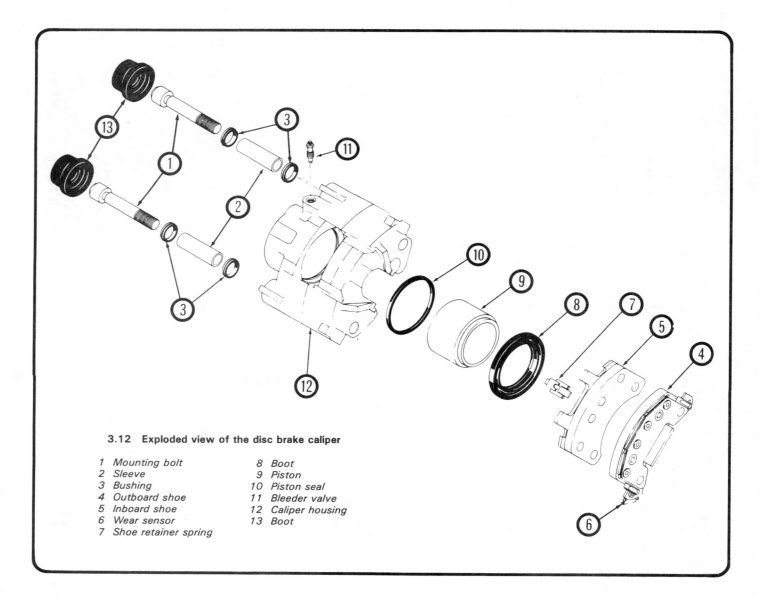

3.12   Exploded view of the disc brake caliper

1 Mounting bolt	8 Boot
2 Sleeve	9 Piston
3 Bushing	10 Piston seal
4 Outboard shoe	11 Bleeder valve
5 Inboard shoe	12 Caliper housing
6 Wear sensor	13 Boot
7 Shoe retainer spring	

3.15   Position the seal in the caliper bore, making sure it is not twisted

3.16   Install the new dust boot in the piston groove with the folds toward the open end of the piston

3.17   Install the piston squarely into the caliper bore

3.18   Use a seal driver to seat the boot in the caliper housing counterbore — if a seal driver isn't available, carefully tap around the circumference of the boot with a drift until it is seated

out of the bore. If the piston is blown out, even with the cushion in place, it may be damaged. **Warning:** *Never place your fingers in front of the piston in an attempt to catch or protect it when applying compressed air, as serious injury could occur.*

10   Carefully pry the dust boot out of the caliper bore **(see illustration)**.

11   Using a wood or plastic tool, remove the piston seal from the groove in the caliper bore **(see illustration)**. Metal tools may cause bore damage.

12   Remove the caliper bleeder valve, then remove and discard the sleeves and bushings from the caliper ears. Discard all rubber parts **(see illustration)**.

13   Clean the remaining parts with brake cleaner or denatured alcohol then blow them dry with compressed air.

14   Carefully examine the piston for nicks and burrs and loss of plating. If surface defects are present, parts must be replaced. Check the caliper bore in a similar way. Light polishing with crocus cloth is permissible to remove light corrosion and stains. Discard the mounting bolts if they are corroded or damaged.

15   When assembling, lubricate the piston bores and seal with clean brake fluid. Position the seal in the caliper bore groove **(see illustration)**.

16   Lubricate the piston with clean brake fluid, then install a new boot in the piston groove with the fold toward the open end of the piston **(see illustration)**.

17   Insert the piston squarely into the caliper bore, then apply force to bottom the piston in the bore **(see illustration)**.

18   Position the dust boot in the caliper counterbore, then use a drift

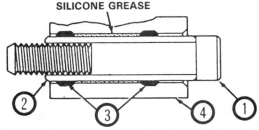

3.20   Pack the area between the mounting bolt sleeve bushings with silicone grease

| 1 Mounting bolt | 3 Bushing |
| 2 Sleeve | 4 Caliper housing |

to drive it into position **(see illustration)**. Make sure that the boot is evenly installed below the caliper face.

19   Install the bleeder valve.

20   Install new bushings in the mounting bolt holes and fill the area between the bushings with silicone grease, supplied in the rebuild kit **(see illustration)**. Push the sleeves into the mounting bolt holes.

Installation

21 Inspect the mounting bolts for excessive corrosion.

22 Place the caliper in position over the rotor and mounting bracket, install the bolts and tighten to the specified torque.

23 Check to make sure the clearance between the caliper and the bracket stops is between 0.005 and 0.012 inch **(see illustration)**.

24 Install the inlet fitting bolt, using new copper washers, then tighten the retaining bolt to the specified torque. It will be necessary to bleed the brakes (Section 9).

25 Install the wheels and lower the vehicle.

26 After the job has been completed, firmly depress the brake pedal a few times to bring the pads into contact with the rotor.

---

4 Brake rotor (disc) — inspection, removal and installation

Refer to illustrations 4.2, 4.3, 4.4a, 4.4b, 4.5a and 4.5b

Inspection

1 Loosen the wheel lug nuts, raise the vehicle and support it securely on jackstands. Remove the wheel and install two lug nuts to hold the rotor in place.

2 Remove the brake caliper as outlined in Section 3. It is not necessary to disconnect the brake hose. After removing the caliper bolts, suspend the caliper out of the way with a piece of wire **(see illustration)**.

3 Visually inspect the rotor surface for scoring or damage. Light scratches and shallow grooves are normal after use and may not always be detrimental to brake operation, but deep scoring — over 0.015 inch (0.38 mm) — requires rotor removal and refinishing by an automotive machine shop. Be sure to check both sides of the rotor **(see illustration)**. If pulsating has been noticed during application of the brakes, suspect rotor runout.

4 To check rotor runout, place a dial indicator at a point about 1/2-inch from the outer edge of the rotor **(see illustration)**. Set the indicator to zero and turn the rotor. The indicator reading should not exceed the specified allowable runout limit. If it does, the rotor should be refinished by an automotive machine shop. **Note:** *It is recommended that the rotors be resurfaced regardless of the dial indicator reading, as this will impart a smooth finish and ensure a perfectly flat surface, eliminating any brake pedal pulsation or other undesirable symptoms related to questionable rotors. At the very least, if you elect not to have the rotors resurfaced, remove the glazing from the surface with medium-grit emery cloth using a swirling motion* **(see illustration)**.

5 It is absolutely critical that the rotor not be machined to a thickness under the specified minimum allowable rotor refinish thickness. The minimum wear (or discard) thickness is cast into the inside of the rotor **(see illustration)**. This should not be confused with the minimum refinish thickness. The rotor thickness can be checked with a micrometer **(see illustration)**.

Removal

6 Remove the two lug nuts which were put on to hold the rotor in place and remove the rotor from the hub.

Installation

7 Place the rotor in position over the threaded studs.

8 Install the caliper and brake pad assembly over the rotor and position it on the steering knuckle (refer to Section 3 for the caliper installation procedure, if necessary). Tighten the caliper bolts to the specified torque.

9 Install the wheel, then lower the vehicle to the ground. Depress the brake pedal a few times to bring the brake pads into contact with the rotor. Bleeding of the system will not be necessary unless the fluid hose was disconnected from the caliper. Check the operation of the brakes carefully before placing the vehicle into normal service.

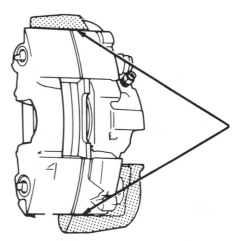

3.23 Measure the clearance between the caliper and bracket stops at the points indicated

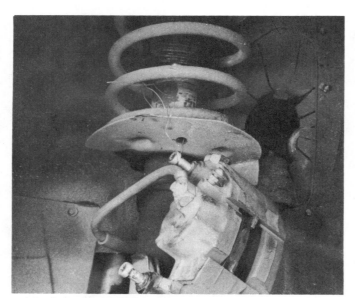

4.2 Suspend the caliper with a piece of wire whenever it is necessary to reposition it. Do not let it hang by the brake hose!

4.3 Check the rotor surface for grooves and scoring

5 Rear brake shoes — inspection and replacement

Refer to illustrations 5.4a through 5.4z and 5.5

Warning: *Drum brake shoes must be replaced on both wheels at the same time — never replace the shoes on only one wheel. Also, the dust created by the brake system contains asbestos, which is harmful to your health. Never blow it out with compressed air and do not inhale any of it. An approved filtering mask should be worn whenever servicing the brake system. Do not, under any circumstances, use petroleum-based solvents to clean brake parts. Use brake cleaner or denatured alcohol only.*

Caution: *Whenever the brake shoes are replaced, the retractor and hold-down springs should also be replaced. Due to the continuous heating/cooling cycle that the springs are subjected to, they lose their tension over a period of time and may allow the shoes to drag on the drum and wear at a much faster rate than normal. When replacing the rear brake shoes, use only high quality nationally recognized brand-name parts.*

1   Loosen the wheel lug nuts, raise the vehicle and support it securely on jackstands.
2   Release the parking brake.
3   Remove the wheel. **Note:** *All four rear shoes must be replaced at the same time, but to avoid mixing up parts, work on only one brake assembly at a time.*
4   Refer to the accompanying photographs and perform the brake shoe inspection and, if necessary, the replacement procedure. Start with illustration 5.4a. **Note:** *If the brake drum cannot be easily pulled off the axle and shoe assembly, make sure that the parking brake is completely released, then squirt some penetrating oil around the center hub area. Allow the oil to soak in and try to pull the drum off. If the drum still cannot be pulled off, the brake shoes will have to be retracted. This is accomplished by first removing the lanced cutout in the brake drum with a hammer and chisel* (**see illustration 5.4a**). With the cutout removed, pull the lever off the adjusting screw wheel with one small

4.4a   Check for runout with a dial indicator, mounted with the indicator needle about 1/2-inch from the outside edge

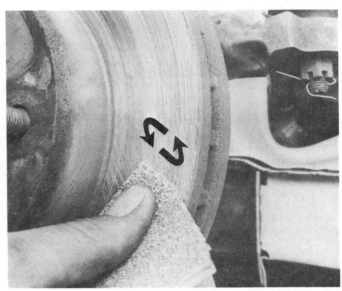

4.4b   If you elect not to have the rotors machined, at the very least be sure to break the glaze on the rotor surface with emery cloth

4.5a   The minimum wear (or discard) thickness (arrow) is cast into the inside of the rotor

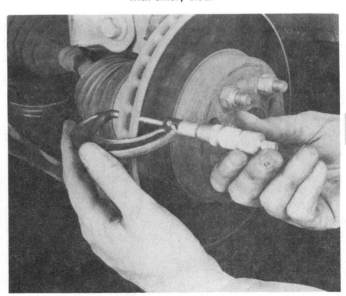

4.5b   Measure the thickness of the rotor with a micrometer

9

5.4a   If the brake drum will not come off easily, it may be necessary to remove the lanced cutout with a hammer and chisel, then turn the adjuster screw to move the brake shoes away from the drum

5.4b   Before removing anything, clean the brake assembly with brake cleaner or denatured alcohol — DO NOT use compressed air to blow the dust from the brake assembly!

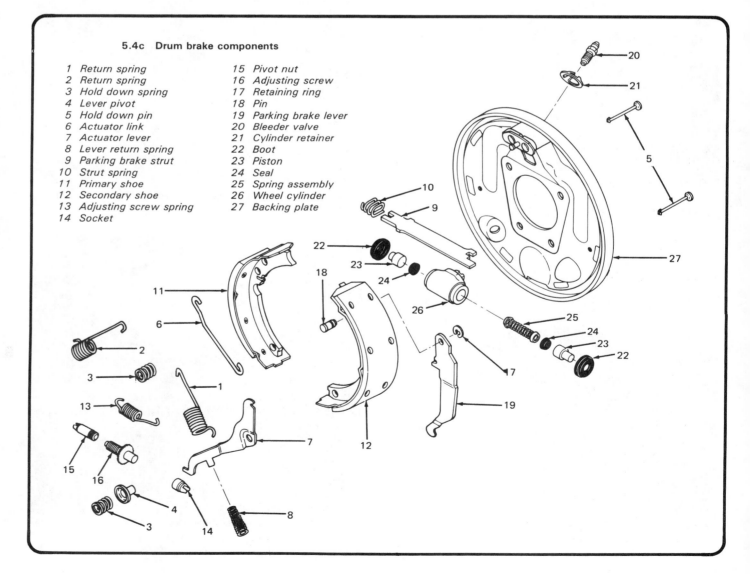

5.4c   Drum brake components

1   Return spring
2   Return spring
3   Hold down spring
4   Lever pivot
5   Hold down pin
6   Actuator link
7   Actuator lever
8   Lever return spring
9   Parking brake strut
10 Strut spring
11 Primary shoe
12 Secondary shoe
13 Adjusting screw spring
14 Socket

15 Pivot nut
16 Adjusting screw
17 Retaining ring
18 Pin
19 Parking brake lever
20 Bleeder valve
21 Cylinder retainer
22 Boot
23 Piston
24 Seal
25 Spring assembly
26 Wheel cylinder
27 Backing plate

5.4d Remove the return springs using a brake spring tool

5.4e Remove the hold down springs and pins by pushing in with pliers and turning (arrows)

5.4f Lift up on the actuator lever and remove the actuating link from the anchor pin pivot along with the actuator lever and return spring (arrows)

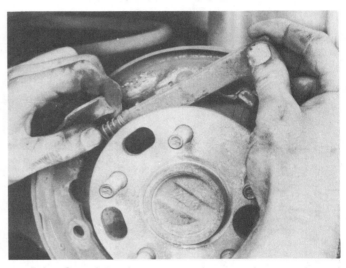

5.4g Spread the shoes apart at the top and remove the parking brake strut

5.4h With the shoe assembly spread to clear the hub flange, lift it from the backing plate

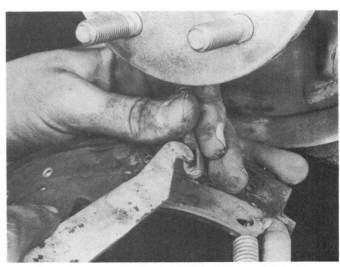

5.4i Disconnect the parking brake lever from the cable and remove the shoe assembly

9

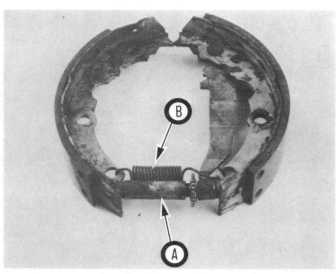

5.4j   Remove the adjusting screw (A) and spring (B) from the shoe assembly, making sure to note the direction in which they are installed

5.4k   Remove the parking brake lever by prying off the C-clip

5.4l   Install the parking brake lever on the new brake shoe and press the C-clip into place with needle nose pliers

5.4m   Lubricate the contact surfaces of the backing plate with white lithium base grease

5.4n   Lubricate the adjuster screw with white lithium base grease prior to installation

5.4o   Connect the parking brake lever to the cable

5.4p Spread the brake assembly apart sufficiently to clear the hub flange and raise it into position

5.4q Install the parking brake strut and spring

5.4r Make sure the parking brake strut is positioned in the shoes properly (arrows)

5.4s Install the hold down pin and spring on the primary brake shoe

5.4t Install the actuator link and lever to the secondary brake shoe

5.4u Install the actuator lever return spring

9

5.4v   Install the hold down pin and spring on the
secondary brake shoe

5.4w   Install the return springs

5.4x   Center the brake shoe assembly so the drum will
slide over it

5.4y   Adjust the star wheel so the drum fits snugly over
the shoes

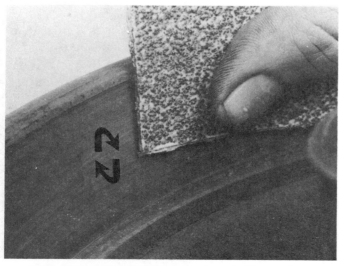

5.4z   Remove the glaze from the drum braking surface
with emery cloth, working in a circular motion

5.5   The drum has a maximum permissible diameter cast into it
(arrow) which is a wear dimension, not a refinish dimension

screwdriver while turning the adjusting wheel with another small screwdriver, moving the shoes away from the drum. The drum may now be pulled off.

5   Before reinstalling the drum it should be checked for cracks, score marks, deep scratches and hard spots, which will appear as small discolored areas. If the hard spots cannot be removed with a fine emery cloth or if any of the other conditions listed above exist, the drum must be taken to an automotive machine shop to have it turned. **Note:** *It is recommended that the drums be resurfaced regardless of the surface appearance, as this will impart a smooth finish and ensure a perfectly round drum, eliminating any brake pedal pulsation or other undesirable symptoms related to questionable drums. At the very least, if you elect not to have the drums resurfaced, remove the glazing from the surface with medium-grit emery cloth using a swirling motion. If the drum will not "clean up" before the maximum service limit is reached in the machining operation, the drum will have to be replaced with a new one. The maximum wear diameter is cast into the each brake drum* **(see illustration).** *This should not be confused with the service limit (the dimension at which the drum should be thrown away).*

6   Install the brake drum on the axle flange.
7   Mount the wheel, install the lug nuts, then lower the vehicle.
8   Make a number of forward and reverse stops to adjust the brakes until a satisfactory pedal action is obtained.

6   Rear wheel cylinder — removal, overhaul and installation

Refer to illustrations 6.4, 6.5, 6.7 and 6.13

Note: *If an overhaul is indicated (usually because of fluid leakage or sticky operation) explore all options before beginning the job. New wheel cylinders are available, which makes this job quite easy. If it is decided to rebuild the wheel cylinder, make sure that a rebuild kit is available before proceeding.*

Removal

1   Raise the rear of the vehicle and support it securely on jackstands.
2   Remove the brake shoe assembly (Section 5).
3   Carefully clean all dirt and foreign material from around the wheel cylinder.
4   Disconnect the brake fluid inlet line **(see illustration).** Do not pull the brake line away from the wheel cylinder.
5   Remove the wheel cylinder retainer by using two screwdrivers to release the clips **(see illustration).**
6   Remove the wheel cylinder from the brake backing plate and place it on a clean workbench. Immediately plug the brake line to prevent fluid loss and contamination.

6.4   A flare nut wrench should be used to disconnect the brake line (arrow)

Overhaul

7   Remove the bleeder valve, seals, pistons, boots and spring assembly from the cylinder body **(see illustration).**
8   Clean the wheel cylinder with brake fluid, denatured alcohol or brake system cleaner. **Warning:** *Do not, under any circumstances, use petroleum based solvents to clean brake parts.*
9   Use compressed air to remove excess fluid from the wheel cylinder and to blow out the passages.
10   Check the cylinder bore for corrosion and scoring. Crocus cloth may be used to remove light corrosion and stains, but the cylinder must be replaced with a new one if the defects cannot be removed easily, or if the bore is scored.
11   Lubricate the new seals with brake fluid.
12   Assemble the brake cylinder, making sure the boots are properly seated.

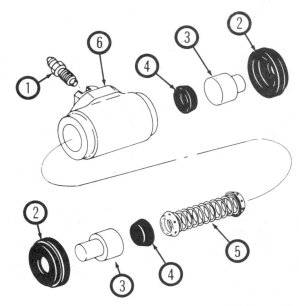

6.7   Wheel cylinder components — exploded view

1 Bleeder valve	*4 Seal*
2 Boot	*5 Spring assembly*
3 Piston	*6 Wheel cylinder body*

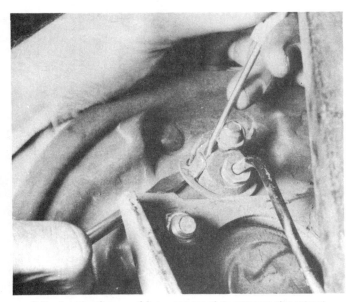

6.5   A pair of screwdrivers are used to remove the wheel cylinder retainer

9

6.13 A wood block (arrow) should be used to hold the
wheel cylinder in position

7.4 Remove the master cylinder mounting nuts (arrows)

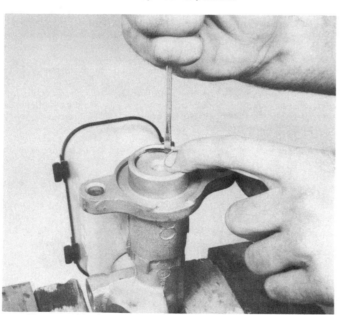

7.7 Press down on the piston and remove the primary
piston circlip

7.8a Remove the primary piston assembly

Installation

13 Place the wheel cylinder in position and use a wooden block
wedged between the axle flange and the cylinder body to hold it in
place **(see illustration)**
14 Install the wheel cylinder retainer over the wheel cylinder using
a 1-1/8 inch 12 point socket to press it into place.
15 Connect the brake line and install the brake shoe assembly.

---

7   Master cylinder — removal, overhaul and installation

---

*Refer to illustrations 7.4, 7.7, 7.8a, 7.8b, 7.10, 7.12a, 7.12b, 7.15,
7.16, 7.18, 7.19a through 7.19f, 7.20, 7.21a through 7.21e and 7.23*
Note: *Before deciding to overhaul the master cylinder, investigate the*

*availability and cost of a new or factory-rebuilt unit and also the
availability of a rebuild kit.*

Removal

1   Place rags under the fluid fittings and prepare caps or plastic bags
to cover the ends of the lines once they are disconnected. **Caution:**
*Brake fluid will damage paint. Cover all body parts and be careful not
to spill fluid during this procedure.*
2   Loosen the tube nuts at the ends of the brake lines where they
enter the master cylinder. To prevent rounding off the flats on these
nuts, the use of a flare-nut wrench, which wraps around the nut, is
preferred.
3   Pull the brake lines slightly away from the master cylinder and plug
the ends to prevent contamination.

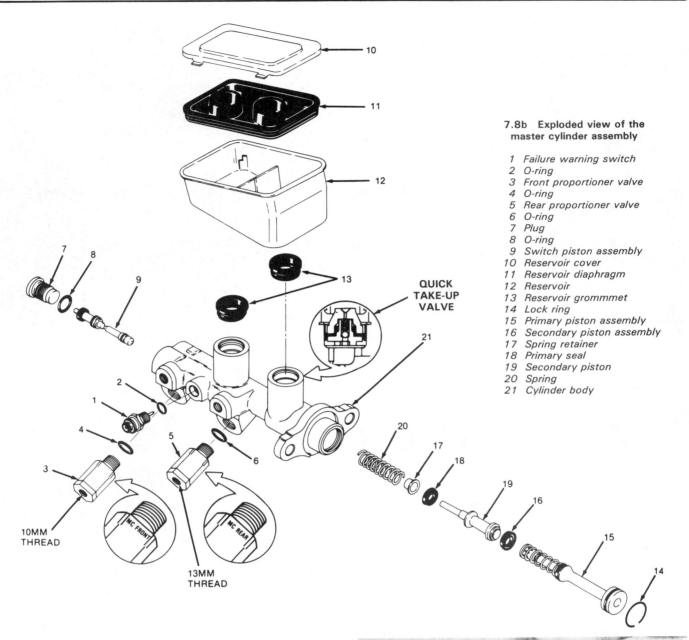

7.8b **Exploded view of the master cylinder assembly**

1   Failure warning switch
2   O-ring
3   Front proportioner valve
4   O-ring
5   Rear proportioner valve
6   O-ring
7   Plug
8   O-ring
9   Switch piston assembly
10 Reservoir cover
11 Reservoir diaphragm
12 Reservoir
13 Reservoir grommmet
14 Lock ring
15 Primary piston assembly
16 Secondary piston assembly
17 Spring retainer
18 Primary seal
19 Secondary piston
20 Spring
21 Cylinder body

4   Remove the two master cylinder mounting nuts **(see illustration)**, move the bracket retaining the combination valve forward slightly, taking care not to bend the hydraulic lines running to the combination valve, and remove the master cylinder from the vehicle.

5   Remove the reservoir cover and reservoir diaphragm, then discard any remaining fluid in the reservoir.

6   Mount the master cylinder in a vise. Be sure to line the vise jaws with blocks of wood to prevent damage to the cylinder body.

7   Remove the primary piston lock ring by depressing the piston and prying the ring out with a screwdriver **(see illustration)**.

8   Remove the primary piston assembly from the cylinder bore **(see illustrations)**.

9   Remove the secondary piston assembly from the cylinder bore. It may be necessary to remove the master cylinder from the vise and invert it, carefully tapping it against a block of wood to expel the piston.

10 Place the master cylinder in the vise once again and pry the reservoir from the cylinder body with a pry bar **(see illustration)**. Remove the reservoir grommets.

11 Do not attempt to remove the quick take-up valve from the cylinder body, as this valve is not serviceable.

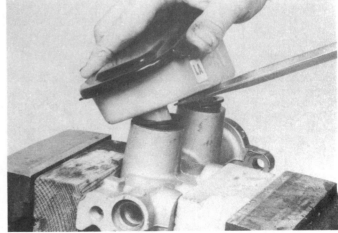

7.10 **Pry the plastic reservoir from the cylinder body**

9

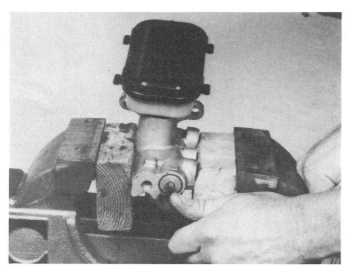

7.12a   Remove the switch piston plug

7.12b   Remove the switch piston assembly

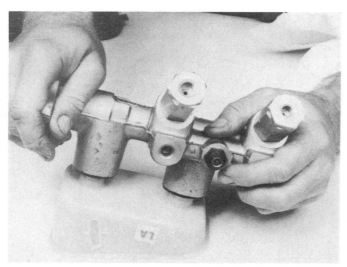

7.15   Use a rocking motion when pressing the reservoir onto the master cylinder

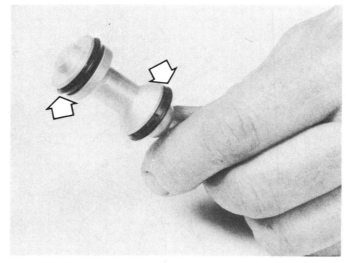

7.16   The secondary piston seals must be installed with the lips facing out as shown

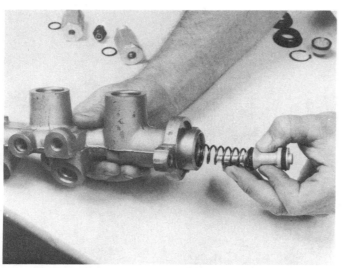

7.18   Install the secondary piston assembly

12 With an Allen wrench, remove the switch piston plug and the switch piston assembly (**see illustrations**). It may be necessary to lightly tap the master cylinder to remove the piston.

Overhaul

13 Inspect the cylinder bore for corrosion and damage. If any corrosion or damage is found, replace the master cylinder body with a new one, as abrasives cannot be used on the bore.

14 Lubricate the new reservoir grommets with silicone lubricant and press the grommets into the master cylinder body, making sure they are properly seated.

15 Lay the reservoir on a hard surface and press the master cylinder body onto the reservoir, using a rocking motion (**see illustration**).

16 Remove the old seals from the secondary piston assembly and install the new seals so that the cups face out (**see illustration**).

17 Attach the spring retainer to the secondary piston assembly.

18 Lubricate the cylinder bore with clean brake fluid and install the spring and secondary piston assembly in the cylinder (**see illustration**).

19 Disassemble the primary piston assembly, noting the position of the parts, then lubricate the new seals with clean brake fluid and install them on the piston (**see illustrations**).

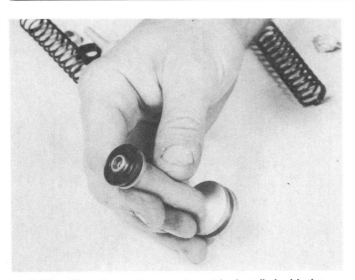

7.19a The primary piston seal must be installed with the lip facing away from the piston

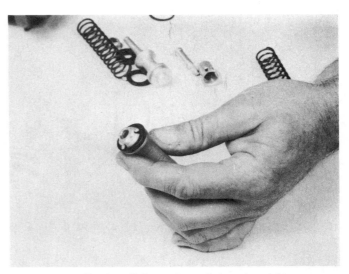

7.19b Install the seal guard over the seal

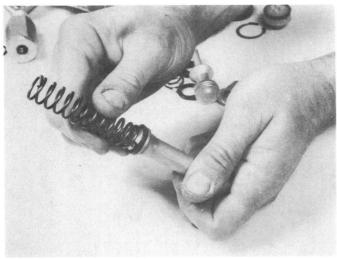

7.19c Place the primary piston spring in position

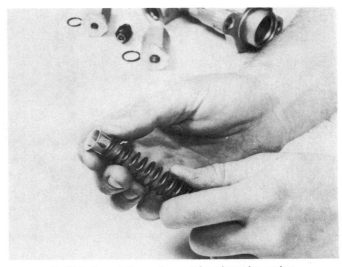

7.19d Insert the spring retainer into the spring

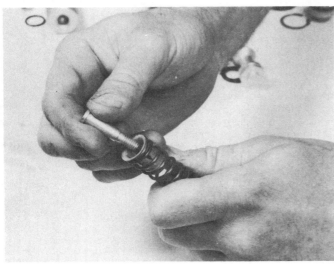

7.19e Insert the spring retaining bolt through the retainer and spring and thread it into the piston

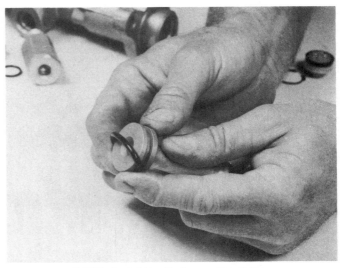

7.19f Install the O-ring on the piston

9

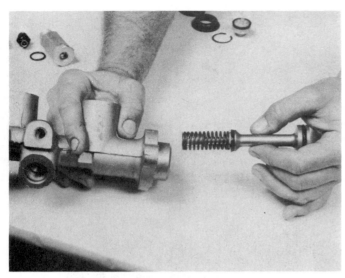

7.20 Insert the primary piston assembly into the body

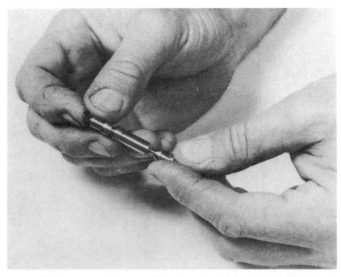

7.21a Install the small O-ring on the switch piston

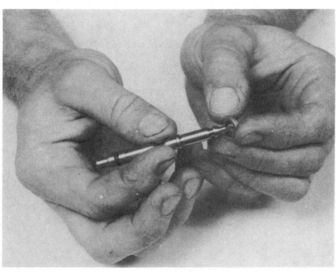

7.21b Place the metal retainer on the switch piston

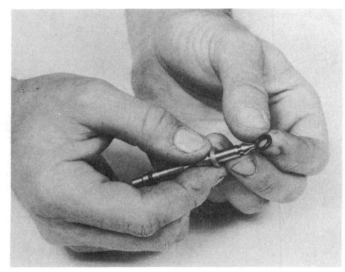

7.21c Slide the large O-ring onto the switch piston

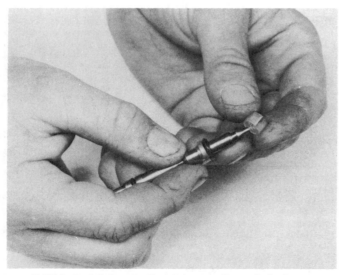

7.21d Install the plastic retainer on the switch piston

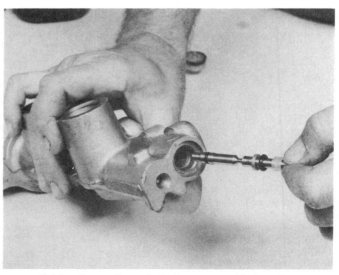

7.21e Insert the switch piston assembly into the
cylinder body

7.23 Install the reservoir diaphragm into the cover

20 Install the primary piston assembly in the cylinder bore (see illustration), depress it and install the lock ring.
21 Install the new O-rings on the switch piston and carefully insert it back into the master cylinder (see illustrations).
22 Install a new O-ring on the piston plug and install the plug.
23 Inspect the reservoir cover and diaphragm for cracks and deformation. Replace any damaged parts with new ones and attach the diaphragm to the cover (see illustration).
24 **Note**: *Whenever the master cylinder is removed, the complete hydraulic system must be bled. The time required to bleed the system can be reduced if the master cylinder is filled with fluid and bench bled (refer to Steps 25 through 28) before the master cylinder is installed on the vehicle.*
25 Insert threaded plugs of the correct size into the cylinder outlet holes and fill the reservoirs with brake fluid. The master cylinder should be supported in such a manner that brake fluid will not spill during the bench bleeding procedure.
26 Loosen one plug at a time and push the piston assembly into the bore to force air from the master cylinder. To prevent air from being drawn back into the cylinder, the appropriate plug must be replaced before allowing the piston to return to its original position.
27 Stroke the piston three or four times for each outlet to assure that all air has been expelled.
28 Since high pressure is not involved in the bench bleeding procedure, an alternative to the removal and replacement of the plugs with each stroke of the piston assembly is available. Before pushing in on the piston assembly, remove one of the plugs completely. Before releasing the piston, however, instead of replacing the plug, simply put your finger tightly over the hole to keep air from being drawn back into the master cylinder. Wait several seconds for the brake fluid to be drawn from the reservoir to the piston bore, then repeat the procedure. When you push down on the piston it will force your finger off the hole, allowing the air inside to be expelled. When only brake fluid is being ejected from the hole, replace the plug and go on to the other port.
29 Refill the master cylinder reservoirs and install the diaphragm and cover assembly. **Note**: *The reservoirs should only be filled to the top of the reservoir divider to prevent overflowing when the cover is installed.*

Installation

30 Carefully install the master cylinder by reversing the removal steps, then bleed the brakes at the wheel bleed valves (refer to Section 9).

---

8 Brake hoses and lines — inspection and replacement

Refer to illustration 8.2

1 About every six months, with the vehicle raised and placed securely on jackstands, the flexible hoses which connect the steel brake lines

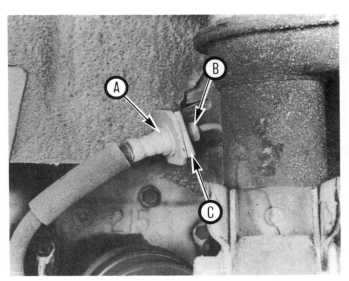

8.2 Using a backup wrench on the flexible hose side of the fitting (A), loosen the tube nut (B) with a flare nut wrench and remove the U-clip (C) from the hose fitting

with the front and rear brake assemblies should be inspected for cracks, chafing of the outer cover, leaks, blisters and other damage. These are important and vulnerable parts of the brake system and inspection should be complete. A light and mirror will prove helpful for a thorough check. If a hose exhibits any of the above conditions, replace it with a new one.

Front brake hose

2 Using a back-up wrench, disconnect the brake line from the hose fitting, being careful not to bend the frame bracket or brake line (see illustration).
3 Use pliers to remove the U-clip from the female fitting at the bracket, then remove the hose from the bracket.
4 At the caliper end of the hose, remove the bolt from the fitting block, then remove the hose and the copper gaskets on either side of the fitting block.
5 When installing the hose, always use new copper gaskets on either side of the fitting block and lubricate all bolt threads with clean brake fluid before installation.
6 With the fitting flange engaged with the caliper locating ledge, attach the hose to the caliper.
7 Without twisting the hose, install the female fitting in the hose bracket. It will fit the bracket in only one position.
8 Install the U-clip retaining the female fitting to the frame bracket.
9 Using a back-up wrench, attach the brake line to the hose fitting.
10 When the brake hose installation is complete, there should be no kinks in the hose. Make sure the hose does not contact any part of the suspension. Check this by turning the wheels to the extreme left and right positions. If the hose makes contact, remove the hose and correct the installation as necessary.

Rear brake hose

11 Using a back-up wrench, disconnect the hose at both ends, being careful not to bend the bracket or steel lines (refer to illustration 8.2 if necessary).
12 Remove the two U-clips with pliers and separate the female fittings from the brackets.
13 Unbolt the hose retaining clip and remove the hose.
14 Without twisting the hose, install the female ends of the hose in the frame brackets. It will fit the bracket in only one position.
15 Install the U-clips retaining the female end to the bracket.
16 Using a back-up wrench, attach the steel line fittings to the female fittings. Again, be careful not to bend the bracket or steel line.
17 Check that the hose installation did not loosen the frame bracket. Tighten the bracket if necessary.
18 Fill the master cylinder reservoir and bleed the system (refer to Section 15).

9

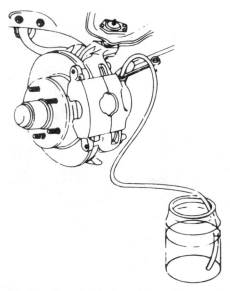

9.8 When bleeding the brakes, a hose is connected to the bleeder valve at the caliper (or wheel cylinder) and then submerged in brake fluid. Air will be seen as bubbles in the container or in the tube. All air must be expelled before continuing to the next wheel

Metal brake lines

19 When replacing brake lines it is important that the proper replacements be purchased. Do not use copper pipe for any brake system connections. Purchase proper brake line from a dealer or brake specialist.

20 Prefabricated brake line, with the tube ends already flared and connectors installed, is available at auto parts stores or dealers. These lines are also bent to the proper shapes if necessary.

21 If prefabricated lengths are not available, obtain the recommended steel tubing and fittings to match the line to be replaced. Determine the correct length by measuring the old brake line (a piece of string can usually be used for this) and cut the new tubing to length, allowing about 1/2-inch extra for flaring the ends.

22 Install the fitting onto the cut tubing and flare the ends of the line with an ISO flaring tool.

23 If necessary, carefully bend the line to the proper shape. A tube bender is recommended for this. **Caution:** *Do not crimp or damage the line.*

24 When installing the new line make sure it is well supported in the brackets and has plenty of clearance between moving or hot components.

25 After installation, check the master cylinder fluid level and add fluid as necessary. Bleed the brake system as outlined in the next Section and test the brakes carefully before placing the vehicle into normal service.

9 Brake system bleeding

Refer to illustration 9.8

Warning: *Wear eye protection whenever bleeding the brake system. If the fluid comes in contact with your eyes, immediately rinse them with water and seek a physician's advice.*

Note: *Bleeding the hydraulic system is necessary to remove any air that manages to find its way into the system when it has been opened during removal and installation of a hose, line, caliper or master cylinder.*

1 It will probably be necessary to bleed the system at all four brakes if air has entered the system due to low fluid level, or if the brake lines have been disconnected at the master cylinder.

2 If a brake line was disconnected only at a wheel, then only that caliper or wheel cylinder must be bled.

3 If a brake line is disconnected at a fitting located between the master cylinder and any of the brakes, that part of the system served by the disconnected line must be bled.

4 Remove any residual vacuum from the brake power booster by applying the brake several times with the engine off.

5 Remove the master cylinder reservoir cover and fill the reservoir with brake fluid. Reinstall the cover. **Note:** *Check the fluid level often during the bleeding operation and add fluid as necessary to prevent the fluid level from falling low enough to allow air bubbles into the master cylinder.*

6 Have an assistant on hand, as well as a supply of new brake fluid, an empty clear plastic container, a length of 3/16-inch plastic, rubber or vinyl tubing to fit over the bleeder valve and a wrench to open and close the bleeder valve.

7 Beginning at the right rear wheel, loosen the bleeder valve slightly, then tighten it to a point where it is snug but can still be loosened quickly and easily.

8 Place one end of the tubing over the bleeder valve and submerge the other end in brake fluid in the container **(see illustration)**.

9 Have the assistant pump the brakes slowly a few times to get pressure in the system, then hold the pedal firmly depressed.

10 While the pedal is held depressed, open the bleeder valve just enough to allow a flow of fluid to leave the valve. Watch for air bubbles to exit the submerged end of the tube. When the fluid flow slows after a couple of seconds, close the valve and have your assistant release the pedal.

11 Repeat Steps 9 and 10 until no more air is seen leaving the tube, then tighten the bleeder valve and proceed to the left rear wheel, the right front wheel and the left front wheel, in that order, and perform the same procedure. Be sure to check the fluid in the master cylinder reservoir frequently.

12 Never use old brake fluid. It contains moisture which will deteriorate the brake system components.

13 Refill the master cylinder with fluid at the end of the operation.

14 Check the operation of the brakes. The pedal should feel solid when depressed, with no sponginess. If necessary, repeat the entire process. **Warning:** *Do not operate the vehicle if you are in doubt about the effectiveness of the brake system.*

10 Parking brake — adjustment

Refer to illustration 10.4

1 Apply the parking brake lever exactly three ratchet clicks.

2 Raise the vehicle and support it securely on jackstands.

3 Before adjusting, make sure the equalizer nut groove is lubricated liberally with multi-purpose lithium base grease.

4 Tighten the adjusting nut **(see illustration)** until the right rear wheel can just be turned rearward with two hands, but locks when forward motion is attempted.

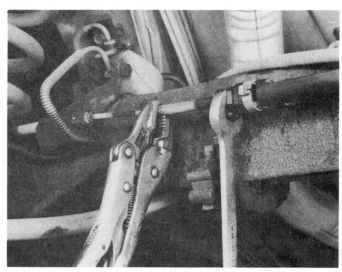

10.4 With a pair of locking pliers clamped to the end of the threaded rod to prevent it from turning, turn the adjusting nut until the right rear wheel can just be turned in a rearward direction but not in the forward direction

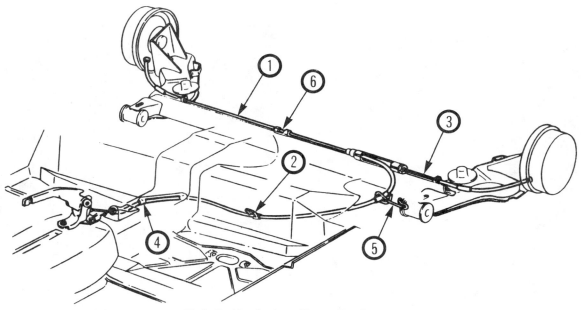

11.4   Parking brake cable routing diagram

1 Right rear cable	3 Left rear cable	5 Bracket
2 Clip	4 Guide	6 Cable joiner

5   Release the parking brake lever and check to make sure the rear wheels turn freely in both directions with no drag.
6   Lower the vehicle.

---

11   Parking brake cables — removal and installation

Refer to illustrations 11.4 and 11.12

Front cable

1   Remove the rear console trim to gain access to the parking brake handle mechanism (refer to Chapter 11).
2   Remove the cable nut from the cable at the handbrake lever and push the cable and casing assembly through the floorpan.
3   Raise the rear of the vehicle and support it securely on jackstands
4   Pull the cable casing from the L-shaped guide just above the rear of the exhaust pipe heat shield **(see illustration)**.
5   Maneuver the cable out of the wire bracket at the left rear suspension pivot.
6   Slide the cable casing out of the equalizer and disconnect the cable from the cable joiner.
7   Installation is the reverse of the removal procedure. Refer to Section 10 for the cable adjustment procedure.

Left cable

8   Raise the vehicle and support it securely on jackstands.
9   Loosen the equalizer adjusting screw and disconnect the left cable from the equalizer.
10 Disconnect the cable casing at the frame mounting bracket by depressing the tangs on the retainer with a pair of pliers.
11 Remove the brake drum and brake shoes as described in Section 5. Disconnect the parking brake cable from the parking brake lever.
12 Using a pair of pliers, depress the tangs on the cable casing retainer and push the cable and casing out through the backing plate **(see illustration)**.
13 Installation is the reverse of the removal procedure. Be sure to adjust the cable as described in Section 10.

Right cable

14 Raise the rear of the vehicle and support it securely on jackstands.
15 Remove enough tension at the equalizer to enable the cable to be removed from the cable joiner.
16 Disconnect the cable casing at the frame mounting bracket by depressing the tangs on the retainer with a pair of pliers.

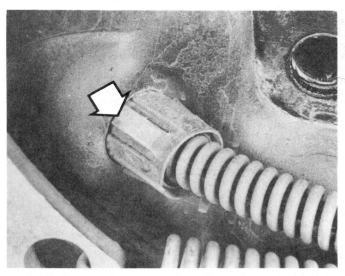

11.12   Depress the tangs on the cable casing retainer and push it through the backing plate

17 Remove the brake drum and brake shoes as described in Section 5. Disconnect the parking brake cable from the parking brake lever.
18 Using a pair of pliers, depress the tangs on the cable casing retainer and push the cable and casing out through the backing plate **(see illustration 11.12)**.
19 Installation is the reverse of the removal procedure. Be sure to adjust the cable as described in Section 10.

---

12   Power brake booster — inspection, removal and installation

Refer to illustration 12.6

1   The power brake booster unit requires no special maintenance apart from periodic inspection of the vacuum hose and the case. Early models have an in-line filter which should be inspected periodically and replaced if clogged or damaged.
2   Dismantling of the power unit requires special tools and is not ordinarily performed by the home mechanic. If a problem develops, it

9

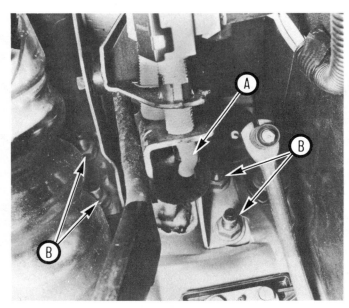

12.6   Remove the retaining clip and slide the power brake
pushrod (A) off of the brake pedal pin, then remove the
booster-to-firewall nuts (B)

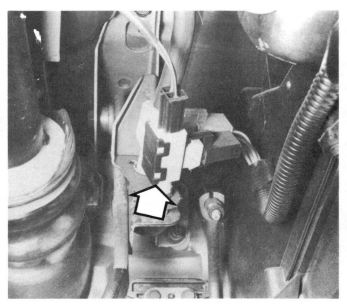

13.3   The brake light switch (arrow) is located to the right
of the steering column at the end of the mounting bracket

is recommended that a new or factory rebuilt unit be used.

3   Remove the nuts attaching the master cylinder to the booster and carefully pull the master cylinder forward until it clears the mounting studs. Use caution so as not to bend or kink the brake lines.

4   Disconnect the vacuum hose where it attaches to the power brake booster.

5   From the passenger compartment, disconnect the power brake pushrod from the top of the brake pedal.

6   Also from this location, remove the nuts attaching the booster to the firewall (see illustration).

7   Carefully lift the booster unit away from the firewall and out of the engine compartment.

8   To install, place the booster into position and tighten the retaining nuts. Connect the brake pedal.

9   Install the master cylinder and vacuum hose.

10   Carefully test the operation of the brakes before placing the vehicle in normal operation.

13   Brake light switch — removal, installation and adjustment

Refer to illustration 13.3

Removal

1   The brake light switch, or stop light switch as it is sometimes called, is located on a bracket at the top of the brake pedal. The switch activates the brake lights at the rear of the vehicle whenever the pedal is depressed.

2   Remove the under dash cover and disconnect the wiring to the courtesy lamp in this panel.

3   Locate the switch at the top of the brake pedal (see illustration). If equipped with cruise control, there will be another switch very similar in appearance. The brake light switch is the one towards the end of the bracket.

4   Disconnect the negative battery cable and secure it out of the way so that it cannot come back into contact with the battery post.

5   Disconnect the wiring connectors at the brake light switch.

6   Depress the brake pedal and pull the switch out of its clip. The switch appears to be threaded, but it is designed to be pushed into and out of the clip and not turned.

Installation and adjustment

7   With the brake pedal depressed, push the new switch into the clip. Note that audible clicks will be heard as this is done.

8   Pull the brake pedal fully rearward against the pedal stop until the clicking sounds can no longer be heard. This action will automatically move the switch the proper amount and no further adjustment will be required. Caution: Do not apply excessive force during this adjustment procedure, as power booster damage may result.

9   Connect the wiring at the switch and the battery. With an assistant, check that the rear brake lights are functioning properly.

Chapter 10 Steering and suspension systems

Contents

Specifications

Front suspension

Torque specifications	Ft-lbs
Control arm pivot bolts............................	60
Suspension support (in the following order)	
center bolts	66
front bolts	65
rear bolts	65
Balljoint-to-steering knuckle nut	45
Stabilizer bar-to-control arm	15
Stabilizer bar bushing clamp nuts	15
Front hub and wheel bearing assembly bolts	70
Strut steering knuckle nuts	133
Strut-to-body nuts	18
Strut damper shaft nut	65
Hub nut	
initial	70
final	185

Rear suspension

Torque specifications	Ft-lbs
Rear hub and wheel bearing assembly bolts	37
Rear axle assembly pivot bolts	63

Steering system

Torque specifications	Ft-lbs
Steering gear-to-firewall clamp nuts	28
Coupling-to-steering column bolt.....................	34
Coupling-to-stub shaft bolt	37
Inner tie rod-to-rack bolts	65
Tie rod end-to-steering knuckle nut	35
Steering wheel hub nut	30
Wheel lug nuts	
steel wheels	80
aluminum wheels	100

1.1 Front suspension components

A Control arm   C Suspension support
B Stabilizer bar   D Balljoint

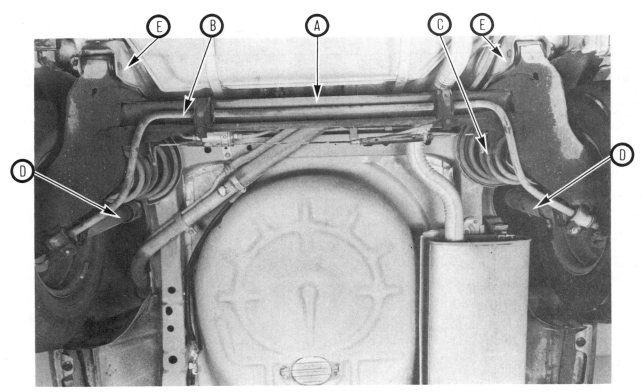

1.2 Rear suspension components

A Rear axle assembly   C Coil spring   E Rear axle-to-underbody
B Stabilizer bar   D Shock absorber   bracket mounting point

1   General information

Refer to illustrations 1.1 and 1.2

Warning: *Whenever any of the suspension or steering fasteners are loosened or removed they must be inspected and if necessary, be replaced with new ones of the same part number or of original equipment quality and design. Torque specifications must be followed for proper reassembly and component retention. Never attempt to heat or straighten any suspension or steering components. Instead, replace any bent or damaged part with a new one.*

The front suspension is a MacPherson strut design. The steering knuckles are located by lower control arms which are mounted to longitudinally positioned, removable frame members. The control arms are connected by a sway bar, which reduces body lean during cornering **(see illustration)**.

The rear suspension is semi-independent with a cross-beam axle with integrated trailing arms, two coil springs and insulator assemblies, two shock absorbers and a stabilizer bar. The axle assembly attaches to the vehicle at two points, one on each side of the vehicle at the underbody side rails **(see illustration)**.

The rack-and-pinion steering gear is located behind the engine/transaxle assembly on the firewall and actuates the steering arms which protrude from the strut housings. Most vehicles are equipped with power steering. The steering column is connected to the steering gear through an insulated coupler. The steering column is designed to collapse in the event of an accident. **Note:** *These vehicles use a combination of standard and metric fasteners on the various suspension and steering components, so it would be a good idea to have both types of tools available when beginning work.*

2   Front stabilizer bar and bushings — removal and installation

Refer to illustrations 2.2, 2.4a, 2.4b, 2.5, 2.6 and 2.7

Removal

1   Loosen the lug nuts on both front wheels, raise the vehicle and support it securely on jackstands. Remove the front wheels.
2   Remove the stabilizer bar-to-control arm bolts, taking note how the link bushings, spacers and washers are arranged **(see illustration)**.
3   Remove the four stabilizer bar bushing clamp nuts through the access holes in the suspension supports **(see illustration 2.4a)**.
4   Working on one side at a time, place a jack under the suspension support then remove the two rear and the two center mounting bolts from the suspension support. Slowly lower the jack and allow the support to drop down. It may also be necessary to slightly loosen the two front support mounting bolts on each side to provide adequate clearance for stabilizer bar removal **(see illustrations)**.
5   Push up on the stabilizer bar while pulling down on the suspension support to separate the bushing clamp from the support **(see illustration)**.

2.2   The stabilizer bar link uses washers, rubber bushings and spacers to connect the stabilizer bar to the control arm

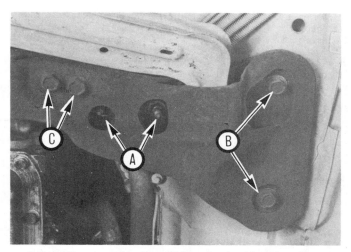

2.4a   After removing the stabilizer bar bushing clamp nuts (A), place a jack under the suspension support and remove the rear (B) and center (C) mounting bolts

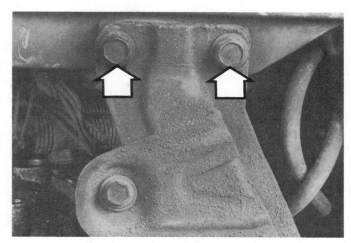

2.4b   If the suspension support doesn't hang down far enough to allow stabilizer bar removal, loosen the two front mounting bolts (arrows) on each suspension support

2.5   Separate the stabilizer bar from the suspension support

10

2.6   Guide the stabilizer bar out through the wheel well

2.7   Pry the stabilizer bar bushing clamp off of the bushing

6   Remove the stabilizer bar through the wheel well **(see illustration)**.
7   Inspect the bushings for wear or damage and replace them if necessary. To remove them, pry the bushing clamp off with a screwdriver **(see illustration)** and pull the bushings off of the bar. To ease installation, spray the inside and outside of the bushings with a silicone-based lubricant. Do not use petroleum-based lubricants on any rubber suspension part!

Installation

8   Assemble the shaft bushings and clamps on the bar, guide the bar through the wheel well, over the suspension supports and into position.
9   Insert the clamp studs through the suspension support and install the nuts finger tight.
10   Raise the suspension supports (one at a time) and install the bolts loosely.
11   Center the bar in the vehicle and install the stabilizer bar-to-control arm bolts, spacers, bushings and washers. Tighten all of the fasteners to the specified torque at this time.

12   Install the wheels and lower the vehicle. Tighten the lug nuts to the specified torque.

3   Balljoint — check and replacement

Refer to illustrations 3.3a, 3.3b and 3.11

Check

1   Raise the vehicle and support it securely on jackstands.
2   Visually inspect the rubber seal for cuts, tears or leaking grease. If any of these conditions are noticed, the balljoint should be replaced.
3   Place a large pry bar under the balljoint and attempt to push the balljoint upwards. Next, position the pry bar between the steering knuckle and the control arm and apply downward pressure **(see illustrations)**. If any movement is seen or felt during either of these checks, a worn out balljoint is indicated.
4   Have an assistant grasp the tire at the top and bottom and shake

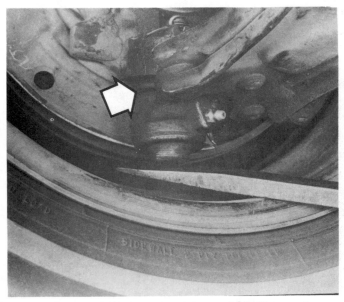

3.3a   Check for movement between the balljoint and steering knuckle (arrow) when prying upward

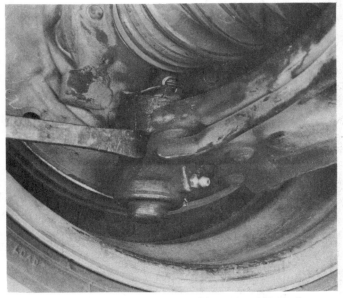

3.3b   With the pry bar positioned between the steering knuckle boss and the balljoint, pry downward and check for play in the balljoint. If there is any play, replace it

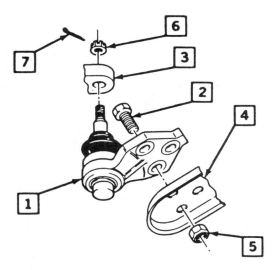

3.11   Replacement balljoint installation details (typical). Be sure to tighten the bolts to the torque specified on the instruction sheet

1   Replacement balljoint   5   Nut
2   Bolt   6   Castellated nut
3   Steering knuckle   7   Cotter pin
4   Control arm

the top of the tire in an in-and-out motion. Touch the balljoint stud castellated nut. If any looseness is felt, suspect a worn out balljoint stud or a widened hole in the steering knuckle boss. If the latter problem exists, the steering knuckle should be replaced as well as the balljoint.
5   Separate the lower control arm from the steering knuckle (Section 4). Using your fingers (don't use pliers), try to twist the stud in its socket. If the stud turns, replace the balljoint.

Replacement

6   Loosen the wheel lug nuts, raise the vehicle and support it securely on jackstands. Remove the wheel.
7   Separate the control arm from the steering knuckle (Section 4).

Temporarily insert the balljoint stud back into the steering knuckle (loosely). This will ease balljoint removal after Step 9 has been performed, as well as hold the assembly stationary while drilling out the rivets.
8   Using a 1/8-inch drill bit, drill a pilot hole into the center of each each balljoint-to-control arm rivet. Be careful not to damage the CV joint boot in the process.
9   Using a 1/2-inch drill bit, drill the head off each rivet. Work slowly and cautiously so as not to deform the holes in the control arm.
10   Loosen (but do not remove) the stabilizer bar-to-control arm nut. Pull the control arm and balljoint downward to remove the balljoint stud from the steering knuckle, then dislodge the balljoint from the control arm.
11   Position the new balljoint on the control arm and install the bolts (supplied in the balljoint kit) from the *top* of the control arm (see illustration). Tighten the bolts to the torque specified in the new balljoint instruction sheet.
12   Insert the balljoint into the steering knuckle, install the castellated nut, tighten it to the specified torque and install a new cotter pin. It may be necessary to turn the nut a bit more to align the cotter pin hole with an opening in the nut, which is acceptable. Never loosen the castellated nut to allow cotter pin insertion.
13   Tighten the stabilizer bar-to-control arm nut to the specified torque.
14   Install the wheel, lower the vehicle and tighten the lug nuts to the specified torque. It is a good idea to take the vehicle to a dealer service department or garage to have the front end alignment checked and if necessary, adjusted.

4   Control arm — removal and installation

Refer to illustrations 4.3, 4.4, 4.5a and 4.5b

Removal

1   Loosen the wheel lug nuts, raise the vehicle and support it securely on jackstands. Remove the wheel.
2   If only one control arm is being removed, disconnect only that end of the stabilizer bar. If both control arms are to be removed, disconnect both ends (see Section 2 if necessary).
3   Remove the balljoint stud-to-steering knuckle castellated nut and cotter pin (see illustration).
4   With a large pry bar positioned between the control arm and steering knuckle, ''pop'' the balljoint out of the knuckle (see illustration).
Caution: *When removing the balljoint from the knuckle be careful not to overextend the inner CV joint or damage to the joint may occur.*

10

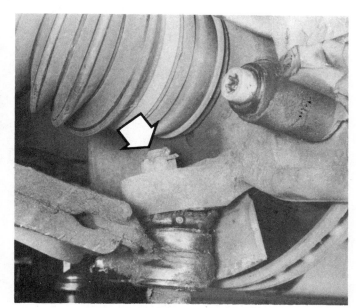

4.3   Remove the cotter pin and castellated nut (arrow) from the balljoint stud

4.4   Pry the balljoint out of the steering knuckle. If it is stubborn and won't come out, strike the steering knuckle boss on both sides (arrow) with a hammer, then try again

4.5a   The control arm mounting bolts are accessible through the reliefs in the suspension support

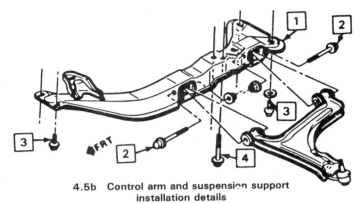

4.5b   Control arm and suspension support installation details

1   *Suspension support assembly*
2   *Control arm pivot bolts*
3   *Front and rear suspension support bolts*
4   *Center suspension support bolts*

5   Remove the two control arm pivot bolts and remove the control arm **(see illustrations)**.
6   The control arm bushings are replaceable, but special tools and expertise are necessary to perform the job. Carefully inspect the bushings for hardening, excessive wear or cracking, and if they appear to be in need of replacement, take the control arm to a dealer service department or repair shop.
7   The suspension support may also be removed if desired. Refer to illustrations 2.4a and 2.4b and remove the mounting bolts and support assembly.

Installation

8   Position the control arm in the suspension support and install the pivot bolts. Do not tighten them fully at this time.
9   Insert the balljoint stud in the steering knuckle boss, install the castellated nut and tighten it to the specified torque. If necessary, tighten the nut a little more if the cotter pin hole doesn't line up with a opening on the nut. Install a new cotter pin.
10   Install the stabilizer bar-to-control arm bolt, spacer, bushings and washers and tighten the nut to the specified torque.
11   Install the wheel and lower the vehicle. Tighten the lug nuts to the specified torque.
12   With the weight of the vehicle now on the suspension, tighten the control arm pivot bolts to the specified torque. **Caution:** *If the bolts aren't tightened with the weight of the vehicle on the suspension, control arm bushing damage may occur.*
13   Drive the vehicle to a dealer service department or an alignment shop to have the front wheel alignment checked and if necessary, adjusted.

5   Front strut and spring assembly — removal, inspection and installation

Refer to illustrations 5.2, 5.4, 5.5 and 5.6

Removal

1   Loosen the wheel lug nuts, raise the vehicle and support it securely on jackstands. Remove the wheel.
2   Using white paint or a scribe, place a mark from the strut to the steering knuckle and also around the strut-to-steering knuckle nuts **(see illustration)**.
3   Separate the tie-rod end from the steering arm as described in Section 15.

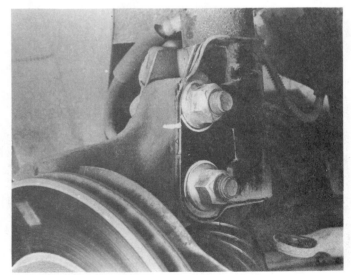

5.2   Mark the relationship of the strut to steering knuckle and around the nuts using paint or a scribe

5.4   Remove the strut-to-knuckle nuts and bolts. The bolts are splined and must be driven out with a brass or plastic faced hammer

5.5   Push inward on the strut while pulling outward on the top of the brake rotor to separate the knuckle from the strut

5.6   Remove the three strut-to-shock tower nuts (arrows) while supporting the strut assembly

4   Remove the strut-to-knuckle nuts (see illustration) and knock the bolts out with a brass or plastic faced hammer.

5   Separate the strut from the steering knuckle (see illustration). Be careful not to overextend the inner CV joint or stretch the brake hose.

6   Support the strut and spring assembly with one hand and remove the three strut-to-shock tower nuts (see illustration). Remove the assembly out from the fender well.

Inspection

7   Check the strut body for leaking fluid, dents, cracks and other obvious damage which would warrant repair or replacement.

8   Check the coil spring for chips or cracks in the spring coating (this will cause premature spring failure due to corrosion). Inspect the spring seat for cuts, hardness and general deterioration.

9   If any undesirable conditions exist, proceed to Section 6 for the strut disassembly procedure.

Installation

10   Verify that the flat in the upper spring seat is in line with the steering knuckle flange. Guide the strut assembly up into the fender well and insert the three upper mounting studs through the holes in the shock tower. Once the three studs protrude from the shock tower, install the nuts so the strut won't fall back through. This is most easily accomplished with the help of an assistant, as the strut is quite heavy and awkward.

11   Slide the steering knuckle into the strut flange and insert the two bolts. These should be positioned with the flats situated horizontally. Install the nuts, align the previously applied marks and tighten them to the specified torque.

12   Install the tie-rod end into the steering arm and tighten the castellated nut to the specified torque. Install a new cotter pin. If the cotter pin will not pass through, tighten the nut a little more, but just enough to align the hole in the stud with a castellation on the nut (do not loosen the nut).

13   Install the wheel, lower the vehicle and tighten the lug nuts to the specified torque.

14   Tighten the three upper mounting nuts to the specified torque.

6   Strut cartridge — replacement

Refer to illustrations 6.4, 6.5a, 6.5b, 6.6, 6.7, 6.11, 6.12, 6.14, 6.15a, 6.15b and 6.15c

1   If the struts exhibit the telltale signs of wear (leaking fluid, loss of dampening capability) explore all options before beginning any work.

The strut cartridges can be replaced. However, rebuilt strut assemblies (some complete with springs) are available on an exchange basis which eliminates much time and work. Whichever route you choose to take, check on the cost and availability of parts before disassembling your vehicle. **Warning:** *Disassembling a strut assembly is a dangerous undertaking and utmost attention must be directed toward the job at hand, or serious bodily injury may result. Use only a high quality spring compressor and carefully follow the manufacturer's instructions furnished with the tool. After removing the coil spring from the strut assembly, set it aside in a safe, isolated area (a steel cabinet is preferred).*

2   Remove the strut and spring assembly following the procedure described in the Section 5. Mount the strut assembly in a vise with the jaws of the vise cushioned with rags or blocks of wood.

3   Following the tool manufacturers instructions, install the spring compressor (which can be obtained at most auto parts stores or equipment yards on a daily rental basis) on the spring and compress it sufficiently to relieve all pressure from the spring seat. This can be verified by wiggling the spring seat.

4   Loosen the damper shaft nut while using a socket wrench on the shaft hex to prevent it from turning (see illustration).

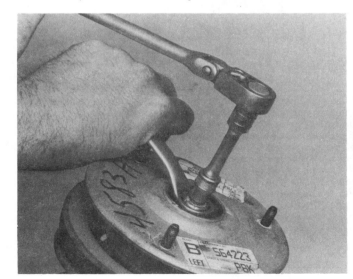

6.4   After the spring has been compressed, remove the damper shaft nut

10

6.5a　Remove the bearing cap . . .

6.5b　. . . and the upper spring seat and insulator from the damper shaft

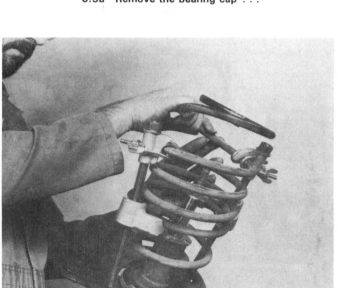

6.6　Remove the compressed spring assembly. Use extreme caution whenever handling the spring

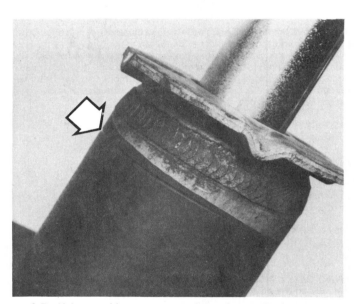

6.7　Using a tubing cutter, cut the end cap off of the strut body at the groove (arrow)

5　Lift the bearing cap, upper spring seat and upper insulator off of the damper shaft **(see illustrations)**. Inspect the bearing in the spring seat for smooth operation and replace it if necessary.

6　Carefully remove the compressed spring assembly and set it in a safe place, such as inside a steel cabinet. **Warning:** *Never place your head near the end of the spring!*

7　Locate the line groove cut in the strut reservoir tube, 3/4-inch from the top of the tube **(see illustration)**. Using a tubing cutter, cut around the groove until the reservoir tube is severed. Lift out the piston rod assembly with the cylinder and end cap. Discard these items.

8　Remove the strut reservoir tube from the vise and pour the damper fluid into an approved oil container.

9　Place the strut back in the vise and lightly file around the inner diameter of the opening to eliminate any burrs that may have resulted from the cutting operation. Be careful not to damage the internal threads that are present in the strut body.

10　Thread the cartridge retaining nut into the reservoir tube, as straight as possible, to establish a clean path in the existing threads. Remove the nut.

11　Install the replacement strut cartridge into the reservoir tube and turn it until you feel the pads on the bottom of the cartridge seat into the depressions at the bottom of the reservoir tube **(see illustration)**.

12　Slide the nut over the cartridge and thread it into the tube **(see illustration)**, tightening it to the torque specified in the kit instructions.

13　Stroke the damper shaft up and down a few times to verify proper operation.

14　Fully extend the damper shaft and hold it in place with a clothes pin placed at the bottom of the rod **(see illustration)**.

15　Assemble the strut beginning with the lower spring insulator and spring, then the upper spring insulator, spring seat and bearing cap. Position the spring seat and bearing cap with the flats facing the steering knuckle flange **(see illustrations)**.

16　Install the damper shaft nut and tighten it to the specified torque. Remove the clothes pin from the damper shaft.

17　Install the strut and spring assembly on the vehicle as outlined in Section 5.

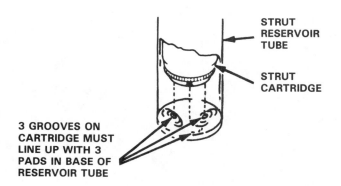

STRUT RESERVOIR TUBE

STRUT CARTRIDGE

3 GROOVES ON CARTRIDGE MUST LINE UP WITH 3 PADS IN BASE OF RESERVOIR TUBE

6.11   Turn the cartridge until it seats in the depressions at the bottom of the tube

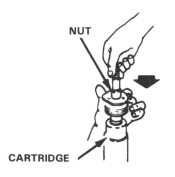

NUT

CARTRIDGE

6.12   Install the cartridge retaining nut, being careful not to cross the threads

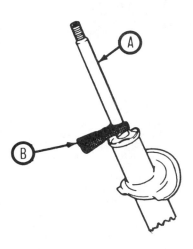

6.14   Extend the damper shaft (A) and hold it in place with a clothes pin (B)

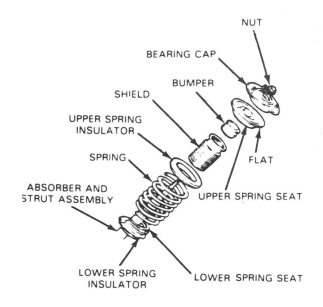

NUT

BEARING CAP

BUMPER

SHIELD

UPPER SPRING INSULATOR

SPRING

ABSORBER AND STRUT ASSEMBLY

FLAT

UPPER SPRING SEAT

LOWER SPRING INSULATOR

LOWER SPRING SEAT

6.15a   Strut assembly details

6.15b   Install the upper spring seat with the flat (arrow) facing the steering knuckle flange

6.15c   The bearing cap must also be positioned with the flat (arrow) facing the knuckle flange

10

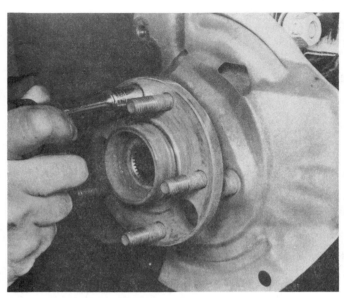

7.6   A No. 55 Torx bit is necessary to remove the hub bolts. Don't use an Allen wrench, as the bolts may be damaged

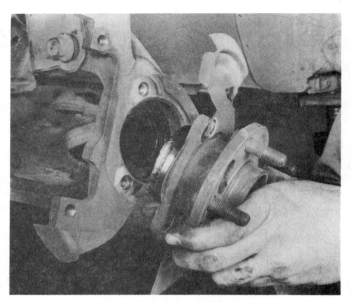

7.7   Pull the hub and bearing assembly and the rotor shield from the steering knuckle

7   Front hub and wheel bearing assembly — removal and installation

Refer to illustrations 7.6, 7.7, 7.8, 7.9 and 7.10

Note: *The front hub and wheel bearing assembly is sealed-for-life and must be replaced as a unit.*

1   Loosen the wheel lug nuts, raise the front of the vehicle and support it securely on jackstands. Remove the wheel.
2   Disconnect the stabilizer bar from the control arm (see Section 2 if necessary).
3   Remove the balljoint-to-steering knuckle nut and separate the control arm from the knuckle (see Section 4).
4   Remove the caliper from the steering knuckle and hang it out of the way with a piece of wire (see Chapter 9).
5   Pull the rotor from the hub and remove the driveaxle (see Chapter 8 if necessary).
6   Using a No. 55 Torx bit, remove the three hub retaining bolts through the opening in the hub flange **(see illustration)**.

7   Wiggle the hub and bearing assembly back-and-forth and pull it from the steering knuckle, along with the rotor shield **(see illustration)**.
8   If the hub and bearing assembly is being replaced with a new one, it is a good idea to replace the dust seal in the back of the steering knuckle. Pry it out of the knuckle using a screwdriver **(see illustration)**.
9   Drive the new dust seal into the knuckle using a large socket or a seal driver **(see illustration)**. Try not to cock the seal in the bore.
10   Install a new O-ring around the rear of the bearing and push it up against the bearing flange **(see illustration)**.
11   Clean the mating surfaces on the steering knuckle and bearing flange, and the knuckle bore. Lubricate the outside diameter of the bearing and the seal lips with high temperature grease and insert the hub and bearing into the steering knuckle. Position the rotor shield and install the three bolts, tightening them to the specified torque.
12   Install the driveaxle (see Chapter 8).
13   Attach the control arm to the steering knuckle (see Section 4).
14   Reconnect the stabilizer bar to the control arm (see Section 2).
15   Install the brake rotor and caliper (see Chapter 9).
16   Install the hub nut and tighten it to the initial torque to seat the driveaxle into the hub. Prevent the axle from turning by inserting a

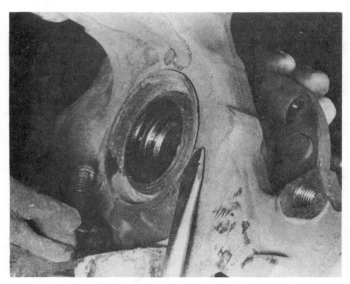

7.8   Pry the seal out of the knuckle with a screwdriver

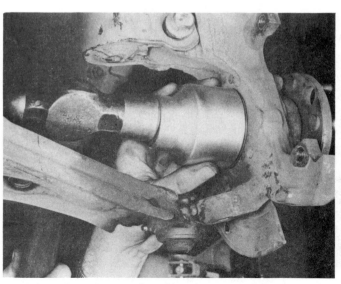

7.9   Using a large socket, drive the new seal into place

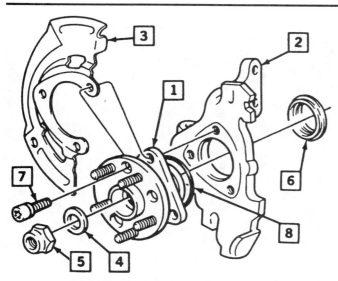

7.10 Hub and bearing installation details

1 *Hub and bearing assembly*   5 *Hub nut*
2 *Steering knuckle*   6 *Seal*
3 *Rotor shield*   7 *Hub and bearing retaining bolt*
4 *Washer*   8 *O-ring*

screwdriver through the caliper and into a rotor cooling vane (see Chapter 8 if necessary).
17 Install the wheel, lower the vehicle and tighten the lug nuts to the specified torque.
18 Tighten the hub nut to the specified final torque.

---

8   Steering knuckle and hub — removal and installation

Removal

1   Loosen the wheel lug nuts, raise the vehicle and support it securely on jackstands. Remove the wheel.
2   Remove the hub nut. Insert a screwdriver through the caliper and into a rotor cooling vane to prevent the driveaxle from turning.
3   Remove the caliper and suspend it out of the way with a piece of wire. Lift the rotor off of the hub.
4   Mark the position of the two strut-to-knuckle nuts and remove them **(see illustration 5.2)**. Do not drive out the bolts at this time.
5   Separate the control arm balljoint from the steering knuckle (see

Section 4 if necessary).
6   Attach a puller to the hub flange and push the driveaxle from the hub (see Chapter 8). Hang the driveaxle with a piece of wire to prevent damage to the inner CV joint.
7   Support the knuckle and drive out the two strut-to-knuckle bolts with a brass or plastic faced hammer. Remove the steering knuckle assembly from the strut.

Installation

8   Position the knuckle in the strut and insert the two splined bolts, with the flats on the bolt heads in the horizontal position. Tap the bolts into place and install the nuts, but do not tighten them at this time.
9   Install the driveaxle into the hub.
10 Connect the control arm to the steering knuckle and tighten the castellated nut to the specified torque. Install a new cotter pin.
11 Align the strut-to-knuckle nuts with the previously applied marks and tighten them to the specified torque.
12 Install the brake rotor and caliper.
13 Tighten the hub nut to the specified initial torque to seat the drive-axle in the hub.
14 Install the wheel, lower the vehicle and tighten the lug nuts to the specified torque.
15 Tighten the hub nut to the specified final torque.

---

9   Rear stabilizer bar — removal and installation

Refer to illustrations 9.2 and 9.3

1   Raise the rear of the vehicle and support it securely on jackstands.
2   Remove the outer stabilizer bar bushing bracket nuts and bolts and remove the brackets from the trailing arms **(see illustration)**.
3   Remove the two inner stabilizer bushing clamp bolts and nuts **(see illustration)** and remove the stabilizer bar.
4   Inspect the bushings for cracking, hardness and other signs of wear, replacing them if necessary.
5   Installation is the reverse of the removal procedure. Before tightening the bolts, make sure the stabilizer bar is centered from side-to-side in the rear axle assembly.

---

10   Rear shock absorber — removal and installation

Refer to illustrations 10.2, 10.3 and 10.4

Caution: *Do not remove both shock absorbers at one time. They limit the downward travel of the rear suspension and damage to the brake hoses and lines may occur if the suspension is allowed to hang.*

1   Loosen the wheel lug nuts, raise the rear of the vehicle and remove the wheel.

10

9.2   Remove the outer stabilizer bar brackets . . .

9.3   . . . then disconnect the the inner bushing clamps and remove the stabilizer bar

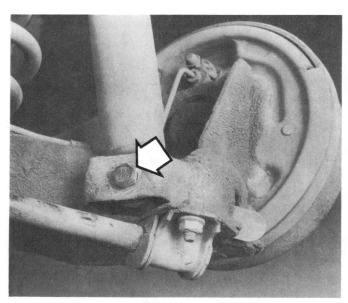

10.2   Remove the lower shock mounting bolt (arrow). Be
sure to support the trailing arm with a jack

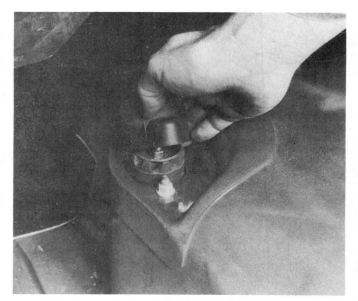

10.3   Locate the upper shock mount behind the trunk
compartment side panel trim and remove the upper
mount cover

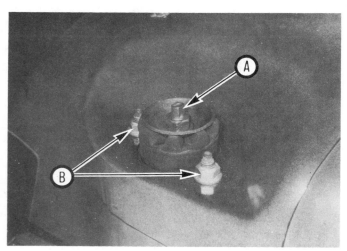

10.4   Using an open end wrench on the damper shaft
flats, remove the shaft-to-upper mount nut (A). The upper
mount is held in place by two nuts (B)

2   Support the trailing arm with a jack and remove the lower shock
absorber mounting bolt (see illustration).
3   Open the trunk lid and peel back the the side trim panel to expose
the upper shock mount. Pull the plastic cap off of the mount (see illustration).
4   Remove the damper shaft-to-upper mount nut and remove the
shock absorber from the vehicle. Inspect the upper mount for cracks,
hardness, separation or other damage. If any of these conditions are
noted, unscrew the two mounting nuts and remove the mount from
the fender well (see illustration).
5   Installation is the reverse of the removal procedure.

---

11   Rear springs and insulators — removal and installation

Refer to illustration 11.5

Removal

1   Loosen the wheel lug nuts, raise the rear of the vehicle and support
it securely on jackstands. Remove both rear wheels.

2   Locate the right and left brake line brackets and unbolt them from
the frame, allowing the lines to hang freely.
3   Place a floor jack under the center of the axle beam to support
it. Remove both lower shock mounting bolts and slowly lower the jack
until the coil spring is fully extended. Keep an eye on the brake hoses
to make sure that they don't become hung-up on anything.
4   Remove the coil spring, compression bumper and the upper spring
insulator. Inspect the rubber components for cracks, hardening and
general deterioration and replace them if necessary.

Installation

5   Position the compression bumpers on the lower spring pockets and
place the coil springs on the axle assembly. Install the upper spring
insulators on top of the springs (see illustration) and raise the axle,
guiding the springs into place. The help of an assistant may be necessary to accomplish this.

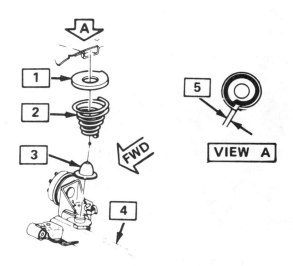

11.5   Rear spring installation details

1   Spring insulator
2   Spring
3   Compression bumper
4   Axle assembly
5   The end of the upper coil
    spring must be within
    15 mm of the spring stop
    in the spring seat

12.3   Remove the four hub and bearing assembly bolts using a No. 55 Torx bit

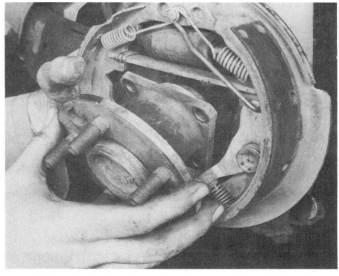

12.4a   Angle the hub and bearing assembly out through the brake assembly

12.4b   Temporarily reinstall two bolts (arrows) to retain the brake assembly to the trailing arm, rather than let it hang by the hydraulic line

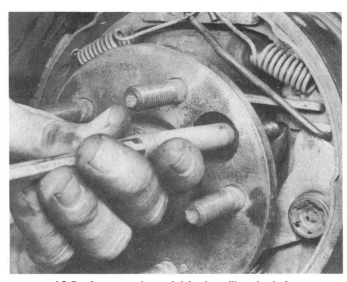

12.5   A magnet is useful for installing the bolts

6   If difficulty is encountered in keeping the upper spring insulators in place, glue them to the contact area on the body with spray adhesive.
7   Install the lower shock absorber mounting bolts.
8   Attach the brake line brackets to the frame.
9   Install the wheels, lower the vehicle and tighten the wheel lug nuts to the specified torque.

12   Rear hub and wheel bearing assembly — removal and installation

Refer to illustrations 12.3, 12.4a, 12.4b and 12.5
Note: *The rear hub and wheel bearing assembly is sealed-for-life and must be replaced as a unit.*

Removal

1   Loosen the wheel lug nuts, raise the vehicle and support it securely on jackstands. Remove the wheel.

2   Pull the brake drum from the hub. If difficulty is encountered, refer to Chapter 9 for the removal procedure.
3   Using a No. 55 Torx bit, remove the four hub-to-trailing arm bolts, accessible by turning the hub flange so that the circular cutout exposes each bolt (see illustration). Save the upper rear bolt for last, because there isn't much clearance between the bolt and the parking brake strut.
4   Remove the hub and bearing assembly from its seat, maneuvering it out through the brake assembly. Reinstall two bolts through the brake backing plate into the trailing arm to avoid hanging the brake assembly by the hydraulic line (see illustrations).

Installation

5   Position the hub and bearing assembly to the trailing arm and align the holes in the backing plate. Install the bolts, beginning with the upper rear bolt. A magnet is useful in guiding the bolts through the hub flange and into position (see illustration). After all four bolts have been installed, tighten them to the specified torque.
6   Install the brake drum and wheel. Lower the vehicle and tighten the wheel lug nuts to the specified torque.

10

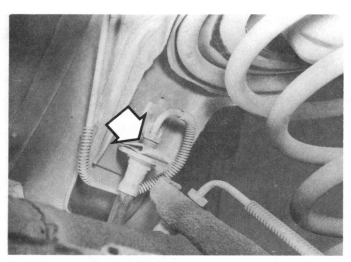

13.6 Loosen the brake line tube nuts and remove the hose retaining clips

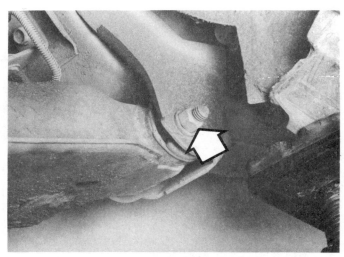

13.7 Remove the rear axle assembly pivot bolt (arrow) and carefully lower the axle to the ground

13 Rear axle assembly — removal and installation

Refer to illustrations 13.6 and 13.7

Removal

1   Loosen the wheel lug nuts, raise the vehicle and support it securely on jackstands. Remove the wheels.
2   If the axle assembly is to be replaced, remove the stabilizer bar as outlined in Section 9.
3   Remove the brake drums from the hubs. See Chapter 9 if any difficulty is encountered.
4   Remove the coil springs (see Section 11).
5   Disconnect the parking brake cable at the equalizer (Chapter 9).
6   Loosen the brake line tube nuts and remove the brake hose retaining clips, disconnecting the brake lines from the rear axle assembly **(see illustration)**.
7   With a floor jack supporting the axle assembly, unbolt the axle from the vehicle at the pivot points on the underbody side rails **(see illustration)**. Lower the axle assembly to the ground.

Installation

8   If a new axle assembly is being installed, transfer the hub and bearing assemblies, the brake assemblies, the parking brake cables and the hydraulic lines to the new axle.
9   Place the new axle on the jack and raise it into position. Install the pivot bolts, but don't tighten them fully yet.
10   Install the coil springs and insulators and connect the shock absorbers (see Section 11)
11   Reconnect the brake lines.
12   Reconnect the parking brake cable to the equalizer and position it in the cable guide.
13   Install the stabilizer bar.
14   Install the brake drums.
15   Bleed the brake system of all air, following the procedure described in Chapter 9.
16   Install the wheels, lower the vehicle and tighten the lug nuts to the specified torque.
17   With the vehicle standing at normal ride height, tighten the axle pivot bolts to the specified torque.

14 Steering system — general information

Warning: *Whenever any of the steering fasteners are removed they must be inspected and if necessary, be replaced with new ones of the same part number or of original equipment quality and design. Torque specifications must be followed for proper reassembly and component retention. Never attempt to heat or straighten any suspension or steer-*
ing components. Instead, replace any bent or damaged part with a new one.

All vehicles covered by this use power rack and pinion steering systems. The components making up the system are the steering wheel, steering column, rack and pinion assembly, tie-rods and tie-rod ends. The power steering system uses a belt-driven pump to provide hydraulic pressure.

In the power steering system, the motion of turning the steering wheel is transferred through the column to the pinion shaft in the rack and pinion assembly. Teeth on the pinion shaft are meshed with teeth on the rack, so when the shaft is turned, the rack is moved left or right in the housing. A rotary control valve in the rack and pinion unit directs hydraulic fluid under pressure from the power steering pump to either side of the integral rack piston, which is connected to the rack thereby reducing manual steering force. Depending on which side of the piston this hydraulic pressure is applied to, the rack will be forced either left or right, which moves the tie-rods, etc. If the power steering system loses its hydraulic pressure it will still function manually, though with increased effort.

The steering column is of the collapsible, energy-absorbing type, designed to compress in the event of a front end collision to minimize injury to the driver. The column also houses the ignition switch lock, key warning buzzer, turn signal controls, headlight dimmer control and windshield wiper controls. The ignition and steering wheel can both be locked while the car is parked to inhibit theft.

Due to the column's collapsible design, it is important that only the specified screws, bolts and nuts be used as designated and that they be tightened to the specified torque. Other precautions particular to this design are noted in appropriate Sections.

In addition to the standard steering column, optional tilt and key-release versions are also offered. The tilt model can be set in five different positions, while with the key release model the ignition key is locked in the column until a lever is depressed to extract it.

Because disassembly of the steering column is more often performed to repair a switch or other electrical part than to correct a problem in the steering, the upper steering column disassembly and reassembly procedure is included in Chapter 12.

15 Tie-rod ends — removal and installation

Refer to illustrations 15.2, 15.3 and 15.4

Removal

1   Loosen the wheel lug nuts, raise the vehicle and support it securely on jackstands. Remove the wheel.
2   Loosen the tie-rod end pinch bolt **(see illustration)**.
3   Disconnect the tie-rod from the steering knuckle arm with a puller **(see illustration)**.
4   Mark the relationship of the tie-rod end to the threaded adjuster

15.2   Before disconnecting the tie-rod end from the
steering arm, loosen the pinch bolt (arrow)

15.3   A two jaw puller works well for separating the tie-
rod end from the steering arm. Do not pound on the stud!

15.4   Using white paint, mark the relationship of the tie-
rod end to the threaded adjuster

16.3   Remove the upper steering coupler pinch bolt
(arrow)

(see illustration). This will ensure that the toe-in setting is restored when reassembled.
5   Unscrew the tie-rod end from the tie-rod.

Installation

6   Thread the tie-rod end onto the tie-rod to the marked position and connect the tie-rod end to the steering arm. Install the castellated nut and tighten it to the specified torque. Install a new cotter pin.
7   Tighten the pinch bolt securely and install the wheel. Lower the vehicle and tighten the lug nuts to the specified torque.
8   Have the front end steering geometry checked by a dealer service department or an alignment shop.

16   Steering gear — removal and installation

Refer to illustrations 16.3 and 16.4

1   Disconnect the cable from the negative battery terminal.
2   Remove the left side under-dash panel.
3   Roll back the boot at the bottom of the steering column to expose the flange and steering coupler assembly. Mark the coupler to the steering column shaft and remove the upper pinch bolt (see illustration).
4   Remove the two left side steering gear-to-firewall clamp nuts and the right upper clamp nut (see illustration).

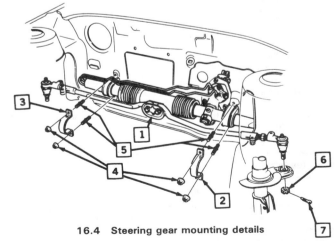

16.4   Steering gear mounting details

1   Steering gear assembly
2   Clamp (left)
3   Clamp (right)
4   Nut
5   Mounting stud
6   Castellated nut
7   Cotter pin

10

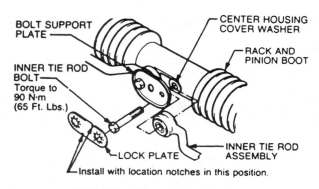

17.2   Tie-rod installation details

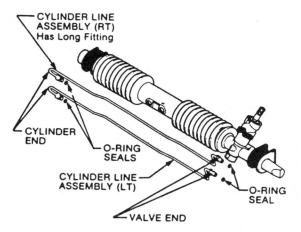

17.3   Hydraulic cylinder line installation details. Upon reassembly, use new O-ring seals

5   Remove the pressure hose retainer from the support bracket at the center of the rack.
6   Place a drain pan or tray under the vehicle, positioned beneath the left side of the steering gear. Using a flare nut wrench, disconnect the pressure and return lines from the steering gear (the two lines closest to the firewall, angled toward the left side of the vehicle). Plug the lines to prevent excessive fluid loss.
7   Loosen the front wheel lug nuts, raise the vehicle and support it securely on jackstands. Remove both front wheels.
8   Remove the lower right side clamp nut.
9   Separate the tie-rod ends from the steering arms (see Section 15).
10 Move the steering gear forward and remove the lower pinch bolt from the coupler. Slide the coupler off of the pinion shaft.
11 Support the steering gear and carefully maneuver the entire assembly out through the left side wheel opening.
12 If any of the mounting studs came out with the clamps, apply a thread locking compound to the firewall side of the threads and install them snugly into the firewall.
13 Pass the steering gear assembly through the left wheel opening into approximate position.
14 Install the coupler and tighten the lower pinch bolt securely.
15 Center the steering gear, ensuring that the dash seal is installed properly. Have an assistant guide the coupler onto the steering column shaft, with the previously applied marks aligned. Position the right side clamp and install the lower clamp nut, tightening it to the specified torque.
16 Install the tie-rod ends in the steering arms and tighten the nuts to the specified torque. Install new cotter pins.
17 Install the front wheels, lower the vehicle and tighten the lug nuts to the specified torque.
18 Install the pressure and return lines to the steering gear. Connect the line retainer to the support bracket.
19 Install the left side clamp and nuts and the upper right side clamp nut, tightening them to the specified torque.
20 Install the upper pinch bolt in the coupler and tighten it to the specified torque.
21 Install the under-dash panel.
22 Reconnect the negative battery cable.
23 Fill the power steering pump with the recommended fluid, bleed the system of air (see Section 19) and recheck the fluid level. Check for leaks.
24 Have the front end steering geometry checked by a dealer service department or an alignment shop.

17   Steering gear boots — replacement

Refer to illustrations 17.2, 17.3 and 17.4

1   Remove the steering gear from the vehicle (see Section 16).
2   Remove the tie-rods from the steering gear **(see illustration)**.
3   Using a flare nut wrench, remove the hydraulic cylinder lines from the steering gear assembly **(see illustration)**.
4   Remove the right mounting grommet from the rack housing **(see illustration)**.
5   Cut off both boot clamps and discard them.
6   Slide the cylinder end (right end) of the boot toward the center

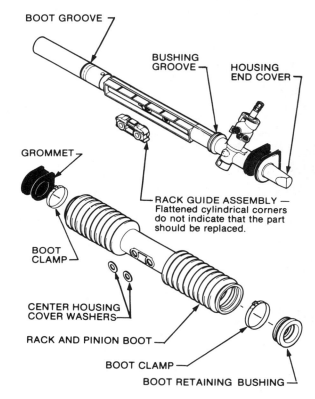

17.4   Steering gear boot installation details

of the steering gear, enough to expose the boot groove. Place a rubber band in the groove to occupy the space then slide the boot off of the steering gear.
7   Install a new clamp on the left end of the boot and insert the boot retaining bushing into the end of the boot. Apply multi-purpose grease to the inside diameter of the bushing and slide the boot onto the steering gear housing.
8   Press the center housing cover washers into the center housing cover.
9   Align the center housing bolt holes with the rack guide assembly and install the two tie-rod bolts. This will ensure proper alignment of the center housing, rack and rack guide.
10 Tighten the left side boot clamp.
11 Slide the right end of the boot onto the housing, remove the rubber band and seat the boot into the boot groove. Install the clamp and tighten it.
12 Install the hydraulic cylinder lines.

18.3 Loosen the return line hose clamp and separate the line from the pump (V6 engine shown)

18.4 Disconnect the pressure hose from the pump. Use a flare nut wrench and a backup wrench to avoid damage to the pipe and fitting (V6 engine shown)

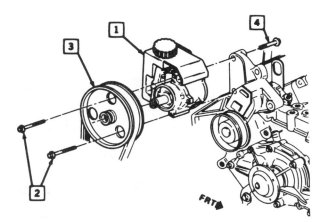

18.5a Power steering pump mounting details (V6 engine)

1	Power steering pump	3	Pulley
2	Bolt	4	Bolt

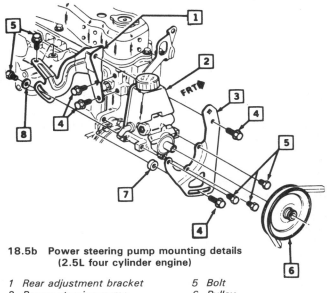

18.5b Power steering pump mounting details (2.5L four cylinder engine)

1	Rear adjustment bracket	5	Bolt
2	Power steering pump	6	Pulley
3	Front adjustment bracket	7	Spacer
4	Bolt	8	Washer

13 Install the tie-rods as shown in illustration 17.2 and tighten the bolts to the specified torque.
14 Install the mounting grommet.
15 Install the steering gear assembly.

---

18 Power steering pump — removal and installation   **10**

Refer to illustrations 18.3, 18.4, 18.5a, 18.5b and 18.5c

Removal

1 Disconnect the cable from the negative battery terminal.
2 Remove the serpentine drivebelt (V6) or the power steering pump drivebelt (four cylinder engines).
3 Position a drain pan under the vehicle. Remove as much fluid as possible with a suction gun, then remove the return line from the pump **(see illustration)**.
4 Using a flare nut wrench and a backup wrench, disconnect the pressure hose at the pump **(see illustration)**.
5 Remove the pump mounting bolts and lift the pump from the vehicle, being careful not spill the remaining fluid **(see illustrations)**.

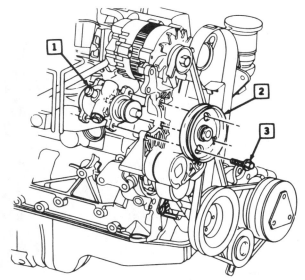

18.5c Power steering pump mounting details (2.0L turbocharged engine)

1	Power steering pump	2	Pulley	3 Bolt

Installation

6   Position the pump on the mounting bracket and install the bolts. On 2.5L four cylinder models, install the front adjustment bracket-to-engine bolt and spacer first, then the front adjustment bracket-to-rear adjustment bracket bolt.

7   Connect the pressure and return lines to the pump.

8   Fill the reservoir with the recommended fluid and bleed the system, following the procedure described in the next Section.

19   Power steering system – bleeding

1   Following any operation in which the power steering fluid lines have been disconnected, the power steering system must be bled of air to obtain proper steering performance.

2   With the front wheels turned all the way to the left, check the power steering fluid level and, if low, add fluid until it reaches the Cold mark on the dipstick.

3   Start the engine and allow it to run at fast idle. Recheck the fluid level and add more if necessary to reach the Cold mark on the dipstick.

4   Bleed the system by turning the wheels from side to side, without hitting the stops. This will work the air out of the system. Be careful that the reservoir does not run empty of fluid.

5   When the air is worked out of the system, return the wheels to the straight ahead position and leave the car running for several minutes before shutting it off. Recheck the fluid level.

6   Road test the car to be sure the steering system is functioning normally and is free from noise.

7   Recheck the fluid level to be sure it is up to the Hot mark on the dipstick while the engine is at normal operating temperature. Add fluid if necessary.

20   Steering wheel — removal and installation

Refer to illustrations 20.3, 20.4, 20.5 and 20.6

1   Disconnect the cable from the negative battery terminal.

2   Pull the horn pad off of the steering wheel.

3   Remove the safety clip from the steering shaft **(see illustration)**.

4   Push down on the horn contact and twist it to allow removal **(see illustration)**.

5   Remove the steering wheel retaining nut then mark the relationship of the steering shaft and hub to simplify installation and ensure steering wheel alignment **(see illustration)**.

6   Use a puller to disconnect the steering wheel from the shaft **(see illustration)**.

7   To install the wheel, align the mark on the steering wheel hub with the mark made on the shaft during removal and slip the wheel onto the shaft. Install the hub nut and tighten it to the specified torque. Install the safety clip.

8   Install the horn contact and press the horn pad into place on the steering wheel.

9   Connect the negative battery cable.

20.3   Remove the safety clip with a pair of snap ring pliers

20.4   Remove the horn contact and spring

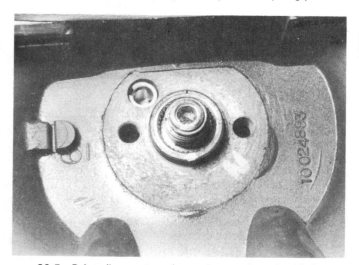

20.5   Paint alignment marks on the steering wheel hub and the shaft

20.6   Use a steering wheel puller to separate the steering wheel from the shaft. Do not attempt to remove the wheel with a hammer!

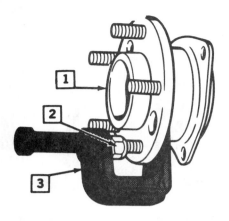

21.3   Use GM tool No. J-6627-A or equivalent to push the stud from the flange

1   Hub   3   Tool
2   Lug nut on stud

21   Wheel studs — replacement

Refer to illustrations 21.3 and 21.4

Note: *This procedure applies to either the front or rear wheel studs.*

1   Remove the hub and wheel bearing assembly (see Sections 7 or 12).
2   Install a lug nut part way onto the stud to be replaced.
3   Push the lug nut from the hub flange using GM tool No. J-6627-A or equivalent **(see illustration)**.
4   Insert the new stud into the hub flange from the backside and install four flat washers and a lug nut on the stud **(see illustration)**.
5   Tighten the lug nut until the stud is fully seated in the flange.
6   Reinstall the hub and wheel bearing assembly.

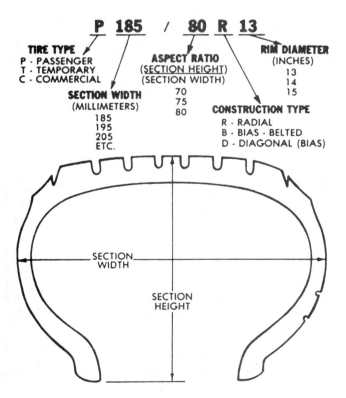

22.1   Metric tire size code

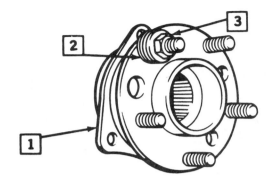

21.4   Install four washers and a lug nut on the stud then tighten the nut to draw the stud into place

1   Hub and wheel   2   Washers installed on stud
    bearing assembly   3   Lug nut

22   Wheels and tires — general information

Refer to illustrations 22.1, 22.4 and 22.6

All vehicles covered by this manual are equipped with metric-sized fiberglass or steel belted radial tires **(see illustration)**. Use of other size or type of tires may affect the ride and handling of the car. Do not mix different types of tires, such as radials and bias belted, on the same car as handling may be seriously affected. It is recommended that tires be replaced in pairs on the same axle, but if only one tire is being replaced, be sure it is of the same size, structure and tread design as the other.

Because tire pressure has a substantial effect on handling and wear, the pressure on all tires should be checked at least once a month or before any extended trips and set to the correct pressure. Tire pressure should be checked and adjusted with the tires cold.

To achieve the maximum life of your tires they should be rotated at 7500 miles and then again at every 15,000-mile interval **(see illustration)**.

The tires should be replaced when the depth of the tread is a minimum of 1/16-inch. Correct tire pressures and driving techniques have an important influence on tire life. Heavy cornering, excessively rapid acceleration and sharp braking increase tire wear. Extremely worn tires are not only very susceptible to going flat but are especially dangerous in wet weather conditions. The tire tread pattern can give a good indication of problems in the maintenance or adjustment of tires, suspension and front end components **(see illustration)**.

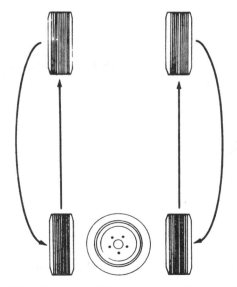

22.4   Tires should be rotated as shown at the recommended intervals

10

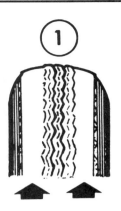
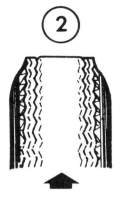

22.6   Common tire wear patterns

1   Wear at outer edges — tire underinflated
2   Wear at center — tire overinflated
3   Wear at one side — incorrect wheel alignment. Check camber and toe-in adjustments

Wheels must be replaced if they are bent, dented, leak air, have elongated bolt holes, are heavily rusted, out of vertical symmetry or if the lug nuts won't stay tight. Wheel repairs that use welding or peening are not recommended, as this can weaken the metal.

Tire and wheel balance is important in the overall handling, braking and performance of the car. Unbalanced wheels can adversely affect handling and ride characteristics as well as tire life. Whenever a tire is installed on a wheel, the tire and wheel should be balanced by a shop with the proper equipment.

All vehicles covered by this manual are equipped with a compact spare tire, which is designed to save space in the trunk as well as being easier to handle due to its lighter weight. The spare tire pressure should be checked at least once a month, and maintained at 70 psi (412 kPa). The compact spare tire and wheel are designed for use with each other only, and neither the tire nor the wheel should be coupled with other types or size of wheels and tires. Because the compact spare is designed as a temporary replacement for an out-of-service standard wheel and tire, the compact spare should be used on the car only until the standard wheel and tire are repaired or replaced. Continuous use of the compact spare at speeds of over 50 mph (80 kph) is not recommended. In addition, the expected tread life of the compact spare is only 3000 miles (4800 kilometers).

23   Front end alignment — general information

Refer to illustration 23.1

A front end alignment refers to the adjustments made to the front wheels so that they are in proper angular relationship to the suspension and the ground. Front wheels that are out of proper alignment not only affect steering control, but also increase tire wear. The only front end adjustment normally required is the toe-in adjustment. Camber adjustments are possible, but only after the strut has been modified.

Getting the proper front wheel alignment is a very exacting process and one in which complicated and expensive machines are necessary to perform the job properly. Because of this, it is advisable to have a specialist with the proper equipment perform these tasks. We will, however, use this space to give you a basic idea of what is involved with front end alignment so you can better understand the process and deal intelligently with shops which do this work.

Toe-in is the turning in of the front wheels. The purpose of a toe specification is to ensure parallel rolling of the front wheels. In a car with zero toe-in, the distance between the front edges of the wheels will be the same as the distance between the rear edges of the wheels. The actual amount of toe-in is normally only a fraction of an inch. Toe-in adjustment is controlled by the tie-rod end position on the inner tie-rod. Incorrect toe-in will cause the tires to wear improperly by making them scrub against the road surface.

Camber is the tilting of the front wheels from the vertical when viewed from the front of the vehicle. When the wheels tilt outward at the top, the camber is said to be positive (+). When the wheels tilt inward at the top the camber is negative (–). The amount of tilt is measured in degrees from the vertical and this measurement is called the camber angle. This angle affects the amount of tire tread which contacts the road and compensates for changes in the suspension geometry when the car is cornering or travelling over undulating surface.

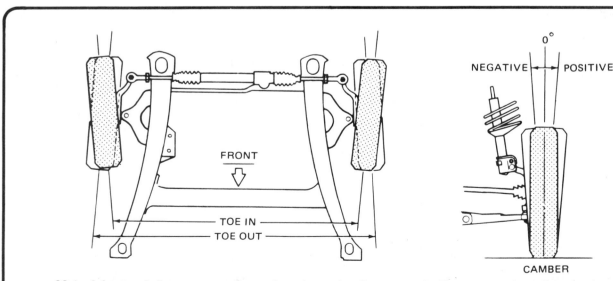

23.1   A front end alignment normally consists of a toe-in adjustment only. However, camber adjustment is possible after strut modification

Chapter 11   Body

Contents

Specifications

Torque specifications

	Ft-lbs
Door hinge-to-body pillar nuts and bolts	36 to 40
Door latch striker bolt	36 to 40
Front seat-to-floor pan nut	15 to 21
Rear seat cushion bolt	14 to 20
Trunk lid latch striker nut	9 to 12

---

1   General information

These models are available in 2-door coupe and 4-door sedan body styles. The vehicles covered in this manual are of unitized construction. The body is designed to provide vehicle rigidity so that a separate frame is not necessary.

Body maintenance is an important part of the retention of the ve-hicle's market value. It is far less costly to handle small problems before they grow into larger ones.

Major body components which are particularly vulnerable in accidents are removable. These include the hood, front fenders, grille, doors, trunk lid and tail light assembly. It is often cheaper and less time consuming to replace an entire panel than it is to attempt a restoration of the old one. However, this must be decided on a case-by-case basis.

2 Maintenance — body

1   The condition of your vehicle's body is very important, because it is on this that the second hand value will mainly depend. It is much more difficult to repair a neglected or damaged body than it is to repair mechanical components. The hidden areas of the body, such as the fender wells, the frame, and the engine compartment, are equally important, although they obviously do not require as frequent attention as the rest of the body.

2   Once a year, or every 12,000 miles, it's a good idea to have the underside of the body and the frame steam cleaned. All traces of dirt and oil will be removed and the underside can then be inspected carefully for rust, damaged brake lines, frayed electrical wiring, damaged cables and other problems. The front suspension components should be greased after completion of this job.

3   At the same time, clean the engine and the engine compartment using either a steam cleaner or a water soluble degreaser.

4   The fender wells should be given particular attention, as undercoating can peel away and stones and dirt thrown up by the tires can cause the paint to chip and flake, allowing rust to set in. If rust is found, clean down to the bare metal and apply an anti-rust paint.

5   The body should be washed as needed. Wet the vehicle thoroughly to soften the dirt, then wash it down with a soft sponge and plenty of clean soapy water. If the surplus dirt is not washed off very carefully, it will in time wear down the paint.

6   Spots of tar or asphalt coating thrown up from the road should be removed with a cloth soaked in solvent.

7   Once every six months, give the body and chrome trim a thorough waxing. If a chrome cleaner is used to remove rust from any of the vehicle's plated parts, remember that the cleaner also removes part of the chrome, so use it sparingly.

3 Maintenance — upholstery and carpets

1   Every three months remove the carpets or mats and clean the interior of the vehicle (more frequently if necessary). Vacuum the upholstery and carpets to remove loose dirt and dust.

2   If the upholstery is soiled, apply upholstery cleaner with a damp sponge and wipe it off with a clean, dry cloth.

4 Vinyl trim — maintenance

Vinyl trim should not be cleaned with detergents, caustic soaps or petroleum-based cleaners. Plain soap and water or a mild vinyl cleaner is best for stains. Test a small area for color fastness. Bubbles under the vinyl can be corrected by piercing them with a pin and then working the air out.

5 Body repair — minor damage

See color photo sequence ''Repair of minor scratches''

1   If the scratch is superficial and does not penetrate to the metal of the body, repair is very simple. Lightly rub the scratched area with a fine rubbing compound to remove loose paint and built up wax. Rinse the area with clean water.

2   Apply touch-up paint to the scratch, using a small brush. Continue to apply thin layers of paint until the surface of the paint in the scratch is level with the surrounding paint. Allow the new paint at least two weeks to harden, then blend it into the surrounding paint by rubbing with a very fine rubbing compound. Finally, apply a coat of wax to the scratch area.

3   If the scratch has penetrated the paint and exposed the metal of the body, causing the metal to rust, a different repair technique is required. Remove all loose rust from the bottom of the scratch with a pocket knife, then apply rust inhibiting paint to prevent the formation of rust in the future. Using a rubber or nylon applicator, coat the scratched area with glaze-type filler. If required, the filler can be mixed with thinner to provide a very thin paste, which is ideal for filling narrow scratches. Before the glaze filler in the scratch hardens, wrap a piece of smooth cotton cloth around the tip of a finger. Dip the cloth in thinner and then quickly wipe it along the surface of the scratch. This will ensure that the surface of the filler is slightly hollow. The scratch can now be painted over as described earlier in this section.

Repair of dents

4   When repairing dents, the first job is to pull the dent out until the affected area is as close as possible to its original shape. There is no point in trying to restore the original shape completely as the metal in the damaged area will have stretched on impact and cannot be restored to its original contours. It is better to bring the level of the dent up to a point which is about 1/8-inch below the level of the surrounding metal. In cases where the dent is very shallow, it is not worth trying to pull it out at all.

5   If the back side of the dent is accessible, it can be hammered out gently from behind using a soft-face hammer. While doing this, hold a block of wood firmly against the opposite side of the metal to absorb the hammer blows and prevent the metal from being stretched.

6   If the dent is in a section of the body which has double layers, or some other factor makes it inaccessible from behind, a different technique is required. Drill several small holes through the metal inside the damaged area, particularly in the deeper sections. Screw long, self tapping screws into the holes just enough for them to get a good grip in the metal. Now the dent can be pulled out by pulling on the protruding heads of the screws with locking pliers.

7   The next stage of repair is the removal of paint from the damaged area and from an inch or so of the surrounding metal. This is easily done with a wire brush or sanding disk in a drill motor, although it can be done just as effectively by hand with sandpaper. To complete the preparation for filling, score the surface of the bare metal with a screwdriver or the tang of a file or drill small holes in the affected area. This will provide a good grip for the filler material. To complete the repair, see the Section on filling and painting.

Repair of rust holes or gashes

8   Remove all paint from the affected area and from an inch or so of the surrounding metal using a sanding disk or wire brush mounted in a drill motor. If these are not available, a few sheets of sandpaper will do the job just as effectively.

9   With the paint removed, you will be able to determine the severity of the corrosion and decide whether to replace the whole panel, if possible, or repair the affected area. New body panels are not as expensive as most people think and it is often quicker to install a new panel than to repair large areas of rust.

10   Remove all trim pieces from the affected area except those which will act as a guide to the original shape of the damaged body, such as headlight shells, etc. Using metal snips or a hacksaw blade, remove all loose metal and any other metal that is badly affected by rust. Hammer the edges of the hole inward to create a slight depression for the filler material.

11   Wire brush the affected area to remove the powdery rust from the surface of the metal. If the back of the rusted area is accessible, treat it with rust-inhibiting paint.

12   Before filling is done, block the hole in some way. This can be done with sheet metal riveted or screwed into place, or by stuffing the hole with wire mesh.

13   Once the hole is blocked off, the affected area can be filled and painted. See the following sub-section on filling and painting.

Filling and painting

14   Many types of body fillers are available, but generally speaking, body repair kits which contain filler paste and a tube of resin hardener are best for this type of repair work. A wide, flexible plastic or nylon applicator will be necessary for imparting a smooth and contoured finish to the surface of the filler material. Mix up a small amount of filler on a clean piece of wood or cardboard (use the hardener sparingly). Follow the manufacturer's instructions on the package, otherwise the filler will set incorrectly.

15   Using the applicator, apply the filler paste to the prepared area. Draw the applicator across the surface of the filler to achieve the desired contour and to level the filler surface. As soon as a contour that approximates the original one is achieved, stop working the paste. If you continue, the paste will begin to stick to the applicator. Continue to add thin layers of paste at 20-minute intervals until the level of the filler is just above the surrounding metal.

16 Once the filler has hardened, the excess can be removed with a body file. From then on, progressively finer grades of sandpaper should be used, starting with a 180-grit paper and finishing with 600-grit wet-or-dry paper. Always wrap the sandpaper around a flat rubber or wooden block, otherwise the surface of the filler will not be completely flat. During the sanding of the filler surface, the wet-or-dry paper should be periodically rinsed in water. This will ensure that a very smooth finish is produced in the final stage.

17 At this point, the repair area should be surrounded by a ring of bare metal, which in turn should be encircled by the finely feathered edge of good paint. Rinse the repair area with clean water until all of the dust produced by the sanding operation is gone.

18 Spray the entire area with a light coat of primer. This will reveal any imperfections in the surface of the filler. Repair the imperfections with fresh filler paste or glaze filler and once more smooth the surface with sandpaper. Repeat this spray-and-repair procedure until you are satisfied that the surface of the filler and the feathered edge of the paint are perfect. Rinse the area with clean water and allow it to dry completely.

19 The repair area is now ready for painting. Spray painting must be carried out in a warm, dry, windless and dust free atmosphere. These conditions can be created if you have access to a large indoor work area, but if you are forced to work in the open, you will have to pick the day very carefully. If you are working indoors, dousing the floor in the work area with water will help settle the dust which would otherwise be in the air. If the repair area is confined to one body panel, mask off the surrounding panels. This will help minimize the effects of a slight mismatch in paint color. Trim pieces such as chrome strips, door handles, etc., will also need to be masked off or removed. Use masking tape and several thicknesses of newspaper for the masking operations.

20 Before spraying, shake the paint can thoroughly, then spray a test area until the spray painting technique is mastered. Cover the repair area with a thick coat of primer. The thickness should be built up using several thin layers of primer rather than one thick one. Using 600-grit wet-or-dry sandpaper, rub down the surface of the primer until it is very smooth. While doing this, the work area should be thoroughly rinsed with water and the wet-or-dry sandpaper periodically rinsed as well. Allow the primer to dry before spraying additional coats.

21 Spray on the top coat, again building up the thickness by using several thin layers of paint. Begin spraying in the center of the repair area and then, using a circular motion, work out until the whole repair area and about two inches of the surrounding original paint is covered. Remove all masking material 10 to 15 minutes after spraying on the final coat of paint. Allow the new paint at least two weeks to harden, then use a very fine rubbing compound to blend the edges of the new paint into the existing paint. Finally, apply a coat of wax.

6 Body repair — major damage

1 Major damage must be repaired by an auto body/frame repair shop with the necessary welding and hydraulic straightening equipment.

2 If the damage has been serious, it is vital that the structure be checked for proper alignment or the vehicle's handling characteristics may be adversely affected. Other problems, such as excessive tire wear and wear in the driveline and steering may occur.

3 Due to the fact that all of the major body components (hood, fenders, etc.) are separate and replaceable units, any seriously damaged components should be replaced rather than repaired. Sometimes these components can be found in a wrecking yard that specializes in used vehicle components, often at considerable savings over the cost of new parts.

7 Maintenance — hinges and locks

Every 3000 miles or three months, the door, hood and trunk lid hinges should be lubricated with a few drops of oil. The door striker plates should also be given a thin coat of white lithium-base grease to reduce wear and ensure free movement.

8 Windshield and fixed glass — replacement

1 Replacement of the windshield and fixed glass requires the use of special fast-setting adhesive/caulk materials. These operations should be left to a dealer or a shop specializing in glass work.

2 Windshield-mounted rear view mirror support removal is also best left to experts, as the bond to the glass also requires special tools and adhesives.

9 Hood — removal and installation

Refer to illustrations 9.1, 9.2 and 9.3

1 Use rags or pads to protect the windshield from the rear of the hood (see illustration).

2 Scribe or paint alignment marks around the hinge bolts (see illustration).

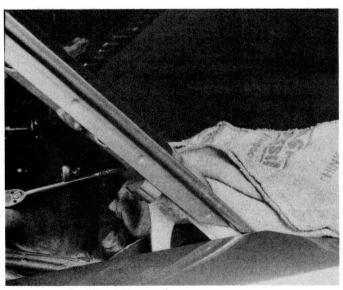

9.1 Pad the back corners of the hood with rags so the windshield won't be damaged if the hood accidentally swings rearward

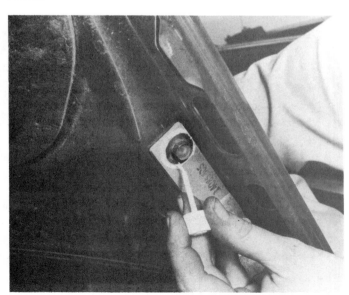

9.2 Use paint to mark the hood bolt positions

This photo sequence illustrates the repair of a dent and damaged paintwork. The procedure for the repair of a hole is similar. Refer to the text for more complete instructions

After removing any adjacent body trim, hammer the dent out. The damaged area should then be made slightly concave

Use coarse sandpaper or a sanding disc on a drill motor to remove all paint from the damaged area. Feather the sanded area into the edges of the surrounding paint, using progressively finer grades of sandpaper

The damaged area should be treated with rust remover prior to application of the body filler. In the case of a rust hole, all rusted sheet metal should be cut away

Carefully follow manufacturer's instructions when mixing the body filler so as to have the longest possible working time during application. Rust holes should be covered with fiberglass screen held in place with dabs of body filler prior to repair

Apply the filler with a flexible applicator in thin layers at 20 minute intervals. Use an applicator such as a wood spatula for confined areas. The filler should protrude slightly above the surrounding area

Shape the filler with a surform-type plane. Then, use water and progressively finer grades of sandpaper and a sanding block to wet-sand the area until it is smooth. Feather the edges of the repair area into the surrounding paint.

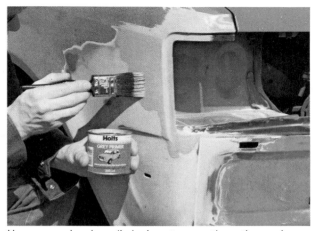

Use spray or brush applied primer to cover the entire repair area so that slight imperfections in the surface will be filled in. Prime at least one inch into the area surrounding the repair. Be careful of over-spray when using spray-type primer

Wet-sand the primer with fine (approximately 400 grade) sandpaper until the area is smooth to the touch and blended into the surrounding paint. Use filler paste on minor imperfections

After the filler paste has dried, use rubbing compound to ensure that the surface of the primer is smooth. Prior to painting, the surface should be wiped down with a tack rag or lint-free cloth soaked in lacquer thinner

Choose a dry, warm, breeze-free area in which to paint and make sure that adjacent areas are protected from over-spray. Shake the spray paint can thoroughly and apply the top coat to the repair area, building it up by applying several coats, working from the center

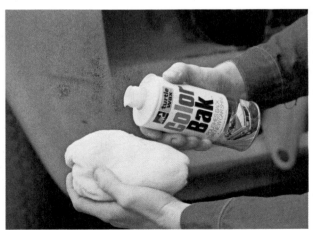

After allowing at least two weeks for the paint to harden, use fine rubbing compound to blend the area into the original paint. Wax can now be applied

11

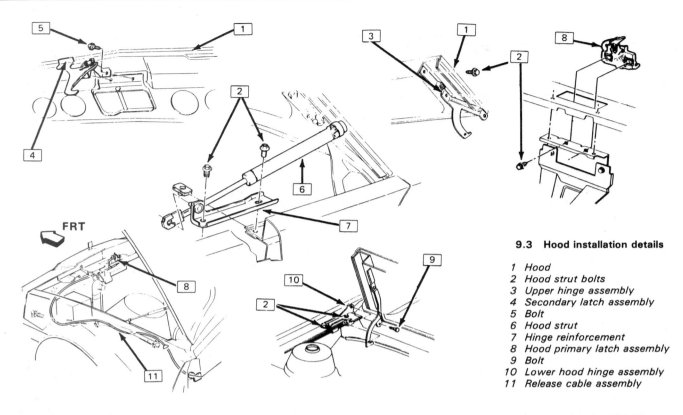

9.3   Hood installation details

1   Hood
2   Hood strut bolts
3   Upper hinge assembly
4   Secondary latch assembly
5   Bolt
6   Hood strut
7   Hinge reinforcement
8   Hood primary latch assembly
9   Bolt
10   Lower hood hinge assembly
11   Release cable assembly

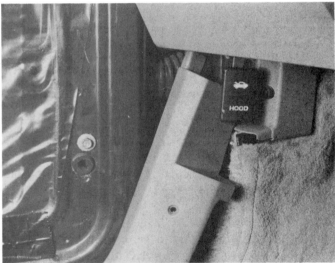

10.1   Pull the trim panel down for access to the two screws behind the hood latch handle

10.2   Remove the two screws with a Phillips head screwdriver

3   On models so equipped, detach the assist strut **(see illustration)**.
4   Remove the bolts and, with the help of an assistant, detach the hood from the vehicle.
5   Installation is the reverse of removal.

---

10   Hood latch cable — replacement

Refer to illustrations 10.1, 10.2, 10.3 and 10.4

1   In the passenger compartment, remove the trim panel **(see illustration)**.

2   Remove the latch handle retaining screws and detach the handle **(see illustration)**.
3   In the engine compartment, pry the cable grommet out of the clip **(see illustration)**.
4   Spread the clip with a screwdriver and detach the end of the cable from the latch **(see illustration)**.
5   Connect a piece of string or thin wire of suitable length to the end of the wire to the cable and pull the cable through into the passenger compartment.
6   Connect the string or wire to the new cable and pull it back into the engine compartment.
7   Connect the cable and install the latch screws and trim panel.

10.3 Pry the hood latch cable up (arrow) to detach it from the clip

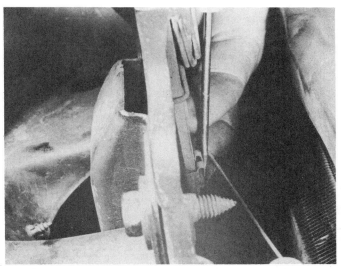

10.4 Pry the clip back and lift the cable up to detach it

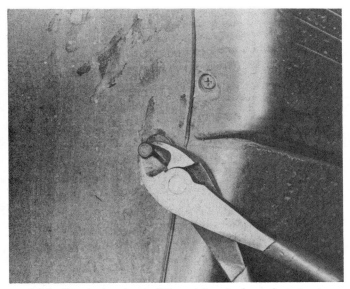

11.2 Pry the head out of the retainer body — do not cut the head off

11.4 Grasp the fender liner and pull the ends inward to detach it from the fender well

11 Front fender liner — removal and installation

Refer to illustrations 11.2, 11.4 and 11.6

1   Raise the vehicle, support it securely on jackstands and remove the front wheel.

2   The fender liner is held in place with special plastic retainers. Use wire cutters or a similar tool to pry the heads of the retainers out of the retainer bodies to release them **(see illustration)**. Pry the heads out, do not cut them off to remove them.

3   Once all of the retainers are released, remove them from the fender liner.

4   Detach the liner and remove it from the vehicle **(see illustration)**.

5   To install, place the liner in position and align the retainer holes.

6   Install the retainers and push the heads in to securely lock them in place **(see illustration)**.

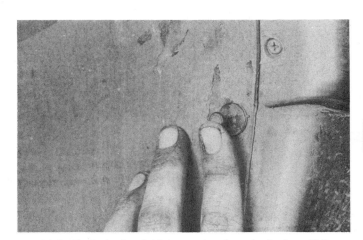

11.6 Push the head of the retainer into the body until it locks in place

11

12 Front fender — removal and installation

Refer to illustration 12.3

1   Raise the front of the vehicle, support it securely on jackstands and remove the front wheel.
2   Remove the front fender liner (Section 11).
3   Remove the retaining nuts and detach the fender from the vehicle **(see illustration)**.
4   To install, place the fender in place and install the retaining nuts. Tighten the nuts securely.
5   The remainder of installation is the reverse of removal.

13 Radiator grille — removal and installation

Refer to illustrations 13.2 and 13.3

1   Open the hood.
2   Remove the retaining screws **(see illustration)**.
3   Rotate the top of the grille out and lift it from the vehicle **(see illustration)**.
4   Installation is the reverse of removal.

12.3   Fender mounting details

1   *Hood insulation retainer*
2   *Hood insulation*
3   *Fender retaining nut*
4   *Fender retaining bolt*
5   *Front end panel retaining bolt*
6   *Fender*
7   *Front end panel*
8   *Radiator grille*

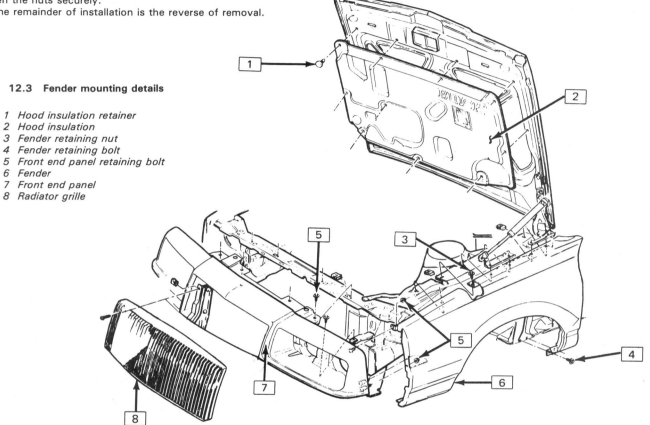

13.2   The radiator grille is held in place by Phillips head screws

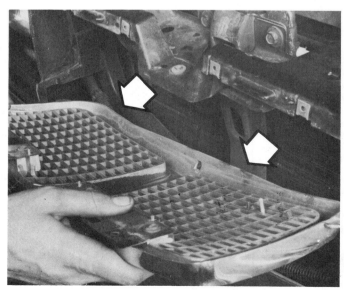

13.3   Tilt the grille forward (arrows) to detach it from the clips

14 Door trim panel — removal and installation

Refer to illustrations 14.1a, 14.1b, 14.1c, 14.2, 14.3a, 14.3b, 14.4, 14.5 and 14.6
1   Remove door glass regulator handle (if equipped) (Section 17), and the visible door panel screws from the door trim panel **(see illustrations)**.
2   Once the screws are removed from the arm rest (if equipped) slide it to the rear to disengage the clips and then lift it off **(see illustration)**.

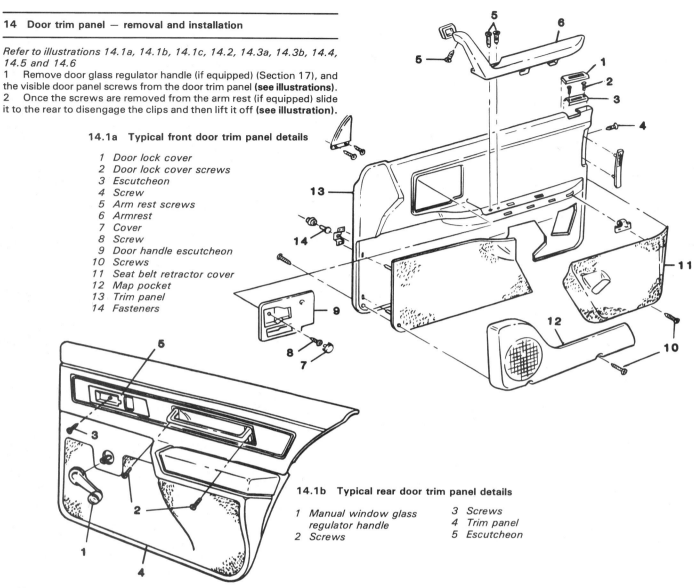

14.1a   Typical front door trim panel details

1   Door lock cover
2   Door lock cover screws
3   Escutcheon
4   Screw
5   Arm rest screws
6   Armrest
7   Cover
8   Screw
9   Door handle escutcheon
10 Screws
11 Seat belt retractor cover
12 Map pocket
13 Trim panel
14 Fasteners

14.1b   Typical rear door trim panel details

1 Manual window glass regulator handle	3 Screws
2 Screws	4 Trim panel
	5 Escutcheon

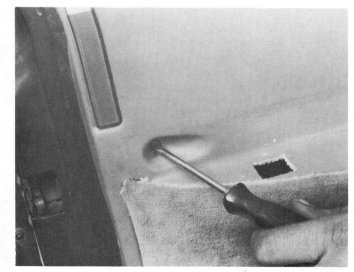

14.1c   Use a Phillips head screwdriver to remove the door panel screws

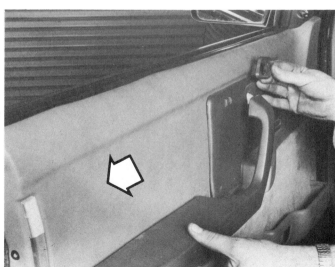

14.2   Move the armrest rearward (arrow) to disengage it

11

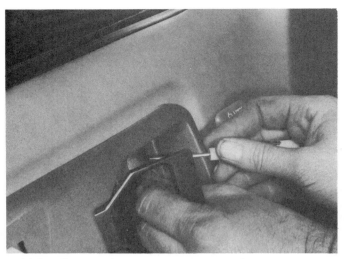

14.3a Use a small screwdriver to pry out the screw covers

14.3b Some screws are hidden under decorative panels

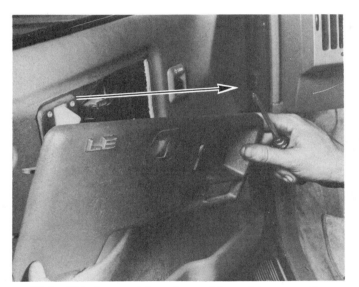

14.4 Slide the escutcheon forward (arrow) to remove it

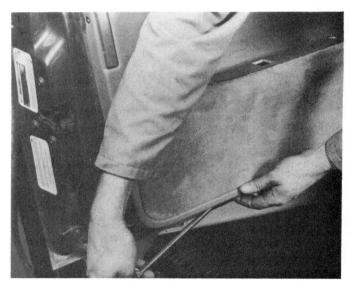

14.5 Pry around the outer circumference of the door panel to disengage the clips

3 Pry out the escutcheon screw covers and remove the screws **(see illustrations)**.

4 Disengage the escutcheon and remove it by sliding it forward off the clips **(see illustration)**.

5 Pry around the outer circumference of the door panel with a pry bar or large screwdriver to disengage the clips **(see illustration)**.

6 Grasp the door trim panel securely and lift upward to disengage it from the door upper edge **(see illustration)**.

7 Unplug any electrical switches and lift the door trim panel from the vehicle.

8 Carefully peel the water shield from the door for access to the inner door components. Take care not to tear the water shield as it must be reinstalled.

9 Installation is the reverse of removal.

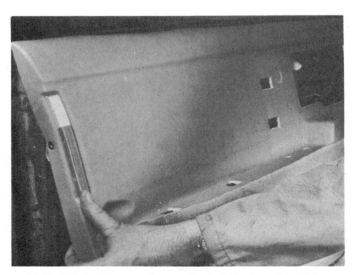

14.6 Lift the door panel up and out of the top edge of the door to disengage it

15 Door lock assembly — removal and installation

Refer to illustrations 15.2a and 15.2b

1 With the window glass in the full up position, remove the door trim panel and water shield (Section 14).

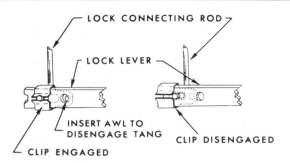

15.2a Door lever rod spring clip installation details

2   Disconnect spring clips from remote control connecting rods rods at the lock assembly **(see illustrations)**.
3   Remove the lock assembly-to-door screws and lift the assembly from the door.
4   To install, place the assembly in position and install the retaining screws.
5   Connect the lock rods.
6   Install the water shield and door trim panel.

---

16 Door window glass — removal and installation

Refer to illustrations 16.3 and 16.10

1   With the window glass in the full up position, remove the door trim panel and water shield (Section 14).

Front door

2   Remove the outside mirror (Section 28).
3   Remove the rubber stop bumper, screws and front run channel **(see illustration)**.
4   Lower the glass to the bottom of the door, slide the window regulator guide block off the sash channel and tilt the glass inboard of the door frame to remove it.
5   To install, insert the glass into the door and engage the regulator guide block to the sash channel. Engage the rear guide clip on the glass to the rear run channel weatherstrip.

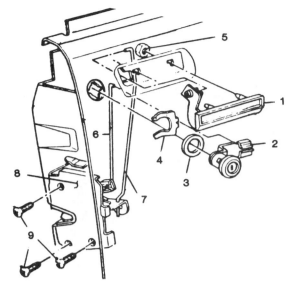

15.2b Door lock component layout

1	Handle	6	Lock cylinder-to-lock rod
2	Lock cylinder	7	Outside handle-to-lock rod
3	Gasket	8	Lock assembly
4	Retainer	9	Screws
5	Nut		

6   Raise the glass to the half way up position and install the front run channel bolts finger tight.
7   Engage the front clip on the glass to the front run channel and tighten the bolts securely.
8   Install the rubber stop bumper.
9   The remainder of installation is the reverse of removal.

Rear door

10 Remove the bolts retaining the regulator block to the window glass **(see illustration)**.

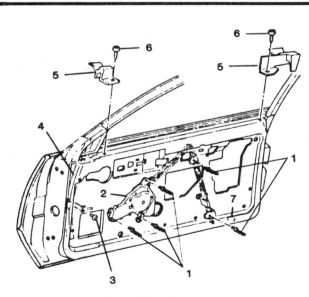

16.3 Typical front door glass details

1	Rivets	4	Front run channel	6	Screws
2	Regulator	5	Fillers	7	Stop bumper
3	Bolt				

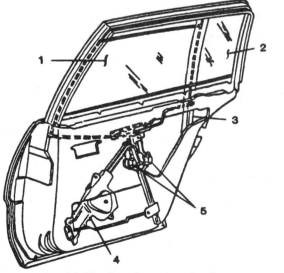

16.10 Rear door glass details

1	Glass	4	Regulator
2	Fixed vent glass	5	Bolts
3	Division channel		

11

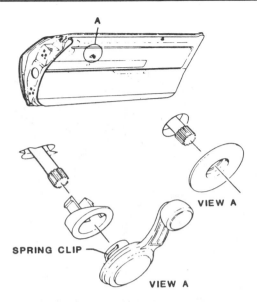

17.2a   Disengage the manual door glass regulator handle spring clip and withdraw the assembly from the door

11   Disengage the glass and lower it to the bottom of the door.
12   Remove the run channel from the door frame at the front and rear of the glass division channel.
13   Lift the glass from the door.
14   To install, insert the glass into the door and connect the division channel, making sure to engage the glass guide securely to the channel.
15   Connect the regulator guide block to the glass sash channel and install the bolts. Tighten the bolts securely.
16   The remainder of installation is the reverse of removal.

---

17   Door glass regulator — removal and installation

Refer to illustrations 17.2a and 17.2b

Removal

1   On power window equipped models, disconnect the negative cable at the battery. Place the cable out of the way so it cannot accidentally come in contact with the negative terminal of the battery, as this would once again allow power into the electrical system of the vehicle.
2   On manual window glass regulator equipped models, remove the handle by pressing the bearing plate and door trim panel in and, with a piece of hooked wire, pulling off the spring clip **(see illustration)**. A special tool is available for this purpose **(see illustration)** but its use is not essential. With the clip removed, take off the handle and the bearing plate.
3   With the window glass in the full up position, remove the door trim panel and water shield (Section 14).
4   Secure the window glass in the up position with strong adhesive tape fastened to the glass and wrapped over the door frame.
5   Punch out the center pins of the rivets that secure the window regulator and drill the rivets out with a 1/4-inch drill bit.
6   On power window equipped models, unplug the electrical connector.
7   Remove the retaining bolts and move the regulator until it is disengaged from the sash channel. Lift the regulator from the door.

Installation

8   Place the regulator in position in the door and engage it to the sash channel.
9   Secure the regulator to the door using 3/16-inch rivets and a rivet tool.
10   Install the bolts and tighten them securely.
11   Plug in the electrical connector (if equipped).
12   Install the water shield, door trim panel and window regulator handle. Connect the battery negative cable.

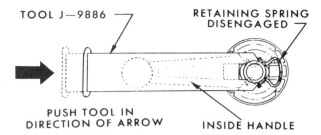

17.2b   A special tool can be used to disengage the the spring clip

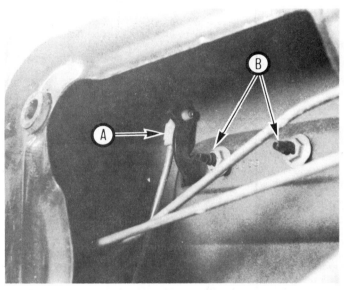

18.2   Push the outside handle rod clip (A) off and remove the two handle retaining nuts (B)

---

18   Door handles — removal and installation

Refer to illustrations 18.2 and 18.4

1   With the window glass in the full up position, remove the door trim panel and water shield (Section 14).

Outside handle

2   Pry the remote rod out of the handle with a small screwdriver, remove the nuts and lift the handle off **(see illustration)**.
3   Installation is the reverse of removal.

Inside handle

4   Disconnect the rod from the handle **(see illustration)**.
5   Punch out the center pins of the rivets that secure the window regulator and drill the rivets out with a 3/16-inch drill bit.
6   Lift the handle from the door.
7   To install, place the handle in position and secure it to the door, using 3/16-inch rivets and a rivet tool.
8   The remainder of installation is the reverse of removal.

---

19   Door lock cylinder — removal and installation

---

1   With the window glass in the full up position, remove the door trim panel and water shield (Section 14).
2   Disconnect the rod from the lock cylinder.
3   Use a screwdriver to pry the retainer off and withdraw the lock cylinder from the door **(see illustration 15.2b)**.
4   Installation is the reverse of removal.

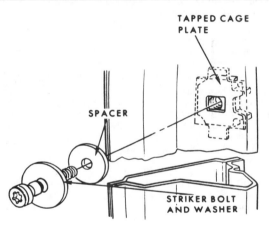

2NE27 STYLE

3NF/NT & 4NJ27 STYLES

18.4 Remote door lock details

1	Lock	7	Locking rod support
2	Inside remote handle	8	Bell crank
3	Remote control	9	Rivet
	handle-to-lock rod	10	Rivet
4	Inside locking rod	11	Rivet
5	Bell crank-to-actuator rod	12	Rivet
6	Actuator	13	Inside locking rod

TAPPED CAGE PLATE

SPACER

STRIKER BOLT AND WASHER

20.2 Door lock striker details

20 Door lock striker — removal and installation

Refer to illustration 20.2

1   Mark the position of the striker bolt on the door pillar with a pencil.
2   It will be necessary to use a special tool to fit the star-shaped recess in the striker bolt head (tool J-23457 or BT-7107). Unscrew the bolt and remove it **(see illustration)**.
3   To install, screw the lock striker bolt into the tapped cage plate in the door pillar and tighten it finger tight at the marked position. Tighten the bolt to the specified torque.

21 Door — removal and installation

Refer to illustration 21.5

1   Remove the door trim panel and water shield.
2   Unplug any wiring connectors.
3   Open the door all the way and support it on jacks or blocks covered with cloth or pads to prevent damage to the paint.
4   Scribe around the hinges to ensure correct realignment during installation.
5   Remove the bolts and nuts retaining the hinges to the door **(see illustration)** and with the help of an assistant lift the door away.

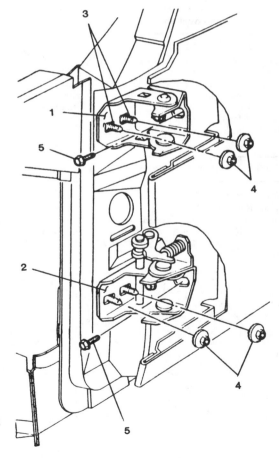

21.5 Door hinge details

1	Upper front door	3	Body studs
	hinge assembly	4	Nuts
2	Lower front door	5	Bolts (2 on each
	hinge assembly		hinge assembly)

11

22.2 Mark the position of the trunk lid bolts with paint before removing them

6   Install the door by reversing the removal procedure. Tighten the nuts and bolts to the specified torque.

22   Trunk lid — removal and installation

Refer to illustration 22.2
1   Open the trunk lid and unplug any electrical connectors and disconnect the solenoid (if equipped).
2   Scribe or mark around the heads of the retaining bolts to mark their locations for ease of reinstallation **(see illustration)**.
3   With an assistant supporting the trunk lid, remove the bolts. Lift the trunk lid from the vehicle.
4   Installation is the reverse of removal.

23   Trunk lock cylinder — removal and installation

Refer to illustration 23.2
1   Open the trunk lid.
2   Punch out the center pin in the retaining clip mounting rivets and drill out the rivets with a 5/32-inch drill bit **(see illustration)**.
3   Pry the retaining clip off and withdraw the lock cylinder from the vehicle.

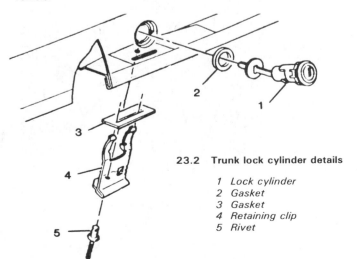

23.2   Trunk lock cylinder details

1   *Lock cylinder*
2   *Gasket*
3   *Gasket*
4   *Retaining clip*
5   *Rivet*

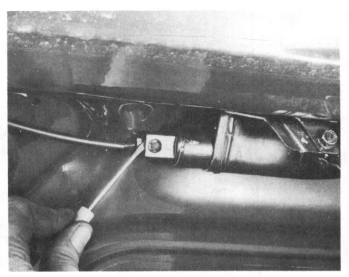

24.2   Insert a small screwdriver into the solenoid connector, depress the retaining tab and then pull the cable out

4   To install, place the lock cylinder in place and secure it with the retaining clip. Use 5/32 by 7/16-inch long steel rivets and a rivet tool to attach the clip to the trunk lid.

24   Trunk latch and striker — removal and installation

Refer to illustration 24.2, 24.3a, 24.3b and 24.4
1   Disconnect the negative cable from the battery. Place the cable out of the way so it cannot accidentally come in contact with the negative terminal of the battery, as this would once again allow power into the electrical system of the vehicle.
2   On models so equipped, disconnect the trunk lock cylinder cable by inserting small screwdriver into the connector to hold the release tab down and them pull the cable out of the solenoid **(see illustration)**.
3   Remove the electronic solenoid (if equipped) and unbolt and remove the latch and (if equipped) the ajar switch **(see illustrations)**.
4   Remove the retaining nut and lift off the striker **(see illustration)**.
5   Installation is the reverse of removal.

25   Rear lens assembly — removal and installation

Refer to illustrations 25.3a and 25.3b
1   Disconnect the negative cable at the battery. Place the cable out of the way so it cannot accidentally come in contact with the negative terminal of the battery, as this would once again allow power into the electrical system of the vehicle.
2   Open the trunk lid.
3   Unscrew the plastic wing nuts, pull the lens assembly out and lean it back **(see illustrations)**. Disconnect the bulb holders (Chapter 12) and lift the assembly from the vehicle.
4   Installation is the reverse of removal.

26   Console — removal and installation

Refer to illustration 26.3, 26.4, 26.5a, 26.5b, 26.6a, 26.6b, 26.7 and 26.8
1   Disconnect the negative cable at the battery. Place the cable out of the way so it cannot accidentally come in contact with the negative terminal of the battery, as this would once again allow power into the electrical system of the vehicle.
2   Remove the ash receptacle and cigarette lighter.
3   Remove the retaining screw at the base of the parking brake handle **(see illustration)**.

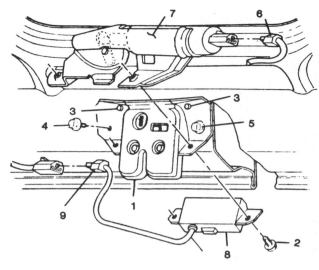

24.3a Trunk latch and solenoid details

1 Latch
2 Bolt
3 Rivet
4 Bolt
5 Bolt
6 Connector
7 Solenoid

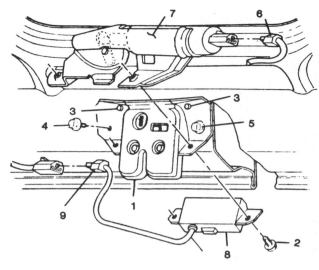

24.3b Trunk latch, solenoid and ajar switch details

1 Latch
2 Bolt
3 Rivets
4 Bolt
5 Bolt
6 Connector
7 Solenoid
8 Trunk lid ajar switch
9 Connector

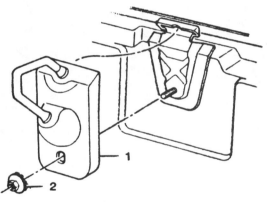

24.4 Trunk latch striker details

1 Striker   2 Nut

25.3a Unscrew the plastic retaining wing nuts and . . .

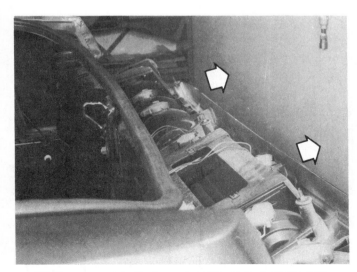

25.3b . . . rotate the lens assembly away from the rear of the vehicle (arrows) for access to the bulb holders

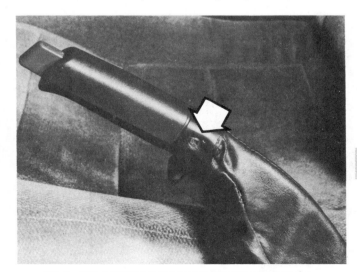

26.3 Use a Phillips head screwdriver to remove the parking brake handle screw (arrow)

11

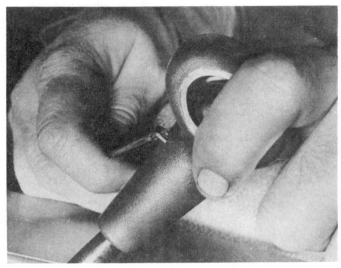

26.4   Pry out the automatic transaxle shift handle
retaining clip

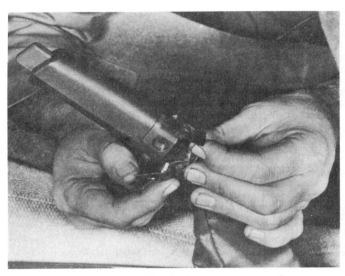

26.5a   Pull the parking brake cover snap retainer
apart and . . .

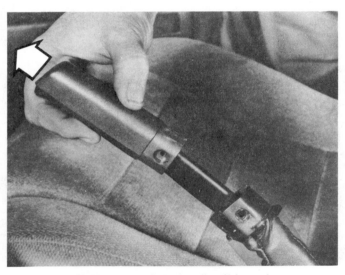

26.5b   . . . pull the handle off (arrow)

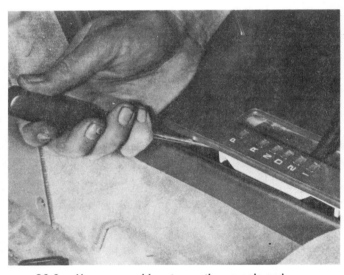

26.6a   Use a screwdriver to pry the console and . . .

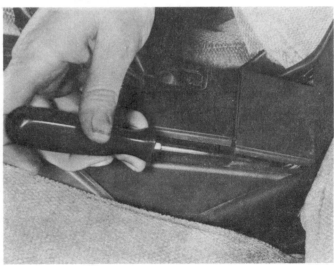

26.6b   . . . the rear cover free of the clips

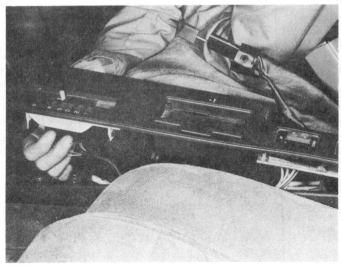

26.7   Raise the console for access to the
electrical connectors

4   Use a small screwdriver to pry the retaining clip out of the automatic transaxle shift handle (see illustration). On manual transaxle equipped models, remove the shift knob retaining screw. Pull the handle or knob off the shift lever.

5   Unsnap the cover and pull the parking brake handle off (see illustrations).

6   Pry around the outer edge of the console until the assembly is free and then pry the rear piece loose and then pull the console up (see illustrations).

7   Lift the console up for access and unplug the electrical connectors (see illustration).

8   Some or all of the retaining clips will probably come out during removal, so be sure to reinstall them prior to console installation (see illustration).

9   Installation is the reverse of removal.

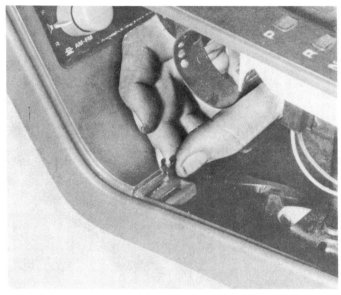

26.8   Insert the retaining clips into their holders before pressing the console into place

---

27   Seats — removal and installation

Refer to illustrations 27.3a, 27.3b and 27.7

Front seat

1   Move the seat all the way forward.

2   Remove the seat track covers and pull the carpet away from the adjuster and retaining nuts.

3   Remove the rear seat adjuster-to-floor panel retaining nuts (see illustrations).

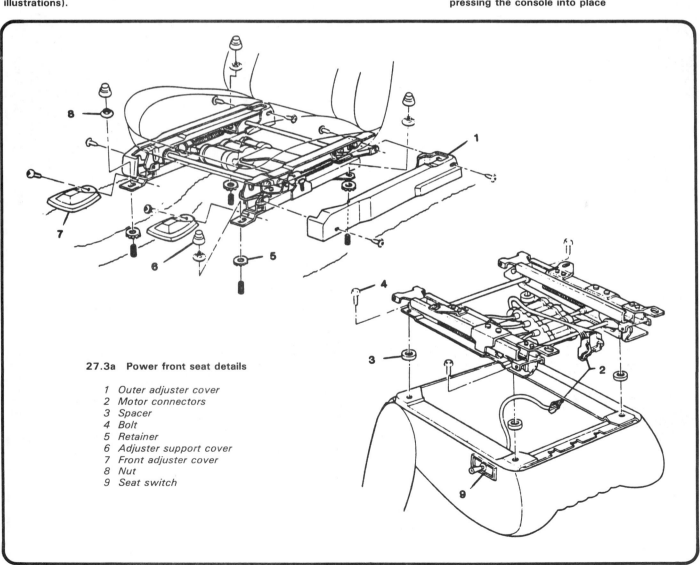

27.3a Power front seat details

1 Outer adjuster cover
2 Motor connectors
3 Spacer
4 Bolt
5 Retainer
6 Adjuster support cover
7 Front adjuster cover
8 Nut
9 Seat switch

11

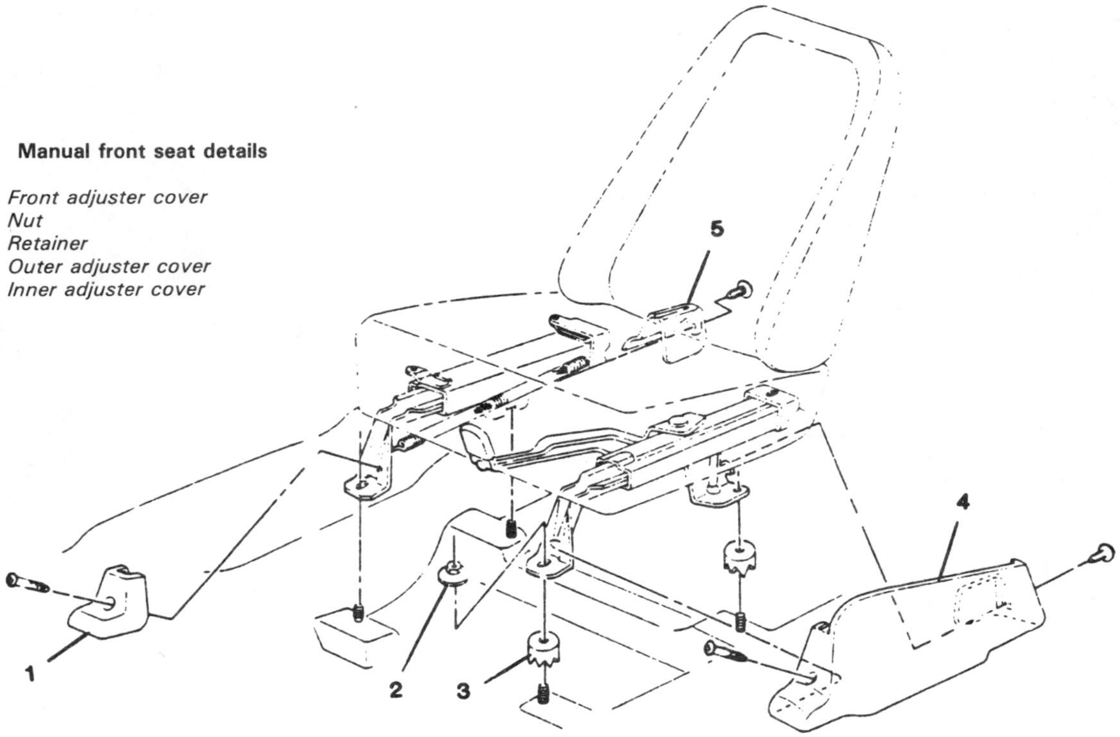

27.3b Manual front seat details

1 Front adjuster cover
2 Nut
3 Retainer
4 Outer adjuster cover
5 Inner adjuster cover

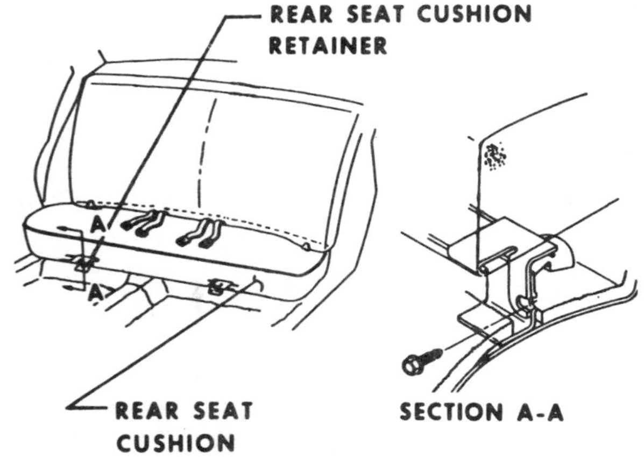

REAR SEAT CUSHION RETAINER

REAR SEAT CUSHION

SECTION A-A

27.7 Rear seat installation details

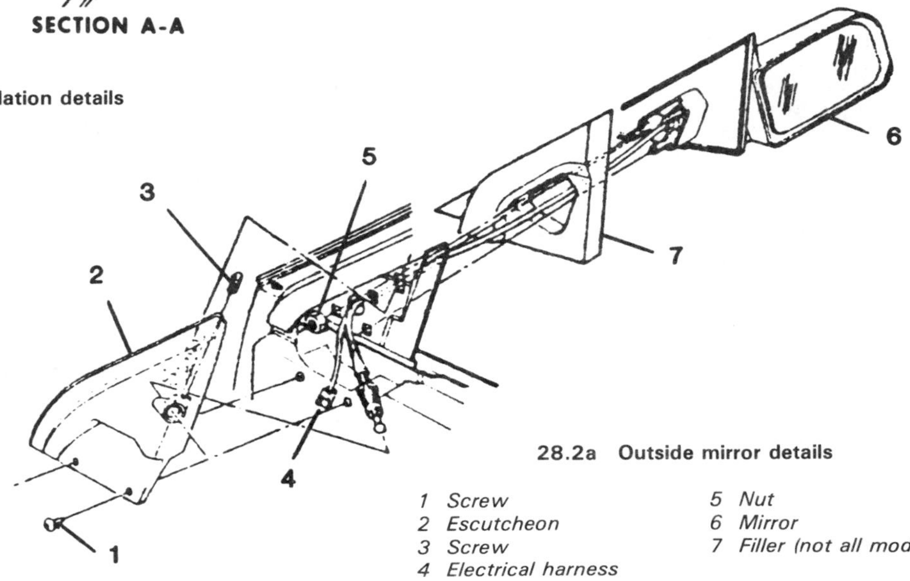

28.2a Outside mirror details

1 Screw
2 Escutcheon
3 Screw
4 Electrical harness
5 Nut
6 Mirror
7 Filler (not all models)

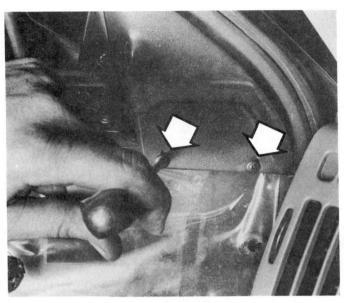

28.2b The mirror escutcheon is held in place by two
Phillips head screws (arrows)

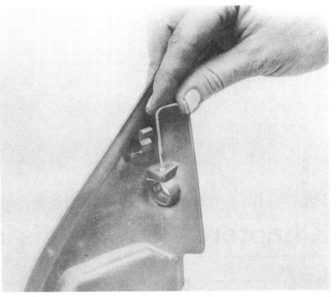

28.3 This Allen head screw must be removed to release
the control cable from the escutcheon

4   Move the seat all the way to the rear.
5   Remove the front seat retaining nuts. On power seats, unplug the
electrical connector. Lift the seat from the vehicle.
6   Installation is the reverse of removal. Tighten the adjuster-to-floor
panel nuts to the specified torque.

Rear seat

7   Remove the seat cushion retaining bolts, detach the seat cushion
and remove it from the vehicle **(see illustration)**.
8   Installation is the reverse of removal.

---

28 Outside mirror — removal and installation

Refer to illustrations 28.2a, 28.2b, 28.3 and 28.6

1   Remove the door trim panel (Section 14).
2   Remove retaining screws and pull the escutcheon back **(see
illustrations)**.
3   On manual mirrors, loosen the Allen screw holding the control on
the escutcheon **(see illustration)**.
4   On power mirrors, unplug the electrical connector.
5   Remove the escutcheon.
6   Remove the three nuts and lift off the mirror assembly **(see
illustration)**.
7   Installation is the reverse of removal.

28.6 Remove the mirror retaining nuts (arrows)

11

Chapter 12 Chassis electrical system

Contents

1 General information

The electrical system is a 12-volt, negative ground type. Power for the lights and all electrical accessories is supplied by a lead/acid-type battery which is charged by the alternator.

This Chapter covers repair and service procedures for the various electrical components not associated with the engine. Information on the battery, alternator, distributor and starter motor can be found in Chapter 5.

It should be noted that whenever portions of the electrical system are serviced, the negative battery cable should be disconnected at the battery to prevent electrical shorts and/or fires.

Note: *Information concerning digital instrumentation and dash related accessories is not included in this manual. Problems involving these components should be referred to a dealer service department.*

2 Electrical troubleshooting — general information

A typical electrical circuit consists of an electrical component, any switches, relays, motors, etc. related to that component and the wiring and connectors that connect the component to both the battery and the chassis. To aid in locating a problem in any electrical circuit, wiring diagrams are included at the end of this book.

Before tackling any troublesome electrical circuit, first study the appropriate diagrams to get a complete understanding of what makes up that individual circuit. Trouble spots, for instance, can often be narrowed down by noting if other components related to that circuit are operating properly or not. If several components or circuits fail at one time, chances are the problem lies in the fuse or ground connection, as several circuits are often routed through the same fuse and ground

connection.

Electrical problems often stem from simple causes, such as loose or corroded connections, a blown fuse or a melted fusible link. Always visually inspect the condition of the fuse, wires and connections in a problem circuit before troubleshooting it.

If testing instruments are going to be utilized, use the diagrams to plan ahead of time where you will make the necessary connections in order to accurately pinpoint the trouble spot.

The basic tools needed for electrical troubleshooting include a circuit tester or voltmeter (a 12-volt bulb with a set of test leads can also be used), a continuity tester, which includes a bulb, battery and set of test leads, and a jumper wire, preferably with a circuit breaker incorporated, which can be used to bypass electrical components.

Voltage checks should be performed if a circuit is not functioning properly. Connect one lead of a circuit tester to either the negative battery terminal or a known good ground. Connect the other lead to a connector in the circuit being tested, preferably nearest to the battery or fuse. If the bulb of the tester lights, voltage is present, which means that the part of the circuit between the connector and the battery is problem free. Continue checking the rest of the circuit in the same fashion. When you reach a point at which no voltage is present, the problem lies between that point and the last test point with voltage. Most of the time the problem can be traced to a loose connection. **Note:** *Keep in mind that some circuits receive voltage only when the ignition key is in the Accessory or Run position.*

One method of finding shorts in a circuit is to remove the fuse and connect a test light or voltmeter in its place to the fuse terminals. There should be no voltage present in the circuit. Move the wiring harness from side-to-side while watching the test light. If the bulb goes on, there is a short to ground somewhere in that area, probably where the insulation has rubbed through. The same test can be performed on each component in the circuit, even a switch.

Perform a ground test to check whether a component is properly grounded. Disconnect the battery and connect one lead of a self-powered test light, known as a continuity tester, to a known good ground. Connect the other lead to the wire or ground connection being tested. If the bulb goes on, the ground is good. If the bulb does not go on, the ground is not good.

A continuity check is done to determine if there are any breaks in a circuit — if it is passing electricity properly. With the circuit off (no power in the circuit), a self-powered continuity tester can be used to check the circuit. Connect the test leads to both ends of the circuit (or to the "power" end and a good ground), and if the test light comes on the circuit is passing current properly. If the light doesn't come on, there is a break somewhere in the circuit. The same procedure can be used to test a switch, by connecting the continuity tester to the power in and power out sides of the switch. With the switch turned On, the test light should come on.

When diagnosing for possible open circuits, it is often difficult to locate them by sight because oxidation or terminal misalignment are hidden by the connectors. Merely wiggling a connector on a sensor or in the wiring harness may correct the open circuit condition. Remember this when an open circuit is indicated when troubleshooting a circuit. Intermittent problems may also be caused by oxidized or loose connections.

Electrical troubleshooting is simple if you keep in mind that all electrical circuits are basically electricity running from the battery, through the wires, switches, relays, fuses and fusible links to each electrical component (light bulb, motor, etc.) and to ground, from which it is passed back to the battery. Any electrical problem is an interruption in the flow of electricity to and from the battery.

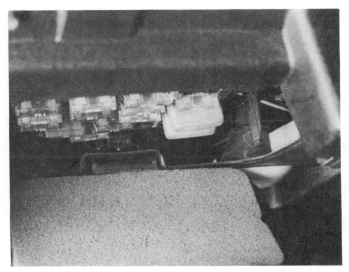

3.1 The fuse box is located above a small swing-down door on the left underside of the dashboard

3 Fuses — general information

Refer to illustrations 3.1 and 3.3

The electrical circuits of the vehicle are protected by a combination of fuses, circuit breakers and fusible links. The fuse block is located under the instrument panel on the left side of the dashboard (**see illustration**).

Each of the fuses is designed to protect a specific circuit, and the various circuits are identified on the fuse panel itself.

Miniaturized fuses are employed in the fuse block. These compact fuses, with blade terminal design, allow fingertip removal and replacement. If an electrical component fails, always check the fuse first. A blown fuse is easily identified through the clear plastic body. Visually inspect the element for evidence of damage (**see illustration**). If a continuity check is called for, the blade terminal tips are exposed in the fuse body.

Be sure to replace blown fuses with the correct replacement. Fuses of different ratings are physically interchangeable, but only fuses of the proper rating should be used. Replacing a fuse with one of a higher or lower value than specified is not recommended. Each electrical circuit needs a specific amount of protection. The amperage value of each fuse is molded into the fuse body. **Caution:** *At no time should a fuse be bypassed with pieces of metal or foil. Serious damage to the electrical system could result.*

If the replacement fuse immediately fails, do not replace it again until the cause of the problem is isolated and corrected. In most cases, this will be a short circuit in the wiring caused by a broken or deteriorated wire.

4 Fusible links — general information

Some circuits are protected by fusible links. These links are used in circuits which are not ordinarily fused, such as the ignition circuit.

Although the fusible links appear to be a heavier gauge than the wire they are protecting, the appearance is due to the thick insulation. All fusible links are four wire gauges smaller than the wire they are designed to protect. The location of the fusible links on your particular vehicle may be determined by referring to the wiring diagrams at the end of this book.

Fusible links cannot be repaired, but a new link of the same size wire can be put in its place. The procedure is as follows:
a) Disconnect the negative cable at the battery.
b) Disconnect the fusible link from the wiring harness.

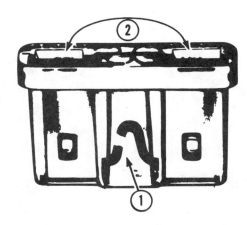

3.3 To check for a blown fuse, pull it out and inspect it visually for an open (1), then with the circuit activated, use a test light across the points shown (2)

c) Cut the damaged fusible link out of the wiring just behind the connector.
d) Strip the insulation approximately 1/2-inch.
e) Position the connector on the new fusible link and crimp it into place.
f) Use rosin core solder at each end of the new link to obtain a good solder joint.
g) Use plenty of electrical tape around the soldered joint. No wires should be exposed.
h) Connect the battery ground cable. Test the circuit for proper operation.

5 Circuit breakers — general information

Circuit breakers, which are located in the main fuse block, protect accessories such as power windows, power door locks and the rear window defogger.

The headlight wiring is also protected by a circuit breaker. An electrical overload in the system will cause the lights to go off and come on or, in some cases, to remain off. If this happens, check the headlight circuit immediately. The circuit breaker will function normally once the overload condition is corrected. Refer to the wiring diagrams at the end of this book for the location of the circuit breakers in your vehicle.

12

6.2a To gain access to the turn signal flasher and convenience center (or the connectors for most instrument panel-related electrical devices), remove the screws from the under-dash panel and allow it to hang down

6.2b Remove the screws from the smaller panel under the steering column and remove it

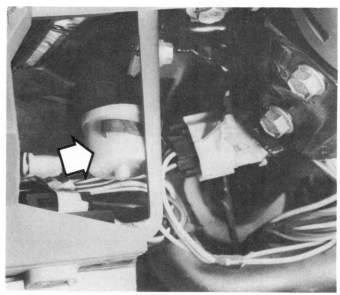

6.4 To remove the turn signal flasher (arrow), pop it loose from its retaining clip and unplug it

6.6 To gain access to the hazard flasher, remove the retaining screws and remove the left side console extension panel

---

6   Turn signal, hazard flasher, chime and convenience center — replacement

Refer to illustrations 6.2a, 6.2b, 6.4, 6.6, 6.7, 6.10, 6.14a and 6.14b

1   Detach the cable from the negative terminal of the battery.

Turn signal flasher

2   The two-piece panel under the instrument panel must be removed to gain access to the flasher unit. Remove the screws retaining the under-dash panel and allow it to hang down **(see illustration)**. Remove the retaining screws **(see illustration)** from the steering column filler plate panel (under the steering column) and remove it.

3   Some vehicles are equipped with a steering column collar and steering column filler plate which must be removed to gain access to the under dash sound insulator panel. If your vehicle is equipped with a collar and filler plate, pinch together the four slide clips along the bottom seam between the collar filler plate and detach them, slide the collar up the steering column and unscrew and remove the filler plate (see the illustration in Section 15). Remove the sound insulator panel as described above.

4   Locate the turn signal flasher **(see illustration)**, remove it from its retaining clip and unplug it.

5   Installation is the reverse of removal.

Hazard flasher

6   Remove the left side console extension panel **(see illustration)**.

6.7   To remove the hazard flasher (arrow), pop it loose from its retaining clip and unplug it

6.10   The chime is located above the glove box on some models — to remove the glove box, remove the mounting screws (arrows)

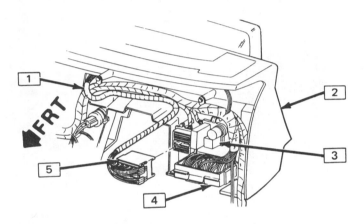

6.14a   If your vehicle is equipped with a "convenience center" for the turn signal flasher, hazard flasher, chime, etc., it is probably located under the dash, in the vicinity of the steering column

1 Cluster pod harness	4 Fuse block
2 Instrument panel assembly	5 Pod transition
3 Convenience center	block connector

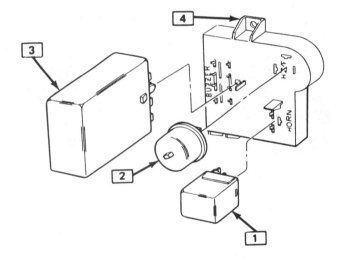

6.14b   Exploded view of a typical convenience center

1 Horn relay	3 Alarm assembly
2 Hazard flasher	4 Convenience center

7   Locate the hazard flasher (**see illustration**), remove it from its retaining clip and unplug it.
8   Installation is the reverse of removal.

Chime

9   On some vehicles, the chime is located immediately above the glove box.
10   Remove the glove box mounting screws (**see illustration**) and remove the glove box.
11   Remove the chime mounting bracket screws and unplug the chime electrical connector.
12   Remove the chime.
13   Installation is the reverse of removal.

Convenience center

14   The turn signal flasher, hazard flasher and chime units are not always located as described above. Some vehicles are equipped with a "convenience center," which is a small junction block, usually located in the vicinity of the steering column, to which the turn signal and hazard flashers, chime and other devices are attached (**see illustrations**).
15   After removing the under dash panel(s), look for a junction block similar to the one in the accompanying illustration.
16   To remove either flasher unit, unplug it and install a new one.

7   Multi-function stalk — replacement

Refer to illustrations 7.4 and 7.6

1   Detach the cable from the negative terminal of the battery.
2   The panels under the instrument panel must be removed to gain access to the multi-function stalk pigtail electrical connector. Remove the two screws retaining the under-dash panel and allow it to hang down (**see illustration 6.2a**).
3   Remove the retaining screws (**see illustration 6.2b**) from the smaller panel under the steering column and remove it (as you remove the panel, note how the tabs along the upper edge fit into the dash).

12

7.4   The multi-function stalk pigtail electrical connector is located under the dash to the right side of the steering column

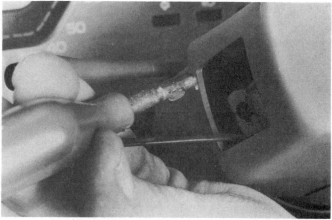

7.6   To detach the multi-function stalk from the steering column, pull straight out

8.3   Remove the shaft lock plate cover

8.4   Depress the shaft lock plate and remove the retaining clip with a scribe or small screwdriver

4   Locate the multi-function stalk electrical connector (see illustration) and unplug it.
5   Attach a suitable length of wire to the pigtail to pull the pigtail back through on installation.
6   Pull the stalk straight out from the steering column (see illustration).
7   Pull the multi-function stalk pigtail lead up through the steering column. Detach the wire from the pigtail lead and attach it to the lead of the new multi-function stalk.
8   Carefully thread the new connector and lead back through the steering column.
9   Installation is the reverse of removal.

---

8   Ignition switch/key lock cylinder — replacement

Refer to illustrations 8.3, 8.4, 8.5, 8.6, 8.7, 8.8, 8.11, 8.12 and 8.13
1   Detach the cable from the negative terminal of the battery.
2   Remove the steering wheel (see Chapter 10).
3   Remove the shaft lock cover (see illustration).
4   Depress the shaft lock plate and remove the retaining clip (see illustration). Remove the shaft lock plate.
5   Remove the the cancelling cam and the spring (see illustration).
6   Remove the hazard flasher button (see illustration).
7   Remove the signal switch arm screw and the signal switch arm (see illustration).
8   Remove the three turn signal switch screws (see illustration).
9   Pull the turn signal switch wire harness up through the steering column until there is sufficient slack to remove the turn signal switch.
10   Pull the turn signal switch out and set it aside.

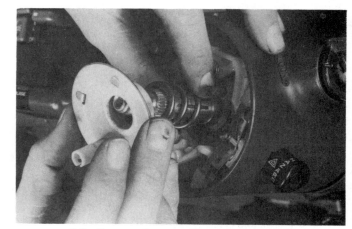

8.5   Remove the cancelling cam and spring

11   Remove the key warning buzzer switch (see illustration). The easiest way to get the buzzer switch out is to use a paper clip to pry it out. Note: Don't lose the small retainer clip that holds the buzzer switch in place. This clip must be installed in exactly the same position it is in in the accompanying photo.
12   Remove the lock retaining screw (see illustration).
13   Turn the ignition switch to the Run position and pull it out (see illustration).
14   Installation is the reverse of removal.

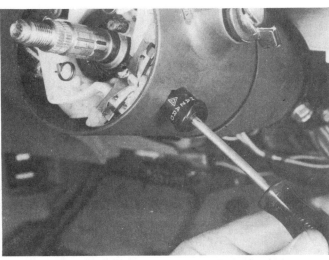

8.6   Unscrew and remove the hazard flasher button

8.7   Remove the signal switch arm screw and the signal switch arm

8.8   Remove the three turn signal switch retaining screws (arrows). Although the signal switch arm screw is still in place in this photo, you should already have removed it before loosening these three screws

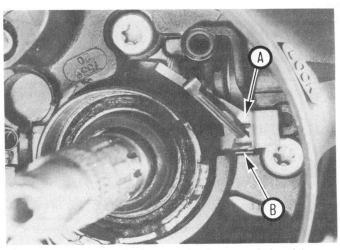

8.11   To remove the key warning buzzer switch, stick a paper clip into the crack (A) between the switch and the steering column assembly and pry it out — don't lose the small retainer (B) underneath the switch

8.12   Remove the key lock cylinder/ignition switch lock screw (arrow)

8.13   Turn the ignition switch to the Run position and pull it out

12

9.3a   If the headlight switch pod on your vehicle looks like this, remove this screw and pull the pod off

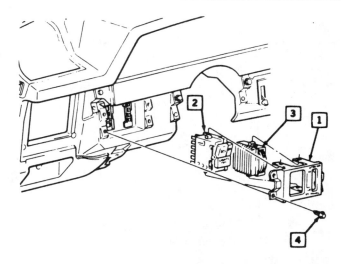

9.3b   Exploded view of another typical headlight switch pod style

1 Trim plate	*3 Dimmer switch*
2 Headlight switch	*4 Trim plate retaining screws*

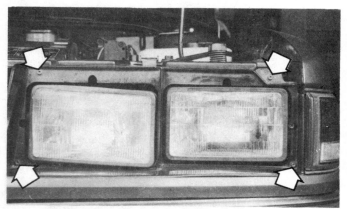

10.2   Remove the headlight trim ring screws (arrows)

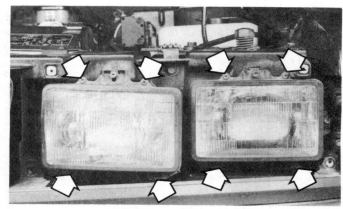

10.3   Remove the headlight bezel screws (arrows)

9   Headlight switch – replacement

Refer to illustrations 9.3a and 9.3b

1   Detach the cable from the negative terminal of the battery.
2   On some vehicles, the steering column collar must be detached to remove the headlight switch pod assembly.
3   Remove the headlight switch pod retaining screw(s) **(see illustrations)** and pull the pod out from the dash.
4   Unplug the electrical connectors and remove the headlight switch.
5   Installation is the reverse of removal.

10   Headlight — removal and installation

Refer to illustrations 10.2, 10.3, 10.12 and 10.13
Note: *Most vehicles are equipped with conventional dual rectangular sealed beam headlights. However, some vehicles are equipped with a single-piece ''composite'' type headlight assembly.*

1   Detach the cable from the negative terminal of the battery.

Sealed beam type

2   Remove the headlight trim ring screws **(see illustration)** and the trim ring.
3   Remove the headlight bezel screws **(see illustration)** and the headlight.

4   Unplug the headlight electrical connector and remove the headlight.
5   Installation is the reverse of removal.
6   Adjust the headlights (Section 11).

Composite type bulb

7   If your vehicle is equipped with composite type headlights, it is not necessary to replace the entire assembly just to change a bulb.
8   Locate the bulb lock ring on the back of the headlight assembly and turn it counterclockwise until it is loose.
9   With a vertical rocking motion, pull the bulb rearward.
10   With one hand, grip the wire harness end of the bulb. Do not grip the wires. With the other hand, grip the base of the bulb. Do not grip the bulb glass. Pull the bulb and base apart.
11   Installation is the reverse of removal.

Composite headlight assembly

12   There are two basic composite headlight types. To remove the first type, loosen the two top thumbscrews **(see illustration)**. Tilt the lamp assembly forward and lift. Unplug the electrical connector, loosen the rotating lock and remove the bulb. **Note:** *The bulbs for high and low beam are the same and have two separate filaments. Instead of using a new bulb for a burned out light, low and high beam bulbs can be interchanged.*
13   On other composite headlight assemblies, it is necessary to remove the headlight bezel, front bumper fascia screws, lens housing bolts and headlight lens assembly screws **(see illustration)**.

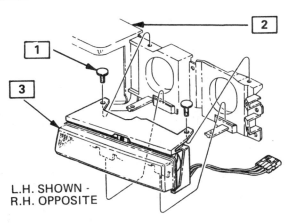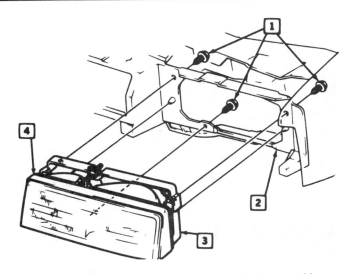

L.H. SHOWN -
R.H. OPPOSITE

**10.12 Exploded view of one type of composite
headlight assembly**

*1 Retaining thumbscrew   3 Composite headlight
2 Headlight housing panel*

14 Installation is the reverse of removal.
15 Adjust the headlights (Section 11).

10.13 Another typical composite headlight assembly

*1 Lens housing bolts   3 Light housing
2 Support panel   4 Light assembly*

---

11 Headlights — adjustment

Refer to illustration 11.2

1 It is important that the headlights be aimed correctly. If adjusted incorrectly they could blind an oncoming car and cause a serious accident or seriously reduce the your ability to see the road. The headlights should be checked for proper aim every 12 months and any time a new sealed beam headlight is installed or front end body work is performed.
2 Each headlight has two spring-loaded adjusting screws, one on the top controlling up and down movement and one on the side controlling left and right movement (**see illustration**). There are several methods of adjusting the headlights. The simplest method uses an empty wall 25 feet in front of the vehicle and a level floor.
3 Park the vehicle on a level floor 25 feet from the wall.
4 Position masking tape vertically on the wall in reference to the vehicle centerline and the centerlines of both headlights.
5 Position a horizontal tape line in reference to the centerline of all the headlights. **Note:** *It may be easier to position the tape on the wall with the vehicle parked only a few inches away.*
6 Adjustment should be made with the vehicle sitting level, the gas tank half-full and no unusually heavy load in the vehicle.
7 Starting with the low beam adjustment, position the high intensity zone so it is two inches below the horizontal line and two inches to the right of the headlight vertical line. Adjustment is made by turning the top adjusting screw clockwise to raise the beam and counterclockwise to lower the beam. The adjusting screw on the side should be used in the same manner to move the beam left or right.
8 With the high beams on, the high intensity zone should be vertically centered with the exact center just below the horizontal line. **Note:** *It may not be possible to position the headlight aim exactly for both high and low beams. If a compromise must be used, keep in mind that the low beams are the most used and have the greatest effect on driver safety.*

---

12 Bulb replacement

Refer to illustrations 12.2, 12.3, 12.12, 12.14, 12.17a, 12.17b, 12.20, 12.22, 12.24, 12.28 and 12.34

1 Detach the cable from the negative terminal of the battery before attempting to replace any of the following bulbs.

Front turn signal/sidemarker lights

2 Remove the outer headlight (refer to Section 11) and remove both turn signal lens retaining screws (**see illustration**).

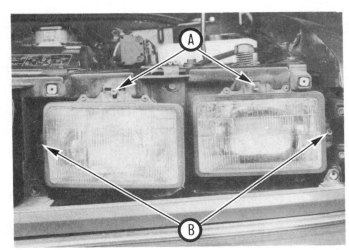

11.2 Each headlight has a horizontal (A) and a vertical (B) adjusting screw

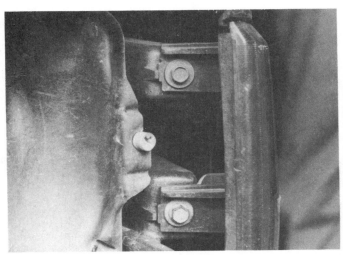

12.2 To replace the turn signal/sidemarker bulb, remove both lens assembly retaining screws

12

3   Pull the turn signal lens assembly forward until the retaining clip **(see illustration)** slides free of the front fender.
4   Turn the bulb holder counterclockwise and remove it from the turn signal lens assembly.

12.3   Pull the lens assembly forward until the retaining clip pops loose from the fender

5   Turn the bulb counterclockwise and remove it from the bulb holder.
6   Installation is the reverse of removal.

Front parking lights

7   Reach under the bumper and locate the bulb holder. Turn it counterclockwise and pull it out of the lamp assembly.
8   To remove the bulb from the holder, depress it and turn it counterclockwise.
9   Installation is the reverse of removal.

Fog lights (if equipped)

10   Some vehicles are equipped with optional fog lights. Bulb replacement requires disassembly of the unit.
11   Unplug the electrical connector from the fog light pigtail lead and remove the fog light assembly from the mounting bracket.
12   Referring to the accompanying exploded view of a typical fog light assembly, disassemble the unit **(see illustration)**, remove the old bulb, install a new one and reassemble the fog light.
13   Install the fog light on the mounting bracket.

Rear turn signal lights

14   If the turn signal lens assembly on your vehicle is similar to the one shown **(see illustration)**, refer to Steps 15 and 16.
15   Raise the trunk lid and remove both turn signal lens retaining screws from the rear taillight trim section.
16   Slide the lens assembly toward the side of the vehicle until it is free.
17   If the turn signal lens on your vehicle is similar to either of the others shown **(see illustrations)**, refer to Steps 18 and 19.
18   Open the trunk lid and remove the plastic wing nuts inside the back wall of the trunk.
19   Pull the lens assembly out of the rear trim section.

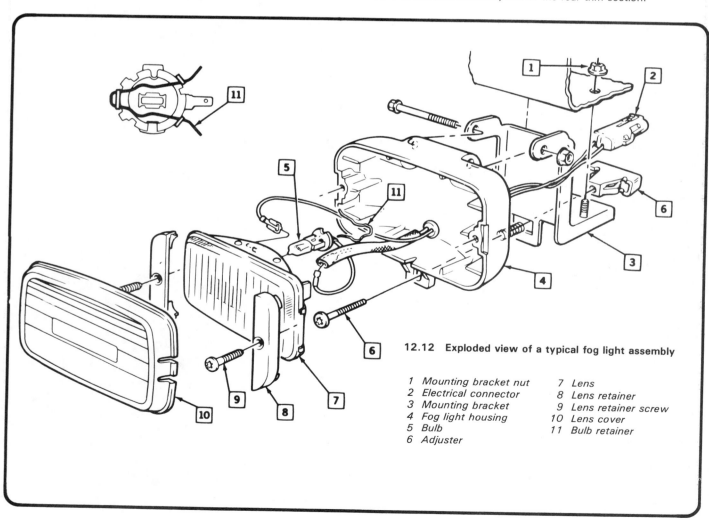

12.12   Exploded view of a typical fog light assembly

1 *Mounting bracket nut*	7 *Lens*
2 *Electrical connector*	8 *Lens retainer*
3 *Mounting bracket*	9 *Lens retainer screw*
4 *Fog light housing*	10 *Lens cover*
5 *Bulb*	11 *Bulb retainer*
6 *Adjuster*	

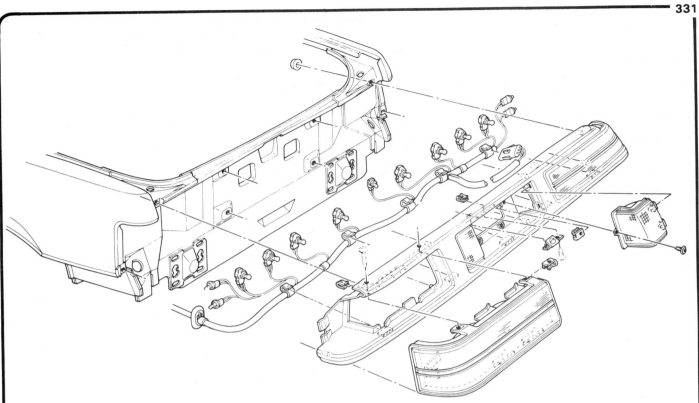

12.14 Exploded view of a typical taillight assembly retained by screws in the top of the rear trim section

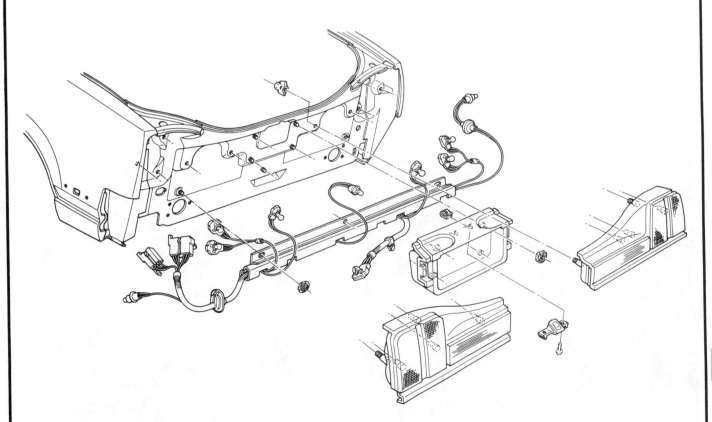

12.17a Exploded view of a typical taillight assembly retained by plastic nuts inside the trunk

12

20 To remove the bulb holder (all types), depress the locking lever with your thumb **(see illustration)** and turn the holder counterclockwise.
21 Turn the bulb counterclockwise and remove it.
22 Installation is the reverse of removal for both types of turn signal assemblies. If you are installing the slide-out type lens assembly, note that the tabs on the bottom of the lens assembly slide into slots in the rear trim section **(see illustration)**.

Backup lights

23 Remove the license plate.
24 Remove the backup lens assembly retaining screw **(see illustra-**

tion) and remove the lens assembly.
25 To remove the bulb holder, turn it counterclockwise.
26 Remove the bulb from the holder.
27 Installation is the reverse of removal.

Dome light

28 Pry off the plastic dome light lens with a small screwdriver **(see illustration)**.
29 Pull the bulb straight out.
30 Installation is the reverse of removal.

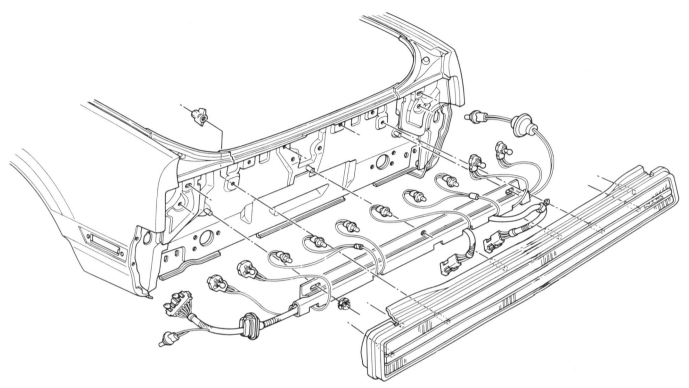

12.17b Exploded view of another typical taillight assembly retained by plastic wing nuts inside the trunk

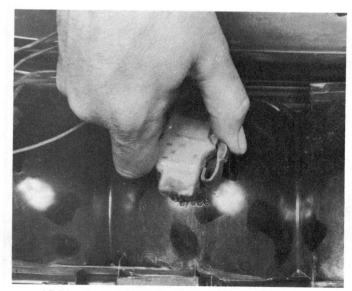

12.20 To release a bulb holder from the taillight lens assembly, depress the locking lever with your thumb and turn the holder counterclockwise

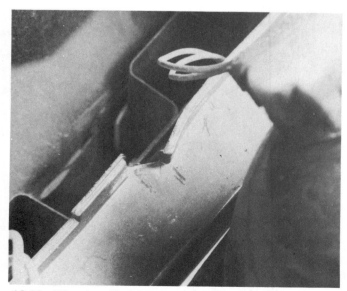

12.22 When installing the slide-out type lens assembly, make sure that the tabs on the bottom of the lens assembly slide into the grooves along the edge of the rear trim section

Courtesy lights

31 Courtesy lights are located in various spots. Most vehicles have a light under the left side of the dash and one in the glove box.
32 To replace a bulb in the glovebox, open the glovebox door, pry loose the lens located in the ceiling of the glove box and pull the bulb straight out. Installation is the reverse of removal.
33 To replace a bulb in the panel under the dash, remove the two screws retaining the under-dash panel and allow it to hang down.
34 Turn the bulb holder **(see illustration)** counterclockwise and remove it from the under-dash panel.
35 To remove the bulb from the holder, turn it counterclockwise and pull out.
36 Installation is the reverse of removal.

Instrument panel lights

37 Remove the instrument panel (Section 15).
38 Turn the instrument panel upside down and lay it down on a clean work surface or shop rag.

39 Turn the bulb holder counterclockwise and pull it out of the back of the instrument panel case.
40 Pull the bulb straight out from the bulb holder.
41 Installation is the reverse of removal.

---

13 Radio and speakers — removal and installation

Refer to illustrations 13.2, 13.3, 13.5, 13.7, 13.8, 13.13, 13.16a, 13.16b, 13.21, 13.22, 13.23 and 13.24
1 Detach the cable from the negative terminal of the battery prior to performing any of the following procedures.

Radio

2 Carefully pry up the forward end of the console trim plate **(see illustration)**. **Caution:** *If you attempt to remove the radio trim plate without loosening the forward end of the console trim plate you will damage the lower end of the radio trim plate.*

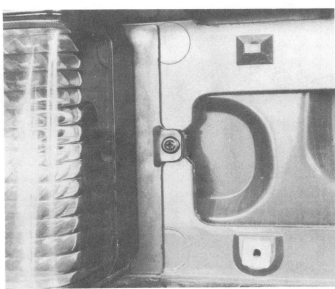

12.24 To remove the backup lens assembly, remove the license plate and this retaining screw

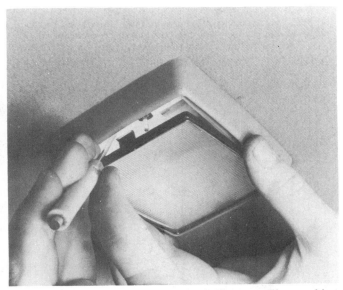

12.28 To replace a dome light, pop the lens cover loose with a small screwdriver and pull the old bulb straight out of the holder

12.34 A typical courtesy light located in the swing-down under-dash panel — turn the holder counterclockwise to detach it from the panel

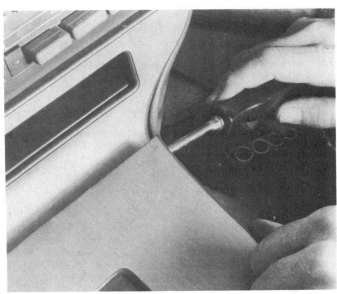

13.2 Prior to removing the radio console trim plate, pop loose the forward end of the console trim plate or you will damage the lower end of the radio trim plate during removal

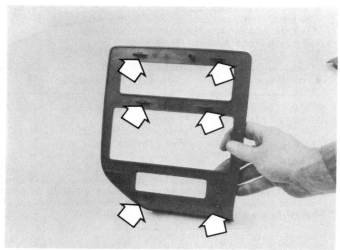

13.3   The radio trim plate has six tabs (arrows) on the back —
when prying it loose from the dashboard, concentrate your prying
efforts to these areas to prevent damage to the plate

13.5   Once the console extension panel is removed,
remove the console heater duct

13.7   To remove the radio, remove the two retaining
screws (arrows)

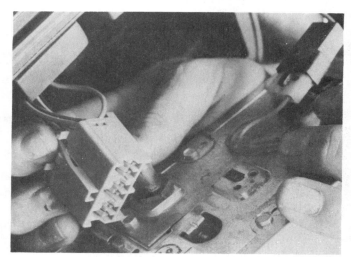

13.8   After pulling the radio out of the dashboard, detach
all electrical connectors

3   Carefully pry the console radio trim plate loose. The back of the trim plate has six tabs **(see illustration)** that must be pried loose from their respective metal clips in the dashboard.
4   Remove the right side console extension panel screws and remove the panel.
5   Remove the console heater duct **(see illustration)**.
6   Reach behind the radio and disconnect the antenna lead.
7   Remove the radio retaining screws **(see illustration)**.
8   Pull the radio out of the console and detach the electrical connectors **(see illustration)**.
9   Remove the radio.
10 Installation is the reverse of removal.

Speakers

Dashboard speakers

11 Remove the pod retaining screws from the pods on either side of the instrument panel and remove both pods.
12 Remove both retaining screws from the instrument panel retaining plate along the upper edge of the instrument panel.
13 Pop loose the dashboard pad above the glove box.
14 Remove the screws from the lower edge of the center heating and air conditioning vent and remove the vent. Remove the retaining screws from the vents at both ends of the dashboard and remove both vents.
15 Pop loose and remove the defroster vent covers from the top of

of the dashboard cover.
16 Remove all dashboard cover retaining bolts **(see illustrations)**. **Note:** *Don't forget the screws hidden in the top of each control pod cavity (not shown in the above illustrations).*
17 Raise the dashboard cover and detach the electrical connectors from both speakers, then remove the cover from the vehicle.
18 Turn the dashboard cover upside down and remove the speaker screws.
19 Installation is the reverse of removal.

Rear speakers

20 Open the trunk lid and locate the speakers (they're affixed to the underside of the package tray).
21 Remove the plastic wing nuts **(see illustration)** from the inner end of the speaker enclosure.
22 The outer end of the speaker enclosure has a hooked lip **(see illustration)** that hangs from a body reinforcement member. To disengage it from the reinforcement member, lift it up. Remove the enclosure.
23 Detach the speaker retaining clip **(see illustration)** from the underside of the package tray.
24 Allow the speaker assembly to swing down, then detach the outer end **(see illustration)** from the reinforcement member.
25 Unplug the electrical connector from the speaker and remove the speaker assembly.
26 Installation is the reverse of removal.

13.16a To remove the dashboard cover, remove the screw from each control pod cavity (not shown) and the bolts from both ends of the dashboard (left end shown) . . .

13.16b . . . and the two bolts (arrows) immediately above the instrument panel (not visible or accessible unless you have removed the retaining plate along the top of the instrument panel)

13.21 To remove either of the rear speaker enclosures, first remove the plastic wing nuts from the inner end of the enclosure

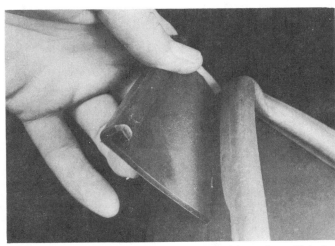

13.22 Lift the outer, hooked end (removed from the vehicle for clarity in this photo) off its corresponding tab on the package tray reinforcement member and remove the enclosure

13.23 To remove the speaker assembly from the vehicle, first disconnect this wire retaining clip from its corresponding hook on the underside of the package tray . . .

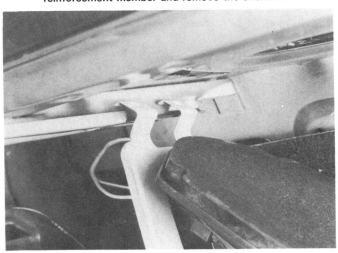

13.24 . . . then unhook the other end of the speaker from the slots in the package tray reinforcement member and lower the speaker far enough to unplug the electrical connector and remove the speaker assembly

12

14   Radio antenna — removal and installation

Refer to illustrations 14.1 and 14.2

Non-extendable antenna

1   Simply unscrew the old antenna mast (see illustration) and install a new unit.

Extendable antenna

2   Remove the locking nut (see illustration).
3   Turn the ignition to ACC and turn the radio on to extend the antenna

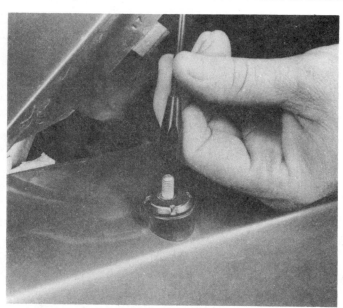

14.1   If the antenna on your vehicle is non-extendable (fixed), simply loosen it with a wrench and unscrew it

and toothed cable out of the motor assembly.
4   Detach the cable from the negative terminal of the battery.
5   Remove the contact spring from the antenna and clean it.
6   Insert the new antenna into the antenna drive assembly. **Note:** *The toothed side of the plastic cable must face the antenna motor to prevent damage to the motor assembly (see the arrow in the accompanying illustration).*
7   Insert the plastic cable into the tube assembly until resistance is felt (about 12 inches).
8   Install the battery cable, turn the radio off and hold the toothed

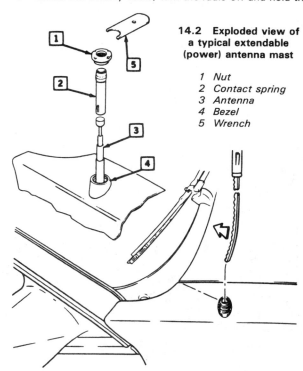

14.2   **Exploded view of a typical extendable (power) antenna mast**

1   Nut
2   Contact spring
3   Antenna
4   Bezel
5   Wrench

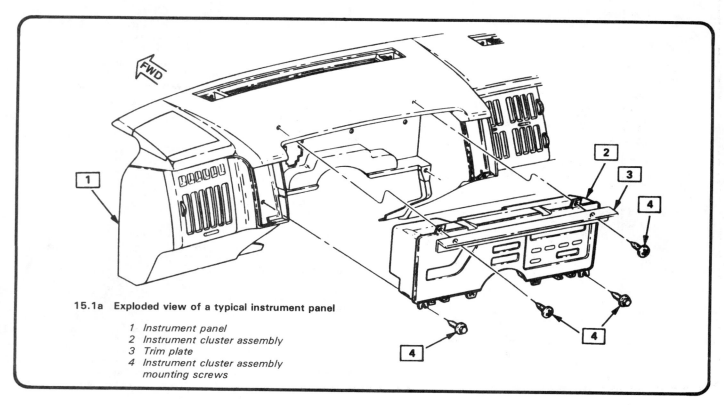

15.1a   **Exploded view of a typical instrument panel**

1   Instrument panel
2   Instrument cluster assembly
3   Trim plate
4   Instrument cluster assembly mounting screws

cable and antenna in position until they retract into the antenna assembly.

9 Insert the antenna into the antenna assembly and install the contact spring with the flanged end facing upward.

10 Install the nut.

11 Cycle the antenna several times to check its operation. At first, the antenna may only extend or retract halfway. Cycle it until it fully extends and retracts.

15 Instrument panel — removal and installation

Refer to illustrations 15.1a, 15.1b, 15.1c, 15.2 and 15.5

1 Remove the instrument panel trim plate **(see illustrations)**.

2 Some vehicles are equipped with a steering column collar and steering column filler plate **(see illustration)** which must be removed before the instrument panel can be removed. If your vehicle is equipped with

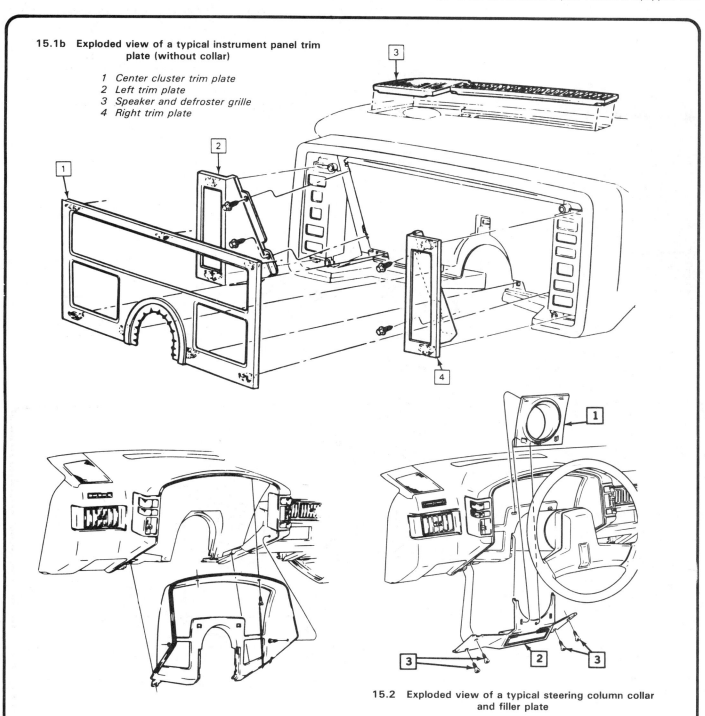

15.1b Exploded view of a typical instrument panel trim plate (without collar)

1 *Center cluster trim plate*
2 *Left trim plate*
3 *Speaker and defroster grille*
4 *Right trim plate*

15.1c Exploded view of a typical instrument panel trim plate (with collar)

15.2 Exploded view of a typical steering column collar and filler plate

1 *Steering column collar*
2 *Steering column filler plate*
3 *Filler plate retaining screws*

12

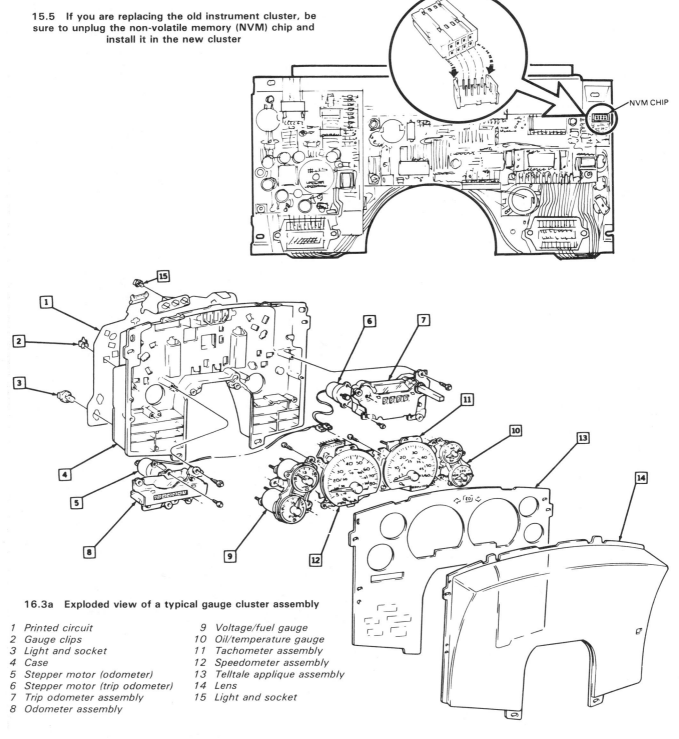

15.5 If you are replacing the old instrument cluster, be sure to unplug the non-volatile memory (NVM) chip and install it in the new cluster

NVM CHIP

16.3a   Exploded view of a typical gauge cluster assembly

1 *Printed circuit*	9 *Voltage/fuel gauge*
2 *Gauge clips*	10 *Oil/temperature gauge*
3 *Light and socket*	11 *Tachometer assembly*
4 *Case*	12 *Speedometer assembly*
5 *Stepper motor (odometer)*	13 *Telltale applique assembly*
6 *Stepper motor (trip odometer)*	14 *Lens*
7 *Trip odometer assembly*	15 *Light and socket*
8 *Odometer assembly*	

a collar and filler plate, pinch together the four slide clips along the bottom seam between the collar filler plate and detach them and slide the collar up the steering column.

3   Remove the instrument panel retaining screws.

4   Pull the instrument panel from its cavity in the dashboard and unplug all electrical connectors, then remove the instrument panel.

5   If you are replacing the old instrument panel with a new one, be sure to remove the non-volatile memory (NVM) chip and install it into the new panel **(see illustration)**. **Note:** *The NVM is usually somewhere near the odometer.*

6   Installation is the reverse of removal.

---

16   Instruments — removal and installation

Refer to illustrations 16.3a, 16.3b, 16.3c, 16.4 and 16.5

1   Remove the instrument panel (see Section 15).

2   Turn the instrument panel upside down and lay it down on a clean work surface.

3   Remove the printed circuit/case assembly screws and separate the case from the cluster assembly **(see illustrations)**.

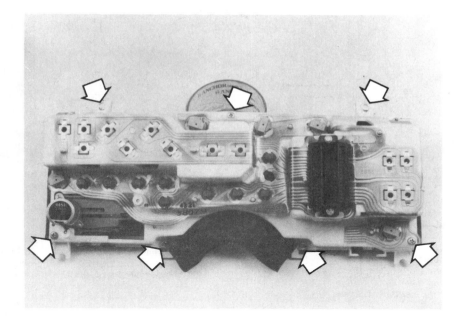

16.3b The printed circuit/case side of a typical instrument cluster assembly — to remove it, take out the screws (arrows)

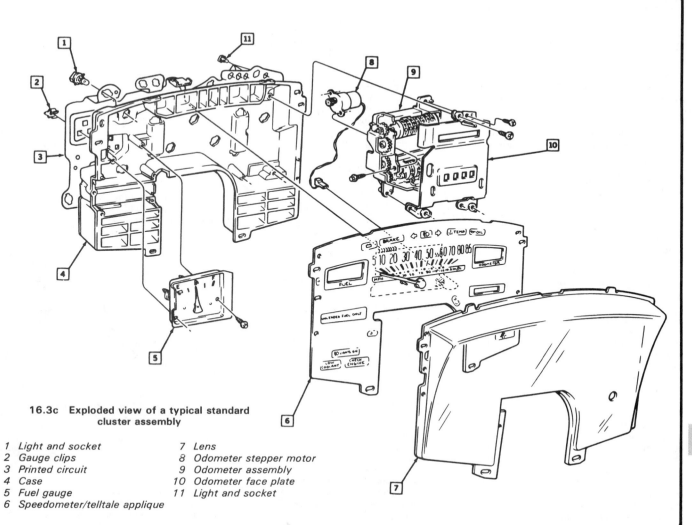

16.3c Exploded view of a typical standard cluster assembly

1 Light and socket
2 Gauge clips
3 Printed circuit
4 Case
5 Fuel gauge
6 Speedometer/telltale applique
7 Lens
8 Odometer stepper motor
9 Odometer assembly
10 Odometer face plate
11 Light and socket

12

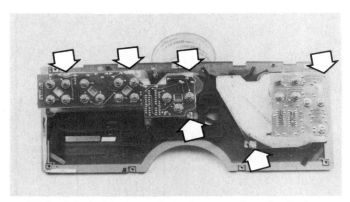

**16.4   A typical instrument panel as seen from the back —
to remove an instrument from the panel, remove the
retaining screws (arrows)**

4   Remove the screws retaining the faulty instrument(s) **(see illustration)**. **Note:** *Some instruments can be replaced individually but others can only be replaced as an assembly. Consult your dealer for information regarding the various replacement gauges for the instrument cluster in your vehicle.*
5   Remove the instrument. **Note:** *If you are replacing the speedometer, there may be a pigtail lead plugged into a spade type terminal on the printed circuit board behind the speedometer. Be sure to unplug it* **(see illustration)**.
6   Installation is the reverse of removal.

17   Rear window defogger — check and repair

Refer to illustrations 17.5 and 17.11

1   This option consists of a rear window with a number of horizontal elements baked into the glass surface during the glass forming operation.
2   Small breaks in the element can be successfully repaired without removing the rear window.
3   To test the grids for proper operation, start the engine and turn on the system.
4   Ground one lead of a test light and carefully touch the other lead to each element line.
5   The brilliance of the test light should increase as the lead is moved across the element **(see illustration)**. If the test light glows brightly at both ends of the lines, check for a loose ground wire. All of the lines should be checked in at least two places.
6   To repair a break in a line, it is recommended that a repair kit specifically for this purpose be purchased from a GM dealer. Included in the repair kit will be a decal, a container of silver plastic and hardener, a mixing stick and instructions.
7   To repair a break, first turn off the system and allow it to de-energize for a few minutes.
8   Lightly buff the element area with fine steel wool, then clean it thoroughly with alcohol.
9   Use the decal supplied in the repair kit or apply strips of electrician's tape above and below the area to be repaired. The space between the pieces of tape should be the same width as the existing lines. This can be checked from outside the vehicle. Press the tape tightly against the glass to prevent seepage.
10   Mix the hardener and silver plastic thoroughly.
11   Using the wood spatula, apply the silver plastic mixture between the pieces of tape, overlapping the undamaged area slightly on either end **(see illustration)**.
12   Carefully remove the decal or tape and apply a constant stream of hot air directly to the repaired area. A heat gun set at 500 to 700 degrees Fahrenheit is recommended. Hold the gun one inch from the glass for two minutes.
13   If the new element appears off color, tincture of iodine can be used to clean the repair and bring it back to the proper color. This mixture should not remain on the repair for more than 30 seconds.
14   Although the defogger is now fully operational, the repaired area should not be disturbed for at least 24 hours.

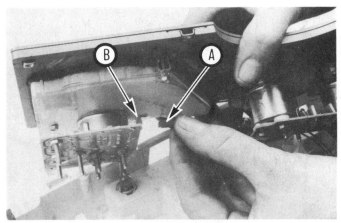

16.5   When removing the speedometer from an instrument cluster, be sure to detach the electrical connector (A) from the spade terminal (B) on the back of the speedometer printed circuit

ZONES OF BULB BRILLIANCE

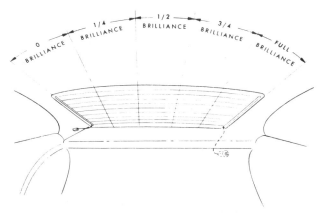

17.5   The brilliance of a test light should vary in brightness when the rear window defogger is functioning normally

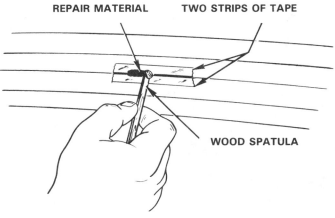

17.11   To repair a broken grid, apply a strip of tape to either side of the grid, then apply the proper mixture of hardener and silver plastic with a small wooden stick or spatula

18.4 Remove the vent grille screws, raise the vent, then remove the washer hose nozzle retaining screw and detach the washer hose and nozzle from the vent grille

18.5 Once the vent grille is out of the way, remove the linkage arm nut and detach the linkage from the windshield wiper motor

18.6 Remove the windshield wiper mounting bolts (arrows) — the third bolt, which is at the bottom of the motor, is not visible in this photo

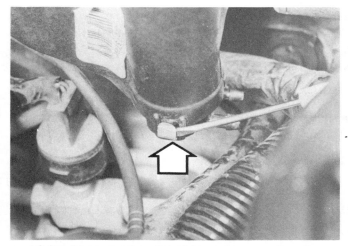

18.9a To remove the windshield washer pump from the wiper motor, pry out the clip (arrow) with a small screwdriver

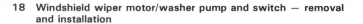

18 Windshield wiper motor/washer pump and switch — removal and installation

Refer to illustrations 18.4, 18.5, 18.6, 18.9a, 18.9b, 18.10a and 18.10b

1 Detach the cable from the negative terminal of the battery before performing either of the following procedures.

Windshield wiper motor/washer pump

2 Unplug the electrical connectors from the motor and the pump.
3 Detach the hoses from the washer pump.
4 Remove the vent grille from the left side of the vehicle. Be sure to detach the washer hose and nozzle **(see illustration)**. Note: *The grilles in some vehicles are retained with plastic pop fasteners instead of screws. Be careful when removing these fasteners or you will break them.*
5 Disconnect the transmission linkage arm **(see illustration)**.
6 Remove the motor mounting bolts **(see illustration)**.
7 Remove the motor. If you are replacing the motor, be sure to switch the washer pump to the new motor (see Step 9 below).
8 Installation is the reverse of removal.
9 If you are just replacing the windshield washer pump, remove the small locking clip **(see illustration)** and pull the pump from the bottom of the motor **(see illustration)**.

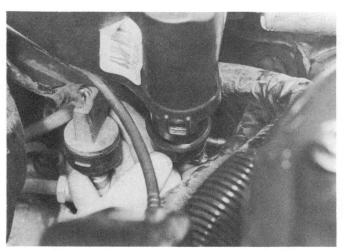

18.9b To detach the washer pump from the windshield wiper motor, pull straight down — the pump is sealed by a rubber O-ring and the top end of the pump is plugged into a socket at the top of the pump cavity so you will encounter some resistance until the pump pulls loose

12

Switch

10 Remove the mounting screw(s) from the windshield wiper motor switch **(see illustrations)**.
11 Remove the switch from the dash and unplug the electrical connectors.
12 Installation is the reverse of removal.

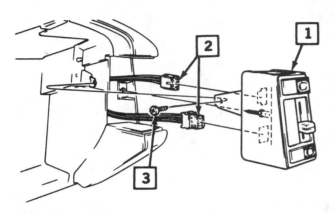

18.10a Exploded view of a typical windshield wiper switch assembly

1 Windshield wiper and rear window defogger switch
2 Wiper and rear window defogger switch electrical connector
3 Attaching screw

19 Horn — removal and installation

Refer to illustration 19.2

1 Detach the cable from the negative terminal of the battery.
2 Locate the horn behind the front bumper **(see illustration)**.
3 Unplug the electrical connector to the horn.
4 Remove the horn mounting bracket bolt.
5 Remove the horn.
6 Installation is the reverse of removal.

20 Cruise control system — general check and repair

Refer to illustrations 20.2, 20.3 and 20.5

1 Servicing the cruise control system is beyond the scope of the home mechanic. However, there are a few simple visual inspections you should make to ensure that the cruise control on your vehicle remains in good working order.
2 Inspect the vacuum hoses **(see illustration)**. Make sure that they are in good condition and firmly attached to their respective fittings. If any hose is cracked or damaged, replace it.
3 Check the electrical connector **(see illustration)** for a tight fit and inspect it for any evidence of dirt, corrosion or moisture. If any of these symptoms are evident, clean the plug thoroughly.
4 Inspect the servo diaphragm for tears or other damage. If such damage is evident, have it replaced.

Cruise release/vacuum release valves

5 If your vehicle's cruise control system fails to release when the brake pedal is applied on a vehicle equipped with an automatic trans-

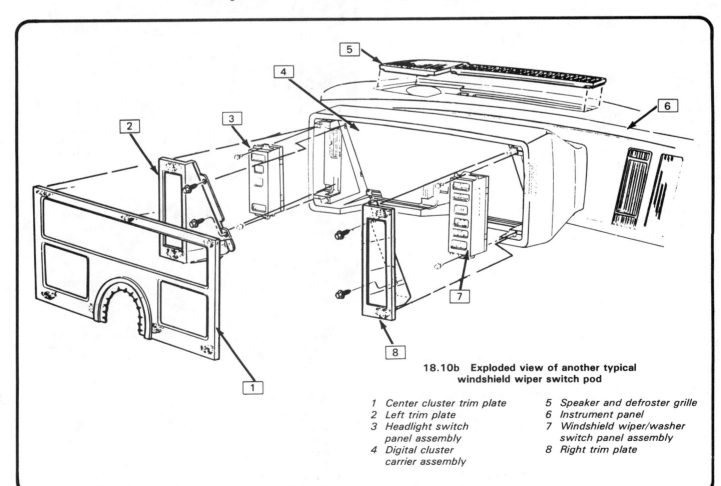

18.10b Exploded view of another typical windshield wiper switch pod

1 Center cluster trim plate
2 Left trim plate
3 Headlight switch panel assembly
4 Digital cluster carrier assembly
5 Speaker and defroster grille
6 Instrument panel
7 Windshield wiper/washer switch panel assembly
8 Right trim plate

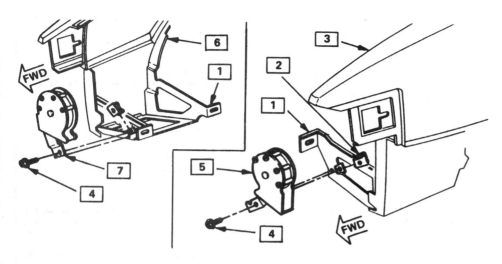

19.2 Exploded view of typical left and right horn assemblies

1 Fender supports
2 U-nut
3 Left fender assembly
4 Retaining screw
5 Left horn
6 Right fender assembly
7 Right horn

axle, or when the brake or clutch pedal are applied on a vehicle equipped with a manual transaxle, check the cruise release valve or vacuum release valve at the pedal **(see illustration)**.

6   If your vehicle is equipped with an automatic transaxle, make sure that the electrical connectors are firmly attached to the vacuum release valve assembly and the switch assembly and the vacuum line is firmly attached to the vacuum release valve assembly.

7   If your vehicle is equipped with a manual transaxle, make sure that the electrical connector is firmly attached to the switch assembly and the vacuum line is firmly attached to the cruise release valve assembly.

8   If everything looks properly attached, the cruise release valve (manual transaxle) or the vacuum release valve (automatic transaxle) is faulty.

9   To remove the cruise release/vacuum release valve, unplug the electrical connector (automatic only) and detach the vacuum hose, turn the retainer counterclockwise and pull out the retainer and cruise/vacuum release valve assembly.

10   Separate the retainer and cruise/vacuum release valve.

11   Install the retainer.

12   With the brake pedal depressed, insert the valve into the tubular retainer until the valve seats on the retainer. Note that ''clicks'' can be heard as the threaded portion of the valve is pushed through the retainer toward the brake pedal.

13   Pull the brake pedal fully rearward against the pedal stop until the ''click'' sounds cease. The valve is now adjusted.

14   Release the brake pedal and repeat Step 11 to verify that no ''click'' sounds can be heard.

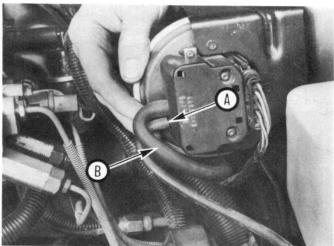

20.2 Periodically inspect the vacuum hoses between the vacuum diaphragm/servo and the intake manifold (A) and the cruise/vacuum release valve assembly (B)

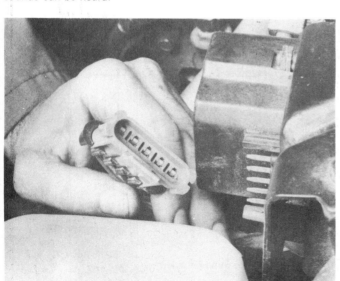

20.3 Inspect the cruise control assembly electrical connector for the presence of dirt, moisture or corrosion

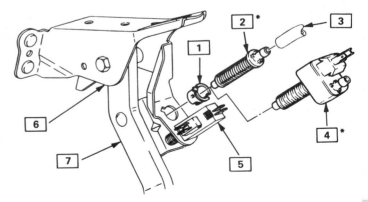

20.5 Exploded view of a typical self-adjusting cruise release/vacuum release valve assembly

1 Retainer
2 Cruise release valve assembly (manual transaxle)
3 Vacuum hose from servo
4 Vacuum release valve assembly (automatic transaxle)
5 Switch assembly
6 Pedal assembly
7 Brake pedal mounting bracket

12

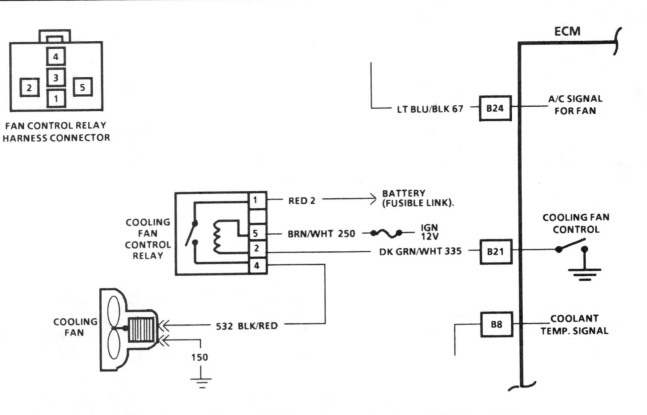

Cooling fan wiring diagram (2.5L four cylinder engine shown, 2.0L turbo similar)

A Pin E8 on 2.0L turbo models   **B** Pin E16 on 2.0L turbo models

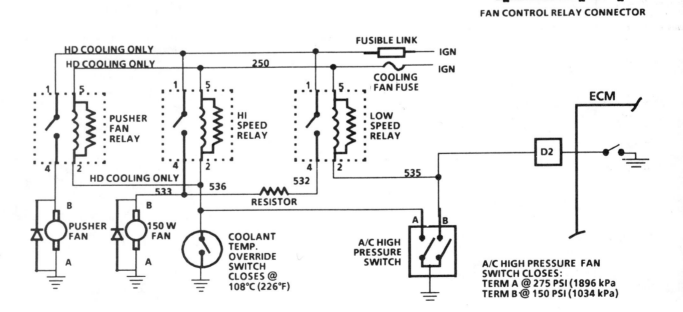

Cooling fan wiring diagram — V6 engine (1987 model shown, others similar)

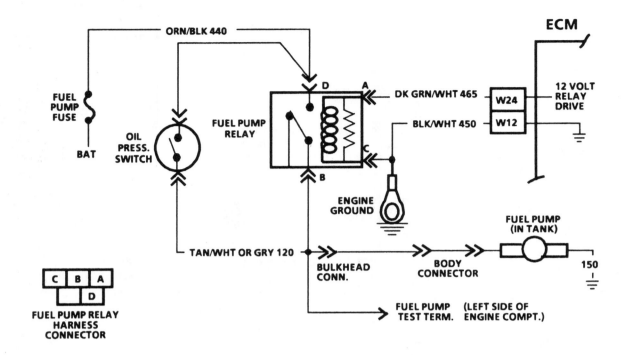

Fuel pump control wiring diagram — 2.5L four cylinder engine (2.0L turbo similar)

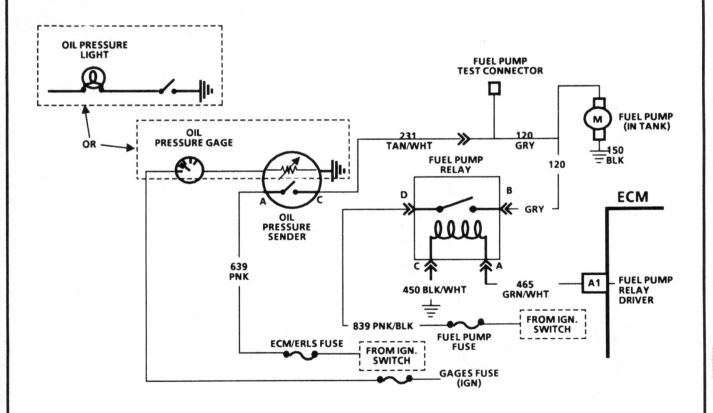

Fuel pump control wiring diagram — V6 engine

12

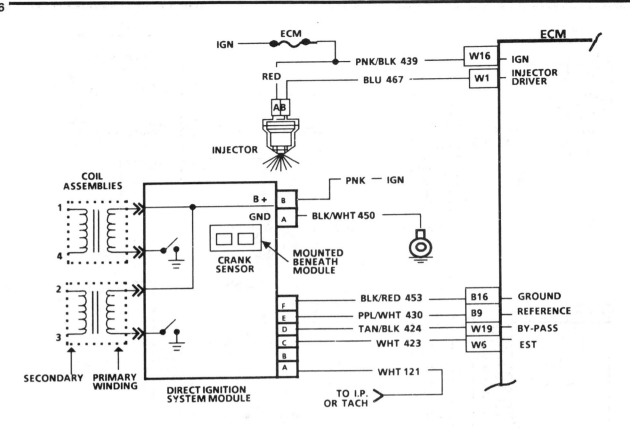

Direct Ignition System (DIS) schematic — 2.5L four cylinder engine

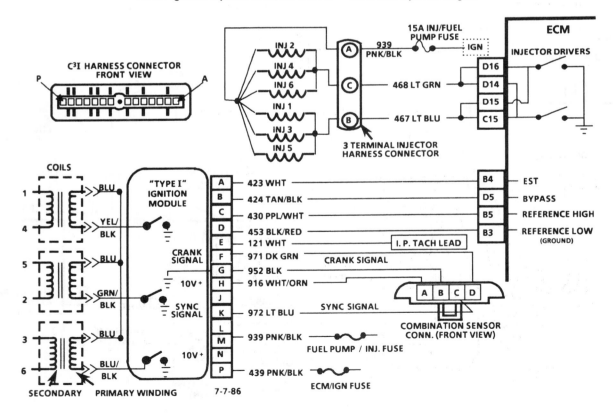

Computer Controlled Coil Ignition system schematic

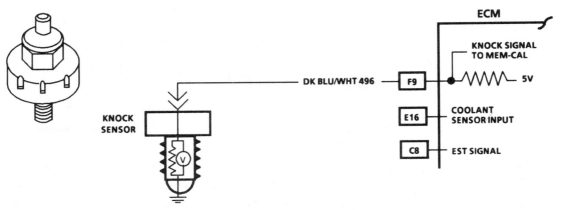

Knock sensor wiring diagram — 2.0L turbo

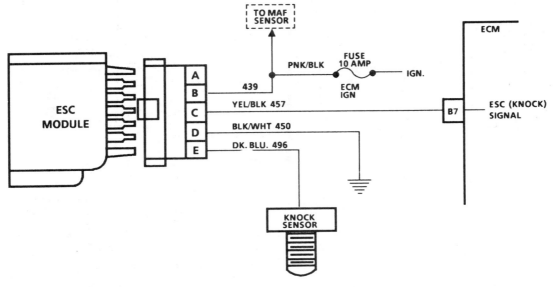

Electronic Spark Control (ESC) wiring diagram

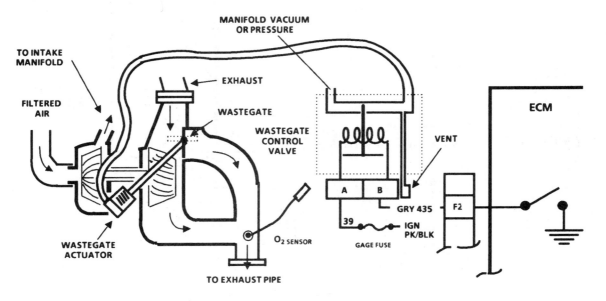

Wastegate control valve wiring diagram (2.0L turbocharged engine only)

Starting system wiring diagram — 4 cylinder models

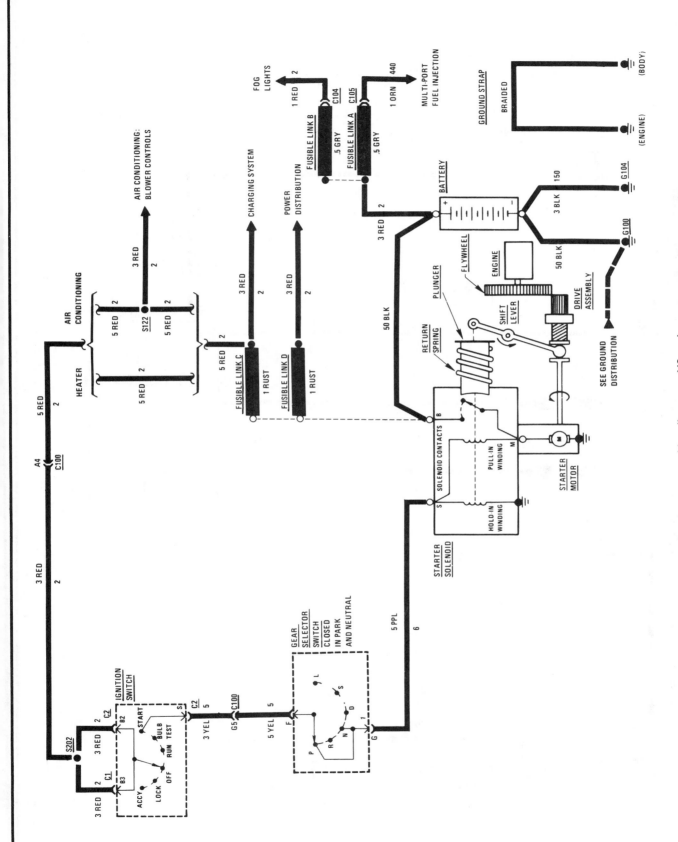

Starting system wiring diagram — V6 engine

12

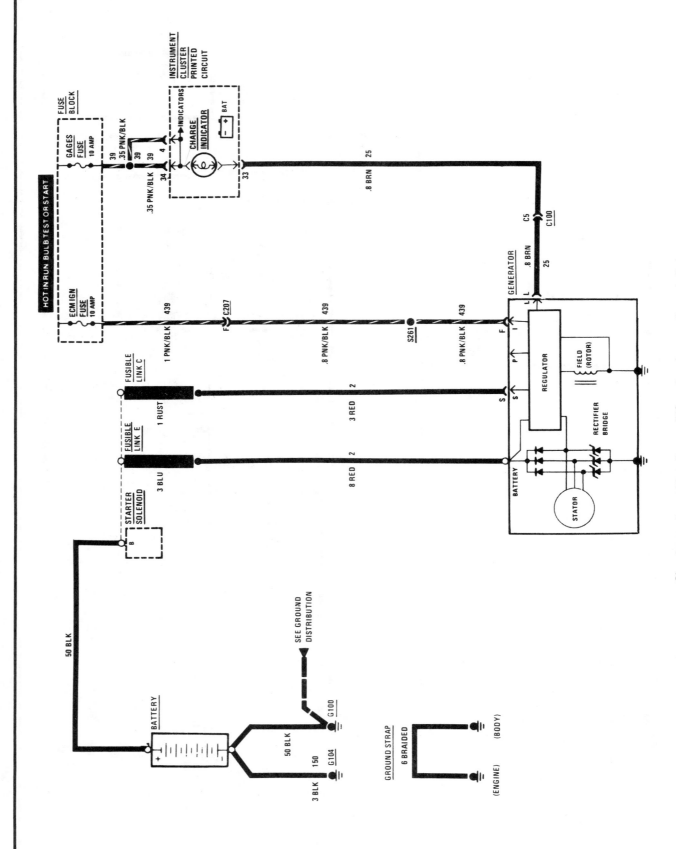

Charging system wiring diagram (V6 engine shown, others similar)

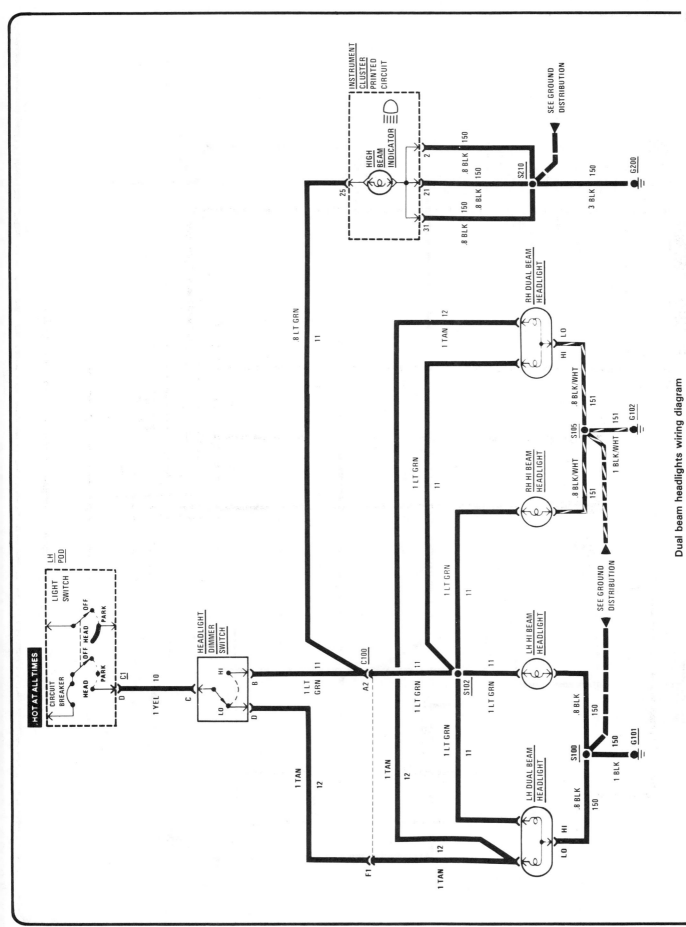

Dual beam headlights wiring diagram

12

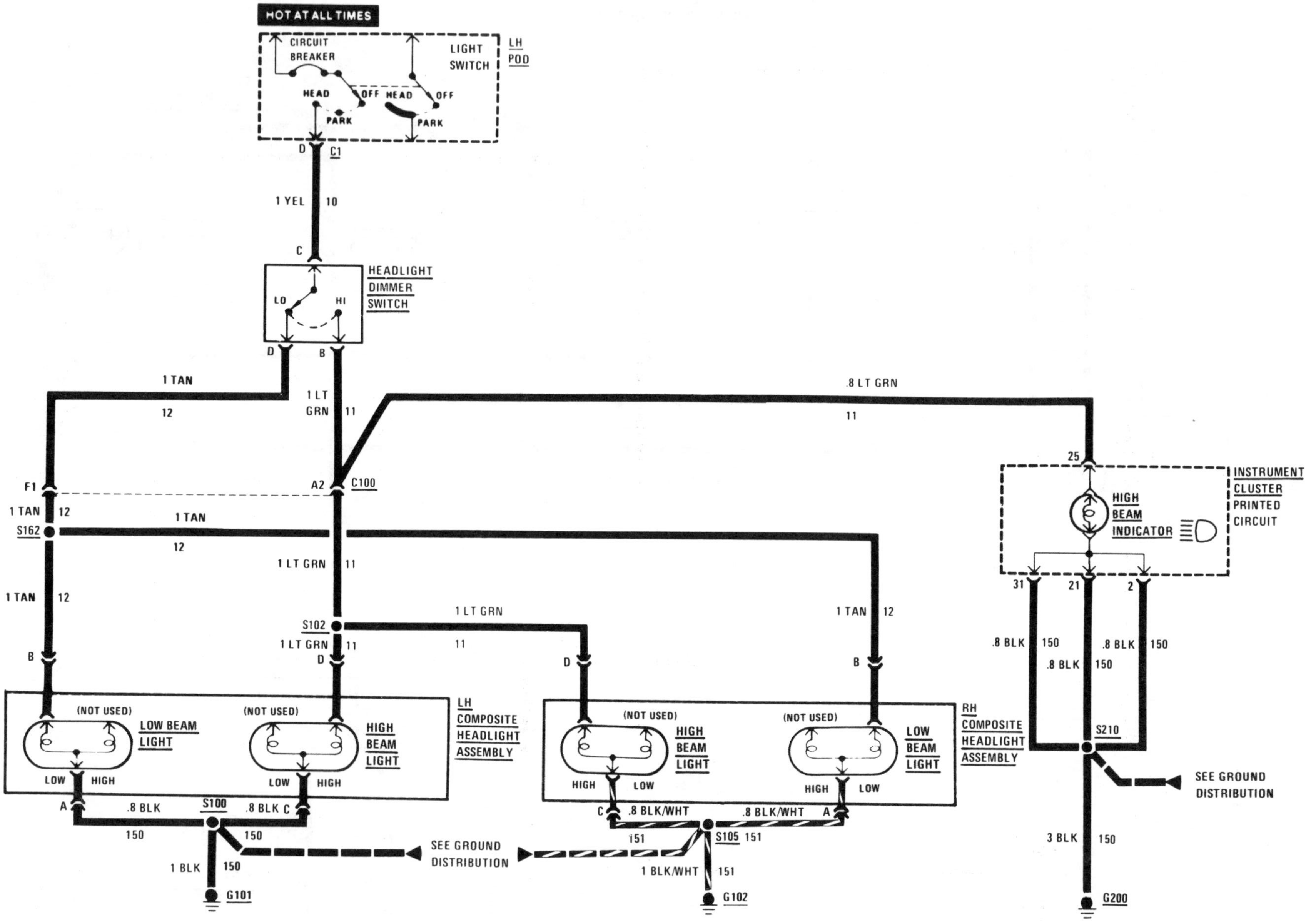

Composite headlights wiring diagram

INSTRUMENT CLUSTER PRINTED CIRCUIT

SEE GROUND DISTRIBUTION

HIGH BEAM INDICATOR

2   .8 BLK   150
21   .8 BLK   150
31   .8 BLK   150

S210

150

G200

3 BLK   150

25

.8 LT GRN

11

RH COMPOSITE HEADLIGHT ASSEMBLY

LOW BEAM LIGHT

1 TAN   12
B

(NOT USED)

HIGH   LOW

HIGH BEAM LIGHT

(NOT USED)

HIGH   LOW

.8 BLK/WHT   A

.8 BLK/WHT   151

S105   151

G102

1 BLK/WHT   151

C

D

1 LT GRN

11

LH COMPOSITE HEADLIGHT ASSEMBLY

SEE GROUND DISTRIBUTION

HIGH BEAM LIGHT

HIGH   HIGH

(NOT USED)

LOW

.8 BLK   C

150

G101

1 BLK   150

S100

.8 BLK   150

LOW BEAM LIGHT

(NOT USED)

HIGH   LOW

A

LH POD

LIGHT SWITCH

OFF   PARK
HEAD
OFF   HEAD   PARK

CIRCUIT BREAKER   HEAD   PARK

HOT AT ALL TIMES

C1   D

1 YEL   10

C

HEADLIGHT DIMMER SWITCH

HI

LO

B   11   1 LT GRN

C100   A2

1 LT GRN   11

S102   1 LT GRN   D   11

D

1 TAN   12

1 TAN   12

F1   12

S162   12

1 TAN   B   12

1 TAN

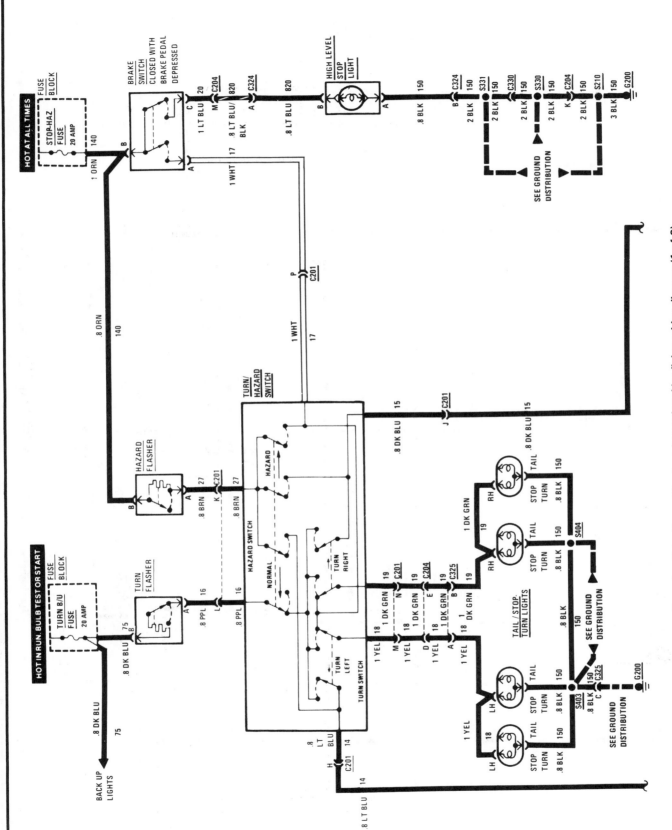

Turn signal/stop/hazard/front marker and parking lights wiring diagram (1 of 2)

12

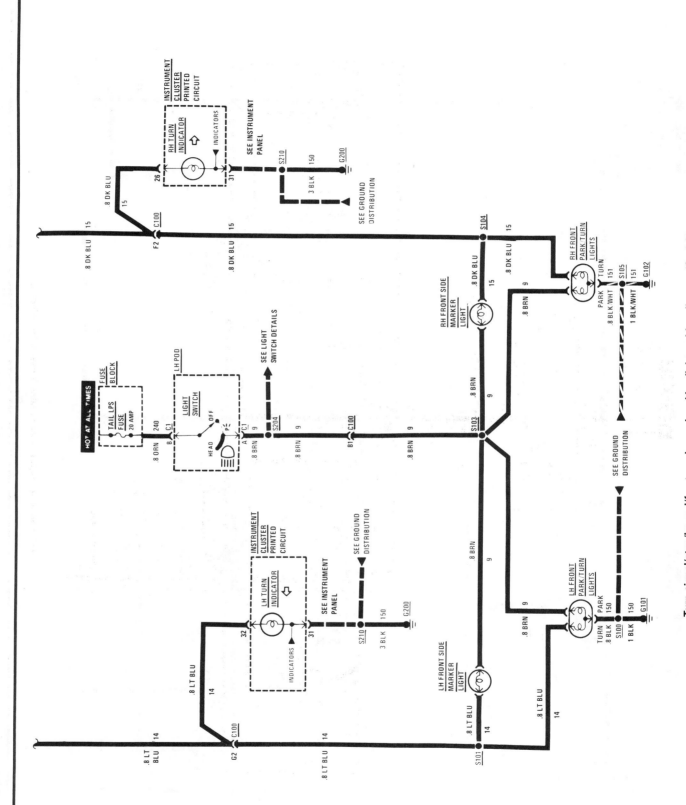

Turn signal/stop/hazard/front marker and parking lights wiring diagram (2 of 2)

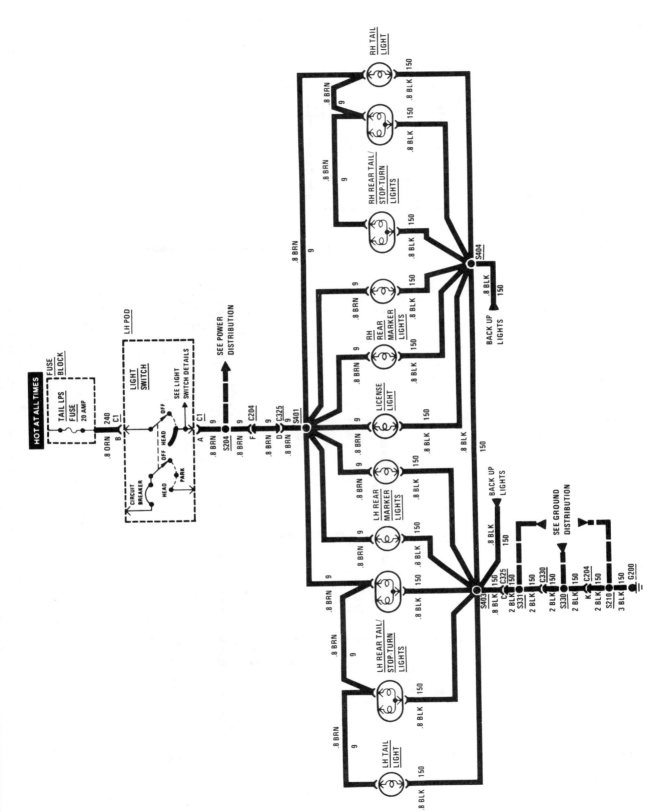

Tail lights/rear marker/license plate lights wiring diagram

12

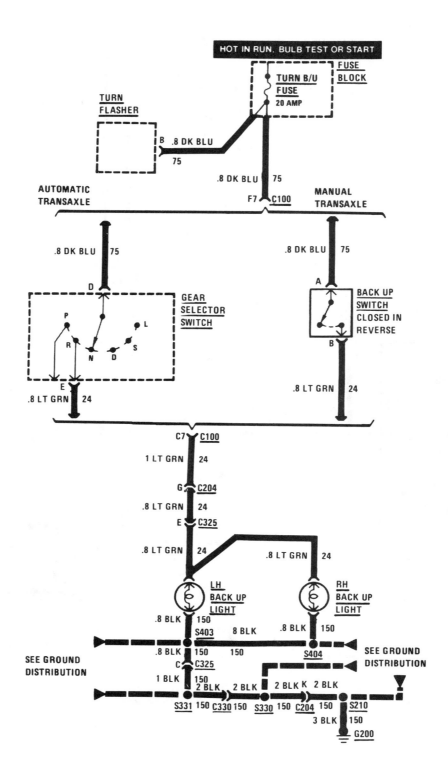

HOT IN RUN, BULB TEST OR START

TURN FLASHER

TURN B/U FUSE 20 AMP

FUSE BLOCK

B .8 DK BLU 75

.8 DK BLU 75

AUTOMATIC TRANSAXLE

MANUAL TRANSAXLE

F7 C100

.8 DK BLU 75

.8 DK BLU 75

D

GEAR SELECTOR SWITCH

P

R

N D S

L

E

.8 LT GRN 24

A

BACK UP SWITCH CLOSED IN REVERSE

B

.8 LT GRN 24

C7 C100

1 LT GRN 24

G C204

.8 LT GRN 24

E C325

.8 LT GRN 24

.8 LT GRN 24

LH BACK UP LIGHT

RH BACK UP LIGHT

.8 BLK 150

S403 8 BLK

.8 BLK 150

SEE GROUND DISTRIBUTION

.8 BLK 150 150

S404

SEE GROUND DISTRIBUTION

C C325

1 BLK 150

2 BLK 2 BLK 2 BLK K 2 BLK

S331 150 C330 150 S330 150 C204 150 S210

3 BLK 150

G200

Interior wiring harness wiring diagram — cigar lighter, door courtesy lights and trunk light

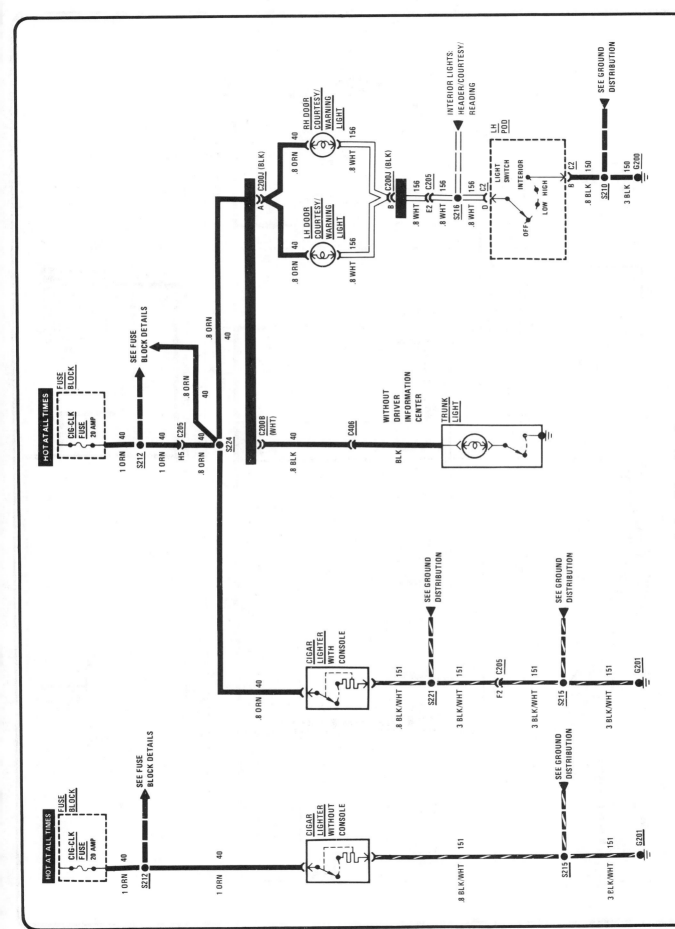

Back up lights wiring diagram

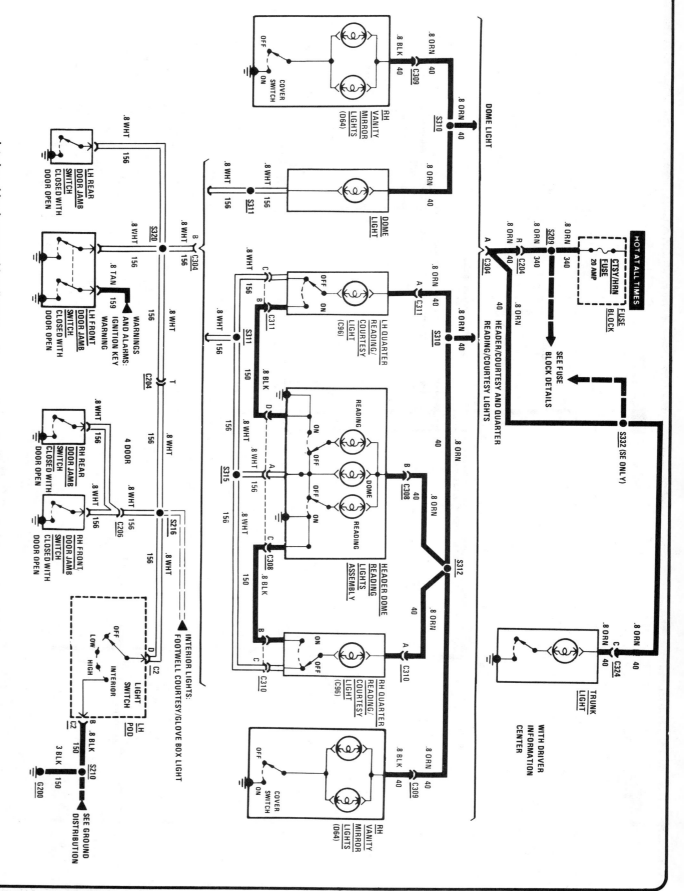

Interior wiring harness wiring diagram — dome, quarter reading/courtesy, vanity mirror and trunk lights wiring diagram

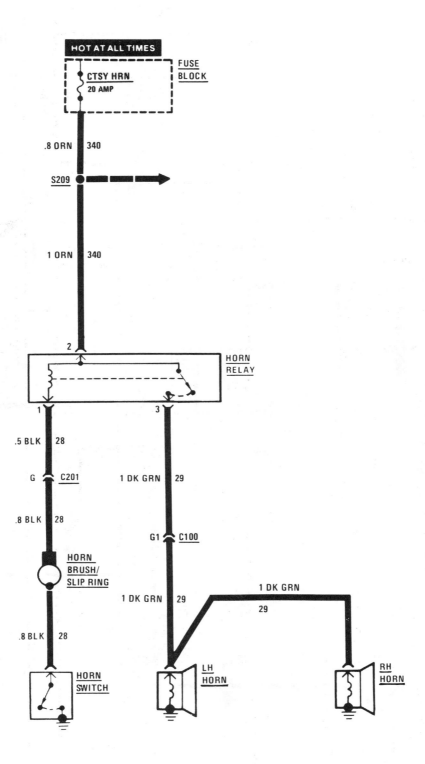

Horn circuit

Power door locks wiring diagram

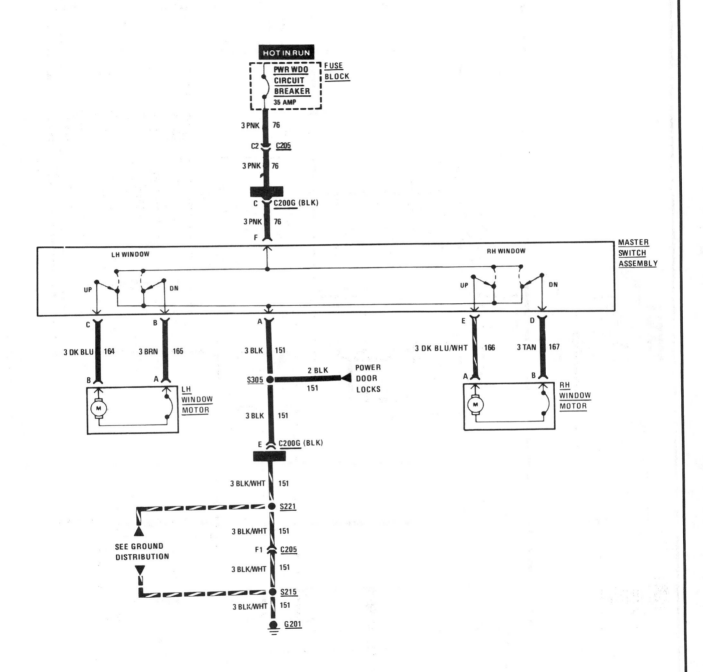

Power window wiring diagram — 2 door models

12

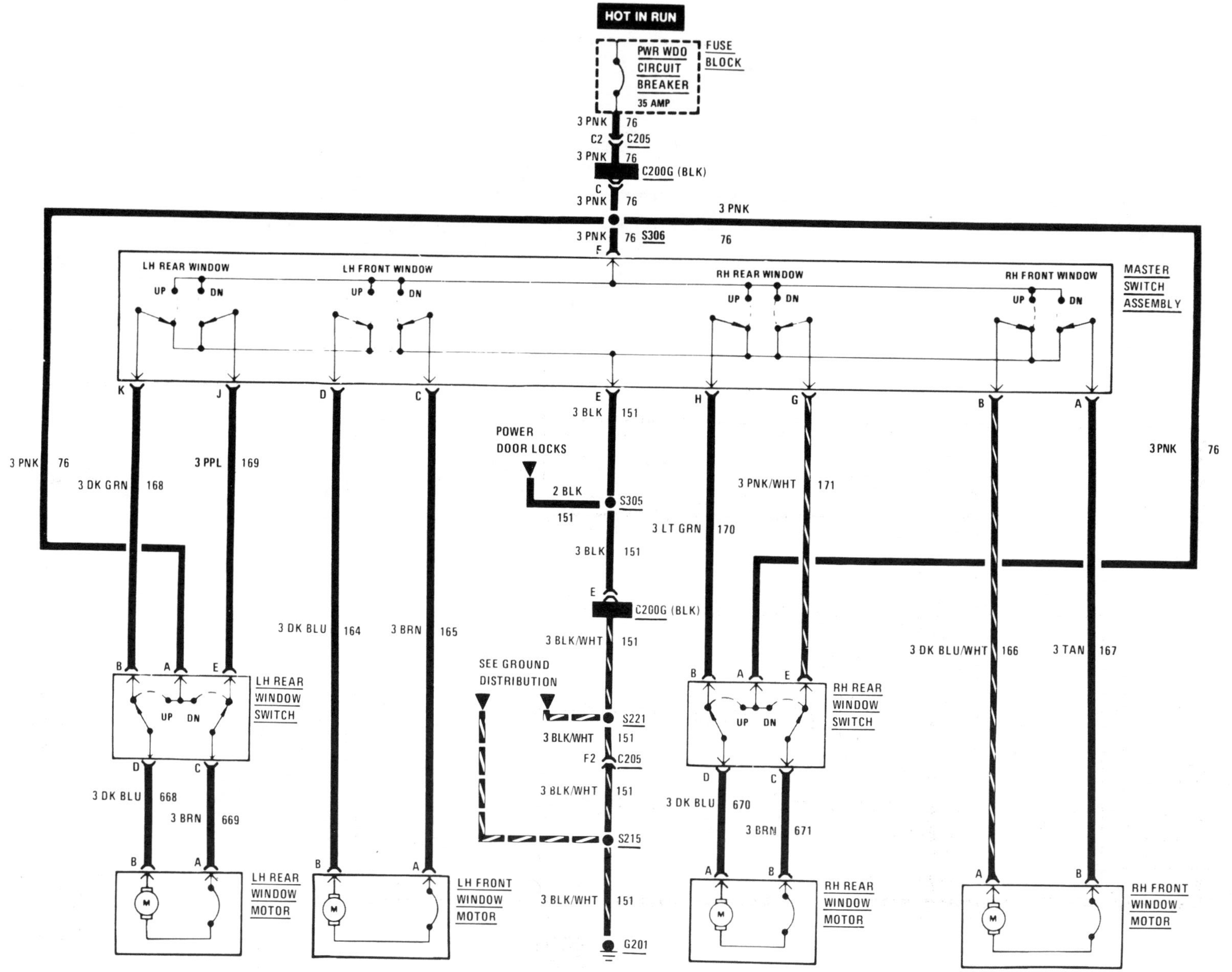

Power window wiring diagram — 4 door models

HOT IN RUN

FUSE BLOCK

PWR WDO CIRCUIT BREAKER
35 AMP

C2 C205

C200G (BLK)

3 PNK
3 PNK
3 PNK
3 PNK
76
76
76
76
76 S306
76
S306

MASTER SWITCH ASSEMBLY

RH FRONT WINDOW

RH FRONT WINDOW MOTOR

DN
UP

A
B

3 PNK
76
167 3 TAN
166 3 DK BLU/WHT

RH REAR WINDOW

RH REAR WINDOW SWITCH

RH REAR WINDOW MOTOR

DN
UP

G
H

171 3 PNK/WHT
170 3 LT GRN

E
A
B
C
D

UP DN

671 3 BRN
670 3 DK BLU

POWER DOOR LOCKS

2 BLK 151

SEE GROUND DISTRIBUTION

151
151
151
151

C200G (BLK)

E BLK
S305
151
3 BLK
E
3 BLK/WHT
S221
3 BLK/WHT
C205
F2
3 BLK/WHT
S215
3 BLK/WHT
G201

LH FRONT WINDOW

LH FRONT WINDOW MOTOR

DN
UP

C
D

165 3 BRN
164 3 DK BLU

A
B

LH REAR WINDOW

LH REAR WINDOW SWITCH

LH REAR WINDOW MOTOR

DN
UP

J
K

169 3 PPL
168 3 DK GRN

E
A
B
C
D

UP DN

669 3 BRN
668 3 DK BLU

A
B

76 3 PNK

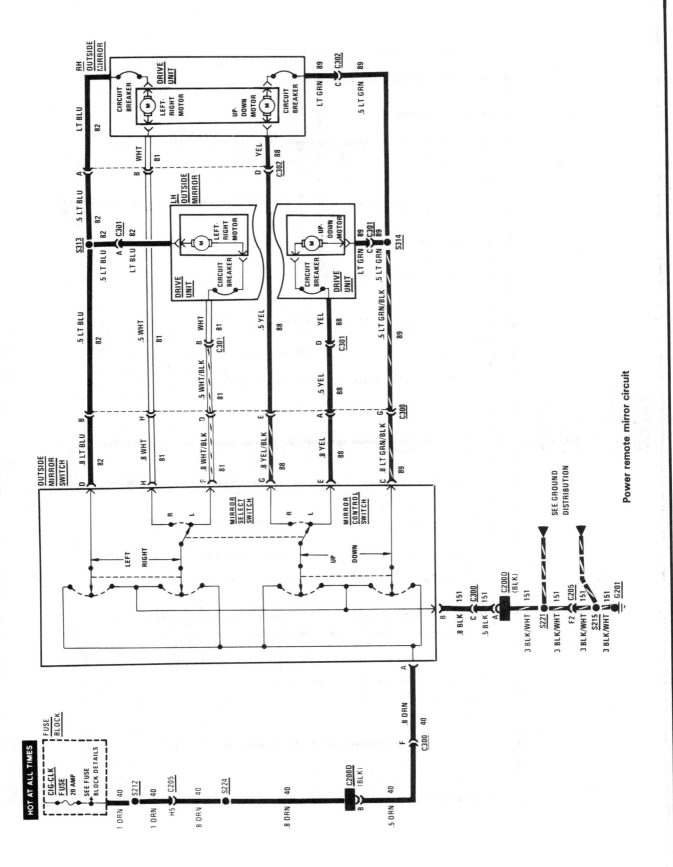

Power remote mirror circuit

12

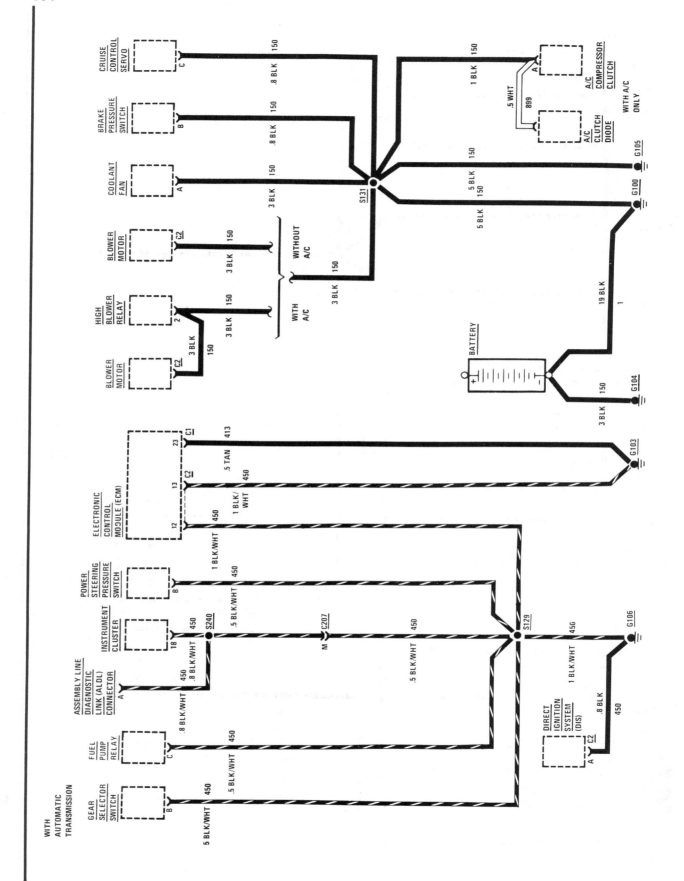

Engine compartment ground distribution wiring diagram (2.5L four cylinder engine shown, 2.0L turbo similar)

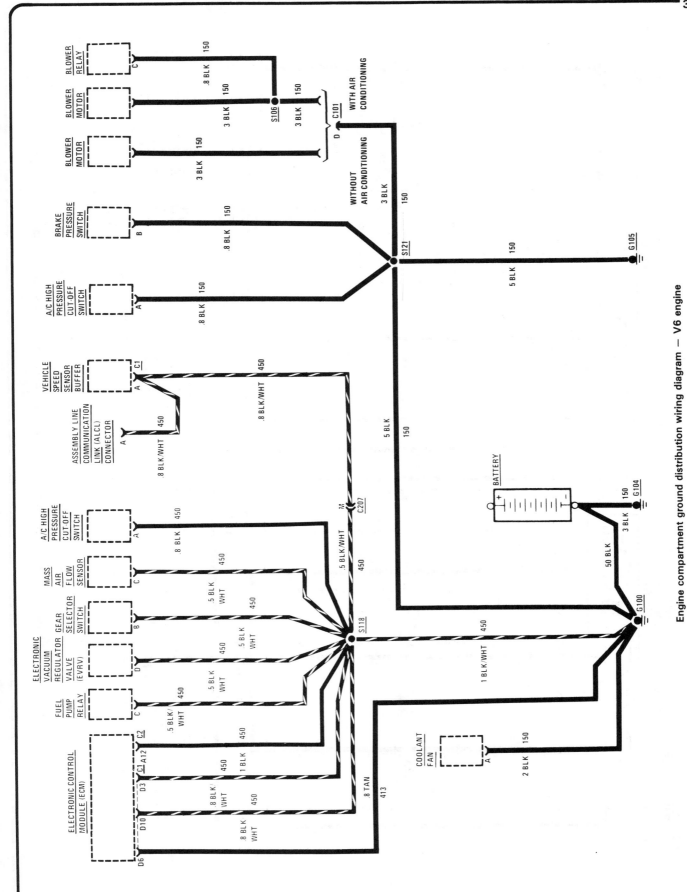

Engine compartment ground distribution wiring diagram — V6 engine

12

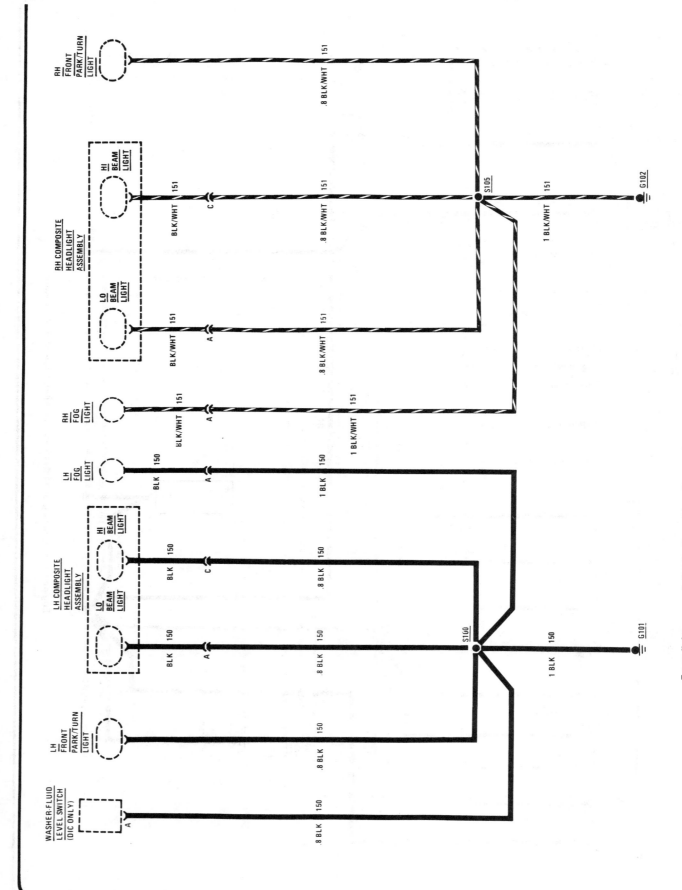

Front lights ground distribution wiring diagram (composite headlights shown, dual beam similar)

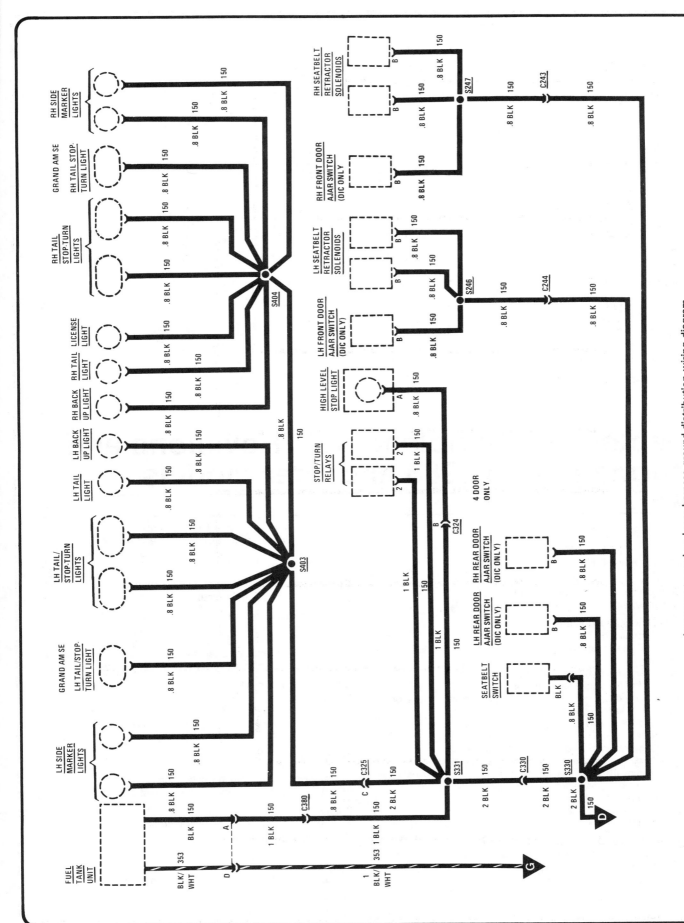

Instrument panel and rear harness ground distribution wiring diagram

Chapter 13   Supplement: Revisions and information on 1988 and later models

Contents

1   Introduction

This Supplement contains specifications and service procedure changes that apply to 1988 and later General Motors N-cars. Also included is information related to previous models that was not available at the time of original publication of this manual.

Where no differences (or very minor differences) exist between 1987 and later models, no information is given. In those instances, the original material included in Chapters 1 through 12, pertaining to 1987 models, should be used.

Before beginning a service or repair procedure, check this Supplement for new specifications and procedure changes. Make note of the supplementary information and be sure to include it while following the original procedures in Chapters 1 through 12.

Specifications

Note: *The following specifications are revisions of or supplementary to those listed at the beginning of each Chapter of this manual. The original specifications apply unless alternative information is included here.*

Fluid capacities (approximate) – 2.3L four-cylinder (Quad-4) engine

Engine oil (with filter change)	4.0 qts
Cooling system	8.0 qts

2.3L four-cylinder (Quad-4) engine

General

Cylinder numbers (drivebelt end-to-transaxle end)	1–2–3–4
Firing order	1-3-4-2
Displacement	138 cubic inches (2300 cc)
Cylinder compression pressure	
Minimum	100 psi
Maximum variation between cylinders	30-percent
Oil pressure	
At 900 rpm	15 psi minimum
At 2000 rpm	30 psi minimum

Camshafts and housings

Lobe lift	
Intake	
VIN D	0.340 in (8.6360 mm)
VIN A	0.410 in (10.414 mm)
Exhaust	
VIN D	0.350 in (8.890 mm)
VIN A	0.410 in (10.414 mm)
Lobe taper limit	0.0018 to 0.0033 inch per 0.5512 in (0.046 to 0.083 mm per 14.0 mm)
Endplay	0.0009 to 0.0088 in (0.025 to 0.225 mm)
Journal diameter	
VIN D (all)	1.3751 to 1.3760 in (34.93 to 34.95 mm)
VIN A	
No. 1	1.5728 to 1.5720 in (39.95 to 39.93 mm)
All others	1.3751 to 1.3760 in (34.93 to 34.95 mm)
Bearing oil clearance	0.0019 to 0.0043 in (0.050 to 0.110 mm)
Lifters	
Bore diameter	1.3775 to 1.3787 in (34.989 to 34.019 mm)
Outside diameter	1.3763 to 1.3770 in (34.959 to 34.975 mm)
Lifter-to-bore clearance	0.0006 to 0.0024 in (0.014 to 0.060 mm)
Camshaft housing warpage limit	0.001 inch per 3.937 in (0.025 mm per 100 mm)

Cylinder head warpage limit   0.008 in (0.203 mm)

Valves and related components

Valve face	
Angle	
Intake	44-degrees
Exhaust	44.5-degrees
Runout limit	0.0015 in (0.038 mm)
Valve seats	
Angle (intake and exhaust)	45-degrees
Width	
Intake	0.0370 to 0.0748 in (0.94 to 1.90 mm)
Exhaust	0.0037 to 0.0748 in (0.094 to 1.90 mm)

13

2.3L four-cylinder (Quad-4) engine (continued)
Valves and related components
Valve margin width . . . .   1/32 in minimum

Valve stem diameter
   Intake . . . .   0.27512 to 0.27445 in (6.990 to 6.972 mm)
   Exhaust . . . .   0.2740 to 0.2747 in (6.959 to 6.977 mm)

Valve stem-to-guide clearance
   Intake . . . .   0.0010 to 0.0027 in (0.025 to 0.069 mm)
   Exhaust . . . .   0.0015 to 0.0032 in (0.038 to 0.081 mm)

Valves
   Length
      Intake . . . .   4.3300 in (109.984 mm)
      Exhaust . . . .   4.3103 in (109.482 mm)
   Installed height* . . . .   0.9840 to 1.0040 in (25.00 to 25.50 mm)
   Stem length exposed beyond retainer . . . .   0.1190 to 0.1367 in (3.023 to 3.473 mm)

Measured from tip of stem to top of camshaft housing mounting surface

Oil pump gear backlash . . . .   0.0091 to 0.0201 in (0.23 to 0.51 mm)

Crankshaft and connecting rods
Crankshaft
   Endplay . . . .   0.0034 to 0.0095 in (0.087 to 0.243 mm)
   Runout
      At center main journal . . . .   0.00098 in (0.025 mm)
      At flywheel flange . . . .   0.00098 in (0.025 mm)
Main bearing journal
   Diameter . . . .   2.0470 to 2.0480 in (51.996 to 52.020 mm)
   Out-of-round/taper limits . . . .   0.0005 in (0.0127 mm)
Main bearing oil clearance . . . .   0.0005 to 0.0023 in (0.013 to 0.058 mm)
Connecting rod bearing journal
   Diameter . . . .   1.8887 to 1.8897 in (47.975 to 48.00 mm)
   Out-of-round/taper limits . . . .   0.0005 in (0.127 mm)
Connecting rod bearing oil clearance . . . .   0.0005 to 0.0020 in (0.013 to 0.053 mm)
Seal journal
   Diameter . . . .   3.2210 to 3.2299 in (81.96 to 82.04 mm)
   Runout limit . . . .   0.0012 in (0.03 mm)
Connecting rod side clearance (endplay) . . . .   0.0059 to 0.0177 in (0.150 to 0.450 mm)

Engine block
Cylinder bore
   Diameter . . . .   3.6217 to 3.6223 in (91.992 to 92.008 mm)
   Out-of-round limit . . . .   0.0004 in (0.010 mm)
   Taper limit (thrust side) . . . .   0.0003 in (0.008 mm) measured 4.173 in (106 mm) down the bore
Block deck warpage limit . . . .   If more than 0.010 in (0.25 mm) must be removed, replace the block
Transaxle mounting bolt boss runout
   limit (rear face-to-crankshaft flange) . . . .   0.008 in (0.203 mm)

Pistons and rings
Piston diameter . . . .   3.6203 to 3.6210 in (91.957 to 91.973 mm) at 70-degrees F (21-degrees C)
Piston-to-bore clearance . . . .   0.0007 to 0.0020 in (0.019 to 0.051 mm)
Piston ring end gap
   Top compression ring . . . .   0.0138 to 0.0236 in (0.35 to 0.60 mm)
   Second compression ring . . . .   0.0157 to 0.0256 in (0.40 to 0.65 mm)
   Oil control ring . . . .   0.0157 to 0.0551 in (0.40 to 1.40 mm)
Piston ring side clearance
   Top compression ring . . . .   0.0027 to 0.0047 in (0.070 to 0.120 mm)
   Second compression ring . . . .   0.00157 to 0.00315 in (0.040 to 0.080 mm)

Torque specifications   Ft-lbs (unless otherwise indicated)
Camshaft housing-to-cylinder head bolts
   Step 1   11
   Step 2 . . . .   Turn bolts an additional 75-degrees
Camshaft sprocket-to-camshaft bolt   40
Connecting rod cap nuts
   1988
      Step 1   15
      Step 2 . . . .   Turn an additional 75-degrees
   1989 on
      Step 1   18
      Step 2 . . . .   Rotate an additional 80-degrees

Cylinder head bolts
   Short bolts
      Step 1 26
      Step 2 .... Turn bolts an additional 80-degrees
   Long bolts
      Step 1 26
      Step 2 .... Turn bolts an additional 90-degrees
Exhaust manifold-to-cylinder head nuts 27
Exhaust manifold-to-cylinder head studs .... 106 in-lbs
Flywheel-to-crankshaft bolts
      Step 1 22
      Step 2 .... Turn bolts an additional 45-degrees
Intake manifold-to-cylinder head nuts/bolts 18
Main bearing cap bolts
      Step 1 15
      Step 2 .... Rotate an additional 90-degrees
Oil pan baffle studs/bolts 30
Oil pan bolts
      6 mm .... 106 in-lbs
      8 mm 17
Oil pump-to-block bolts 33
Oil pump cover-to-oil pump body bolts .... 106 in-lbs
Oil pump screen assembly-to-pump bolts 22
Oil pump screen assembly-to-brace bolts .... 106 in-lbs
Crankshaft rear main oil seal housing bolts .... 106 in-lbs
Timing chain cover-to-housing bolts .... 106 in-lbs
Timing chain housing bolts 19
Timing chain housing-to-block stud 19
Timing chain tensioner .... 115 in-lbs
Vibration damper-to-crankshaft bolt
      Step 1 74
      Step 2 .... Turn bolt an additional 90-degrees
Water pump-to-timing chain housing bolts/nuts 19
Water pump-to-water pump cover bolts .... 106 in-lbs
Water pump cover-to-block bolts 19
Thermostat housing bolts 19

2.5L overhead valve (OHV) four-cylinder engine

Camshaft lobe lift (intake and exhaust) .... 0.232 in (5.8882 mm)

Torque specifications   **Ft-lbs (unless otherwise indicated)**
Camshaft thrust plate-to-block bolts .... 90 in-lbs
Camshaft sprocket-to-camshaft bolt (1990) 43
Timing chain tensioner-to-block bolt 18
Cylinder head bolts
   Step 1 – all bolts, in sequence 18
   Step 2
      All bolts, except 9, in sequence 26
      Bolt 9 18
   Step 3 – all bolts, in sequence .... Tighten an additional 90-degrees (1/4-turn)
Main bearing cap bolts 70

3.0L V6 engine (1988)

General
Valve spring pressure .... 175 to 195 lbs at 1.340 in
Piston-to-bore clearance .... 0.001 to 0.0045 in
Piston ring side clearance
   Compression rings .... 0.001 to 0.003 in
   Oil ring .... 0.0005 to 0.0065 in

Torque specifications   **Ft-lbs**
Crankshaft balancer bolt 219

3.3L V6 engine (1989 on)

General
Cylinder bore diameter .... 3.70 in

13

3.3L V6 engine (1989 on) continued

Camshaft lobe lift	
Intake	0.250 in
Exhaust	0.255 in
Piston ring side clearance	
Compression rings	0.0013 to 0.0031 in
Oil ring	0.0011 to 0.0081 in
Crankshaft main bearing journal diameter	2.4988 to 2.4998 in
Oil pump	
End clearance	0.001 to 0.0035 in
Inner gear tip clearance	0.006 in
Outer gear diameter clearance	0.008 to 0.015 in
Pressure regulator valve-to-bore clearance	0.0015 to 0.003 in
Gear pocket depth	0.461 to 0.4625 in
Gear pocket diameter	3.508 to 3.512 in

Torque specifications   Ft-lbs (unless otherwise indicated)

Crankshaft balancer bolt	219
Timing chain sprocket-to-camshaft bolt	26
Connecting rod bolts	20, plus an additional 50-degrees rotation
Main bearing cap bolts	90
Cylinder head bolts	
Step 1 – all bolts in sequence	35
Step 2 – all bolts in sequence	Tighten an additional 130-degrees
Step 3 – four center bolts only	Tighten an additional 30-degrees
Exhaust manifold-to-cylinder head bolts	30
Flywheel-to-crankshaft bolts	60
Intake manifold-to-cylinder head bolts	88 in-lbs
Oil pan-to-cylinder block bolts/nuts	124 in-lbs
Oil pan-to-front cover bolts/nuts	124 in-lbs
Rocker arm cover-to-cylinder head bolts	88 in-lbs
Rocker arm bolts	37
Lifter guide retainer bolts	22
Water pump-to-front cover bolts	84 in-lbs

Fuel and exhaust systems (Quad-4 engine)

Fuel pressure

Engine stopped, system pressurized	40.5 to 47 psi
Engine idling	Lower than above measurement by 3 to 10 psi

Torque specifications   Ft-lbs (unless otherwise indicated)

Fuel rail-to-cylinder head bolts	19
Return line clamp bolt-to-fuel pressure regulator	53 in-lbs

Brakes

Torque specifications   Ft-lbs

Proportioning valve caps	20

---

3   Tune-up and routine maintenance

Engine oil and filter change (2.5L four-cylinder models)
Refer to illustration 3.1

1   Some later models with the 2.5L four-cylinder engine are equipped with a drain plug **(see illustration)**. Follow the oil and filter change procedure described in Chapter 1, but before removing the filter access plug, remove the drain plug and allow the oil to drain.

---

4   2.0L overhead cam (OHC) four-cylinder engine

Timing belt – removal, installation and adjustment
Refer to illustration 4.6
Note: *This procedure applies to 1989 models only.*

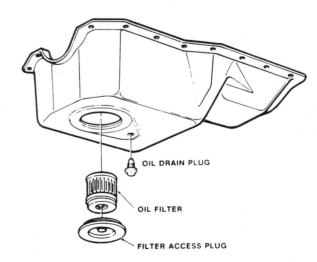

3.1   Later model 2.5L four-cylinder engines are equipped with a drain plug next to the oil filter access plug

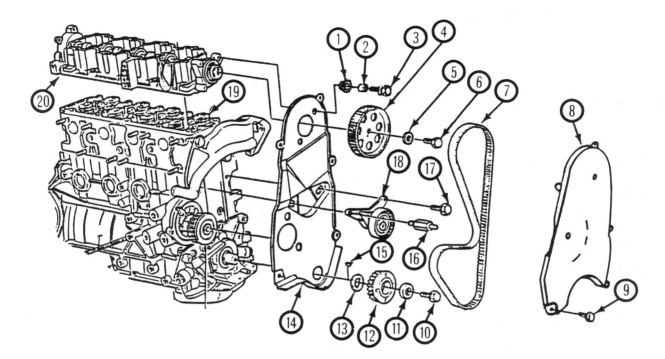

4.6   1989 2.0L OHC engine timing belt details

1	Grommet	8	Front cover	14	Rear cover
2	Sleeve	9	Bolt (front cover)	15	Woodruff key
3	Bolt (rear cover-to-camshaft housing)	10	Bolt (crankshaft sprocket-to-crankshaft)	16	Stud (tensioner-to-block)
4	Camshaft sprocket	11	Washer	17	Bolt (tensioner-to-block)
5	Washer	12	Crankshaft sprocket	18	Tensioner
6	Bolt (camshaft sprocket-to-camshaft)	13	Washer	19	Cylinder head
7	Timing belt			20	Camshaft housing

Removal

1   Follow Steps 1 through 6 of the timing belt removal procedure in Chapter 2 Part A.
2   Rotate the crankshaft and camshaft until the marks on the timing belt sprockets are aligned with the marks on the rear cover.
3   Loosen the water pump bolts and rotate the water pump to release the belt tension (see Chapter 2 Part A, Step 11).
4   Remove the bolts and detach the pulley from the crankshaft.
5   Remove the timing belt.

Installation and adjustment

6   Recheck the alignment of the crankshaft and camshaft sprockets. Install the timing belt, routing it properly around the tensioner pulley **(see illustration)**. There should be tension on the belt between the camshaft and crankshaft pulleys, with the marks on the sprockets still in alignment with the marks on the rear cover.
7   Rotate the water pump eccentric clockwise until the tensioner makes contact with the high torque stop. Tighten the water pump bolts enough to hold the pump in position.
8   Rotate the crankshaft two full revolutions, then bring the timing marks back into alignment.
9   Loosen the water pump bolts slightly, then turn the pump counterclockwise until the hole in the tensioner arm is aligned with the hole in the tensioner base.
10   Tighten the water pump bolts to the torque specified in Chapter 3, while making sure the tensioner holes are still in alignment.
11   The remainder of installation is the reverse of the removal procedure. Refill the cooling system (see Chapter 1) and check for leaks.

5   2.3L four-cylinder (Quad-4) engine

General information

The Quad-4 engine was first offered as an option on the Oldsmobile Calais in 1987. In 1988, this engine was made available on the Pontiac and Buick models.

The Quad-4 engine utilizes a number of advanced design features to increase power output and improve durability. The aluminum cylinder head contains four valves per cylinder. A double-row timing chain drives two overhead camshafts – one for intake and one for exhaust. Lightweight bucket-type hydraulic lifters actuate the valves. Rotators are used on all valves for extended service life.

Intake manifold – removal and installation

Removal
Refer to illustrations 5.6 and 5.8

1   Relieve the fuel system pressure as described in Section 9.
2   Disconnect the negative battery cable from the battery, then refer to Chapter 1 and drain the cooling system.
3   Remove the throttle body (see Chapter 4).
4   Label and disconnect the vacuum and breather hoses and electrical wires.
5   Remove the oil/air separator (see Section 11).

13

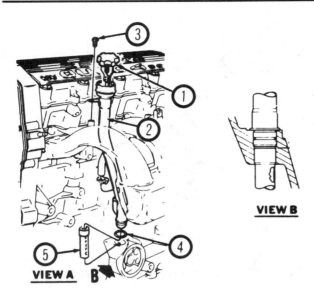

5.6   Oil fill tube mounting details

1	Oil fill cap and dipstick	4	O-ring
2	Oil fill tube	5	Guide
3	Bolt		

5.8   Intake manifold brace mounting details

1	Intake manifold brace	4	Stud
2	Bolt	5	Washer
3	Nut	6	Spacer

6   Remove the oil fill cap and dipstick assembly **(see illustration)**.

7   Unbolt the oil fill tube and detach it from the engine block, rotating it as necessary to gain clearance between the intake tubes.

8   Remove the intake manifold brace **(see illustration)**.

9   Loosen the manifold mounting nuts/bolts in 1/4-turn increments until they can be removed by hand.

10   The manifold will probably be stuck to the cylinder head and force may be required to break the gasket seal. If necessary, dislodge the manifold with a soft-face hammer. **Caution:** *Don't pry between the head and manifold or damage to the gasket sealing surfaces will result and vacuum leaks could develop.*

Installation

Refer to illustration 5.16

Note: *The mating surfaces of the cylinder head and manifold must be perfectly clean when the manifold is installed. Gasket removal solvents in aerosol cans are available at most auto parts stores and may be helpful when removing old gasket material stuck to the head and manifold (since the components are made of aluminum, aggressive scraping can cause damage). Be sure to follow the directions printed on the container.*

11   Use a gasket scraper to remove all traces of sealant and old gasket material, then clean the mating surfaces with lacquer thinner or acetone. If there's old sealant or oil on the mating surfaces when the manifold is reinstalled, vacuum leaks may develop.

12   Use a tap of the correct size to chase the threads in the bolt holes, then use compressed air (if available) to remove the debris from the holes. **Warning:** *Wear safety glasses or a face shield to protect your eyes when using compressed air. Use a die to clean and restore the stud threads.*

13   Position the gasket on the cylinder head. Make sure all intake port openings, coolant passage holes and bolt holes are aligned correctly.

14   Install the manifold, taking care to avoid damaging the gasket.

15   Thread the nuts/bolts into place by hand.

16   Tighten the nuts/bolts to the torque listed in this Chapter's Specifications following the recommended sequence **(see illustration)**. Work up to the final torque in three steps.

17   The remaining installation steps are the reverse of removal. Start the engine and check carefully for leaks at the intake manifold joints.

Exhaust manifold – removal and installation

Refer to illustrations 5.20, 5.21, 5.22 and 5.27

Removal

Warning: *Allow the engine to cool completely before performing this procedure.*

18   Disconnect the negative battery cable from the battery.

19   Unplug the oxygen sensor electrical connector (see Chapter 6).

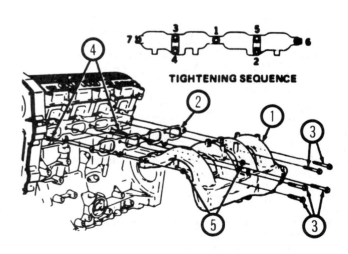

5.16   Intake manifold fastener tightening sequence

1	Intake manifold	4	Studs
2	Gasket	5	Nuts
3	Bolts		

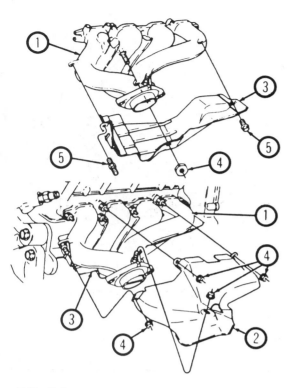

5.20 Exhaust manifold heat shields – exploded view

1	Exhaust manifold	4	Nut
2	Upper heat shield	5	Bolt
3	Lower heat shield		

5.22 Exhaust manifold brace mounting details

1	Brace	2	Mounting nut

20 Remove the manifold heat shields **(see illustration)**.
21   Raise the vehicle and support it securely on jackstands, then remove the exhaust pipe-to-manifold nuts. The nuts are usually rusted in place, so penetrating oil should be applied to the stud threads before attempting to remove them. Loosen them a little at a time, working from side-to-side to prevent the flange from jamming **(see illustration)**.
22 Remove the exhaust manifold brace **(see illustration)**.
23 Separate the exhaust pipe flange from the manifold studs, then pull the pipe down slightly to break the seal at the manifold joint.

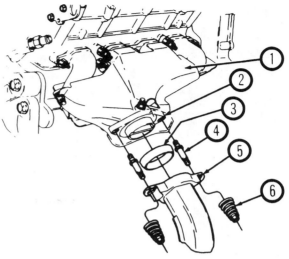

5.21 Exhaust pipe-to-maniofld mounting details

1	Heat shield	4	Stud (2)
2	Exhaust manifold	5	Exhaust pipe flange
3	Seal	6	Spring nut (2)

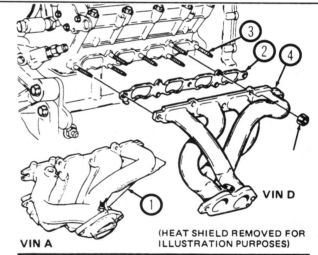

VIN A   **VIN D**

(HEAT SHIELD REMOVED FOR ILLUSTRATION PURPOSES)

TIGHTENING SEQUENCE

5.27 Exhaust manifold nut tightening sequence

1	Exhaust manifold	3	Stud (7)
2	Gasket	4	Nut (7)

24 Loosen the exhaust manifold mounting nuts 1/4-turn at a time each, working from the inside out, until they can be removed by hand.
25 Separate the manifold from the head and remove it.

Installation

26 The manifold and cylinder head mating surfaces must be clean when the manifold is reinstalled. Use a gasket scraper to remove all traces of old gasket material and carbon deposits.
27 Using a new gasket, install the manifold and hand tighten the fasteners. Working from the center out following the recommended sequence **(see illustration)**, tighten the bolts/nuts to the torque listed in this Chapter's Specifications.
28 The remaining installation steps are the reverse of removal.

13

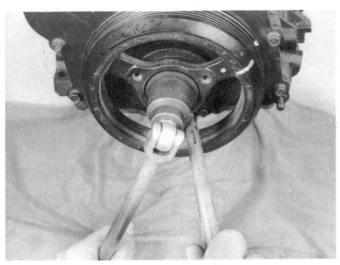

5.32   The vibration damper can be kept from turning with a bar while the bolt is loosened/tightened

5.33   Use a bolt type puller that applies force to the damper hub as shown here – don't use a jaw type puller that applies force to the outer edge; it will damage the damper

Vibration damper – removal and installation

Refer to illustrations 5.32, 5.33 and 5.36

29 Remove the cable from the negative battery terminal.

30 Remove the drivebelt (see Chapter 1).

31 With the parking brake applied and the shifter in Park (automatic) or in gear (manual), raise the front of the vehicle and support it securely on jackstands.

32 Remove the bolt from the front of the crankshaft. A breaker bar will probably be necessary, since the bolt is very tight. Use GM special tool J-38122 (or equivalent) to keep the crankshaft from turning. If the special tool isn't available, insert a bar through a hole in the damper to prevent the crankshaft from turning **(see illustration)**.

33 Using a puller (tool J-24420-B or equivalent), remove the vibration damper from the crankshaft **(see illustration)**.

34 Check the oil seal and replace it if necessary. Refer to Steps 40 through 43.

35 Apply a thin layer of multi-purpose grease to the seal contact surface

of the vibration damper hub.

36 Position the damper on the crankshaft and slide it through the seal until it bottoms against the crankshaft sprocket. Note that the slot (keyway) in the hub must be aligned with the Woodruff key in the end of the crankshaft **(see illustration)**. The crankshaft bolt can also be used to press the damper into position.

37 Tighten the crankshaft bolt to the torque and angle of rotation listed in this Chapter's Specifications.

38 The remaining installation steps are the reverse of removal.

Crankshaft front oil seal – replacement

Refer to illustrations 5.40 and 5.43

39 Remove the vibration damper (see Steps 29 through 33).

40 Pry the old oil seal out with a seal removal tool **(see illustration)** or a screwdriver. Be very careful not to nick or otherwise damage the crankshaft in the process and don't distort the timing chain cover.

41 Apply a thin coat of RTV-type sealant to the outer edge of the new seal. Lubricate the seal lip with moly-base grease or clean engine oil.

5.36   Align the keyway in the vibration damper hub with the Woodruff key in the crankshaft

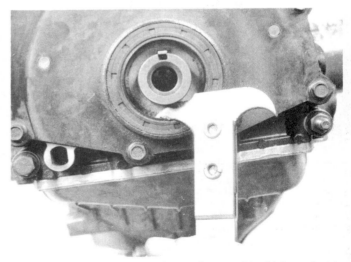

5.40   Pry the old seal out with a seal removal tool (shown here) or a screwdriver

5.43   Install the new seal with a large socket or piece of pipe and a hammer

5.48   Remove the vent hose and engine lifting bracket bolts

1   Vent hose fitting   *2   Engine lifting bracket bolts*

42   Place the seal squarely in position in the bore with the spring side facing in.
43   Carefully tap the seal into place with a large socket or section of pipe and a hammer **(see illustration)**. The outer diameter of the socket or pipe should be the same size as the seal outer diameter.
44   Install the vibration damper (see Steps 35 through 38).
45   Start the engine and check for oil leaks at the seal.

Timing chain and sprockets – removal, inspection and installation

Note: *Special tools are required for this procedure, so read through it before beginning work.*

Removal

Refer to illustrations 5.48, 5.50, 5.53, 5.55, 5.56, 5.57, 5.58, 5.59, 5.62, 5.63 and 5.65

46   Disconnect the negative battery cable from the battery.
47   Remove the coolant reservoir (see Chapter 3).
48   Detach the timing chain cover vent hose and unbolt the engine lifting bracket at the drivebelt end of the engine **(see illustration)**.
49   Remove the vibration damper (see Steps 29 through 33).
50   Working from above, remove the upper timing chain cover fasteners **(see illustration)**.
51   Working from below, remove the lower timing chain cover fasteners.
52   Detach the cover and gaskets from the housing.
53   Slide the oil slinger off the crankshaft **(see illustration)**.
54   Temporarily reinstall the vibration damper bolt to use when turning the crankshaft.

5.50   Timing chain cover fastener locations (arrows)

5.53   Note how it's installed, then remove the oil slinger (arrow) from the crankshaft

13

5.55   Insert 8 mm (5/16-inch) bolts (arrows) or pins to hold the camshaft sprockets

5.56   The mark on the crankshaft sprocket must align with the mark on the block (arrows)

5.57   The timing chain guides are wedged into the housing at four points (arrows) – just pull them out

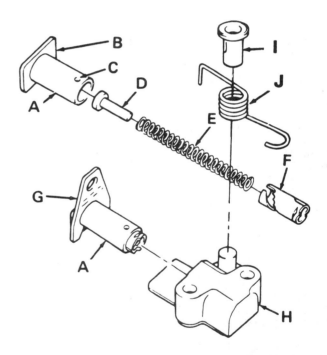

5.58   **Timing chain tensioner components – exploded view**

A	Plunger assembly	F	Restraint cylinder
B	Long end	G	J-36589 (anti-release device)
C	Peg	H	Tensioner body
D	Nylon plug	I	Sleeve
E	Spring	J	Spring

55   Turn the crankshaft clockwise until the camshaft sprocket's timing pin holes line up with the holes in the timing chain housing. Insert 8 mm pins or bolts into the holes to maintain alignment **(see illustration)**.
56   The mark on the crankshaft sprocket should line up with the mark on the engine block **(see illustration)**. The crankshaft sprocket keyway should point up and line up with the centerline of the cylinder bores.
57   Remove the three timing chain guides **(see illustration)**.
58   Detach the timing chain tensioner sleeve and spring **(see illustration)**.
59   Make sure all the slack in the timing chain is above the tensioner assembly, then remove the chain tensioner shoe **(see illustration)**. The timing chain must be disengaged from the wear grooves in the tensioner shoe in order to remove the shoe. Slide a screwdriver blade under the timing chain while pulling the shoe out. **Note:** *If difficulty is encountered when removing the chain tensioner shoe, proceed as follows:*

   a)   Hold the intake camshaft sprocket with tool J-36013 (or equivalent) and remove the sprocket bolt and washer.

b)   Remove the washer from the bolt and thread the bolt back into the camshaft by hand.
c)   Remove the intake camshaft sprocket, using a three-jaw puller in the three relief holes in the sprocket, if necessary. **Caution:** *Don't try to pry the sprocket off the camshaft or damage to the sprocket could occur.*

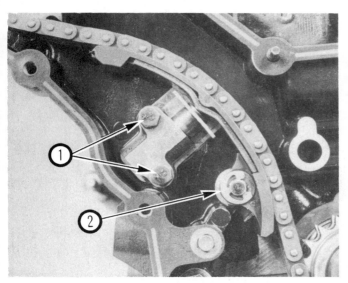

5.59   The timing chain tensioner shoe is held in place by an E-clip

1   Tensioner mounting bolts   2   E-clip

5.62   Begin removing the chain at the exhaust camshaft sprocket

60   Remove the tensioner assembly retaining bolts and tensioner. The spring can be caged with GM tool J-36589, or equivalent. **Warning:** *The tensioner plunger is spring loaded and could come out with great force, causing personal injury.*
61   Remove the chain housing-to-block stud (timing chain tensioner shoe pivot).
62   Slip the timing chain off the sprockets **(see illustration)**.
63   To remove the camshaft sprockets (if not already done), loosen the bolts while the pins are still in place. Mark the sprockets for identification **(see illustration)**, remove the bolts and pins, then pull on the sprockets by hand until they slip off the dowels.
64   The crankshaft sprocket will slip off the crankshaft by hand.
65   The idler sprocket and bearing **(see illustration)** are pressed into place. If replacement is necessary, remove the timing chain housing (see

Steps 80 through 92) and take it to a dealer service department or automotive machine shop. Special tools are required and the bearing must be replaced each time it's pressed out.

Inspection
66   Visually inspect all parts for wear and damage. Look for loose pins, cracks, worn rollers and side plates. Check the sprockets for hook-shaped, chipped and broken teeth. **Note:** *Some scoring of the timing chain shoe and guides is normal. Replace the timing chain, sprockets, chain shoe and guides as a set if the engine has high mileage or fails the visual parts inspection.*

5.63   Mark the sprockets (arrows), then remove the bolts and pull the sprockets off

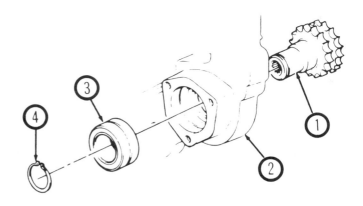

5.65   Timing chain idler sprocket, bearing and snap-ring

1   Idler sprocket   3   Bearing
2   Timing chain housing   4   Snap-ring

13

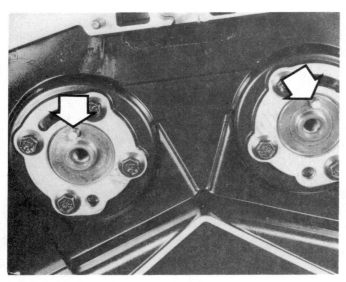

5.67   The camshaft sprocket dowel pins should be near the top (arrows) prior to sprocket installation

Installation

Refer to illustrations 5.67, 5.68 and 5.76

67   Turn the camshafts until the dowel pins are at the top **(see illustration)**. Install both camshaft sprockets (if removed). Apply GM sealant 12345493 (or equivalent) to the camshaft sprocket bolt threads and make sure the washers are in place. Keep the camshaft from turning with tool J-36013 (or equivalent, such as 8 mm bolts). Tighten the bolts to the torque listed in this Chapter's Specifications.

68   Recheck the positions of the camshaft and crankshaft sprockets for correct valve timing **(see illustration)**. **Note:** *If the camshafts are out of position and must be rotated more than 1/8-turn in order to install the alignment dowel pins:*

   a) The crankshaft must be rotated 90-degrees clockwise past Top Dead Center to give the valves adequate clearance to open.

   b) Once the camshafts are in position and the dowels installed, rotate the crankshaft counterclockwise back to Top Dead Center. **Caution:** *Do not rotate the crankshaft clockwise to TDC (valve or piston damage could occur).*

69   Slip the timing chain over the exhaust camshaft sprocket, then around the idler and crankshaft sprockets.

70   Remove the alignment dowel pin from the intake camshaft. Using tool J-36013 (or equivalent), rotate the intake camshaft sprocket counterclockwise enough to mesh the timing chain with it. Release the special tool. The chain run between the two camshaft sprockets will tighten. If the valve timing is correct, the intake cam alignment dowel pin should slide in easily. If it doesn't index, the camshafts aren't timed correctly; repeat the procedure.

71   Leave the dowel pins installed for now. Working under the vehicle, check the timing marks. With slack removed from the timing chain between the intake cam sprocket and the crankshaft sprocket, the timing marks on the crankshaft sprocket and the engine block should be aligned. If the marks aren't aligned, move the chain one tooth forward or backward, remove the slack and recheck the marks.

72   Install the chain housing-to-block stud (timing chain tensioner shoe pivot), and tighten it to the torque specified in this Chapter.

73   Reload the timing chain tensioner assembly to its "zero" position as follows:

   a) Assemble the restraint cylinder, spring and nylon plug in the plunger. While rotating the restraint cylinder clockwise, push it into the plunger until it bottoms. Keep rotating the restraint cylinder clockwise, but allow the spring to push it out of the plunger. The pin in the plunger will lock the restraint cylinder in the loaded position.

   b) Position tool J-36589 on the plunger assembly.

   c) Install the plunger assembly in the tensioner body with the long end toward the crankshaft when installed.

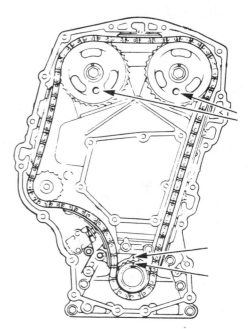

5.68   Recheck the timing mark alignment (arrows)

74   Install the tensioner assembly in the chain housing. Tighten the bolts to the torque specified in this Chapter. **Note:** *Recheck the plunger assembly installation – it's correctly installed when the long end is toward the crankshaft.*

75   Install the tensioner shoe, spring and sleeve.

76   Remove tool J-36589 and squeeze the plunger assembly into the tensioner body to unload it **(see illustration)**.

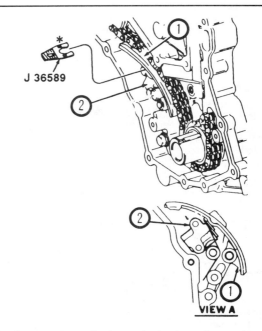

5.76   Remove the anti-release device from the tensioner and depress the shoe once to release the tensioner

1   Timing chain tensioner shoe   *2   Tensioner*

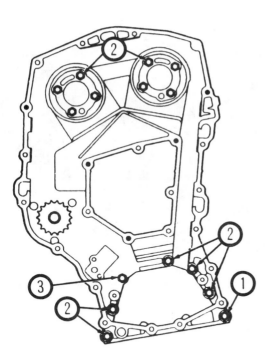

5.85   Timing chain housing mounting details

1 Bolt	3 Stud (timing chain
2 Bolt (chain housing-to-block	tensioner shoe pivot)
and camshaft housings)	

77   Remove the alignment pins.

78   Slowly rotate the crankshaft clockwise two full turns (720-degrees). Don't force it; if resistance is felt, back up and recheck the installation procedure. Align the crankshaft timing mark with the mark on the engine block and temporarily reinstall the 8 mm alignment pins. The pins should slide in easily if the valve timing is correct. **Caution:** *If the valve timing is incorrect, severe engine damage could occur.*

79   Install the remaining components in the reverse order of removal. Check fluid levels, start the engine and check for proper operation and coolant/oil leaks.

Timing chain housing – removal and installation

Refer to illustrations 5.85 and 5.93

80   Remove the timing chain and sprockets (see Steps 46 through 63).

81   Remove the exhaust manifold (see Steps 18 through 25).

82   If you're installing a replacement timing chain housing, remove the water pump (see Section 8).

83   Remove the timing chain housing-to-belt tensioner bracket brace.

84   Remove the four oil pan-to-timing chain housing bolts.

85   Remove the timing chain housing-to-block lower fasteners **(see illustration)**.

86   Remove the lowest cover retaining stud from the timing chain housing.

87   Remove the rear engine mount nut.

88   Loosen the front engine mount nut, leaving about three threads remaining in contact.

89   Remove the eight chain housing-to-camshaft housing bolts.

90   Position a floor jack under the oil pan, using an 18-inch long piece of wood (a 2x4 works well) on the jack pad to distribute the weight.

91   Raise the engine off the front and rear mounts until the front mount bracket contacts the nut.

92   Remove the timing chain housing and gaskets. Thoroughly clean the mating surfaces to remove any traces of old sealant or gasket material.

5.93   Position a new gasket over the dowel pins (arrows)

93   Install the timing chain housing with new gaskets **(see illustration)**. Tighten the bolts to the torque listed in this Chapter's Specifications.

94   The remaining steps are the reverse of removal.

Camshaft(s), lifters and housing(s) – removal, inspection and installation

Note: *Special tools are required for this procedure, so read through it before beginning work.*

Removal

Refer to illustrations 5.101a, 5.101b, 5.104, 5.105, 5.106 and 5.108

Intake (front)

95   Disconnect the cable from the negative battery terminal.

96   Remove the timing chain and sprockets (see Steps 46 through 63).

97   Remove the timing chain housing-to-camshaft housing bolts **(see illustration 5.85)**.

98   Remove the ignition coil and module assembly (see Section 10).

99   Disconnect the idle speed power steering pressure switch.

100 Remove the power steering pump and brackets.

101 Remove the power steering pump drive pulley **(see illustrations)**.

Caution: *The power steering pump drive pulley must be removed following this procedure or damage to the pulley will result. If any other removal procedure is used, a new pulley must be installed.*

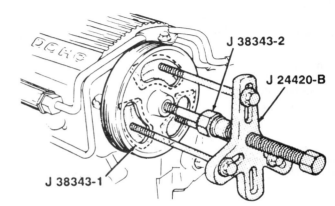

5.101a   The power steering pump drive pulley must be removed with a puller like this one . . .

13

5.101b   . . . or an aftermarket tool like this one – don't use any other tools

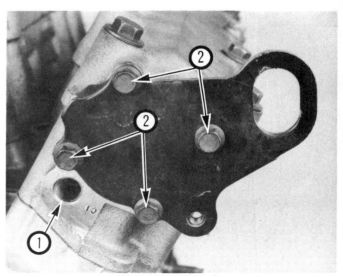

5.104   Oil pressure sending unit mounting hole (1) and engine lifting bracket bolts (2)

5.105   Gently lift the camshaft housing off the cylinder head and turn it over so the lifters won't fall out

102 Remove the oil/air separator as an assembly, with the hoses attached (see Section 11).

103 Remove the fuel rail from the cylinder head and set it aside (see Section 9).

Exhaust (rear)

104 Unplug the oil pressure sending unit wire and unbolt the engine lifting bracket **(see illustration)**.

Intake and exhaust

105 Loosen the camshaft housing-to-cylinder head bolts in 1/4-turn increments, following the tightening sequence in reverse **(see illustration 5.122)**. Leave the two cover-to-housing bolts in place temporarily. Lift the housing off the cylinder head **(see illustration)**.

106 Remove the two camshaft cover-to-housing bolts **(see illustration)**. Push the cover off the housing by threading four of the housing-to-head bolts into the tapped holes in the cover. Carefully lift the camshaft out of the housing.

107 Remove all traces of old gasket material from the mating surfaces and clean them with lacquer thinner or acetone to remove any traces of oil.

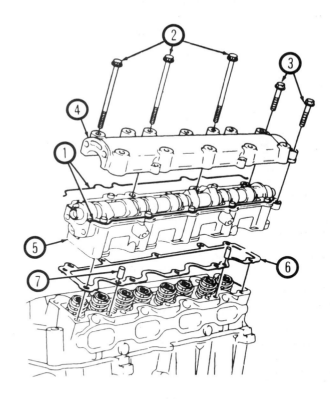

5.106   Camshaft, housing and related components (exploded view)

1   *Side seal*
2   *Camshaft housing-to-cylinder head bolts*
3   *Camshaft cover-to-housing bolts*
4   *Camshaft cover*
5   *Camshaft housing*
6   *Gasket*
7   *Dowel pin*

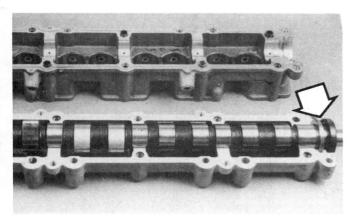

5.108   Remove the oil seal (arrow) from the intake camshaft

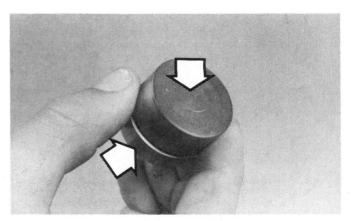

5.111a   Check the camshaft lobe surfaces and the bore surfaces (arrows) of the lifters for wear

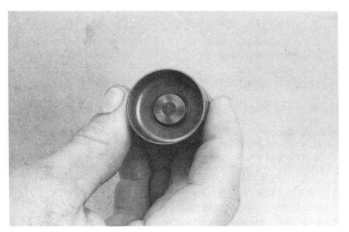

5.111b   Check the valve-side of the lifters too

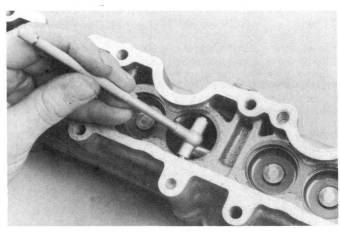

5.112   Use a telescoping gauge and micrometer to measure the lifter bores, . . .

108 Remove the oil seal from the intake camshaft **(see illustration)** and discard it.
109 Remove the lifters and store them in order so they can be reinstalled in their original locations. To minimize lifter bleed-down, store the lifters valve-side up, submerged in clean engine oil.

Inspection

Refer to illustrations 5.111a, 5.111b, 5.112 and 5.113

110 Refer to Chapter 2, Part D, for camshaft inspection procedures, but use this Chapter's Specifications. Do not attempt to salvage camshafts. Whenever a camshaft is replaced, replace all the lifters actuated by the camshaft as well.
111 Visually inspect the lifters for wear, galling, score marks and discoloration from overheating **(see illustrations)**.
112 Measure each lifter bore inside diameter and record the results **(see illustration)**.
113 Measure each lifter outside diameter and record the results **(see illustration)**.
114 Subtract the lifter outside diameter from the corresponding bore inside diameter to determine the clearance. Compare the results to this Chapter's Specifications and replace parts as necessary.

Installation

Refer to illustrations 5.118, 5.120, 5.121, 5.122 and 5.123

115 Using a new gasket, position the camshaft housing on the cylinder head and temporarily hold it in place with one bolt.

5.113   . . . then measure the lifters with a micrometer – subtract each lifter diameter from the corresponding bore diameter to obtain the lifter-to-bore clearances

116 Coat the camshaft journals and lobes and the lifters with GM Camshaft and Lifter Prelube (no. 12345501) or equivalent and install them in their original locations.
117 On the intake camshaft only, lubricate the lip of the oil seal, then position the seal on the camshaft journal with the spring side facing in.

13

5.118   The dowel pins (arrows) should be at the top (12 o'clock position)

118 Install the camshaft in the housing with the sprocket dowel pin up (12 O'clock position) **(see illustration)**. Position the cover on the housing, holding it in place with the two bolts, as described above.
119 Apply Pipe Sealant (GM no. 1052080) or equivalent to the threads of the camshaft housing and cover bolts.
120 Install new housing seals **(see illustration)**.
121 Install the camshaft cover and bolts while positioning the oil seal (intake side only). Be sure the seal is installed to the depth shown **(see illustration)**.
122 Tighten the bolts in the sequence shown **(see illustration)** to the torque and angle of rotation listed in this Chapter's Specifications.
123 Install the power steering pump pulley with GM tool no. J-36015 or equivalent **(see illustration)**.
124 Install the remaining parts in the reverse order of removal.
125 Change the oil and filter (see Chapter 1). Add GM engine oil supplement 1052367 (or equivalent). **Note:** *If new lifters have been installed or*

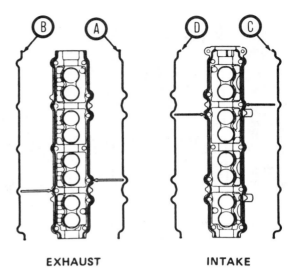

5.120   Each housing side seal is different

| A | Inner exhaust (red) | C | Outer intake (blue) |
| B | Outer exhaust (red) | D | Inner intake (blue) |

the lifters bled down while the engine was disassembled, excessive lifter noise may be experienced after startup – this is normal. Use the following procedure to purge the lifters of air:
   a) Start the engine and allow it to warm up for five minutes.
   b) Increase engine speed to 2000 rpm until the lifter noise is gone.
126 Road test the vehicle and check for oil and coolant leaks.

Valve springs, retainers and seals – replacement
Refer to illustrations 5.130, 5.131 and 5.144
Note: *Broken valve springs and defective valve stem seals can be replaced without removing the cylinder head. Two special tools and a com-*

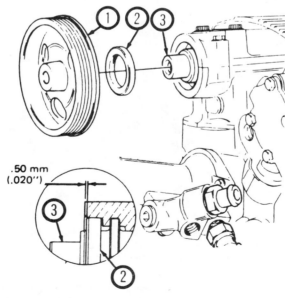

5.121   Intake camshaft pulley and seal mounting details

| 1 | Power steering | 2 | Seal |
| | pulley | 3 | Intake camshaft |

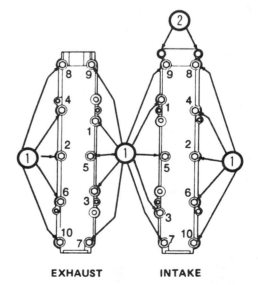

5.122   Camshaft housing-to-cylinder head bolt tightening sequence

| 1 | Housing-to-cylinder head bolts |
| 2 | Cover-to-housing bolts |

5.123   The power steering pump drive pulley must be pressed on with a special tool

5.130   Timing marks (arrows) on the Quad-4 engine

pressed air source are normally required to perform this operation, so read through this Section carefully and rent or buy the tools before beginning the job. If compressed air isn't available, a length of nylon rope can be used to keep the valves from falling into the cylinder during this procedure.

127 Remove the spark plug from the cylinder which has the defective part. Due to the design of this engine, the intake and exhaust camshaft housings can be removed separately to service their respective components. If all of the valve stem seals are being replaced, all of the spark plugs and both camshaft housings should be removed.

128 Refer to Section 10 and remove the ignition coil assembly.

129 Remove the camshaft(s), lifters and housing(s) using the procedure beginning with Step 95.

130 Turn the crankshaft until the piston in the affected cylinder is at top dead center on the compression stroke. This can be accomplished by removing the number one spark plug and placing your finger over the hole, then having an assistant turn the crankshaft with a socket and ratchet until until pressure is felt at the spark plug hole. Align the timing mark on the crankshaft pulley with the "0" mark on the timing chain cover **(see illustration)**. Top dead center for any of the other pistons can be found by rotating the engine 180-degrees (one-half turn) for the next cylinder in the firing order. If you're replacing all of the valve stem seals, begin with cylinder number one and work on the valves for one cylinder at a time. Move from cylinder-to-cylinder following the firing order sequence (see this Chapter's Specifications).

131 Thread an adapter into the spark plug hole **(see illustration)** and connect an air hose from a compressed air source to it. Most auto parts stores can supply the air hose adapter. **Note:** Many cylinder compression gauges utilize a screw-in fitting that may work with your air hose quick-disconnect fitting.

132 Apply compressed air to the cylinder. **Warning:** The piston may be forced down by compressed air, causing the crankshaft to turn suddenly. If the wrench used when positioning the number one piston at TDC is still attached to the bolt in the crankshaft nose, it could cause damage or injury when the crankshaft moves.

133 The valves should be held in place by the air pressure. If the valve faces or seats are in poor condition, leaks may prevent air pressure from retaining the valves – in this case a "valve job" is needed.

134 If you don't have access to compressed air, an alternative method can be used. Position the piston at a point just before TDC on the compression stroke, then feed a long piece of nylon rope through the spark plug hole until it fills the combustion chamber. Be sure to leave the end of the rope hanging out of the engine so it can be removed easily. Use a large ratchet and socket to rotate the crankshaft in the normal direction of rotation (clockwise) until slight resistance is felt.

135 Stuff shop rags into the cylinder head holes adjacent to the valves to prevent parts and tools from falling into the engine, then use a valve spring compressor to compress the spring. Remove the keepers with small needle-nose pliers or a magnet.

136 Remove the retainer and valve spring, then remove the valve guide seal and rotator.

137 Wrap a rubber band or tape around the top of the valve stem so the valve won't fall into the combustion chamber, then release the air pressure. **Note:** If a rope was used instead of air pressure, turn the crankshaft slightly in a counterclockwise direction (opposite normal rotation).

138 Inspect the valve stem for damage. Rotate the valve in the guide and check the end for eccentric movement, which would indicate the valve stem is bent.

139 Move the valve up-and-down in the guide and make sure it doesn't bind. If the valve stem binds, either the valve is bent or the guide is damaged. In either case, the head will have to be removed for repair.

140 Reapply air pressure to the cylinder to retain the valve in the closed position, then remove the tape or rubber band from the valve stem. If a rope was used instead of air pressure, rotate the crankshaft in the normal direction of rotation until slight resistance is felt.

141 Reinstall the valve rotator.

142 Lubricate the valve stem with engine oil and install a new guide seal.

143 Install the spring in position over the valve.

5.131   This is what the air hose adapter that threads into the spark plug hole looks like – they're commonly available from auto parts stores

13

5.144   Apply a small dab of grease to each keeper before installation to hold it in place on the valve stem until the spring is realeased

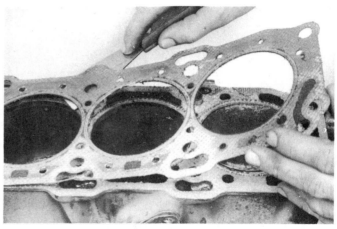

5.158   Remove the old gasket and clean the head thoroughly

144 Install the valve spring retainer. Compress the valve spring and carefully install the keepers in the groove. Apply a small dab of grease to the inside of each keeper to hold it in place if necessary **(see illustration)**. Remove the pressure from the spring tool and make sure the keepers are seated.

145 Disconnect the air hose and remove the adapter from the spark plug hole. If a rope was used in place of air pressure, pull it out of the cylinder.

146 Refer to Steps 115 through 122 and install the camshaft(s), lifters and housing(s).

147 Install the spark plug(s) and the coil assembly.

148 Start and run the engine, then check for oil leaks and unusual sounds coming from the camshaft housings.

Cylinder head – removal and installation

Removal

149 Disconnect the negative cable from the battery.

150 Refer to Steps 1 through 10 and remove the intake manifold. The cooling system must be drained to prevent coolant from getting into internal areas of the engine when the head is removed.

151 Refer to Steps 18 through 25 and detach the exhaust manifold.

152 Remove the camshafts and housings as described in Steps 95 through 109.

153 Make a holder for the head bolts. Using the new head gasket, outline the cylinders and bolt pattern on a piece of cardboard. Be sure to indicate the front of the engine for reference. Punch holes at the bolt locations **(see illustration 10.14** in Chapter 2 Part B**)**.

154 Loosen the head bolts in 1/4-turn increments until they can be removed by hand. Work from bolt-to-bolt in a pattern that's the reverse of the tightening sequence **(see illustration 5.163)**. Store the bolts in the cardboard holder as they're removed – this will ensure they are reinstalled in their original locations.

155 Lift the head off the engine. If resistance is felt, don't pry between the head and block, as damage to the mating surfaces will result. To dislodge the head, place a block of wood against the end of it and strike the wood block with a hammer. Store the head on blocks of wood to prevent damage to the gasket sealing surfaces.

156 Cylinder head disassembly and inspection procedures are covered in detail in Chapter 2, Part D.

Installation

Refer to illustrations 5.158 and 5.163

157 The mating surfaces of the cylinder head and block must be perfectly clean when the head is installed.

158 Use a gasket scraper to remove all traces of carbon and old gasket material **(see illustration)**, then clean the mating surfaces with lacquer thinner or acetone. If there's oil on the mating surfaces when the head is installed, the gasket may not seal correctly and leaks could develop. **Note:**

Since the head is made of aluminum, aggressive scraping can cause damage. Be extra careful not to nick or gouge the mating surface with the scraper. Use a vacuum cleaner to remove debris that falls into the cylinders.

159 Check the block and head mating surfaces for nicks, deep scratches and other damage. If damage is slight, it can be removed with a flat mill file; if it's excessive, machining may be the only alternative.

160 Use a tap of the correct size to chase the threads in the head bolt holes. Mount each bolt in a vise and run a die down the threads to remove corrosion and restore the threads. Dirt, corrosion, sealant and damaged threads will affect torque readings.

161 Position the new gasket over the dowel pins in the block.

162 Carefully position the head on the block without disturbing the gasket.

163 Install the bolts in their original locations and tighten them finger tight. Following the recommended sequence **(see illustration)**, tighten the bolts in several steps to the torque and angle of rotation listed in this Chapter's Specifications.

164 The remaining installation steps are the reverse of removal.

165 Refill the cooling system and change the oil and filter (see Chapter 1, if necessary).

166 Run the engine and check for leaks and proper operation.

Oil pan – removal and installation

Refer to illustrations 5.172, 5.177 and 5.181

Note: *The following procedure is based on the assumption the engine is in place in the vehicle. If it has been removed, simply unbolt the oil pan and detach it from the block.*

5.163   Cylinder head bolt TIGHTENING sequence

5.172 On manual transaxle-equipped models, remove the nut, stud and spacer

| 1 | Nut | 2 | Stud | 3 | Spacer |

5.177 The oil pan baffle is held in place by four bolts (arrows)

Removal

167 Disconnect the negative battery cable from the battery, then refer to Chapter 1 and drain the oil.
168 Remove the lower splash shield.
169 Detach the lower bellhousing cover.
170 Unbolt the exhaust manifold brace.
171 Remove the radiator outlet pipe-to-oil pan bolt.
172 On manual transaxle equipped models, remove the transaxle-to-oil pan nut and stud with a 7 mm socket **(see illustration)**.
173 Gently pry the spacer out from between the oil pan and transaxle.
174 Remove the oil pan-to-transaxle bolt.
175 Remove the oil pan mounting bolts.
176 Carefully separate the pan from the block. Don't pry between the block and pan or damage to the sealing surfaces may result and oil leaks may develop. **Note:** *The crankshaft may have to be rotated to gain clearance for oil pan removal.*
177 If you need to get at the crankshaft or other lower end components, remove the oil pan baffle **(see illustration)**.

Installation

178 Clean the sealing surfaces with lacquer thinner or acetone. Make sure the bolt holes in the block are clean.
179 The gasket should be checked carefully and replaced with a new one if damage is noted. Minor imperfections can be repaired with GM silicone

sealant (no. 1052915) or equivalent. **Caution:** *Use only enough sealant to restore the gasket to its original size and shape. Excess sealant may cause part misalignment and oil leaks.*
180 Reinstall the oil pan baffle, if removed. With the gasket in position, carefully hold the pan against the block and install the bolts finger tight.
181 Tighten the bolts in three steps to the torque specified in this Chapter **(see illustration)**. Start at the center of the pan and work out toward the ends in a spiral pattern. Note that the bolts are not all tightened to the same torque figure.
182 The remaining steps are the reverse of removal. **Caution:** *Don't forget to refill the engine with oil before starting it (see Chapter 1).*
183 Start the engine and check carefully for oil leaks at the oil pan.

Oil pump – removal, inspection and installation

Refer to illustrations 5.185, 5.187, 5.188, 5.190a and 5.190b

Removal

184 Remove the oil pan as described in Steps 167 through 176.
185 While supporting the oil pump, remove the mounting bolts **(see illustration)**.
186 Lower the pump from the engine.

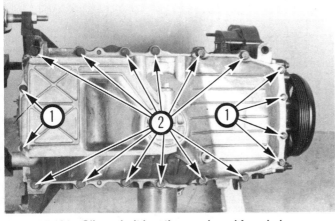

5.181 Oil pan bolt locations – viewed from below

| 1 | 6 mm bolts | 2 | 8 mm bolts |

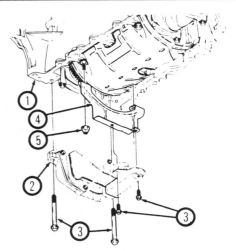

5.185 Oil pump mounting details

| 1 | Engine block | 3 | Bolt | 5 | Nut |
| 2 | Oil pump | 4 | Brace | | |

13

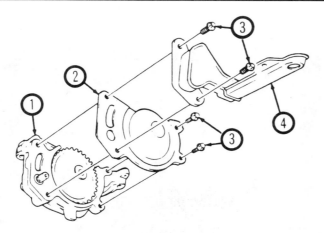

5.187   Oil pump components – exploded view

1	Oil pump	3	Bolt
2	Oil pump gear cover	4	Screen assembly

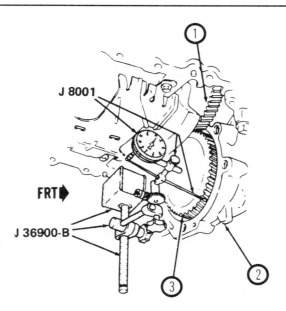

5.190a   Measuring the oil pump driven gear backlash with a dial indicator

1   Oil pump drive gear
2   Oil pump (gear cover removed)
3   Oil pump driven gear

Inspection

187 Clean all parts thoroughly and remove the cover **(see illustration)**.
188 Visually inspect all parts for wear, cracks and other damage **(see il-lustration)**. Replace the pump if it's defective, if the engine has high mile-age or if the engine is being rebuilt.

Installation

189 Position the pump and shims on the engine and install the mounting bolts. Tighten them to the torque specified in this Chapter.
190 Oil pump drive gear backlash must be checked whenever the oil pump, crankshaft or engine block is replaced. Mount a dial indicator (GM tools J-26900 and J-8001, or equivalents) on the engine with the indicator stem touching the oil pump driven gear **(see illustration)**. Check the backlash and compare it to the Specifications in this Chapter. Add or sub-tract shims **(see illustration)** to obtain the desired backlash.

5.188   Check the oil pump drive gear (arrow) and driven gear for wear and damage

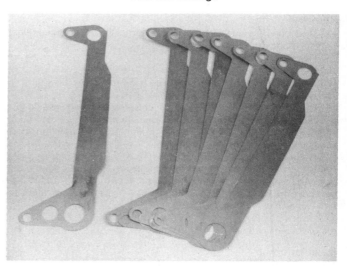

5.190b   Shims between the oil pump and engine block allow for adjustment of gear backlash

191 Install the oil pan (and baffle, if removed).
192 Add oil and run the engine. Check for oil pressure and leaks.

Flywheel – removal and installation

193 This procedure is essentially the same for all engines. Refer to Chap-ter 2 Part A and follow the procedure outlined there. Be sure to use the bolt torque specified in this Chapter.

Rear main oil seal – replacement

Refer to illustrations 5.198, 5.199, 5.200 and 5.201

Warning: *A special tool (GM no. J-28467) is available to support the en-gine during repair operations. Similar fixtures are available from rental yards. Improper lifting methods or devices are hazardous and could result in severe injury or death. DO NOT place any part of your body under the engine/transaxle when it's supported only by a jack. Failure of the lifting device could result in serious injury or death.*

Note: *The rear main (crankshaft) oil seal is a one-piece unit that can be replaced without removing the engine. However, the transaxle must be re-moved and the engine must be supported as this procedure is done. GM special tool no. J-36005 is available for seal installation, but the procedure outlined here was devised to avoid having to use the tool.*

5.198   Remove the seal housing bolts (arrows)

5.199   After removing the housing from the engine, support it on wood blocks and drive out the old seal with a punch and hammer

5.200   Drive the new seal into the housing with a block of wood or a section of pipe, if you have one large enough – don't cock the seal in the housing bore

5.201   Lubricate the seal journal and lip, then position a new gasket over the dowel pins (arrows)

194 Remove the transaxle (see Chapter 7).
195 Remove the pressure plate and clutch disc (see Chapter 8).
196 Remove the flywheel (see Chapter 2, Part A).
197 Remove the oil pan (see Steps 167 through 176).
198 After the oil pan has been removed, remove the bolts **(see illustration)**, detach the seal housing and peel off all the old gasket material.
199 Position the seal housing on a couple of wood blocks on a workbench and drive the old seal out from the back side with a punch and hammer **(see illustration)**.
200 Drive the new seal into the housing with a block of wood **(see illustration)**.
201 Lubricate the crankshaft seal journal and the lip of the new seal with multi-purpose grease. Position a new gasket on the engine block **(see illustration)**.
202 Slowly and carefully push the new seal onto the crankshaft. The seal lip is stiff, so work it onto the crankshaft with a smooth object such as the end of an extension as you push the housing against the block.
203 Install and tighten the housing bolts to the torque listed in this Chapter's specifications.
204 Install the flywheel and clutch components.
205 Reinstall the transaxle.

Engine mounts – check and replacement
Refer to illustrations 5.212 and 5.219
Warning: *A special tool (GM no. J-28467-A) is available to support the engine during repair operations. Similar fixtures are available from rental yards. Improper lifting methods or devices are hazardous and could result in severe injury or death. DO NOT place any part of your body under the engine/transaxle when it's supported only by a jack. Failure of the lifting device could result in serious injury or death.*

206 Engine mounts seldom require attention, but broken or deteriorated mounts should be replaced immediately or the added strain placed on the driveline components may cause damage or wear.
Check
207 During the check, the engine must be raised slightly to remove the weight from the mounts.
208 Raise the vehicle and support it securely on jackstands. Support the engine as described above. If the special support fixture is unavailable, position a jack under the engine oil pan. Place a large block of wood between the jack head and the oil pan, then carefully raise the engine just enough to take the weight off the mounts. **Warning:** *DO NOT place any part of your body under the engine when it's supported only by a jack!*

13

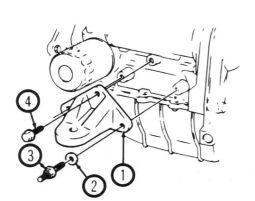

5.212   Front engine mount – exploded view

1	Bracket	4	Bolt
2	Washer	5	Nut
3	Stud	6	Mount

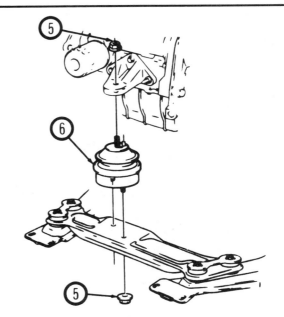

209 Check the mounts to see if the rubber is cracked, hardened or separated from the metal plates. Sometimes the rubber will split right down the center.

210 Check for movement between the mount plates and the engine or frame (use a large screwdriver or pry bar to attempt to move the mounts). If movement is noted, lower the engine and tighten the mount fasteners.

211 Rubber preservative should be applied to the mounts to slow deterioration.

Replacement
Front mount
212 Detach the negative battery cable from the battery. Remove the upper mount nut **(see illustration)**.

213 Raise the engine off the mount.

214 Remove the two lower mount nuts.

215 Remove the mount.

216 Place the new mount in position and install the nuts. Gently lower the engine and tighten the nuts securely.

217 Reconnect the negative battery cable.

Rear mount
218 Detach the negative battery cable from the battery. Remove the right lower splash shield.

219 Working under the mount, remove the nut from the through-bolt **(see illustration)**.

220 Raise the engine off the mount.

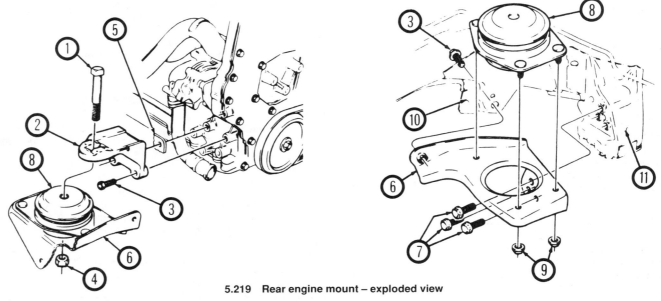

5.219   Rear engine mount – exploded view

1	Bolt	5	Transaxle support	8	Mount
2	Bracket		(partial view)	9	Nut (3)
3	Bolt	6	Bracket assembly	10	Right frame rail
4	Nut	7	Bolt (4)	11	Cowl assembly

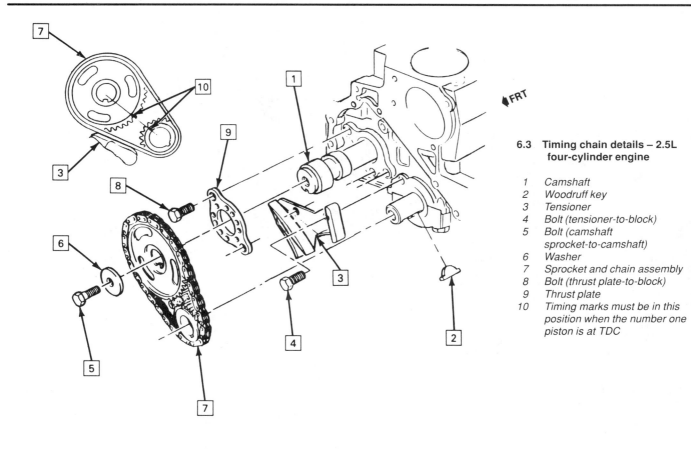

6.3   **Timing chain details – 2.5L four-cylinder engine**

1   *Camshaft*
2   *Woodruff key*
3   *Tensioner*
4   *Bolt (tensioner-to-block)*
5   *Bolt (camshaft sprocket-to-camshaft)*
6   *Washer*
7   *Sprocket and chain assembly*
8   *Bolt (thrust plate-to-block)*
9   *Thrust plate*
10   *Timing marks must be in this position when the number one piston is at TDC*

221   Remove the four mount-to-bracket nuts.
222   Remove the mount from the vehicle.
223   Installation is the reverse of removal.
224   Gently lower the engine.
225   Tighten the nuts securely.
226   Reconnect the negative battery cable.

6   2.5L overhead valve (OHV) four-cylinder engine

Timing chain, sprockets and tensioner – removal and installation
Refer to illustration 6.3

Removal
1   Beginning with the 1990 model year, the timing gears have been replaced with a timing chain and sprockets.
2   Remove the front cover (see Chapter 2, Part B).
3   Loosen, but do not remove, the camshaft sprocket bolt **(see illustration)**.
4   Align the timing marks on the camshaft sprocket and the crankshaft sprocket, with the engine at Top Dead Center (TDC) for number one cylinder. This can be confirmed by removing the spark plug from the number one cylinder and turning the engine in the normal direction of rotation while holding your finger over the spark plug hole. When you feel compression building up, the number one cylinder is approaching TDC. Continue turning the engine until the timing marks are aligned as in illustration 6.3.
5   Remove the camshaft sprocket bolt, then slip the timing chain and camshaft sprocket off the camshaft. **Note:** *If the timing chain is to be replaced, also replace the camshaft sprocket and the crankshaft sprocket.*
6   Check the tensioner for signs of wear and replace it if necessary. The tensioner is retained by a single bolt.

Installation
7   Installation is the reverse of the removal procedure, but make sure the timing marks are in alignment and tighten the camshaft sprocket bolt to the torque listed in this Chapter's Specifications.

Cylinder head bolt tightening procedure
8   1988 and later 2.5L engines require a slightly different cylinder head bolt tightening procedure.
9   Install all of the bolts finger tight, then tighten them, using the sequence shown in Chapter 2 Part B (illustration 10.25), to 18 ft-lbs.
10   Repeat the sequence, tightening all bolts except number nine, to 26 ft-lbs. Tighten bolt number nine to 18 ft-lbs.
11   Repeat the sequence again, tightening all the bolts an additional 90-degrees (1/4 turn).

Main bearing cap tightening procedure
12   When tightening the main bearing cap bolts, work from the front of the engine to the rear, tightening the bolts to the torque listed in this Chapter's Specifications.

7   V6 engines

General information
3.0L V6 engine
1   The 3.0L V6 engine remained basically unchanged through the 1988 model year, aside from a few specifications which are listed at the beginning of this Chapter.
3.3L (3300) V6 engine
2   Beginning with the 1989 model year, a 3.3L V6 (commonly referred to as the "3300") was made available, taking the place of the 3.0L engine.

13

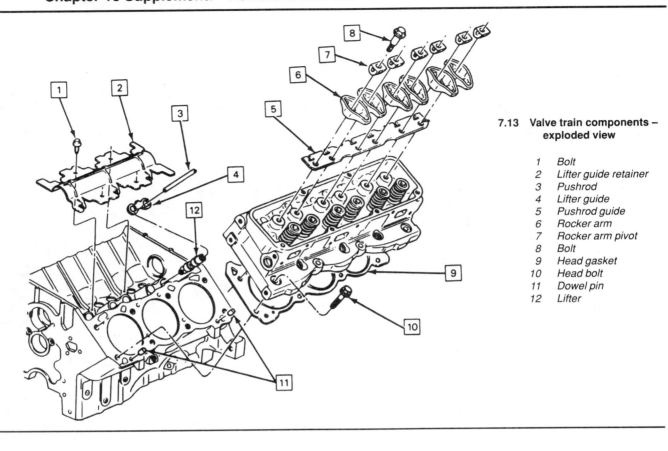

**7.13   Valve train components –
exploded view**

1   Bolt
2   Lifter guide retainer
3   Pushrod
4   Lifter guide
5   Pushrod guide
6   Rocker arm
7   Rocker arm pivot
8   Bolt
9   Head gasket
10   Head bolt
11   Dowel pin
12   Lifter

Essentially it is a bored-out 3.0L V6 with roller-type hydraulic lifters. Most of the service procedures and specifications described in Chapter 2 Part C and Part D will also apply to this engine, but the procedures that differ will be described here. Any specifications that have been changed will be listed at the beginning of this Chapter.

Cylinder head(s) – removal and installation

Note: *A torque angle meter (GM tool no. J-36660, or equivalent) is required to properly tighten the cylinder head bolts on this engine.*

3   Follow the removal, installation and bolt tightening sequence described in Chapter 2 Part C, but use the tightening procedure outlined below and the torque listed in this Chapter's Specifications.
4   Tighten the cylinder head bolts to 35 ft-lbs in sequence **(see illustration 8.20** in Chapter 2 Part C).
5   Using a torque angle meter, turn each head bolt, in sequence, an additional 130-degrees.
6   Rotate only the four center bolts an additional 30-degrees.
7   The remainder of installation is the reverse of the removal procedure.

Hydraulic lifters – removal, inspection and installation

Refer to illustration 7.13

8   As stated earlier, the 3.3L V6 engine is equipped with roller-type hydraulic valve lifters. Lifter guides and retainers are used to prevent the lifters from rotating on the camshaft lobes. The cam lobes are ground with no front-to-rear taper.
9   Remove the rocker arm covers (see Chapter 2 Part C).
10   Remove the intake manifold (see Chapter 2 Part C).
11   Loosen the rocker arm bolts and rotate the rocker arms away from the pushrods.
12   Remove the pushrods and store them in order so they can be reinstalled in their original positions.
13   Remove the lifter guide retainer bolts, then lift the retainer from the engine **(see illustration)**.
14   Remove the lifter guides.

15   Remove the lifters. A special lifter removal tool is available, or a scribe can be hooked into the groove at the top of the lifter and used to pull the lifter up. Don't use pliers or other tools on the outside of the lifter body, as they will render the lifter useless.
16   The lifters should be kept separate for reinstallation in their original bores.
17   Inspect the lifters as described in Chapter 2, Part D.
18   Installation is the reverse of the removal procedure.

Piston/connecting rod assembly – installation and rod bearing oil clearance check

Note: *A torque angle meter (GM tool no. J-36660, or equivalent) is required to properly tighten the connecting rod bolts on this engine.*

19   Follow the piston/connecting rod installation procedure described in Chapter 2 Part D, but use the following connecting rod bolt tightening method.
20   Tighten the connecting rod bolts to the torque listed in this Chapter's Specifications.
21   Using a torque angle meter, tighten the bolts an additional 50-degrees rotation.

---

8   Cooling, heating and air conditioning systems

Water pump (Quad-4 engine) – removal and installation

Refer to illustrations 8.5 and 8.13

Warning: *Wait until the engine is completely cool before beginning this procedure.*

Removal

1   Disconnect the cable from the negative terminal of the battery.
2   Drain the cooling system (see Chapter 1). Also disconnect the heater hose from the thermostat housing to ensure complete coolant draining. If the coolant is relatively new or in good condition, save it and reuse it.

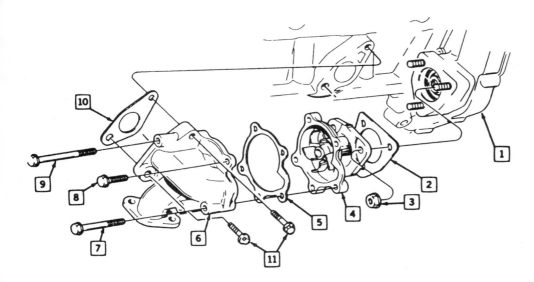

8.5   Quad-4 engine water pump components – exploded view

1	Timing chain housing
2	Gasket
3	Nut (3)
4	Water pump body
5	Gasket
6	Water pump cover
7	Bolt
8	Bolt
9	Bolt
10	Gasket
11	Bolts

3   Remove the exhaust manifold (see Section 5).

4   Remove the readiator outlet pipe-to-water pump cover bolts, leaving the lower radiator hose attached. Pull down on the radiator outlet pipe to disengage it from the water pump and detach the pipe from the oil pan and transaxle.

5   Remove the water pump cover-to-block bolts **(see illustration)**.

6   Remove the bolts/nuts and detach the water pump from the engine.

Installation

7   Clean the fastener threads and any threaded holes in the engine to remove corrosion and sealant.

8   Compare the new pump to the old one to make sure they're identical.

9   Remove all traces of old gasket material from the engine with a gasket scraper.

10   Clean the engine and water pump mating surfaces with lacquer thinner or acetone.

11   Apply a thin coat of RTV sealant to the engine side of the new gasket.

12   Apply a thin layer of RTV sealant to the gasket mating surface of the new pump, then carefully mate the gasket and the pump.

13   Lubricate the splines of the water pump drive with chassis grease prior to installation **(see illustration)**. Carefully attach the pump and gasket to the engine and start the bolts/nuts finger tight. Lubricate the O-ring

on the radiator outlet pipe with antifreeze before installing.

14   Tighten the fasteners in 1/4-turn increments to the torque figure listed in this Chapter's Specifications. Don't overtighten them or the pump may be damaged. Tighten the bolts in this sequence:

   Pump-to-chain housing
   Pump cover-to-pump assembly
   Cover-to-block, bottom bolt first
   Radiator outlet pipe-to-water pump cover

15   The remainder of reassembly is the reverse of disassembly.

16   Refill the cooling system (see Chapter 1). Run the engine and check for leaks.

9   Fuel and exhaust systems

Fuel pump relay (Quad-4 engine) – removal and installation

Refer to illustration 9.1

1   The fuel pump relay on models with the Quad-4 engine is located in the engine compartment on the firewall **(see illustration)**.

8.13   Lubricate the splines of the water pump drive with grease

9.1   Relay location – models with Quad-4 engine (exact placement of relays may vary)

1	Fuel pump relay	3	Coolant fan relay
2	A/C compressor relay	4	A/C blower relay

13

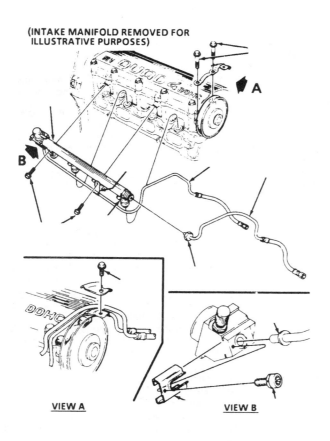

(INTAKE MANIFOLD REMOVED FOR ILLUSTRATIVE PURPOSES)

VIEW A   **VIEW B**

9.16   Fuel rail installation details – Quad-4 engine

2   Disconnect the cable from the negative terminal of the battery.
3   Detach the relay from its mounting bracket, then lift up on the retaining tab and unplug the relay from its electrical connector.
4   Installation is the reverse of removal. If a new relay is being installed, make sure it is the correct part number.

Fuel pressure relief procedure (Quad-4 engine)

Warning: *Gasoline is extremely flammable, so extra precautions must be taken when working on any part of the fuel system. Don't smoke or allow open flames or bare light bulbs near the work area. Also, don't work in a garage where a natural gas-type appliance with a pilot light is present. If you spill any fuel on your skin, rinse it off immediately with soap and water. Have a fire extinguisher rated for gasoline fires handy and know how to use it!*

5   Before servicing any component on a fuel injected vehicle, it is necessary to relieve the fuel pressure to minimize the risk of fire or personal injury.
6   Disconnect the cable from the negative terminal of the battery.
7   Unscrew the fuel filler cap to relieve any pressure built up in the fuel tank.
8   Connect a fuel pressure gauge, equipped with a bleed valve and hose (GM tool J-34730-1 or equivalent) to the Schrader valve on the fuel rail (wrap a rag around the fitting while doing this). Place the end of the bleed tube into an approved gasoline container.
9   Open the valve on the gauge to relieve the pressure. The fuel system may now be serviced.

Fuel rail and injectors (Quad-4 engine) – removal and installation

Refer to illustration 9.16

10   Disconnect the cable from the negative terminal of the battery.
11   Relieve the fuel system pressure (see Steps 5 through 9).
12   Remove the crankcase ventilation oil/air separator (see Section 11).
13   Detach the vacuum hose from the fuel pressure regulator.

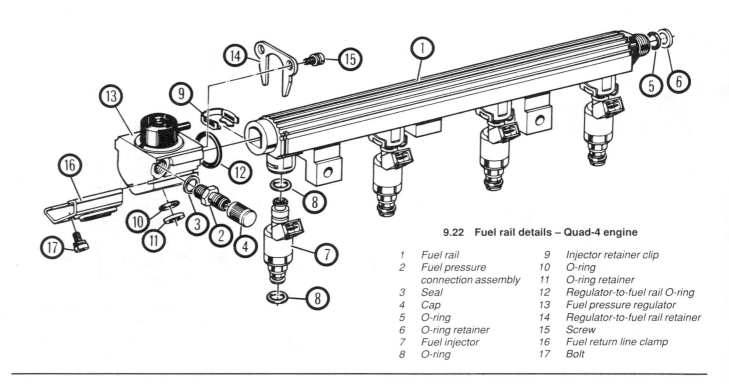

9.22   Fuel rail details – Quad-4 engine

1	Fuel rail	9	Injector retainer clip
2	Fuel pressure connection assembly	10	O-ring
		11	O-ring retainer
3	Seal	12	Regulator-to-fuel rail O-ring
4	Cap	13	Fuel pressure regulator
5	O-ring	14	Regulator-to-fuel rail retainer
6	O-ring retainer	15	Screw
7	Fuel injector	16	Fuel return line clamp
8	O-ring	17	Bolt

14   Remove the fuel rail-to-cylinder head bolts. Remove any fuel line clamp bolts, if necessary.

15   Carefully lift the fuel rail and injectors from the cylinder head, then disconnect the electrical connectors from the injectors. To disconnect the electrical connectors, push in on the wire clips, then pull the connector from the injector.

16   Remove the fuel return line clamp bolt and clamp from the fuel pressure regulator **(see illustration)**, slide the clamp off, then separate the line from the regulator.

17   Disconnect the fuel inlet line from the end of the fuel rail, using a back-up wrench on the fuel rail fitting.

18   Lift the fuel rail from the engine.

19   Refer to Chapter 4 for the fuel injector removal and installation procedure. Be sure to replace the O-rings with new ones.

20   Installation of the fuel rail is the reverse of the removal procedure, but be sure to tighten the return line clamp bolt and the fuel rail mounting bolts to the torque figures listed in this Chapter's Specifications.

Fuel pressure regulator (Quad-4 engine) – removal and installation

Refer to illustration 9.22

21   Remove the fuel rail (see Steps 10 through 18).

22   Remove the screws from the fuel pressure regulator retainer, slide the retainer off the fuel rail, then separate the regulator from the rail **(see illustration)**.

23   Installation of the fuel pressure regulator is the reverse of removal, but be sure to use a new O-ring between the regulator and the fuel rail.

---

10   Engine electrical systems

Integrated Direct Ignition (IDI) system – general information

Refer to illustrations 10.1a, 10.1b and 10.1c

1   The Quad-4 engine uses an Integrated Direct Ignition (IDI) system, which operates in a similar manner to the Direct Ignition System described in Chapter 5. The IDI system uses two ignition coils, an ignition module, a crankshaft sensor, and a secondary conductor housing, which takes the place of the spark plug wires. The crankshaft sensor is mounted on the bottom of the engine block, just above the oil pan rail **(see illustration)**. This sensor picks up signals from a reluctor ring cast into the crankshaft, which acts as a signal generator for the ignition timing. The IDI unit is mounted between the camshaft housings **(see illustrations)**.

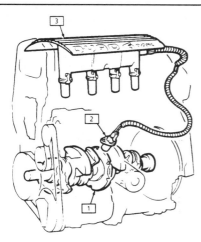

10.1a   The crankshaft sensor sends impulse signals to the ignition module

1 Crankshaft reluctor ring	3 Ignition coil and
2 Crankshaft sensor	module assembly

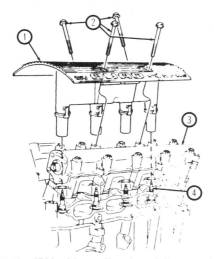

10.1b   IDI ignition coil and module assembly

1 Ignition coil and	3 Camshaft housing and cover
module assembly	4 Spark plug
2 Bolts	

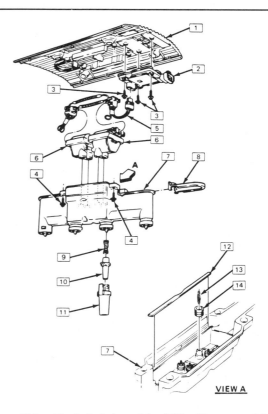

10.1c   Exploded view of the IDI ignition assembly

1	Ignition module cover	8	Cover
2	Module assembly	9	Connector
3	Bolt	10	Boot
4	Bolt	11	Retainer
5	Module wiring harness	12	Spacer
6	Coil assembly	13	Contact
7	Housing assembly	14	Seal

13

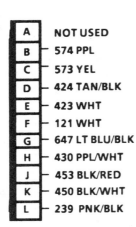

A	NOT USED
B	574 PPL
C	573 YEL
D	424 TAN/BLK
E	423 WHT
F	121 WHT
G	647 LT BLU/BLK
H	430 PPL/WHT
J	453 BLK/RED
K	450 BLK/WHT
L	239 PNK/BLK

10.3   IDI unit electrical connector details

10.16   A typical spark tester

Integrated Direct Ignition (IDI) system – check

Warning: *Because of the very high voltage generated by the ignition system, extreme care must be taken whenever an operation involving ignition system components is performed.*

Note: *These tests require a special fuel injector harness test light (GM tool J-34730-2 or equivalent), which is available at most auto parts stores. Also, a digital multi-meter will be needed (analog meters may damage some of the sensitive components).*

Engine cranks over but won't start

Refer to illustration 10.3

2   Check all the fuses.

3   Disconnect the 11-wire electrical connector from the IDI unit. Turn the ignition to the On position and connect a test light between terminals K and L **(see illustration)**. The test light should come on.

4   If the light doesn't come on, check the wiring harness for an open circuit condition.

5   If it does come on, connect the test light to the battery positive terminal. Unplug an electrical connector from one of the fuel injectors and install the special injector connector test light. Touch the test light to terminal H of the IDI unit electrical connector. The light in the fuel injector connector should blink. If it doesn't, check for an open or shorted circuit in the IDI wiring harness or the fuel injector harness. There is also the possibility that the ECM is malfunctioning. Have the vehicle checked by a dealer service department or other repair shop.

6   If the light in the injector connector does blink, connect a digital multi-meter, set on the 2-volt A.C. scale, between terminals B and C of the IDI unit electrical connector. Crank the engine and read the voltage (an assistant would be helpful here). The voltage should be more than 20-mV. If it is, a defective IDI module is indicated.

7   If the voltage is less than 20-mV, remove the crankshaft sensor from the cylinder block. Connect the digital multi-meter, set on the 2K-ohm scale, across the terminals of the sensor. The reading should be between 500 and 900 ohms. If not, replace the sensor.

8   If the resistance reading is OK, check the sensor to make sure it is still magnetic. If it isn't, replace it. If it is, check the wiring to the sensor for an open or shorted sircuit condition.

9   If these checks still don't pinpoint the problem, take the vehicle to a dealer service department or other repair shop for further diagnosis.

Engine runs but misfires

Refer to illustration 10.16

Note: *These checks assume that the engine is in good mechanical condition.*

10   Remove the crankcase ventilation oil/air separator (see Section 11) for access to the injector electrical connectors.

11   Disconnect the Idle Air Control (IAC) valve electrical connector from the IAC valve (mounted on the throttle body).

12   Start the engine and momentarily disconnect each injector electrical connector, one at a time. As an injector is disconnected, the engine rpm should drop noticeably. If it doesn't, the particular injector that was disconnected wasn't working to begin with.

13   Connect the special fuel injector harness test light to the electrical connector of the injector that didn't result in an rpm drop when it was disconnected. Start the engine and watch the light – it should blink, indicating the signal to the injector is present.

14   If it doesn't blink, there is a problem with the harness to the injector, a faulty ECM or a malfunctioning (shorted) fuel injector. Check the resistance of all the injectors. The resistance reading should be between 1.8 and 2.2 ohms. If any injector measures less than 1.8 ohms, replace it. If the problem persists, take the vehicle to a dealer service department or other repair shop for further diagnosis.

15   If the light does blink, as it's supposed to, the signal to the fuel injector is OK. Check the resistance value of that injector – the resistance reading should be as stated in the above Step. If not, replace the injector.

16   If the injector resistance is OK, remove the IDI unit from between the camshaft housings and connect spark plug jumper wires between the IDI unit and the spark plugs. Disconnect the spark plug wire from the spark plug of the affected cylinder and attach a spark tester (available at most auto parts stores) **(see illustration)**.

17   Crank the engine over and see if there is spark present at the tester. If there is spark, there may be a problem with the fuel injector. Check the rest of the cylinders with the spark tester in the same way, but if they all spark normally it is recommended the vehicle be taken to a dealer service department or other repair shop for further diagnosis.

18   If there isn't any spark present, detach the spark plug boot assemblies from the affected coil. Using a digital multi-meter set on the 20K-ohms scale, measure the resistance between the coil terminals (pair for cylinders one and four, or cylinders two and three). The resistance should be less than 10K-ohms – if it's higher, replace the coil.

19   Now check the resistance between the coil terminals to the cover plate – the reading should be infinite. If it isn't, replace the coil.

20   If the resistance values are OK, disconnect the coil electrical connector at the module. Connect a test light (at the module) between the battery positive terminal to the coil (terminal A) and terminal B or C. Crank the engine over and watch the light. If the light blinks, check for an open or shorted circuit in the coil wiring harness, or a faulty coil or boot.

21   If the light doesn't blink, check for a bad connection between the coil and the module. If the connection is OK, the IDI module is defective.

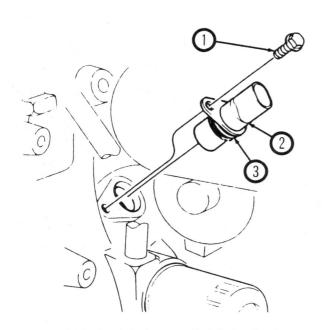

10.36   Crankshaft sensor installation details

1	Bolt	3	O-ring
2	Crankshaft sensor		

Integrated Direct Ignition (IDI) system – component removal and installation

IDI unit

22   Disconnect the cable from the negative terminal of the battery.
23   Unplug the electrical connector from the IDI unit.

24   Remove the four bolts that retain the IDI unit to the camshaft housings **(see illustration 10.1b)**.
25   Pull the IDI unit straight up, disconnecting it from the spark plugs.
26   Installation is the reverse of removal.

Ignition coil(s)
27   Remove the IDI unit from the engine.
28   Remove the coil housing-to-cover screws and remove the cover **(see illustration 10.1c)**.
29   Unplug the electrical connectors from the coil. Lift the coils from the housing.
30   Installation is the reverse of the removal procedure.

Ignition module
31   Remove the IDI unit from the engine.
32   Disconnect the module-to-coil electrical connector.
33   Remove the module-to-cover screws and separate the module from the cover **(see illustration 10.1c)**.
34   Installation is the reverse of the removal procedure.

Crankshaft sensor
Refer to illustration 10.36
35   Unplug the electrical connector at the sensor.
36   Remove the bolt that retains the sensor to the engine **(see illustration)**.
37   Pull the sensor from the cylinder block.
38   Installation is the reverse of the removal procedure, but be sure to check the O-ring for hardness, cracking and general deterioration, which may cause a leak. Replace the O-ring if necessary. Lubricate the O-ring with engine oil before installing the sensor.

---

11   Emissions control systems

Trouble codes

1   Along with the new engines and modified fuel, ignition and emissions control systems, are some additional or altered trouble codes. When accessing trouble codes, check the chart in this Chapter first, to see if any stored codes are listed here. If not, refer to the trouble code chart in Chapter 6.

Trouble code	Circuit or system	Probable cause
Code 16 (3.3L V6) (1 flash, pause, 6 flashes)	System voltage high	Check voltage across battery terminals with the engine running above 800 rpm. If the voltage is above 16-volts, the alternator/voltage regulator is faulty. If the reading is below 16-volts, the ECM is malfunctioning.*
Code 26 (2 flashes, pause, 6 flashes)	Quad–driver circuit	Take the vehicle to a dealer service department or other repair shop for diagnosis.
Codes 27 or 28 (3.3L V6) (2 flashes, pause, 7 or 8 flashes)	Gear switches circuits	Check the wiring harness and electrical connector to the transaxle for an open or shorted circuit condition. Furtherdiagnosis must be performed by a dealer service department or transmission repair shop.
Code 31 (3.3L V6) (3 flashes, pause, 1 flash)	Park/neutral switch circuit	Adjust the park/neutral switch (see Chapter 7). Clear code and see if it resets. If it does, either the switch, ECM or wiring is defective.*
Code 34 (3.3L V6) (3 flashes, pause, 4 flashes	MAF sensor	Open or shorted circuit condition in sensor wiring harness, loose electrical connector, faulty MAF sensor or malfunctioning ECM.*
Code 35 (Quad–4) (3 flashes, pause, 5 flashes)	Idle speed error	Check IAC valve wiring harness for an open or shorted circuit condition. If OK, IAC valve or ECM is faulty.*
Code 38 (3.3l v6) (3 flashes, pause, 8 flashes)		Adjust brake switch and clear code. If code resets, check wiring harness to switch. If OK, replace switch*. Also could be faulty ECM or TCC solenoid.*
Code 39 (3.3L V6) (3 flashes, pause, 9 flashes)	TCC circuit	Check wiring harness to transaxle for an open or shorted circuit condition. Further diagnosis must be left to a dealer service department or other repair shop.

13

Trouble code	Circuit or system	Probable cause
Code 41 (Quad–4) (4 flashes, pause, 1 flash)	1X reference circuit	The ignition module sends a signal to the ECM, once per crankshaft revolution, to tell the ECM when to pulse the fuel injectors. Check the wiring to the ignition module. If OK, the ECM or ignition module could be at fault.*
Code 42 (Quad–4) (4 flashes, pause, 2 flashes)	Electronic Spark Timing	Check the wiring harness from the ECM to the ignition module for an open or shorted circuit condition. If OK, the ECM or the ignition module is defective.*
Code 46 (3.3L V6) (4 flashes, pause, 6 flashes)	Power steering pressure switch	Check the wiring from the switch for an open or shorted circuit condition. If OK, the switch or the ECM may be faulty.*
Code 48 (3.3L V6) (4 flashes, pause, 8 flashes)	Misfire diagnosis	Check the spark plugs and wires (see Chapter 1) and replace if necessary. Check for proper fuel pressure and fuel injector operation (see Chapter 4). Check the compression of all cylinders. Replace the oxygen sensor.*
Code 62 (Quad–4) (6 flashes, pause, 2 flashes)	Gear switches circuit	See codes 27 and 28.
Code 65 (Quad–4) (6 flashes, pause, 5 flashes)	Fuel injector circuit	Check fuel injection wiring harness and electrical connectors. Check the resistance of all the injectors, replacing any that aren't to specification. Further diagnosis should be performed by a dealer service department or other repair shop.
Code 66 (6 flashes, pause, 6 flashes)	A/C pressure sensor circuit	Check the wiring harness from the sensor for an open or shorted condition. If OK, the sensor or the ECM may be at fault.*

Component replacement may not cure the problem in all cases. For this reason, you may want to seek professional advice before purchasing replacement parts.

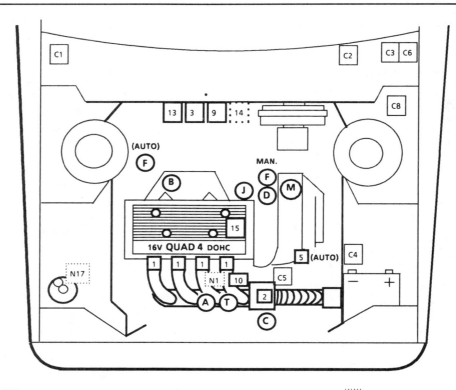

11.2   Emission control and related component locations – Quad-4 engine (1990 model shown, others similar)

☐ **COMPUTER HARNESS**	☐ **CONTROLLED DEVICES**	◯ **INFORMATION SENSORS**	⋯ **NOT ECM CONNECTED**
C1 Electronic Control Module (ECM)	**1** Fuel injector	**A** Manifold pressure (M.A.P.)	**N1** Crankcase vent oil/air separator
C2 ALDL diagnostic connector	**2** Idle air control valve	**B** Exhaust oxygen	**N17** Fuel vapor canister
C3 "SERVICE ENGINE SOON" light	***3** Fuel pump relay	**C** Throttle position	***N14** A/C High speed fan relay
C4 ECM power (2)	**5** Torq. converter clutch connector	**D** Coolant temperature	
C5 ECM harness ground	***9** Engine coolant fan relay	**F** Vehicle speed	***** Exact placement of relays may vary.
C6 Fuse panel	**10** Canister purge solenoid	**J** ESC knock (below manifold)	Circuit diagrams and wire colors may
C8 Fuel pump test connector	***13** A/C compressor relay	**M** P/N (Park/Neutral Switch) (Auto)	be used for positive identification.
	15 IDI module (under IDI cover)	**T** Manifold air temperature	

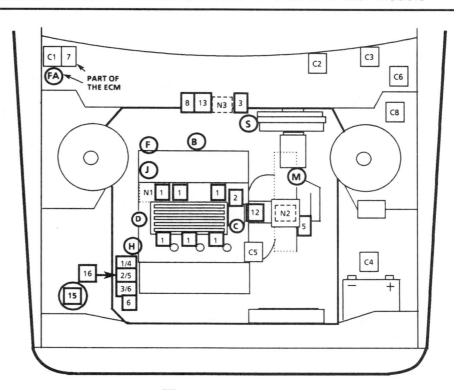

11.3   Emission control and related component locations – 3.3L V6 engine (1990 model shown, others similar)

☐ CONTROLLED DEVICES

1   Fuel injector
2   Idle Air Control valve (IAC)
*3   Fuel pump relay
5   Torque Converter Clutch connector (TCC)
6   Computer Controlled Coil Ignition(C^{3}I)
7   Electronic Spark Control module (ESC)
*8   Engine coolant fan relay
12   Mass Air Flow Sensor (part of TBI)
*13   A/C compressor relay
15   Fuel vapor canister solenoid
16   Coil Assemblies

☐ COMPUTER HARNESS

C1   Electronic Control
C2   ALDL diagnostic connector
C3   "SERVICE ENGINE SOON" light
C4   ECM power fusible link
C5   ECM harness ground
C6   Fuse panel
C8   Fuel pump test connector

⬜ NOT ECM CONNECTED

N1   Crankcase vent valve (PCV)
N2   Air Cleaner
*N3   Blower Motor Relay

* EXACT ORDER OF RELAYS MAY VARY.

◯ INFORMATION SENSORS

B   Oxygen Sensor
C   Throttle Position (TPS)
D   Coolant Temperature
F   Vehicle Speed (VSS)
Fa   Vehicle Speed Sensor Buffer
H   Dual Crank Sensor
J   ESC knock sensor
M   P/N switch
S   P/S switch

11.4   Quad-4 engine oil/air separator

1   *Oil/air separator*
2   *Intake duct-to-air cleaner hose*
3   *Chain housing-to-separator hose*
4   *Fill tube-to-separator hose*
5   *Retaining bolts*
6   *Intake-to-separator hose*

Emissions control component locations
Refer to illustrations 11.2 and 11.3

2   The 2.3L four-cylinder (Quad-4) engine uses many of the emissions control components described in Chapter 6 (**see illustration**).
3   Although similar to the 3.0L V6 engine, some of the emissions control component locations on the 3.3L V6 engine have been changed (**see illustration**).

Positive Crankcase Ventilation (PCV) system (Quad-4 engine)

General information
Refer to illustration 11.4

4   Instead of a ventilating the crankcase the conventional way, using a PCV valve, the Quad-4 engine uses an oil/air separator crankcase breather arrangement. Blow-by gases are continuously drawn through a crankcase ventilation oil/air separator and into the intake manifold. The oil/air separator causes oil droplets, which may be suspended in the blow-by gases, to be separated from the gases and allows them to drain back into the crankcase through a hose (**see illustration**).
5   If the oil/air separator becomes clogged, it must be replaced as a unit.

Oil/air separator – removal and installation
6   Label and remove all hoses from the oil/air separator.
7   Remove the mounting bolts and detach it from the engine.
8   Installation is the reverse of the removal procedure.

13

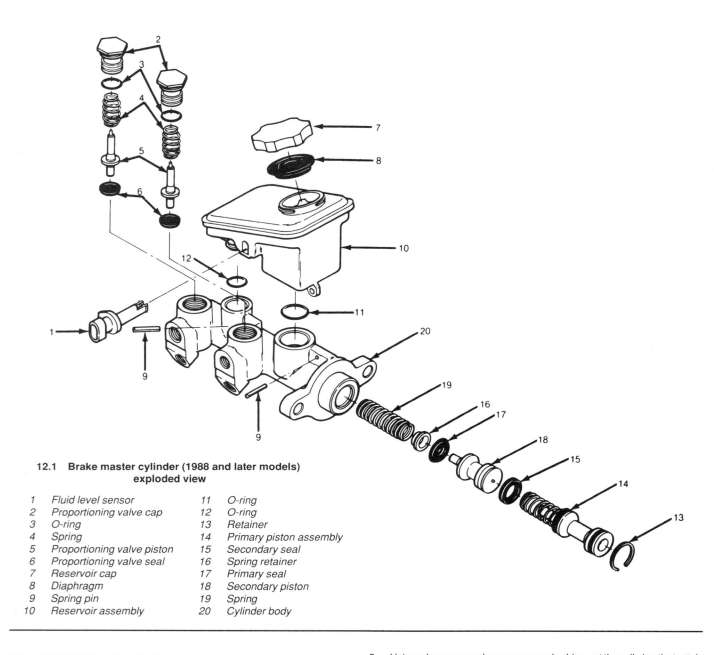

**12.1   Brake master cylinder (1988 and later models)
exploded view**

1	Fluid level sensor	11	O-ring
2	Proportioning valve cap	12	O-ring
3	O-ring	13	Retainer
4	Spring	14	Primary piston assembly
5	Proportioning valve piston	15	Secondary seal
6	Proportioning valve seal	16	Spring retainer
7	Reservoir cap	17	Primary seal
8	Diaphragm	18	Secondary piston
9	Spring pin	19	Spring
10	Reservoir assembly	20	Cylinder body

12   Brakes

Brake master cylinder – general information
Refer to illustration 12.1

1   The brake master cylinder on 1988 and later models is similar to the one shown in Chapter 9, with the exception of the location of the proportioning valves and the mounting of the fluid reservoir **(see illustration)**. When overhauling the master cylinder, follow the procedure outlined in Chapter 9, but use the reservoir and proportioning valve removal and installation procedure described here.

Master cylinder fluid reservoir – removal and installation
Refer to illustration 12.3

2   Drain all of the fluid from the master cylinder, then mount the cylinder in a vise, as described in Chapter 9 (Master cylinder – removal, overhaul and installation).

3   Using a hammer and a narrow punch, drive out the roll pins that retain the reservoir to the cylinder **(see illustration)**.
4   Carefully pry the reservoir from the cylinder body.
5   To install the reservoir, push it down into the grommets in the cylinder body, then tap in the roll pins. If the roll pins are loose, replace them with new ones.

Proportioning valves – removal and installation
Removal
6   Remove the fluid reservoir.
7   Unscrew the valve caps from the master cylinder body **(see illustration 12.1)**.
8   Remove the O-rings and springs, then pull the pistons from the bores with needle-nose pliers. **Note:** *Be careful not to scratch the stems of the pistons.*
9   Check the proportioning valve pistons for corrosion or other signs of damage, replacing them if necessary. Clean all parts in denatured alcohol or brake system cleaner. Dry them off with compressed air, if available.

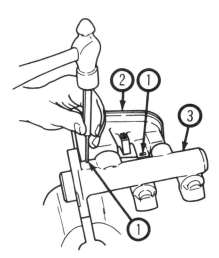

12.3   Drive the roll pins out with a hammer and a narrow punch

1	*Roll pin*	*3*	*Cylinder body*
2	*Reservoir*		

Installation

10   Using the silicone grease supplied in the overhaul kit, lubricate the new O-rings, proportioning valve seals and and the proportioning valve pistons.

11   Install the new seals to the proportioning valve pistons, with the lips of the seals facing up **(see illustration 12.1)**.

12   Install the piston assemblies to the master cylinder body, followed by the springs.

13   Install new O-rings in the grooves of the proportioning valve caps. Install the caps, tightening them to the torque listed in this Chapter's Specifications.

14   Install the reservoir and bench bleed the master cylinder (see Chapter 9).

15   Install the master cylinder and bleed the brake system (see Chapter 9).

13   Body

Automatic shoulder harnesses – general information

Many late model vehicles are equipped with automatic front seat shoulder harnesses. They are termed automatic because you don't have to buckle them – the shoulder harness automatically positions itself when the door is closed. On some vehicles, an emergency release lever allows the harness to be manually removed for exit in an emergency. **Warning:** *Be sure to fasten the manual seatbelt as well. The automatic shoulder harness will not work properly unless the seatbelt is fastened.*

Most systems have a warning light and buzzer that indicate the emergency release lever has been pulled up, releasing the shoulder harness. Make sure the release lever is down and the light/buzzer are off to ensure proper operation of the automatic shoulder harness. Also, if you disconnect any wires or remove any automatic shoulder harness components when performing repair procedures on other vehicle components, be sure to reinstall everything and check the harness for proper operation when the repairs are complete.

Since the automatic shoulder harness is operated by several electrical switches, diagnosis and repair must be done by a dealer service department. Do not jeopardize the safety of front seat occupants – if the automatic shoulder harness malfunctions, or you have questions regarding the proper use or operation of the system, contact a dealer service department.

14   Chassis electrical system

Wiring diagrams

Included in this Supplement are selected wiring diagrams that apply only to those circuits which differ significantly from earlier models. If a particular circuit is not included here, refer to the wiring diagram for the latest model in Chapter 12.

Wiring diagrams
begin on next page

13

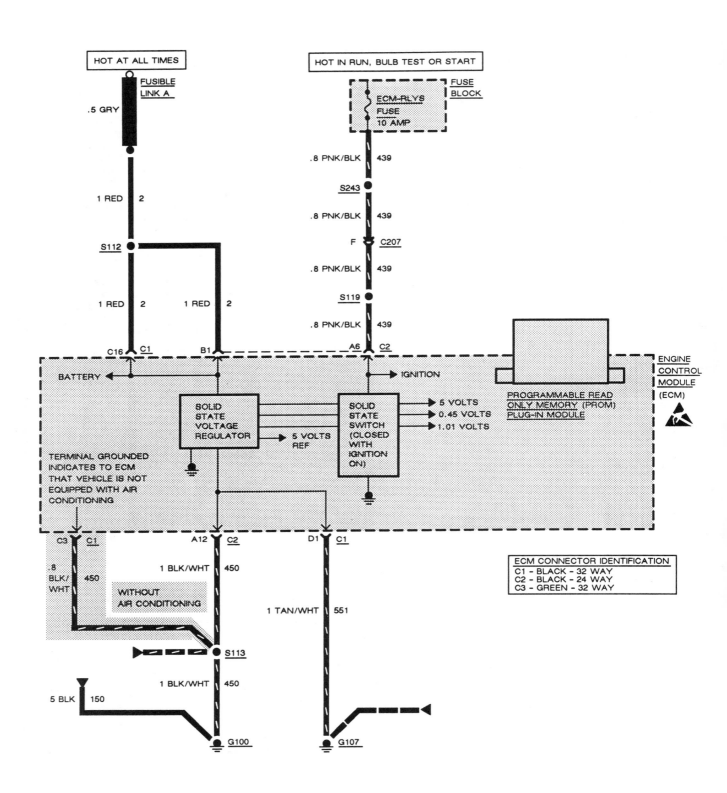

Multi-port fuel injection power distribution (Quad-4 engine) – 1990 shown, others similar

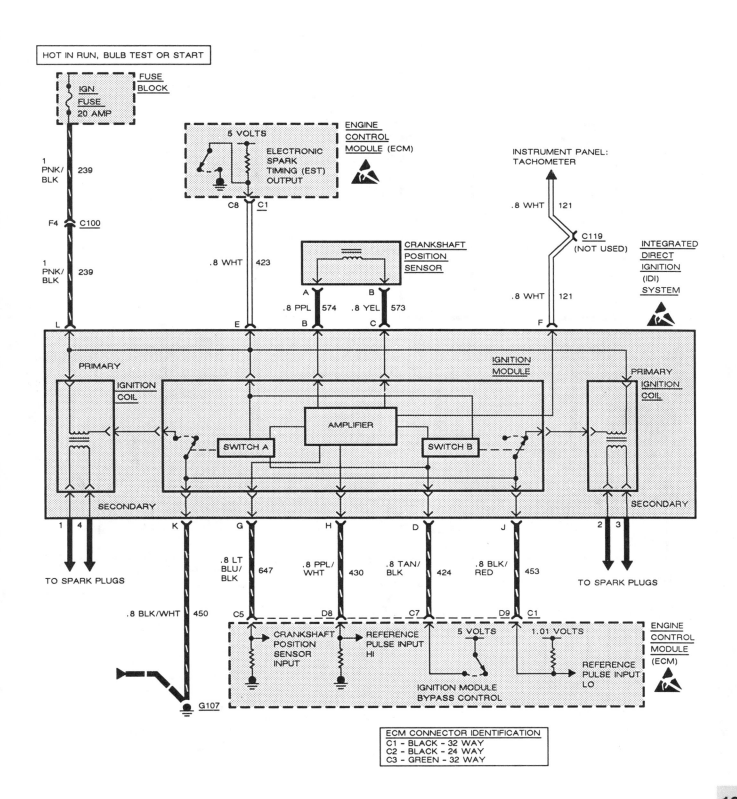

Integrated Direct Ignition (IDI) system (Quad-4 engine) – 1990 shown, others similar

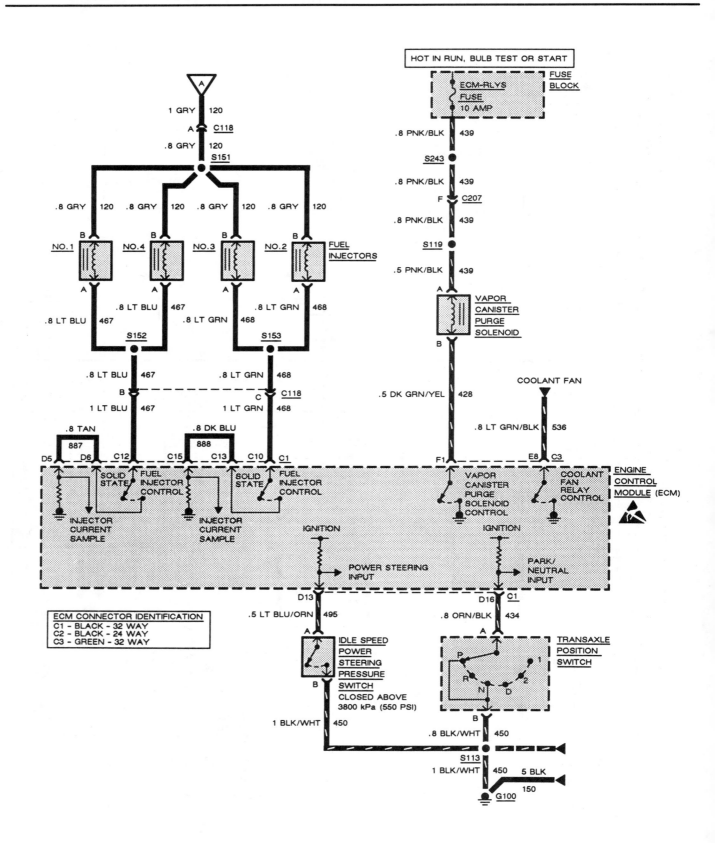

Fuel injectors and engine data sensors (Quad-4 engine) – 1990 shown, others similar (1 of 3)

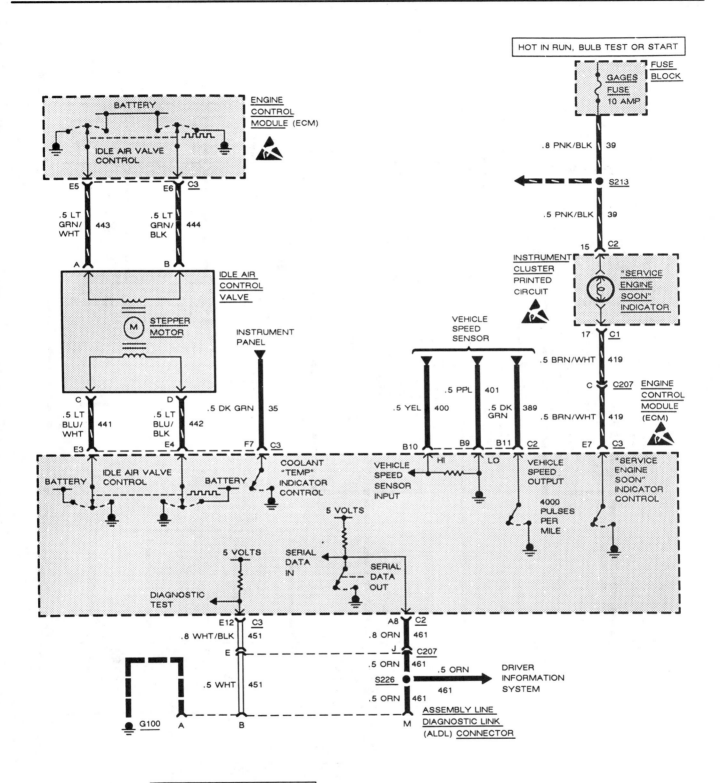

Idle air control valve and engine data sensors (Quad-4 engine) – 1990 shown, others similar (2 of 3)

13

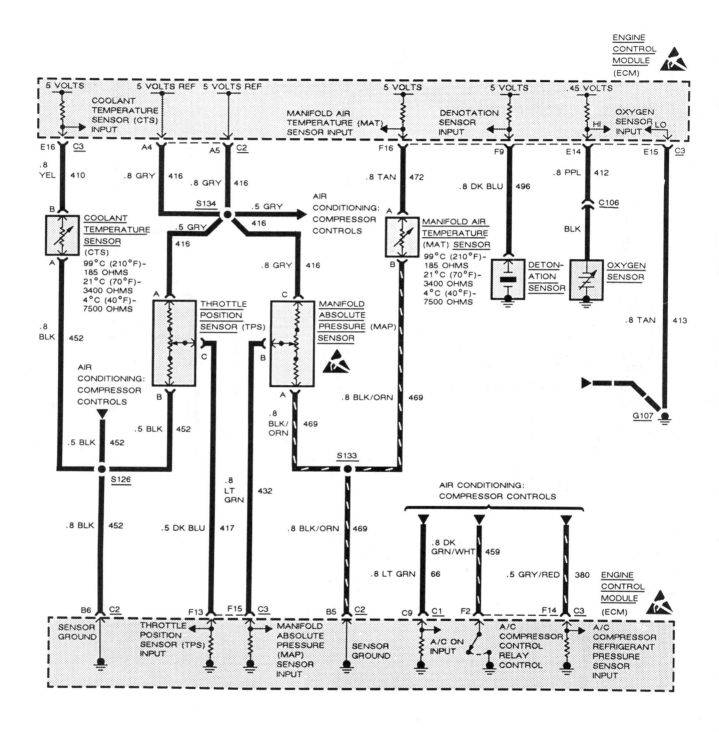

Engine data sensors (Quad-4 engine) – 1990 shown, others similar (3 of 3)

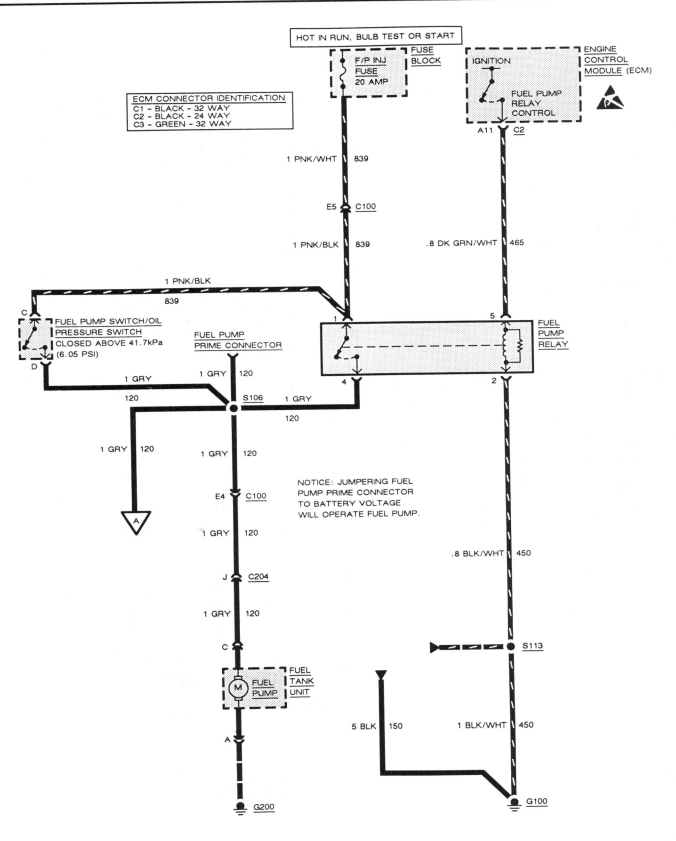

Fuel pump circuit (Quad-4 engine) – 1990 shown, others similar

13

Index

HAYNES AUTOMOTIVE MANUALS

NOTE: New manuals are added to this list on a periodic basis. If you do not see a listing for your vehicle, consult your local Haynes dealer for the latest product information.

ALFA-ROMEO
531	Alfa Romeo Sedan & Coupe '73 thru '80

AMC
	Jeep CJ – see JEEP (412)
694	Mid-size models, Concord, Hornet, Gremlin & Spirit '70 thru '83
934	(Renault) Alliance & Encore '83 '87

AUDI
615	4000 '80 thru '87
428	5000 '77 thru '83
1117	5000 '84 thru '88
207	Fox '73 thru '79

AUSTIN
049	Healey 100/6 & 3000 Roadster '56 thru '68
	Healey Sprite – see MG Midget (265)

BLMC
260	1100, 1300 & Austin America '62 thru '74
527	Mini '59 thru '69
*646	Mini '69 thru '88

BMW
276	320i all 4 cyl models '75 thru '83
632	528i & 530i '75 thru '80
240	1500 thru 2002 exceptTurbo '59 thru '77
348	2500, 2800, 3.0 & Bavaria '69 thru '76

BUICK
	Century (front wheel drive) – see GENERAL MOTORS A-Cars (829)
*1627	Buick, Oldsmobile & Pontiac Full-size (Front wheel drive) '85 thru '90 Buick Electra, LeSabre and Park Avenue; Oldsmobile Delta 88 Royale, Ninety Eight and Regency; Pontiac Bonneville
*1551	Buick, Oldsmobile & Pontiac Full-size (Rear wheel drive) Buick Electra '70 thru '84, Estate '70 thru '90, LeSabre '70 thru '79 Oldsmobile Custom Cruiser '70 thru '90, Delta 88 '70 thru '85, Ninety-eight '70 thru '84, Pontiac Bonneville '70 thru '86, Catalina '70 thru '81, Grandville '70 thru '86, Parisienne '84 thru '86
627	Mid-size all rear-drive Regal & Century models with V6, V8 and Turbo '74 thru '87
	Regal – see GENERAL MOTORS (1671) Skyhawk – see GM J-Cars (766)
552	Skylark all X-car models '80 thru '85

CADILLAC
*751	Cadillac Rear Wheel Drive all gasoline models '70 thru '90 Cimarron – see GM J-Cars (766)

CAPRI
296	2000 MK I Coupe '71 thru '75
283	2300 MK II Coupe '74 thru '78
205	2600 & 2800 V6 Coupe '71 thru '75
375	2800 Mk II V6 Coupe '75 thru '78
	Mercury Capri – see FORD Mustang (654)

CHEVROLET
*1477	Astro & GMC Safari Mini-vans '85 thru '90
554	Camaro V8 '70 thru '81
*866	Camaro '82 thru '90
	Cavalier – see GM J-Cars (766) Celebrity – see GM A-Cars (829)
625	Chevelle, Malibu & El Camino all V6 & V8 models '69 thru '87
449	Chevette & Pontiac T1000 '76 thru '87
550	Citation '80 thru '85
*1628	Corsica/Beretta '87 thru '90
274	Corvette all V8 models '68 thru '82
*1336	Corvette '84 thru '89
704	Full-size Sedans Caprice, Impala, Biscayne, Bel Air & Wagons, all V6 & V8 models '69 thru '90
	Lumina – see GENERAL MOTORS (1671)
319	Luv Pick-up all 2WD & 4WD '72 thru '82
626	Monte Carlo all V6, V8 & Turbo '70 thru '88
241	Nova all V8 models '69 thru '79
*1642	Nova & Geo Prizm front wheel drive '85 thru '90
*420	Pick-ups '67 thru '87 – Chevrolet & GMC, all V8 & in-line 6 cyl 2WD & 4WD '67 thru '87
*1664	Pick-ups '88 thru '90 – Chevrolet & GMC, all full-size (C and K) models, '88 thru '90
*1727	Sprint & Geo Metro '85 thru '91
*831	S-10 & GMC S-15 Pick-ups '82 thru '90
*345	Vans – Chevrolet & GMC, V8 & in-line 6 cyl models '68 thru '89
208	Vega except Cosworth '70 thru '77

CHRYSLER
*1337	Chrysler & Plymouth Mid-size front wheel drive '82 thru '89
	K-Cars – see DODGE Aries (723) Laser – see DODGE Daytona (1140)

DATSUN
402	200SX '77 thru '79
647	200SX '80 thru '83
228	B-210 '73 thru '78
525	210 '78 thru '82

206	240Z, 260Z & 280Z Coupe & 2+2 '70 thru '78
563	280ZX Coupe & 2+2 '79 thru '83
	300ZX – see NISSAN (1137)
679	310 '78 thru '82
123	510 & PL521 Pick-up '68 thru '73
430	510 '78 thru '81
372	610 '72 thru '76
277	620 Series Pick-up '73 thru '79
	720 Series Pick-up – see NISSAN Pick-ups (771)
376	810/Maxima all gas models '77 thru '84
124	1200 '70 thru '73
368	F10 '76 thru '79
	Pulsar – see NISSAN (876) Sentra – see NISSAN (982) Stanza – see NISSAN (981)

DODGE
*723	Aries & Plymouth Reliant '81 thru '89
*1231	Caravan & Plymouth Voyager Mini-Vans '84 thru '89
699	Challenger & Plymouth Saporro '78 thru '83
236	Colt '71 thru '77
419	Colt (rear wheel drive) '77 thru '80
610	Colt & Plymouth Champ (front wheel drive) '78 thru '87
*556	D50 & Plymouth Arrow Pick-ups '79 thru '88
*1668	Dakota Pick-up all models '87 thru '90
234	Dart & Plymouth Valiant all 6 cyl models '67 thru '76
*1140	Daytona & Chrysler Laser '84 thru '89
*545	Omni & Plymouth Horizon '78 thru '90
*912	Pick-ups all full-size models '74 thru '90
*349	Vans – Dodge & Plymouth V8 & V6 cyl models '71 thru '89

FIAT
080	124 Sedan & Wagon all ohv & dohc models '66 thru '75
094	124 Sport Coupe & Spider '68 thru '78
310	131 & Brava '75 thru '80
479	Strada '79 thru '82
273	X1/9 '74 thru '80

FORD
*1476	Aerostar Mini-vans '86 thru '90
788	Bronco and Pick-ups '73 thru '79
*880	Bronco and Pick-ups '80 thru '90
014	Cortina MK II except Lotus '66 thru '70
295	Cortina MK III 1600 & 2000 ohc '70 thru '76
268	Courier Pick-up '72 thru '82
789	Escort & Mercury Lynx all models '81 thru '90
560	Fairmont & Mercury Zephyr all in-line & V8 models '78 thru '83
334	Fiesta '77 thru '80
754	Ford & Mercury Full-size, Ford LTD & Mercury Marquis ('75 thru '82); Ford Custom 500, Country Squire, Crown Victoria & Mercury Colony Park ('75 thru '87); Ford LTD Crown Victoria & Mercury Gran Marquis ('83 thru '87)
359	Granada & Mercury Monarch all in-line, 6 cyl & V8 models '75 thru '80
773	Ford & Mercury Mid-size, Ford Thunderbird & Mercury Cougar ('75 thru '82); Ford LTD & Mercury Marquis ('83 thru '86); Ford Torino, Gran Torino, Elite, Ranchero pick-up, LTD II, Mercury Montego, Comet, XR-7 & Lincoln Versailles ('75 thru '86)
*654	Mustang & Mercury Capri all models including Turbo '79 thru '90
357	Mustang V8 '64-1/2 thru '73
231	Mustang II all 4 cyl, V6 & V8 models '74 thru '78
204	Pinto '70 thru '74
649	Pinto & Mercury Bobcat '75 thru '80
*1026	Ranger & Bronco II gasoline models '83 thru '90
*1421	Taurus & Mercury Sable '86 thru '90
*1418	Tempo & Mercury Topaz all gasoline models '84 thru '89
1338	Thunderbird & Mercury Cougar/XR7 '83 thru '88
*1725	Thunderbird & Mercury Cougar '89 thru '90
*344	Vans all V8 Econoline models '69 thru '90

GENERAL MOTORS
*829	A-Cars – Chevrolet Celebrity, Buick Century, Pontiac 6000 & Oldsmobile Cutlass Ciera '82 thru '89
*766	J-Cars – Chevrolet Cavalier, Pontiac J-2000, Oldsmobile Firenza, Buick Skyhawk & Cadillac Cimarron '82 thru '90
*1420	N-Cars – Buick Somerset '85 thru '87, Pontiac Grand Am and Oldsmobile Calais '85 thru '90; Buick Skylark '86 thru '90
*1671	GM: Buick Regal, Chevrolet Lumina, Oldsmobile Cutlass Supreme, Pontiac Grand Prix, all front wheel drive models '88 thru '90

GEO
	Metro – see CHEVROLET Sprint (1727) Tracker – see SUZUKI Samurai (1626) Prizm – see CHEVROLET Nova (1642)

GMC
	Safari – see CHEVROLET ASTRO (1477) Vans & Pick-ups – see CHEVROLET (420, 831, 345, 1664)

HONDA
138	360, 600 & Z Coupe '67 thru '75
351	Accord CVCC '76 thru '83
*1221	Accord '84 thru '89
160	Civic 1200 '73 thru '79
633	Civic 1300 & 1500 CVCC '80 thru '83
297	Civic 1500 CVCC '75 thru '79
*1227	Civic all models '84 thru '90
*601	Prelude CVCC '79 thru '89

HYUNDAI
*1552	Excel '86 thru '89

ISUZU
*1641	Trooper & Pick-up all gasoline models '81 thru '90

JAGUAR
098	MK I & II, 240 & 340 Sedans '55 thru '69
*242	XJ6 all 6 cyl models '68 thru '86
*478	XJ12 & XJS all 12 cyl models '72 thru '85
140	XK-E 3.8 & 4.2 all 6 cyl models '61 thru '72

JEEP
*1553	Cherokee, Comanche & Wagoneer Limited '84 thru '89
412	CJ '49 thru '86

LADA
*413	1200, 1300. 1500 & 1600 all models including Riva '74 thru '86

LAND ROVER
314	Series II, IIA, & III all 4 cyl gasoline models '58 thru '86
529	Diesel '58 thru '80

MAZDA
648	626 Sedan & Coupe (rear wheel drive) '79 thru '82
*1082	626 & MX-6 (front wheel drive) '83 thru '90
*267	B1600, B1800 & B2000 Pick-ups '72 thru '90
370	GLC Hatchback (rear wheel drive) '77 thru '83
757	GLC (front wheel drive) '81 thru '86
109	RX2 '71 thru '75
096	RX3 '72 thru '76
460	RX-7 '79 thru '85
*1419	RX-7 '86 thru '89

MERCEDES-BENZ
*1643	190 Series all 4-cyl. gasoline '84 thru '88
346	230, 250 & 280 Sedan, Coupe & Roadster all 6 cyl sohc models '68 thru '72
983	280 123 Series all gasoline models '77 thru '81
698	350 & 450 Sedan, Coupe & Roadster '71 thru '80
697	Diesel 123 Series 200D, 220D, 240D, 240TD; 300D, 300CD, 300TD, 4- & 5-cyl incl. Turbo '76 thru '85

MERCURY
See FORD Listing

MG
475	MGA '56 thru '62
111	MGB Roadster & GT Coupe '62 thru '80
265	MG Midget & Austin Healey Sprite Roadster '58 thru '80

MITSUBISHI
*1669	Cordia, Tredia, Galant, Precis & Mirage '83 thru '90 Pick-up – see Dodge D-50 (556)

MORRIS
074	(Austin) Marina 1.8 '71 thru '80
024	Minor 1000 sedan & wagon '56 thru '71

NISSAN
1137	300ZX all Turbo & non-Turbo '84 thru '89
*1341	Maxima '85 thru '89
*771	Pick-ups/Pathfinder gas models '80 thru '88
*876	Pulsar '83 thru '86
*982	Sentra '82 thru '90
*981	Stanza '82 thru '90

OLDSMOBILE
	Custom Cruiser – see BUICK Full-size (1551)
658	Cutlass all standard gasoline V6 & V8 models '74 thru '88
	Cutlass Ciera – see GM A-Cars (829) Cutlass Supreme – see GM (1671) Firenza – see GM J-Cars (766) Ninety-eight – see BUICK Full-size (1551) Omega – see PONTIAC Phoenix & Omega (551)

PEUGEOT
161	504 all gasoline models '68 thru '79
663	504 all diesel models '74 thru '83

PLYMOUTH
425	Arrow '76 thru '80 For all other PLYMOUTH titles, see DODGE listing.

PONTIAC
	T1000 – see CHEVROLET Chevette (449) J-2000 – see GM J-Cars (766) 6000 – see GM A-Cars (829)

1232	Fiero '84 thru '88
555	Firebird all V8 models except Turbo '70 thru '81
*867	Firebird '82 thru '89
	Full-size Rear Wheel Drive – see Buick, Oldsmobile, Pontiac Full-size (1551) Grand Prix – see General Motors (1671)
551	Phoenix & Oldsmobile Omega all X-car models '80 thru '84

PORSCHE
*264	911 all Coupe & Targa models except Turbo '65 thru '89
239	914 all 4 cyl models '69 thru '76
397	924 including Turbo '76 thru '82
*1027	944 including Turbo '83 thru '89

RENAULT
141	5 Le Car '76 thru '83
079	8 & 10 with 58.4 cu in engines '62 thru '72
097	12 Saloon & Estate 1289 cc engines '70 thru '80
768	15 & 17 '73 thru '79
081	16 89.7 cu in & 95.5 cu in engines '65 thru '72
598	18i & Sportwagon '81 thru '86
	Alliance & Encore – see AMC (934)
984	Fuego '82 thru '85

ROVER
085	3500 & 3500S Sedan 215 cu in engines '68 thru '76
*365	3500 SDi V8 '76 thru '85

SAAB
198	95 & 96 V4 '66 thru '75
247	99 including Turbo '69 thru '80
*980	900 including Turbo '79 thru '88

SUBARU
237	1100, 1300, 1400 & 1600 '71 thru '79
*681	1600 & 1800 2WD & 4Wd '80 thru '89

SUZUKI
1626	Samurai/Sidekick and Geo Tracker '86 thru '89

TOYOTA
*1023	Camry '83 thru '90
150	Carina Sedan '71 thru '74
229	Celica ST, GT & liftback '71 thru '77
437	Celica '78 thru '81
*935	Celica except front-wheel drive and Supra '82 thru '85
680	Celica Supra '79 thru '81
1139	Celica Supra in-line 6-cylinder '82 thru '86
361	Corolla '75 thru '79
961	Corolla (rear wheel drive) '80 thru '87
*1025	Corolla (front wheel drive) '84 thru '91
*636	Corolla Tercel '80 thru '82
230	Corona & MK II all 4 cyl sohc models '69 thru '74
360	Corona '74 thru '82
*532	Cressida '78 thru '82
313	Land Cruiser '68 thru '82
200	MK II all 6 cyl models '72 thru '76
*1339	MR2 '85 thru '87
304	Pick-up '69 thru '78
*656	Pick-up '79 thru '90

TRIUMPH
112	GT6 & Vitesse '62 thru '74
113	Spitfire '62 thru '81
028	TR2, 3A, & 4A Roadsters '52 thru '67
031	TR250 & 6 Roadsters '67 thru '76
322	TR7 '75 thru '81

VW
091	411 & 412 all 103 cu in models '68 thru '73
159	Beetle & Karmann Ghia all models '54 thru '79
238	Dasher all gasoline models '74 thru '81
*884	Rabbit, Jetta, Scirocco, & Pick-up all gasoline models '74 thru '89 & Convertible '80 thru '89
451	Rabbit, Jetta & Pick-up all diesel models '77 thru '84
082	Transporter 1600 '68 thru '79
226	Transporter 1700, 1800 & 2000 all models '72 thru '79
084	Type 3 1500 & 1600 '63 thru '73
1029	Vanagon all air-cooled models '80 thru '83

VOLVO
203	120, 130 Series & 1800 Sports '61 thru '73
129	140 Series '66 thru '74
244	164 '68 thru '75
*270	240 Series '74 thru '90
400	260 Series '75 thru '82
*1550	740 & 760 Series '82 thru '88

SPECIAL MANUALS
1479	Automotive Body Repair & Painting Manual
1654	Automotive Electrical Manual
1480	Automotive Heating & Air Conditioning Manual
1763	Ford Engine Overhaul Manual
482	Fuel Injection Manual
1666	Small Engine Repair Manual
299	SU Carburetors thru '88
393	Weber Carburetors thru '79
300	Zenith/Stromberg CD Carburetors thru '76

See your dealer for other available titles

Over 100 Haynes motorcycle manuals also available

4-1-91

Listings shown with an asterisk (*) indicate model coverage as of this printing. These titles will be periodically updated to include later model years — consult your Haynes dealer for more information.

Haynes North America, Inc., P.O. Box 978, Newbury Park, CA 91320 • (818) 889-5400 • (805) 498-6703